Plato

International Library of Philosophy and
Scientific Method

Editor: Ted Honderich

A Catalogue of books already published in the
International Library of Philosophy and Scientific Method
will be found at the end of this volume.

Plato
The Written and Unwritten Doctrines

J. N. Findlay F.B.A.

University Professor of Philosophy,
Boston University

Formerly Professor of Philosophy
at the Universities
of London and Yale

New York

HUMANITIES PRESS

First Published
in the United States of America 1974
by Humanities Press Inc.
450 Park Avenue South
New York, N.Y. 10016

Copyright © J. N. Findlay 1974

Library of Congress Cataloging in Publication Data

Findlay, John Niemayer.
Plato: the written and unwritten doctrines.

(*International library of philosophy and scientific method*)
1. Plato.   I. Series.
B395.F49   184   73–16065
ISBN 0–391–00334–8

Printed in Great Britain

To
my students at Yale
who always drew from me
far more ideas than
I ever knew I had

CONTENTS

Preface   ix

I   Introductory and Biographical   1

II   General Sketch of the Eidetic Theory and of its Arithmetized Version   29

III   The Socratic Dialogues   81

IV   The Ideological Dialogues: The *Meno*, *Phaedo*, *Symposium* and *Phaedrus*   122

V   The Ideological Dialogues: The *Republic*   159

VI   The Stoicheiological Dialogues: The *Cratylus*, *Theaetetus* and *Parmenides*   210

VII   The Stoicheiological Dialogues: The *Sophist*, *Statesman*, *Philebus* and *Epistles*   255

VIII   Plato's Philosophy of the Concrete: The *Timaeus*, *Critias*, *Laws* and *Epinomis*   302

IX   Appraisal of Platonism and its Influence   350

Contents

Appendix I: Translated Passages Illustrating
Plato's Unwritten Doctrines   413

Appendix II: Critical Note on the Views of
Harold F. Cherniss   455

Index
                                                   475

PREFACE

This book is the final expression of a set of convictions which first formed themselves in me in 1926–7, in a period of leisure spent at Oxford after my completion of Greats in 1926. These convictions were borne in on me by a close, combined study of Plato, Plotinus and the *Metaphysics* of Aristotle. The scholarly climate of the time, the limitations of my own scholarship, and the need to find immediate employment, did not then favour the further elaboration of these convictions, but after nearly half a century of continued meditation on them, and in a changed scholarly climate – particularly on the Continent, after the publication of works by Krämer, Gaiser and others – I have ventured to set these convictions forth in the present interpretative study of Plato's written and reported teachings.

My first and most fundamental conviction is that the Platonic Dialogues are not, taken by themselves, the sort of works in which anyone's views on any matter could be clearly set forth: they point beyond themselves, and without going beyond them they are not to be understood. Plato's deepest insights are of course present in them, but, like the Sea-God Glaucus, these insights require to be freed from a vast incrustation of barnacles and manneristic reflexes, as well as from a vast number of deliberate literary, historical, polemical and other disguises. The historical sequence of the Dialogues, painstakingly arrived at by stylistic investigations, is also no clear document of the development of Plato's thought. It rather documents, on the view to which I came, Plato's ever-changing willingness to divulge parts of a long-held, profound programme, unclear as regards both goal and method, to which he felt ever varying attitudes of confidence and criticism, of impassioned defence and despairing retreat, all inspired by the vivid controversies in the Academy of which we can have only the dimmest imagination. A study of Plato which confines itself to the letter of the Dialogues, such as has been attempted by most scholarly interpreters in the past two centuries, has ended by stripping Plato of his philosophical dignity and interest, has set him before us as a brilliant, but basically frivolous player-about with half-formed, inconsistent notions and methods, and has failed to explain the persistent, historical sense of him as a deeply engaged thinker, to whom we owe one of the most important, most coherently elaborated, most immensely illuminating ways of regarding the world.

My second conviction was that *some* of the systematizations of Platonism by Ammonius Saccas and Plotinus, and particularly the doctrine of the Three Hypostases, represented what almost anyone with any interpretative flair must arrive at, if he read the main speculative passages in the Dialogues and Epistles with some care, and was willing to 'put two and two together'. My remark does not, of course, apply to those unable or unwilling to draw conclusions from more or less palpable hints, or constitutionally unable to understand metaphysical or mystical utterances, or to enter into mystical feelings, but such classes of persons should certainly *never* engage in the interpretation of Plato.

My third conviction is concerned with the Aristotelian evidence regarding Plato's attempt to give a purely numerical account of the Eide or Ideal Meanings. This evidence is scattered throughout the Aristotelian corpus, the writings of the Aristotelian commentators and some other sources, and was first classically summed up by Robin in his *Idée Platonicienne des Idées et des Nombres d'après Aristote* as far back as 1908 (also exhaustively, but less coherently, by Ross in his *Plato's Theory of Ideas* in 1951). It is my view that this evidence provides the most precious documentation of 'what Plato really thought' that we have, that it permits, despite vast difficulties at certain points, a fairly clear elucidation once the tangles of Aristotelian misunderstanding have been resolutely cut through, that it alone provides the key to the sustained *drame à clef* of the Dialogues, and that it provides, moreover, an illuminating and defensible view of experience and

existence. I work, further, on the hypothesis that the accounts of
Platonism which are to be found in *Metaphysics* I and elsewhere
represent the teaching that Aristotle encountered when he first
joined the Academy in 367, and by which he was indelibly
impressed and shocked, but that this teaching went back to at
least the time of the writing of the *Republic*, and perhaps earlier,
and was the basic programme of Plato's teaching in the Academy.
And it remained unwritten, not because it was thought to be too
high or too deep to be communicated to the many, but because
it never became more than a programme, one that inspired all
Plato's efforts, but that he was never able to implement fully.
What he was unable to communicate to others was also what he
was unable to say clearly to himself, the predicament of many
great thinkers. But, despite this, it is a thoroughly intelligible
programme: the determination to see in complex, many-
dimensional Numbers and Ratios, all transparently harking back
to one or two ultimate Principles, the explanatory essence of
everything – of Mind as much as of Matter, and of Value as
much as Fact – the qualitative content of our experience being
then regarded as a mere surface decoration on this numerical
substructure. Aristotle never understood Plato's programme,
and elaborately spoke and wrote out his many objections to it,
but the Academy was not the sort of place where such dissidence
was unwelcome, as the *Parmenides* and the *Sophist* amply bear
witness. This view of the Aristotelian evidence throws a critical
light on Jaeger's view of Aristotle's twenty years of reverential
conformity in the Academy: the Academy was not, we may hope,
a place where such orthodoxy was encouraged. And it of course
also cuts across the views of Cherniss as to the derivation of
Aristotle's accounts of Platonism from Aristotle's own incredibly
wilful distortions of things said in the Dialogues. I have not
troubled to argue against these latter views in my book, since
they have to my mind been conclusively refuted by Ross in
Plato's Theory of Ideas.

A fourth conviction regarding Platonism that has grown on
me over the years is that it is incredibly wrong to treat Platonism
as a form of dualism, as involving the postulation of a *second*
world of detached meanings over against the solid world of
particular things. If Plato believed or disbelieved anything, he
disbelieved in the genuine being of particular things: eternal

Natures may for him be changeably and inadequately instantiated, but there is nothing substantial, nothing ontically ontic, in such instantiations. They enter merely into the description of what Eide are and what they *do*. I have also come to believe in a very illuminating Category-doctrine in Platonism for which there is independent evidence in Simplicius and Sextus Empiricus: on this doctrine the Prime Forms are models of *self-existent* Excellence, but there are secondary, interstitial or '*relative*' patterns of the deviant and defective, and there are also tertiary quasi-patterns of an *opposing* Formlessness. Quite apart from this documentation, the three Categories in question, the Self-existent, the Relative or Approximate and the merely Opposed, reveal themselves in what Plato says in the Dialogues.

My book is aimed at achieving a unified presentation of a unified view of Plato, developed in relation to the full span of the Platonic writings, and the ancient writings on Plato. It does not profess to demonstrate its conclusions cogently, but to rest its case on their overall coherence, and on their accordance with the whole range of the evidence. It has not involved itself in tedious detailed controversy with alternative interpretations: these must be as indemonstrable as itself, and subject to the same standards of judgment. They will not, however, win the day by ignoring half the evidence, or by explaining it wildly. We have not, further, concerned ourselves with any facts or theories about Plato which are of no philosophical interest.

This book begins with two introductory chapters sketching the main landmarks in Plato's life and activity, the influences which shaped his opinions and the main structure of his views. It contains, in Chapter II, a long section in which my own, tentative interpretation of the Aristotelian material is expounded. A chapter on the Socratic Dialogues then follows, which tries to make plain the nature of the morally inspired, brilliant sophistry which Socrates practised, and, despite our admiration of it, to divide it off from the authentic contributions of Plato. Two chapters on the 'Ideological' or Middle Period Dialogues follow, and thereupon two chapters on the Stoicheiological or Later Critical Dialogues, where the accent is on the Principles behind the Eide, rather than the Eide themselves. There is then a chapter on Plato's Theory of the Concrete, which covers the *Timaeus* and the *Laws*, and a final chapter appraising Platonism and its historical influence. Let no one suppose that my all too sketchy treatments of the Platonic element in Neoplatonism, Thomism and many modern movements is an irrelevance. Platonism is only understood when it is seen as providing a background or framework within which the arbitrarinesses of religion can be restrained and religion consequently given its fullest, most rational development, and in which the scientific outlook can likewise be restrained from a too radical, too self-destructive empiricism. At the end of my book I have imitated Gaiser in including an Appendix of passages, mainly following his own excellent selection, which illustrate the Unwritten Doctrines of Plato as known to us only by report. Many students of Plato have no familiarity with these documents, or have never considered them *en somme*. I have translated these passages as carefully as I could, avoiding, as far as possible, the un-English abracadabra of many Aristotle translations.

There are many requirements for a good interpreter of Plato: the ability to follow intricate arguments and fill in their gaps, the ability to feel the drift of speculative passages and see where they tend without going off into speculative excursions of one's own, the deep feeling for an ultimate mysticism which is not incompatible with clearness and commonsense, the grasp of the nuances of Plato's wonderful Greek style and use of words, and deep and thorough knowledge of that very small part of the almost infinitely extended secondary literature on Plato, both ancient and modern, which really deserves close study, and, finally, an understanding of Greek mathematics, and of mathematics generally, which is quite essential to the understanding of Plato. In my own equipment for interpreting Plato some of the above qualifications are much less strong than I could wish them to be, but when I contrast my equipment with that of some others who none the less have not been deterred from interpreting Plato, I do not feel that I have been too presumptuous.

Boston J. N. FINDLAY

Postscript In response to a request from the Editor of this series I have added, as Appendix II to this book, a Critical Note on the Views of Harold F. Cherniss.

I also wish to express my especial gratitude to Professor

Reginald Allen of the University of Toronto who, though approving neither of my method nor of my conclusions, encouraged me to persist in preparing my work at a time when I felt gravely discouraged about it.

I

INTRODUCTORY AND BIOGRAPHICAL

I

The aim of this book can be said to be to make sense, in a comprehensively general manner, of a philosophy which itself seeks to make sense of every phenomenon, fact or side of reality that it considers, and also seeks to weave all its separate exercises of sense-making into a single, comprehensive fabric of sense, dependent throughout on the operations of a single supreme unifying Principle or set of Principles. The philosophy we are to consider is that of Plato, which, despite the fact that it interprets everything in terms of what is common or generic or capable of being present in many vastly differing cases, is itself very hard to characterize in a general manner. The common run of philosophies are concerned principally with the existent world and with the large number of particular things that play a part in it, whose extraordinary juxtapositions and collisions form the pathos and comedy and absurdity of the world's history: if concepts or types or general patterns then come, at a second remove, to be considered, they are thought of as categories embodied in the existent world, or as notions that *we* apply to this world in order to understand it or to master it. The focus of interest remains fixed on the items which parade before us in direct encounter, and which, elusive and half-glimpsed as they often are, are felt to be all that is worth understanding or changing, all that, with more zeal than that of the mere ontologist, we are ready to speak of as 'real'. For Platonism, on the other hand, the world of particular existence is never a central topic: what for it are centrally thematic are always the types, the natures, the characters and general structures which are or might be embodied in the realm of particular existence, or to which particular existence can in varying degrees approximate. It is Equality as Such or the Equal Itself, or what it is or means to be equal, which is interesting to the Platonist, rather than the things which happen to be equal or nearly equal to one another, and the same holds of being triangular, being spherical, being a harmonic mean, being swift, being slow, being hot, perceptive or alive, being this or that sort of plant or animal or elementary substance, and also being just, being self-controlled, being beautiful, being truly cognizant of this or that, and so on.

The Platonist, moreover, is not concerned with the actual juxtapositions of instances of this or that general type with one another, but with the nearnesses or affinities, or with the remotenesses and incompatibilities of the types themselves: he is more concerned to see how being equal stands to being unequal, or to being the same, or to being one, or to being indivisible or divisible and so forth, than to see in what circumstances things actually tend towards or achieve complete equality. And he is concerned to *arrange* all the *sorts* of things that there are or might be, and all the characters and relationships that they might show forth or embody, into an all-comprehensive map of the possibilities of being this or that, or of being thus or thus characterized or related or situated, in which all that is specific will be seen as a particular case of something more generic, and will be ranged in orderly fashion alongside other specifications of the same general sort, and in which genera, ranged under ever higher genera, will tend towards the smallest possible number of highest kinds, within and beneath which any and every possible sort of thing will find its appointed place. (We shall later see reason to think that Plato placed the Principles or Principle of order governing the whole system of ideal types at an altogether higher level than those types themselves.) The cosmos of Platonism therefore differs as deeply from the cosmos of ordinary thought as the systematic order of some vast, card-indexed library differs from the shelf-order of the volumes listed in it, or from the inconceivable scattering of the items mentioned in those volumes. It is a world of notional headings, a true conceptual or logical geography, rather than a world of things as they exist, or as they happen, or as they are put together. To change from the normal world of 'cases' to the ideal world of characters is, however, a difficult and painful operation, even if the 'association by similarity' which leads to it is as natural and basic as the 'association by contiguity' out of which ordinary world-construction develops.

This difficulty is increased for all those thinkers, mainly Anglo-Saxon, who feel that there is something dangerous, even intellectually unprincipled, in thinking about 'being equal as such', or being anything as such, or finding an abstract name to cover it: to do so is to run the risk of hypostatization, of turning a mere aspect of something into a self-subsistent entity, of violating Ockham's rule of economy, or what not. To do so is also to postulate an identity or an invariance of meaning, corresponding to an expression like 'equal' or 'equality', which is very far from obtaining. These fears are increased when it is found that Plato actually encouraged hypostatization, and that Platonism is in fact hypostatization conducted as a systematic policy, with the added oddity that ordinary names for individual things are 'dehypostatized', and made to cover mere 'reflections', mere outward communions or instantiations of the new, hypostatized class of entities. For the ordinary ontologist equal things are the basically real entities in which 'Equality as Such' parasitically inheres that it connects, whereas for the Platonist Equality as Such is more straightforwardly and paradigmatically selfsame and real than the vanishing things that it seems, in our inaccurate estimates, to connect. We shall not here attempt a full defence of the great ontological inversion in which Platonism consists, the seeing of what primarily is, not in the instances which exemplify or nearly exemplify being equal, but in the type, the nature, the pattern that they exemplify: the whole of this book is an attempt to understand, and with qualifications to adopt, a Platonic ontology. Here we need only stress the profound psychological difference, almost one of Eidos or type, between those, mainly of Mediterranean extraction, to whom universal Meanings are practically 'old friends', living objects of personal acquaintance, while others of a more passive, observational, perhaps 'northern' type, see rather the variable impedimenta of sense-experience, imagery, outward instrumentality than the ensouling Meaning Itself. Between Socrates and Moore, on the one hand, to whom

3

universal Meanings were livingly present, and Wittgenstein and Hume, on the other, for whom they dissolve in a fine spume of experienced irrelevances, there would seem to be a great gulf fixed. The Platonic inversion was as easy and natural to the former as it was difficult and against the grain for the latter.

The difficulty of understanding and expounding Plato lies then in the difficulty of turning one's mind from the actual concrete cases of certain conceptual Meanings and *their* contingent, factual relations, to the conceptual Meanings themselves, and to *their* ideal, necessary relationships. But there are other deep difficulties which spring from the manner in which Plato expounded his basic insights. He did so in three manners, none of which alone suffices for the understanding of his deeper drifts, but which it takes patience and insight to fit together so as to obtain from them a single, coherent, philosophically illuminating message. The three manners in which Plato expounded his insights were, in the first place, the written Dialogue, varying from the extreme of dramatic vividness to cases where dialogue-form merely serves to mask what had better been put as continuous exposition, the written Epistle, of which the main specimens are now held to be of definite authenticity – if not written by Plato they were written by a forger of equal profundity – and the Unwritten, Oral Teachings of which elaborate, fairly uniform, if deeply unsympathetic reports are given by Plato's greatest pupil, Aristotle, who thoroughly knew, though he may not always have thoroughly understood, the basic drift of Plato's Unwritten Teaching. Other sources – Theophrastus, Sextus Empiricus, Proclus, the Aristotelian commentators – also add impressively to the testimony as to Plato's Unwritten Doctrines, whose content, up to a certain point, is not in any way unclear, though beyond that point it is to the last degree obscure. The trouble with the three ways in which Plato chose to express himself is, as we have said, that none, taken alone, tells us with sufficient clearness and depth what Plato really thought, and that all together raise conflicts which only the most persistent probing can compel into harmony. If the Platonic maker of the world (in the *Timaeus*) found it infinitely hard to fit together the sharply quarrelling notes of Sameness, Difference etc. which he wished to accommodate in the World-Soul, but reached a richer harmony in the outcome, the interpreter of Plato must fit together his dramatic, his formally expository, his epistolary and his unwritten, reported teaching if he is to take full measure of his achievement.

The trouble with those of Plato's Dialogues which careful stylistic examination has established as 'earlier' is that they are primarily a picture of Socrates 'made young and beautiful', and of his argumentative activities in the company of the young and not so young, and that, while they may indicate the soil in which Plato's opinions grew, and some early growths in that soil, they do not express the full luxuriance of his mature opinions. There is, of course, the possibility, raised by the great intuitive interpreters, John Burnet and A. E. Taylor, that some part of the theory of Ideal Meanings, usually attributed to Plato, and some of the mystical Pythagoreanism that went with it, may have been played about with by Socrates: we have the problem as to where precisely Socrates ends, and Plato begins. This Socratic problem is also a Platonic problem, since whatever we give to Socrates we also take away from Plato. The wisest reaction to this round of questions is to be indifferent to their precise answer: philosophically it is unimportant which part of the doctrine of Ideal Meanings first developed in the mind of Socrates, and which in the mind of Plato. As Plato progressed in his Dialogue-writing, he continued to use the *persona* of Socrates for the expression of opinions and the conducting of arguments which cannot plausibly be thought of as Socratic. The question still remains: are they authentically Platonic? The Dialogue-form permits Plato to put forth points of view tentatively, to put them through their paces, as it were, without being personally committed to their content or their method. Many of Plato's mature Dialogues wear an outer face of enigma: it is not clear when they are being literal and when figurative, when they are being tentative and when assertive, when they are holding absurdities up to ridicule, or hinting at a mystical sense behind such absurdities, nor is it always clear what positive contentions or what malign absurdities they are concerned with. The setting of the discussions is at times historically impossible, the course of the argument incredible, and only the immense genius which breathes through every word persuades one to continue the examination of what is, from many points of view, an 'abyss of nonsense'. One has but to refer to the mature Dialogue *Parmenides*, perhaps with the

Phaedo the most magnificent product of Plato's genius, to document what we are saying: the interpretations of its content cover the widest of spectra, and so do the disgusted reactions of those who, to tell the truth, refuse to interpret it at all. If we consider the Dialogues alone, we are faced with a range of ideas which Plato considered, but which he neither firmly endorsed nor even worked out with any approach to a rounded treatment. Many are satisfied with this tentative, suggestive thought-fragmentation which is certainly worth a pack of low-grade systematization, but the *nisus* of Plato's thought is none the less towards systematic completion, and if we lose the willingness to run along with this *nisus*, the fragments lose all their meaning, become even trivial and ridiculous. A Plato who merely played around with notions and arguments is a Plato corrupted, a Plato unworthy of serious study.

If we turn to the *Epistles*, they have, in the main cases, a philosophical depth which vouches for their authenticity: none but a Plato or a second Plato could have written them. But apart from documenting the mystical fringes which necessarily and profitably surrounded Plato's central sense-making activities, they throw little light on the main points in his doctrine. The documentation of Plato's Unwritten Teaching in Aristotle and in other sources is in a different case: full, detailed and to a certain extent coherent, it raises countless questions. While it makes plain that Plato intended to give all Ideal Meanings a mathematical explication, and to derive all such mathematicized meanings from two, and perhaps in the end, one single primitive notion or super-notion, it does not make plain, in its use of strange metaphors, what the reduction to Number was really meant to compass, or how Plato imagined that it could in detail be carried out. We have, further, the vast difficulty of connecting the countless qualitative, valuational, psychological, ordinarily descriptive and culturally derived Meanings of the Dialogues – for example, the shuttles and beds of frequent mention – with the austerely empty Numbers or numerical Ratios in which the significant essence of everything is in this Unwritten Teaching held to consist. We have the further problem, a complete stumbling-block to many, as to why it was necessary to operate in this two-level manner, backing an overt, written type of exposition with an Unwritten Teaching which did not plainly

6

square with it at all. This difficulty leads to the relegation of the reported mathematicization to Plato's successors or to his senility or to Aristotle's wanton misconstructions etc., etc. All these difficulties are compounded by the complete lack of sympathetic understanding which Aristotle displays even in his most carefully worded accounts of the mathematicizing tendencies of Plato and the Platonists. To Aristotle, with his qualitative, piecemeal, descriptive orientation, all these tendencies amounted to near-madness: while he could accept some of the results of the Platonic mathematicization, as in his accounts of sensation or his doctrine of the virtues, he could not accept the mathematicization itself. The reason for all this mystery and misunderstanding undoubtedly lay in the unworkable grandeur of Plato's basic enterprise: to reduce all basic 'senses' to one (or at most two) basic senses, having in themselves an infinite fecundity of differentiation and specification, which can obviously only be sought in the region of Quantity and Number, since there alone can the simple and uniform differentiate itself into an infinity of species of unimaginable complexity. The grand design behind Plato's oral teaching could obviously never become more than a grand design: the insightful knowledge in which it would be consummated was itself a Platonic Idea, a transcendent Ideal Meaning, towards which school opinion could advance, but to which it could never attain. From such an aspiration towards finished intellectual vision Aristotle turned aside: he was content with a high form of the piecemeal, full of many gulfs and gaps, and with only a few meaninglessly cut-off remnants of the crowning unities of Platonism (God, the Active Intelligence etc.). But though many would approve of Aristotle's lowered level of aspiration, they cannot, in so doing, be satisfactory interpreters of Plato. For Plato's aspirations are of the essence of his teaching, and without the projected mathematicization of all Meanings, and their incorporation into a single closely-knit meaning-structure, covering all possibilities of the specific and the instantial, his teaching would not make any important sense at all. The interpreter of Plato has therefore the supremely difficult task of grasping the aspiration behind its imperfect elaboration, seeing this aspiration through the hostile reports of those who did not share it, and then seeing how this aspiration illuminates the assertions and silences of the Dialogues. The task involved is severe, but

7

it can be carried out if one sees that its carrying out is the one way to give concrete meaning to what we feel to be the 'greatness' of Plato.

II

We follow this exordium with an account of the main probabilities of Plato's life and philosophical activity, hardly any of which are beyond controversy. But since the controversy is, to a very large extent, philosophically unimportant, we shall only enter into it sparingly.

Plato was born in Athens in Olympiad 88 in the month of Thargelion (in May–June of the year 428–7 B.C. of our era): he was the son of Ariston, an aristocratic figure who claimed descent from the old kings of Attica, and of Perictione, a highborn lady closely related to anti-democratic figures such as Charmides (her brother) and Critias (her uncle), both involved in the short-lived tyranny of the Thirty which took place at the end of the Peloponnesian War (404–3). After Ariston's death, Perictione married her uncle Pyrilampes, a friend and strong supporter of Pericles: Plato was accordingly brought up in a political household, dedicated to democracy as Athens understood it, however much his aristocratic descent and subsequent experience may have pushed him in an anti-democratic direction. Plato was subjected to many philosophical influences in his formative years, from 428 till the death of Socrates in 399, but he directed himself, as we know from his Seventh Letter, to a political rather than a philosophical career. Only the mad policies of Athens in the latter part of the Peloponnesian War, the evil actions of the Thirty Tyrants among whom his own relatives were prominent, and, finally, the trial and death of Socrates at the hands of the restored democracy – a man who to Plato was not merely wise and good, but practically sacred – turned Plato from the political life, henceforth judged vain except in miraculously ordained circumstances, to the life of a practical teacher of philosophy.

In these first three decades of Plato's life, Socrates must plainly have been the supreme formative influence. Plato must have heard him discoursing on many occasions, and felt the fascination of his personality and style of thought long before he really understood either. Plato's elder brothers were close associates of Socrates, and are depicted as his interlocutors in the *Republic*, and Plato must have had the spiritual lineaments of Socrates graven on his soul long before he could make full sense of them. He picked up Socraticism as children pick up languages from their nurses, and only so can we understand his ability to use the manner and method of Socrates as if it were his own, to project it into historical contexts in which he, Plato, could not have been present, and to continue using it, with considerable vividness and verisimilitude (for example in the *Theaetetus*), in imagined situations and arguments in which the historical Socrates could not have been engaged. So remarkable is the 'identification' thus achieved, and so capable of sliding seamlessly over from the authentically Socratic to the definitely Platonic, that some have attributed to Socrates the theory of 'Forms' or Ideal Meanings, while others have supposed that even those writings usually taken to be most revelatory of Socratic stances (for example the *Apology* of Socrates) really reflect crises and cruces in the life of Plato (see Gilbert Ryle in *Plato's Progress*, 1966). Plato's familiarity with the philosophical manners of Socrates must have been paralleled by his familiarity with the philosophical manners of the Sophists, the teachers of an unprofound practical wisdom, against whom he may on some occasions have seen Socrates pitted, if not, alas, on those very great occasions about which some of his finest Dialogues are written (for example the *Protagoras* and the *Gorgias*). But Plato was as unrelentingly unsympathetic to the sophistical opponents of Socrates as he was sympathetic to Socrates, and is responsible for the excessively bad reputation from which these valuable thinkers still suffer. He is also responsible for blurring the very considerable community between the sophistical and the Socratic techniques of argument.

Socrates was further a supreme influence on Plato in directing his mind to the analysis of Meanings which are *valuational* rather than merely descriptive: the nature of Courage, Self-control, Justice, Piety, of true Knowledge as opposed to mere Opinion etc. To Socrates these valuational meanings were living presences which immediately declared themselves for or against the superficial identifications of his interlocutors, but they were also living presences inextricably integrated into an ideal of reasoned living which could not be separated from one's own inner apprehension of it, and which further resisted the precise definition which would make such apprehension a case of Knowledge rather than Opinion. All these characteristics of Socratic doctrine and procedure remain in Plato's later doctrine of Ideal Meanings: these Meanings always carry with them a strong note of the excellent and the well-formed, the ill-formed and deviant having at best a derivative or interstitial status: they are, despite the opinion of those who would make them all rigorously separate from one another (for example Harold Cherniss in some utterances), no more than the distinguishable facets of a single total Meaning in which they, and the total Meaning they form, never receive final, formal definition.

Of other philosophical influences in this first period of Plato's life we should not go far wrong in listing the various pre-Socratic philosophers of Nature, who are gestured at in the *Phaedo*, 95e–102a, as having had an influence in the intellectual development of Socrates, the early Ionian and Sicilian physicists, Alcmaeon etc., and finally Anaxagoras who declared Mind to be the motive power behind all things. Plato and Socrates – for they must obviously have been in profound sympathy – felt that this *ought* to mean that the arrangements of nature are all subject to the rule of the absolutely Good, that all in nature is geared to the exigencies of the Best. For them the great error of Anaxagoras and the pre-Socratic cosmologists lay precisely in their use of purely efficient mechanical causation (which is not fully explanatory by itself) in the place of the teleological explanation by ideal goals which alone seemed to them truly satisfactory. The reasoned Good that we pursue in all our actions, and which inspires the varied patterning of the human virtues, must in some obscure fashion lie behind the physical universe also, even if we cannot in detail say how. This last is of course the faith of Plato in his later cosmological writings, but it obviously had its roots in the profound, rational piety of Socrates.

This profound rational piety also made Socrates, and after him Plato, sympathetic to the mystical otherworldliness taught and practised by the Pythagoreans: Simmias and Cebes, two Theban disciples of the Italian Pythagorean Philolaus, were among the devoted associates of Socrates, and joined in the discussions on immortality which, however transformed by Plato, almost certainly took place in some form on the last day of Socrates's life. (Their association with Socrates is independently confirmed by Xenophon.) The Pythagorean faith in a Divine Justice which punishes wickedness and rewards purity of life in posthumous states of bliss or torment, served as a problematic reinforcement of the Socratic faith in the inherent unprofitability of unjust living, and its inferiority, even from the point of view of personal advantage, to the mere undergoing of Injustice. Socrates did not know if there was an afterlife, but he did see it to be impossible that evil should be the lot of the good man, and he doubtless also thought that, if there were such a thing as an afterlife, it would probably be after the wise of the Pythagorean stories. His feeling also for the ordered harmony of a disinterested, reasoned life, and for the virtues which were its members, possibly made him not unreceptive to the Pythagorean numerical harmonies in terms of which the Soul and its virtues were interpreted. If one may hazard a guess, the arguments against the view of the Soul as a harmony which occur in Plato's *Phaedo* are the genuine protests of Socrates against a too abstract Pythagorean analysis: they are not the protests of Plato, for whom a harmony, being incorporeal and ideal, would be just the right sort of thing to be timeless and immortal. Be this all as it may, Plato, if not Socrates, certainly felt the analogy between the Socratic excellences radiating from a half-glimpsed, reasoned Good, and the Pythagorean Number-patterns, all of which were after their impersonal fashion virtues, and all of which radiated from Principles more august and obscure than themselves. It must, in fact, have been this felt analogy which later led to that comprehensive Pythagoreanization of Ideal Meanings, whether valuational, physical, political or psychological, in which the characteristic contribution of Plato may be held to consist.

Aristotle in his historical sketch of the origins of Platonism in *Metaphysics*, I, 6, connects it both with Socrates and the Pythagoreans, giving greater prominence to the latter. But he also connects it closely with the teaching of Heraclitus of Ephesus, as mediated by his contemporary disciple Cratylus. The degree to which Plato's basic positions were influenced by Cratylus also appears in two of the Platonic Dialogues, the *Cratylus* and the *Theaetetus*. Heraclitus may have taught a doctrine of continuous, flowing change from one pole of burning, mobile Fire through

Air and Water down to the congealed coldness and dullness of Earth, and then back again through Water and Air to Fire, but this doctrine was balanced by a doctrine of more or less constant *measures* which went with this flux, so that whatever was lost on the way up from Earth to Fire was compensated for on the way down, the face of things remaining thereby more or less unchanged. And a Divine Wisdom, which would and also would not permit itself to be called by the religious name 'Zeus', lay behind all this preservation of constancy in flux, and imparted itself to the human mind in its brighter, 'drier' moods. In all this vivid theorizing, flux and constancy play an opposed but integrated role, but the 'message' that popularizing thought distilled from this doctrine was that everything was so absolutely in flux that nothing like a thing or a property remained fixed for an instant, and that all attempts to characterize the state of things as being thus or thus were therefore necessarily false and senseless. Such at least was the doctrine of Cratylus, who seems to have mixed the flux-doctrine he derived from Heraclitus with a subjectivism which he read into the teaching of the great sophist Protagoras, so that all mental life became a flux of the impacts of external objects upon our sense-organs, with no truth in regard to the vanishing sensations and sense-qualities thus evoked that would extend beyond the person and the instant. (See *Theaetetus*, 156–7.) Cratylus in his stricter moments in fact cultivated a form of aphasia, no doubt prefaced by much verbal justification: he refused to name objects and properties, and merely gestured in their direction. To Plato, who had lived with Socrates and his analyses and arguments over a long period, the absurdity of the Cratylean position was plain: it made knowledge and reasoned assertion impossible. If nothing can be pinned down as being this or that, or as being this or that sort of thing, or even as *having* for a moment been this or that sort of thing, then one cannot say anything true or false about it, and there cannot even be an abiding state of understanding or opinion which may or may not be correct. Plato was, in fact, irresistibly led by the Cratylean view of the world (see for example *Cratylus*, 440) to the notion that the virtues and other fixed Natures and Meanings which Socrates was attempting to circumscribe and pin down, had a being different from the sensible things in which they were vanishingly illustrated: there were, and must be, eternal Meanings, no doubt after a fashion flickeringly reflected on the surface of flux, but having in addition a being in and for themselves, the being of being precisely the sort of Meanings or Ideal Contents that they were. And for Plato they did not even include the *qualities* of sense, which were entirely vanishing and unreliable, but only the constancies which can be established by counting, measuring and weighing, and which are accordingly quantitative rather than qualitative. (See, for example, the of course much later passage in *Republic*, 602d.) Plato may very well have proclaimed the being of these 'Ideas', these reliable, notional 'Shapes', to the master who spent all his time investigating them without making them or their being the *theme* of his discourse – Socrates was a moralist and not an ontologist – and Socrates may very well have extended his indulgence to the 'hypostatizations' of his young friend. Socrates who lived always in the presence of the virtues and the other forms of excellence, to whom they were more real, more objects of reverent acquaintance, than the friends with whom he discoursed about them, would have been sympathetic, if not altogether receptive, to Plato's ontological leanings. To Socrates the virtues, whether analysed or unanalysed, remained a practical path towards perfected human goodness, and towards participation in a goodness more perfect than that of man, whereas to Plato they had become things to be contemplated and argued about, and so leading on to a more than Socratic philosophy.

If Plato was repelled by what he took to be the teaching of Heraclitus, this automatically caused him to lean to the teaching of Parmenides, the great South Italian philosopher, and to those, like the philosophers at neighbouring Megara, who derived from him. Aristotle did not stress the association of Plato with this Eleaticism, but it is clear from Plato's works (for example the late Dialogues *Parmenides* and *Sophist*), and also from such facts as that he took refuge with the Megarian Eleatic Euclides after the death of Socrates. Parmenides taught the impossibility of truly talking or thinking about anything unreal, anything without being, and this led to the denial of the possibility of real change (which involves the passage of that which is not into that which is, or *vice versa*) and even to a denial of differentiation (since for one thing to be different from another involves the presence of a differentiating feature other than being itself) or any kind of separative gulf or void (for quite obvious reasons). The change-able world of the senses therefore existed not in truth but only in the 'Opinions of Mortals', a view which probably did not mean that it was just nothing: it had perhaps a certain shadowy, dependent half-being of which Plato was later to make use in his own theory. Obviously this Being Itself which has nothing to distinguish itself from the thought of itself (as would be the case if this thought could be directed to other features than the being it grasps), is therefore the one and only entity that there really is or can be, its Unity not being taken to be anything other than the Being it is. Parmenides was far from realizing the implicit contradiction involved in attributing Unity and other characters to something so unitary as to be no more than Being itself. He was also so little critical as to liken his unique existent to a well-rounded sphere, extending equally in every direction. Later Eleatics, such as Euclides of Megara, sublimated this materialistic picture or image into a pure conception of Unity or Being which they further identified with the Socratic Good, holding, however, that there was no internal difference in it which corresponded to the differing names applied to it. Whatever one might say of it, one was always in effect affirming Being to be Being, Unity to be Unity, the Good to be the Good. A new form of aphasia therefore replaced the aphasia of the Heracliteans: they could predicate nothing of anything since all was in flux, whereas the Eleatics could predicate nothing of anything since what there was was only itself. All these difficulties were afterwards to be made thematic in the late Dialogues *Parmenides* and *Sophist*, but Plato's whole thought was, from the very beginning, a partial protest against it. Changeless being must be retained, and its unity asserted, but this being must be that of the endlessly distinct 'senses', the Ideal Contents, which, however much built into a single system of significance, none the less represent different facets of it. And one must also recognize various sorts of secondary, derivative and as-it-were-being or near-nothing, to accommodate the changeable qualities of sense and the vague medium or field in which they were projected. The whole of Platonism represents a careful modification of Eleaticism which prevents it from being as absurd as the flux-physics and flux-logic of Cratylus. And as Plato's thought developed, he became inclined to stress rather than minimize the parasitic reality of flux and movement, and they even gain a frozen admittance into the changeless realm of his ideal 'senses'.

What we have so far done is simply to locate in the long thirty years of Plato's early life the influences that cannot have failed to impinge on him during that period. The period came to an end in 399 B.C. when Socrates, the inspired analyst and exemplar of the virtues, was tried and condemned for corrupting the young and for seeking to introduce foreign cults into Athens. So strange and paradigmatic are the circumstances of this trial, which is so much a confrontation between pure Wisdom and Goodness, on the one hand, and confusion, narrowness and resentment, on the other, that it has been held by some to be no more than an edifying myth, an inspirational fable dreamt up by the Sophists or by Plato. We need not, however, reject the occasional irradiation of our sad sphere by paradigmatic personalities from a somewhat higher level, an irradiation which may very well give rise to paradigmatic hatreds, especially when it transcends the pieties and prescriptions of society, and especially when it can be abused so as to undermine those pieties and prescriptions. The execution of the paradigmatic man by the community which he had sought to enlighten was, however, enough to turn Plato from what seemed the plain hopelessness of political life to the life of a philosophical teacher, and there seems little reason to question that it first moved him to write those unique documents, the early Dialogues, in which Socrates lives and discourses again without the intrusion of those systematic viewpoints which internal evidence of style and content, as well as Aristotle's testimony, relegates to a different, Platonic stratum. These Socratic Dialogues will be considered in some detail in our third chapter. Here we may merely mention the *Charmides* in which Socrates attempts an analysis of the Greek virtue of Self-control (σωφροσύνη), the *Laches* in which he tries to do the same for Courage (ἄνδρεια), the *Hippias Major* in which he attempts it for the Fine (καλόν) in conduct, the *Hippias Minor* which considers the possibilities of evil which are inherent in the exclusion of evil by good, the *Euthyphro* in which some puzzles which surround true Piety (ὁσιότης) are considered, the *Lysis* which studies the nature of Love or Favour (φιλία), the *Ion* which deals with the rapt understanding of the poets, and the *Meno* which deals with the Knowledge and Right Opinion which are part and parcel of the true Good. Somewhat different are the *Euthydemus*, the *Gorgias* and the *Protagoras*, where Socrates is seen pitting his analytic capacities and moral commitment against the great and less great Sophists of the period, and the amusing eristics or 'wranglers'. The first book of the *Republic* also belongs here, whether written separately or not. There are also the Dialogues which describe the trial and death of Socrates: the *Apology* or Defence of Socrates, the *Crito* which exhibits him in prison, to which we may probably also add an *Ur-Phaedo* which dealt with Socrates's discussions of immortality on the last day of his life, to which Plato afterwards added his incomparable enrichments. It is important to stress, as Ryle has done in *Plato's Progress*, that the production of dialogues in antiquity was not like the production of literary works in modern times. They were probably first performed or read aloud in chosen assemblies, a few copies were at first made or circulated, the contents were modified in successive copyings or presentations; only at a late stage, and sometimes never, did they become widely available as things that one might buy, or have specially copied for one's own use. Hence even intimates of Plato, for example Aristotle, never knew much of the contents of certain of the Dialogues: they were absent when they were read, and had perhaps never been zealous enough to borrow a copy or have one made for themselves. (Unless indeed, in the case of the *Parmenides*, the jesting exposition of their own objections to Platonism so offended them as to render the Dialogue unmentionable.) The period of the writing of these Socratic Dialogues may plausibly be placed in the time between 399 and 387, after which Plato went on his first visit to Italy and Sicily. It is not, however, necessary to confine them to this period. Plato may have written some of his Socratic Dialogues within the lifetime of his great friend, though the latter is not represented as commenting on such Boswellian activities. And what he wrote after he returned from Italy certainly had much continuity with what went before. The Dialogues held to be Socratic sometimes employ Plato's technical term Eidos or Ideal Meaning or Pattern, and they shade gradually into the so-called Middle Period or mature Dialogues (the *Phaedo*, *Republic*, *Symposium* and *Phaedrus* etc.) in which straightforward exposition, sometimes thinly veiled in question and answer, often replaces true Socratic analysis. The *Meno* likewise contains Pythagorean touches regarding our knowledge of the relations of Ideal Meanings in some epoch prior to our descent into this flesh, the *Protagoras* hints at a true metric of good and evil which suggests Plato's mature tendency towards arithmetization, and so on.

III

If 'watersheds' are legitimately to be sought in a development so continuous as Plato's, the visit to Southern Italy and Sicily in 388–7 B.C. may be regarded as such a 'watershed'. Plato became deeply intimate with Dion, the son-in-law of Dionysius I, the tyrant of Syracuse, and was at a later date led by the latter into high-minded but ill-judged intrusions into Sicilian politics. More importantly, he came into contact with Archytas, Philolaus, Eurytus and other Pythagoreans in Tarentum. Plato, as we have held, had at this time long given an ontological meaning to the Notional Shapes of the virtues and excellences which Socrates examined, and he was no doubt willing to range the concepts of the mathematicians, the exact Numbers, Angles and Figures whose applications they problematically studied (conceived however in their notional purity and uniqueness and not even in the ideal applications of the mathematician), as Notional Shapes of precisely the same dignity as the virtues. What he may be held to have taken over from the Italian Pythagoreans is not so much the general concept of such Notional Shapes, as the grandiose project of mathematicizing them all, of making them all part of a vast arithmetic, so that the true essence of *everything*, whether explicitly mathematical, or physical, or biological, or having to do with the psychic or moral life of man, should be given a purely mathematical analysis, should be shown to be nothing but a vast prolongation and complication of the simple processes through which the Number-series was generated. This project was of course infinitely far from execution by the Italian Pythagoreans – Eurytus is said to have ranged pebbles round the crudely drawn figure of a man and to have determined Man's Number by counting them – and all modern physics has failed to bring it to perfection. Arguably, further, it is impossible of execution, there being categorial and qualitative 'leaps' in the world, of which, however, Plato later took notice in his accounts of the geometrical

Essences that 'came after the Numbers', or the mathematical instances which multiplied them, or the sense-qualities which rested on a mathematical basis. Plato, however, may be taken to have seen, even at this early stage, that it was only in the direction of such comprehensive mathematicization or arithmetization that the whole realm of Ideal Meanings could develop itself understandably out of the Unity which was alike the foundation of all numerical meanings and of the virtues as analysed by Socrates. In both fields we have great specific distinctness with an evident but not readily formulable or understandable Unity of Principle: both, further, arouse an identity of emotional response to which the Greeks were particularly sensitive. It is not remarkable that the great design should at this time have assumed a dominant place in Plato's mind, even if its working out was to take place over many successive stages, and never with any conclusiveness, and to be relegated in the end to the unattainable rather than the perfectly achievable.

It is in the time after Plato's return from Italy and Sicily that we must probably place the writing or the revision of the great mature Dialogues in which Pythagorean Soul-theory and Number-theory, and the belief in a transcendent source of all the Notional Shapes and of our knowledge of them, play an important part, and in which various arguments for an ontology of Notional Shapes begin to assume definiteness. The *Meno* with its doctrine of a reminiscence of the relations of what must plainly have been Notional Shapes, the *Phaedo* with its proof of immortality based on the close relation of the Soul to the Notional Shapes and to the Very Life Itself which cannot admit death or non-existence, the *Symposium* or Banquet which culminates in a mystical ascent from Notional Shapes to their almost ineffable Principle, the *Republic* or Ideal State, an ideal Pythagorean community whose virtue and whose mathematics are two sides of one Wisdom, and whose pathology also receives a notional, Pythagorean handling, and finally the *Phaedrus*, a strange amalgam probably written for a special occasion, in which rhetoric and love and the ideal essences are all intertwined. The *Timaeus*, or a version of it, a comprehensive cosmological study of the natural world in time and space, and its relation to its ideal original, has by some (for example Professor G. E. L. Owen of Harvard) been referred to this period, with which it agrees in doctrinal tone, though cross-references to late Dialogues, and stylistic communities with them, have more convincingly referred it to the latest period of Plato's writing, where we ourselves shall place it. Since, in our view, the main lines of Platonism were fixed at a fairly early date, and since Plato's 'development', in so far as he had one, lay in a clearer and more detached view of the methods and assumptions of his whole approach, and a growing sense of the great difficulties that attended upon it, it does not matter precisely when the *Timaeus* was written. The Dialogues we have mentioned will all be examined in subsequent chapters.

In the same period after Plato's return from his visit to Italy we may place the foundation of the philosophical school known as the Academy. The organization of this school and its studies has been a subject of endless debate: Harold Cherniss in his *Riddle of the Early Academy* (1945) has amusingly pointed out how each historian of philosophy has seen it as anticipating the university schools of his own age and country. To some, it was a complete university embracing various schools of mathematical, logical, astronomical, biological, physical and metaphysical research, to some it was an advanced school in geometry with some philosophical frills added, while to yet others it was basically a religious group organized about a special cult etc. What seems clear about it (despite doubts raised by some) is that it must have been organized around the philosophical teaching of Plato himself, which, however tentative, problematic, programmatic, undogmatic, obscure and widely tolerant, none the less gave it all the unity and direction that it had. This teaching cannot have been confined to a study of the Dialogues, on which in fact it seems that Plato commented little, though some like the *Phaedo*, and later the *Timaeus*, were closely studied. But the whole gist and thrust of Plato's main thinking is not to be found in the Dialogues taken alone, however much some have tried to find it there. The Dialogues themselves (for example *Phaedrus*, 275–6) proclaim the superiority of oral over written exposition, the latter consisting of words that resemble life-like paintings that maintain an august silence when interrogated, and are unable to defend themselves if attacked or abused, whereas the former create living 'writings' in the soul, that are able to speak for and defend themselves. And the Dialogues themselves constantly refer to a more thorough treatment that must occur 'elsewhere', and would be hollow productions were these promises themselves hollow. Thus Socrates in the *Republic* says (506) that he must 'now leave the question as to what the Good Itself is, for it seems to be beyond my present powers to bring out what I have in mind on the present occasion', or that, despite all effort, a great deal is being left out and must be left out in the development of the likeness of the Sun (509c). The whole account of the Good in the *Republic*, in fact, points to a missing elucidation, and is unintelligible without it, and so do such statements as that about the soul as being something whose uniformity or triformity can only be established by methods more accurate than those followed in the Dialogues (435d, 612a). The missing elucidation is, however, largely available, even if it itself demands further elucidation, and the task of this book will be to show that, carefully used as a background to the mainly literary Dialogues, it can throw on the latter a flood of philosophical light.

An outline sketch of the presumed content of Plato's whole teaching will be given in the next chapter. Here we need only say that the general trend of that doctrine was at first to establish the being of the Eide or Notional Shapes by arguments more systematic and thorough than those given in the other-purpose Dialogues, and at the same time to develop and name various antinomies that arose in the course of such systematic argumentation, and then, at a later period, to consider the feasibility of a complete 'mathematicization' or arithmetization of all these Notional Shapes, a systematic derivation of them from more ultimate 'Principles' (ἀρχαί). Both of these stages in the development of Platonic doctrine are documented concisely in Aristotle's *Metaphysics*, and the former stage was more elaborately dealt with in Aristotle's lost treatise *On the Ideas*, possibly written in the Academy (a treatise which lay before Alexander of Aphrodisias when he wrote his commentary on Aristotle's *Metaphysics* in the second century A.D., and whose contents are consequently partially known to us) while the latter was dealt with in Aristotle's lost treatise *On the Good*, the gist of whose three books seems to be the basis of a long passage in Sextus Empiricus's *Against the Mathematicians* which will be considered later. It is not the minutiae of these teachings which it is important to consider, nor the detailed accuracy of our knowledge of them, but the immense project that they represent: first, the placing at the centre of reality of a number of paradigms in which intelligibility and excellence were pre-eminent, and around which all other possibilities and actualities cluster like notional detritus, then the attempt to arrange them according to principles intrinsic to themselves and then, after the envisaging of all this ordered richness, the endeavour to reduce it to the formality and purity which could, on Plato's view, only be found in a philosophically transformed mathematics, and lastly the attempted derivation of all this ordered purity from Principles or a Principle of such meta-mathematical purity as to achieve, on Plato's view, the necessary ineffability of a mystical Ultimate. This project was not a piece of *Spätphilosophie*, a product of Plato's old age: the *Laws* will show what he was capable of at that stage. It was essentially the background of Plato's mature work: it hovers behind the *Phaedo*, but the *Republic*, above all, is unintelligible without it. We cannot, for example, imagine that the advanced scheme of mathematical studies prescribed in Book VII should terminate in a Dialectic which quite fails to crown and connect their contents, and that men should have to wait till the age of fifty in order to be schooled in jejune analyses of the common virtues such as Socrates had practised on young men and boys. One may in fact hold that Plato, as he developed, did not advance towards a mathematicizing doctrine of the Notional Shapes but rather retreated from it or became less completely confident regarding it. As time went on, and the grandiose programme yielded few definite fruits, the critical attitude of later Dialogues like the *Parmenides* became possible, and it also became possible to give inadequate sketches of the mathematicizing programme, or some of its details, as is done in the Second Part of the *Parmenides*, or hintingly in the *Philebus*. It was therefore in the heyday of the Notional Shapes theory that the mathematicizing project was also in its heyday, or more or less approaching its heyday, and Aristotle must have encountered both in full florescence when he entered the Academy in 367. It is the philosophy of that period that he documented in his two lost treatises, and which appears in truncated form in the *Metaphysics*, and which is uniformly reported in all Aristotle has to say of Plato. We cannot understand anything that is said in the mature or late Dialogues without taking full account of it.

Some of course have refused to believe that Plato could have attempted anything so silly as a reduction of all concepts to Numbers and numerical relations; they have refused to hold that he would have taught a doctrine that did not at all points square with what he publicly propounded in his writings; they have rejected as spurious the references in the Epistles (for example Epistle II, 312d) to matters that must be obscurely put lest they fall into the hands of the unsuitable; they have attributed the mathematicizing doctrines to Plato's old age or to his pupils Speusippus and Xenocrates; or, lastly, they have explained Aristotle's detailed account of these doctrines as due to systematic distortions of statements in the Dialogues by the high refractive index of Aristotle's extraordinary intelligence. This last mode of rejection is the one followed by Harold Cherniss in his fascinatingly unpersuasive *Riddle of the Early Academy* (1945) and his *Aristotle's Criticism of Plato and the Academy* (1944), both works which display complete mastery of the evidence and the greatest skill in reacting to it all. But all the brilliance of Cherniss has not sufficed to give plausibility to an incredible thesis, and his detailed sponsorship of it has only brought out its extreme weaknesses. We shall not be concerned to refute it in these pages: both Cherniss's view and the view which attributes the mathematicizing doctrine to Plato's pupils are conclusively disposed of in the ninth chapter of Ross's *Plato's Theory of Ideas* (1951). It is in any case impossible to refute any view of Plato except by showing that it yields us an incredible and not respectable philosopher (both points on which there might be differences of opinion), or to establish a view except by showing that, with due respect for the evidence, it yields the opposite. If our treatment succeeds in doing just that, it will have achieved its purpose.

Plato may therefore be held to have functioned in a bifurcated or two-tier manner in the Academy, and that from the first. He wrote and held public readings of Dialogues for the general philosophical public, and he also conducted intensive methodological and systematic discussions for smaller groups of participants. This bifurcation was not the incomprehensible, unmotived thing that it might appear to be, especially when we consider the ridiculing notice that surrounded philosophers in the brilliant small towns of antiquity, and which is quite absent in our modern conurbations. Socrates was mercilessly ridiculed by Aristophanes, and the biological investigations of the Academy were likewise ridiculed in a well-known comic fragment. There was, moreover, nothing specially arcane about Plato's oral discussions: they were not kept closed to the general public because Plato had some highly elaborate, secret doctrine to impart in them, but precisely because he had not. All that he had to impart and to discuss was a programme, a project, every aspect of which was surrounded with problems and difficulties. Nor is there good reason to think that Plato arbitrarily excluded people from his oral assemblies: they excluded themselves by the discouragement which attendance at those assemblies soon engendered. Aristoxenus in a well-known passage (Appendix I, 2) tells us of the dismay felt by those who attended a certain discourse on the Good, probably the first lecture of the course, to which they came expecting to hear 'about the commonly recognized human goods, such as wealth, health, strength or some marvellous form of happiness' and instead, found that Plato was 'only to speak about mathematical studies, geometries and astrologies, and to identify goodness with unity, and how all then felt smitten with paradox, and some scorned, whereas others reproved the whole undertaking'. A few, however, must have persisted in their attendance and begun to see the sense of what Plato was attempting, and we, after more than two millennia, can see that he was striving after nothing less than the exact or inexact quantification of empirical data in which all empirical science consists, and in the formalization of the principles according to which those data were processed. Only Plato had a place in this total design for much that is thought too imprecise, too subjective, too tinged with valuation, too reaching out towards the transcendent, to be incorporated in any modern scientific and logical picture.

The Academy must of course have included many other teaching members besides Plato, and there is no reason to think that there was not wide difference of interest and even controversial opposition among them. It included mathematicians like Theaetetus, Leodamas and Philip of Opus, the first of whom contributed to the theory of irrationals and of the regular solids, while the last-named either edited or wrote the *Epinomis*, a short sequel to Plato's last long work, the *Laws*. It included mathematical astronomers like Eudoxus, Menaechmus, Callippus and Heracleides, who elaborated those wonderful attempts to 'save the phenomena' of the heavens by the theory of a series of immaterial spheres to which Aristotle was afterwards to give a more solid constitution, and who were sufficiently homely to conceive of some of the more extraordinary, lemniscate wanderings of the planets in terms of a 'hippopede' or ordinary horse-fetter. There also were the ontological Number-theorists and Cosmologists of what we may call the Platonic 'Right', Speusippus and Xenocrates who afterwards succeeded Plato as Heads of the School, and who, with their entourage, may well have been the 'Friends of the Ideas' referred to in the *Sophist*, to whom Plato was sympathetic but with whom he could not wholly associate himself. Finally, of course, we have Aristotle, around whom a considerable party may well have gathered, which may perhaps correspond to the 'Giants' or down-to-earth men, who were critical of any attempt to separate the Notional Meanings from the concrete instances in which they were embodied or the minds that conceived of them.

Aristotle's activities in the Academy may well have been as two-tiered as Plato's: while he could write a Dialogue like the *Eudemus* which included many echoes of the *Phaedo*, and a very Platonic *Protrepticus* or *Exhortation to Philosophy*, of both of which works excerpts survive, he may very well, in the discussions of Plato and in other assemblies, have uttered many of the trenchant criticisms of Platonism which he afterwards stated at length in the *Metaphysics* and elsewhere. There is an old tradition reported by Proclus according to which Aristotle was, almost from the first, critical of the doctrinal trends of the Academy, a role which fits in well with his origins in a remote colony and his being the son of a no doubt empirically-minded physician. But the tradition has since been clouded by modern developmental studies (for example, that of Jaeger) which stress the fact that Aristotle must have been for a long time a committed Platonist, and that it can only have been in his 'years of wandering' through Assos, Lesbos and other places that he could have acquired that independence from Platonism that made the institution of his own school and the production of his own corpus of original writings possible. The solution to this conflict lies in accepting and reconciling both sides of it: Aristotle *was* a committed member of the Academy, but the Academy was not the sort of reverential, monolithic place, built around a study of the Dialogues, that some have supposed. It must have included the cut and thrust of lively internal controversy, and Dialogues like the *Parmenides* and the *Sophist* bear witness to this fact. And if Aristotle could write a school-exercise on the model of the *Phaedo*, in memory of the departed Eudemus, we must remember that he never lost the transcendental tones that he had learnt from Plato. In speaking of the 'spectacles yonder' (τὰ ἐκεῖ θεάματα) that Eudemus would see, he may have been envisaging spectacles in the Active Intelligence, or in whatever ancestor of this conception his fertile mind had devised. It is not possible, in the present work, to speculate on the mental development of Aristotle: only it remains a possibility that very much more of his Logic, his Theology, his Psychology, his Ethics and other branches of his thought, should have been worked out fairly fully in the controversial atmosphere of the Academy, and under the benign tolerance of Plato, than in the less stimulating atmosphere of Assos and Lesbos.

To the later years of Plato's activity in the Academy we may ascribe the writing of a number of Dialogues in which the whole doctrine of Notional Patterns is considered from above (as it were), and in which Notional Patterns become central which are, we may say, the Notions *of* Notional Patterns and their structure, rather than any Notion that is to be found at their level. Plato became clear in these writings, as he was far from clear in earlier expositions, that to discourse about Ideal Meanings and their relations to one another, to their instances and to the Principles under which they fall, is to go *outside* the *first* order of Ideal Meanings altogether, and to embark on discussions of a new type in which wholly new notions will make their début. Plato, we may say, making use of the later language of the Middle Ages, became aware of 'transcendentals', notions like Unity, Being, Goodness, Number etc. which straddle widely differing territories of Reference, or, using the language of Russell, we may say that he became aware of Type-differences, or talking the language of Kant and Henry Jackson, we may say that he became concerned with Categories and categorial questions rather than with any notions or questions that fell under them. The technical terms which describe his new orientation are ἀρχαί, Principles and στοιχεῖα, Elements: Plato was interested in the Principles and Elements of his (mathematicized or unmathematicized) Meanings, and we have accordingly called some of the Dialogues of this period 'the Stoicheiological Dialogues'. This new direction of interest went with an interest in the role of language in illuminating or confusing issues. It is in this period that the puzzling Dialogue *Cratylus* must probably be placed, where, veiled in jest, the point is made that all meanings must have a constancy that enthrones them above the range of flux, and yet that their content must, very paradoxically, be nothing but the features of this flux which is thus brought to arrest. Here too belongs the great *Parmenides*, a legendary confrontation of historical figures, where the first part rehearses Academic controversies raging over the doctrine of Ideal Meanings, and their relations to their sensible instances, while the second part points to the even deeper difficulties surrounding those Ideal Meanings considered for themselves, or in their relations to the Principles from which they are to be derived. These Principles are seen, in antinomic fashion, on the one hand in abstract self-containment, and, on the other hand, in rich fulfilment in a whole world of 'generated' Notional Meanings, and Plato thereby both divulges some of the lines of the general 'mathematicization' that he was projecting, and also, by exhibiting the cleavages that it sets up and reconciles, shows up the triviality of the puzzles raised in the first part of the Dialogue. (Our interpretation of the Dialogue is of course controversial.)

Here we also have the *Theaetetus*, harking back in style to the earliest Socratic Dialogues, but laying its stress on structuring categorial notions such as Unity and Plurality, Likeness and Unlikeness, Identity and Difference rather than on the specific notions which they structure, and wrestling through a sensuous model with the terrible problems of Falsehood and Non-being which infect the realm of pure Meanings as much as the realm of sense. The *Sophist* continues this tale, and manages to find room both for eternal Motion and eternal Falsehood in the timelessly true realm of Ideal Meanings, and also establishes the same sort of interpenetration among these Meanings which was once seen as a hallmark of illusion among the qualities of sense. There is also the *Statesman*, with its fascinating doctrine of a total temporal reversal, and of a necessary alternation between periods in which instances approximate closely to, and in which they fall far short of, their ideal originals.

We here also have the *Philebus* in which discussion of purely

Socratic, ethical themes goes hand in hand with an advanced version of Plato's later Theory of Principles, these Principles being however seen, not in their operation on the ideal plane, where they 'generate' eternal Notional Patterns, but in their parallel operation among the qualities and motions of the things of sense. In general, the mathematicizing tendencies of Plato's thought, which lurk in the background in a Dialogue like the *Republic*, become more and more overt and explicit, possibly because Plato had become more critical towards them: in the Second Part of the *Parmenides*, and in the *Philebus*, the tiers of his thinking are practically amalgamated. And Plato's later work is rounded off by the production of the immensely significant *Timaeus*, in which the whole force of the doctrine of Ideal Meanings is brought to bear, in creatively explanatory fashion, on the appearances of our instantial world. Here, veiled in pictures, but shining clearly through them, we see what a world patterned according to Notional Shapes and Numbers really amounts to, and how the 'works of Mind', the patterns of inorganic, organic and psychic excellence, which are the objects of an Ideal Thought or rather Thinkingness, are adjusted to fit in with the fortuitous, instantial exigencies which Plato calls the 'Works of Necessity'. The long series of Plato's fine works ends, however, in anti-climax: if we ignore a very few interesting and brilliant passages, it is hard to see anything but sheer deterioration in Plato's last long work, the *Laws*, published after his death in 347 B.C. All the works listed above, and some others, will be commented upon in the following chapters, so that our present accounts may stand as merely provisional.

We may conclude this chapter with a brief notice of Plato's two abortive excursions to Syracuse in 367–6 and in 361–60. The details of these visits are to be found in Plato's Seventh Epistle, which also contains an important account of his philosophical method. The main body of scholars believes this Letter to be genuine, and it is not easy to know what confabulations we are to embark on if we reject this prime source of Sicilian history over a brief period in the fourth century. Plato was invited by Dion, the son-in-law of the recently dead Dionysius I, to preside over the education of the young Dionysius II, and to make of him a true philosopher-ruler, trained in the mathematical sciences and in the Dialectic of Goodness which is mathematics transfigured:

raised to this elevation, he was to unite Sicily and Italy under one government, and to drive back the barbarous Carthaginians. Plato accepted the invitation, after a great deal of hesitation, because, as he says in his Letter, 'he felt a pressing obligation to go, since if ever a carrying out of his ideas regarding laws and the state were to be undertaken, this was the time' (328b). The noble project was, however, a failure, like the even more noble mathematicization of all Meanings on which it was based. Dionysius was a clever but not sufficiently assiduous student of geometry, he professed a complete understanding of the nature of the Superessential Good which profounder thinkers had, after years of reflection, found wholly incomprehensible, he treated his uncle Dion, who had summoned Plato to Syracuse, with jealous injustice, he lionized Plato but also subjected him to many indignities. On Plato's second visit, it was only through the intervention of Archytas of Tarentum, who had an embassy sent to assist him, that Plato was able to leave Syracuse. These sad incidents were followed by further violence and disaster after Plato's departure, and confirmed his view that only a divine intervention, absent in this case, could make possible the institution of a state founded on a mathematicizing ideology.

II

GENERAL SKETCH OF THE EIDETIC THEORY AND OF ITS ARITHMETIZED VERSION

I

In the present chapter we shall attempt to give a rounded account of the doctrine of 'Eidē' ($\epsilon \check{\iota} \delta \eta$) or Ideal Meanings as presented both in the Platonic Dialogues, and in the Unwritten Doctrines which form their background, and whose contents are known to us through the reports of Aristotle and other writers. There will be a certain necessary dogmatism in our immediate procedure, which will receive further documentation and confirmation in ensuing chapters where we shall comment on the detail of various Platonic writings. It is vain to pretend that our statement of basic Platonic doctrine will be acceptable to all interpreters of Plato, and, in particular, to those who think that the presumptive order in which Plato's Dialogues were written reflects the precise order and development of Plato's full thought. In our view it only reflects his willingness to put more and more of that full thought into writing, in the midst of a mass of fascinating but peripheral discussion. Our aim will be to give a unified, positive presentation rather than one merely ending in queries or alternatives. For it is on the joint force of innumerable mutually confirming indications that a viable interpretation of Plato must rest: there never was, and cannot now be, an authoritative, explicit account of his doctrine.

The Greek word Eidos ($\epsilon \check{\iota} \delta o s$, plural Eidē, $\epsilon \check{\iota} \delta \eta$), as well as the cognate word Idea ($\imath \delta \acute{\epsilon} a$), both derive from the verb $\imath \delta \epsilon \hat{\iota} \nu$ (to see), and had originally the sense of the form or figure, the characteristic look that a thing presents to vision: from this it took on the more abstract senses of 'constitution' or 'nature', and also the sense of the various *species* or sub-varieties of this or that. For Plato an Eidos is a common look or stamp or character which a number of cases, whether seen or thought of, display to the contemplating intelligence, and which is felt to be one and the same in all of them: our experience of an Eidos is an experience of Oneness-in-Manyness, of an identity or unity multiply illustrated, or at least capable of multiple illustration. This common look, stamp or character is what we normally express by a single descriptive word such as 'pious', 'equal', 'human', but Plato is aware that not every word always has as its sense precisely the same character, and he is even doubtful, in the case of at least some meaningful descriptive words or verbal combinations, whether they express any genuine Eidos at all. But whether or not an Eidos is present must be decided by a direct understanding or mental grasp (νοῦς): we must directly encounter the unity, the identity pervading a set of particulars, and it must in fact be the Eidos which makes the things it pervades be of the character or sort that we say they are, i.e. pious, equal, human, and which justifies us in calling them so.

A good expression of what it is to be an Eidos or Idea occurs in the early Dialogue *Euthyphro* (6d, e). Socrates says: 'Do you remember that I did not ask you to tell me one or two out of many pious things, but that very Eidos itself in virtue of which pious things are pious? For you said that there was one Idea in virtue of which impious things are impious and pious things pious. . . . Tell me therefore what this Idea itself is, that, looking at it, and using it as a paradigm, I may declare what is such, if done by you or another, to be pious, and if not such, deny it to be pious'. It is very possible that Socrates himself used 'Eidos' or 'Idea' in this manner, but, if not a user of the word, he was certainly acquainted with what it stands for, and with the unique experience which brings it before the mind. Some, it would seem, have small aptitude for the experience in question, but Socrates and Plato, and in modern time Moore, Husserl and others, were plainly not of their number. For some thinkers indeed a 'mere meaning' is a more genuine object of contemplation than a thing of sense.

An Eidos is not by Plato taken to be some sort of subjective distillation, varying from man to man, and not having *being* in the fullest sense of the word: things of themselves, we read in the *Cratylus*, 356 d, e, 'have their own firm essence, not relative to us, nor produced nor dragged hither and yon by our imaginations, but of themselves and by nature stand related to their essence'. Even the thought that apprehends and enjoys an Eidos, though related to it in the most intimate and necessary manner, is not thought by Plato (as it later was by Aristotle) to achieve identity with it, much less to constitute it or make it: the Eidos is revealed in appropriate acts of thinking, which parallel some of its structure, but the revelation can still be distinguished from the thing revealed (see for example Epistle VII, 42a). Eide are likewise approached through names and the stringing of names together in ordered speech, and it is not therefore wrong to refer to them as 'Ideal Meanings', as we did for convenience in the previous chapter. But Eide are more than the senses of words or expressions, and are none other than the firm Natures which the application of words to cases brings to mind, and when words thus bring these Natures to mind, the Natures alone lend sense to the words. Eide, in fact, are for Plato the heritors of Eleatic being: they are the true self-constant things which make discourse and judgment possible, and in default of which we should have nothing definite to talk or think about, and no possibility even of consummating an act of speaking or thinking or knowing.

Even if the senses reflect only the varied clash of the world on our bodies, which is only by accident selfsame from one instant to another, and even if what they put before us is unintelligibly qualitative, or oscillates restlessly from type to type, or combines divergent types in what can only be characterized as an absurd manner – what exhibits unity also exhibits plurality, etc., etc. – still it remains possible to think of some types that have been thus perishingly illustrated, and to recur to the thought of them on many occasions, and to prise them loose from what the senses offer us in profusion and confusion, so as to have before us distinct Natures which have nothing confused or fluctuating and unintelligibly qualitative about them at all. The Eide thus discriminated are the only firm being with which we are acquainted, and they alone confer what imperfect approach to firm being can be attributed to other entities, and they alone enable us to have such fluctuating and imperfect knowledge as we can have even of such other entities.

The fact that Plato is willing to make the Eide (and, later, what they ultimately spring from) the only absolutely real entities that there are, shows up the deep wrongness of the characteristic Aristotelian interpretation and criticism which has coloured practically all subsequent evaluations of Platonism. In the Aristotelian ontology, in at least a representative section of its divergently tending utterances, the individual instances of sorts or species – this man, that dog, that star, etc., etc. – are certainly given a privileged ontological status. They alone *are* in an absolutely straightforward and primary sense, whereas other things only *are* in a sense which derives from their primary being, and which is altogether 'parasitic' upon it. (We are using some modern terms, but are not misrepresenting ancient thought.) Thus qualities may be said to *be* in so far as individual members of species are thus and thus qualified, quantities and relations may be said to *be* in so far as individual members of species are thus and thus quantified and related and so on. Having this sort of view of what absolutely is, Aristotle could only think of Plato, in his doctrine of Eide, as positing the existence of a *second* world of quasi-individual entities, a world necessarily separate from this world since not sharing all of its properties, and merely increasing the population of the total cosmos without explaining what was already there. In addition to equals there was the Equal Itself or the Eidos of Absolute Equality, in addition to dogs there was What-it-was-to-be-a-dog or The Dog as Such and so on. Aristotle very properly objected that other-world entities thus conceived could have nothing to do with the coming into being or the active functioning of this-world things. Even if the things in our world were more or less exact replicas of the Things Yonder, the latter need not therefore have anything to do with their being or origin, any more than a man who happened to resemble Socrates need have been begotten by Socrates or modelled on Socrates by someone. And our knowledge of the things in this world, whether as regards their intrinsic nature or their origin, would not be assisted by the knowledge of these other-world duplicates that merely corresponded to them. There would further be a danger, if this world of duplicates were once admitted, that the postulation of further duplicates would be in order and without end, the famous argument of the Third Man (or one of its forms) which, with the arguments *for* the being of the Eide, was among the commonplaces of Academic discussion. The realm of the Eide will in fact readily become rent with the same schisms which already separate it from the realm of the senses, since Eide are both specific cases, and also in some cases instances, of higher Eide. Moreover to talk of 'participation' or 'presence' or 'causation' or 'modelling' where such separated entities are concerned is merely to charm men with pictures instead of satisfying them with thoughts.

The arguments in this famous polemic, first stated in Aristotle's Academic treatise *On the Ideas* and briefly summarized in two places in the *Metaphysics* (I, 9 and XIII, 4, 5), and thereafter wearisomely repeated and endorsed throughout the history of philosophy, are, however, among the most total *ignorationes elenchi* in the whole of philosophical history. For they assume that Plato believed, in full seriousness, in a world of firmly identical, particular existents, sorted into classes by their intrinsic character and behaviour, and that he then gratuitously invented a second world of detached Eide to take care of their common features (whether for existence or for knowledge) without seeing that these Eide could do nothing towards fulfilling such an absurd task. Whereas the whole thrust of Platonism (despite its manifold metaphors), the thrust derived from its origin in the flux-theory of Heraclitus and Cratylus, and from its yearning towards a reformed version of Eleatic constancy, was to *deny* that there was anything genuinely seizable and knowable, or anything truly causative and explanatory, in the flowing realm of particular things and matters of fact as such: what was seizable, what was knowable, what could truly imprint itself on and maintain itself in flux, and give purchase to our recognition, was always an Eidos, a nature or constitutive pattern, and it was only because our minds realized or maintained a corresponding cognitive pattern that they could understand or know anything, even concerning the realm of flux. And this Eidos always had the firmness, the immunity from change, which its embodiments never could have, and it was therefore Eide, and only Eide, that could be identified on many occasions and by many individual thinkers, and identified in acts that themselves embodied unchanging, repeatable patterns of understanding and insight.

We might exaggerate the central point of Platonism and say that for Plato nothing but Ideas existed: in the strict sense of 'existence', this was really for him (as in a different sense for Berkeley) the 'obvious though amazing truth'. He was not, however, willing to go as far as the Eleatics and make the changeable sense-world exist only in the 'Opinion of Mortals'. It had to have being *of a sort*, even if not the fully-fledged being of the Eide, just as Aristotle had to give qualities, quantities etc. being of a sort, though not the primary, fully-fledged being of an individual thing or of its specific nature. This being of a sort becomes, as the sequence of Dialogues progresses, a status that Plato locates halfway *between* Absolute Being and Absolute Nothingness: 'the many things thought by the many regarding beauty and the rest roll around somewhere halfway between what is not and what purely is' (*Republic*, 479d). In the *Timaeus* (28a) this status is said to be that of something always in process of arising and being destroyed, and never (unlike the Eide) absolutely there at all. This notion of a status intermediate between Being and Non-being only makes sense if we realize it to be an essentially *dependent*, a *parasitic* status: changeable, sensible things are nothing *in themselves*, they only have being in the sense of embodying, multiply mirroring or illustrating, imperfectly and dispersedly sharing in, or, as we should now say, *instantiating* an Eidos or set of Eide. All that there really is to instances is the fact of instantiation, of which Eide are really the sole logical subjects: instances are really instantiations, things undergone by the Eide, mere modalities *of* them. Though Plato may not precisely use this language, such is the logical purport of what he does say.

The total dependence on the Eide of changing sensibles is moreover brought out by that doctrine of the *causality* of the Eide which Aristotle finds so completely objectionable. The Eide *make* changing sensibles be what they are, they are the only true causes of any sensible thing's being what it is (*Phaedo*, 100d), and whatever other factors enter into the causation of the being so-and-so of anything are only subsidiary, occasional, ancillary. Man may beget man, to use the well-worn Aristotelian slogan, but the true begetter of man is the Eidos of humanity, and behind this that Intelligible Animality on which the whole cosmos was shaped in the *Timaeus*, and behind that perhaps Life Itself, and the Goodness or Unity that is beyond life. In this long line of ancestry, one's instantial father has a very humble last place. Souls are likewise the sources of motion in the cosmos, but souls, we know, are a mere structure of harmonic and other ratios, and what they effect in the world likewise stems from a supra-instantial original. There is, indeed, in the *Timaeus*, the great empty receptacle of Space, the seat of strange shakings and other irregular disturbances, in which the images of the Eide appear distortedly: this it might seem is a causative factor distinct from the Eide, and its strange shakings may well be privy to those 'Works of Necessity' with which the causality of the Eide has, positively or negatively, always to reckon. But this empty Space or Mirror of Becoming is by Plato accorded a nullity even more profound than that of the changing sensibles: for it is said to be arrived at by a species of bastard reasoning, and to be no fit object of faith (*Timaeus*, 52b), so that it seems indistinguishable from the utter Non-being which in the *Republic* serves as the object for a wholly unknowing state of mind (*Republic*, 478c), a diagnosis confirmed by what Aristotle says at various points in the *Metaphysics*. The ontology of Plato accepts, in fact, two sorts of ontological status for what contrasts with the only true being, that of the Eide, and which, as we would say, are necessary to make it meaningful: the status of what *utterly* is not, on the one hand, i.e. the sheer emptiness which contrasts with the Eide, and which is also the mere possibility of all instances, and the status of what only *relatively* is not, on the other, the imperfect instances which hang about the Eide and which only approximately illustrate them. There is strong evidence, based on a passage in Sextus Empiricus (*Against the Mathematicians*, 263–75) which is backed up by a fragmentary citation from Hermodorus, a friend of Plato (Simplicius on the *Physics*, 247–8, Diels), that Plato believed in precisely these three categories: the being of what is conceived absolutely (ἀπολύτως) or for itself (καθ' ἑαυτό), the being of what is conceived oppositely (ἐξ ἐναντιώσεως) and the being of what is conceived only relatively (πρός τι). These passages will be considered below (pp. 73–6) and will be connected with the distinctions we are at present establishing. Our interpretation does not, however, rest on isolated passages, whether early or late: it is plain from the whole drift of innumerable statements that for Plato instances are merely accidental modalities of the Eide, which derive all their force and substance from the latter, while in their mere possibility they provide the element of sheer Otherness and Inauthenticity in contrast with which the Eide appear as alone truly authentic. These may not be modern ways of thinking, but we shall not get far in our understanding of Platonism if we are incapable of entering into them.

Since sensible changing things have this merely peripheral, attributive and dependent ontological status in relation to Eide, it is plain that the much-asked Aristotelian questions as to whether the latter exist *in* their instances or *apart from these* in a world of their own, are questions that cannot, except in a mere skirmish of metaphor, be raised at all. Where what one is supposed to be present *in*, or *apart from*, only exists in a manner of speaking and is really only one's own contingent, surface modality, one cannot properly be said to exist in it or apart from it, or rather *both* of these things can with a suitable grain of salt be said. Sensible things are Eide inadequately, multiply and changeably mirrored, shared in or carried into effect, but Eide have in addition a being for themselves, their being in fact the Natures or Essences that they are, and are not as such shared in by, or present in, anything. But if one asks whether an Eidos instantiated is the same or different from an Eidos as it in itself is, or whether an Eidos instantiated here or now, is the same or different from that Eidos instantiated there and then, the answer is of course that it is and it isn't, according to the inappropriate analogy one cares to use, or the aspect of the matter on which one chooses to insist. This we shall argue is the true moral of the First Part of the Dialogue *Parmenides*, in which the clash of mature Platonic wisdom with the young, logic-chopping wits of the Academy is vividly portrayed.

Plato at no time gives us a clear explanation of the why and the how of instantiation, except to project before us a number of pictures whose variety really shows that any question as to this why and how is really senseless and inadmissible. God is said in the *Timaeus* to have constructed the world of instances out of an absence of envy and a desire to make everything as excellent as possible. Here we have, when pictures are stripped away, the conception of an instantial status which stands in some sort of necessary relation of contrast to the status of the Eide, which is capable of falling short of the latter in various ways, but also of approximating to the latter, and we have also the conception of an eternal, necessary *nisus* seeking to bring the Instantial into line with the Eidetic, making the former come to be, or more nearly come to be, what the latter in its eternal perfection always is. Of this vision of how things are no explanation is offered: this (we may say) is how things are and can only be. And, as to the relations between Eide and their instances, Plato provides a number of detailed metaphors, some suggesting 'immanence', some 'transcendence', some an active making and some a more mysterious 'luring' or inspirational influence, and so on. What these various metaphors show is that Plato does not really care how instantiation is pictured: instantiation is a 'last thing' which can be elucidated for the mind, not made vivid to the imagination. There is the family of metaphors which suggest the total otherness and beyondness of the Eide, their existence by themselves or yonder or in a heavenly or supra-heavenly place, and which make instances mere icons or likenesses of these transcendent existences, things which in fact only *try* or want to be like them, without ever being capable of being so. This type of talk is summed up under the rubric of Mimesis or Imitation, and is said by Aristotle to have been borrowed from the Pythagoreans, who thought of the whole Cosmos as 'modelled upon numbers', and in fact so well modelled as to be itself 'a harmony and a number'. This Pythagorean way of conceiving the relation of Eide to instances obviously has its justification: intimate and necessary as is the relation between Being Just as Such and the manifold cases of being just, there is also a great gulf set between them, since the primary way in which being just is just, and the secondary, derivative way in which a case of justice is just, are obviously irreducible to one another. And to this gulf of ontological type may of course be added the gulf between the perfection of Justice Itself, and the mere approach to perfect instantiation of such perfection in every case of so-called 'justice'.

Another way of conceiving the relation of sensible instances to Eide is covered by a family of terms such as 'sharing', 'possession', 'participation', 'communion' etc. The term Methexis, Participation, has been used to cover them all. They connote a closer relation of the Instance to the Eidos, and are therefore more truly Platonic than the Pythagorean Mimesis: the Instance really has something of the Eidos in it, if not the Eidos in its full purity, or as it is in and for itself. This metaphor can be travestied by imagining the Eidos to be cut up into little parts in the instantial multiplication. We see from the *Parmenides* how the logicians of the Academy exploited these absurdities to the full. A yet closer relation of Eidos to instance is achieved in cases where Plato talks of the Eide as being 'present in', 'coming to be in', 'coming to be added to', or 'supervening upon', or 'entering into' their instances, to all of which the term Parousia, Real Presence, seems appropriate. Here we have a doctrine of an indwelling presence which with a little pressing could become a doctrine of identity: the Instance *is* the Eidos present or instantiated. A retreat to a somewhat more eminent distance is involved in the doctrine of the Eide as the true causes ($\alpha\dot{\iota}\tau\dot{\iota}\alpha\iota$) which impart characters to their instances, which make them human or just or liquid or odd or living etc. This doctrine of eidetic causality is the foundation of the Aristotelian notion of formal causes which, with material, efficient and final causes, exhaust the Aristotelian theory of explanation. Only whereas, in the Aristotelian theory, the formal cause (in ordinary cases) only effects results *in virtue* of its incarnation in instances, Plato's Eide are themselves the ultimate causes of their own incarnation in instances, and are in fact the only truly efficient causes that there are or can be.

If instances thus are approximations to, or participations in, or the real presences or the causal results of their Eide, they can also be regarded from points of view in which their *difference* from their Eide is emphasized. The Eide are first of all, as seen above, predicable *of themselves* in a true or primary manner to which the manner in which they are predicable of their instances is essentially secondary and derivative. (Not, we may stress, the other way round, as in modern accounts where instances of Justice are taken to be just in the primary manner, and the self-predication of Justice of Justice is thought to be a 'confused' misapplication of this primary predication, as if Plato was silly enough to think of Justice Itself, which is just in the sense of simply *being* Justice, as merely another extraordinary *case* of Justice. Identity with Justice, is, however, the transcendent limit of being instantially just, in a logic which regards Identity as in series with, and yet also as a transcendent limit to, the ordinary copulative 'is'. That Plato did not make the confusion of which he is accused is shown, for example, in his insistence that the eidetic Number Three does not, like its instances, contain three members, but is what it is to have them.

Instantiation is, further, actually or potentially *multiple* where the Eidos instantiated cannot be other than single, and it is actually or potentially *changeable* while it does not make sense to conceive of the Eidos itself as changing into anything other or different. And these possibilities of multiplication and change are, in the mature Dialogue *Timaeus*, connected with the mysterious something called Time, which is change reduced to, or at least documented by, recurring measures dependent on the regular motions of the heavens, in which we have a 'moving image of eternity'. (We shall see reason to maintain that Space and Time are, considered in the full light of everything Plato says of them, little more than what, with some paradox, we may call Instantiality as Such.) The Instance is further distinguished from the Eidos by its actual or potential *sensuousness* or *qualitativeness*: it can reveal itself in qualities which represent the changing clash of external things on our sense-organs, and which, try as we will, we cannot wholly reduce to anything intelligible. The Eidos, on the other hand, is something that we can understand with our minds, that we may be incited to conceive by the senses, but which involves constancies of Measure and Number which the senses cannot present adequately: it is this connection of the Eide with pure, non-sensuous thought that in the end led Plato to give a purely mathematical account of them.

But not only are the instantiations of Eide thus multiple, localized, changeable and sensuous: they also involve another sort of multiplicity, since a given localized, changeable, sensuous thing may instantiate *many* Eide, giving them a union with one another which is as little essential as their instantial multiplicity. As put in *Republic*, 476a, 'each Eidos itself is one, but by the apparent communion with actions, bodies *and one another* which is everywhere occurring, they each seem to be many'. Eide have, of course, many necessary communions with one another, as Unity imports Being, or Fieriness Heat, but the majority of instantial connections are not of this character, and are matters of Chance Fact, which is always changing and which also differs from case to case. And not only are instantial conjunctions thus variable, but they also in many cases involve something which comes close to conflict or inconsistency: thus the many equals, looked at a little narrowly, betray shimmering side-flashes of inequality, while the many units similarly scrutinized reveal hidden seams of disunity definitely excluded by the notion of Unity as Such (see *Republic*, 523–4). It is, in fact, not merely the contingency, but the inner contrariety of the Instantial that leads our minds upwards to the Eide, which are each always one single, uniform, undiluted thought-appearance, not flashing iridescently from semblance to semblance, but always presenting the same notional face to our thought. And the instantiation of Eide is in many cases not merely ambiguous but definitely defective: instances fall short of the 'Natures' under which we must none the less range them, and to which, in some metaphorical sense, they may be said to 'aspire' (see for example *Phaedo*, 74–5). The whole instantial realm is, in virtue of being instantial, full of declensions and deviations from set ideals: the stars fail to arrive on schedule (*Republic*, 530a), the shapes of the atoms are in certain cases disrupted or distorted (*Timaeus*, 81), and men and cities obviously often fail to live up to the ideal pattern of Justice. Excess and defect, the going beyond the ideal, beyond the equalizing, just-right standard in one direction or another, are in fact a prime mark of the Instance, though we shall argue later that such a prime mark has a secondary place even among the Eide.

II

It would have been a strange thing if Plato, who derived his first impulse towards the eidetic theory from the Socratic examination of the virtues, and who was further moved in its direction by a form of Eleaticism (the Megarian) which was itself Socratically influenced, identifying its unchanging unified Being with the Socratic Good, should not have carried over an ethical or value-interest into his Eidos-theory. The Eide have in fact always a strain of the Good about them: if we speak of them as 'Ideal Meanings', then they are, in the modern phrase, cases of evaluative as well as descriptive meaning. (Though to Plato the two sorts of meaning would have seemed so deeply welded together that he would have been incapable of drawing the modern distinction.) The Eide most saliently mentioned in the best known Platonic Dialogues are in fact either the virtues of Justice, Piety etc.

studied in the Socratic investigations, or mathematical patterns characterized by superior cognitive eligibility from *our* point of view, as they are also characterized by simplicity, unity-in-variety and 'Goodness of Form' from their own. The Unit, the Integers and their essential properties, the Straight Line, the Right Angle and the various simpler sorts of angle, the Arithmetical, Geometrical and Harmonic Ratios, the regular Figures and Solids: these are the prime candidates for the status of Eide rather than the infinitely various and twisted structures of the instantial world. If the strictly ethical Eide are the patterns of Goodness for men and societies, the mathematical Eide are plainly a set of models for things in Space and also in Time (the ideal Velocities of the heavenly bodies to which they do not always perfectly conform). Eide of natural species, inorganic and organic, are less unequivocally in evidence in the early Dialogues, and there is some question about them even in a Dialogue like the *Parmenides*: in the *Timaeus*, however, they assume pride of place, particularly the Eide of living creatures, and there is a passage in Aristotle (*Metaphysics*, 1070a 13–19) which confirms the priority of the Eide of living creatures. To talk of an Eidos is clearly, in almost all cases, to talk of a model of perfection, something which not only *is* in some absolute sense, but which also is, in some absolute sense, beautiful or good. The whole account in the *Timaeus* of the construction of the instantial world as the best possible approximation to the best and most beautiful of originals, implies that the ideal model on which it was constructed was good and pure throughout, and did not contain all the defective and deviant forms of which the realm of instantiation is full. And the *Timaeus* is here in harmony with such an earlier Dialogue as the *Phaedo*, where explanation by Eide is said to be a secondary substitute (δεύτερος πλοῦς) for explanation by way of the Best, or with the *Republic* where the being of all the Eide is said to owe its genesis to the Idea of the *Good*. These passages imply that the Eide are specifications of Goodness, particular ways of being good. Even the Eide of artefacts mentioned in the Dialogues, beds, shuttles, etc., are always the Eide of good and useful objects, and not of broken-down appliances or chance assemblages of items of which no good use can be made.

There was, however, a tradition in the Academy, probably dominant when Aristotle joined it, and given great prominence in his criticisms of Platonism (see Appendix I, 11), according to which there were Eide, intelligible models or patterns, only in the case of certain sorts of privileged and excellent things in the world: of other things there were no such intelligible patterns, and they existed and were understood only as failing to embody certain ideal patterns, or as embodying them imperfectly, or as embodying them impurely or confusedly and so on. They would represent the divergence of the Instantial from the Eidetic order, or the divergence of Imagination and Perception and Sophistical Persuasion from True Insight, rather than anything genuinely rooted in the Eidetic Order. A classical exposition of this tradition occurs in the comments of the fifth-century Academic Scholarch Syrianus, the predecessor of Proclus, on certain relevant statements by Aristotle in *Metaphysics*, 1078b 32 and elsewhere. (See last two excerpts in Appendix I). Syrianus tells us that there were held to be no Eide of (1) Bad or Base things, these being what they are by departure from Eide; nor of (2) Negations, since these overrun the eidetic boundaries which set things apart from other things; nor of (3) Changeables, which must derive their changes from moving causes and not from unmoving Eide; nor of (4) Parts which are not themselves wholes, such as hands, heads or fingers; nor of (5) Sensible Qualities such as sweetness and whiteness (in their case what is eidetic is a λόγος or Ratio); nor of (6) Composites such as Being a Wise Man – Aristotle certainly took up this point; nor of (7) Hybrids, such as mules or grafted trees; nor of (8) Imitative Arts whose products are only of use in this life; nor of (9) the outcomes of arbitrary choices or chance combinations of factors. The reasons for denying Eide to these nine classes of instances is plain: they can be regarded as having a defective or multiple eidetic allegiance. And Syrianus goes on to hold that there were only Eide of perfect substances (e.g. Man), and of what contributes to their natural state (e.g. Wisdom). Elsewhere he denies the Eide of accidental Relations (e.g. right and left) and of purely bodily attributes. The programme of exclusions agrees with Aristotle's statements that independent Eide were denied of the parts and even elements of natural substances (*Metaphysics*, 1070a), of Relations (*Metaphysics*, 990b), and of artefacts such as a house or a ring (*Metaphysics*, 991b).

With this extremely selective, dualistic opinion Plato would not seem to have finally aligned himself, and it is in fact clear that it could not recommend itself to anyone who carefully thought out the implications of an eidetic theory like his. For it is plain that each form of ethical or ontological excellence is necessarily two-edged: it is what it is only by excluding or ruling out what it is not at all, or what, while not entirely opposed to it, none the less falls short of it in certain definite manners or directions. A realm of Ideal Contents from which negation and defect and artificial composition were excluded, would be a realm of contents full of lamentable gaps, and forming no ordered, total scheme of thought-possibilities. It would also be a realm which only made sense in *conjunction* with that experience of changeable, instantial things which it was introduced exhaustively to explain. And Plato in fact shows his sensitiveness to the badness of such selectivity by often in the Dialogues mentioning Eide of Impiety, Injustice and other patterns of defect, always, however, in close conjunction with the accompanying excellences. (See, for example, the passage from the *Euthyphro* quoted above, p. 30.) And there is, of course, a too much quoted because rather casual passage in *Republic*, X, 596a, where it is suggested that there must be an Eidos corresponding to *any* name that we happen to apply generally, a suggestion that however conflicts with the immense solemnities needed for the postulation of an Eidos of this or that, for example Lines, Angles etc., in an earlier part of the Dialogue (*Republic*, 510c). That evil and defect have a place in the realm of the Eide is further shown by the prominence there of Numbers, the very type of instantiation rather than eidetic unity, and, in the later development of the eidetic theory, the location in the realm of the Eide of a material Principle of Indefinite Quantity or Excess and Defect, through the limitation of which by a principle of Unity the Eide are produced. And if one desires further evidence from the Dialogues one has only to consider the argument in *Republic*, 333e–334b to the effect that knowledge is always of opposites – to know how to keep is to know how to steal – a principle afterwards taken over by Aristotle and generally credited to him, but undoubtedly Socratic and Platonic, and pointing to the necessary presence of what we may call un-Forms as foils or contrasts to the Forms or Eide. And the long treatment of the perversions of the State in the *Republic*, a treatment as eidetic as anything in Plato, shows also how the perversions of political Justice are but the shadow cast by its substance. The late Dialogue *Sophist*, too, can be regarded as dwelling on the same point: that every eidetic Nature is what it is by excluding what it is not, and this gives false connections a place even among the august Eide, a place which makes it possible for a Sophist to persuade us that a Nature or Eidos includes what it really excludes, so that we may end, e.g., by believing Justice to be the interest of the stronger, and so on.

The practice of Plato, we may say, rather than his official utterances, plainly shows that he admitted a duality of membership in the realm of Eide. This realm embraced, on the one hand, patterns of characteristic excellence and simplicity and good form – the Straight, the Single, the Just, the Harmonically Proportioned etc. – to which eidetic status was unhesitatingly accorded, but it also embraced patterns of more dubious lineage – the Deviant, the Hybrid, the Intermediate, the Fragmentary, the Composite, the Artificial, the merely Negative, etc., etc. – whose claim to an eidetic status was plainly less evident. If we admit such things at all, they will be admitted as the Opposites of the Eide, or as the Intermediates between them, or as the imperfect Approximations to them, or as mere Admixtures of them, etc., etc.: their position will be essentially parasitic and derivative. Their status in the ideal realm is, if one likes, that of prisoners handcuffed between warders, or of vulgarisms and solecisms kept out of certain styles of diction: in the realm of instantiation, however, these prisoners and these solecisms achieve their freedom, it being the distinguishing prerogative of the Instance that it can deviate from its Type. In a sense therefore there are Eide of everything, and in a sense only of certain privileged cases of excellence. Such detailed questions, then, as whether or not Plato believed in Eide of artificial objects themselves become artificial: very probably, since the State is a case of excellence and corresponds to a prime Eidos, the various necessary instruments of civilized social life, such as knives, beds etc., correspond to prime Eide, while some intensely arbitrary and defective artefacts have merely an interstitial position in the Eidetic Order. They are deviant, wanton forms that civilized, social living *can* take, but does not typically and excellently take, much as certain arbitrary and ugly musical chords and intervals have an interstitial place among the regular musical harmonies. In such a way we can understand *both* the marriage of the Eide to the excellent, and their necessary coverage of anything and everything: in being married to the former, they also necessarily cover the latter. All this is not, however, mere interpretation, but is to some extent documented by the passages (from Sextus Empiricus and Simplicius) referred to previously, the outcome of which arguably is that Plato believed in the three basic categories of what exists absolutely (ἀπολύτως) or for itself (i.e. the prime Eide), of what exists merely *in opposition* to such Eide, and of what exists merely *in relation* to such Eide (the various forms of the Intermediate and the Defective). The passages in question, which involve mathematical considerations, will be dealt with below (pp. 73-6).

If the Eide have therefore a firm and necessary marriage to Value or Goodness, it is equally plain that they have a firm and necessary marriage to System. They may be distinct pieces of pure significance, each representing an ideal character in its purity, and so unlocalized, changeless, self-identical in their manifestations, and more truly accessible to pure understanding and thought than to the confused, variable, instantially conditioned commerce of the senses. But these pieces of pure significance cannot be separated islands, but must be built together into a complete continent of sense, bound together by relations other than those that derive from joint instantiation. It cannot be doubted that in this relation of the Eide to one another that of Species to Genus must be central: the same notion of the One-over-many which led to the Eide, must of necessity lead on from the more specific Eide to the more generic ones. And just as the specific Eide, though having their pure Being-on-their-own which transcends instantiation, and also being what they are in a manner to which an instance can only approximate, none the less are present in, are genuinely shared by, and are causally active in their instances, so the generic Eide may be taken to be both beyond and yet also actively present in their Species, and so that one does not progress to what is ontologically more derivative and parasitic as one rises from the more specific to the more generic, but rather progresses to what is more substantial and ontologically prior. For an instantialist like Aristotle, the most specific account of the nature of anything comes closest to what is primarily real, whereas the most generic is also the most remote from reality: the former is also the richest in content, and the latter the poorest and thinnest. Whereas, for one who thinks eidetically, the disjunctive mode in which the Genus branches out into its various Species is not inferior to the conjunctive mode in which the Species or the Instance embraces its various characters, and in fact embraces a much richer range of variety. In *virtue*, in fact, the Genus covers all that is covered by the Species and the Instance, and very much more besides.

And that Plato thought in this generically oriented manner cannot be in doubt. For in the *Republic* he makes the Idea of Good, a notion so purely generic as hardly to count as an Eidos at all, and afterwards promoted from the ranks of the Eide to the more august standing of a Principle, none the less the active source of all the Eide and of all the knowledge that can be had of them. Plainly the Idea of Good transcends all the Eide in the richness of its efficacy. And in the much later Dialogue *Timaeus* the whole sensible Cosmos is seen as instantiating an intelligible Cosmos which is also a Living Creatureliness *in genere*, in which all forms of Living Creature are systematically contained. For Plato, accordingly, we do not lose by going up, in classificatory ascent, from the Species to the Genus: we rather achieve the synoptic, dialectical view of the affinity of all things with one another, and with the nature of Being, which is spoken of in *Republic*, 537c. And Plato's preoccupation with what is generic, must necessarily have made him look in the direction of a single, supremely generic Nature, a descendant of Socratic Goodness and Eleatic Unity, however much he may afterwards have been led to place that Nature beyond, rather than in, the Eidetic Order. And in such a grasp of what is generic, a capacity to go down to more specific levels would of necessity be involved, since to know the Genus is to know it as the source of all the Species into which it can be differentiated, and to know all this in a purely eidetic, or, as we should now say, *a priori* manner. Empirically known Species can be fitted into the eidetic specification of a Genus, but their place in that order could not be established empirically. One of the major events in the history of the Academy must have been the proof by Theaetetus that there are five and only five Regular Solids, the Tetrahedron, the Cube, the Octahedron, the Dodecahedron and the Icosahedron. This, the perfect articulation of a generic Eidos into its Species, is obviously the exemplar which Plato hoped to extend to any and every territory of thought, whether physical, biological, psychological, ethical, political or theological. It is a far nobler programme than any-thing merely empirical, though it may take its initial material from experience, and it is the interpretative base of the *Phaedo*, the *Republic*, the *Phaedrus*, the *Parmenides*, the *Timaeus*, the *Sophist*, the *Statesman* and the *Philebus*, though not all have found it there.

There seems little doubt, therefore, that the system of Eide must at all stages of Plato's thought have been that of a classi-ficatory hierarchy, ranging from patterns of the most specific to patterns of the most generic, and tending towards unity at the summit, as it also tended to number and variety at the lower levels. Propositions, theorems, arguments, inferences might be necessary to establish the whole hierarchy or to work out its details, but they were not themselves the central themes of Plato's thought: they had, in fact, to wait for their full recognition till the work of Bolzano in the nineteenth century. Nor had Plato even the interest in the interrelations of assertions that was afterwards to be elaborated in the Aristotelian theory of Demon-strative Science or ἐπιστήμη. The centre of Platonic interest lay throughout in the Eide: what else was true, or what had to be true, of all their instances was the subject-matter of the mathe-matical and other sciences, not of the eidetic Dialectic which illuminated their concepts. It is therefore quite wrong to imagine that Plato had at any time the thematic interest in deduction and deductive systems which some have read, for example, into the accounts of Dialectic in the *Republic*. It is of course true that Plato in later life wrote Dialogues that were explicitly about classification and its implications: the *Sophist*, *Statesman* and *Philebus* are signal in this. But only a fixed determination to force a 'development' on the organically related notions in Plato's outlook, would deny that these classificatory notions were present at an earlier period – they are explicit in the *Phaedrus* – or would hold that Plato, who had heard Socrates reducing the virtues to subspecies of a single Knowledge which was also Goodness, and who believed that Knowledge consisted in finding a λόγος or eidetic characterization of something in which Genus and Species certainly figured, and who had been an intimate of Euclides and Hermogenes with their belief in a Unity which was also Being and Goodness, should have rested content with a realm of isolated Meanings, externally held together by a mere set of axioms or demonstrated theorems. Plato certainly had a place for axioms and demonstrations in his total view of Knowledge, but it was more in the explicitly mathematical than in the philosophical realm. The philosophical task *par excellence* was to take the various Eide which occur in the mathematical and other sciences, and which are for those sciences 'primitive', and to show how all of them were but specifications of more generic Eide, differentiated in this way or that, and so make progress towards some supremely generic Eidos or Eide, from which one could then go down, not along one, but a thousand different and divergent ladders, till one was back at the level of not further specifiable Eide, beneath which would be only those chance combinations of characters which we find in the vanishing things of sense. In this passage up and down, and also no doubt from side to side at various levels, the whole range of ideal possibilities was to be exhaustively mapped, and in all of it, no doubt, one would only have differentiations of Goodness, the Defective or Evil having a place in the hierarchy merely as something which is *not* part of it, and which, by being thus excluded, is also after a fashion comprehended. In all this classificatory arrangement deductive argument would only have served to place the Eide in the hierarchy, and was only a means to eidetic classification, and not of interest for its own sake. And in many cases intuition, rather than proof, would have been all that could be mustered in the construction of the hierarchy, and sometimes no doubt Plato, like his pupil Aristotle, based his postulations of Eide on intimations gotten from the vanishing things of sense, as in those biological classifications in which we know that the Academy engaged. Ideally, however, all this was to be replaced by a rigorous establishment that these were all the Eide there were or could be, and it must have been the demand for such rigour that drove Plato in the direction of a complete mathematicization of all the Eide.

In the dialectical arrangement of the Eide it is important that we should not import notions of mutual exclusion borrowed from the things of sense. Plato may at times have set something of a gulf between the Eide and their sensible instances, but there is nowhere a similar gulf set or implied between Eidos and Eidos, though some have held that Plato meant there to be one. Plato never could have argued as does Aristotle in *Metaphysics*, 991a, that if there is a distinct Eidos of the two-footed in general, it cannot be the same as the two-footedness which enters into the nature of Man. Plato did indeed hold that there was a confused, contingent, joint presence of Eide in an instance to which there is nothing parallel in the relations of Eide among themselves. Eide are not eidetically associated in the external and contingent manner in which a man seems great or small in different contexts, or exemplifies unity from one chosen point of view and plurality from another (see for example, *Parmenides*, 129). But this does not mean that Eide do not have genuine eidetic associations, whether as entering into one another as components, or as conjoined with other Eide in compound Eide, or as participating in other Eide in the sense of instantiating them. All these manifold eidetic relations are explored in mature dialogues like the *Parmenides* and the *Sophist*, and are shown to involve paradoxes which have only an appearance of self-contradiction, though seemingly similar paradoxes may have established the genuinely self-contradictory and so merely apparent character of the things of sense. The Eide may therefore have many forms of overlap or communion with one another, and may have one form of overlap or communion with one another while not having another form, and so on, all of which will readily engender an appearance of self-contradiction which the dialectician must learn to discount. All this has been viewed as a late piece of Platonic wisdom, Plato having previously held to a mutual separation of the Eide parallel to their strict separation from the things of sense. Arguably, however, both these types of separation were the invention of groups of thinkers in the Academy who, whether of the Eidetic Right or the Instantialist Left, felt forced to think of the Eide on an analogy with the mutually external things of sense. This, however, could never have been the tendency of Plato, nor of anyone capable of genuine eidetic experience, and these controversies merely served to provoke him to a clearer and more carefully qualified expression of the Unity-in-plurality which was always basic to his thought.

Three points in the eidetic theory remain to be considered before we pass on to the arithmetized version of the theory. The first concerns the increasing 'concreteness' or richness of content of the Eide as Plato meditated longer and longer on the problem of what sorts he should allow them to be. As his thought developed, he became less and less disposed to number highly abstract notions like Equality or Unity or Difference among the prime Eide: in so far as they were considered, they were dealt with in the higher-order Stoicheiology or Theory of Elements, which studied the organizing Principles of the Eide rather than the Eide themselves. What was a prime Eidos then tended to become a fully rounded natural pattern, such as Being a Man, or Being a Plant, or Being a Particle of Fire or Water. And the biological patterns began to take precedence over the purely physical patterns, the 'Works of Necessity', in which no goodness or purpose is dominant, being subordinated to the Works of Mind in which goodness and purpose are supreme. That Plato's eidetic doctrine developed in this manner is clear not only from a previously mentioned passage of Aristotle (*Metaphysics*, 1070a 13–19), but from the whole drift of a Dialogue like the *Timaeus*, where the sensible cosmos is modelled on an 'intelligible living creature' in whose generic embrace, as in a Noah's ark, every species of living creature is contained (*Timaeus*, 31a). Fire and Air and Earth and Water have their own intelligible natures, but these natures are ancillary to that of the living creatures whose being they subserve, either the Great Living Creature whose moving principle is the Soul of the World, or the subordinate living creatures whose moving principles are our own Souls or those of the animals. It is only to be regretted that Plato never took the step afterwards taken by Plotinus, of allowing there to be Eide of at least some individual things. If instances, in a Platonic ontology, are vanishing nothings, the being of a complex individual, for example Socrates, is not in this position. It is, in fact, a profoundly united, many-sided pattern, rather than a loose assemblage of unrelated cases. For such a pattern there should be an eternal place in the realm of Notional Shapes, and perhaps also an unending instantiation in time. Plato might have found a better proof of individual immortality by dwelling on Socraticity than on the generic pattern of Soulfulness or Life. It is clear, however, that he did not move in this direction.

The second point that requires mention is the remarkable Mind-theory which, unemphatic in the Dialogues, and nowhere stressed in Aristotelian accounts of Platonism (though it must certainly have been the foundation of Aristotle's own Mind-doctrine), is none the less an integral part of the eidetic theory, and is certainly implied by some of Plato's best-considered statements and accounts. This is the doctrine that there are not only Eide of sorts of *things*, circles, plants, men, cities etc., but also Eide of the acts of understanding, perceiving, reasoning, knowing etc. which are correlated with such Eide, and which are the Eide of the Apprehensions *of* such things. As Proclus was afterwards to phrase the distinction, we require *noeric* as well as *noetic* Eide, patterns (in modern terminology) of subjectivity as well as of objectivity. Aristotle, with his relatively crude theory of the literal presence of Eide in the intelligence, might not require such Eide, but Plato, with his carefully drawn parallelism between faculties and acts of cognition, on the one hand, and types of object cognized, on the other, would certainly want them. And as the Eide form a single classificatory hierarchy, so the Eide of the Apprehensions of the Eide must form an eidetic system of Apprehensions, an eternal timeless Mind or Mind as Such, which is the perfect Givenness or Thinkingness of everything. Such a doctrine is plainly stated in *Parmenides*, 134 a–d, where there is said to be a Knowledge Itself correlated with every form of Being Itself, and the question is whether an instantiation of such knowledge will not necessarily be confined to the imperfect instantiations of Being, and eidetic knowledge be for ever denied us, being the sole privilege of an essentially *non*-instantial being, i.e. God. The doctrine is also implied by the much misunderstood passage in the *Sophist* (248e–249a), in which Mind, Life, Soul and Movement are said to have a place in eternal Being. The Mind, Life, Soul and Movement that are thus placed among the Eide are, however, obviously not our own miserable instantiations of these august originals, but the originals themselves, a view borne out by the whole subsequent discussion of Movement among the Major Kinds. And the Soul and Mind of a King attributed to Zeus in *Philebus*, 30d may well be Soul and Mind as Such rather than any instance, even a cosmic one, of these same perfections. All this is further borne out by the identity of structure between knower and known postulated in the construction of the Soul in the *Timaeus*, and in a similar numerical parallelism between mental faculties and spatial dimensions mentioned by Aristotle in *De Anima*, 404b 16–27, as also by the whole notion of the Demiurge in the *Timaeus*, who is obviously timeless Thinkingness as Such as opposed to the instantial thinking of the World-Soul or of our own Souls. Obviously Plato was able to draw a distinction between a thought which could be said timelessly to *make* the

Eide, because it was on their level, and a thought which only followed the Eide and was illuminated by them in its proceedings, and with a little willingness to exercise understanding one can read such a doctrine back into those early passages in the *Republic* where the Idea of Good is said to be responsible, not only for the being of the Eide, but also for the Knowledge of them (508e). The Knowledge here mentioned is of course instantial knowledge in Souls, but such Knowledge must instantiate a Knowledge which is as eternal and eidetic as the essences that it 'contemplates'. And there seems no reason, in the light of all this evidence and these compelling implications, why we should not follow the Neoplatonists and see a reference to this eternal Mind in Plato's Second Epistle where, after telling us of a King of All (the Principle of Good) 'for whose sake all is, and who is cause of all things lovely', he goes on to speak of 'secondary things' surrounding a Second Being, and tertiary things surrounding a Third (Epistle II, 312e). Obviously the 'Second Being' here referred to is Mind as Such, as the Neoplatonists rightly saw, while the Third Being is the thinking and active World-Soul. Why, if Plato thus believed in a Paradigmatic Mind, did he not make his belief more explicit? Possibly because Aristotle, or some like-minded predecessor, had already psychologized it, turning Mind as Such into a supreme instantial mind, which is also a last refuge and line of retreat for those who must at all costs deny the absolute Being of the Eide.

A third point must, however, be briefly dwelt upon before we go on to consider the mathematicized version of the Eide. The eidetic system and the principles of its construction inevitably became an object of interest and discussion in the Academy, and this led to the formation of a higher sort of ideology involving concepts that could not be placed among what we may call the first run of the Eide. The notion of an Eidos as Such, the authentic being which is common to all the Eide, is obviously not an Eidos on the same level as the Eide which exemplify, or, as we may correctly say, instantiate it, and it as much transcends them (while being also present in them) as the common-or-garden Eide which instantiate it transcend their instances. Even in the *Republic* the transcendent nature of the Good is recognized, and while it is styled an Idea, and at times said to be an object of knowledge, it is, in a crucial passage, said to transcend eidetic being in dignity and power (*Republic*, 509c), and the censure of Dionysius for writing freely about it and claiming to understand it (Epistle II, 313a–c) shows that it was also a pattern that in some sense transcended knowledge. The Aristotelian doctrine of the transcendental or non-generic character of certain highest universals – Being, Unity, Goodness and the like – was obviously in process of development in the Academy, and the Goodness and Beauty which are so freely discussed in the early Dialogues are obviously being elevated to a higher plane of discourse, or perhaps to a plane that transcended discourse altogether. The possible difficulties arising from the fact that it might then be necessary to postulate yet higher universals in which these higher universals participated, and so on without end, was not one that could have occurred to Plato, nor would he have liked to evade an ultimate mysticism by taking refuge in an endless series of meta-meta-Eide. It is clear, however, that many of the notions discussed even in earlier Dialogues belong really to the level of Meta-Eide or Principles and not really to the level of first-order Eide. Thus not only the notion of an Eidos as Such, but the notion of a Genus or Species and their mutual relations fall into this class, and so does the notion of an Instance, or of the relations of Participation, Imitation etc. in which it stands to its Eidos. Plato showed a recognition of the problems raised by such higher-order Eide by denying that there were Eide that spanned entities of which some stood in relations of priority to others: thus there could be no generic Eidos of Number as Such, since the notion of each of the Numbers except the first presupposed the notion of some of its predecessors (see *Nicomachean Ethics*, 1096a 16–19). It was probably owing to some similar scruple that Plato refused, at some point in his thought-development, to include Relations among his first-order Eide. These relations may not have been the unessential relations which Syrianus mentions, but Relations among the Eide proper, such as Likeness, Difference, Compatibility etc. These Relations obviously belong to a higher level of discourse or being than the Eide which they connect and across whose order they cut, and it may have been for this reason that Plato wanted to deny that there were Eide of them. It is odd to think that Likeness and Unlikeness, such typical Eide in the early Dialogues, should have been edged out of the whole order of the Eide by Plato's later interest in eidetic Principles. The hesitation to use the word 'Eide' of notions that themselves apply to Eide, and are therefore of higher order, is however evident in many of the later Dialogues, and points to Plato's consciousness of a new discipline concerned with the Principles or Elements, or, as we should say, the Categories of the Eide rather than the Eide themselves. The examination of this higher side of Platonism, its Stoicheiology or Theory of Elements, must now be embarked upon. It runs through all the later Dialogues of Plato, but it is also deeply inwound with those mathematicizing or arithmetizing doctrines of which we have information mainly through the reports of Aristotle. As, in our view, these doctrines form the unwritten background of all the mature thought of Plato, we shall have to give what account of them we can in our present introductory chapter.

III

The mathematicization and arithmetization of the Eide is plainly a natural extension of the eidetic theory, and one that coheres with its basic tendencies. For if the Eide are not to be a set of disjoined communities of character, casually garnered from the vanishing things of sense, and if they are themselves to exhibit communities and distinctions which order them in an intelligible manner, then it is much more reasonable to pin down their nature and content in regions at least bordering on the arithmetical and geometrical than in regions marked out by sensuous quality, or by what perception reveals as casually going together. Plato probably had, at the same period at which he conceived an epistemological and ontological contempt for the changeable things of sense, also conceived a like contempt for the qualities that they vanishingly exhibited. These were conceived to be the perishing products of an interaction among motions, a swift motion in a sense-organ and a slower motion originating in some outside object: whiteness in the object and white-seeingness in the sensitive organ were the passing creations that originated in this manner, it being impossible to characterize anything firmly in terms of such qualities, since they were always in flux. This sort of view of sensation and the sense-qualities is most fully expressed in the fairly late Dialogue *Theaetetus* (156a–157c), where it is dubiously tied up with a criticism of Protagoras and

Heraclitus, but in some form it must have been Plato's own view from the earliest times as Aristotle makes plain in the *Metaphysics* (987a 30–987b 15), when reflection on the endless fluctuation of the sense-world directed Plato's thought to the notion of the unchanging Eide. Plato did not, however, confidently pass from the fluctuations of sense to any notion of 'the White Itself' or 'the Warm Itself', as many modern Platonists have done: while he speaks in some passages of Eide of Warm and Cold etc. he was disposed to see the Eidos behind the shows of sense as essentially something measurable, something in the nature of a Number or a Ratio or a geometrical pattern, and so for example in *Republic*, 602d, counting, measuring and weighing are specified as the ways in which we pass beyond the inconstancies of sense to what alone is worthy of reliance (πίστις) even in the vanishing sense-world. (It is somewhat odd, incidentally, that Plato's teaching on these points should have so impressed even Aristotle when he entered the Academy that, though his whole interpretation of nature is basically qualitative rather than quantitative, he should none the less have retained the Platonic doctrine that makes the sense-qualities merely the 'pathetic' outcome of the interaction of sense-organ and external influence, and that he should have been willing to analyse the qualities of sense in terms of mathematical ratios. See *Categories*, 9a 28–9b 8; *De Anima*, 425b 26–426a 30.) If for sense-qualities it was somehow possible to substitute Numbers and numerical Ratios and the relations of Measure which occur in geometry it is obvious that a great increase in perspicuity in the content, order and deductively necessary pattern of the Eide would result, and that the Eide would have been rendered eidetically, explanatorily one-over-many, to the highest possible degree.

Plato had also, quite early in his development, become interested in problems connected with the nature of Number and the relations of Numbers. Even in an early Dialogue like the *Hippias Major* (300–302), certain peculiarities of numerical concepts are noted: they as it were straddle the instances which embody them, and are present in them jointly, but not severally. Thus while only unity is instantiated in each of the members of a couple, Duality is paradoxically instantiated in both of them taken together, thus seemingly coming from nowhere. Similar strangenesses are mentioned in the early but mature Dialogue *Phaedo* (197a, b), where it is pointed out how *both* addition and division can generate a case of Duality out of Unity, thus showing that neither process is 'of the essence' of being twofold. These reflections and others must early have led Plato to draw a delicate distinction, clearly reported by Aristotle (for example in *Metaphysics*, 987b 14–19), between the eidetic and the mathematical numbers: of this no explicit statement is to be found in the Dialogues, though there are quite a number of transparent references to it for those who do not expect Plato to be explicit. The tentativeness and obscurity of the whole distinction, framed to meet difficulties since made more familiar to us through the work of Russell, Frege and Husserl, is quite sufficient to account for its non-statement in smooth literary products like the Dialogues. Mathematical numbers, Plato held, were 'many alike': thus in the simple assertion that $2 + 2 = 4$ we have *two* quasi-instances of Duality which, taken together, give rise to a quasi-instance of Quadruplicity. We use the word 'quasi-instances' because obviously we are not dealing with instances of Duality and Quadruplicity as when we say that these two drachmae taken together with those two drachmae yield four drachmae: our reference is to shadowy particulars of a sort, but obviously purged of the individuating content which distinguishes particulars. The doubtful status of these shadowy intermediates, half-way between 'Natures' and instances, may very well have given Plato pause. But plainly the Eidos Duality and the Eidos Quadruplicity do not occur explicitly in mathematical reasonings, which make use of them without applying to them. Quadruplicity is, further, not constituted by adding Duality to Duality, since there are not in fact two Eide of Duality to add to one another, and Quadruplicity is in fact a unitary concept which, while necessarily related to Duality, and standing to it in a relation which is in fact Duality doubled or the second power of Duality, none the less excludes and is incomparable ($\dot{\alpha}\sigma\nu\mu\beta\lambda\dot{\eta}\tau\eta$) with the Duality which it presupposes. Plato is often accused of having thought of his Eide as glorified instances of themselves: this he at least certainly did not do in the case of numerical Eide such as Duality, which he explicitly denied to have two members or to be a case of Twoness. These, the commonplaces of eidetic theory, and wholly understandable in modern disciplines like set theory or semantics, were as obscure to Aristotle as to most interpreters of Plato up to this century, and Plato must have despaired of putting higher-order thought across to those determined at all costs never to leave ground-level. The same uniqueness and absence of constructibility applies also to the mathematical concepts which, as Plato said, 'come after' the Numbers, the geometrical patterns, for example, which have a more complex dimensional structure than the natural numbers. In a geometrical reasoning we may have two or more triangles of precisely the same triangular structure, and they may be constituted out of other triangles which enter into them as parts. These geometrical triangles are not, however, the imperfect triangles of sense-perception, but equally they are not the generic pattern of Being a Triangle as Such, nor the more specific patterns of being a right-angled triangle etc., each of which is wholly unique and which does not consist of, though it may imply the concepts of, the parts into which a case of such Triangularity might be divided. There is then a mathematical world of quasi-instantiation, which preserves the multiplicity of the sensuous image while stripping it of its sensuousness, and this world hovers perplexingly between the realm of Eide or Ideal Meanings and the region of genuine instantiation.

The main development of Plato's mathematical philosophy was, however, inspired by Pythagoreanism, and consisted in looking for basic Principles (ἀρχαί or στοιχεῖα) of Number, and of constructing or *generating* the Numbers out of these. The Pythagoreans thought of these Principles and this generation in a quasi-physical manner: in their queer thought-mixture of the conceptual and the naturalistic, they thought of mathematical patterns, and after these the world, as being almost literally made out of certain materials in the course of certain processes. Plato, though he was willing to use this Pythagorean language, particularly in dialogues like the *Timaeus*, certainly did not physicalize his basic concepts in this manner, but rather purged them of all sensuous content. What the Pythagoreans meant by the principles of Number and reality comes out in a well-known table or inventory (συστοιχία) of opposites which they drew up, and on which Aristotle reports in *Metaphysics* I, 5. This table ran:

Limit (πέρας) – Unlimited (ἄπειρον)
Odd (περιττόν) – Even (ἄρτιον)
One (ἕν) – Multitude (πλῆθος)

Right (δέξιον) – Left (ἀριστερόν)
Male (ἄρρην) – Female (θῆλυ)
Resting (ἠρεμοῦν) – Moving (κινούμενον)
Straight (εὐθύ) – Twisted (καμπυλόν)
Light (φῶς) – Darkness (σκότος)
Good (ἀγαθόν) – Bad (κακόν)
Square (τετράγωνον) – Oblong (ἑτερομῆκες)

Though brief, this table is almost incredibly revelatory of Pythagorean, Platonic and Greek thought in general. It is in the first place through and through axiological: the members on one side are 'good', on the other side 'bad'. And the good members are in the main characterized by definiteness of nature and structure, while the bad are indefinite, sprawling, patternless, inchoate. Unity is supremely good because it is the most absolutely restricted of all things, whereas Multitude is bad, not only because it departs from Unity, but because there is no limit to such departure. The Odd is good because it is rounded off by a unity which does not fall into either of the halves into which we might divide it, and also because the sum of the first *n* odd numbers is always a perfect square, a Pythagorean discovery, whereas the sum of the first *n* even numbers yields 'oblong' products of ever varying dimensions. What we have said also explains why 'square' is a term of praise, while 'oblong' is a term of abuse. That it should be good to rest in one position and bad to move in the innumerable ways in which one might deviate from rest, and that the straight, single direction is good and the infinitely varied forms of crookedness and twistedness bad, are obvious applications of Pythagorean values. Less obvious, but none the less understandable, are the connection of Goodness with the Male and Badness with the Female, or with the Right and the Left, or with Light and Darkness respectively. What is remarkable in all this Pythagorean Stoicheiology is the systematic bringing of Badness into the picture, a view based in part on the tragic discovery that some magnitudes are not rationally related to one another. The Pythagoreans had achieved a proof that the diagonal of a square was not rationally related to the magnitude of its sides, they had discovered that while certain sets of magnitudes have rational relations among one another, there is not necessarily a rational relation between the members of one set and those of

another. For revealing this awesome secret Hippasus of Metapontium was said to have been drowned at sea, but what it led to
was the acceptance of a dualism of factors in which one was
discrete, finite and good, while the other was essentially continuous, unmeasured, irrational and in itself evil. The abstract
world of Numbers and the real world of space and motion
depended for their health and goodness, and ultimately for their
being, on the imposition of Limit on the Unlimited Principle, in
which imposition the Unlimited played a yielding and essentially
female part. Provided the yielding was complete, which it
unfortunately never could quite be, there would be no evil in
notions or existence. How deeply these Pythagorean conceptions pervaded the thought of Plato is shown throughout the
Dialogues, but in none more clearly than in the late dialogue
Philebus. The mathematicized Platonic Stoicheiology was further
a mere modification of this Pythagorean Stoicheiology, in which
the Principle of Limit was given the new designation of One or
Unity, while the Pythagorean Unbounded or Infinite received the
strange, new, double designation of the 'Great and Small'.

Before we consider the details of Plato's reduction of the Eide
to Numbers, we must, however, stress that it was an exceedingly
obscure process, as imperfectly understandable to those who
heard Plato expound it as it is to us. It was not some well worked
out secret theory of which only garbled reports have come down
to us. Here of course we have the previously cited account of
Aristoxenus (see Appendix I, 2) as to the amazement of those
who came to hear Plato discourse on the Good, and who,
instead of hearing something about wealth, health, strength or
some marvellous happiness, were provoked to scorn and censure
by a discourse that only dealt with Numbers and geometry and
astronomy, and culminated in the statement that Unity was the
Good (ὅτι τἀγαθόν ἐστιν ἕν). And here we also have the com-
plaint of Theophrastus (*Metaphysics*, 6a 15–6b 17), that the
Pythagoreans, Plato and the Platonists only went up to a certain
point in explaining how the numbers, surfaces and bodies
followed from or were generated by Absolute Unity and the
Indefinite Dyad and 'there came to a stop' (μεχρὶ τινὸς ἐλθόντες
καταπαύονται). And that they came to a stop at this and at many
other points explains how Aristotle, who wrote two elaborate
treatises *On the Ideas* and *On the Good* concerning Plato's oral

teaching in the Academy, should have been quite unclear as to whether the reduction of Eide to Numbers meant their simple identification with Numbers, which gave rise to many problems (see for example *Physics*, 206b 32–33, *Metaphysics*, 1084a 12–17), or whether it meant their reduction to *Ratios* of Numbers (*Metaphysics*, 991b 13–21), in which case his problem became of *what* they were the Ratios. And he was quite unclear what Plato meant by his Pythagorean confinement of the eidetic numbers within the Decad, or even if such a confinement was invariably and seriously meant by Plato (*Metaphysics*, 1073a 18–21). And the extreme obscurity of Plato's exposition comes out in Aristotle's complete inability to understand the nature of the eidetic Numbers and what Plato meant by holding them to be mutually incomparable (ἀσύμβλητοί), and not containing one another as parts or elements. He could best interpret this doctrine as involving that each Number consisted of unique units which were not to be found in any other Number (*Metaphysics*, 1080a 15–35), an elementary misunderstanding that a good exposition should surely have averted. Had the doctrine been well expounded, it should also not have been possible for Aristotle to ask, as according to Syrianus (Kroll, p. 159f.) he did ask, 'which of us common men' (τίς γὰρ τῶν γε πλείστων ἡμῶν) could have any understanding of Numbers other than the mathematical, such as the Eide are held to be. The position of the eidetic Lines, Planes and Solids in Plato's system, whether identical with Numbers or in some sense 'coming after them', and having distinct Principles, is also a point which Aristotle does not understand (*Metaphysics*, 992b 13–17, 1085a 7–14), and which cannot have been clear in Plato's exposition. In view of all this primal obscurity, it is plain that our interpretation of the reduction of Eide to numbers must not be too narrow and inelastic, nor is there any profit in ingenious detailed theories of the arithmetization for which not a jot of evidence will ever be available. The reduction to Numbers must allow for their possible reduction, not merely to specific Natural Numbers, but to various Ratios or sets of Ratios among the Natural Numbers, and it must in fact be stretched to cover a reduction to many-dimensional measures and proportions such as those which the Demiurge is said to have imposed on the emptiness of Space when in *Timaeus*, 53b he shaped things according to shapes and numbers. It must in fact be given an interpretation which accords with Plato's whole expository practice, not with some narrowly philological view of the meaning of the word ἀριθμός (Number) in isolation or in non-philosophical contexts.

As to the 'Principles' (ἀρχαί) out of which Plato generated his arithmetized Eide, Aristotle tells us or implies that they were basically the same as those of the Pythagoreans. The Pythagoreans, as we saw, had made their Principles the Limit (πέρας) and the Unlimited (ἄπειρον), which are the Principles also attributed to the Pythagoreans and invoked in the *Philebus*. But whereas the Pythagoreans had hedged between treating Unity as on a level with Limit and Oddness (in their Table of Opposites), and on the other hand as something which secondarily 'proceeds' from the Limit and the Unlimited as the Principles of the numbers (*Metaphysics*, I, 986a 15–21), Plato had simply made Unity or the One one of his Principles. And whereas the Pythagoreans had made the Unlimited their second Principle, Plato had been original in positing a Dyad in its place, and in composing the Unlimited out of the *Great* and the Small (*Metaphysics*, 987b 25–6). It is plain, however, from what Aristotle and others say, that there was not that difference between the Pythagorean and the Platonic doctrine that these terminological changes suggest. For the Absolute Unity which lay behind the Numbers, Lines, Surfaces and Solids and served as their common Principle, is plainly something different from the Unity which is the First Principle and Source of the Numbers, and there is a report from Sextus Empiricus, arguably based on Aristotle's lost three-book work *On the Good* (*Adversus Mathematicos*, X, p. 276), which suggests that Plato did in fact distinguish between a Unity which belongs to Numbers (τὸ ἐν τοῖς ἀριθμοῖς ἕν), and a more ultimate primal Unity (πρώτη μόνας) from which this springs. In any case the One of Plato has the same property of setting bounds to vanishing or burgeoning Quantity, and bringing it to fixity and equality, that the Limit had in Pythagorean thought. And the Great and Small, though dualistically named, plainly was little more than the Pythagorean Unlimited: it was dualistically named because it connoted alike the possibilities of going on infinitely in the direction of Increase and the direction of Reduction (ἐπὶ τὴν αὔξην ὑπερβάλλειν καὶ εἰς ἄπειρον ἰέναι καὶ ἐπὶ τὴν καθαίρεσιν, *Physics*, 220b 27–8), or because the Great and Small do not cease going on in the direction of ἐπίτασις, extension, and ἄνεσις, relaxation, but proceed into the indefiniteness of infinity (Simplicius quoting Alexander on the above passage). The Great and Small are also described as a plastic medium out of which the Numbers can be neatly formed (εὐφυῶς ἐξ αὐτῆς γεννᾶσθαι ὥσπερ ἔκ τινος ἐκμαγείου, *Metaphysics*, I, 987b 34–5), and the action of Unity on the Great and Small is said in many passages to be one of equalization (ἰσάζειν, e.g. *Metaphysics*, I, 1091a 25), all of which yields an idea of Indefinite Magnitude having its tendencies to increase or diminution stopped by the imposition of a definite and uniform limit. With such a view go the equations of the Great and Small with underlying Matter as opposed to Form, Difference as opposed to uniform Sameness, Motion as opposed to Fixity, Inequality (i.e. Excess or Defect) as opposed to Equality, Plurality as opposed to Unity, Non-being as opposed to Being and Badness as opposed to Goodness. (See for example *Physics*, 187a 12–21, *Metaphysics*, 1091b 13–15, 26–35, *Metaphysics*, 1087b 4–12, *Metaphysics*, 1004b 27–1005a 2, *Physics*, 201b 16–26.) Everywhere the One imposes itself on the Unbounded and Unlimited, and brings forth those definite patterns which are at once eidetic and numerical. As to the nature of the acts by which the arithmetized Eide are engendered, Aristotle is willing to argue, for dialectical reasons, that if the generation of Numbers means anything it means a generation in time (*Metaphysics*, 1091a 23–9), but Xenocrates made plain, with more cogency than in the case of the generation of the instantial Cosmos, that the generation is merely an expository device (διδασκαλίας χάριν καὶ τοῦ γνῶναι, Pseudo-Alexander on Aristotle's *Metaphysics*, 1091a 12), putting into time eidetic relations which are of necessity eternal. The Eide are simply Unbounded Quantity, capable of indefinite expansion and shrinkage, and variously bounded by Unity. If one is puzzled as to how the series of generations involved in the case of some Eide can be achieved 'all at one blow' – Aristotle worries as to how the One can generate all the Eide together while men only generate many offspring in a long series of copulations (*Metaphysics*, 988a 1–8) – it is merely the case that any number of iterations of the same operation need be as little drawn out in time as a single performance. All may resemble the timeless manner in which certain modern formalists try to coax the numbers out of zero by the simple act of 'stroking' it.

At the threshold of discussions as to the generation of the arithmetized Eide out of their Elements one is confronted by the major problem as to what Plato can have meant by limiting his Number Series to the Decad. This limitation is often attested by Aristotle, and causes him boundless perplexity, though he also declares such a limitation not to have been invariable (*Metaphysics*, 1073a 20). Seemingly such a limitation excludes from eidetic status any number greater than 10, and even forbids us to conceive of ratios whose member-numbers exceed 10. Aristotle rightly finds this an impossible situation: the Eide will soon run short, and it is grotesque that there can be no Eidos of the Number 11 (*Metaphysics*, 1084a 10–26). It is moreover absurd to introduce a Great and Small which is said to be capable of being indefinitely reduced and exceeded, if it stops short at Unity in the one direction and at Ten in the other (*Physics*, 206b 29–33). Obviously also, we may add, a restriction of the Numbers within the Decad cannot be harmonized with the indefinite doublings, triplings etc. postulated in the *Parmenides* (143d–144a), nor with the Numbers running up to 27 used in the generation of the Soul in the *Timaeus*, nor even with the ratio $\frac{256}{243}$ which is the arithmetized Eidos of a semitone in the generation in question (*Timaeus*, 35b–c, 36b). Nor have modern attempts like those of Gaiser (see *Platons Ungeschriebene Lehre*, 1963, pp. 125–36) to keep the arithmetized Eide within the Decad, inspired confidence: it is immensely artificial to try to connect the Eidetic Numbers with divisions of classes like those in the *Sophist*, and it turns the whole arithmetization-programme into an arbitrary and silly correlation of numerical ratios with the extension of specific classes. Obviously we have to take our cue and our clue from another group of statements that are of constant recurrence, statements which equate the Decad with the *sum* of the Numbers 1, 2, 3 and 4, the traditional Pythagorean Tetractys, and which make plain that these Numbers are really of an elder stock than the Natural Numbers, that they are, in fact, archaic Numbers presupposed alike by the Natural Numbers and by 'the things that come after the numbers', the Lines, Planes and Solids that are the eidetic backing of geometry.

Aristotle tells us (*Metaphysics*, 1090b 20–4) that the believers in the Ideas make Magnitudes out of Matter and Number, Lengths out of the Dyad, Planes perhaps from the Triad, and

Solids from the Tetrad or other numbers, and he also tells us (*De Anima*, 404b 16–22) that in the lost work *On Philosophy* it was laid down as Platonic doctrine that the Archetypal Living Creature (αὐτὸ τὸ ζῷον) was constituted out of the Idea of Unity and the first Length, Breadth and Depth. The four 'dimensions' of (1) the Natural Numbers, corresponding to Unity, and (2) the Lines, corresponding to the Dyad – two points are necessary for a Line – and (3) the Planes corresponding to the Triad – three points are necessary for the simplest plane figure – and (4) the Solids corresponding to the Tetrad – four points are necessary for the simplest solid figure – are also set forth as successively generated by Absolute Unity and the Indefinite Dyad in the third part of the comprehensive report on the arithmetized eidetic theory summarized by Sextus Empiricus (*Against the Mathematicians*, pp. 276–83), and thought by some (for example Wilpert), on account of its correspondence with references in Alexander's comments on *Metaphysics*, 987b 37, which attribute similar doctrines to Aristotle's lost treatise *On the Good*, to be a summary of the Third Book of that treatise. The Numerical, the Linear, the Superficial and the Solid are accordingly, by these lines of converging evidence, the Primal Four, and they amount to a Decad because the continuous linear dimension involves the discrete arithmetical dimension, because two-dimensional Superficiality involves both the Linear and the Arithmetical, and because three-dimensional Solidity involves all of its three predecessors. (In Platonism what it is often convenient to call a series of 'dimensions' are really a series in which the higher members presuppose and incorporate the lower.)

If it now be pertinently asked how cases of number up to Four or up to Ten are possible, if one has not already got the Natural Numbers which still remain to be 'generated', the answer might be that an enumeration which stops short absolutely at 4 or at 10 has not yet reached the level of the Natural Numbers at all, that it is setting forth primal forms of pure Diversity or Multiplicity which have yet to give rise to the varied Numbers and Figures. The difficulty is there in any case, since his basic Principles, Unity and Indefinite Multiplicity or Quantity, are undoubtedly two in number, and yet Twoness is a product of their interaction or synthesis, a difficulty like that raised by Aristotle when he repeatedly asks whether Plato's views do not involve the postulation of a Two before the Primal Two (990b 17–20). That Plato's Primal Four (=Primal Ten) are simply Natural Number plus the three forms of Linear, Superficial and Solid Spatiality, is further shown by the fact that Plato employed, on some Aristotelian assertions, *four* distinct species of the Great and Small to generate them, the Many and Few for Numbers (τὸ πολὺ καὶ τὸ ὀλίγον, *Metaphysics*, 1087b 16), while the Long and Short, the Broad and Narrow and the Deep and Shallow (τὸ βραχὺ καὶ μακρόν, τὸ πλατὺ καὶ στενόν, τὸ βαθὺ καὶ ταπεινόν, *Metaphysics*, 992a 10–15) are the 'raw material' for the three forms of spatiality. Plato ultimately came to believe, as witnessed by the *Laws* (819d–820c), that deep gulfs of incommensurability severed the members of the Primal Four from one another, and that the passage from one to another involved what Aristotle was later to call the passage from one Categorial Kind (γένος) to another. Plato also believed that the same radical transitions of sense which generated the Primal Four also generated four mental faculties which corresponded to them and which were equally irreducible (see *De Anima*, 404b 16–27). To the monadic dimension in which the Natural Numbers arose, the mental faculty of Intellection (νοῦς) corresponded: it would probably intuit the essence of each single Eidos and go no further. To the bi-directional linear range, Knowledge (ἐπιστήμη) corresponded, which probably discerns the necessary relations among the Eide. To the three-point range of Surfaces, Opinion (δόξα) corresponded, a faculty which discerns relations among Eide which are vouched for by well-warranted sense-perception, whereas to the four-point solid world Sense-experience (αἴσθησις) corresponds, which is both solid and wholly unreliable. The four mental faculties must *not* be understood as anything belonging to actual instantial minds: they are all ideal possibilities, instantiated in the case-world, but prefigured in the type-realm. There is therefore an eidetic original, Primal Quadruplicity, for the sheer sense-experience which, as an instantial phenomenon, is as far as possible from the realm of the Eide. The realm of the Eide therefore anticipates everything, even that which departs as far as possible from itself. It anticipates all that is spatial, in the form of a peculiar structure of mutually irreducible numbers, without itself being spatialized. And, as we have said, it prefigures the subjective as much as the objective. There is therefore of necessity a pure Conceivingness, a pure Knowingness, a pure Believingness and a pure Sensitiveness in which instantial experiences participate, and which have the same dimensional structure as their objects. So much is implicit in the doctrines we have just examined, and they make plain how the eidetic Mind or Mind as Such could be held by the Platonists to be the all-comprehending Place (τόπος) of the Eide. (See *De Anima*, 429a 27–9, a reference said by Philoponus to be Platonic.)

Plato stops short at the Tetractys or Decad because Sensible Solidity is for him the terminal form of being. Being in the concrete terminates there, whether in Instance or in eidetic anticipation. Why does not Plato recognize the additional dimension of temporality, and mention such additional forms of the Great and Small as the Brief and the Lasting, or the Swift and the Slow? The answer is that he does in fact do so, as will be plain if one reads the passages on astronomy in Book VII of the *Republic*, or the passages on the various cosmic and Soul-motions in the *Timaeus*, or the enumeration of the Species of Motion in Book X of the *Laws*. It will also be plain if one meditates on the fact that Motion is one of the five Primal Kinds selected for detailed study in the *Sophist*. Plato would have raised his insights to their highest peak if he had explicitly recognized the need to add an idealized Temporality to the three forms of Idealized Spatiality which, with his basic dimension of Natural Number, yield his Primal Four. But he would then have found himself believing in a Primal Five which would have seemed impious in the face of 'him who gave us the Tetractys'. There are however tendencies to burst the bonds of the Tetractys elsewhere in Plato, for example in the *Philebus*, and also in the *Epinomis* with its fifth natural element. The notion of Numbers which, though commensurable within each Primal Kind, none the less fall into irreducible and incommensurable Primal Kinds, is undoubtedly of the highest importance, and it is a notion to which, in his obscure deference to the Tetractys and the Decad, Plato unquestionably attained.

IV

We have now to develop the 'generation' or construction of the Natural Numbers and dimensional entities which come after the 'Numbers' in more detail, and to proceed therefrom to consider the intermediate world of the Soul, with the intermediate Mathematical Objects which are arguably its special concern, and then on to the concrete instantial world with its three-dimensional Space mirroring the higher eidetic dimensions, and its Time providing a mobile, instantial image of eidetic eternity, all moreover diverging from the perfect regularity of the eidetic order, in which deviations are only included *qua* excluded.

The Greek word ἀριθμός, which we may render as 'Number', is confined in its application to the Integers from the Dyad onwards: it is not applied to Unity, and of course not to the Nought or Zero below Unity, of which the Greeks had no notion beyond the ordinary notion of Nothing. It is not applied to any of the fractions such as we conceive as lying below Unity, or as occupying the interstices between Unity and the Dyad or any other pair of integral numbers. (*Republic*, 525e tells us how strenuously mathematicians resisted any attempt at fractionalization.) Number is therefore, *a fortiori*, not extended to cover any surds that might arise in the attempt to measure one geometrical Magnitude in terms of another incommensurable Magnitude, of which of course many interesting instances had been unearthed by Pythagoreans, Theodorus of Cyrene and other mathematicians. Plato or Philip of Opus was making an altogether revolutionary demand when in *Epinomis*, 990–991b it was suggested that *Irrational Numbers* should be recognized as applying to such cases. While the Greeks were very ready to geometrize arithmetic, and to speak, as Theaetetus does, of 'Oblong Numbers', 'Square Numbers' etc., they seem to have had an odd unwillingness to arithmetize geometry completely, and to recognize that, in a higher sense, one has a Number wherever one has a defined numerical task, even if one cannot bring it to a straightforwardly precise outcome. The notion of λόγος, Ratio or Proportion, or what we now call Relation Number, therefore becomes central in Plato's eidetic theory, both on account of its happy terminological identity with the Socratic λόγος of definition, and also because it could perform more tasks, for example those now performed by fractional and irrational and complex magnitudes, than the narrowly restricted common-or-garden concept of Number. The notion of a bond or relation between magnitudes, whether harmonic, arithmetical or geometric, is always of the greatest interest to Plato, and it is extremely odd that Aristotle, while recognizing it as a perfectly possible interpretation of Plato's arithmetization of the Eide (*Metaphysics*, 991b 13–21), should have considered it so slightly, and that so great a Platonic-Aristotelian commentator as Robin should have simply followed him in this. (See *La Théorie Platonicienne des Idées et des Nombres d'après Aristote*, 1908, pp. 355–6.) It is, however, on account of his essentially relational and operational concept of Number that Plato's generation of the Natural Numbers is multiplicative and divisive rather than monotonously additive: it is doubling, tripling, halving, squaring etc. that is of interest to Plato, rather than any outcome of such proceedings. Of our modern concepts of Negative Numbers, Real Numbers, Complex Numbers etc. the Greeks and Plato were of course not possessed, but in their methods of exhaustion, and their stress on absolute dimensional differences etc., they had of course the rudiments of such concepts, and perhaps the rudiments of alternative better concepts, concepts not so enslaved to some ultimate, intuitive 'cash-value', or summing-up of results.

The Natural Numbers begin to arise for Plato in so far as the Indefinite Dyad, with its two indefinite tendencies towards expansion and contraction, is so 'equalized' by the force of the Principle of Unity or Uniformity, that it becomes just as expansive as it is contractive: the outcome of this 'equalization' is Definite Duality or the Number Two, the first of the Natural Numbers. In the Number Two the indefinite tendency towards excess becomes channelled into a precise act of doubling, while at the same time the indefinite tendency towards diminution becomes channelled into a precise act of halving: this halving and this doubling are of course the same proceeding regarded from two different points of view. Alexander, quoting Aristotle *On the Good*, and commenting on *Metaphysics*, 987b 33, says that 'when limited by the One the Indefinite Dyad becomes the numerical Dyad, ... its Principles are the Exceeding and the Exceeded since in the first Dyad one has a double and a half which are exceeding and exceeded respectively', and Simplicius commenting on *Physics*, 202b 36, and quoting Porphyry citing what is probably the same passage, says: 'The first even number is the Dyad and in the nature of its evenness it embraces the double and the half, the double in excess and the half in defect'. Had Plato recognized a strictly arithmetical form of Unity, he might have seen in this generation of Duality a simultaneous generation of this strictly arithmetical Unity. Duality is of course an eidetic, not a mathematical Number: it is Twiceness which 'comes after' Singleness and presupposes it, but does not contain it, and it does not really differ from the doubling operation which is merely itself in action. Duplication and Duplicity would, in fact, seem to be only two metaphorically different ways of regarding the same timeless procession. But Plato holds that that the operation which generates and *is* Doubleness, can be reiterated indefinitely: after Duplication, we can have Duplication of Duplication, Duplication of Duplication of Duplication, all the powers, in short, of Twiceness. What in the mathematical instance is drawn out into many like cases of the same Eidos, is in the Eidos merely the same Eidos exercising itself characteristically on itself alone.

The generation of Number will, however, require other resources besides mere duplication, which will only yield us the powers of Two. It will have to make an appeal to the other Principle of Unity or Uniformity, and the latter will have to exercise itself characteristically in finding an arithmetical mean between two numbers, a number which will exceed one of them to the same absolute extent in which it is exceeded by the other, and will so equalize any gaps between the first generated numbers which might otherwise be widely different and irregular (see Robin, *La Théorie Platonicienne*, 1908, pp. 442–50). Such 'splitting the difference' is obviously no more than a second exercise of the 'equalization' by which the Number Two was itself brought into being. The first result of this process of 'splitting the difference' will obviously be Thriceness or the eidetic Number Three, something which is equally removed from Twiceness as from Twice-twiceness. But, given Thriceness, and the power to use it on itself, and on Twiceness, and *vice versa*, one obviously has all the powers of Three and all the multiples of Three and Two. It is only when one comes to the next Prime Number after Three, i.e. Five, that one will again have to invoke the equalizing, mean-striking power of Unity, which will locate Fiveness in the gap between Twice-twiceness and Thrice-twiceness (or alternatively between Twice-twiceness and Twice-thriceness). This it would seem is the meaning of the enigmatic statement of Aristotle that Plato thought that the Numbers apart from the Primes (ἔξω τῶν πρώτων) could be simply generated from the Indefinite Dyad as from some plastic medium (*Metaphysics*, 987b 33–5). The One sets the type on occasion after occasion, and the printing press of the Dyad then goes indefinitely into action. The generation of the factorizable numbers is all routine, all a turning of the crank: they are twice two, and thrice two, and five times seven etc. as suggested in the *Parmenides*, 143e. But the generation of the Prime Numbers which, apart from Definite Duality, are all odd, involves a going back on one's tracks and a filling-in of gaps. These gaps, it would seem, never exceed the first gap between Two and Twice Two, and like that first gap they are filled by a single act of splitting the difference, since every Prime Number is half-way between two even multiples of Two. Aristotle, we may note, gives no clear account of the generation of Primes, but plainly it must involve the same 'equalization' already involved in the generation of Twiceness.

It may seem odd that Plato should have wished to order his generation of the Natural Numbers in a manner different from its final outcome, but it certainly accords with his procedure at higher levels, as when, in the generation of Soul in the *Timaeus*, Harmonic and Arithmetic Means are inserted in among a first series of Numbers. In any case Plato may have been deliberately obscure on many points in his generation, since in a timeless proceeding many alternative generations might yield the same result. Sextuplicity, for example, is indifferently Thrice-twiceness and Twice-thriceness. As opposed to the minimally additive generation of the integers by Peano and his successors, Plato's generation has certain superiorities, in that it both high-lights the innovation involved in the generation of each new Prime Number, and lumps all the other generations into sets of transfinite progressions which originate in such Primes. By so doing it stresses a fundamental bifurcation in the eidetic order.

The next step in the eidetic genesis is that of Linear Patterns. Here it would appear that two theoretical possibilities were canvassed. On one of these the first Principles of Lines were Points (σημεῖα or στιγμαί) which were defined by Plato as 'units having position' (see Simplicius on *Physics*, 202b 36), and there would appear to have been Platonists who imagined that such Points had an inherent fluxion or positional variability, which was their form of the Great and Small. Fluxion in respect of length generated Lines, fluxion of such Lines in respect of breadth generated Surfaces, and fluxion of such Surfaces in respect of depth generated Solids. The transcendental 'motions' involved in such fluxions are also outlined in *Laws*, 894a. But, on another account Plato rejected the notion of Point in favour of the notion of Indivisible Line (*Metaphysics*, 992a 20–22), his reason being that the incommensurability of certain lines must be due to their constitution out of mutually incommensurable linear minima (see Pseudo-Aristotle, *De Lineis insecabilibus*, 968b 5–22). We need not concern ourselves with the detailed working out of this interesting doctrine, which reflects embarrassments that are certainly perennial. Suffice it to say that what the advent of Linearity really means is the passage from the discrete series of the Natural Numbers to the compact series of the Ratios or Relation-numbers, all capable of illustration by Linear Magnitudes. On the new infinity of the Long and Short, Unity exercises its equalizing role by finding lengths, not necessarily corresponding to integral measures, which exemplify certain salient Ratios: the Geometric Mean, in which something is as many times something else as a third something is many times this second something, the Arithmetic Mean in which something is as much more than something else as a third something is more than this second something, and the Harmonic Mean, in which the proportionate distance of the Mean from two extremes is also the Ratio of the two extremes to one another.

Having given rise to the Lines, the Great and Small expands into a second dimension in the Broad and Narrow, and into a third dimension in the Deep and Shallow. There is no elucidation of this dimensional development: the Tetractys or Decad enshrines it among the absolute Principles of Being. There is here no tradition to the effect that Plato believed in Indivisible Surfaces as he believed in Indivisible Lines, but consistency would have forced him to do so. Incommensurability and irrationality were by Plato associated with difference of dimension in whose context problems concerning them first arose, as we can see from references in *Laws*, 819e, where it is suggested that Length is by nature commensurable with Length, Breadth with Breadth, and Depth with Depth, though they need not be commensurable with one another. There are no clear data regarding the generation of the regular polygons or the circle, nor how less regular figures were to be inserted among them. In the case of the Solids, we have of course the interesting generation of Tetrahedron, Cube, Octahedron and Icosahedron out of elementary triangles in the *Timaeus*, and their use as the eidetic pattern of the elementary bodies: though the Dodecahedron is not used for this purpose in the *Timaeus*, the *Laws* and *Epinomis* show Plato tending to use it for his fifth element Aether. The proof that there are five and only five regular solids was of course due to the crowning researches of Theaetetus, and may have inspired the whole Platonic programme of 'generation'.

On the generation of irregular solids, and their due insertion in the interstices of the regular Solids and beyond them, we have no clear data. On the pure theory of Solids in Motion there are theorems to be culled from the *Timaeus* and the *Laws*, though no discussion of the various simple and complex forms of regular circular and rectilineal motion, or of the descent from these to some treatment of irregular motions, can be attempted here. Suffice it to say that for Plato rational, or as he would have called it eidetic Dynamics, must crown the whole series of eidetic sciences that precede it, and must lead on, with perfect continuity, to rational or eidetic Psychology, the study of the forms of Self-movingness and Self-organization and eidetic governance and direction in which Life, and Soul and Mind, in their eidetic essence, consist. Plato did not, it is plain, think of the governing patterns of Life in any fundamentally different manner from the simpler, more purely geometrical governing and moving principles of their elements: the Eide of Livingness are in fact the complexly constituted patterns of eidetically governed Self-motion which necessarily take precedence over the simpler non-self-moving patterns of their component elements. (See *Metaphysics*, 1070a 18–20 and the *Timaeus*, passim.) And if the extremely fundamental Eide which are the Natural Numbers are generated from certain ultimate Principles in a necessary fashion, and the same is true of the regular Polygons and Solids and their regular Motions, we must not doubt that this will be true of the various species of Living Creature, and of their characteristic functions, virtues and cognitive powers, from Polyp to Man. Aristotle, in fact, in *De Anima*, 414b 20–35, compares the relations of different psychic activities and psychic species to that of a series of ever more complex figures each of which includes its predecessors, a comparison which must come straight from the

Academic treatments which almost everything else in the treatise directly or indirectly reflects. Life and Intelligence are plainly for Plato highly complex, higher-order sets of Ratios, far exceeding Plato's or our power to work them out, though possibly the modern molecular geneticist may be beginning to move into this field. The numerical and geometrical ratios built into the great Cosmic Living Creature and its eternal functioning must be necessary for lower living creatures of every sort. The biological classifications attempted in the Academy, out of which Aristotle's Natural History later grew, were not mere empirical exercises: they must have been the preparatory amassing of material out of which an arithmetico-eidetic biology was to grow, of which it was hoped that it would 'save the phenomena' as had been done for the starry heavens by Eudoxus and Callippus. In our age such a mathematicized biology is not the absurd project that it must have seemed in Plato's age, and in all ages between his time and our own.

It will be profitable at this point to return to a passage from Sextus Empiricus (*Adversus Mathematicos*, 263–75) which has been mentioned previously, and which throws very considerable light on Plato's arithmetization of the Eide. This passage, though vaguely referred to 'Pythagorean groups' as well as to Plato by Sextus, to whom all these metaphysical mathematicians are birds of one colour, nevertheless has close Platonic connections which are attested by some closely parallel passages in Alexander commenting on *Metaphysics*, 987b 37, and in Simplicius commenting on *Physics*, 202b 36. There seems little doubt, as for example Wilpert (*Zwei aristotelische Frühschriften über die Ideenlehre*, 1949) and Gaiser (*Platons Ungeschriebene Lehre*, 1963, 1968) persuade us, that these sources are, as they say they are, summarizing material from Aristotle's lost treatise *On the Good*: Alexander commenting on *Metaphysics*, 1003b 12 even refers one most crucial passage to the *Second* Book of this treatise. Sextus's long, stupid summary falls into three parts, presumably corresponding to the Three Books of the lost work in question.

In the first of these parts there is a long critique of those who locate the First Principles of phenomena in other phenomena: as words are constituted out of syllables and letters which are not words, so everything phenomenal must be constituted out of what is not phenomenal. The atomists went some distance in this direction, but they erred in making their invisibles bodies: one is involved in an infinite regress if one thus explains bodies by bodies. Rather do bodies refer us to incorporeal solid patterns as their Principles, which in their turn refer us to prior plane patterns, while these last in their turn refer us to Lines, which refer us to Numbers. But Numbers all refer us to the Monad, by participation in which every entity is made unitary or single, and also to the Indefinite Dyad, the Principle which differentiates entities from one another. Passing to the Third Book, we find the argument worked in reverse: the Numerical One arises from the Prime Monad (suggesting that Plato drew a distinction between them), and the Definite Dyad from the Monad and the Indefinite Dyad. The generation is said to go on *in infinitum*, though Sextus does not clearly say that each new generation builds on prior ones. The Prime Monad now generates the Point, while Lines, which always involve two points, also involve the Indefinite Dyad as Principle; this Principle then generates Surfaces which involve at least a triad of Points, and Solids which involve at least a tetrad of Points. We then pass on to the *Sensible* Elements and the Cosmos, in which Arithmetical, Geometrical and Harmonic means play a prominent part.

It is, however, in the Second Book that we have Plato's interesting doctrine of categorial distinctions. Some things, we are told, are conceived *by themselves* (καθ'ἑαυτά) or absolutely (ἀπολύτως) or by their peculiar description (κατ'ἰδίαν περιγραφήν), things such as Man, Horse, Plant, Earth, Water, Air, Fire. Others are conceived through the *opposition* of one thing to another (ἐξ ἐναντιώσεως ἑτέρου πρὸς ἕτερον) such as Good-Bad, Just-Unjust, Moving-Resting etc. Yet others are conceived by their *Relation* to something (πρός τι) such as Right and Left, Above and Below. Opposites are distinct from Relatives, inasmuch as they are mutually destructive, whereas Relatives are mutually compatible: where there is Good, Bad is not, but where there are Doubles there are always Halves etc. They also differ in that there is no Mean between true Opposites, whereas there always is a Mean, which is also a position of excellence, between two Relatives. The three Kinds just mentioned depend, however, on more ultimate Principles. The things thought of absolutely or by themselves depend on the One, which is the Principle of sufficient, distinct being. The things thought of through Opposition have as principles the Equal and Unequal, the one opposite representing a position of equilibrium and natural perfection, while the other represents states that exceed it or fall short of it. Equality, however, plainly points to the One which is primarily self-equal, while Inequality always abides in Excess and Defect and so points to the Indefinite Dyad. Relatives, however, all fall under Inequality, and so stem from the Indefinite Dyad.

What this garbled exposition implies is (a) a reference of *one* Opposite to Excess and Defect and the Indefinite Dyad, while the other expresses the central equilibrium of the One: (b) relatives are merely special cases of Excess or Defect either in relation to the central equilibrium or to each other; (c) the eidetic realm has three categories of members: first-category members which are the Eide proper, the essences of natural things and their essential components and virtues; second-category members which are what the Eide altogether exclude, for example, Impiety, Injustice, and which in being thus opposed to the Eide are the shadows which always accompany them; and third-category members which depart from the eidetic norm by way of Excess and Defect and which thereby claim a tertiary place in the realm of the Eide. In a passage of Simplicius commenting on *Physics*, 192a 3 which quotes what must be this very same passage, we read 'Of things which are some are said to be by themselves like Man and Horse, some relatively to others, and of these latter some to Opposites as Good is to Bad, some to Relatives, and of these last some definite and some indefinite'. There are in short definite relatives, such as spending twice as much as one should or being twice as tall as one should be, and indefinite relatives which are merely being extravagant or over-tall. The indefinite relatives are said to be 'borne about in a certain unjudgeableness' (ἐν ἀκρισίᾳ τινὶ φέρεσθαι). If we are not wrong, these passages solve the discrepancy between the statements of Aristotle and commentators like Syrianus as to cases, e.g. Negatives, Relatives etc., in which there are no Eide, and the practice of the Dialogues. Prime category Eide there are indeed only in certain privileged cases, but there are second-category and third-category Eide which necessarily attend upon and environ the former. The realm of the first class Eide is one of unalloyed good form, but unalloyed good form presupposes both a sheer Opposition to and an infinitely varied Declension from itself. The procedure of inserting

Arithmetical, Geometrical and Harmonic Means between the Integers must therefore be carried further: we must insert further interstitial components which are topheavy and one-sided, and some even which are quite irregular or boundlessly irrational. All is part of the eidetic order, and remains fixed in the confining embrace of the Good. It is only in the instantial realm that the Bad works free from this confining embrace, and is instantiated in defective form and irregular movement. All this can be seen as implied in these citations by writers who certainly failed to understand them, and to be documented by the general practice of Plato.

The Eide seen as infinite specifications of definite pattern imposed on an indefinite, shifting base, are further seen as having an intermediate quasi-instantiation in the Objects of Mathematics previously mentioned, and a second or full instantiation in the changeable things of sense. The Unwritten Sources merely describe in terms of timeless fact what in the *Timaeus* is an expression of free demiurgic grace. Plato must, however, have been clear that, while application in this or that case is not and cannot be of the pure essence of the Eide, a general applicability to cases *is* of their essence – the goodness of the Demiurge means just this – and hence that the Soul, that great mediator between the eidetic and the instantial, is necessarily confronted by an indefinitely numerous, purged set of idealized instances, to which, in default of actual instances, it can apply its eidetic insights. Insight into Triangularity as Such and into a peculiar sub-species of Being Triangular, can lead one to see the ideal congruence of two possible triangles of such a sub-species. The Mathematical Objects thus arrived at are a necessary element in an eidetic epistemology: they are the Noemata of Husserl, the Incomplete Objects of Meinong, perhaps the Senses of Frege and Church. They are in a sense the images of concrete sensuous instances, rather than the other way round, since they represent a half-way house towards instantiation rather than a full arrival there. If the paradigm of Eidetic Status is in the highest Eide, the paradigm of Instantial Status lies in the things of sense. It is perhaps because the Mathematica are such shifting phantasmal things, multiplied to suit the problems and hypotheses of the mathematician, and not even having the measurable reliability of the proven things of sense, that Plato is so chary of saying anything definite about them in the Dialogues, where they are so often peeping round the corner yet never allowed to come fully into view. But their presence is certain since it is theoretically necessary: mathematics is not about Eide nor about sensible instances of Eide. Plato could see the obvious even if some of his commentators cannot.

If we turn to the instantial sense-order, the Unwritten Sources tell us little about it beyond the fact that the *very same material Principle*, the Great and the Small, which together with the One yields the Eide, also yields the particular, changeable instances of sense, in co-operation with the Eide and ultimately with the One which is their Principle. As Aristotle tells us in *Metaphysics*, 998a 8:

> This is what Plato laid down in regard to the matters in question. It is clear from the above that he made use of only two Principles, one of essence (τοῦ τί ἐστι) and one material (the Eide are the essential cause of other things, and the One of the Eide). It is also clear what the underlying cause is of which the Eide are predicated in the case of sensible things, and of which the One is predicated in the case of the Eide, that it is a Dyad, the Great and the Small. It is further clear that he assigned causality for Good and causality for Evil to his two Principles respectively.

Similarly Simplicius, commenting on *Physics*, 207a 18, writes:

> Plato speaking in his discourses on the Good said that the Great and Small, which he also called the Infinite, were the matter out of which all sensible things were assembled, and that they were rendered unknowable through their material, infinite and flowing nature. It followed from this notion, however, that even among intelligibles there was a Great and Small which is there called the Indefinite Dyad, and which is the source with the One of all Number and all Beings. For the Eide are Numbers.

The physical Great and Small is identified by Aristotle with the Space (χώρα) of the *Timaeus* (*Physics*, 209b 11–17), with an explicit reference to Plato's Unwritten Doctrines. The Great and Small was also associated with Difference and Inequality and Movement and Irregularity. (See Simplicius in his comments on *Physics*, 201b 16 citing Eudemus, Plato's pupil and Aristotle's close friend.) The Receptacle of the *Timaeus*, with its irregular shakings which the Demiurgic Thinkingness has to reduce to limit, is merely the Great and Small which, having assumed various eidetic and mathematical avatars, is now dancing its final dance of death in the sensible world. The continuity of all these proceedings means, for example, that we can take everything said in a late Dialogue like the *Philebus* about the Limit and the Unlimited in the sense-world as applying also in the realm of the Eide. And it means finally that the whole appearance of a two-world doctrine, that an injudicious reader might collect from, for example, the *Phaedo*, is radically un-Platonic. The generation goes on unbrokenly through the eidetic, mathematical and sense-levels, and involves the same principles throughout. This means that it is no less essential for the Eide to have imperfect changeable instances than it is essential for the One and the Great and Small to be variously specified in the Eide. The whole fabric is of one piece and whatever is above is below and vice versa. The most defective instantial arrangements have an interstitial reflection at the eidetic level, and the Principles of the Eide are at work among instances.

And since the Great and Small is further identified with What is Not (*Physics*, 201b 20 and elsewhere), with the emptiness of Space and the illusory being of sensible instances, and with the corresponding emptiness and possibility of sophistry which even infect the region of the Eide, we see that the Second Principle in the Platonic Ontology is really no more than the pervasive Nothingness which is also the ever-present presupposition of Specification and Instantiation, the Nothingness called into a simulacrum of being by the formative activity which is Unity Itself. The Wisdom of Elea, as Plato understood it, therefore both confirms and overturns the Opinions of Mortals, and the arts of the Sophist. These statements may appear wild and un-Hellenic, but no one who studies the direct and reported material with care can doubt that they describe the final drift of Plato's thought. Though hard and clear at the centre, and delightful to those who like what is hard and clear, it melts into mists at the extremities, which are very fortunately just as delightful to others.

V

Any further treatment of Plato's unwritten arithmetization of the Eide is too controversial and technical a task to be carried on in the present volume. Our aim is philosophical understanding, and philosophical understanding would not be further assisted by closer study of the limited documentary material and by framing daring hypotheses to deal with their detailed difficulties. Some of the hypotheses so framed have been much too daring and too arbitrary, and they have attributed to Plato correlations of Eide with Numbers that are about as silly as the procedure of Eurytus the Pythagorean, who tried to determine the number of Man by counting pebbles assembled along the outline of a roughly drawn human figure. If Plato was guilty of such theories, and some of the speculations of Stenzel and Gaiser, for example, suggest that he was, his theories are certainly not worth exploring. What we have been concerned to show is that the arithmetization of the Eide was a programme rather than a finished doctrine, and that, on a suitable interpretation, it was a magnificent and not a silly programme. A suitable interpretation is one that does not follow Aristotle in supposing that the equation of Eide with Numbers means the one-for-one equation of each Eidos with a Natural Number – an interpretation which even the statements of Aristotle do not force upon us, a connection with Ratios being given as an alternative. And a suitable interpretation is not possible if we imagine that the pre-eminence of the Tetrad-Decad in Plato's theory meant that the Eidetic Numbers stopped short at the Number Ten. This latter view, also, is not forced upon us by the Aristotelian testimony, which says that not all Platonic statements fit in with it. The view that the arithmetization did not preclude the introduction of the 'Things that come after the Numbers', i.e. the many-dimensional numerical ratios involved in geometrical and dynamic patterns, is also one that fits in with the Aristotelian testimony and the teaching of the Dialogues. If further study of the scholarly treatment of the arithmetization is desired, the student is referred above all to Robin's classic *La Théorie Platonicienne des Idées et des Nombres d'après Aristote* (1908), to Stenzel's *Zahl und Gestalt bei Platon und Aristoteles* (1924, 1959), to Ross's *Plato's Theory of Ideas* (1951), to Wilpert's

Zwei aristotelische Frühschriften über die Ideenlehre (1949), to Gaiser's *Platons Ungeschriebene Lehre* (1963, 1968) and to Krämer's *Arete bei Platon und Aristoteles* (1959) and the follow-up in *Der Ursprung der Geistesmetaphysik* (1964, 1967). If some of these works provide exhaustive coverage of material from which none the less nothing that is psychologically credible or philosophically viable is allowed to emerge, they yet all bear witness to an all-important side of Plato's teaching, and works like those of Gaiser and Krämer concur with our systematic hypothesis that the arithmetization was an early rather than a late development of Plato's thought, which though never adequately expressed in the Dialogues, on account of its essentially unfinished, programmatic character, none the less formed the unwritten background of all the mature Dialogues from at least the time of the *Republic*. When Aristotle came to the Academy in 367 the arithmetization was already in full swing, and the reports on Platonism in the *Metaphysics* and elsewhere reflect the doctrines of this period. Of Plato's later, more critical attitude to his own programme, and his turning away to more purely analytical or concrete studies, there is much less notice in Aristotle. It is therefore as a background to the Written Dialogues that the Unwritten Doctrines will henceforth be treated by us, and we shall try to show that they at every point throw light on what is explicit in the Dialogues, and that the hypothesis of their background presence is in every way feasible and helpful.

Note: The two Appendices to the present volume provide most of what is *essential* to the understanding of Plato's Unwritten Teaching. The first provides translations of most of the most relevant Greek passages; the second hopefully refutes Cherniss's misinterpretations of the same, and of other Platonic material.

III

THE SOCRATIC DIALOGUES

I

In the present chapter our aim will be to comment, with some sketchiness, on those writings of Plato in which, it may be presumed, his main concern was to paint a picture of Socrates in the full flush of his intellectual vigour and brilliance, conducting those famous discussions to which the name 'dialectical' has been given. This name indicates an investigation conducted by two interlocutors, a major and a minor, in which the former never proceeds without first exacting a positive, or at least an assenting, response from the latter. These Dialogues are presumed to be the earliest written by Plato, and though they often imply the theory of Eide or Ideal Meanings, and at times even use the language afterwards pre-empted to express the latter, they do not make the Eide an actual topic of discussion. What they are concerned with is an analytical circumscription of the various Virtues or moral Excellences recognized in fifth- and fourth-century Athens, and a consideration of their relation to one another and to the intelligent persons and communities who accept them and cultivate them, as well as an examination of various notions and practices relevant to such virtues and excellences as were embodied in the teachings of various professional teachers and practitioners of argument, of Practical Wisdom and general knowledge, who are classifiable as 'Sophists', Rhetoricians and Eristics, and who were a main force in the intellectual and moral ferment of the period. We shall consider Dialogues which attempt analyses of aesthetic and moral 'Fineness' (*Hippias Major*), of Courage, Self-control and Piety (*Laches, Charmides* and *Euthyphro*), or which consider the nature and necessary conditions of Love or Friendship (*Lysis*). We shall also see Socrates defending himself before his judges (*Apology*), or refusing to escape from the prison and death to which they had condemned him (*Crito*), and we shall see him confronting the Sophist Protagoras with a theory of Virtue as a kind of exact calculus of what will truly satisfy the Soul, the rhetorician Gorgias and his pupils with a theory of what, contrary to common opinion, will truly tend to the Soul's advantage, while the contentious verbal tricksters Euthydemus and Dionysodorus are met with a 'protreptic' discourse designed to turn the Soul from the lesser goods of common esteem to the authentic if nebulous goals of truly reasoned and virtuous living.

All these Dialogues acquaint us with the methods and conclusions of the Socratic Dialectic, but they also reveal a stage in the thought of Plato, for it was in trying to give expression to Socrates's incomparable manner and person that Plato himself developed his characteristic opinions, though, as we have seen, Pythagorean, Heraclitean and above all Eleatic influences also played a part in their origin. Sometimes indeed what is arguably Platonic, rather than Socratic, shines through these early writings, and sometimes even the rudiments of the 'mathematicization', that most characteristic contribution of mature Platonism, can be found in them. We are therefore justified in treating these earlier writings as authentic expressions of philosophical Platonism, and not merely as literary reflections of a Socraticism to which it was only historically related. At the same time the dominant intent to portray Socrates makes these early Dialogues of less interest for Platonic interpretation than those, regarded as later, in which this intent is absent or less pronounced. We shall therefore set forth their content in much less detail than in the case of the more mature, indefeasibly Platonic treatments. In general we shall avoid the pitfall of following all the windings of the imagined or reported discussions. To do so involves burying issues of substance, difficult to define and lay hold of, in difficulties of detail that will never be satisfactorily resolved, and adding one more unsatisfactory restatement of Plato's infinitely delicate and wandering argument to the many made in the past. There are so many analyses and interpretations of the Platonic Dialogues which merely rewrite them blunderingly, linking them irrelevantly with transient contemporaneity, that a more selective though careful oversight may well be in place, and can always be filled out by recourse to the analyses in question, or, better still, to the cleaner detail of Plato's actual text.

A general comment on the Socratic arguments is here in place: that they are as brimful of fallacy as are the ordinary or sophistical positions to which they oppose themselves, often more so. The interlocutors whom Socrates demolishes by his carefully slanted questions, and by the conclusions he draws from their unthinking utterances, often show a better grasp of the ways in which ordinary words are used, and the ways of the living concepts behind them, than their brilliant interrogator, with his various fixed logical, semantic and philosophical prepossessions. They illustrate their meanings with confidence, but are hesitant and diffident in offering definitions and analyses of them, except in those cases where they have themselves been schooled in some type of precise analysis. They are not afraid or ashamed to say things inconsistent with what they previously said when their feeling for an actual meaning demands this, and they have in general no rigid, preconceived doctrines of logical consequence, exclusion and compatibility which regiments all their utterances. Socrates, on the other hand, not only assumes that to every well-established ethical term some uniform, self-consistent, clear-cut notion corresponds, but is also guided by a host of principles of shaky authenticity, such as that every predicate can have only a single contrary, or such as that what is in all cases a necessary condition of A is also in all cases a sufficient condition of A, and is in fact the whole analysis or essence of A. (*Virtue is Knowledge* rests, for example, on this last, shaky principle.) He also in general shows a defective sense of the varied senses and uses of negation in living thought and speech, that 'not-just', for example, may stand for the simple lack or absence of justice, or for that lack conjoined with other characters which are widely different or even opposed to justice, or that it may stand, lastly, for the presence of characters *other* than justice which none the less do *not* entail its lack. As modern logicians seldom consider these Protean differences in the sense of negation, we may perhaps excuse Socrates for failing to do so, and for arriving at conclusions even more narrowly rigorous than theirs.

Socrates clearly realized the considerable gulf between the endemically vague, profitably directive and emotive concepts of Virtue and Value, and the more precisely geared, narrowly descriptive concepts which occur in mathematics and in ordinary life and discourse, and much of his dialectic consists in bringing such differences out. Thus Socrates sees that value-notions like those of the Virtues have a closer relation to feelings of satisfaction and to choice and action than do concepts like 'surface' or 'circular', which are only by accident stirring or directive. He believes that it is impossible to be wholly clear as to where the Good lies, and not to move in its direction. He is also clear as to the higher-order, universalistic character of value-concepts: that they urge us on, not merely to compass one more or less definite result, as do certain forms of pandering or flattery (e.g. cookery, persuasion), but to coordinate all our tasks and wants 'wisely', and to coordinate all the tasks and wants of various persons 'fairly', and that such coordination involves a particularization Protean in its variety, and finely adjusted to the variations of circumstance, so that hardly anything that is just or sensible or moderate or brave for one person in one set of circumstances, will be just or sensible or moderate or brave for another person in other circumstances. But the endeavour of Socrates to exclude from the concepts of the virtues whatever varies from case to case, and to give them a rigidity of profile by analogy with the definite tasks and arts, ends by making them almost wholly indefinite and void of content: they become a mere being deeply wise or judicious in conduct in which no separate emphases are allowed to distinguish themselves. Plato was later willing to make virtue a One-over-many in which the separate emphases of being Sensible or Wise, Firm or Brave in adhering to the dictates of such Wisdom, Moderate in the control of one's personal wants, and Fair in one's dealings with the other members of one's community, were allowed to distinguish themselves, but for Socrates all tended to lose itself in a dialectical mist, in which 'Knowledge' or Wise Living alone cast a vague illumination, a general obfuscation to which his less logical interlocutors seldom fell victim.

Socrates was therefore in many ways a Sophist, the professor of an emptily general Wisdom which gives little concrete guidance, though it was noble and high-minded in tone rather than concerned with personal aggrandisement and advantage, and he was also an Eristic, an argumentative wrangler who uses principles of argument having only a vague initial plausibility, and often leading to absurd or disastrous conclusions when applied too widely. But Socrates infused into his Sophistry and his Eristic a moral passion which his interlocutors and competitors did not share at all, and a deep feeling for the elusive meaning of moral terms which invariably guided him in the right direction despite the roughnesses and the hazards which his own logical obsessions everywhere threw up. And his feeling for moral meanings was unerring because he himself embodied them all, sharing both the acceptance of concrete, existent obligations, without which the moral life would be void of content, and the endless willingness to criticize and reflect on them impartially and in the company of others, without which they would lack the intersubjectivity and the claim to validity which makes them moral. And though Socrates may not have been successful in outlining the *corpus mysticum* of the Virtues, his very failure to do so itself introduced a new higher set of Virtues: the Virtues of Impartiality, of Tolerance of the opinions of others, of Willingness to pursue Enquiries indefinitely, together with an acceptance of the duties of an existent society which all meaningful criticism presupposes. Socrates was very remarkably both an incarnation of the humane conventionalism which the better Sophists also accepted, and also of the criticism of which they only knew the beginnings. And he irradiated this all with a mystical holiness in the light of which the ancient world found it possible to live through the long iniquities of the later Roman Empire, and the fanaticisms and cruelties of much early Christianity, for the 'wise man' whom Stoics, Epicureans, Sceptics and Neoplatonists alike strove to be was in all cases a reflection of Socrates. If we desire an incarnation of the Logos or reasoned argument, then Socrates was that incarnation, and it is as such that he is presented in the earlier Dialogues of Plato, and continues as an abiding presence and inspirational background in all the Platonic writings.

II

Our consideration of Plato's Dialogues may well start with two extremely immature exercises, both of which present Socrates discoursing with the famous Sophist Hippias of Elis, one who specialized in imparting encyclopedic information, and who claimed expertise in mathematics, astronomy, mythology, history, linguistics, harmonics etc. In the hands of Socrates he appears as the veriest child, being wholly ignorant of what it is to isolate and define a universal meaning. The authenticity of the two Dialogues, the *Hippias Major* and the *Hippias Minor*, is vouched for by references in Aristotle, and, authenticity being conceded, their great immaturity as exercises is very revealing: we realize how far Plato had to go from such rude portrayals of Socrates to the accomplished drama of the *Charmides*, *Protagoras* etc., and how much of art, and of the transformation involved in art, these later writings presuppose.

In the *Hippias Major* the excellence to be analysed is the one pinned down by the commendatory Greek adjective καλόν, a word covering both the beauty and dignity which seems to reside in the objects of the nobler senses of sight and hearing, and also the loftiness or nobility or moral beauty which is felt to inform human characters and actions. The beauty of abstracted theoretical meanings such as those of mathematics is not here included: it will be later brought up in the *Symposium* and other Dialogues. Though the Dialogue is early and immature, Socrates formulates his problem in advanced terms: there is, he holds, such a thing as Justice through which just men are just, such a thing as Wisdom through which the wise are wise, and, in the third place, such a thing as Beauty or the Beautiful through which beautiful things are beautiful, and we wish to enquire, in the case of the last, not what things are beautiful, but what Beauty or the Beautiful itself is (*Hippias Major*, 287-8). Here we have three initial assumptions: (a) that there *is* a Beautiful Itself or as Such (real being of the Eide); (b) that it is in some manner responsible for anything's being beautiful (efficacy of the Eide); (c) that it is possible and profitable to ask what this Beautiful Itself may be, and that this is *quite* a different question from asking what a beautiful thing may be (independent analysability of the Eide).

Hippias's reply to this invitation to elucidate Beauty is merely to illustrate it: a lovely girl, he says with confidence, is a beautiful thing. But so, too, are horses and lyres and pieces of pottery, and if one holds that these last lose their semblance of beauty when set beside a girl, then the girl herself loses her semblance of beauty

when set beside a goddess. One's concern is not here with semblant beauty, which may very well go together with semblant
ugliness, but with the Beauty Itself which by being present to
things makes them appear beautiful. (Here one has the doctrine
of the inadequate illustration of the Eidos by the Instance: an
instance of Beauty is not as purely beautiful as its Eidos, and
appears, rather than is, truly beautiful. Modern critics will argue
that Beauty is not properly self-predicable: its self-predication is
certainly rather that of self-identity than of self-participation.)
Hippias now makes a further *gaffe* by identifying the Beautiful
with the golden or with gold: wherever gold is laid on something, it imparts beauty to it. Obviously, however, there are
other cases of beauty than the golden, and obviously gold may be
unsuitable to certain objects, for example domestic implements.
This suggests that suitability (τὸ πρέπον) is a suitable account of
Beauty, but obviously, though suitability may be a necessary, it
cannot be a sufficient condition of being beautiful. Hippias's final
gaffe is to suggest that Beauty unmixed with even a semblance of
the unlovely is to be found in the death of a rich man who has
given appropriate funeral honours to his parents and who now
receives such honours from his own offspring. Obviously there
are many quite different cases of Beauty than this unfortunate
example, and above all it is not the 'Beauty Itself' of which we
are in quest.

The Suitable (τὸ πρέπον) mentioned above is now more
seriously tried out as a candidate to be Beauty Itself, but is
rejected for the curious reason that it only makes objects *appear*
beautiful – i.e. in a context that they happen to suit – and not
really to *be* beautiful, which everyone agrees cannot be a matter of
context. The Useful (τὸ χρήσιμον) meets with a similar rejection:
it would make beautiful things merely instrumental to some
further good, and not good in themselves as they obviously are.
(It is here assumed as axiomatic that 'a cause cannot be a cause of
itself' (297a), and that if being beautiful is being productive of
good, it cannot itself be a higher-order cause of good.) A remaining suggestion connects beauty with pleasure, though not
with pleasure derived from every source: the Beautiful is arguably
the object of visually and auditorily aroused pleasure. Even laws
and occupations, it is pointed out, have a connection with what
we see and hear, and can therefore be enjoyed as 'fine' whereas

the objects of sexual and nutritive pleasures have not. Obviously, however, it is unsatisfactory to differentiate objects of pleasure in respect of something quite extrinsic to pleasure, i.e. the particular sense from whose stimulation pleasure arises. The ingenious suggestion is then made that there may be some property pertaining to things heard and things seen *taken together* which pertains to neither singly. If it be doubted whether any such property can exist, we have only to consider the case of Numbers and numerical properties which pertain to things *taken in the plural* and not to any such things taken singly. Thus Twoness and Evenness pertain to two objects in the plural, though only Unity and Oddness pertain to each single object, and being both an object of sight and hearing obviously depends on both properties, and not on either of them singly. This remarkable suggestion, basically valuable for the philosophy of Number, is however inapplicable to the theory of Beauty: Beauty does not work like the Number Two, and if both of two objects are beautiful, each is so and vice versa. A further suggestion that objects are beautiful if they give *harmless* pleasure once more reduces beauty to a case of the profitable, which involves the divorce between beauty and intrinsic goodness which was previously rejected.

The final reaction of Hippias to all this vain argumentation is understandable: it is only really beautiful to come out on top in forensic or political debate, thus winning security for one's person, property and friends, and 'bidding farewell to these verbal pettinesses and so avoiding the appearance of utter silliness which comes from messing about with such rubbishy twaddle' (304b). Socrates, however, has to satisfy 'a man within' who will not allow him to pursue even plain cases of the Beautiful unless he can say what the Beautiful Itself is. What this Dialogue shows, rather than asserts, is the higher-order or 'transcendental' character of Beauty: it is plainly an eidetic *Principle* rather than a specific Eidos such as being golden or being young and feminine. And what it also shows is that, despite the manifold connections of the Beautiful with the Useful, the Pleasing, the contextually Suitable etc., it still is a distinct facet of that ultimate Unity of the Virtuous, the Profitable and the Wise into which Socrates makes all excellences melt. What the aesthetic emphasis specifically is neither Socrates nor Plato ever succeeded in saying. Which does not mean that, at a sufficient distance from the concrete, the place of Beauty in an economy of interlaced 'transcendentals' cannot be adequately stated.

The *Hippias Minor* deals with a much slighter but highly exciting question: whether the deliberately and consciously wicked, who for instance tell lies knowing them to be lies and knowing it to be bad to tell them, are or are not better than those who tell such falsehoods ignorantly, not knowing them to be falsehoods and perhaps not seeing any evil in telling a falsehood. Hippias takes the ordinary view that those who deliberately tell lies about something, or otherwise transgress, are quite different from, and much baser people than, those who deliberately tell the truth or in some other manner go straight, and that those who fall short of rectitude and truth owing to ignorance are neither virtuous nor base, but deserve compassion rather than condemnation. Socrates points out, however, how every art or science is of opposites. The good mathematician or astronomer who can hit upon the right answer to some problem, is also unerringly able to answer wrongly, and will never accidentally give a right answer when he aims at being wrong. The runner who can run very fast and so win a race, is also unfailingly able to lose the same race. If every intelligent power is therefore of opposites, and there is no absolute gulf set between those who exercise such a power in a right or a wrong way, they are in either case better men than those who lack such a power and who merely achieve what is good or bad by accident. A man, therefore, who voluntarily compasses what is evil is better than one who compasses it involuntarily, since the former was capable of achieving the good, whereas the latter, except by accident, could not. In the Socratic-Platonic thought-world, where the sciences are shot through with values, and the virtues are themselves sciences which impel to action, the man who goes astray voluntarily must possess more of the saving science of Virtue than the man who does so involuntarily.

It would be easy to dismiss the exercise as a piece of pure sophistry and so the sound moral sense of the Sophist Hippias not unjustifiably regarded it. And it would be easy to see it as inconsistent with the characteristic Socratic opinion that it is impossible to have Knowledge of the Good and also to swerve from it into Evil. There would appear, however, to be merit in this early exercise, and it is in fact the first statement of a doctrine without which the whole doctrine of the Eide would fail to make sense: that there is no need for *separate* Eide of the impious, the unjust, the ill-formed and for the many other contraries of the well-formed and intelligible and excellent. Their being is in fact part of the being of the Eide which exclude them, and which by excluding them also give them a parasitic contrast-status. And arguably those whose imperfect feeling for the absolutely Good enables them with some accuracy to fall short of it, are further advanced on the road towards entire virtue than those whose efforts are wide of the mark and only accidentally hit it. The Marquis de Sade, with the compassion which he overcame, and respect for innocence which he systematically violated, was therefore less remote from the ultimate goal of Virtue than those who had no such sensitivenesses to violate. I should not, however, myself wish to argue for such a view, and feel in this discussion nearer to Hippias than to Socrates.

Our treatment of these early exercises may be rounded off by a consideration of the *Ion* in which Socrates questions an Ephesian rhapsode who claims to be expert at interpreting Homer, though he practically goes to sleep when any other poetic writings are in question. Socrates points out, implying the same principle that we have commented on in the case of the *Hippias Minor*, that those who have an expert understanding of Homer, the best of poets, ought necessarily to have an expert understanding of all who fall short of Homer's excellence in various ways, but who are throughout doing the same sort of thing as Homer and working on the same religious and mythic material. The fact that Ion's interpretative flair is limited to Homer shows that it cannot be a true interpretative capacity: there are no principles on which it works and certainly none of which the rhapsode is conscious or can formulate for the benefit of others. There is a passage in the *Iliad* where a charioteer is counselled to be careful at the turns of the course, so as not to scrape its stone boundaries, and only a charioteer, and not Ion, could judge of the appropriateness of Homer's prescription. The like applies to passages where food is provided for invalids, and where only a doctor, and not a rhapsode, could possibly judge of its suitability. Ion contends that he, and all rhapsodes, at least thoroughly understand generalship, but this claim is refuted by the fact that the Athenians, who have often put foreigners in charge of their armies, have not done so in the case of such as Ion.

Obviously then, Socrates reasons, poets and interpreters of poets are like magnets tenanted by a divine power which can be communicated to a long chain of attached rings and pieces of iron, or like the Corybantes dancing in delirium because of the God in them. The value of the Socratic theory of poetic interpretation, like that of Anamnesis or Recollection, is that it emphasizes the existence of vague total consciousnesses which lead up and are capable of being developed into clearly analysed knowledge, the latter not being arrived at by the steady piecing together of clearly envisioned fragments. The empiricist theory of knowledge follows the latter pattern, and so do many modern theories of meaning, but all fail totally to explain the variety and depth of what we can come to understand and know. We shall see Plato showing up the emptiness of all such gradualistic, elementaristic theories in later Dialogues like the *Cratylus* and the *Theaetetus*.

III

The *Charmides*, *Laches* and *Lysis* are three very perfect attempts at analysing a virtue or excellence which, by their failure, reveal the higher-order character of the meanings involved, the variability of their relation to specific contents, and the difficulty of separating them from one another in an ordered scheme of well-considered living. The *Charmides* deals with the Greek virtue of σωφροσύνη, whose scope may be rendered by such English words as 'moderation', 'restraint', 'self-control' or 'temperateness'. ('Temperance' does not now render the notion since in the nineteenth century it became the name of a form of intemperate fanaticism. None the less, it will often be convenient to use the word.) Obviously it will mainly be in cases where there is a strong tendency to go 'too far' in one direction or another that well-considered living will assume this moderating form: in other cases moderation will lack significant application. The *Laches* deals with the Greek virtue of ἀνδρεία, which may be fairly rendered by such terms as 'courage', 'bravery', 'firmness' or 'endurance'. Well-considered living will assume this form where there is a strong but unsuitable tendency to run away from some situation –

otherwise it will have no significant application. The *Lysis* deals with that excellence of feeling in which one thing or person is *dear* (φίλον, φίλος) to someone or when something or someone cherishes or is cherished by something or someone. The 'dear', though seemingly simple, reveals itself to be an extraordinarily elusive, many-sided notion, spanning the most commonplace and the most abstract and exalted affections. All this shows itself rather in the manner in which the Socratic Dialectic turns and moves in our three cases than in the imperfect analyses that it successively throws up for our consideration.

In the *Charmides* Socrates interrogates a young man, Plato's uncle, who afterwards became one of the Thirty Tyrants, but who is still a youth and held by all to be an examplar of that σωφροσύνη or quiet drawing-the-line-in-conduct whose analysis is the theme of the Dialogue. At a later stage the older and more sophisticated Critias, a cousin of Charmides and later also one of the Thirty, becomes Socrates's interlocutor. Charmides is told that if σωφροσύνη, Moderation is present in him, he will be able to form a view regarding it, for being *in* Charmides it will necessarily give rise to an experience or perception of itself which will lead Charmides both to believe *that* it exists and to know what sort of thing it is. Knowing Greek, he will then be able to say just how it appears to him (158e–159a). The view of the speech-side of Charmides's responses is not that of a mere casting about among what is commonly said of Moderation, but casting about among established usages for words that express how the virtue feels to the virtuous person and to hint at its actual felt quality. Charmides examining himself first dredges up Quietness (ἡσυχιότης) as the distinguishing mark of temperate action: the temperate, moderate man walks, talks and generally conducts himself in a subdued, quiet fashion. Obviously, however, such Quietness would not be appropriate in the countless skilled performances, boxing, running, reading, writing, learning etc., in which its application, if made at all, would carry with it inappropriate suggestions of languor. Socrates acting on the tacitly accepted principle that what it is to be temperate cannot include a reference to context, and so be at times inapplicable, and taking it that a virtuous person must necessarily be virtuous in all ways at all times, therefore dismisses the subdued and restrained as the mark of the temperate. Charmides, again dredging his sense of the virtue and the Greek language, next puts forward Shame (αἰσχύνη) as the mark of the temperate: the temperate man draws the line at certain performances because he would be ashamed to do them. Obviously, however, there are many cases in which shame would be quite 'false' and inappropriate, and (granted we refuse to add to the notion of Shame the circumstances in which shame would be inappropriate) Shame is not suited to circumscribe the Temperate.

Charmides now borrows from his cousin Critias the sophisticated definition of the Temperate as 'doing one's own thing' (τὸ τὰ ἑαυτοῦ πράττειν), a definition which the *Republic* will afterwards try to fit to the nature of Justice. Temperate people are those who stay within the limits of the role assigned to them by nature or society, and do not officiously trespass on the duties and provinces of others. This sophistical definition is sophistically rejected by pointing out that men with roles carry them out in relation to the demands of others: it would not be temperate to weave and wash only one's own cloak, cobble only one's own sandals etc. and not those of others. Critias now replaces Charmides, and imitates the subtle word-distinguisher Prodicus by drawing a distinction between making (ποιεῖν) and doing (πράττειν). In *doing* what is one's own, one need not necessarily *make* what is one's own, and it is the former and not the latter which must be good if one is to be classed as temperate (163e).

Socrates now sees a chance to bring in his favourite doctrine that the good performer of some praxis or action must necessarily *know* how it should be done and also *that* it has been done as it ought, a line of argument that is to lead to the exaggerated identification of Virtue with Knowledge. It leads Critias, however, to a further sophistical definition: Knowing Oneself is what it is to be temperate, it is, in short, having a perfect understanding of one's role. Socrates, however, is unclear as to the precise scope of this peculiar sort of Knowledge, so unlike the knowledge of a builder or a doctor, and is met with the new suggestion that Knowledge of Self is simply Knowledge of Knowledge, a knowledge which embraces among its objects, not only other forms of knowledge, but also the very Knowledge of Knowledge which it itself is. Socrates adds to this the point that he has made very familiar, that a Knowledge of Knowledge will necessarily *also* be a Knowledge of Ignorance, so that the temperate man will both know when he knows something and also when he is ignorant of something. This knowledge, for reasons unstated, is further not introspective, but general: the temperate man will not only know when *he* knows or does not know something, but he will also know when *other* people know things and when they are exceeding their knowledge (167a). The peculiar logical status of this supposed Knowledge of Knowledge and Ignorance is, however, productive of difficulty. No other conscious approach, for example sight, hearing, desire, opinion, love, is directed exclusively to itself and to things of like type with itself: all are exclusively directed to objects other than and other in type than themselves. To believe in a knowledge which is only of knowledge and its contrary would be as absurd as believing in something greater than itself and also greater than all things that are greater than anything. If such a knowledge is possible, it is, moreover, doubtful whether there can be any profit in it, and Temperateness is certainly held to be a profitable and excellent thing. For if a man has a knowledge of knowledge, it will only inform him *that* he knows something and not exactly *what* he knows: this latter will only be revealed to him through the special sciences of medicine, music, architecture etc. Here, we may note the argument is brazenly sophistical: it assumes that the higher-order Knowledge of Knowledge cannot be built upon, and in a sense contain the knowledge which is its object, so as to have that knowledge's object as its secondary object. In knowing how to build I am also in a position to know that I know how to build, and I can know the latter in so far as in knowing it I also know the former. These are plain truths and we must adjust our principles of argument to fit them, not mishandle the truths in order to fit the principles. Socrates has engineered himself into a position where neither the knowledge of *X* nor the knowledge of that knowledge, can teach us that we know *X*, yet plainly we are often very clear that we know something.

Socrates passes on, however, to a further demonstration of the total uselessness of the supposed Knowledge of Knowledge. For it is obviously quite useless to know whether one knows something or not, unless one also knows whether what one knows is worth knowing, i.e. is intrinsically good. The knowledge of Good and Evil, of what is profitable to man, is therefore necessary to make the knowledge of knowledge profitable, and yet this answer cannot give enlightenment since we have connected a good life with a life guided by knowledge (174c). Even apart from this, the notion of a Knowledge of Knowledge involves the great difficulty of an attendant Knowledge of Ignorance, for how without knowing something can we know that we do *not* know it? The dilemma of Socrates rests on his acceptance of the principle that a universally necessary condition of X must also be the true and sufficient condition of X, and that since the knowledge of goodness is a necessary condition of the good life, it is also the *only* element which gives excellence to that life, and that there cannot be other contributory elements which are only in the full sense good when perfected by knowledge. Plato in the *Republic*, *Philebus* etc., was to become clear as to the necessary many-sidedness of the human good, and to temper the moral Eleaticism of Socrates with graded differentiations. Socrates, further, in making Knowledge not merely the crowning but the only element in the human Good, also necessarily makes that Good and that Knowledge abstract and empty. But, as the *Charmides* shows, Socrates was perfectly conscious of the impossibility of finding an answer to his questions within the framework of his own method and assumptions. His method is not, therefore, merely destructive of superficial definitions and analyses, but of the whole method of definition and analysis. That it is defective, and that it points to something better, may be said to be the 'unspoken doctrine' of Socrates.

In the *Laches*, Socrates has succeeded in turning the practical anxieties of two parents, Lysimachus and Melesias, concerning the advisability of submitting their sons to a training in fighting in armour given by a military expert Stesilaus, into a discussion of the nature of Courage. In this discussion Laches, who has innocently brought Socrates into this practical discussion, will have to serve as a respondent in talk that moves further and further from the practical. Nicias, who is not so innocent of the wiles of Socrates, will afterwards also take part in the discussion. Obviously the aim of a course in fighting in armour is to develop virtue in the trainees, and that special part of virtue that is known as ἀνδρεία or Courage. Only if we know what Courage is, shall we be able to decide whether Stesilaus is able to impart it by imparting the art of fighting in armour. Laches has no difficulty in saying what Courage is: it is remaining within one's ranks and defending them against the enemy and not taking to flight (190e). This definition is far from bad provided 'the ranks', 'the enemy' and 'flight' are given a sufficiently wide and metaphorical sense. Socrates, however, is able to invalidate it, if taken quite literally, by pointing to the Scythians and other brave fighters who fight flying, or fight by retreating strategically etc. We are, as Socrates says, not merely concerned with the bravery of heavily armed foot-soldiers, but with the bravery of cavalry, or of men at sea, or of those fighting against disease or poverty or political power, or against their own strong lusts and pleasures.

Socrates now puts forward as a model the clear-cut definition of swiftness – a power which performs much in a little time – and Laches thereupon defines Courage as a perseverance (καρτερία) or firmness of the soul, a 'sticking it out'. This is obviously inadequate, as the 'sticking it out' may be perverse or harmful: only a wise, balanced 'sticking it out' can amount to that beautiful thing Courage. Wise persistence would not, however, appear to be courageous in cases where such persistence comes easily, and it would even seem that those who do not know how to do things, and who are therefore *not* wise about them, are more courageous in attempting them than those who do have such wisdom. Obviously, however, some sort of wisdom is necessary to the circumscription of Courage. Laches becomes intellectually exhausted, and hands over his role to Nicias, who suggests that the Wisdom or Knowledge which is a part or the whole of Courage can only be a wisdom regarding what is truly dangerous (δεινόν) or truly 'safe' (θαρραλέον) whether in war or in any other situation. This Wisdom or Knowledge is not merely a knowledge as to how to do this or that, but also a knowledge as to whether something is worth doing or achieving, or whether, that is, it is good or bad, a knowledge which no animal can achieve, and hardly any child, no matter how daring and fearless it may be. It seems an arguable opinion that Courage is concerned with the goods and evils that lie *in the future*, and not with those that are to be found in the present or the past: a courageous man will be one who knows what is really dangerous or 'safe', and both the dangerous and the safe lie in the future, and are the concern of attitudes that are oriented towards the future. Socrates, however, cannot believe that

in regard to such things as can be known, there is one
science that knows how the past happened, another science
that knows how what is happening is happening,
another science which knows how what has not yet happened
may best come to be, and continue to come to be, but
rather that the same science knows all these things. Just as
medicine being one and not different considers what
is happening in the realm of health, and how what
happened happened, and how what will happen will happen.
(198d, e)

The science which is Bravery is not therefore confined to dangers
and salvations which lie exclusively in the future, but to forms of
Good and Evil which are located at any time. We are therefore
unable to draw a dividing line between Courage and other forms
of Virtue: all are absorbed in the Knowledge of Good and Evil,
and the use of this conclusion to resolve doubts as to the desirability of training one's sons to fight in armour remains as far as
ever.

Socrates has therefore deliberately dissolved the ordinary
concept of Courage, to which a context of difficulty and persistence in the face of difficulty are essential – as well as a reference
to merely possible future goods and evils – into the wider, vaguer
concept of reflective living, which certainly only expresses itself
in Courage on appropriate occasions. Without lapsing from
virtue or becoming uncourageous, one cannot, as Socrates
plainly sees, be positively courageous in situations which pose no
threat. But the Unity of Virtue, and the necessity of insight and
reflection in its perfected forms, need not imply that it may not
have to take the form of Courage in circumstances of special
difficulty and danger, and that this is as much 'of its essence' as
what is common to all the cases in which one is virtuous. Socrates,
it is plain, is victim to an axiom of abstract universality which
makes him see and feel a puzzle in what we may call the essential
alternativity of certain higher universals – that it is part of their
sense, while including something that is invariant and generic,
to be specified in this way in these circumstances and in that
different way in that – though this essential alternativity is what
all the instances adduced in the argument bring out. The necessary, structured alternativity of reasoned living is the true outcome

of the Dialectic, which can have no outcome of the sort it is seeking. Plato in some later Dialogues, for example the *Timaeus*, considering the inclusion of all the specific forms of living creature in the generic pattern of the Living Creature as Such, sees the sense of this alternativity which for Socrates always remained a difficulty.

If we now turn to the *Lysis*, we sample the Protean many-sidedness and internal conflict of the concept of Loving or Liking. The Dialogue is set in an environment of homosexual 'crushes' among young men and boys in an Athenian gymnasium, but its logical structure is well adapted to a much austerer setting. Lysis, a very young boy, and the beloved of one of the young men, is the first respondent of Socrates. Menexenus his friend takes his place in the more abstruse part of the discussion. The Dialogue begins by enquiring into the love which the parents of Lysis feel for Lysis: they desire Lysis to be happy, but this does not mean that they let Lysis do just what he likes. They, in fact, allow him to do much less than the hirelings or slaves who are entrusted with driving their chariots and other similar tasks: even the teaching of Lysis is entrusted to a slave-pedagogue. Lysis is, however, allowed to read and write and play the lyre whenever he chooses, the reason being, not that he is of an age to do such things, but that he *knows* how to do them. Plainly then, tasks are entrusted to those who know how to do them, but are kept from those who do not have this knowledge even by those who love them, and who leave those they love in the leading strings of those who, even if unloved, do know how to do the things in question.

From this Socrates proceeds, by a transition not wholly lucid, to the contention that a person can only be loved if he is in some way useful or profitable to the person who loves him. The wise will therefore be loved by all because he is profitable to all, whereas the unwise will be loved by no one. This contention, which flies in the face of the facts, only seems to follow from what has gone before: we do not entrust tasks to those who have no wisdom to perform them, but we may none the less love them by keeping them in leading strings. Menexenus, the friend of Lysis, with some reputation as an eristic or verbal wrangler, now takes over from Lysis. Socrates asks him where, in a relation of loving, does the 'Dearness' reside: is it located in the person to whom someone is dear, or in the person who is dear to this person? Menexenus correctly replies that it belongs to both, though he does not add that it belongs differently to each of them, and Socrates is therefore able to argue that, on this admission, the relation of loving is necessarily mutual or symmetrical, which is plainly not the case, though Menexenus tries half-heartedly to hold that it is. The hypothesis is now tried out that 'the Dear' belongs primarily to beloved persons, not to those who love them, and whether or not this love is reciprocated. The 'Hateful', similarly, belongs primarily to the hated, and not to those who hate them. This, however, has the paradoxical consequence – paradoxical only when the logical working of relation-concepts is imperfectly understood – that a man may be hateful to those who are dear to him, and dear to those who are hateful to him, which, by its appearness of conflict, seems to remove Dearness from lovers and beloved alike.

A new start is now made, with an appeal to Lysis and the poets, and the position taken up that Love or Friendship depends always on a *likeness* between the friendly parties. This is in conflict with the fact that the wicked are not endeared to the wicked by their common wickedness, but are rather at odds with one another, a state which reflects their own inward instability and conflict with themselves. The true sense of like befriending like must therefore lie in the attraction of the good for the good. But this too has its difficulties, since it has been agreed that friends will be profitable to friends, and the good, being good, are to that extent self-sufficient, and can derive no profit from those who also are good. That the profit may consist in mutual reinforcement and encouragement, or in the simple delight of multiplied selfhood, is not considered, but the Hesiodic suggestion it canvasses is that it is rather the unlike or even opposed that are friendly to the unlike, the dry affecting the moist, the cold the warm, the sour the sweet, the vacuum the plenum and so on. This, however, will have the unacceptable consequence that enmity will be favourable to love, and vice versa, or that the various forms of badness will be friendly to the corresponding forms of goodness. Yet another suggestion is that it is not the good that are friendly to the good, nor the bad to the bad, nor the good to the bad, but that it is those that are neither good nor bad who are friendly to the good, and, perhaps also, to what is neither good nor bad. Thus the sick man values the doctors whom he does not value in health, and he also values the ordinary state of his body which in itself is neither good nor bad. This intermediate state of being neither good nor bad involves a presence (παρουσία) of goodness and badness in the thing which is none the less not an authentic, thoroughgoing presence: it resembles the whiteness of powdered hair rather than the whiteness of hair that age has bleached. Being thus intermediate, the half-and-half good desires the through-and-through good, which it would not desire if it were to become through-and-through bad. (It will be noted that Socrates does not suppose that the intermediate desires the bad as well as the good, and he thereby concedes the secondary, parasitic character of the bad.)

A new line of thought, however, intrudes, and a distinction is drawn between things that are dear to someone for their own sakes, and things that are only dear for the sake of something else. These latter are not really dear at all, but are as it were images of that which is dear for its own sake. Socrates, however, argues that all lines of instrumental Dearness must terminate in a single First Dear, for the sake of which all other dear things are dear. No argument is given to show that there may not be an irreducible plurality of such Ultimate Dears: Eleaticism in the realm of values is the inevitable result. The difficulty, however, arises that, as all specific Dears are as it were parasitic upon the One First Dear, for the sake of which we pursue them, the one First Dear must be parasitic upon the evils for which it provides the remedy, and in the absence of which it would not be profitable. It can, however, be argued that, even in the absence of positive evil, there would still be a dearness attaching to what is positively desired, in opposition to what is neither good nor evil. It is desire, therefore, that underlies Dearness rather than vice versa. But desire, it would appear, is necessarily of that which is congenial (οἰκεῖον) to the desirous person, and which in some manner completes him, a view which has as a consequence a deep tendency towards mutuality in all cases of genuine love. But if the congenial is identified with the like, we shall have to face our previous refutation of the view that the Dear is always the like, and if the congenial is identified with the good, we shall face the rejected consequence that only the good will be congenial and dear to one another.

The Dialogue here breaks up in an array of negations: neither the loved nor their lovers, nor things like nor unlike, nor things good, nor things which are congenial, have plainly shown themselves to be what is truly Dear, and no positive answer is in sight. Plainly the positive answer would lie in seeing that the One First Dear must necessarily specify itself in a variety of ways, and that there is something diversified and disjunctive as well as unifying about it. Altogether the Dialogue is an interesting first essay in value-theory, and touches on almost all the essential questions of the subject.

IV

In the present sub-section we shall consider the three Dialogues *Euthydemus*, *Protagoras* and *Gorgias*. In the first of these Socrates is seen expounding his theory of reasoned living on a background of undisciplined Eristic or verbal wrangling, while in the second he pits himself against the great teacher of a mundane good life, who also backed his teaching with an incoherent philosophy. In the third, finally, he preaches a mystical, other-worldly moralism against the philosophically unbacked rhetoric of the defender of a rhetoric which could prove anything regarding anything (or regarding nothing) with equal facility.

In the *Euthydemus* Socrates attends a display of verbal pugilism given by the brothers Euthydemus and Dionysodorus, elderly foreigners from Chios and Thurii who have been living for some years in Athens, and who have in the last year perfected a new method of fighting with words as they previously had perfected methods of fighting in armour or in the law-courts. The Dialogue is held together by the professed concern of Socrates for the education of the young and beautiful Cleinias: are the brothers able to teach virtue both to someone who believes them capable of doing so, and also to someone who doubts whether virtue is teachable at all or teachable by them? And will the art they teach also teach the taught that virtue is teachable, and that they themselves, the teachers, *are* teachers of it? The brothers reply that their art is indeed capable of endorsing and validating itself (274e). Socrates therefore requests that they will postpone the other parts of their exhibition and confine themselves to exhorting Cleinias to turn to philosophy and the cultivation of virtue.

Euthydemus then asks Cleinias whether those who learn are the wise or the ignorant. Obviously, one has to reply, it will be the wise who learn, since it is a wise thing to do so, but obviously also it will be the ignorant who learn, since no one can learn what he already knows. This double argument, only a little sillier than many used by Socrates, could have a gloss put upon it as showing that we do after a fashion know what we do not know and have to learn, and so on. In the brothers, however, no profound meanings lurk beneath the simple desire to confound and confute. This leads Euthydemus to his next question: whether those who learn, learn what they know or what they do not know? Obviously when wisdom is dictated by a teacher, no unknown words or letters are dictated, and the pupil therefore learns nothing that he does not already know: on the other hand, learning is by definition the acquisition of knowledge, and an acquisition of anything implies that he who acquires it does not as yet possess it. We again have a triumphant antinomy, and Socrates is well able to argue that all their Eristic has in truth been no more than an intellectual initiation. Having been made aware of the misleading traps set by words, and of the rules which govern their correct use, the pupil may now be given a true protreptic discourse, one that will turn him to virtue and philosophy. Of such a protreptic discourse Socrates, with ironic suitability to the occasion, now gives a consummate specimen.

All men, it is readily granted, desire to do or fare well (εὖ πράττειν). In what way, however, can this well-doing or well-faring be achieved? Obviously many good things must accrue to us. Of these it is not hard to offer many instances. Wealth obviously is a good thing and a part of 'doing well', and so is good health and personal beauty and other bodily advantages. Good birth, and positions of power and honour in one's own country are likewise incontestably good. The virtues of being temperate, just etc. are even more obviously good, though Socrates violates our usual conceptions and language in implying that they count among a man's personal advantages or contribute to his 'welfare'. Wisdom now makes its inevitable, crowning appearance, but is as yet simply set alongside of the other good things of life. We require, however, a good fortune (εὐτυχία) which will adjust these goods with a happy hand, and it is not hard to argue from this that such good fortune is inseparable from wisdom: it is trained, i.e. knowing flute-players who have the happiest mouth and breath on the flute, trained grammarians who have the happiest turns of speech, trained pilots who have the happiest touch with the rudder, experienced generals who give the happiest orders in battle, etc., etc. The argument now proceeds to the assertion that the so-called goods which are other than wisdom, only uniformly profit us if directed by wisdom, if we know, that is, how to use them. The abuse of such so-called goods is much worse than their non-possession, and their possession, unguided by wisdom, leads as readily to abuse as to proper use. From this it is concluded, by a gross *non sequitur* (281e), that the so-called goods other than wisdom are in reality not goods or evils at all, and that wisdom *alone* is good and ignorance evil. Socrates has not and cannot prove that, because a wise use of certain things is indispensable to good living, the presence of those things themselves is not equally essential, that they are not as much a part of true 'prosperity' as the wisdom which co-ordinates them. Socrates now turns his persuasion upon Cleinias: wisdom being the sole and sufficient condition of 'prosperity', it must be sought from all sources, and by all not dishonourable efforts. All this depends, however, on a belief that virtue can be taught, and, since Cleinias is willing to concede that it can, further hypothesizing or testing of hypotheses becomes unnecessary. Socrates offers this fine specimen of his moralizing and of his argument as a model to the brothers: they may now exhort Cleinias even more competently.

Dionysodorus now proves that those who desire Cleinias to become virtuous, necessarily desire him to become what as yet he is not, and to cease being what he as yet is, both of which amount to a desire for his 'destruction', which of course in a limited sense they do. Ctesippus, the lover of Cleinias, is moved to give him the lie, whereupon Euthydemus proves, in long-established Eleatic fashion, that since it is impossible to say nothing at all, or to do anything that involves this, and since it is only possible to say one or other among the things that are, all speech is necessarily true and lying is impossible. Socrates now calms the troubled situation by pointing out that the sort of destruction effected by the brothers, if indeed they do effect it, which can turn the wicked and foolish into the worthy and sensible, is a wholly desirable sort of destruction, which they should be allowed to practise on everyone. Ctesippus then says that his contradiction of Dionysodorus is not to be taken as abuse. Dionysodorus hereupon proves the impossibility of contradiction: it can occur neither when two men say the same thing, nor when two men both say nothing, nor when one man says something and the other nothing, nor when one man says one thing and another man some quite other thing. The impossibility of false utterance, thus proved, is widened to include false belief and even ignorance. What then, asks Socrates, is the value of the brothers' instruction, for which such high claims have been made? Dionysodorus says that Socrates is 'in a quandary' (does not know what words to use) because he is harking back to previous utterances, which leads Socrates to ask what is meant by the phrase 'in a quandary', which leads Dionysodorus to say, with a fine anticipation of modern semantics, that he means precisely what he says, and that it is moreover absurd to attribute meaning to a phrase that does not think, and can therefore not mean anything. It is not necessary to say that there is substance in the difficulties here raised by the brothers, and that just how that which is not the case can none the less contribute to the being and character of what is the case, and so in a sense parasitically *is*, is to raise one of the deepest of categorial questions, on which Plato himself will make many pronouncements.

The Dialogue now again passes from the riotous scherzo of the brothers to the serene andante of Socratic exhortation. The brothers have been fooling in their Corybantic initiation: it is time to make Cleinias turn towards the virtuous, philosophic life. Philosophy, however, is the obtaining of such knowledge as will be of profit to us, and this knowledge is one that will teach us, not only to produce, but also to *use* other so-called goods. The precise character of this knowledge however requires further elucidation. It is not a particular knowledge like that connected with musical instruments, where making and using are distinct. Nor is it a verbal art which would involve the same separation, as also do generalship and the art of hunting. (In 290b, c Socrates anticipates the *Republic* by holding that the philosophers and their Dialectic are necessary for the full interpretation of the results hunted out by the mathematicians.) The royal art (ἡ βασιλικὴ τέχνη), which is also the political art, is a plausible candidate for the required science, since it is the art which can use the contributions of all the other arts and sciences. The way in which it will use them remains, however, obscure, and we are not helped by saying that it will make men wise and good, i.e. by imparting *itself* to them. We are, as in the *Charmides*, entrapped in the Socratic circle of a knowledge which is no knowledge since it is only of itself, and since it has been emptied of all the specific aims that might have given content to it.

The riot of the brothers is now resumed and we need not follow it in detail. Dionysodorus makes use of the Law of Contradiction, with no more fallacy than many others in their employment of it, to prove that since Socrates has knowledge he cannot also lack knowledge, and must therefore know everything, including the royal art. In the same manner, Euthydemus proves Socrates to be omniscient by the fact that he knows everything with whatever he knows it, an argument which perhaps masks the logical insight that every reference to everything specific is, in concealed fashion, a reference to everything whatever. A proof is also given that anyone's father or other relative is also everyone's father or other relative, since he cannot *not* stand in the relation in which he stands. In the same way it is argued that since Socrates has an Apollo, a Zeus and an Athene in his house, and since these are Gods and therefore have souls and are therefore animals, Socrates has certain divine animals in his house which he can use in all the ordinary and sacrificial ways in which animals can be used. The Dialogue ends with a brilliant ironic speech by Socrates, counselling the brothers to keep their wisdom to themselves, since its tricks will otherwise be too easily learnt by others. It is important to remember that Socrates too has his tricks, not so easily learnt nor so consciously deceptive, but not saved from gross fallacy by the insight and moral purpose that lies behind them.

In the *Protagoras*, next to be considered, we have the by now familiar picture of a youth, Hippocrates, who is seeking to be schooled in wisdom and virtue by Protagoras of Abdera, and a dialogue between Socrates and Protagoras in which the claims and competence of the latter are dialectically investigated, and found to be extremely shaky. There is as usual much more good sense, though less accurate argument, and of course less ultimate depth of wisdom, in the views of Protagoras than in those of Socrates. The dramatic construction and background of the Dialogue are superb: with the *Phaedo* and the *Symposium* it is the most vivid of Plato's writings. The description of Socrates being awakened at dawn by the ardent Hippocrates, the ironically serious discussion of the dangers of confiding one's soul to the care of someone who professes Sophistry, the arrival of the men at the house of Callias the Sophist-lionizer, where the disgusted door-keeper wishes to slam the door in the faces of yet another pair of Sophists, the three incomparably described Sophists, Hippias of Elis, Prodicus of Ceos and Protagoras himself, each surrounded by their wonderfully well-behaved, deferential entourage, are among the highest points in European literature (314d–316a).

To Socrates enquiring what after all Hippocrates will learn if he associates with Protagoras, the answer is given that he will not be instructed in a whole repertory of irrelevant sciences, but in a Good Counsel ($\epsilon\dot{v}\beta ov\lambda\acute{\iota}a$) which will enable him to manage both his private and public affairs whether in word or deed. Socrates, however, doubts whether such an $\epsilon\dot{v}\beta ov\lambda\acute{\iota}a$ or political Good Counsel is teachable, since Pericles, and other men of good political counsel, were quite unable to teach their specific cunning to their sons, or to have it taught them by others, though they succeeded quite well in imparting other accomplishments to them. To these objections to the possibility of his instruction Protagoras replies by an elaborate and eloquent myth (320c–328d), in which persuasion covers up the cracks and leaps in the argument. It may very well be taken from discourses actually given by Protagoras. In this myth Epimetheus is said to have distributed various built-in bodily endowments to the animals to provide for their survival ($\sigma\omega\tau\epsilon\rho\acute{\iota}a$), while Prometheus sought to mitigate the physical helplessness of men by the gifts of fire and technological wisdom. Technology was, however, of no account without the political art which enables men to live and work together, and which is rooted in reverence ($a\mathring{\iota}\delta\omega s$) and the inner rule of right ($\delta\acute{\iota}\kappa\eta$). Society could not, however, have been a success, had these two qualities only been imparted to *some* men and not to all, and hence *all* share in them to some degree, and hence one is not thought modest and truthful, but absurd and mad, if one professes a complete lack of reverence and justice. But though everyone has them, everyone also teaches them to everyone – Protagoras suggests but does not explicitly state the *reinforcing* role of such teaching – and this teaching of all by all proceeds regularly from admonition to punishment, which latter has always a reformatory aim, and looks to the future and not to the past. That good fathers often fail to impart their political wisdom to their sons is due both to differences of natural capacity and to the multiplicity of practising teachers: if all played the flute, good flute-players would have sons as inferior to themselves as politicians now have. By this loosely rambling, not very consequent argument Protagoras seeks *both* to make political wisdom a thing popular and universally shared, and *also* to ground his claim to be a superior teacher of it.

Socrates now guides the discussion into familiar paths: Is the teachable political wisdom or virtue which Protagoras professes, and in which he vaguely distinguishes such things as reverence, justice and self-restraint, really one and the same thing differently named, or does it consist of a number of specific parts or virtues? And do the various virtues merely differ circumstantially, as one piece of gold differs from another, or are they also different in character and function like the parts of a face? Protagoras opts for the second, structured view of virtue, which he backs by the more questionable assertion that some have one species of virtue and some another: those who are courageous are not necessarily just, nor those who are just necessarily wise, thereby giving Socrates an opportunity to demolish him by some very questionable and some less questionable arguments.

The logical relations of the five virtues Wisdom, Justice, Bravery, Self-restraint and Piety are now examined, and Socrates begins by making the hypothesis that Justice is a definite *thing* ($\pi\rho\hat{a}\gamma\mu a$), the basic existential assumption, and then making Protagoras concede that this *thing* is itself just and not unjust. Obviously being just can be said to be just in an 'eminent' though not in an ordinary instantial sense – Socrates has no words for this distinction – since it is indeed Justice Itself, but one may well question the exhaustiveness of the dichotomy between Justice and its contrary Injustice. The same procedure is now repeated in the case of Piety, and we establish that Piety is a *thing*, and an eminently pious and not an impious thing. Socrates now asks whether Piety Itself is not a just *thing*, and whether Justice Itself is not a pious thing, or whether on the other hand Piety is to be rated as unjust, and Justice as impious. The question is vitiated by the assumption that Piety cannot be other than Justice, without having that specific incompatibility with Justice which would make it coincide with Injustice, and the like, *mutatis mutandis*, in the case of Justice and Impiety. Socrates, however, being unable to make Piety and Justice logically exclusive, is forced by his inadequate dichotomy to make them coincident or very nearly so. Protagoras refuses to be bullied by this bad logic, and contends that Piety and Justice are analogous rather than fully identical; when pressed, he admits that they are *closely* analogous, and not merely 'like' in the empty sense in which everything is like everything. Presumably such analogy would involve some tendency to go together, even if it did not involve the invariable going-together entailed by the complete coincidence of the two notions. Socrates, however, prefers to steer the discussion in other directions, and to enquire whether there are not two such *things* as Folly and Wisdom, and whether the latter is not the complete contrary (ἐνάντιον) of the former. When, however, men act properly and profitably, they are said to act with σωφροσύνη or Self-restraint, and Self-restraint is accordingly also contrary to Folly. A new axiom is introduced: that to each distinct Eidos or meaning there can be only a single contrary, from which it follows that Wisdom and Self-restraint, being alike contrary to Folly, are necessarily one and the same. The unacceptability of this conclusion should have been allowed to invalidate the axiom from which it was deduced, but Socrates seldom sacrifices logic for truth. Protagoras, however, has not the expertise to put forward axioms or to question them, and is therefore dragged uncomfortably in the wake of Socrates's superior skill. Socrates is now going on to prove the identity of Self-restraint with Justice by way of the key notions of Profit and Knowledge, but Protagoras vents his confused vexation in a long series of irrelevances centring in the point that what profits one creature in one situation will not necessarily profit another (334a–e).

The discussion breaks down, but is renewed after gravely amusing, conciliatory speeches from the various sophistic auditors. Protagoras is now permitted to do the questioning, while Socrates has to make the responses, the analysis centring on some singularly asinine lines from Simonides in which the statement that 'It is hard to be good' is both made in one context and reproved in another. Socrates then gives an ironic exegesis, as abounding in myth as the Protagorean account of the gifts of Prometheus, which disposes of this 'discrepancy': to *become* good is humanly difficult, but to *be*, i.e. remain, good is superhumanly so, since time, toil, disease and other chances may always deprive a man of his knowledge and of his power to exercise it. Socrates then adds to the exegesis by making Simonides fully aware of the truth of the Socratic doctrine of the involuntariness of all evil. The whole exhibition reduces the hermeneutics of Protagoras to the absurd, and ends by comparing it to the flute-girls hired to enliven the dull drinking of extremely vulgar persons (347d, e).

After some persuasion of the much disarrayed, reluctant Protagoras by the company, the investigation into the unity of Virtue is resumed, Socrates taking over the interrogation. The question under discussion is whether 'Wisdom', 'Self-restraint', 'Bravery', 'Justice' and 'Piety' are but five names for a single *thing* ($\pi\rho\hat{a}\gamma\mu a$), or whether, alternatively, 'a peculiar essence ($o\vec{v}\sigma\acute{\iota}a$) or *thing*, having in each case its own power, and not being like any other such *thing*, underlies each such name' (349b). Protagoras is asked whether he still believes that the virtues differ like the parts of a face, and he replies, somewhat carelessly, that while four of them are more or less similar, Courage is very different from the others, since the most unjust, impious, uncontrolled and ignorant men can be very courageous. He is now an easy prey to Socrates, who can hardly wait to point out that Courage is an admirable thing, and that a guidance by Wisdom is plainly essential to its being admirable, and that those whose daring is unguided by Wisdom deserve to be called 'mad' rather than courageous. The false conclusion is thereby insinuated that it is a guidance by Wisdom which *alone* renders Courage admirable, a conclusion that Protagoras rightly hesitates to accept.

Socrates now turns the whole discussion into a direction which could be interpreted as 'hedonistic', but which in fact bears quite a different interpretation. He enquires whether anyone can be held to 'live well' if he lives in pain, or whether, if he has lived out his life pleasurably ($\dot{\eta}\delta\acute{\epsilon}\omega s$), he has not lived well? To these suggestions Protagoras sensibly replies that he will have lived well if he has taken pleasure in fine and worthy things. Socrates, however, with his secret persuasion that only the life of virtue can be truly sweet, is not afraid to suggest that things are good in so far as they are pleasurable, and bad in so far as they are painful, a hypothesis which Protagoras, with considerable reluctance, consents to 'try out' (351e). Socrates maintains that when pleasurable outcomes are said to be bad or base, the reason must be that, while pleasurable at the moment, they have in the long run many painful consequences: if the consequences were as pleasurable as the activities, there could be no baseness or badness in the latter. In the same way, when painful activities are said to be good, the meaning is that, while they may be painful at the moment, they will lead to consequences that outweigh them in pleasurableness. The pleasurable and the painful are, in fact, identical (respectively) with the Good and the Bad, except that, in the case of the latter, we consider only overall pleasurableness and painfulness, and not merely the pleasurableness and painfulness of the moment.

Since pleasurableness and goodness (and painfulness and badness) have this close relation, Socrates rejects the view that we can be deflected from the pursuit of Good and the avoidance of Evil by the overwhelming blandishments of pleasure or torments of pain. This would be as absurd (?) as saying that we were deflected from the Good by the Good, or from the Evil by the Evil. What these statements really mean is that we may be deflected from the greater good or the more pleasurable by the less good and the less pleasurable, and the same *mutatis mutandis* in regard to the shunning of pain. And these last statements only become intelligible if we admit that we may for some reason be ignorant of what is the overall good or evil (i.e. pleasurableness or painfulness) implicit in a given activity. For Knowledge is essentially something strong, directive and governing, one that guides activity if it is present at all: of its very nature it cannot be pushed around by passion, by pleasure and pain, or by love and fear (352b). It is therefore only by an absence of knowledge that men opt for the immediate pleasure or good, or avoid the immediate pain or evil, and thereby bring on themselves a greater overall pain or lessened pleasure. The art, therefore, that is supremely needed to guide life aright, is a *metric* art, one that will measure the more and the less, the greater and smaller, and the more remote and more immediate among pleasures and pains, and determine the extent to which they exceed or fall short of or are equal to one another (357a, b). This art is needed to correct the immediate appearances, just as, in the case of sense-perception, we require a metric art to correct immediate perceptual impressions of size, distance, speed etc. If it were as important for life to assess distances and sizes as it is to assess 'values', the perceptual metric would be as important as the metric concerned with pleasures and pains (356c, d).

The whole tone and context of these passages shows that Socrates, in identifying the Good with the pleasurable, is in effect identifying the pleasurable with the Good. It is not a vanishing feeling that measures Goodness, but Goodness that gives whatever substance there may be to a vanishing feeling. It is when we exercise the divine metric that Socrates is here speaking of, that we not only grade all satisfactions in the life of reason, but also see that the life of reason embraces the only real joys that there are or can be, that it sums up and transfigures all other types of good. The belief in a life which is thus at once scientific and purely delightful, and which is the one only in so far as it is also the other, will continue to be the theme of many of Plato's later discussions. But in the present treatment we also see the more or less accomplished acceptance of the 'mathematicization' of the Eide, and even of its language, in which Plato's mature philosophy was to consist. Everywhere we have a More and a Less, a Greater and a Smaller, an Exceeding and a Falling short, and the divine art consists in striking a Measure, finding a point of equilibrium in all this confused variability.

The Dialogue ends by applying the notion of the satisfaction-metric to the special case of Courage. Fear is admitted to be the expectation of future evil which it is sought to avoid. Both the brave and the cowardly seek to avoid future evil by their actions, and the only difference between them is that the former apply a right metric to the situation while the latter ignorantly apply a wrong one. The brave know that going to war, and enduring certain immediate pains, will lead to a better and finer and happier condition of things than running away from such immediate pains and evils, whereas the cowardly confusedly suppose that greater danger resides in such immediate pains and evils, which must at all costs be avoided. The drift of the argument (359–60) is to assume some sort of ultimate, necessary unity among the Good, the Beautiful and the Delightful, even though immediate appearances may belie this. Socrates comments on the strange fact that his reduction of Virtue to Knowledge has ended by making it teachable, contrary to his own initial doubts, whereas Protagoras's pluralistic theory of the virtues would render virtue unteachable. Protagoras then retreats politely and in good order from the intolerable barrage of argument to which he has been subjected by the Divine Sophist, Socrates.

We turn, finally, to the third of our Socratic confrontations with the success-philosophy of the period, the Dialogue *Gorgias* in which Socrates discourses with the famous Sicilian professor of Rhetoric. Dramatically the Dialogue is poor, and Socrates is depicted as uttering majestic sermons which are 'not his style', and which are charged with a high-flown sense of 'mission' and not with half-ironic Socratic modesty. The Dialogue falls into three parts: in the first Socrates tries to ascertain from Gorgias what he holds to be the role of the rhetorician, and gives his own, very unflattering picture of that role, in the second he continues the argument with Polus, an ardent young disciple of Gorgias, and propounds several unworldly moral axioms which to such as Polus seem utterly ridiculous, while in the third he continues the defence of these axioms against the much more radical objections of Callicles, and also buttresses his principles with the transcendental visions of Pythagorean eschatology.

After some preliminary skirmishing with Polus, Gorgias is asked by Socrates what the art of Rhetoric concerns itself with, and receives the answer that it is concerned with speech. What sort of speech? Speech functioning on its own, is the reply, and not merely ancillary to some other performance, and speech aiming not to impart this or that sort of information, but directed to persuading judges in the law-courts, senators in the senate and assemblymen in the assembly, speech, in short, through which a man achieves the greatest and best of goods, freedom for himself and political power over others, however expert in their own art they may be (452e). The rhetorician is therefore rightly described as the creator of persuasion. But the professors of other arts are also creators of persuasion when they tell us how this or that matter in their art stands or must be, for example when the arithmeticians persuade us of the truth of certain numerical principles. It seems to follow that the rhetorician is one able to persuade even when he lacks all specialist knowledge, and that, if we distinguish between knowledge and belief, the distinguishing mark of the rhetorician is that he is able to create belief about objects, the just and unjust in particular, without either having or imparting knowledge regarding them (455e–455a). Gorgias dilates upon the marvellous power conferred by Rhetoric, but adds, in mitigation of its obvious dangers, that the rhetorician must not be blamed if this power is abused: it is for all who have learnt the art of persuasion to use it responsibly, and not to subvert morality by its means nor the dicta of the specialist sciences. Does this mean that the rhetorician will impart knowledge concerning just and unjust, fine and base, good and bad, to prevent such abuse? Gorgias, with a naïve confidence in established values, answers that, if someone happens to be untrained in such matters, he, Gorgias, will have to train him in them. This, says Socrates, involves an inconsistency. The rhetorician is, on the one hand, presented as capable of abusing his art, on the other hand, as having a standard which prevents such abuse. Where and how does Rhetoric possess itself of such a standard?

Polus now takes over the discussion and asks Socrates what sort of an art *he* believes Rhetoric to be. Socrates replies that it is not an art at all, but a sort of empirical trick (ἐμπειρία) proceeding without a λόγος or explanatory concept (462a), which engenders gratification, making us feel benefited when we really are not, and is therefore a form of pandering or flattery (κολακεία). To medicine with its guiding concept of the health of each sort of body, to which that body is led back, cookery stands opposed as the corresponding form of pandering: it makes one *feel* in health, instead of really being so. To gymnastic, likewise, with its scientific building-up of bodily health, the trick of adornment stands opposed, building up an *appearance* of health and beauty which has no real foundation. These forms of pandering attend upon the body, but there are two others which attend upon the soul: to the legislative art, which trains men in real Justice and the health of their souls, and which corresponds to gymnastic in the realm of the body, we have the corresponding pandering tricks of Sophistry which enable men to cast a show of Justice over their actions and proposed actions, while to the judicial art which corrects men's injustices, and which corresponds to medicine in the realm of the body, correspond the pandering tricks of Rhetoric which enable a man to get away with his injustices. The notion of a geometrical proportion is applied in a complex manner to the relations of the four arts and their counterfeits, showing that the project of a mathematicization of all meanings is already at work in the mind of Plato (465b, c).

Polus is outraged at this characterization of Rhetoric as a form of pandering, and points to the great repute and power of rhetoricians in the various city-states. Socrates replies that there is no soundness in their reputation, and that they have no real power, since they only achieve what *seems* to them best, and not what they really want, i.e. what is really best. What is wanted in all actions is not the actions themselves – these are neither good nor bad – but the ultimate Good for the sake of which the actions are done. 'In pursuit of the Good, we walk when we walk, thinking it better to do so, and contrariwise stand when we stand still, for the sake of the same Good' (468b). It follows that when a tyrant or rhetorician despoils, exiles or kills a man, he does so believing that Good will accrue to him through this deed: it is this Good that he wants, and if it is not to be had in this way, then he is not acting as he wants to act. Socrates now utters the first of his great paradoxes: that while both doing injustice and suffering injustice are evils, the former is a greater evil than the latter. Polus admits that doing injustice may be worse than suffering it owing to the penalties which attach to the former, but holds that when these penalties are absent, as in the case of a great tyrant, there is no evil in doing injustice. Socrates then utters his second paradox: that to do injustice and get away with it is worse than to do injustice and be punished for it (472e).

This utterance awakens derision in Polus, but Socrates none the less gets him to admit that doing injustice, though less bad than suffering injustice, is baser than the latter. The base (τὸ αἰσχρόν) is, however, the contrary of the fine and the beautiful (τὸ καλόν). Of beauty there are two accounts: that it consists in advantage or profit, or in being a source of pleasure to the beholder. Sounds, shapes, colours, laws, practices are all reckoned fine and beautiful for one or both of these reasons, and, on one or other account, baseness will consist in disadvantage or in giving pain. (The reference to the beholder is tacitly dropped, making the argument sophistical.) But doing injustice is not base in virtue of giving pain: it gives little pain to the unjust. (But it does give pain to the beholder.) It is therefore base in virtue of being disadvantageous or evil, and no man can knowingly prefer it to the less base suffering of injustice. It is clear, further, that to punish justly is to do something fine and beautiful, since the just has been admitted to be of the nature of the fine and beautiful. But, if an action has a property, the corresponding undergoing will have the same property – if I hit someone hard and quick, he will get hit hard and quick – and it is therefore clear that if someone punishes someone justly, the man he punishes will be punished justly. And if to punish justly is fine and beautiful, to be punished justly will likewise be fine and beautiful. But it is not fine and beautiful in virtue of giving pleasure to the sufferer – the beholder is again left out – it must therefore be fine and beautiful in virtue of being advantageous to the sufferer. His soul must be bettered if his punishment is a just one, and he must be freed from that worst of evils, injustice, just as other forms of betterment will free him from the less base, and therefore less evil – since certainly more painful – states of disease and poverty. As money-making saves a man from poverty, and as medicine saves a man from disease, in both of which pain predominates over disadvantage, so the punitive judicial act will save a man from injustice, in which disadvantage prevails over pain. It would, of course, have been better still if a man had been rich enough not to need to make money, and healthy enough not to need medical care, and just enough not to require punishment, but whenever there is poverty, disease or injustice, the state of a man is improved by the arts which go against them. The unjust man who is justly punished is therefore better off than if he goes unpunished, and vastly better off than an unpunished tyrant whose injustices are also vast.

Socrates now advances to the third of his great moral paradoxes: that if one has committed injustices, then one must invoke the aid of rhetoricians, not to secure one's acquittal or reduce one's sentence, but to ensure that it is appropriately severe. And if one has reason to be anyone's enemy – he does not suggest that one can have such a reason – then and then alone should one employ rhetoric to exempt him from the penalties of his unjust deeds. Polus is dumbfounded by these arguments, and it is hard for us not to be dumbfounded by their brilliant rhetoric. For they pass from a sense of baseness as being painful to the observer, to a sense in which it is painful to the agent. And they pass from the lower, ordinary sense of advantage and disadvantage, in which it is connected with the person and his contingent personal aims, and in which being virtuous often involves the sacrifice of personal advantage, to a new, 'higher' sense of advantage and disadvantage, in which virtue and advantage coincide, and in which there can be nothing more profitable to the individual than having a virtuous soul. These persuasive redefinitions of 'advantage' certainly have their deep illumination, but they involve a blurring of differences between what is good in itself and good for myself. Certainly one should not prove the spiritual profitability of virtue, true and absolute as it is, by simply blurring the difference between the higher prerogatives and the lower advantages which they often override. Polus and Gorgias understandably see something warped and unfair in all these Socratic subtleties.

The argument now passes over to Callicles, who asks whether Socrates can be serious in all these preposterous contentions, which run against everyone's views and practice (481b). Conventionally, indeed, it is wrong and base to take advantage of others, even if one has the power, and it is in deference to such convention that Gorgias said he would instruct his pupils in justice if they came to him knowing nothing about it, and that Polus likewise said that it was baser to do injustice than to suffer it. There are, however, a natural fineness and baseness, good and bad, which run contrary to the conventional, and naturally it is baser and worse to suffer injustice, to be pushed around like a slave, than to do injustice. We may in fact say that it is naturally more just to do what is conventionally unjust than to suffer what is conventionally unjust, and that the inversion of the natural meanings of these words has come upon us through a continuously applied sort of verbal enchantment, whose real foundation lies in the inferiority and weakness of the enchanters. Philosophy is a continuation of the same sort of enchantment, and, while it is delightful in the very young, it is quite ridiculous in a mature man at grips with the hard realities of political life (482c–486d).

As we study this speech, with its crude acceptance of natural meanings and values, we cannot fail to anticipate how its contentions will collapse under the questioning of Socrates. He at once argues that, if what is naturally best and just is what is best and just for the stronger element in a state, then, since the law-givers in a state represent this stronger element, and since the laws they set up follow the patterns of conventional justice, natural and conventional justice are *not* at odds, but in complete harmony. Callicles replies that by the stronger element in a state he does not mean the physically stronger, but those who are better and more knowing. These, he maintains on further questioning, are not those who practise self-restraint and the other conventional virtues, but who allow their desires to increase without limit, and who use all their knowledge and courage in their gratification (491e–492a). The majority of men are not in a position to emulate these strong, wilful souls, and therefore condemn their insatiability, praising the moderation and equality which protects their own mediocrity. Socrates asks whether it is not better to have a soul that remains suitably full for a fair time, than to have a leaky soul that requires continual replenishment, and which suffers agony if replenishment is delayed. Callicles, probably a Heraclitean, prefers his leaky condition: the filled condition, he says, is lacking in 'life'. Socrates argues, however, on logical rather than psychological grounds, that the leaky condition involves both the pain of desire and the pleasure of replenishment, and both simultaneously. (In actual fact desire ceases to be painful when it is being satisfied at a pace which corresponds to its urgency.) Socrates argues that, since pleasure and pain are thus compatible, whereas good living and bad living are not, the former cannot be identified with the latter. He also points out that good living has been admitted to involve bravery and intelligence, which do not vary concomitantly with pleasure and pain, the latter pair being as much present in the cowardly and foolish as in the brave and intelligent. Callicles then concedes that good and bad, since they involve bravery and intelligence (or their opposites), are not the same as pleasure and pain, and Socrates immediately rushes him on to the distinction made with Polus between forms of pandering such as cookery and adornment which minister only to pleasing appearances, and the genuine arts such as medicine and gymnastic which conduce to the real good of health. In the life of the soul, similarly, there are genuine arts which minister to true goods – Callicles is too exhausted to deny that justice and temperance are among such true goods – while there are forms of spiritual pandering which minister only to pleasure. Rhetoric, if it is to be a true art, will therefore be one that will aim at all times to implant justice and temperance in men's souls, and to turn them away from being unjust and unrestrained. Each thing has its characteristic excellence, which will correspond to a form of order (τάξις) and correctness (ὀρθότης) and art. It is not only we men, but the whole cosmos of gods and men, heaven and earth that is held together by analogues of temperance and justice (506d, e; 508a).

The Dialogue ends in a long argument by Socrates, the gist of which is that none of the previous political leaders has really made the Athenians better, the proof being that they attacked the same leaders, which could not have happened had the leaders been good and the citizens improved. Socrates, in his endeavours to make the Athenians intelligently virtuous, has been the only true professor of the political art (521d). The argument is rounded off by a magnificent Pythagorean myth, in which the seeming discrepancy between external power and success and inner injustice and intemperance is rectified, in which souls are purified (if indeed they admit of purification) of their soul-evils by sufferings which as it were make them know how evil they have been, or in which they rise to enjoy the blessedness which is but the completion of their virtue. Just allocations of suffering and bliss are meted out by the divine measurers Minos, Rhadamanthus and Aeacus, judges and souls being alike 'naked', i.e. free from the deceits of bodily instantiation. It is not necessary that we should regard these eschatological passages as mystical irrelevances: if the world depends on Ideal Meanings radiating from an Absolute Good, something like them is arguably true. The Dialogue shows the increasing Pythagoreanization of Plato's thought – the Socratic logic-chopping is becoming a reflex – and this is shown also by the use of the concept of unbounded quantity in the treatment of the life of mere pleasure, while the life of virtue always involves Limit and Order and Measure imposed upon such unbounded quantity.

V

We shall end our treatment of Plato's Socratic Dialogues by considering three Dialogues – the *Euthyphro*, the *Apology* and the *Crito* – which all report discourses set in the last days of Socrates's life. They lead up to the *Meno*, *Phaedo* and *Republic* where Pythagorean otherworldliness and a poetically stated Eidos-theory serve to shadow forth, as well as is exoterically possible, the new mathematicizing Eidos-conceptions of Plato.

The *Euthyphro* is a very simple Dialogue, an attempted analysis of the virtue Piety, very much like the *Charmides* or the *Laches* or the *Lysis*, and with as many lightly touched-upon profundities as these latter Dialogues. Socrates, about to face prosecution by Meletus on the charge of corrupting the young and of introducing alien cults into Athens, meets Euthyphro who is about to prosecute his own father for cruelly allowing a field-labourer of his to die in chains in a ditch of hunger and cold, while a diviner was consulted as to what should be done with him. This crime, as heinous as many of the atrocities of tyrants that Socrates so eloquently condemns, has rightly seemed very impious to Euthyphro, but to Socrates it is no more than a stepping-off place for a discussion of Piety. Does Euthyphro know so much about Piety as to be quite sure that, in prosecuting his own father, he may not be doing something more impious than the father's act in allowing the field-labourer to perish? And *is* there an Eidos of Piety, the same in all pious actions, and does Euthyphro know it, and what does he say it is? Euthyphro can at first only say that Piety consists in prosecuting crimes no matter who has done them, just as Zeus punished Cronos for eating his own offspring, and Cronos punished Uranus for the same reason. Obviously, however, this only presents us with a species of Piety, and not with the Eidos or Ideal Meaning which makes all pious actions pious (6d, e). Euthyphro then gives the theological definition that Piety consists in being dear to the Gods whereas Impiety consists in being odious to them. The Gods are, however, depicted in myths such as that which Euthyphro has just cited, as being often at odds with one another, and these divine differences must be due to differing opinions as to what is just and unjust, good and evil, noble and base. If this is the case, what is dear to some of the gods may be odious to others, and the same act may accordingly be both pious and impious. We may endeavour to meet this difficulty by saying that the Pious is what is dear to *all* the Gods, the Impious what is odious to *all* of them, but still the question arises whether Piety simply *is* the being dear to all the Gods, or, contrariwise, whether Piety is not something *different* from being dear to all the Gods, and whether, moreover, it is not something that *justifies* the divine love, so that it is *because* acts are pious that all the Gods love them, and not *vice versa*? Obviously the second view is alone acceptable, and this leaves us with a definition of Piety still to find.

After some prompting by Socrates, Euthyphro comes forward with another definition of Piety: it is that part of Justice which concerns doings towards the Gods, whereas the rest of Justice deals with our doings towards men. This seems to suggest that there is some way in which we can benefit the Gods or improve their life, just as we can benefit or improve the life of men and animals, yet it is not clear *what* benefit we can possibly confer on the Gods. It remains that, while we cannot benefit the Gods, we can none the less please them, and this brings us back to our unacceptable definition of Piety as what is pleasing to the Gods. What the Dialogue really shows is that there can be no other satisfactory object of Piety or Reverence but Absolute Goodness Itself, whether in itself or in one of its instances, and that it is only from this source that can come that self-communication of the Good to ourselves and to our deeds which (metaphorically) amounts to a sacred approval. In the *Euthyphro*, however, the Platonic Theology is only in its beginnings.

The *Apology* is a magnificent piece of writing on which we need not spend many words. Obviously it is a more finished piece of oratory than Socrates can have given in an Athenian court-room, but there is no reason to believe that it is merely some sophistical picture of the perfectly good man standing trial before unworthy accusers or some displaced crisis in the philosophical career of Plato. The perfectly good man that it reveals is also one endowed with a human as well as a paradigmatic nature, and one in whose humanity there are touches of the playful and the divinely naughty, which no form of philosophical didacticism nor personal self-justification could have counterfeited. Reading the *Apology* we get an extraordinary sense of the conscious and unconscious motivation of the man. There have been compulsive speakers before and after Socrates, and many as brilliant in their personal exhibitionism and determination to outshine all others, but not many in whom the compulsion was felt as a divine voice and humbly accepted as a sacred mission. There have likewise been many radical critics and many passionate moralists before and after Socrates, but not many who combined the extreme of criticism with the humblest submission to accepted duties and pieties. All this is evident in the light-hearted incorrigibility of his last defence: he is putting on his greatest personal show, but it is also the show that will glorify not himself but the lovely Shapes of Virtue of which he has talked, and not merely talked of but embodied. Particularly to be admired are the passages towards the end where he maintains a serious suspense of mind towards the Pythagorean promise of the after-life. What the Pythagoreans relate, or something like it, is what the dedicated man *has* to believe in; it represents an inevitable extension of the whole plan of his life, but it does not represent anything about which he can have *knowledge*. The inimitable suggestion that Socrates may spend his time in eternity tormenting the shades with his questions is so moving as almost to compel faith: we see it happening. This is what the Divine Man will be doing and doing to all eternity, and so expressing the eternal self-criticism which, though ignored by theologians, is plainly a vital aspect of Godhead as Such.

The *Crito* is scarcely less moving than the *Apology*, since it shows us the man who could be so critical of all the leaders and policies of the Athenian state, and in fact of all moral and political ideas and customs, also expressing his deep, simple loyalty and love for that state, in the face of the fact that, through a malfunctioning of its institutions, it has unjustly and foolishly condemned him to death. His seventy years spent in Athens have constituted an unspoken pact with the laws and customs of that city, from which he cannot now draw apart merely because it is to his personal disadvantage to remain there. He will therefore refuse to repay evil with evil, and will listen to the voice of the living spirit behind the Athenian laws, which, like the flutes heard by the Corybantic mystics, seems always sounding in his ears.

IV

THE IDEOLOGICAL DIALOGUES: THE *MENO*, *PHAEDO, SYMPOSIUM* AND *PHAEDRUS*

I

It will be our task in the present chapter and the next to set forth and comment on the content of the Dialogues of Plato's Middle Period, the *Meno, Phaedo, Symposium, Phaedrus* and *Republic*, Dialogues which go beyond a lifelike evocation of the Socratic philosophy-by-conversation, and which explicitly give an ontological status, a status superior to that of the vanishing things of sense, to the Ideal Meanings or Eide which the examinations of Socrates were intended to circumscribe. The Eide have been the non-thematic background of the previous Dialogues: now they become the explicit theme, or at least one of the explicit themes, of the new set of Dialogues. These, further, tend towards losing their question-and-answer character, and become, to an increasing extent, continuous expositions punctuated by not very considered expressions of assent. This was already the pattern of the *Gorgias*; in the *Phaedo, Symposium* and *Republic* it will become the pattern of most of the Dialogue. The Dialogues we are examining are also to be understood, on the more-than-mere-hypothesis on which we work, as a public, written reflection of doctrinal and methodological phases in the thought of Plato, mainly concerned with the 'mathematicization' of all concepts, to which no full written, but only an oral exposition was given. These unwritten opinions were not kept from the public for any mystery-mongering reason, but solely because they were difficult, imperfectly worked out, and above all tentative: it was not clear what form they would have to take in detail nor even how fruitful they would in the end prove to be. They were like those colossal, never completed palaces which confront us all over the world, and which raise special problems because much of their structure never went beyond the mind. But though obscure in their final outcome, they were clear in their tendency, in the complete transparency that they sought to achieve, and, if we fail to take account of them, Dialogues like the *Republic* and even the *Phaedo* remain largely unintelligible. We should be deeply grateful to Aristotle for at least providing us with the outline of these wonderful opinions, instead of being, as is the case with some, signally ungrateful.

The *Meno*, which we shall first consider, is in most respects an ordinary Socratic Dialogue. But it contains passages full of otherworldly Pythagoreanism, and this other-worldliness is by implication such as to give a real status to Ideal Meanings, and to the relations which hold among them or flow from them. Socrates is shown discoursing with Meno, a young man from Larissa in Thessaly, a friend of Aristippus, the hedonistic disciple of Socrates, and much influenced by the latest Thessalian sensation, the rhetorical displays of Gorgias. Meno is keen to raise the question, much debated in Thessaly, whether Virtue is teachable or not, but Socrates says that at Athens they are not as yet clear what Virtue *is*, and so cannot hope to answer further questions regarding it. Meno then gives an account of Virtue, derived from Gorgias, which merely outlines its species: if one is a man, Virtue consists in engaging in politics, benefiting one's friends and injuring one's enemies, and in all circumstances saving one's own skin, if one is a woman, Virtue consists in running one's house well, caring for all in it, obeying one's husband and so on. Definition by specification is a less contemptible proceeding than Socrates, with his passion for definition by invariant abstraction, will, of course, allow: Socrates complains that, looking for one Virtue, he has been offered a swarm. In the case of health and size and strength we recognize the existence of a single Eidos (72d) whether in man or woman, young or old: why should the case be different in regard to Virtue? Surely Self-restraint and Justice are necessary for men and women, young and old, and are one and the same for all of them? (It might have been argued against Socrates that the different specific forms of these Virtues for differently placed people are as important as what is abstractly common to them all.) Self-restraint and Justice and Bravery and Wisdom are, however, only specific Virtues, and we wish to discover what is common to all Virtue *qua* Virtue.

To help the discussion further Socrates then gives as an example of the One-over-many, or Sameness-in-Differentiation, that he is looking for, the definition of Figure, as being first of all, an end (τελευτή or ἔσχατον) or limit (πέρας), and in the second place the limit of a solid (στέρεον). This definition is acceptable because the notion of a limit and of a solid must necessarily be understandable to anyone who can hope to rise to the conception of a figure, whereas such a definition as 'Figure is what invariably accompanies Colour' raises questions as to the nature of Colour, which might be felt to be as unclear as Figure. Certainly no one would maintain that Colour elucidated Figure in the way in which Limit and Solid do so. (Plato is not here appealing, as some would suppose, to what ordinary speakers would say, but to the deeply felt rightness that leads them to say this or that: in saying (75d) that it is 'most truly dialectical not merely to say what is true, but to say it by way of what the interrogated person would confess that he knew', he is testing his Dialectic, not by what certain interrogated persons *happen* to confess, but by what any interrogated person *must* confess. The definition is interesting, further, in pointing straight to the 'mathematicization' in which Plato must even at that time have become interested: the Eide called Solids arise when limits are set to continuous three-dimensionality (the Deep and Shallow), these limits being themselves *Surfaces*, or not further divisible Solids, just as what the vulgar call 'Points' are really Indivisible Lines.) Meno, however, asks Socrates what may be meant by 'Colour', and Socrates playfully gives an answer in harmony with the Empedoclean theories of Gorgias, according to which Colour is an effluence from Figure commensurate with sight and therefore perceptible. Meno, pressed to give a similar definition of Virtue, hazards the poetic 'to rejoice in what is fine and to be able to realize it' (77b). This suggests that it is possible to rejoice in what is *not* fine, i.e. not good, knowing it to be not good, and this Socrates is at all times willing to argue to be impossible, largely owing to his refusal to distinguish Goodness as Such from Goodness for Me. If, however, everyone rejoices in what is fine and good, it becomes useless as a definition of

Virtue: the mark of Virtue must therefore lie in the capacity for realizing good. But obviously it can only be virtuous to realize good if one does so in a just and self-restrained manner, and this is to make Virtue depend on a part of itself, a self-contradictory and circular mode of characterization (79b, c).

After some arrests, Socrates proposes to go in quest of Virtue in company with Meno, but Meno now raises the quibble of the Wranglers that, if one is ignorant of what Virtue Itself is, one cannot very well go in search of it, nor will one recognize it if one does come upon it: it is impossible to look for what one knows or for what one does not know. This quibble challenges Socrates, as did the inspiration of Ion, to argue for the existence of forms of knowing that are not explicit, that guide us in life, and guide us in the activity of question and answer, without being such as one could clearly formulate and acknowledge. The existence of such implicit knowledge is then attested in the case of Meno's slave-boy who, understanding in relation to a diagram what it is to be square, and what it is to have a side, and to have sides standing as regards their lengths in the proportions $1:2$, $1:3$, $2:3$ etc., and to have areas standing in the continuous proportion $1^2:2^2:3^2:4^2$ etc., and what it is finally to be the diagonal distance of a square's corner from its opposite corner, is enabled to see, after several false starts, that being a square of twice the area of another square entails having a side of length equal to the diagonal of the other square (and not, as one might at first imagine, a side twice or $1\frac{1}{2}$ times as long as that of the first square).

Socrates does not here say that all this knowledge rests on a deep understanding of being square as such, of having such and such a length, of standing in such and such a ratio to another length, of being a diagonal distance etc., but it is plain that he *does* postulate such an understanding, since he certainly does not think that the particular square in the diagram, even if it were a perfect instance of being square, which of course it is not, is sufficient to establish these conclusions. He in fact supposes that we must have had a fully-developed geometrical understanding *before* becoming embodied human beings, and that the instances or rather approximate illustrations of the various Ideal Meanings involved in such understanding merely *recall* the latter, and their various ideal relations, when we are questioned in the face of a diagram. And the procedures of Socrates, if not his precise words, certainly give ontological status to the Square as Such etc., since there certainly would not have been diagrams in the disembodied state before we were men. There might, of course, have been, and in fact certainly must have been, *perfect* instances of being square etc. which Plato (later or earlier) called the Objects of Mathematics, for the being of these is entailed by the being of the Eide and vice versa, it being impossible to consider the content and relations of Eide without considering their possible instantiation, just as it is impossible to consider instances, perfect or imperfect, except in relation to the Eide that they instantiate. The passage in question therefore implies the ontology of the Eide, and perhaps also that of the Objects of Mathematics, and while it does not explicitly endorse the doctrine that *all* Ideal Meanings have a purely mathematical analysis, the examples of definition given at other points in the Dialogue certainly tend in that direction. The notion of a thinking existence in which, shorn of bodily particularity, though not of the residual particularity of life and mind, we should come livingly into contact with Ideal Natures or Senses, seeing them in relation to purely possible examples, and then later be led to remember them and their idealized instantiation, through their imperfect instantiations 'down here', are views no doubt repugnant to 'modern thought', with its belief in universal meanings as pale abstractions from the particulars given to sense. But on a Platonic ontology, it is instances that are the pale reflections of living idealities, and there is no reason why we should not apprehend these latter without seeing them in and through actual instances, as we do in fact apprehend them whenever we deeply understand anything even in this life. The notion of a pre-incarnate or post-incarnate grasp of the 'gist' of complicated thought-contents and relations is in every way defensible, even if *we* should wish to stress its intrinsic relation to *possible* instantiation rather more than Plato does. One does not, of course, in a properly understood Platonism, suppose the being of anything other than the Eide if one thinks of them as being actually, or (as they necessarily are) possibly instantiated. What the doctrine of reminiscence at least shows, as will be more elaborately argued in the *Phaedo*, is that we as thinkers have access to a world of unchanging Meanings, which at least suggests that, though inexpugnably instantial even in our acts of thought, we in some degree rise above such instantiality and achieve a certain communion with 'deathlessness' in such acts of thinking.

Socrates, having disposed of the difficulties involved in our ignorance of the precise analysis of Virtue, is now willing to investigate the teachability of Virtue without professing to know exactly what Virtue is. Instead of hypothetically assuming that to be virtuous is to be *X*, and then seeing what secondary attributes of teachability or non-teachability flow from this assumption, he assumes, contrariwise, that Virtue *is* teachable, and then sees what consequences regarding the *nature* of Virtue follow from this assumption. It might then be possible to give unconditional acceptance to what one is now only accepting *on* a certain hypothesis. Obviously if Virtue is teachable, it must be some form of Knowledge, for only a form of Knowledge could be teachable. (In the text, 87c, Socrates talks as if being a species of Knowledge were only a sufficient and not a necessary condition of being teachable, but his next sentence makes plain that it is to be understood as being necessary as well as sufficient: so that *either* the teachability of Virtue or its knowledge-status can be regarded as the substantive hypothesis, from which the other follows. This explains subsequent shifts in the extremely confusing argument.) We have therefore to see whether this consequence, that Virtue is Knowledge, stands up to further examination. This consequence entails, since both Virtue and Knowledge are certainly goods, that Virtue is either made good simply and solely because it is Knowledge, or alternatively that it is made good because it is either wholly or in part something *other* than Knowledge. Socrates now argues in his accustomed fashion that some so-called good things other than Knowledge, only profit us so far as we *know* their use, and that virtues like bravery, self-restraint etc. only profit us because intelligence is part of them. From this he draws the invalid conclusion that it is Knowledge alone which confers all the good that can be found in anything, but retreats from this to the sounder position that Virtue consists either wholly or at least in part in Knowledge (89a); which latter alternative would not, however, yield him the right consequence. The argument is further held to be weakened by the fact that, if Virtue is Knowledge (or if Virtue is teachable) there should be universally recognized teachers of Virtue, and the fact that there are no such universally recognized teachers makes it a likely inference (89c) that Virtue is not after all Knowledge (or not teachable). The absence of universally recognized teachers of Virtue is now attested by the opportune arrival of Anytus, the principal prosecutor of Socrates at his forthcoming trial. Anytus contumeliously rejects the view that the Sophists, the only professed teachers of Virtue, really make anyone better: any decent, cultivated Athenian will give better instruction in Virtue than such Sophists. But were any of the great good men venerated in Athens able to train their sons in Virtue? It would appear doubtful. Anytus departs in anger.

Socrates now points to the fact that there is such a thing as Right Opinion which will lead to the same profitable results as knowledge as long as a man definitely has it. Meno suggests that Right Opinion, since it is only opinion, will sometimes lead to correct action, sometimes to the reverse: Socrates replies that the latter is impossible as long as the opinion remains right. But even if an opinion is right, the man who has it will not be sure of its rightness, as he will be when he knows something. And since he will not be sure of his opinion, he will be readily seduced from it, and will then be as likely to act wrongly as rightly. He must turn his right opinion into real knowledge by tying it down with 'the reason why' ($\alpha i\tau i\alpha s \lambda o\gamma\iota\sigma\mu\hat{\omega}$), which is also what was described as recollection. If one is clear, it is suggested, what it is to be square and twice the size of another square, and what it is to pursue the profitable in dangerous circumstances, one will know how to construct the double of a square or how to be brave in those circumstances. Whereas the man who is not clear on these fundamental notional issues, will not do the right thing infallibly and will be readily persuaded not to do it. Socrates holds therefore that what is *ordinarily* called Virtue cannot be Knowledge, and, what is equivalent, that it cannot be taught. (It is not made clear, however, why there should not be a communication of opinion similar to the imparting of knowledge.) The great good men of the Athenian past were, therefore, divinely inspired like the poets: they enacted the right policies without knowing that and why they were right. Virtue accrued to them by a divine fate, being neither natural nor acquired by instruction. Socrates fails to note how what he is now saying is in contradiction with his previous proof that Virtue must consist, either wholly or in part, in Knowledge. It seems that he is veering towards a view in which, in addition to Virtue Absolute, which involves clear knowledge of the Good, there is also a weakened simulacrum of the same in which true opinion takes the place of knowledge.

II

We now turn to the *Phaedo*, the most beautiful and moving of all the Dialogues of Plato. In it Phaedo, a very dear associate of Socrates, describes the happenings and speeches on the last day of Socrates's life, when he, Socrates, tried to determine by argument what would happen when the hemlock separated his 'Soul', his own personal instance of vitality and thought, from his 'body', his own instance of gross, palpable, sensibly apparent humanity. Certainly the latter would for some time survive its loss of Soul, but could Soul reasonably be held to survive its loss of body? Socrates attempts to argue that there are features of being a Soul that make it, a Soul, more eminently capable of survival, less capable of being merely dissipated or attenuated, than is the case with the instances of other universal meanings: fires may be extinguished, and snows melted, but the fugitive fabric of thought and vital control is made of more resistant stuff. The arguments of Socrates are by no means trivial or archaic, to those at least to whom there is a rational *a priori* in this field as in every other field. The deeply Pythagorean character of the arguments is shown by the two men with whom Socrates mainly discourses: Simmias and Cebes, pupils of the Italian Pythagorean Philolaus, who has recently been a visiting teacher at Thebes, but who have been lured to Athens by the voice of Socrates. Among those present are impassioned devotees like Apollodorus, Epigenes and Phaedo himself, Megarians like Euclides and Terpsion, but Plato expressly tells us that he himself was absent. This has led some to think that none of the reported arguments for immortality could have been Socratic, and that Plato merely grafted his Eidos-theory and his Pythagorean Soul-doctrine on to the historical circumstances of Socrates's death. This is not in any way plausible. Socrates, we learn from Xenophon, *did* have the Pythagoreans Simmias, Cebes and Phaidondas among his associates, and he would certainly have been willing to lend tentative credence to the sublime Pythagorean vistas of the after-life, even if he did not go so far as to affirm them confidently. And if we take a little trouble, we can very well separate out in the arguments in the Dialogue an original deposit which may well have been Socratic, that is free from definite ontological commitments in regard to the Eide, but only stresses the timeless character of the issues that come up in Dialectic, to which we can oppose other Platonic and Pythagorean strata in which the Eide are central and thematic. Beneath both of these strata probably lie, on the view that we have taken, movements towards that comprehensive mathematicization of the Eide to which Plato was at all times tending. All these strata are, however, blended in a unique conceptual and literary whole, in which countless questionable logical moves are throughout transfigured by profound ontological insight.

After many vivid preliminaries, among which the most magnificently authentic is perhaps the picture of Socrates rubbing the leg from which the fetters have just been removed, and commenting on the close marriage of pleasure with pain that he is now experiencing, we find Socrates arguing that it would involve a complete abandonment of the philosophical character to do anything but rejoice in the present approach of death. For philosophy is in fact nothing but the practice of dying, and it would be an odd thing if, when the goal of all philosophizing drew near, those who sought that goal should draw back in fear or anger (64a). Death, moreover, is definable as the separation of Soul from body, in which each of these factors exists on its own, but for the Soul to be thus separated merely consummates a process that has been going on all the time in the philosophic life. The philosophical man is not keen on bodily pleasures whether these be those of the table or the couch, nor does he care to adorn his body in any noteworthy fashion. But the philosophical man is keen to possess knowledge and insight, and this always involves going beyond the confusing, variable appearances of the senses to an accurate, invariant structure that approves itself to reason: it is only when he theorizes that the various facets of being declare themselves to his soul. Is there something which can be called the Just Itself, or the Beautiful Itself, or the Large, the Healthy, the Strong Itself, and so on, and has any such thing ever declared itself to our senses (65d)? Obviously there *are* all these things, they are what it is to be each sort of thing, but they are accessible in their true exactitude only to the understanding functioning in its purity, and ridding itself of all sensuous admixture. It is arguable that the total removal of the body with all its confusing sensuousness will enable us to penetrate directly to the defining Natures of things. In death we may see what things in their true being are, as in life we cannot hope to do (66e). Those who fear death are men of counterfeit virtue who restrain themselves only in the hope of future bodily enjoyments, or who are brave only out of fear of future bodily evils. They are, that is, temperate out of intemperance and courageous out of fear. The truly philosophical man, however, does not seek to barter gratification for gratification, nor pain for pain, but is ready to sacrifice all for insight, that pearl of great price, and, since he hopes to enjoy this perfectly when dead, he will not be afraid of death (69). All this, we may say, is superbly beautiful, but we cannot help feeling a strain of exaggeration in it. For surely the shows of sense illustrate as well as distort? And surely what there is of substance in the instances of sense are the Eide manifest in them, so that they are not as despicable as Socrates here suggests? And if the instances of sense are not to be realities independent of the Eide, and so members of some second, equally real order, what alternative is there but for them to be the mere 'efflorescences' of the Eide, in which those Eide exert their causative efficacy, and become in the fullest sense active and real? All these are points that in later Dialogues like the *Sophist* or the *Timaeus* will be stated or implied. Here we are in the grip of a more or less world-fleeing hysteria. But the pure insight of the philosopher must have a relation to instances as well as to Eide even if in that insight the generalized 'Objects of Mathematics' have to replace concrete sensuous instances.

Cebes the Pythagorean now remarks that many men doubt whether the Soul-side of the living man really outlasts death or its separation from the body-side. It is widely held that, when death occurs, the Soul-side of the living man is simply dispersed like smoke or like a breath of wind, and is not to be found anywhere at all (70a). Socrates then proposes that they should 'tell each other a story' about all these matters: no one, at least, could say that he is now chattering about what does not really concern him.

The first argument advanced by Socrates is the Heraclitean one that there is perpetual change from one opposite to another, but in such fashion that the total quantity or measure of each opposite and of the world in action is always preserved. This means that change is not unidirectional but circular: the large is always being reduced, but the small, on the other hand, is always growing, the strong is losing force but the weak is becoming stronger, the more excellent is deteriorating but the less excellent improving, the aggregated is being dispersed and the dispersed aggregated, those asleep are awaking and the awake falling asleep, the hot is losing heat and the cooler becoming warmer etc. (70d–71b). If there were not this circularity or perpetual compensation of opposite by opposite, the whole universe would run down irretrievably in one direction: everything would be infinitesimally reduced, or hopelessly enfeebled, or most closely aggregated or profoundly asleep etc. (72a, b). Socrates is implying, but not clearly saying, that there cannot be a generation of an opposite from or into nothing, but only from or into its opposite: otherwise there would not be the one-sided running-down that he premises. And he is also suggesting the opposites in the world require one another, and that they can only *be* if a rough balance can be struck between them. The conclusion of this universal dependence of opposite on opposite is then applied to life and death. If life is a togetherness of body and soul, of corporeal and psychic function, then such togetherness must arise out of a state in which body and Soul exist apart, and it must pass away into a state in which body and Soul again exist apart, which must pass away into a state of renewed togetherness and so on indefinitely. The alternative that body passes from a state in which it for a time has psychic functions associated with it to a state in which these are simply absent or non-existent, would not, it is correctly implied, involve the generation of opposite from *opposite* which the doctrine postulates, but the generation of something from its mere absence or privation. For this reason we are justified in believing in the old myth of the Souls in Hades which return after a time to life in the flesh, go back to Hades and so on. If *per impossibile* there were not this compensation, the whole world would run down into a state of death, body having no source from which it could replenish its 'Soul'. The arguments of this passage are by no means contemptible, though they involve the unmodern beliefs that nothing can *be* except in an opposing context against which it sets itself off, and that the presence of Life and Mind somewhere are as much required by the dead parts of the universe as the latter are required by Life and Mind. A regular alternation between deeply engaged embodiment and disembodied understanding of what has thereby been undergone, would likewise seem to reduce, rather than increase, the strangeness of the empirical marriage between the living and thinking, on the one hand, and what is lifeless and unthinking, on the other.

Cebes then strengthens Socrates's argument by recurring to the argument stated in the *Meno*: that men properly interrogated tell us exactly how things stand in some geometrical or dialectical situation, proves that such knowledge has been left in them from some former state, and is now merely being recalled. Simmias asks to be reminded of the purport of the argument mentioned by Cebes, and Socrates gives a more concrete sense to the 'reminiscence' mentioned in it by likening it to the manner in which seeing or hearing something recalls something which is like it or otherwise associated with it. Thus the lyre of a person we care for leads our thought to the cared for person, seeing Simmias carries our thought to his companion Cebes, and seeing a picture of Simmias makes us think of Simmias himself. In all such reminiscence there is a sense of the likeness, but also of the unlikeness, of the thing remembered to the thing which makes us remember it. All this is conspicuously the case when our minds are carried from the imperfect illustrations of Eide to the Eide themselves. Pieces of wood and stone are never exactly and constantly equal, but suggest equality or inequality according as we or others look at them. The Equal Itself, on the other hand, is always paradigmatically equal, and its instances are both wholly different from it, and yet in a curious tendentious way like it. In seeing those instances we are both aware of the paradigm they are 'of', and also that they fall short of it and cannot be as it is, that they after a fashion 'want' to be as it is and yet cannot achieve this (74d–75b). The whole being of instances, it is here suggested, in so far as being can be predicated of instances at all, is simply the forthshadowing of a being which not being itself a forthshadowing is quite unlike that which shadows it forth, which, being thus forthshadowed, can in that sense be said to be like what thus shadows it forth. And our awareness of instances as instances is thus always a carrying back of our minds to what they instantiate, and of which we must have a clearer grasp than we can ever have of an instance. How do we achieve this grasp? The Platonic-Pythagorean suggestion is that we must have had this grasp *before* we became men, before we had ever heard or seen anything, and the argument, of course, applies not only to the Equal, but to the Greater or Less, the Beautiful, the Good, the Just and the Holy, and to every standard Meaning that enters into Dialectic: to all of these Meanings, which are also the real foundation of every possible instance, we must have had a pre-natal exposure. The soul-functions of life and thought must therefore have antedated their association with a body, and it must almost certainly have been at the moment of birth that this pre-natal experience was forgotten, to be later recalled, since we cannot at birth or for a long time afterwards give a rational account of the various ideal contents with which Dialectic and mathematics are concerned. The argument of course only proves the pre-existence but not the post-existence of the Soul, but, together with the previous argument of the generation of opposites from opposites, it will, says Socrates, prove the latter point as well. The reminiscence-argument has the merit of suggesting that beings capable of the instance-transcendence which takes off from imperfectly representative instances must be capable of having the more radical transcendence of instances involved in seeing Eide as the mere foci of possible instances, and that something so remarkable as to be capable of the second type of transcendence may very well have exercised it, if indeed in instances of thinking, yet in instances that borrowed no objects from the instantial world.

This leads on to a third line of proof for spiritual survival, one explicitly based on the place of Soul in the eidetic-instantial structure of things. The universe contains as central, non-sensuous realities the Ideal Meanings of the Beautiful as Such, the Equal as Such etc., of which each is unique, exactly what it is and cannot significantly be thought to alter from being what it is. The universe also contains the peripheral instantiations of these Ideal Meanings, which are essentially manifold, never perfectly illustrative because not necessarily so, and in fact always in a state of flux. The latter announce themselves to sense, the former only to the reasoning mind. Soul, however, occupies a curious intermediate place in the cosmic economy: it is itself instantial rather than eidetic, and it veers towards the confused sensuous sphere of instantiation and is closely associated with the perturbations of body. It is, however, also capable of thinking Ideal Meanings without sensuous admixture, and so after a fashion liberating itself from its instantial status, and sharing the fixity and incapacity for dispersion of the things it contemplates (79c, d). Soul, we may say, without being an Eidos, is as it were eidetic, and it shows its quasi-eidetic status by the dominion it has over bodily particularities, the sort of divine dominion that an Eidos has over its instances (79e, 80a). Soul therefore has something of the character of the Pure Natures, which, when it draws most thoroughly into itself, it can apprehend and obey, and it may, therefore, be presumed to have a lastingness and an incapacity for dismemberment which is found in these Natures. If even the body holds together for a while after death, how much more will a Soul, whose nature is like that of the unshatterable things of thought, last indefinitely? The Soul, in fact, lives on a scale or on a spectrum between the sensuous and the eidetic, and can go up and down this spectrum both in this life and the life to come, veering towards sensuous, somatic dispersion, on the one hand, or ascending towards true eidetic unity and fixity, on the other. The pleasures, pains and desires of the lower regions hold it captive, but it is also capable of being drawn up aloft, and finding true satisfaction in the knowledge of what things truly are.

This third proof by 'affinity' is magnificent and crucial. It is not demonstrative, since Soul is not taken to be *itself* an eternal Eidos, and is admitted to have essential business with the changeable sensuous realm of instantiation. But it is much *better* than a demonstration since it appeals, not to some rigid, trivial identity, but to an affinity which genuinely, if problematically, widens its sphere of application to cover a new range of cases. Instantiation is never really anything *per se*, but has its whole substance in what it instantiates, and in Soul this becomes as it were explicit: the instance as it were rises above its instantial status, and takes on the character of the ideal unities that it contemplates. There is something absurd in supposing that something which can thus take on the character of what without qualification is, which can almost cease to be a particular at all, should be dependent on what is most peripherally particular, and should share the divisibility and dispersion of the latter. This absurdity, we may remark, is present in all those modern theories which seek to build patterns of meaning and interpretation into the structure of the brain or cortex, and hope that the former will be controlled (rather than disturbed) by the graftings, extirpations and other manipulations which they practise on the latter.

At this point Simmias and Cebes feel that the three merely probable arguments that Socrates has adduced are insufficiently compelling. Something more ineluctable must be produced if the terrors of dispersion are themselves to be dispersed. Simmias puts forward the Pythagorean view of Soul as a harmonic attunement of the various bodily elements, the hot and the cold, the moist and the dry etc.: when certain proportions among these elements are maintained, life and soul are present, when there is considerable departure from such proportions disease results, and yet further departure results in death. This view is, in all essentials, Plato's own view of the nature of Soul, that it is a set of geometrical and dynamic Ratios corresponding to the various sorts of state and object that the living, thinking being can control and know, to its whole repertoire of sensitivity and reactivity: here, however, Simmias objects to it on the non-Pythagorean ground that such a set of ratios and proportions must vanish into nothing when the organism is out of tune or dismembered, just as the marvellous tuning of a lyre, despite its fine exactitude, vanishes altogether when the lyre is neglected or allowed to go to pieces. The argument that, if the bodily elements outlast death, the beautiful, incorporeal attunement of those elements should be even more durable, is, Simmias says, as vacuous as a similar argument in the case of a lyre. No one argues that the excellent tuning of a lyre exists incorporeally when the lyre is broken or out of tune. This argument of Simmias is not without force, for though, on a Platonic-Pythagorean view, Ratios have a reality far more indisputable than any instrument or body which manifests them, this is not true of the instances of such Ratios: these may depend on the state of instruments and bodies. All the same, a true Pythagorean or Platonist should be indulgent even to the instances of such divine things as Ratios, which ought to count as Objects of Mathematics if not as Eide, and the view that Ratios are nothing if not embodied in an assemblage of bodily elements is possibly an objection raised by the historic Socrates in his last discussion, and one that would not have been approved by someone so Pythagorean as Plato. The objection raised by Cebes is more fundamental: it is simply that the three arguments given by Socrates are not enough to lend substance to the view that the Soul that perhaps functioned before and will perhaps function after its association with body will in fact always do so. We must show that Soul is inherently imperishable, that it can *never* be dispersed or reduced to nothing. Otherwise Soul may be no different from the weaver who, after outlasting many of his woven garments, is none the less outlasted by the last of them.

To the harmonic-ratio objection of Simmias, Socrates replies that it makes Soul wholly dependent upon bodily constituents and their mutual relations: it arises only when they enter into certain Ratios, and is the first to vanish when such Ratios cease to hold among them. Such a dependent, secondary status is incompatible with the prior existence of Soul proved in the reminiscence-argument which Simmias still finds compelling (92d). And it is also incompatible with the magisterial position of the Soul over against the desires which spring from the body: the Soul, schooled in medicine and the virtue of self-restraint, resists these desires as a harmonic Ratio could not resist the elements on which it is founded (94b–e). And it is incompatible with the fact that virtue is an attunement of Soul, and vice a departure from attunement, which must entail, either that one attunement, Soul, is capable of another, or that all Souls are of necessity equally virtuous, or, if that is absurd, that one Soul, being less virtuous, can also be less of a Soul than another (93a–94a). All these alternative consequences of the hypothesis that Soul is a harmonic Ratio among bodily elements are unacceptable: Soul cannot therefore be such a Ratio. The argument is well-marshalled, and has much of the deceptive prettiness of a genuine Socratic argument. One wonders, however, whether an acceptance of the Eidos-theory would not involve that an Eidos will have precisely such a magisterial, causative relation to the instances to which it lends character as the Soul is supposed to have to the body it organizes, and also whether the notion of some soul-instances being less adequate soul-instances than others is not quite in keeping with the eidetic theory. The defects of the argument suggest, as we have said, that it is an original piece of Socratic logic-chopping, perhaps credited to Socrates in a first version of the Dialogue, and now preserved even though

Socrates has to be the mouthpiece of later, more Platonic conceptions. The argument also probably reveals, even though the Socratic argument may discount it, how the mathematicizing goal had already become the unwritten background of Plato's published work: both the soul and its virtues are thought of in terms of attunements, and both attunements have their ultimate analysis in a set of numerical Ratios.

In reply to the demand of Cebes for an out-and-out proof of Soul's indestructibility, Socrates begins by giving an autobiographical account of the mental history which led up to his acceptance of the Eidos-theory: in this account Socratic and Platonic elements are certainly intertwined, but equally clearly the Platonic elements predominate. Plato in his intimate companionship with Socrates took over the latter's recounted past, in which such things as a temporary interest in physical philosophy (confirmed by Xenophon) probably figured, but he also wove into that past his own Pythagorean and Eleatic interests, and his own explicit ontology of the Eide, none of which can have been carried far by Socrates. The account of the Socratic-Platonic mental development stresses the notion of causation: Socrates-Plato was concerned to discover the causes of each thing, that through which it arises and perishes and in fact is. Such views are mentioned as that living things originate in a rotting of the hot and the cold (Archelaus of Athens), that thought stems from the mixture of elements in the blood (Empedocles), from the air (Diogenes of Apollonia), or from the brain (Alcmaeon of Croton), that organic growth stems from the various elements taken in in food and drink (Anaxagoras) (96a–d). The problems raised by growth led on to more abstract problems involving the greater and smaller, the more and the less, and here we have plainly a piece of Platonic rather than Socratic autobiography, since the notions of definitely and indefinitely increasing and diminishing quantity were to become key-notions in the mature thought of Plato. Socrates-Plato, we are told, had thought it reasonable to hold that one man or horse was bigger than another *by a head*, or that the number Ten exceeded the number Eight by the added number Two, or that two cubits in height exceeded one cubit by half of itself, and so on. He became clear, however, that there were not one, but countless operations converging on the same quantitative result – it could be obtained by addition, but also by subtraction and division – and it was, moreover, mysterious how separate ones could generate a duality by merely coming together, or which of the ones was thereby raised to two. (Plato was afterwards, or perhaps even at this time, to believe in a unique, standard 'generation' of the numbers by the continued intercourse of his two Principles of Unity and Indefinite Quantity acting on prior products of such intercourse, but in the present context no such unique, standard mode of 'generation' is suggested.)

From what is probably a later insertion regarding quantitative problems, we return to physics (97b), and Socrates-Plato tells us of the impression made on him by reading in Anaxagoras's book *On Nature* a statement to the effect that Mind orders and causes all. This Socrates thought, and it may well be Socrates who is now speaking, meant that Mind would have had to look to the Best in its ordering, and that everything in nature would have been ordered for the best. We need therefore only to have meditated on what was good or better or best – Socrates here parenthetically makes the immensely important admission (97d) that there is no separate science, and hence no separable Eidos, of the bad or worse, but that in knowing the best or better or good we *ipso facto* know what it would exclude – in order to answer all the questions of the physicists. We should be able to determine whether the earth is round or flat or at the centre of the cosmos by asking whether it is good for it to be thus, and the same regarding the heavenly bodies, and their velocities and turnings and other affections. (This last touch involves an incomparable Socratic-Platonic admixture. Socrates probably did put foward a naïvely moralistic, teleological view of natural arrangements – he certainly does so in Xenophon – but for Plato Goodness is Ratio, the One dominating and limiting Indefinite Quantity, and the goodness of the starry velocities lies, not in some copy-book conformity to imaginary stellar proprieties, but in their steadfast subjection to fixed laws and proportions. Human virtue of course has precisely the same structure.) Anaxagoras, however, quite by-passed the Best in his physics, and in his explanations made use mainly of airs, ethers and waters and suchlike strange inventions (98b, c). It is as if one explained the fact that Socrates had chosen to stay in prison, and not run away to Thessaly, not by the fact that it seemed best to him to do so, but by various facts regarding the set-up and state of his bones and muscles. The physical philosophers have in general seen no explanatory power, no causative force in the Best (99c), yet it is only the Good that can ultimately effect anything.

Socrates-Plato now says that he would have liked to explain all things through the Good, but feels unable to do so: as a second best, he will try to consider the world in the light of thinkingly-used-words (λόγοι), much as a man, unable to look at the sun in the sky, contemplates its image in water. (Socrates-Plato does not, however, admit that one is truly going away from things as they are in reality when one studies them through the medium of thinkingly-used-words: the reverse is rather the case.) Hypothetically one will assume the existence of these or those Eide or patterns of excellence and clear meaning: the Beautiful Itself, the Good Itself, the Great Itself and so on. Socrates-Plato assumes that we know the sort of entities that will be thus taken to exist, and can therefore sum up our postulation of their being in general terms, i.e. that there are Eide, but nothing rules out the view that each Eidos must be separately and momentously postulated, and that (despite *Republic*, 596a) they will all, as the context necessitates, represent patterns of *excellence* or *goodness*, the bad or defective consisting merely (97d) in what they exclude. *How* they are to be derived from the Good or supreme Principle of Platonic thought, is in the context left unclear – the whole of Dialectic and of the projected generation of the mathematicized Eide from the One and the Great and Small here looms obscurely in the background – but somehow they do so derive, and if we accept *their* existence, we shall be able, Socrates-Plato promises, to prove the immortality of the Soul. This proof requires, however, the additional postulate that the Eide are the *only* true causes of the presence of any characters in instances: deriving from the Good, it is implied, they explain what exists as in a more ultimate manner the Good Itself will explain them. It is Beauty Itself which renders things beautiful whether by its presence or self-communication or in some other manner: it is not, for example, a colour or a shape which is the true cause of beauty. In the same way it is Greatness Itself or Smallness Itself, or perhaps a specific degree of Greatness or Smallness, that makes things be of the great or small size that they are, and not circumstances like addition or division which are mere conditions of

size. (Socrates is much puzzled by relative magnitudes, as when
A is small in relation to *B* but large in relation to *C*: it is far from
clear how he resolves his difficulties, but would seem to hold that
such relative magnitudes always have a foundation in other
absolute magnitudes. Relational properties, it is plain, occasioned
great difficulty for Plato both when, as here, he is dealing with
relations among sensuous instances, and also when he is dealing
with relations that obtain among the Eide. See *Metaphysics*,
990b 15–22, *Nicomachean Ethics*, 1096a 17–19.)

The whole introduction of the Eide as a second-best to an
explanation in terms of the Good only makes sense, as we have
said, on the assumption that the Eide are all special cases of
Goodness, derivable in some not as yet specified manner from the
nature of Goodness Itself. And the derivation of the Eide from
Goodness itself arguably points to the beginnings of that mathematicizing project without which such a derivation would be
unintelligible, would in fact be no more than a vulgar piece of
Xenophontic edification. Plato uses the language of hypothesis
in this connection: we postulate specific Eide and participation
in such Eide to cover specific facts about instances. If the postulations fail to cover those facts – as the harmonic theory of Soul
failed to cover the facts of self-control – we alter the postulations.
If the postulations fit the instances, we make higher postulations
which cover the lower postulations until ultimately we arrive at a
postulation which appears wholly satisfactory, not only to the
interlocutors, but also in and for itself (101c–e). The context
implies that the postulation of an Ultimate Good was meant to be
the last postulation in the whole series. It is important in this
context not to bring in the whole modern machinery of the
deductive system which Plato could not have conceived or found
interesting. What he was constructing was a comprehensive,
transparent hierarchy of *conceptions*, based throughout on necessary
rather than empirical principles, in which a single generic or
supra-generic root was thought of as ramifying in an ordered
range of necessary differentiations, under which empirical
instances would ultimately be arranged.

The Eide having been established as the true causes of anything's having certain properties or being of a certain sort,
Socrates-Plato goes on to prove the Soul's immortality. He first
postulates that opposites will never admit opposites in their

instances or cases, but that their instances will depart or perish when such opposites approach. Thus an instance of Warmth cannot admit Cold, an instance of Largeness cannot admit Smallness etc. but must vanish or depart when such an opposite approaches, though an instance of Coldness could very well admit of an approaching Largeness or Smallness since neither is opposed to being cold. There are, however, certain sorts of things whose natures involve, without being identical with, one of a pair of opposites: things of such sorts will not admit the approach of the other member of the relevant pair of opposites, but will, like the instance of the opposite that they contain, retreat or vanish on such approach. Thus snow having Coldness as part of the sort of thing it is will either vanish or depart when the Warm approaches; a case of triplicity, having Oddness as part of what it is, will either vanish or depart when threatened with the Even etc. Soul, however, is related to Life as snow is to Coldness or the triple to Oddness: Soul is what by its presence gives Life to a body, it carries Livingness with it as part of what it is, and it is quite impossible for it to admit what is opposite to Life, namely Death. Soul is therefore intrinsically deathless, as snow is intrinsically warmthless, and as a case of being three is intrinsically uneven, and when the opposite of its intrinsic Life, Death, approaches, Soul must either retreat or be destroyed. There is, however, a difficulty in Soul's being destroyed on the approach of Death, which does not arise in the case of the approach of other opposites, for to be destroyed is after a fashion to admit Death, which is Life's opposite, and this is what Soul, being intrinsically living and life-giving, cannot possibly do. The intrinsically living would seem in fact to be of necessity the intrinsically lasting, and the intrinsically lasting to be incapable of destruction. Soul, therefore, being inherently alive and inherently life-giving, is inherently incapable of destruction: it in fact shares the indestructibility which one must of necessity accord to the Eidos of Life Itself (106d). If death therefore approaches, Soul can only depart and not be destroyed, and the souls of the dead must therefore live on in some sort of Hades.

This strangely brilliant argument is also strangely obscure. It can be regarded as an unsatisfactory sort of ontological argument, imperishability or necessary persistence having been made part of the defining essence of Soul, and therefore capable of being read out of it with unhelpful triviality. It can also be held to be built on ambiguities in the notion of Death, this being either taken to be an incapacity for vital functioning or the total cessation of existence: Soul might be held to be deathless in the former sense but not in the latter. It is best, however, to see in it an argument of the same sort as those which have led up to it, one which does not trivially or fallaciously compel, but which builds on deep mutual connectednesses and affinities of notions, which it would not be self-contradictory, but deeply misguided and irrational to deny. For the Eidos of Life which is mentioned in 106d occupies a very special place in or beyond the hierarchy of the Eide: in a system like Plato's, where the whole Cosmos is a living creature containing countless other living creatures, and where lifeless structures are all incorporated into living creatures, Life is the Principle which gives the Cosmos and all its subordinate structures unity, which is the necessary complement of its dispersion and its transience. And Thought as Such, which for Plato and all the Greeks goes together with Life, cannot, even at this stage, have been without a uniquely significant place in the realm of the Eide: it, as an Eidos or Principle of Eide, must have represented that in which all the Eide come together, are wrought into a single ordered system. This paradigmatic thought is, of course, no one's thought, not even the thought of a God: it is the Eidos of Thinking as Such, which all thinking Souls instantiate, and which is the connective tissue of the ideal cosmos. Such a Life involving such a Thought will be unique among Eide, and its instances, Souls, including that sovereign Soul which steers the world, will likewise be unique among instances. If anything in the changeable realm of instances effectively copies the timeless and systematic endurance of the Eide, souls in their endless temporal persistence would be such. There is good reason, therefore, to suppose that souls will not only be incapable of that attenuation of function known as dying, but also of the total annihilation in which such an attenuation *seems* to end. They must be the most enduring entities in the cosmos, a reasoning not trivially cogent, but which is not without its rational persuasiveness. The instantial world must in some manner manage to illustrate the *difference* between the eidetic and the instantial order.

A magnificent eschatological account follows, outlining the glories and miseries of the life to come. Heaven, the home of philosophers and virtuous non-philosophers, is literally heaven: it lies at the upper bounds of the air, and it breathes the ether, just as we who live at the upper bound of the sea breathe polluted air. We are submarine creatures in relation to the dwellers on the 'true earth' above, in the same relation to them as creatures in the sea stand to us. And the shape of the lower cosmos there appears as a marvellous dodecahedron, that noblest of solids, tricked out in luminous colours. The joys and beauties of this philosophical Heaven are described in terms which accord with the Mahayana Buddhist descriptions of Paradise: if Mind as Such occupies the place in the Cosmos given it in either system, probably such descriptions adumbrate truth. The descriptions of the underworld rivers and the sufferings endured in or near them are interesting: they have at least deeply influenced Christian eschatology. We should in general treat the eschatological side of Plato with respect: it is only absurd if it is right to base one's view of the universe on the string of phenomena that for Plato are only shadows in a Cave. The eschatological passages are followed by a wonderful account of the hemlock-drinking and last acts and words of Socrates. There is nothing more elevated and elevating in the whole range of human literature.

III

The *Symposium* takes up the theme of Love which had been broached in the *Lysis,* and which was to be carried further in the *Phaedrus.* As in these other Dialogues, the severe, notional, Socratic-Platonic analysis of Love is put forward on a background of upper-class homosexuality: Socrates deals with the passion for the ultimately Beautiful and Good, while the other speakers deal with passions for beautiful persons, who are for the most part male rather than female. The Dialogue shows Socrates wholly tolerant of this fashionable homosexuality, as in fact playfully adopting its language, but as adhering in his personal relations to the severer rule of his city's customs and laws, and as only really interested in forms of love that range far beyond the love of persons, though persons can be united through this very person-transcending love. The central passages in which Socrates describes the ascent of the loving, contemplative mind to the vision of Beauty and Goodness Itself, are rightly thought to enshrine everything that is central in the teaching of Plato, and to be in addition, to those able to enter into them and use them, mystical scriptures without price.

The Dialogue is a report of a number of discourses in praise of Love held at a drinking-party given by the young and beautiful Agathon in celebration of the success of his prize-winning tragedy. Phaedrus the rhetorician, Pausanias, a vague cultivator of philosophy, Eryximachus a physician, Aristophanes the comic poet, Agathon himself and Socrates, contribute to the symposium, and the Dialogue is rounded off by an extraordinary encomium of Socrates, mixed up with personal confessions, from the mouth of the drunken Alcibiades. The Dialogue is also remarkable for its report of the trance which suddenly beset Socrates on his way to the dinner, and which delayed his arrival there, and which probably took the form of an elevation to that Absolute Beauty of which Socrates was afterwards to speak. It also contains a report from Alcibiades of a similar trance that befell Socrates during the campaigns of the Peloponnesian War. Socrates, it is plain, was not only a name-dropper and logic-chopper about Absolutes, he also consorted with those Absolutes Themselves.

The speech of Phaedrus, after a brief reference to the place of Love in poetic cosmogonies, is mainly concerned with the inspiring effect of homosexual love on military prowess. Achilles was moved to all the efforts which ended in the slaying of Hector, and to his own subsequent, voluntary death, by his love for his slain lover Patroclus, and it is thus apparent that lovers are everywhere infinitely concerned to appear brave and honourable in the eyes of the beloved. Even women can be part of the inspiring influence of love, as when Orpheus went to Hades in quest of Eurydice, or as when Alcestis was willing to die for the sake of her beloved husband Admetus.

The speech of Pausanias rises a little above this extremely low level. There are, he holds, not one, but two species of Love, one the Uranian or heavenly, born from Aphrodite the motherless daughter of Cronus, and the other the Pandemian or vulgar, born from Aphrodite the daughter of Zeus and Dione. The Pandemian love is the love practised by inferior men, and is as readily directed to women as to men and boys: it is concerned with bodies rather than souls, and sets no store by the intelligence of its objects.

Uranian love, on the other hand, is directed to men and maturing boys alone, loves them for their strength and intelligence as well as their bodies, and continues to love them even when they become grown up men. Societies differ in their attitude to such homosexual love; in some places it is held honourable, and in others dishonourable. In Athens it is thought honourable if it is combined with faithfulness and personal respect, dishonourable if faithless and promiscuous. There are in short circumstances in which the love of men and boys can be virtuous and not vicious, and it is this virtuous homosexuality which goes by the name of 'Uranian Love'.

In the speech of Eryximachus there is a yet further elevation of content. Love is not merely a human affection, but is a principle that dominates the whole of organic and inorganic nature. It also governs the whole art of medicine, which is concerned at all times with the body's love of fulfilment or 'evacuation', healthy or depraved, and which can arouse and satisfy healthy bodily loves while refusing satisfaction to depraved appetites. The medical art, like gymnastic, music and agriculture, is an art which induces love and friendship among opposites, including such extreme opposites as the hot and the cold, the acid and the sweet, the moist and the dry etc. In the well-doctored organism these opposites no longer are at war but are reconciled in harmony, as notes of differing pitch are reconciled by music. The arts of reconciliation are in fact all rightly described as erotic arts. In man alone these erotic arts break up into the two divisions mentioned by Pausanias, the Uranian and the Pandemian, the former restraining all appetites in an overall harmony, while the latter gives rein to separate appetites which it is important should not be let go too far. Even in nature there is a contrast between well-tempered harmonies of opposites which bring health to all living things, and tendencies to encroachment and disorder among such opposites which lead to pestilence, frosts, hail, blight and other disastrous conditions. This speech makes explicit reference to Heraclitus and his view of a harmony arising out of the tension of opposites, and it also plainly has connections with the medical views of the school of Empedocles and with the stress on 'isonomy' held by Alcmaeon of Croton. But it is more than a medical passage: it is one of the earliest passages in which the notion of the healthy or right state of the body is regarded as a sort of physical Justice and Temperance, one connected also with the preservation of certain precise *Ratios* among various opposed constituents. This notion is not one that Plato borrowed from medical sources: medical sources rather borrowed it from the philosophers, and Plato's teaching may very well have reinforced such borrowings. The mathematicization of the Eide, and of the characteristic values that are part of the Eide, are here seen in their origins.

Eryximachus is succeeded by Aristophanes, who has got rid of a hiccup which previously halted his performance. He gives vent to a long, brilliant, mythological extravagance, in which men are depicted as having arisen through the cutting in twain of extra-ordinary double creatures with faces, backs, limbs and sexual organs facing both ways. Some of these double creatures were doubly male, some doubly female, some male-female in structure. The creatures were split into two by Zeus to repress their danger-ous contumacity, their heads were turned round and they were given new fronts with the skin drawn together at the navel, and their sexual organs moved into a frontal position. The two halves of these double creatures then craved sexual union with one another, in some cases males with females, in which case the continuation of the race was also secured, in other cases males with males, or females with females, in which case there was only an appeasement of erotic tension. But in all cases the real aim of such sexual union was a return from separation to an original unity: Love therefore is always the desire and pursuit of the Whole (192e). This speech is in many ways merely comic, but it is also true to the phenomenology of sex in which each person feels himself into the position of the other, and so moves some distance towards a transcendence of his own specific, instantial separateness, feeling also that the goodness of sex lies in doing so. It also suggests that homosexuality is as inevitable a form of such transcendence as heterosexuality, even if, contrary to Greek judgment, there may be greater richness in the latter than in the former. The Eleatic implications of everything that is worthwhile in sex are plainly suggested, and though the speech is put in the mouth of a comic poet, it has undoubted touches of true Platonism.

From Aristophanes the word passes to Agathon, who con-structs an extremely artificial speech, not unlike Gorgias's *Encomium of Helen*, first praising Love for its essential youth, and then quibblingly demonstrating its connection with virtue. In Love there is never injustice since Love willingly submits to anything and everything; Love is temperate since it can master all pleasures and desires; Love inspires boundless courage; Love is wise since it inspires cunning poems and is responsible for the cunning shapes of plants and animals, and for most of the cunning exploits of the Gods, etc., etc.

After all this clever after-dinner speaking, Socrates undertakes to give a not necessarily flattering account of Love. Love it is plain is always *of* something: it necessarily has an object. It is plain, further, that it desires what it is *of*, and that it does not itself *have* what it desires. When it is said that someone both *has* something and also desires it, what is really meant is not that he has it now and does desire it now, but that he desires to *go on* having it in the future. Love therefore is always in need of what it loves, and does not actually possess it. But what it is thus in need of cannot be base ($\alpha i\sigma\chi\rho\acute{o}\nu$): it is therefore necessarily fine and beautiful ($\kappa\alpha\lambda\acute{o}\nu$). Love is therefore nothing but the need of Beauty, which Love itself does not possess. Beautiful things are, however, necessarily good, and Love is therefore also in need of what is good.

From this strange conclusion Socrates goes on to quote what, he says, was taught him by a wise woman, Diotima of Mantinea, who visited Athens once in the past, and was able to ward off a threat of plague. This woman (in whose reality it is impossible to believe) proved to Socrates that Love was neither good nor beautiful, but refused to conclude from this that Love was therefore base. For just as there is something called Right Opinion which is not Knowledge, since it can give no adequate reason for what it believes, and yet is not Ignorance, since it is of real Being, and just as this is intermediate between Knowledge and Ignorance, so there is something which is not beautiful without being base, and not good without being bad, and which is intermediate between these extremes. Love should therefore not be regarded as divine, since the Gods in their blessedness possess goodness and beauty, but as daemonic, and as having a status between the mortal and the immortal. And while Love's father was Plenty ($\Pi\acute{o}\rho os$), an accredited member of the Gods, his mother was Poverty ($\Pi\epsilon\nu\acute{\iota}\alpha$), a beggar at the Olympian gates, and

Love accordingly always alternates between brief spells of flourishing possession and long spells of hopeless need. Not all forms of the desire for the Good and Beautiful will, however, count as Love, but only such as long for a perpetuation of goodness and beauty, a perpetuation which necessarily involves a *begetting* of something in the beautiful. Such perpetual begetting is the only manner in which a mortal creature can approach immortality, which is accordingly the secret goal of all love. Such begetting may be offspring like oneself, but it may also be of one's own bodily and spiritual state which one seeks to maintain against the inroads of change: it may also be a begetting of the reputation which will survive one indefinitely. But it may also take the form of a begetting of wisdom and virtue in a younger person whom one seeks to instruct and inspire.

All these procreative desires are, however, mere adumbrations of a higher form of Love in which one steadily rises above things beautiful and good, whether in oneself or in others, and seeks to lay hold of the absolutely Beautiful as Such. One begins with the admiration of beautiful bodies, and then rises to the admiration of the bodily beauty which they all have in common. One then goes on to admire the invisible beauties of souls which exceed the beauties of bodies, and the more exalted beauties of laws and social practices, and the yet more exalted beauties of the ideas and principles which one finds in the sciences. Ultimately one becomes aware of a wonderful Nature or Principle, specified in all these forms of beauty, but admitting of no diversity of aspect or variation of degree, a Nature or Principle which is simply the Beauty Itself in which all instances and species of beauty share. In this commerce with Beauty Itself Love reaches its supreme form, and becomes infinitely fruitful of virtue and wisdom, both in a man himself, and in others to whom he communicates his vision.

No one who reads these passages carefully can doubt that they teach the supremely real existence of something which is not so much a specific Eidos, a specific case of excellent visible or invisible form, but rather something which all such cases specify, and which is itself rather a Principle of Eide than another Eidos. This supreme Principle is in a sense all that one has in all the Eide: they are all *It* in one or other specific guise, and in a sense it is also all that one has in all the instances of the Eide. No account is offered of the existence or conceivability of what is base and defective, but it is plain that such things play no part in the ascent: it is not by contemplating base or deformed possibilities or realities that one rises to the Beautiful Itself. Some sort of theory according to which there is but one science, and consequently one Eidos, of the species of Beauty and of what they exclude, is accordingly again indicated. It is also clear that Plato draws no harsh line between the Beautiful Itself and the Good Itself: they are, if one likes, the same thing reached along a somewhat different route, just as Unity Itself will, in a late Dialogue like the *Parmenides*, be ready to take the place of either. The passage moves us, further, because it not only connects the vision of Beauty Itself with an ascent to the same, but also with a corresponding descent: the man who has seen the Highest will be infinitely fruitful in good works, thoughts and acts of love. All that one misses in the whole account is the sense of a 'Love' outpoured from Plenitude to Poverty, a 'Love' which necessarily gives itself to the specifications and instantiations which also necessarily fall short of it, but which are not to be regarded as having any substance or shadow of true Being apart from it. This other Love is recognized in the *Timaeus* where Plato speaks of the Divine absence of envy, which must always desire everything to be as good as possible. There are, however, a few shreds of a philosophical theology which were left for the Christians to emphasize, and which are underemphatic in Plato.

The discourses on Love are now disturbed by the entry of the drunken Alcibiades who utters an encomium, not in praise of Love, but of Socrates. We have the comparison of Socrates to a bust of Silenus, familiar in the shops of statuaries, which opens and reveals gods within, or to Marsyas the satyr, in that the sweetness of his discourse makes the heart leap up and tears pour from the eyes. (One is reminded in this account of some of the first sermons of Buddha, so surpassingly sweet that one could only tear oneself away from listening to them by stopping up one's ears.) Socrates alone has made Alcibiades ashamed of his life of political flattery of the multitude, which has often led him far from the paths of virtue. We then receive the extraordinary confession as to how Alcibiades, fascinated by the strange charm of Socrates, sought to entrap him into a homosexual relationship with himself, and even spent a whole night holding the amazing 'monster' in his arms. Socrates, we know, was not indifferent to the glorious body then embracing him, whose beauty he had so often praised, but Alcibiades spent the night as in the bed of a father or elder brother. For Socrates, though infinitely radical in exploring the nature of the Good Itself, preferred not to innovate in regard to the laws and customs and 'right opinions' of the community to which he belonged. He preferred to show his love for Alcibiades by saving his life in battle, and by soliciting for him honours which he, Socrates, more richly deserved.

IV

The *Phaedrus*, to which we now turn, is one of those thoroughly unsatisfactory, multi-purpose writings of Plato which none the less contain some extraordinarily beautiful and insightful passages. Concerned to score off the contemporary rhetoricians, and concerned to prove that even their poor art of persuasion requires a backing in philosophy, it earns for us the uninterest and slight repugnance that attaches to anything that we should call 'rhetorical'. It begins with a deplorable speech by Lysias, with as little style as morals, which Phaedrus reads aloud to Socrates, and which praises coolly calculating sensuality in contrast with deeply committed and often tiresome love (221a–234c). The content of this speech is then restated by Socrates in a slightly less deplorable Socratic manner (327b–241d). Socrates then repents of his blasphemies against the divine madness of Love, and delivers a magnificent Pythagorean speech containing, among much that is sublime or sensual, an account of the pre-natal vision of the Eide by the Soul, and of the structure of the Soul and its position as the supreme motive and organizing force in the Cosmos. The discussion then returns to Rhetoric as the art of persuasion, and Socrates-Plato seeks to show that the rhetorician, even if he is concerned to mask truth in persuasive probabilities, must none the less know the truth, and particularly the truth concerning the human psyche, and that he must organize his discourse in a manner which shows deference to true divisions and communities in the nature of things.

The speech of Lysias (by some regarded as authentic) is an ugly, heartless, ill-contrived piece of incoherence. A man of pleasure is trying to win a boy's favours with the unusual plea that he is not in love with him, and that he, the man of pleasure, will therefore undergo no reverses of attitude towards the boy, paying the due price for his favours without subsequent regret and without loading him with reproaches for his own excessive expenditures. He will, he says, cause no public scandal nor seek to isolate his favourite from any with whom he wishes to associate, he will be patient and benevolent towards his friend and not violent and moody, and he will avoid all the boastings, belayings and other vexatious proceedings to which passionate lovers are so prone. Socrates, professing to be able to give a much better speech, based on what he has learnt from Sappho, Anacreon and others, lessens the heartlessness of the Lysian oration by making its speaker really *be* a lover who hopes to 'make' his boy by pretending *not* to be one. Before one can decide whether it is better to gratify a lover or a non-lover, one must however be clear as to the defining essence (οὐσία) and power (δύναμις) of Love. Love, he argues, is a species of desire, which stands opposed to the sort of desire which pursues what is opined to be best and which reason can guide: it is a form of insolent passion or ὕβρις which pushes us towards bodily beauty in a totally un-reasoning manner. It will desire the beautiful object to be wholly subservient to the lover's desires, and so make or keep it ignorant, cowardly, slow and inarticulate rather than the reverse: it will keep its love-object away from every association or influence that might improve it and render it superior to the lover. It will also make its beloved soft and effeminate, rather than manly and vigorous. It will further impose on its beloved the torment of the perpetual presence of one who is no longer blooming and youthful, and then, when love has departed, will leave the beloved to the sour dregs of unseasonable prudence and temperance. Lovers, in short, love boys as wolves love sheep, and wise boys will therefore prefer non-lovers to them.

Socrates has therefore brought in the ordering power of an Eidos, Desire, differentiated into a number of subordinate Eide, to provide the justifying background for the disordered prescriptions of Lysias. He is, however, deeply ashamed of the *content* (not the form) of his previous argument, and feels that he must now offer a propitiatory retraction to the divinity of Love. He points out, therefore, that Love is a form of madness, and that the Lysian argument would only have been valid if all forms of madness, being opposed to self-restraint, were evil. There is, however, a divinely inspired form of madness of which Oracular Divination is one species, Ritualistic Purgation another, Poetry a third, and Love a fourth: the nature of the divine, erotic madness requires, however, a longer explanation.

Socrates at this point introduces the notion of Soul, and sees its being (οὐσία) and definition (λόγος) in Self-movingness. Bodily existences are essentially made to move by what is external to themselves, but things ensouled move themselves, and require no further explanation for their motion beyond the fact that they are thus ensouled and self-motived. Socrates-Plato is here defining Soul in terms of its universal motive power: in other places, for example the *Phaedo, Timaeus* and later in the *Phaedrus*, it will also be characterized by its twofold mode of cognition. It will embrace all Eide and instances of Eide in its awareness, and will thereby determine where and how such Eide will be instantiated. Soul, being thus as it were a radiating point of the power and wisdom which streams from the Eide, is necessarily immortal: it is the fountain and principle of all motion, and without it the universe would grind to a halt, and would be unable to recharge itself again. Socrates-Plato now glides, without clearly indicating the transition, from the cosmic to the human soul, and the latter is likened to a strange composite creature, a human charioteer fused in body with two steeds that he drives through the heavens, one noble and taking direction from the charioteer, and the other baseborn and recalcitrant. What is here being inculcated is doubtless a picture used by the Pythagoreans: they thought of the Soul as having three parts or aspects, one rational and fully human, one leonine and full of daring, and one serpentine and grossly appetitive (see *Republic*, 588c–e). Here a somewhat different picture is being introduced, the charioteer with his two horses replacing the three closely cemented animals. To this a touch is added which is probably Plato's: that the well-behaved horses of non-human Souls have 'wings' by which they can travel through the whole circuit of the heavens. In the human Soul these wings have fallen away, though there are still expedients which can lead them to sprout once more.

Soul, however, is not only the principle of all motion in the universe: it also enjoys a comprehensive vision of the Eide, the eternal patterns of excellence, or at least it did so in its pure state.

Its exposure to those patterns is described in terms of a procession of twelve divisions, each headed by a God in a winged chariot: all who will and can may join the procession, since there is no envy in divinity (247a), but human souls, hampered by one recalcitrant horse, often find difficulty in keeping up with the rest. Beyond the circuit of the heavens, if 'beyond' is the correct term, the members of the procession see, and have true knowledge of, a colourless, shapeless, intangible, really real essence (ἀχρώματος τε καὶ ἀσχημάτιστος καὶ ἀναφὴς οὐσία ὄντως οὖσα), only visible to the mind which pilots the soul (247b). As the universe wheels about, they behold Justice Itself, Self-restraint Itself and Knowledge Itself and all the other Eide, among which, we may note, nothing evil or base is included, it being further insinuated that all are no more than facets of the single intangible essence that is then being contemplated. It will be noted that Plato in this passage not merely affirms the existence of the instances of knowledge present in given souls, but also of an eternal Eidos of Knowledge Itself. This, unlike our knowledge, 'involves no becoming, and is never different nor in a different member of what we now call real things, but is Real Knowledge in the realm of Real Being' (247d, e). This Knowledge is of course nobody's knowledge, being simply Knowledge as Such enjoyed by Mind as Such, but it is also a Knowledge in which everybody can share, in virtue of the Mind that they instantiate. Many of the Souls, however, only rise intermittently to such Knowledge, and some sink entirely beneath it, and are only able to form true opinions. The Souls which sink beneath True Knowledge have a variety of destinies in human and animal bodies, with bodiless periods between, but none rises to human form unless he has glimpsed the Eide in the divine procession, and can now be led to recollect them. 'It is necessary that a man should understand what is spoken of eidetically (κατ'εἶδος), going from many sense-perceptions to something comprehended in unity by reason' (249e). Socrates-Plato also brings God into this account: the philosopher is said always to converse in memory, to the extent that he is able, with the objects in relation to which God is divine (249c). God is here plainly Mind as Such, the eternal Knowingness eternally correlated with all the eternal Knowables. In sharing this eternal Knowingness, the philosopher is deemed mad by the multitude, but he remains a man possessed, divinely inspired.

The reminiscence of the pre-natal vision of the eternal, intangible Essence assumes the form of Love where what we are contemplating is a case of personal beauty, a beauty which recalls that of the God who led a division of souls to the ultimate vision. Both the horses are involved in such Love, the unruly horse urging the soul on to carnal performance, the noble horse and the charioteer resolutely holding it back. There will then be two species of lovers, some in the modern sense Platonic, who *never* indulge the leanings of the baser horse, and some who have occasionally been dragged into carnality by the baser horse and have accordingly lost their wings. The penalties for such lapses are not, however, severe: the lovers will live radiantly after death, and will ultimately receive their wings back. The eroticism of these passages (252c–257b), despite their homosexual accent, is repressed and romantic.

The speeches having been made, the Dialogue turns to the consideration of Rhetoric and style, and particularly in the case of written discourse. Socrates suggests that successful speech-writing demands a knowledge of truth, but Phaedrus rejoins that all that is required is a knowledge of what will *appear* true to the multitude. Socrates shows that Rhetoric in this sense is not confined to political assemblies and the law-courts, but extends even to the arguments of such as Zeno of Elea, who can prove that the same things are like and unlike, one and many, at rest and in motion (261d). If Rhetoric is to contrive an appearance of truth, it must be thoroughly aware of the true similarities and dissimilarities of things (262a), for deception can only be successful if it blurs comparatively *small* differences. Rhetoric therefore demands knowledge of things as they truly are, and not merely as they will appear to the many. And Rhetoric will be greatly benefited by following the canons of philosophical Dialectic which Socrates has followed in his own second speech: these make a speech into an ordered whole like a living body, having head and middle parts and terminal feet. Dialectic of this sort proceeds in two manners. At one time it gathers scattered cases together under a single Eidos, as when Love is placed, together with other forms of madness, under a special sort of madness which is divinely inspired. At another time it divides an Eidos into subordinate species, as when we divide the same inspired madness into a divinatory, an initiatory, a poetic and an erotic sub-species (265d–266a). (The collecting and dividing aspect of Dialectic often merely traverse the same territory in an opposite sense, but it makes a difference whether one's interest lies in discovering a common pervasive Eidos, or whether it lies in dividing such an Eidos into sub-species.) Socrates-Plato emphasizes the non-arbitrary character of the division into species: it should be determined by what is divided, not by the predilections or whims of the carver. A good dialectician must cut his material at its natural joints (κατ᾽ ἄρθρα ᾗ πέφυκεν) and must try not to break up anything after the fashion of a bad cook (265e). This has been presumably done in Socrates's distinction of the various forms of inspired madness: Socrates in this division has certainly followed the bent of our minds and what seemed natural to us, but he has also seemed to be led by real differences and resemblances, breaks and continuities, in the material he was considering.

The short passage we are considering is one of the most important in Plato, since it brings us up against that intuitive element essential in an eidetic philosophy: we must simply *see* that this or that really *is* a fundamental community running through a gamut of cases, and that there really *is* a difference of principle dividing this from that. The postulation of an Eidos is an hypothesis, a postulation of being, and the being it involves is of a kind to involve non-sensuous intuition. Modern philosophers who wish above all things to dispense with non-sensuous intuitions have nothing to put in their place. They cannot find a basis for distinguishing between real affinities, real communities, and merely conventional, verbal ones, nor between deep-cutting differences and merely trivial, external ones. Formally and linguistically anything can be said to be of the same or a different sort with everything: we can find trivial resemblances and artificial distinctions to justify any and every alignment of thought-material. Platonism holds that there are discernible rifts and communities in all that we can think of, and that it is all-important and not arbitrary to say just where they lie. There are not genuine Eide corresponding to any artificial way in which we may choose to regard things or to talk about them. Plato here says that the rhetorician cannot wholly close his eyes to such genuine Eide, and the same would apply to the modern formal analyst some of whose creations have an alleged 'convenience' which has certainly nothing eidetic about it. What Aristotle has to say about the action of *Noûs* in discovering, among other things, the primary, non-verbal definitions of the various species in nature, bears on the same point that is here being emphasized by Plato.

The rhetoricians, however, follow a variety of devices and prescriptions which have little apparent connection with the dialectical procedures outlined by Socrates-Plato. They have their exordia, their marshallings of fact, their proofs, their likelihoods, their innuendoes, their studied ambiguities, their appeals to emotion or to correct usage, and their final summings-up of the whole argument, but they do not lay stress on the isolation of general matters of principle, nor on the division of thought-material into a complete system of mutually exclusive species. And since they do not dig down to the defining principles from which their various rules and classifications should be made to follow, they are also unable to apply these rules and classifications to the detail of practice. They are like doctors who lack the guiding concept of bodily health, or musicians who lack the guiding concept of harmony, or tragedians who lack the guiding concept of the tragic, and who are accordingly unable to say when and to whom and to what extent etc., this or that should be introduced or performed (268a). If there is then a genuine art of Rhetoric, and not merely a set of empirically successful tricks and devices, it must base itself on a true knowledge of Soul in General and of various species of Soul, and must deduce from such knowledge the kinds of argument likely to persuade this or that sort of Soul (271b–272b). The various probabilities or like-nesses of truth, which are held to be of more importance to the rhetorician than truth itself, can only be discovered by the rhetorician if he knows the truth of which they are the likenesses.

All this leads up to a strong plea for the inwardly embraced and understood, rather than the externally recorded, written shape of a doctrine: if Rhetoric effects anything, it must effect this inner understanding, not the external embrace of verbal formulae. For verbal formulae are dead things like paintings, unable to defend or explain themselves, whereas a living understanding can always assume infinitely varied forms in order to fit different types of question or questioners (275c–276a). This passage shows why Plato divided his teaching into a written and an unwritten part.

The written part could not hope to secure that living understanding of difficult, many-sided subject-matters that could only
be achieved in living, face to face discourse. Of course Plato did
not mean to dispense with words altogether, or to have recourse
to some more direct form of communication: words are wholly
essential to Dialectic, but they must be varied and rubbed together with other words, and with presented or imagined cases,
before they can generate an understanding that goes quite beyond
what they conventionally stand for. (Compare Epistle VII 342–4.)
Even quite simple meanings often involve for their communication a varied suggestion of what is strictly unshowable, and
this, Plato imagines, the invariantly written symbol cannot hope
to achieve. If Plato had anticipated the profoundly different
effects on different readers of his written works, and the completely evanescent character of the illuminations that stemmed
from his oral discourses, he would perhaps have taken a less
unfavourable view of written as opposed to unwritten communications.

V

THE IDEOLOGICAL
DIALOGUES: THE *REPUBLIC*

I

The *Republic* is the most widely studied of Plato's writings, and studied for so long and so closely, that it may be dealt with a little more summarily than its length and rich content would otherwise demand. We shall, in particular, spend little time in approving or disapproving its various Utopian proposals, and finding that they tend towards Fascism or Communism, or are 'in principle' deeply democratic. Plato was deeply concerned to make his eidetic theory, with its profound and necessary marriage between ideal meaning-content (in the last resort mathematical), on the one hand, and value-patterns on the other, a guiding norm for politics, but the cast of his mind, and the disastrous practical excursions into which it was later to lead him, show him to have had very little understanding of the arbitrarinesses, the roughnesses and the compromises which are most of what there is to political life. There is little even of inspirational value in a series of recommendations so remote from the actual or even the possible, and it has been a mistake to argue for or against any practical implications of the doctrine: all these were discredited when he tried to turn Dionysius into a philosopher-king by instructing him in Dialectic and geometry. Plato is best regarded as having constructed an imaginary Pythagorean commune, hanging in the pure ether of hypothesis, in order to show how political life derives from the metaphysical Ultimates of the universe, and how the same Unity which everywhere disciplines variety into excellence and limit, and which expresses itself in cosmic and individual Life, Soul and Mind, is also expressed in the mutual regard that different individuals and groups of individuals have for one another in an ordered social whole. It is in the notion of this mutual regard among persons, and their alignment into a structure as beautiful, in its own way, as that of a dodecahedron or a system of moving spheres, and the derivation of this beautiful order from the Unity which is also Goodness, that Plato makes his fundamental contribution: the principles underlying these fine structures have a philosophical and phenomenological interest quite lacking in any possible applications that may be given to them. If his sketches are of interest, it is in illustrating what it is to be socially integrated with others, in a deliberately abstract, and, because abstract, vivid and telling manner: we become aware of Social Space in reading the *Republic* much as we become aware of Geometrical Space in reading of the strange events and transactions which take place in that old fantasy, Flatland.

The *Republic* was very possibly written in sections at various times and in progressively extended forms. Of its ten books, the first is an ordinary, logic-chopping, Socratic discourse on Justice, quite possibly published as such before the later books were written. Books II, III and IV form a fairly self-sufficient unit and a supplement to I: they deal with the four cardinal virtues of Wisdom, Courage, Self-restraint and Justice. Books V, VI and VII belong together and work out Plato's theory of the metaphysical foundations of the world, knowledge and society: they are at many points nothing but a fine web of hints and pictures, and clearly point to the Unwritten Doctrines with which Aristotle and others have made us acquainted, and without which as a background these books would be largely unintelligible. Books VIII and IX are a study in Political Pathology, in the pattern of decline which communities follow as they become less and less perfect exemplifications of what it is to be a Community or Social Unity: this pattern of decline is in a sense included, *qua* departure, in the perfection from which it steadily departs. Book X sums up the whole, and includes a by no means valueless argument for immortality and a magnificent Pythagorean vision of the after-life.

Book I is, as said, a Socratic discussion of the nature of Justice: in it Socrates discourses first with the aged Cephalus, his host, then with Cephalus's son Polemarchus, then with the theoretically daring but dialectically inexpert Thrasymachus of Chalcedon. Cephalus says that the supreme advantage of having been wealthy is that it has made it possible for him to avoid cheating and lies and the neglect of his obligations to the Gods and his fellows, so that he can now face approaching death without fear of post-mortem penalties. This raises questions as to the nature of Justice, for which Polemarchus first offers the Simonidean definition that it consists in rendering to each man what is owing to him (τὰ ὀφειλόμενα ἑκάστῳ ἀποδιδόναι). This does not, how-ever, mean that a man's possessions should necessarily be restored to him if, for example, he asks for them when he is out of his mind: 'what is owing to him' is a meaning of higher generality and more varied application than at first seemed to be the case. Polemarchus, instead of improving the vague but not essentially misguided definition of Simonides, is induced, by vague notions of just requital, to define Justice as the art which enables one to do harm to one's enemies as one does good to one's friends. Socrates is easily able to show that practically every art or form of expertise enables one to help or harm others, and that if one supposes, for example, the just man to be particularly expert in keeping what is entrusted to him, one will also have to credit him with the contrary capacity of theft (334a, b). This is one of the many passages in which Plato teaches that the knowl-edge of deviant evil is part and parcel of the knowledge of the good from which it deviates, and that evil, therefore, has no independent subsistence. Socrates further argues that we are often mistaken as to who really are our friends or our enemies, or, what is taken to be the same, as to who really are, and do not merely appear, good or bad: this provokes the amended defi-nition that Justice is doing good to those who both are and appear to be good, and who are, it is implied, 'our real friends', and also in harming those who both are and appear to be bad. Socrates then retreats to 'higher ground', and asks whether Justice, being a good thing, can ever be or involve the production of evil, the contrary of good, and whether, since Justice is done to men, whose characteristic virtue is Justice, this evil does not necessarily amount to Injustice, so that Justice is absurdly connected with the production of Injustice. As heat cannot chill, nor drought moisten, so the work of Justice cannot consist in making those on whom it is exercised less just (335). This argument is, of course, highly sophistical, in ways that it would not profit us to unravel in detail, and it involves above all the Socratic confusion between what is good for a person in the sense of representing what is personally advantageous for him, and what is good for or in a person in the sense of representing a virtue that all can impersonally endorse and admire. But the argument none the less expresses our deep sense of the affinity of these different values, of there being something abnormal and requiring special explanation in the fact that the virtuous is not the profitable, and that the profitable for me is not quite the same as the profitable for you. Somehow or at some level these different values belong together and should come together, and it is this, rather than the much too simple, confused identification put forward by Socrates, which the argument is really aiming at.

The argument now passes to Thrasymachus, who intrudes rudely into the discussion, attacking Socrates for the way in which he has connected Justice with the advantageous, the profitable, the beneficial or the useful. On *his* view Justice is not what is to the advantage *of anyone*, but only what is to the advantage *of the stronger* (τὸ τοῦ κρείττονος συμφέρον), which Socrates at first affects to misunderstand as meaning that it is just for us, who are not so strong as the Olympic champion Polydamas, to eat what and as much as he eats. The definition means, Thrasymachus explains, that Justice in any state, whether it be tyrannical, democratic or aristocratic, is always what is to the advantage of the rulers in that state, and is what those rulers have embodied and imposed in its laws. To this definition Socrates, with his eyes set on some goal of 'real' or 'true' advantage, objects that the rulers may be in error as to what is to their advantage, and may impose laws that do not reflect this at all. Will it then be right and just for the subjects to do what the laws enjoin but what is *not* to the rulers' true advantage? Thrasymachus replies, meeting a quibble with a quibble, that, in so far as a ruler fails to pursue his true advantage, he is not acting as a true ruler: strictly speaking (κατὰ τὸν ἀκριβῆ λόγον) he is not, in thus failing, a ruler at all. In so far therefore as a ruler *is* a ruler, he will organize all things in the state to his own advantage. Socrates now asks whether this does not mean that a ruler, considered as a ruler, is strangely different from others who perform seemingly similar functions and activities. For a doctor is not truly a doctor, does not act *as* a doctor, in so far as he earns fees for himself, but in so far as he ministers to the sick, in so far, that is, as he does what is to the advantage, not of himself or his art, but of the sick body. An art or performance like doctoring has, in fact, nothing which can be considered its advantage or disadvantage since, in so far as it really *is* doctoring, it cannot be further corrected, protected or perfected: the advantage that it pursues is therefore exclusively that of the body it treats (341e–342c). The same holds of an art of horsemanship: it is not concerned with itself as an art, but with what is advantageous to horsemen and horses. It seems true, in general, that every art or performance has its scope defined by the interests of those it directs and presides over, by the interests, that is, of the weaker and not of the stronger (342c). It would be strange indeed if this were not the case with ruling also: here it would seem that it is the advantage of the ruled that defines the art and not that of the ruler. Thrasymachus is completely floored by this argument, but it is not clear that he need have been so. For it is possible to construct the conception of arts whose scope is defined by the advantage of the performer: the arts of boxing, of swordsmanship, of showmanship are cases in point. Nor is it true that the art of ruling is as firmly connected with the interests of the ruled as medicine is with the interests of its patients: it is possible to say that Catherine the Great was a great ruler without implying that what she did was best for the governed. The error of Thrasymachus lies in connecting Justice, as ordinarily under-stood, with his own Machiavellian art: Justice as ordinarily understood precisely excludes that ruling self-interest which is the mainspring of such Machiavellianism.

This error is retracted by Thrasymachus in the next phase of the discussion, after Socrates has vainly tried to buttress his notion of the art of rule, by pointing to the fact that men are paid for assuming political offices, and that, where they are not paid, they so dread the possible rule of unsuitable people as to be forced to accept those offices themselves. Thrasymachus admits that he is overturning ordinary concepts: he is in effect defining Injustice and not Justice, the only difference being that, for him, Injustice, when successfully practised, is a virtue, a case of being well-advised (εὐβουλία), whereas Justice is a case of high-minded simplicity (γενναία εὐήθεια: 348c). Socrates pretends to be 'struck all of a heap' by this new turn of the discussion, but he soon rallies, and asks Thrasymachus whether he does not think that the unjust man, supposedly wise and virtuous, will not try to get the better of the just and the unjust man alike, whereas the just man will only try to get the better of the unjust man. This Thrasymachus admits, but Socrates points anew to the lack of analogy between the practitioners of Justice or Injustice and the practitioners and malpractitioners of the other arts. For the musically trained and knowing does not try to get the better of another musically trained and knowing man, but only of one who is untrained in music. And the trained medical man does not try to get the better of other trained medical men, but only of those who are untrained. (There may, of course, be rivalries among musicians and doctors, but not *qua* practitioners of their art.) From these cases it would seem that the 'knowing' or 'good' in a field only try to get the better of the ignorant and bad in that field, and not of other knowers, whereas the ignorant try to get the better of everyone, whether knowing or ignorant. This would suggest that just men are like knowers, and therefore wise and good, whereas unjust men are like the ignorant, and therefore foolish and bad. But if Socrates had considered the competitive arts, he would have seen that *their* practitioners prefer to get the better of equally good or better practitioners, and that they have no interest in getting the better of the inexpert or bad.

Socrates now goes on to argue that, so far from Injustice being stronger than Justice, it is necessarily weaker. For Injustice creates enmity and hatred among those who treat each other unjustly, and that an unjust man or group only can be strong if it confines its Injustice to outside persons. The notion, finally, that 'doing well' can be possible for the unjust is scotched by a general argument concerning the work (ἔργον) of each thing. Everything has its own peculiar work to do, and it 'does well' if it performs that work properly, the eyes if they help us to see, the ears if they help us to hear, etc., etc. The Soul, too, must have its peculiar work to do, and will 'do well' only if it performs that work fitly. The work of the Soul is then readily equated with looking after things and governing things and taking counsel about them, and to do this work properly is to exercise the Soul's peculiar virtue, Justice. The just Soul is therefore the properly working Soul, and therefore the Soul that does well, and therefore, by a further verbal slide, the Soul that is blessed or happy, the unjust Soul being the contrary of all these (353d–354a).

It is hard not to admire the extraordinary mixture of depth and sophistry in all these arguments. Though they affect rigour by playing on the ambiguities of the term 'doing well', they exploit affinities which override the differences of the term's uses. One can do well in the manner in which a thief does well who makes a big haul, or in the manner in which he does it with great aplomb and adroitness, or one can do well in the manner of the good bishop in the story who gave the stolen candlesticks back to the apprehended thief etc., and it is easy to say that the term 'doing well' has a wide range or family of different uses, some concerned with successful performances of any sort, some only with socially acceptable performances, some only with performances having highly disinterested, social motivation, etc., etc., and that it is wrong to pass from one case or use of 'doing well' to quite another. It is also possible to point to the widely varied use of the concept of function or work: if it is the work of the eye to see, it is the work of the cancer-cell to destroy an organ, of a prostitute to seduce etc. By and large, however, we do move towards the notion of a comprehensively good life, in which all these forms of 'doing well' will press towards a general integration, some being eliminated in the process, and in which free variables will everywhere replace bound variables, so that whatever is pursued is pursued by everyone for everyone etc. And we do move towards a conception of our task or work or duty which accords with such a comprehensively good life. So that the Socratic sophistries rest on a substrate of eidetic truth. It is a pity, none the less, that it exacts so much patience with surface-fallacy to dig down to this substrate.

II

In Book II of the *Republic* Glaucon, Plato's brother, reopens the question of the superiority of Injustice over Justice which Thrasymachus has argued in a confused manner, using words which retain the savour of the impersonal values that he is intent on rejecting. Glaucon suggests that Thrasymachus has a better case than his tendentious, ill-stated arguments would suggest.

For it seems arguable that Justice falls, not among things desirable in themselves, such as health, knowledge, sight etc., but among things burdensome in themselves but useful in respect of their consequences. For there seems a good case for saying that, while it is fine and good to do what is unjust, it is much more miserable to undergo it, and that it is therefore worthwhile to sacrifice the advantages of doing injustice in order to avoid the miseries of suffering it, and to agree with others to this effect. That everyone thinks thus, is shown by the fact that everyone would be ready to take unjust advantage of others if he could be certain of doing so quite undiscovered (359), and that no one would prefer to have the reality of Justice, with every appearance of consummate Injustice, rather than have the reality of Injustice, with every appearance of consummate Justice (361). We all want to get away with Injustice, and only wish to seem, not to be, just. Adeimantus, Glaucon's brother, reinforces this argument by pointing out how all exhortations to Justice turn on rewards and penalties rather than on the intrinsic goodness of being just, and how the Gods, who at times figure as the authorities behind Justice, are none the less willing to condone the gravest Injustice at the cost of a few mystical acts of propitiation. These arguments show that the goods and evils of personal advantage and disadvantage are the only real goods and evils, and that the so-called goods and evils of impartial Justice have only a fraudulent purchase on our wills, all that really recommends them being the personal advantages that flow from them or the personal disadvantages that they help us to avoid (367).

Socrates, faced with these fundamental objections, refuses to consider the desirability that a single individual should be just or unjust without first considering the desirability that a whole city or society of such individuals should be just or unjust. Justice or Injustice, he contends, will be 'written larger' in the society than in the individual, and having seen their pattern in the large structure of a society we shall be able to discern it repeated in the more minute structure of the human individual or Soul (369a). This line of argument is both profound and confused: in refusing to consider Justice in the isolated individual, it obscurely recognizes the social nature of Justice, and that a man can only be just in his dealings with others and with men at large, and not in actions that concern himself alone. The recognition is, however, blurred, since it is implied that Justice in the individual, while illuminated by Justice in the larger social whole, could none the less exist in the individual alone, and from this implication many of the bad errors of the subsequent treatment are derived. The argument is further at fault since it obscures the fact that, while Justice has to do with the social dealings of men, it is, in the sense which interests the discussion, a virtue of separate individuals, and that its application to a whole society involves a change of sense and not solely one of scale. By and large, however, there are deep analogies between the manner in which individual attitudes and virtues are reflected in the whole pattern of society, and the manner in which the whole pattern of society reproduces itself in individual attitude and performance, so that the Socratic determination to consider the two types of structure together is not quite the superficial, fallacious thing that it would at first appear to be. If it fails to bring out what is highly specific in the individual virtue of Justice, or in certain vaguely correlated excellences of society, it at least puts both into connection with higher, generic patterns of excellence, in the end reducible to number, on which reality, society and the individual Soul alike repose.

Socrates goes on to give what appears at first to be a purely naturalistic account of the genesis of an actual city-society, though it soon becomes plain that what he is leading up to never was on sea or land, but is the pure Eidos of the City-Society as Such, the Pythagorean Commune set in the ether of pure thought, and based, not on the chance interchanges of men, but on the necessary patterns which underlie all reality. A city-society arises, we are told, owing to men's lack of self-sufficiency, owing to the need which each man has of the services of others (369). This leads at first to the 'most necessary of city-societies', one based on a division of labour into such basic occupations as that of farmer, builder, weaver, cobbler etc., the population of many Socratic language-games, each limiting himself to his own occupation and not meddling with that of others. But even here there will be interstitial occupations concerned with marketing and trade, with the export and import of goods to and from other city-societies, and with the money which is the inevitable medium of such exchanges. The wants that give rise to the most necessary society are, however, such as to press onward beyond necessity, and to do so indefinitely: the most necessary society becomes the luxurious and the increasingly luxurious and greedy society. (This tendency towards overweening expansion is at all times, we may hold, one of the basic Principles in the thought of Plato, and was, in more technical contexts, called the Indefinite Dyad or the Great and Small: it can be curbed, but it cannot be wholly eliminated.) With the growth of luxury go inevitable tendencies towards territorial expansion and hence to war, and the consequent development of a military establishment. Socrates-Plato does not explicitly approve of war, but he sees its origin in the limitless expansion of lower-grade wants (373e). The whole Dialogue is henceforth concentrated on the life and education of the military establishment, both throughout characterized by an extreme austerity, which has no plain justification either in the tendencies towards luxury which it will have to restrain, even in the case of civilians, nor in the external dangers from other societies, some of which may be as austerely military as the society we are sketching. How is all this to be explained?

The explanation probably lies in a pervasive Pythagorean background, already dominant in the thought of Plato, and destined to become more and more explicit as the Dialogue progresses. On this view, it may be argued, there are exact sets of Ratios, constituting anything's privileged pattern of excellence, which are necessarily surrounded by a vast rabble of deviant or deficient possibilities, which exceed or fall short of such a privileged pattern. Thus Ratios like the double and triple etc. have a vast unprincipled population of rational and irrational proportions between them, regular polygons and solids are surrounded by countless irregular variants, etc., etc. After this manner the ideal City-Society we are constructing necessarily stands surrounded, as part of what it is, by countless more or less degenerate societies which it sternly excludes, but which in the relaxed medium of instantiation will come to have a quasi-reality equal to its own (see 445c). The relation of an instance of near-perfect city-society to degenerate societies may be a temporal one, and this side of the matter is set forth in the patterns of degeneration studied in Books VIII and IX. But it may also be a pattern of coexistence, since instantiation always involves multiplication, and so even the near-perfect society will stand surrounded by numerous other societies more or less perfect. But it must maintain itself against all these other imperfect instantiations of state-life, and against tendencies towards similar degeneration in itself: this it does in and through the military class which is a necessary expression of its active integrity. And this military class must culminate in a class of knowers or military intelligence, men who understand and so can apply the precise patterns of structure and behaviour which distinguish the true polity from the innumerable deviant versions which depart from it and which surround it. Seen in the light of the foregoing suggestions, which certainly must dot some i's and cross some t's, the strange intrusion of militarism at this point in the *Republic* can be rendered less inexplicable and less ugly. It is possible, too, that the philosophic militarism of the *Republic* has its roots in actual Pythagorean practice. For in the first half of the fifth century the Pythagorean Order not only governed the city of Croton, but tried also to take over the government of other South Italian cities. It was these expansive excesses that led to the burning of the Pythagorean lodges and the persecution of their members in the middle of the fifth century. The Pythagorean sodality, like the Society of Jesus, must have seen itself as a sort of intellectual and spiritual soldiery in an intellectually and morally degraded world.

Socrates-Plato at this point deviates into a long account of the elementary education of the soldier-guardians of his polity and of their auxiliaries. This education is to be in music, which includes literature and the arts, and in gymnastics. The most intelligent of the guardians are later to have an education in mathematics and in mathematical philosophy and this will be considered in Books V, VI and VII of the *Republic*. The account of the elementary education begins with mythology: myths are said to mould the soul more effectively than bodies are moulded by sculptors' hands (377c). Myths as told to the military class must eliminate all the colourful warring, wrangling and discreditable actions attributed to the Gods in the established mythology: Divinity must be depicted as being incapable of imposture or deception and as being only a source of what is good in the world. If the Gods ever inflict pains on men, it must be to profit them by punishment (380b). The life after death, for soldiers ready to die, must not be depicted in melancholy colours, at least not for virtuous and vicious alike: Socrates-Plato here seems to wish to eliminate all talk of Styx, Cocytus etc. (387), despite their place in his own vivid eschatology. As regards written works, the style must be narrative rather than dramatic, and, if there is to be dramatic representation at all, it must in the main be of noble and sensible persons, and only to a small extent of the impassioned, the unworthy or the ridiculous (396c–e). An all-imitative actor, despite any brilliance he may have, must be kept out of the pure state that is being constructed (398a, b), and will not, presumably, be allowed to diversify the dull life even of the merchant and working classes.

From discourse and its content Socrates-Plato goes on to consider the musical modes through which discourse is expressed or accompanied, and rejects the use of all mournful, relaxed or over-gay modes in his state: only the Dorian mode which imparts courage, and the Phrygian mode which imparts self-restraint, will be tolerated. Socrates-Plato believes in some deep community, rooted, no doubt, in Numbers and Proportions, between the harmonic relations of musical notes and corresponding relations in the experience and action of the living, thinking Soul. This correspondence also obtains in respect of rhythms, and is likewise present in the visual rhythms and harmonies found in painting, textiles, decoration and architecture. There is a good form and a deformity in all these fields, which is necessarily akin to excellence and depravity in speech and manners, so that to live surrounded by certain sorts of good form in the arts is to be pushed insensibly towards similar good form in behaviour (see 401b, c). Socrates-Plato even goes so far, at a later stage in the Dialogue (424c), as to suggest that the introduction of new styles in music is a potent cause of political revolution and degeneration.

The gymnastic education of the soldiery is next considered, and is said not to be directed to the mere strengthening of the body, but to the disciplining of the audacious, spirited side of the soul, which is the needed complement to the gentler, thoughtful side trained by music: an exclusively musical education would make the soldiery soft, as an exclusively gymnastic education would leave them harsh and fierce. A blend of both tendencies is required in those required to guard the institutions and secure the continued existence of the state, for they will have to be as gentle to friends as they are harsh to enemies. The complete devotion of the soldier-guardians to their state will further be secured by the mythical faith created by a 'noble lie', to the effect that their souls are of gold or of silver (officers and auxiliaries), whereas the souls of merchants and workmen are of iron and copper. This 'noble lie' will no doubt be recognized as such by the inner circles of the guardians, and will be less vicious than the name suggests, since it will not be used to create imaginary divisions among men, like certain modern racial theories, but to recognize differences that the Pythagoreans imagined to be actually there. The offspring of golden, silver, iron or copper parents will not automatically be ranked as of the same metal as their parents: scientific 'tests' will decide where they stand (see 415a–c). If the tests were as valid, and the human differences as genuine, as Pythagorean science supposed, there would not be the objection to this 'noble lie' that modern critics have felt. Plato also tells us, more or less in passing (417a), that the members of the ruling class of guardians must have no private possessions, a provision not extended to the members of the subordinate classes. These presumably will be allowed to accumulate wealth, and to enjoy such luxuries and comforts, and such limited cultural fare, as their rulers permit them.

Having built up his state around a mystico-military Pythagorean sodality, Socrates-Plato looks around to find just where in this structure the main virtues recognized by the Pythagoreans, and also, as seems likely, by most contemporary Greeks, had their principal seat. Plato thinks that if we first use our eidetic intuition to find the relatively clear place of the Wisdom, the Courage and Self-restraint in the ideal community, it will be a less difficult task to locate the more elusive and pervasive place of Justice. The Wisdom of the Commune, *qua* Commune, is, however, plainly located, not in the knowledge and skill of carpenters and the like, but in the guiding sense of the small band of guardians who take counsel for the survival and expansion of the *whole* city-society rather than of any special part of it. The Bravery or Courage of the Commune, *qua* Commune, is as plainly located in the firmness of soul of the whole class of auxiliary protectors who preside over it, and who save it from external assault or internal subversion. The Self-restraint and Temperance of the Commune, *qua* Commune, is more pervasive: it consists in a silently felt agreement among the members of all classes as to who should rule in the state and who submit to rule. It is manifest in the ready submission of the commercial and labouring classes to their guardians and protectors, and in the quiet exercise of authority by the latter. What place is there left for Justice in this ordered class system? Disembarrassed of confusion by the hiving off of the other virtues, Justice immediately tumbles forth before our eidetic insight (432d): it has been implicit in the whole construction of the Commune, and now disengages itself plainly. Justice lies, Socrates-Plato holds, solely in the performance by each class of its appropriate function and the refusal to meddle with the functions of others (τὸ τὰ αὑτοῦ πράττειν καὶ μὴ πολυπραγμονεῖν), or at least in some special form of such non-meddlesomeness. This exclusively functional conception of Justice, not quite in harmony with our ordinary conception, is brought closer to that conception by being made to cover possessions and enjoyments as much as functions. Not only must the just man not *do* what another should do, but he must also not *have* what another should have, and of which that other ought not to be deprived. Justice, in fact, may be agreed to be the having and doing of what is a man's very own (433e). Such Justice will of course apply to the relations of men *within* a class as well as to the relations of classes to one another: a farmer, for example, must not attempt to do the work of a shoemaker or another farmer, nor to take over the instruments and living-space with and within which the other man works and lives. At a later stage of the discussion (443a) Socrates-Plato thinks that his account of Justice, whose application to the individual as such corresponds to its application to classes and class-members as such, covers the ordinarily recognized exclusion by Justice of such things as thefts, embezzlements, betrayals, adulteries, neglect of elders, etc., etc. and this on the whole may be conceded. Socrates-Plato's account readily suggests to the modern mind an arbitrarily stratified society, in which just behaviour is lamentably limited to accepting one's station in society and its duties. It must, however, be remembered that Plato believes both in the actuality and desirability of great differences of psychic capacity and orientation, for which arguments can no doubt be offered, and that he also believes in the scientific discoverability and even legitimate eugenic production of such differentiations. All this being premissed, he is merely anticipating Marx in demanding from each what lies within his ability, and providing for each what he specifically needs. If there is fault to be found with this notion, it lies not in the preference for difference over sheer uniformity, but in the lack of stress on the specific tastes and wants of individuals, and on their freedom to have or do what they *like*, for no other reason than that they like it, and of course provided that their having or doing it does not infringe the equal right of others. In the austere Socratic-Platonic-Pythagorean conception of Justice there is insufficient recognition of what in another Dialogue (*Timaeus*, 48a) is called the unreliable or wandering cause, the necessary descent into random particularity which is part and parcel of instantiation, and which here would take the form of the infinite variability of personal taste. Such variability and particularity is not something lying quite beyond the reach of the Eide and their normative perfection, but is rather the material which the latter must limit and order, perfectly at the level of the Eide as Such, imperfectly in their dependent instantiations. Nowhere, however, is there room in a Platonic ontology for the independent world of real particulars in which instantialists believe, and it is accordingly impossible to analyse or understand what Justice may be in and for Itself without taking account of the range of possible instantiation which is merely Justice in action.

Socrates-Plato now turns to the last part of his successfully performed task: the location of Justice and the other virtues that have been pinned down in the large script of the state, in the small script of the individual man. He pursues this investigation on the assumption that the various distinct types of character and function which distinguish classes in the state, and which determine their virtues, must all also be found in individuals, considered as individuals. It is, in fact, he somewhat un-Platonically argues, only because they are present in individuals *qua* individuals that they can be present in individuals as members of classes and hence in those classes themselves (435d). He is not dogmatic as to the precise analogy between individual and community: he will simply see if the same differentiations which obtain in the state also obtain in the individual, and will go back and forth between them till this is firmly established. Justice will be made to flash forth by the rubbing together of individual and state in our talk, and will then become clearly fixed in our minds (434e–435a), a fine description of eidetic intuition. Individuals must certainly have something in their 'Souls' which corresponds to the reflective counsel-taking element which characterizes the guardians of the state, though in individuals this element may concern itself with private problems and not with those of the whole state. They must likewise have something which corresponds to the daring and dash of the auxiliary guardians who surround the counsel-taking protectors. They must have something, finally, which corresponds to the boundlessly diversified wants of the merchant and labouring classes, though it may not be as diversely split as in the case of the needs and activities of cooks, shoemakers etc. And to the relationships of these 'somethings' in the soul, there must correspond virtues which correspond to the various virtues found in the state.

Socrates-Plato is, however, led on to ask whether these distinct Eide unquestionably instantiated in the Soul are separately or conjointly instantiated: is it with our total Soul that we take counsel, perform deeds of daring and have multitudinous wants, or are there as it were separate Soul-parts by which these distinct functions are exercised (436a, b)? The Pythagoreans, it would seem, made use of myths and pictures which suggested the latter alternative: they conceived of the Soul as having various lower attachments added on to it, attachments which tied it close to the body, and which might drop from the mathematicizing and philosophizing Soul-segment once the body was discarded. And it is to the Pythagoreans that Plato undoubtedly owes his account of the threefold soul which we find in the *Phaedrus* and the *Timaeus* as well as in the present passage. None of these pictures or accounts are, however, decisive as to whether the Soul is really one or three, and it seems clear that the only acceptable answer would be that, like the Trinity, it is both. Socrates-Plato, however, tries at this point to emphasize pluralism rather than monism, though neither here (see 435c, d) nor elsewhere (see 612e) does he consider the matter completely settled. He says in fact that a longer road (435d) will have to be trodden if an accurate account of the matter is to be attained, and the longer road is later (504b *et seq.*) shown to point to an ontological distinction between absolute eidetic being on the one hand, and parasitic instantial being on the other. Only on the basis of such a distinction shall we be able to draw valid distinctions between Soul-functions and corresponding Soul-parts.

In the present context Socrates-Plato tries to solve his problem by means of a misguided use of what would afterwards be called the Law of Non-contradiction. He gives this principle a concrete and ontological meaning, rather than a legitimately formal and quite trivial use. He accepts as a principle that 'the same thing will not at once do or undergo opposites in respect of the same thing (κατὰ ταὐτόν) and towards the same thing' and illustrates his principle by the example of a whirling top which can elliptically be said to be both at rest and in motion, but which is in fact at rest only in respect of its central axis, and in circular motion in all the surrounding parts. This use of the Principle of Non-contradiction is innocuous if it means no more than that, in so far as the top illustrates differences of velocity ranging between a certain maximum and zero, it also concomitantly illustrates differences of location: it is a vicious, ontological use if it leads us to turn its central axis or any other difference of location discernible in it into a distinct something which can be legitimately isolated. The principle is further defective in that it concerns 'opposites' rather than strict logical contradictories: opposites are characters certainly tending towards mutual exclusion, but quite as definitely not always achieving it. It is in fact only as capable of contending for joint presence in the same instance that opposites can be said to be opposed, a point which Socrates-Plato himself obscurely admits when he says in 439b that '*the same thing* will not at a single time act oppositely towards the same thing with the same thing in itself' (οὐ γὰρ δὴ τό γε αὐτὸ τῷ αὐτῷ ἑαυτοῦ περὶ τὸ αὐτὸ ἅμα ἂν τ'ανάντια πράττοι). As regards the Soul, Socrates-Plato argues, with much misguided panache (437–8), that each desire or aversion in the soul can be directed only to one uniform object – for example hunger to food, thirst to drink as such – and that it can only acquire specificity of direction through the addition of another Eidos to it, for example the Hot added to thirst will make it a thirst for the hot, while the Much added to it will make it a thirst for much drink etc. It follows that opposition among desires cannot spring from their concurrent direction to opposing objects, but only to their separate source in different Soul-elements. Thus if one wants one's drink to be both hot and cold, this cannot be a simple want directed to an object involving conflict, but must consist of two desires springing from two different Soul-parts.

On this shaky logical basis, covertly instantialist rather than eidetic, but helped out by many fine phenomenological illustrations (for example the one of Leontius drawn to a sight by sadistic voyeurism, but repelled from the same by his nobler reason), Socrates-Plato builds up an argument for three distinct Soul-things or Soul-parts, a reflective, reasoning part which considers facts and values generally and in the cool (τὸ λογιστικόν), a multifarious appetitive part (τὸ ἐπιθυμητικόν) and an intermediate combative or spirited part (τὸ θυμοειδές), which can both act in concert with the reflective, reasoning part and impose the latter's directives on the multifarious appetites, but which can also act *against* rational reflection in the case of the rash and quick-tempered. We thereby arrive by argument at what must have been an established Pythagorean triplicity – cf. the Pythagorean doctrine of the 'three lives' – though the arguments used could also have led to any number of Soul-parts, since rational considerations need not always agree with one another, and since there are infinite antagonisms in the realm of appetite. But Socrates-Plato's view does not rest on logical argument but on phenomenological insight: there are these three profoundly distinct Eide instantiated together in every instance of psychic life, and their distinction and conflict is quite different from the relatively trivial distinction between hunger and thirst, or the quite trivial distinction of thirst directed to different sorts of drink. And that the distinction is profound and important is shown by its analogy with the similar divisions of such master-phenomenologists as Sigmund Freud and Bishop Butler.

From the eidetic distinctions within the soul, Socrates-Plato goes on to distinguish Soul-virtues on lines similar to those on which virtues were established in the larger structure of the state. A man will have the virtue of Wisdom in so far as the reflective, reasoning element directs his behaviour, he will have the virtue of Courage in so far as he acts firmly in defence of the conceptions of the truly safe and dangerous which he derives from this reflective, reasoning element, he will have the virtue of Self-restraint in so far as there is inward harmony among his constitutive Soul-parts (442c), and an agreement as to which principle should direct and which should accept direction. Finally we proceed to Justice which, in the context of the individual, is not described in terms very different from Justice in the Commune: it is the performance by each Soul-part of its appropriate function without any attempt to take over that of other parts. In all this Socrates-Plato is not really, as many have emphasized, giving a good circumscription of the ordinary concept of Justice, whether in the individual or the state: he is seeing both in the light of a higher identity of kind. It is easy to point out that he has turned Justice in the individual into a sort of internal Temperance, just as he has turned Temperance in the state into a sort of inter-personal Justice. Obviously his analogies are exaggerated: there are obvious specific differences between state-parts and state-excellences on the one hand and Soul-parts and Soul-virtues on the other. Plato is not, however, primarily interested in Souls or states, but in the divine patterns, the 'Numbers', that they instantiate, and which alone give them sense or substance. It is only if we ourselves can think in this abstractedly structural manner that we can hope to see the point of his extraordinary comparisons and provisions.

III

We now enter upon Books V, VI and VII of our Dialogue, the Books of the 'three waves', which also contain the core of the whole work. The 'three waves' are three objections to the ideal construction that has been proceeding: the first an objection to the association of women with men in the education of the guardians, the second an objection to the community of wives and children which is to obtain in the case of the guardians, and the third a general difficulty as to the desirability and feasibility of building up a case of Ideal Community in the realm of instantiation. The way Socrates-Plato meets the first two waves does not merit very great attention. In the case of the first the objection is to the association of women with men in the training of the guardians, when the whole principle of our ideal society is that beings differing in nature ($\phi\acute{\upsilon}\sigma\iota\varsigma$) should have a different work ($\acute{\epsilon}\rho\gamma\upsilon$) to do in society, and should not attempt to do the work of those who have a different nature. Socrates-Plato meets this objection by holding it to be eristic, based on words rather than notional realities: it considers sameness and differences of nature in respect of arbitrarily selected performances or characters, for example making shoes or being bald, instead of seeing the deeper gulfs and communities of social performance which alone are relevant in the context. Women certainly differ from men in bearing the children which men only beget, but this difference, it is suggested, is too trivial to be regarded as a difference in nature. In all social contexts barring the procreative, there is no difference between male and female nature as such. Both exhibit the genuine differences underlying the republic's class-stratification, but they differ, in other respects, only in degree. Human nature in the female is, in general, feebler in capacity than human nature in the male, though some cases of the former surpass some cases of the latter (455d, e). It is therefore mere prejudice which sees absurdity in the association of women with men in the same educational and social tasks: this association is beautiful and not ridiculous, because it is essentially profitable (457b). We need not here consider whether Socrates-Plato is right in regarding the antithesis between what is called masculinity, and what is called femininity, as playing a merely peripheral, quantitative role in the structure of human nature: being Greek, Socrates-Plato knew that the whole antithesis is as much represented in the single individual as in the whole society. The main point is that it is eidetic insight which alone can decide whether or not there is a genuine difference of Eidos or Phusis – the two are deeply associated in the thought of Plato – in the difference between men and women: procreative, grammatical and conventionally social distinctions do nothing to decide the issue. And logic-chopping or Eristic is precisely the sort of reasoning that confounds genuine distinctions of Eidos or Phusis with conventional, verbal or contingently factual distinctions.

The second wave is the general strangeness of the plan to share wives and offspring: to this Socrates-Plato responds by working out the plan in more detail and giving general reasons for its desirability. There are to be annual festivals at which sexual unions will be consummated for the sake of maintaining the Commune's sacredly proportioned numbers. The offspring which occur outside of such sanctioned unions will not be reared, but an ingenious system of spurious lots will give an appearance of chance to the system of family-planning. None will know which offspring from each festival are his natural children, nor will the offspring know their natural parents: all members of a populating group will regard all offspring springing from it as *their* offspring, and all the offspring will regard all the parents as *their* parents. Ineffective devices are proposed to ward off the ancient miasma of incest: the Delphic Pythoness and the Rulers will know how to relax these. But that this strange form of contrived sharing maintained by deception is truly desirable is argued on the ground that there is an equation between Unity and Goodness: there can be no greater evil in a state than what dirempts it into many instead of making it one, and no greater good than what binds it together and unifies it (462a, b). The community of parents and children creates a wider community of joy and grief and a more extended sense of what is one's own: it brings a group closer to the condition of a single man, who overcomes bodily dispersion through the unity of his Soul, so that he is *as a whole* affected by each pain or pleasure in each bodily part (462c, d). Just as a man suffers in his finger, so will the Commune suffer in each injured member. It seems clear that the Platonic ideal is noble: it neither subordinates the individual to the Commune nor the Commune to the individual. Both are forms of that self-articulating Unity, that pervasive structuralism, that in its most abstract form underlies the Numbers and the many-dimensioned structures of mathematics. It is only questionable whether the natural family is not also an admirable pattern claiming a place in this ordered hierarchy, just as triangles build themselves out of lines, and are themselves built into the higher polygons and solids.

The third great wave now looms upon the horizon: the practical possibility of achieving all this, at least to the extent that practice (πρᾶξις), however perfect, necessarily falls short of the perfection sketched in notional discourse (λέξις, 473a). This practical possibility, Socrates-Plato affirms, with the sickening experiences of the folly and wickedness of the unguided Athenian democracy to back him, is bound up with the practical possibility of making true philosophers into state-rulers, or state-rulers into true philosophers (473e), an aim reasserted in Plato's famous Epistle VII (326a, b), which sets forth his dealings with a state-ruler whom he did *not* manage to turn into a true philosopher. The nature of the true philosopher, and the mode of rearing him, then become the main themes of the discussion which occupies what remains of Books V, VI and VII.

What is the true philosopher? Like the impartial paederast, who loves young male beauty in all its forms, or like the impartial *aficionado* of other forms of excellence, the true philosopher is enamoured of Wisdom in all its species, and this means that he is desirous of knowing the true and absolute Being which Ideal Natures alone possess. He is interested in knowing what it is to be just or unjust, or beautiful or ugly, and in short, what it is to be each thing that anything can be: he is interested, as we would put it, in the single sense which each of these notions embodies, not in the multiple cases in which each may be instantiated, and thereby give itself a seeming multiplicity. For it is by their unessential association with actions and bodies, and with each other in such actions and bodies, that such Natures appear, but are not, many and not single (476a). The true philosophers therefore differ entirely from the φιλοθεάμονες, the *aficionados* of sensible sights and sounds: the philosophers direct their love to the ideal, non-sensible Natures embodied in these sights and sounds, i.e. the numerical Ratios in them, whereas the spectacle-lovers are only interested in the sensibly worked out instances of such Natures. The lovers of sights and sounds are like dreamers, for they attribute to insubstantial sense-pageants the substantial being which they only share in or vaguely mimic.

Socrates-Plato now advances to the magnificent climax of his revisionary ontology: that the being of Ideal Natures is the *only* being in the full and strict sense, and that the knowledge of such Natures (and presumably that of their relations and their possibilities of instantiation) is the only Knowledge in the full and strict sense. What in the fullest sense is, is in the fullest sense knowable, just as what lacks being is in every way inaccessible to knowledge (477a). There may, however, be something which, while falling short of Being in the full sense of the word, yet is not simply nothing at all, and there may be something which while falling short of Knowledge, is none the less not the ἀγνωσία, the complete Unknowingness, which is the relation of mind to what is simply nothing. Doxa, Opinion, Empirical Judgment, seems to occupy this intermediate position, having an object which falls short of absolute Being, but which yet instantiates or exemplifies it, and which itself falls short of the Knowledge which has the inimitable firmness of the Natures that it knows. The argument is developed in terms of a logic of powers and faculties (δυνάμεις): powers and faculties are a non-sensible genus of entities defined solely in terms of their objects and what they

effect (477a: ἐφ'ᾧ τε ἔστι καὶ ὃ ἀπεργάζεται). On such a basis
Knowledge (ἐπιστήμη, γνῶσις), Opinion (δόξα) and Unknowingness (ἀγνωσία, ἄγνοια), are plainly distinct powers or faculties,
for they differ in the manner in which they approach their objects,
and they also differ according to the objects which are given
to them. Knowledge is infallible and demands absolutely real
objects, whereas Opinion is fallible and is of objects which,
though each may be a single something (ἕν τι), and so not
nothing, none the less faces a dispersed multiplicity in which
Knowledge can discern nothing firmly real nor clearly graspable. Unknowingness, it may be presumed, has as its object the
Non-being (μὴ ὄν), which is not any sort of definite single
something.

It is easy to be scornful of the remarkable piece of ancient
ontology and epistemology here confronting us, especially if we
are fully persuaded that there *are* particular real entities, and that
we are in contact with them through the senses, both propositions
of which Platonism is the entire negation. It is also easy to argue,
on a basis of ordinary diction, that Knowledge and Opinion have
precisely the same objects, i.e. particular things and facts in the
world, and only differ in their reliability, whereas Unknowingness
is no faculty at all, and its object, Non-being or Nothing, only a
pseudo-object. The Platonic ontology, however, implies that there
really are no things but the Eide, and that to talk of their instances,
the things of common diction, is merely to talk of Eide in the
instantial mode, as characters instantiated or illustrated. It is part
of what we understand by being an Eidos that it can be multiply
instantiated, and we recognize nothing but Eide in recognizing
them to be instantiated here or there or in this or that company.
Particulars, we may say, are only Things by courtesy, being
merely the modalities of true Things. Doxa, Opinion, is then the
unreliable knowledge of the variable instantiation of the Eide: it
is in modern terms empirical as opposed to *a priori* knowledge.
And, being empirical, it can never reach the upper limit of
infallible, unshakeable grasp which is entirely stationed in the *a
priori*, and concerns the being and relations of universal essences.
Hence Socrates-Plato is right in recognizing the eidetic gulf
between the two modes of conscious approach, the gnostic
approach to the unshakeable Eide, and the doxastic approach to
their wavering instantiations. And in treating Unknowingness

as a faculty, and its object as Non-being or Nothing, Socrates-Plato is not being merely bewitched by language. He is recognizing that all Knowledge, and also all Opinion, is two-sided, and that in knowing any Nature, one *ipso facto* knows, in a left-handed, squinting fashion, the lack or privation which is its shadow, and all the distortions which misrepresent it, and that in knowing the whole nature of the Ideal Forms as Such, we *ipso facto* know the Great Formlessness with which they contrast, as well as all the illusory distortions that could be made to people this. This great unshaped possibility of pattern has not the definite character which could make it an object of Knowledge, nor even of Opinion, but the Unknowingness and the Unopiningness with which it floods in on us is yet not the total absence of a state of mind. The great unshaped possibility appears in the Unwritten Doctrines as the Indefinite Dyad or the Great and Small which underlies both the Eide and their instantiations: in the *Timaeus* it appears as a sort of universal recipient of sensible being, having some of the properties of pure Space, but yet with rudiments of irregular shape and movement, and given neither to sense-experience nor pure thought, but to a sort of spurious, non-sensuous insight. Obviously we may say there are different orders of object, and as in modern logic the Null-class of individuals becomes one individual among others at the next highest level of discourse, so the Utter Formlessness which all Forms exclude, is itself from a higher point of view a sort of Form, and its presence to mind a queer sort of notional apprehension.

The question of the nature of the true philosopher and of true philosophy comes up again towards the end of Book VI, after many questions, interesting in themselves but not important for our purposes, and relating to the qualities and difficulties of the philosophic temper, have been discussed in great detail. Socrates-Plato now tells us that we have to start on that longer circuit (μακρότερα πέριοδος: 504c) for which a short-cut was substituted in the previous discussion of Soul-parts and Soul-virtues: we have, it now appears, to distinguish the structures and faculties of the Soul in relation to the ontological differences with which they are connected. There is, Socrates-Plato maintains, a greater lesson (μάθημα) than Justice and the Virtues, practised as the guardians have learnt to practise them, and sketched as they have so far been sketched in the Dialogue: we have to see the roots of such structures in something that is greater than them all. It is, however, commonly asserted that the Idea of Good is the greatest of all lessons, since it is by the use of this Eidos that all other things become profitable and useful. To know or possess all other goods would plainly be quite profitless if we could not know and possess the Good Itself. The Good Itself is, however, identified with Pleasure by the vulgar, and with Knowledge or Understanding (φρόνησις) by subtler spirits. But neither of these identifications is viable, since there are evil as well as good pleasures, and since the Knowledge that is supremely precious can only be defined as a Knowledge *of* the Good. Knowledge of this Good, which is itself more than Pleasure and Knowledge, but which lends itself to Pleasure and Knowledge and to many other things as well, must however be compassed by the guardians if they are to guide the state aright. What then is the nature of this Good? Socrates-Plato here takes refuge in a figure suitable to exoteric discourse: he will elucidate the role of the Good in the realm of Ideal Natures by considering the parallel role of an 'offspring' (ἔκγονος) which supremely instantiates the Good in the realm of visible instances. This offspring is the Sun, and it has this supremely excellent position in the visible world because it dispenses light in that world, a light which enables the eye, which resembles the Sun in its lovely sphericity, to *see* the objects around it, as it also enables the objects in that world to reveal themselves in all their shapes and colours. This Sun, as the source of light, is, however, a more noble thing than the eye or the objects it sees, or than the light it dispenses or the sight that it imparts to the eye. The Idea of Good stands, however, in a precisely analogous relation to the Ideal Objects that thinking Mind discerns, and to the discerning Mind itself, to that in which the Sun stands to visible objects and to the seeing eye. It is the source of the pervasive intellectual 'light', as it were, by means of which the Ideal Natures become perspicuous to Mind, and by means of which the Mind is able to lay hold of them intellectually. It is the source of the 'truth', the unhiddenness of the Eide from the Mind, as it is also the source of the cognitive grasp (γνῶσις or ἐπιστήμη) which the Mind has of the Eide. Lovely and worthy of honour as are both light and sight, the sun which dispenses them is yet lovelier and more honourable, and the same holds of the Good in relation to the knowledge and the perspicuous givenness that it dispenses. The surpassingness of the Good goes yet further: as the Sun is responsible for the origin, growth and nurture of all visible instances, so the Idea of Good is responsible, not only for the perspicuous givenness of the Eide, but even for their Being as Eide, for their very substantial Being itself (τὸ εἶναι τε καὶ τὴν οὐσίαν). And being itself the author of all such ideal Being, it is itself beyond all such being in hierarchical seniority and power (πρεσβείᾳ καὶ δυνάμει: 509b).

This most remarkable passage bears all the marks of the exoteric. It can be read as a nebulous, if glorious effusion, to be hastily compared to certain fine passages in St Paul or St John and then dismissed and forgotten: it can also be regarded as a statement, in very condensed, cryptic, figurative language, of a very definite doctrine, clear in its programmatic structure if not worked out in all detail, which is known to us independently from the Aristotelian accounts of Academic doctrine, and of which certain other implications filtered through to those first Neo-platonists – Ammonius Saccas and Plotinus – who were determined to make sense of the Platonic texts, and who used certain Aristotelian doctrines to throw light on their origins in Plato. What lies behind the whole passage is that Mathematics lies behind Ethics as it lies behind everything else in the world: the Goodness which is the foundation of all deep delight, and is all that enables us to make reliable sense of anything, is essentially a matter of Unity and of the endless numerical offspring into which it burgeons, in the Ratio and Proportion which it everywhere establishes, and in endlessly diversified, many-dimensioned structures which are merely its specifications. It is this formal structure which is shown forth in the differences of qualities, and their variously proportioned compromises, colours being based on the proportionate combinations of the light and the dark, sounds of the high and the low and so on, the only truly graspable thing in the qualitative pageant of the senses. It is likewise shown forth in the shape-differences of the natural elements and their varied behaviour, in the movements and arrangements of the heavenly bodies, in the beautiful growing patterns of the various sorts of organisms, in the intelligent perceptions and activities of souls, and in the stratification of classes in society. It is as much present in the skill of the shoemaker or the adroit moves of the rhetorician or the disciplined kindness of gracious women, as in the elementary theorems which relate to Numbers or geometrical figures. It is this that the rulers of the state must understand if they are to administer it rightly. And Socrates-Plato further believes that there is some sort of long argument which will show all these conceivable structures of duly proportioned Being to be derivable from a Principle of Absolute Unity which is present in them all, which is fully responsible for all they have and are, but which, as so universally present and responsible, cannot be ranked with any of them, but necessarily overtops them at all times and in all ways. It is, if one likes, what it is to be an Eidos, what it is to be a pattern of Numbers and Proportions, and what it is to be an Eidos is plainly a universal higher than the Eide, which, by its presence, enjoy eidetic status. This Principle of Unity or Goodness in a sense lies beyond the unhiddenness of truth or the clarity of the penetrating mind or the definite structures which specify it: we in a sense transcend ordinary knowledge in talking of it. Socrates-Plato does not rise to the Neoplatonic conception of a form of identification or direct contact superior to knowledge, but he is certainly not far from it.

The Principle of Unity is also one of Goodness, for at every point it excludes the unruliness, the lack of precision, the absence of clear limitation with which it contrasts, and to which by such exclusion it necessarily gives a certain shadowy status, not only in the instantial, but also in the intelligible sphere. In that latter sphere, we may say, as in a well-ordered family, certain things are not done, not said and not even thought of, but in being thus relegated to the undone, unsaid, unthought of, they remain in a sense everywhere present. And they of course run riot in the sphere of instantiation as they are curbed and disciplined in the ideal order. All this the ruler of the ideal state must know if he is to be a good administrator: he must see what are the authentic patterns of excellence which specify Absolute Unity and he must also, in doing so, take general cognizance of the innumerable possibilities of deviation from these authentic patterns which he will only too frequently encounter in the realm of practice.

It is also important to realize that Socrates-Plato's account implies a view of the knowing Mind and its relation to the knowable Eide which is the foundation of Aristotle's view of the Active Intelligence, and which led to the Neoplatonic doctrine of the all-embracing Absolute Mind. For Socrates-Plato, who has just developed such an elaborate eidetic treatment of the knowing, opining and unknowing aspects of the soul, and has related them all to appropriate objects, and who is also on the point of carrying this treatment further in his account of the Divided Line, cannot have failed to see that the various mental acts which exist in the soul, must themselves instantiate eidetic originals, so that there must, in addition to the instantial minds which exist in you, myself or the Divine World-Soul, be a Pattern Mind or Mind Itself which they all exemplify, and which represents the eternal vision and enjoyment of all the perspicuous Eide. And all our thinking must be, as it were, the overflowing action of this Pattern Mind, which, as in the account of Aristotle, raises our souls into ever more perfect instantiation of its Pattern-Vision. All this is what Aristotle may have misunderstood in his doctrine of the Active Intelligence, and what the Neoplatonists may have been right in reading into a passage like the present, as also into passages such as that in the Second Epistle (312e).

The Sun-analogy is forthwith succeeded by two other equally famous likenesses, the Line and the Cave, which are to be the foundation of the long account of the philosophic education which follows. In the Line (509d–511e) a division is made *within* Knowledge and Opinion and their respective objects which is parallel to the division *between* these faculties and their respective objects. Knowledge will have an inferior mode which has something of the unreliability of Opinion, and its objects something of the sheer multiplicity of Opinion's objects, while Opinion will have a superior mode which has something of the reliability of Knowledge, and its objects something of the unity and fixity of the objects of Knowledge. The doctrine is confused by an attempt to proportion the relative clearness of the two main segments of the whole line in the same ratio as the relative clearness of the two subsegments in each of these two main segments, an attempt which, though attractive in itself, leads to consequences that Plato obviously did not intend, i.e. the equal illumination of the lower segment of Knowledge and the upper segment of Opinion. The inferior mode of Opinion, which in this particular context is given the name of εἰκασία, Guesswork, is the type of Opinion which does not go beyond sensible and other appearances, and whose most salient examples are what we see presented in a mirror or by way of a shadow (509e–510a), though subsequent references suggest that all appearances, and even the semblances of Justice which Rhetoric conjures up in the law-courts (517d), are among the objects of Guesswork. What is important is that Guesswork is unreliable, and that it further gives us a multiplicity of seeming objects where only one is looked for, and that this desired unity and stability is achieved in πίστις, Reliable Judgment, where we go beyond multiple appearances to an invariant 'reality'. Elsewhere (602e) it is suggested that counting, weighing and measurement are the means through which such reliability and unity are achieved, so that even here Number is all-important. But πίστις, Reliable Judgment is not reliable in an absolute sense: the best measurements may prove to be inaccurate and biassed, and nothing can bring to fixity and finality the elusiveness and obscurity of the instance.

There is, however, also a lower form of Knowledge which, in comparison with genuine eidetic Knowledge, has many of the properties of Opinion and of its lower segment: it has a certain unreliability based on an absence of firm foundation, and it also has a multiplicity of objects which assimilates it to empirical instance-knowledge. The mathematical sciences, developed without a firm foundation in mathematical ontology, were a case of this inferior species of Knowledge: they built on what Socrates-Plato called 'hypotheses', which in this context mainly mean the postulation of the being of certain Ideal Natures, the Natural Numbers, the various types of Lines, Angles and Figures etc. of which being a derivation from certain ultimate Principles *could* be given – a derivation no doubt showing their origin through the repeated application of the same procedures to the results educed from the same basic Elements – but of which they provided no such derivation. They took for granted the being of certain ideal primitives of which a long recursive definition *could* be given. But mathematical science has the further peculiarity of not considering its Eide in and for themselves, but only in certain postulated instances, which need not, however, belong to the instantial realm at all. In our actual passage in the *Republic* it is only said that the mathematician studies his Eide through *sensible* illustrations (510d, e), but we know from the testimony of Aristotle that it was one of the central doctrines of Plato that there were special Objects of Mathematics which differed from sensible objects in being non-sensuous and unchanging, but which resembled sensible objects in being 'many alike', in offering many specimens of the same ideal nature (*Metaphysics*, 987b). The distinction is indeed an obvious one, and Plato would have been a dolt not to draw it, every case of mathematical reasoning being full of dealings with hypothetically assumed multitudes of units, couples, lines, triangles, segments etc. which are the conceived instances of Eide to which no actual sensuous Illustration need correspond. *Two units and two units make four units*, is neither about Eide nor about actual sensuous instances of Eide, but about instances conjured up by the mathematician in the interests of some problem. So central were these strange intentional objects in the discussions of the Academy, that Speusippus diverged from Plato in holding that they, and not numerical Eide, would do all the work required in an ontology of mathematics, whereas Xenocrates held the more obscure but challenging doctrine of an *identity* between the Eide of numbers and their purely conceived instances (*Metaphysics*, 1083a). It is, moreover, clear that the whole context *requires* special Mathematical Objects: the modes of cognition distinguished are said to differ in *object* as well as manner (509e) and there is no such objective difference if the mathematician merely studies Eide through sensuous illustrations. There are also other passages where the doctrine of the Mathematical Objects is transparently suggested (e.g. 516a, 525e–526a), and 534a even gives us the *reason* why the doctrine has not been spelt out, namely that it would greatly lengthen the present discussion. Those who would deny that the *Republic* implies the doctrine of special Mathematical Objects do so on the assumption that the most parabolic and hinting of philosophical exponents is 'nothing if not explicit' (see Ross, *Plato's Theory of Ideas*, 1951, p. 59). The result of such an assumption is to make Plato a fool, and so happily to render itself absurd.

The upper segment of Knowledge is now said to be Intellection Proper (νόησις) and its objects the Eide or pure intelligibles (νοητά). It is further characterized as having no mere postulations which admit of, but do not receive, further justification: it treats the postulations of the mathematical sciences as the mere postulations they are, and, making them the taking-off places and springboards (ἐπιβάσεις τε καὶ ὁρμάς) for dialectical investigations, it proceeds from them to an absolute starting-off place, which is in no sense postulational but wholly self-justifying. From this self-justifying starting-off place, which it cannot be doubted is the existence (or more-than-existence) of the Idea (or more-than-Idea) of Good, it will then proceed step by step to construct the whole hierarchy of the Eide, making no use of sensuous illustration, and proceeding from Eide to Eide by way of Eide, and terminating in what, though to the last degree specific, is yet utterly eidetic (511b). It cannot be doubted that what is here being projected as the programme of Dialectic is the complete mapping of all the possible patterns of mathematical being, arithmetical, geometrical, chronometric and dynamic, which for Socrates-Plato are as much normative and axiological as merely ontological – a mapping based, moreover, on principles that are wholly self-justifying, and which leave nothing to mere postulation or unreliable conjecture. In contrast to the *Noûs*, the true Understanding which can do all this penetration and derivation from ultimates, the merely postulational mathematical sciences are said to be cases of mere διάνοια or Mathematical Understanding, a condition of mind inadequate to its intelligible material because lacking in a justifying base, and hovering obscurely between mere Opinion and true Understanding.

The Line is now succeeded at the beginning of Book VII by the more beautiful and pictorial Cave. Here we have the famous likeness of the imprisoned men held in a fixed position in a cavern by the chains of a delusive ontology and epistemology, which leads them to hold the absurd belief that the blurred instantiations of Eide alone have authentic being and that there is firm and reliable knowledge to be had regarding them. They are completely the slaves of the 'natural attitude', as Husserl might have called it, and they see the instantiating shadows cast by the real objects at the mouth of the Cave – shadows which break the light of a fire, an image of the Sun, stationed at a yet further point beyond the objects – as having the full being that they will afterwards learn to attribute only to the fully real things which cast such shadows. To tear such beings from their intercourse with shadows and echoes (the last also introduced into the account), and from the guessing-games that they play with their fellows regarding the sequence of such half-real objects, and to place them suddenly among real objects in the full blaze of the true sun, would engender complete dazzlement: they need to pass gradually from the upper-world shadows which resemble those of their Cave (geometrical figures and illustrations?), to the reflections of upper-world objects seen in water (the intentional Objects of Mathematics?, called θεῖα, divine in 532c), and thence to the same objects seen in reality (the grosser, more empirical Eide?), and thence to the heavenly bodies seen in the sky at night (the more principial, categorial Eide?) and then at last, in full daylight, to the Sun itself (the Principle of Unity or Goodness), seen in its proper place and as it truly is (516b), but with a vision that is probably meant to retain some of the dazzlement appropriate to an object that is more than existent, more than one definite, substantial Eidos among others. The passage to upper world exploration and vision is plainly meant to be a parallel to the great ontological turn of the mind, whereby it ceases to attribute substantial being to particular things as such, and locates it rather in what seemed at first to be the mere characters of those things, and then begins to acquire skill in seeing how the members of this new order of true 'things' are hierarchically ordered, until at last it sees them all as having their explanatory source in something more than themselves, in a Principle of Order, or Unity, or Goodness which 'generates' them all, in that they are all special cases of it, constructible out of it and by it in a standard manner, and that they in their turn, but in a looser manner, 'generate' the instances in which they are present. This great revisionary turn of the soul is not some new wisdom poured into the soul from without, but the simple exercise of a power inherent in it (418d–519a), and only requiring an exorcism from that exclusive preoccupation with the Instance, the source of lust and pleasure, by which eidetic vision is obscured. Socrates-Plato completes the account by describing the temporary blindness which overwhelms the soul when returning to the trivialities of instantiation from the radiant perspicuity of eidetic principle. The philosopher returning to such trivialities is at first quite in the dark and certainly ridiculous: after a while, however, he becomes quite as good an empiricist as those around him, better in fact, since he remembers the eidetic structures which observed instances only dimly shadow forth, and of which those around him see nothing. The philosopher who is to rule in the state must be able and willing both to take the at first painful turn of soul which puts Eide before instances, and also later to take the reverse turn, with its painful renunciation of insight, and must then be ready and able to apply the remembered rules and principles which obtain among the Eide in the merely approximate divination and improvisation which is all that is possible 'down here'. The latter parts of Book VII contain detailed prescriptions as to how the life of the philosopher-ruler must alternate between periods of deep thought on eidetic principles, and periods of carrying them out in the inferior medium of practice. And what they *suggest* is that it is wrong and purblind to think that it would have been better to have remained 'aloft'. The illuminated man must have a sense of 'mission', which is plainly a reflex of the eternal mission of instantiation of which the *Timaeus* will speak more plainly.

The allegory of the Cave leads on, however, to an account of the mathematical sciences which form the first part of the training in eidetic understanding necessary for the philosopher-ruler, and which lead on to Dialectic, now utterly remote from the question-and-answer techniques of Socrates and the Sophists, which will justify the mere postulations of the mathematical sciences in terms of a self-justifying First Principle. This whole account is deeply interesting as showing that there is nothing at this level of study but mathematics and the foundations of mathematics: despite the use of the term 'Good' for the self-justifying First Principle, there are no ethical concerns, *as ordinarily understood*, in the Platonic programme of studies. Ethical concerns, such questions, for example, as to whether one ought to prosecute one's own father for impiety because he allowed a slave to perish, or the various details of state-laws, are not a matter for Νοῦς or Philosophical Understanding, not even a matter for διάνοια or mathematical Understanding. They are a matter for πίστις, well-founded Judgment, and so are all the analogies and persuasive arguments in the *Republic* itself, which, despite much opinion to the contrary, is not an essay in philosophical Dialectic at all, but only an exoteric adumbration of the same. There would indeed be a place for what is now called Deontic Logic among the mathematical sciences, and the same holds for the Axiological Axiomatics which some moderns have developed: the inexactly topological character of these disciplines would not matter. It is, for example, a good postulate that the obligatory excludes the permissibility of the contrary, or that merit increases with difficulty faced, and in proportion to value achieved. But the higher Dialectic would be nothing beyond an establishment of the foundations of *all* these mathematical sciences, a derivation of all of them from First Principles, and as such it would effectively comprehend Principia Ethica and Principia Philosophiae Naturalis as well as Principia Mathematica. Plato, we see, was firmly wedded to what Moore called the Naturalistic Fallacy: to him the good form of anything was also the natural form of that thing, and that natural form depended in the last resort on a vast complex of Products, Ratios and other functions of Number. This good, natural, numerical form of everything included the defective and bad only as its inherent contrast, but in the realm of instantiation being and good fell apart, irregularity superseded right ratio, and naturalism really became the fallacy that Moore held it to be. This plainly is the drift of the treatment of the mathematical sciences as leading up to Dialectic in this part of the *Republic*; it would be incredible that after long courses in these sciences the guardians should descend to such adolescent puerilities as, for example, the arguments bandied to and fro in a Dialogue like the *Protagoras*. The Socratic argumentations had their place in history, and so had those of the Sophists, but Plato, despite his use of Socrates as a covering device, had plainly quite different provender to offer. Some might imagine that the reference in 538c–539d to the unsettling effects of Dialectic on the too young, was an indication that Dialectic involved the sort of treatment of moral questions that occurred in the Socratic Dialogues. We may agree that Socrates-Plato wished to give this impression to exoteric audiences, while really referring to the ὕβρις of the young mathematicizing philosopher, perhaps known in the Academy and certainly known in our own time, who tried to tear the principles of the sciences from their axiological roots, and who then perhaps sought to reorganize society in a supposedly scientific, but arbitrarily bad, manner. It is the danger of being the wrong sort of mathematicizing Utopian against which Plato was perhaps concerned to guard.

The mathematical sciences which Socrates-Plato prescribes for the first part of the higher education of his philosopher-rulers are Arithmetic, Plane Geometry, Solid Geometry, Celestial Dynamics and Harmonics. They are all sciences in which sensuous instantiation and illustration is necessarily defective, as it is not in the case of purely sensuous quality and what it establishes. There is, and can be, no perfect sensuous illustration of Number or Shape or Size or Solidity or Speed. The unitary dissolves on examination into endless multiplicity, as a purely conceived unit does not (526a), the visible stars as instances of movement (530a) are never absolutely constant in speed, direction and so on. Instances which in a partial manner illustrate such Eide draw us beyond themselves to the true Being that they illustrate, but we cannot identify this true Being with what they draw our minds towards, since the instances obviously illustrate them imperfectly, and illustrate many contrary Eide as well. We are therefore called upon to cease looking and to think instead. In Arithmetic the mind is drawn to consider as it were perfect illustrations of Unity, beyond the reach of the senses, all exactly equal to one another, and incapable of indefinite division into parts (525d, e). The mathematician is here primarily dealing with eternal mathematical instances rather than the pure Eide they exemplify: the Eide are only being grasped in and through such instances, and it is only the philosopher who will later deal with them in and for themselves. From Arithmetic the study proceeds to Plane Geometry, which Socrates-Plato emphasizes should not be spoken of in terms of human activity, for example squaring, applying, extending etc., but solely as presenting perfect instances of eternal Eide which will lead the soul to the vision of the Idea of Good (526e). The generic geometrical patterns that are thus indirectly studied, and the Principles that help to constitute them, will of course be left to the philosopher rather than the mathematician. But Plane Geometry, Socrates-Plato insists, is to be rounded off by a study of Solids; this being a field in which the Academy achieved one of its most spectacular triumphs, the demonstration by Theaetetus that there are five and no more than five regular Solids. The further analysis of Solidity and its Species is of course a matter for the philosopher rather than the mathematician, but in establishing propositions about imagined instances of Solidity the mathematician indirectly illuminates Solidity Itself. From Geometry Socrates-Plato proceeds to mathematical sciences which involve a fourth dimension of temporality: we have Celestial Dynamics or Astronomy, the mathematical study of Solids in Motion, of whose multifarious problems the actual arrangements of the decorated sky afford only a single, not wholly accurate illustration. Another temporally involved science is Harmonics, where not only distance but also velocity becomes relevant, and we study the numerical basis, long laid bare by the early Pythagoreans, of the harmonic delights of sensuous music.

What is most remarkable in all this is the gathering into the region of the Eide, through their perfected mathematical instances, of the multiplicity, the spatiality and the temporality which are also most emphatically present in the genuinely imperfect, instantial world. But in the eidetic realm they are domesticated, mastered, wholly subordinated to the Principle which sets limits to them, and so distinguished from the chaotic Infinite of the realm of instantiation, which is never completely subordinated to Form and Number. What has also been frequently remarked upon is Plato's disdainful attitude to the empirical sciences of dynamics, harmonics etc. which apply mathematical ideals to the facts of Nature. Plato is not, however, so wholly disdainful of the world of empirical fact as some have supposed: the *Timaeus* bears ample witness to his interest in it. But the dianoetic sciences must study the accurate types to which sensuous instances only approximate, and they must also study the whole round of ideal possibilities in which the facts of Nature occupy only a single place. The 'problems' of the dianoetic scientist presumably include the construction of other celestial systems than our own, and perhaps the construction of other geometrical particles and other organic patterns than those in our world.

The place of Dialectic as the θριγκός or coping-stone of the mathematical sciences is now set forth with more fullness. Dialectic arises because the mathematical sciences make various Postulations (ὑποθέσεις) which they do not further question, and for which they offer no justifying reason (533c). These Postulations, as we have already seen, are postulations of the existence of 'primitive Ideas', Eide such as Linearity, Oddness, Rectangularity etc. and their species, though obviously there will be other axioms than these – for example, if equals are added to equals etc. – if the mathematical sciences are to be developed completely. It may seem odd that ideal existence-postulates should be thus necessary, especially on the view, suggested by one obviously exoteric remark in 596a, that there will be an Eidos corresponding to every name applicable to many things. But in the Ideal Ontology there are plainly Prime Eide, paradigms of rational perfection, which set the standard in terms of which both privative and defective meanings are to be conceived and applied. Dialectic is not, however, satisfied with the mere Postulation of Linearity Itself, Oddness Itself etc.: it feels presumably that some sufficient reason must be given as to *why* such Postulations are necessary. This questioning of mathematical Postulations is called by Socrates-Plato their lifting or destruction (533c): we have to abandon them as fixed starting-points and proceed to find a truly unquestionable First Principle from which they all can be derived.

There can be no doubt, if we consult the reports of Aristotle, as to the way in which Socrates-Plato conceived the construction of his dialectical supra-mathematics. It would survey the vast variety of variously dimensioned mathematical patterns, and would try to find Principles looking to which the existence of all such patterns could be rendered perspicuous and comprehensively demonstrated: it could also re-establish confidence in the already proven relations of all such patterns to one another, for example the relation of being a right angle to being the summed angular magnitude present in any triangle. The Principles by which the whole range and structure of the mathematical field could be thus established, were a Principle of Unification, on the one hand, and of Indefinite Increase and Decrease on the other, the latter Principle having a hydra-like variety of forms corresponding to more and more complexly dimensional patterns – the Many and Few, the Long and Short, the Broad and Narrow, the Deep and Shallow, and, we may add, with a view to Astronomy and Harmonics, the Swift and the Slow. The manner in which these two Principles generated the mathematical patterns must have been by mutual saturation or notional co-operation: such and such a pattern was Unity going so far, for so long, to such a breadth and thickness, at such a rate, etc., etc. It was like hitting off points on a graph through their various co-ordinates. And the patterns of living creatures in nature, and the excellences and virtues which represented their natural functions, all of which came to occupy a central place in the Platonic ideology, are to be conceived as no more than extremely complex cases of such co-operation or symphysis, in which Numbers, numerical Ratios, Dimensions, and intercalations of Arithmetical, Geometrical and Harmonic Means, beggared all description. Experience will at best offer us only a few twisted specimens of all this eidetic wealth. We may further note that the *supremacy* ascribed to the Principle of Unity or Good in the proposed dialectical deduction, shows that the system to be elaborated was only in appearance dualistic: the multidimensional media in which Unity disported itself must in the end prove to be wholly a reflex and an internal avocation of Unity Itself. The Dialogue *Parmenides* goes some distance in suggesting how this can be so, and how in the most aloof notion of Unity Itself all multiplicity and variety is necessarily locked up. All this, in all its dazzling combination of the most difficult issues in mathematics with the most difficult issues in philosophy, must have been what the philosopher-guardians were required to meditate on in the periods when they were not absorbed by the practical problems of the state. Small wonder then that they saw nothing difficult in the adjudications of the law-courts or in the strategy and tactics of their campaigns.

IV

Books VIII and IX deal with the παρεκβάσεις, the departures from, or perversions of, the ideal community sketched in Books II to VII. These are: Timarchy or Timocracy, the rule of the spirited, but uncultivated, military element; Oligarchy, the rule of the propertied minority; Democracy, the rule of all and sundry, in which the lazy, vicious and stupid have quite as much influence as the industrious, spirited and intelligent, and finally Tyranny, in which all becomes subordinated to a single mad individual, who becomes madder and madder as his situation becomes worse and worse. There are, following the analogy on which the whole Dialogue works, parallel perversions of the individual person, in which the dominance of different psychic elements answers to the dominance of different classes in the state. What is most important in these books is the light it throws on Plato's eidetic theory. The ideal state and man are in a sense the prime Eide, the point of departure for the whole series: they are in a sense more truly and absolutely eidetic than the departures from them. But the departures are also Eide, and not merely corruptions found in the realm of Becoming, and the transitions from one polity or psychic condition to another are also eidetic transitions, implicit in fact in the Eide from which they deviate, and capable of being explored by ideal vision and experiment, though doubtless also instantiated over and over again in Greek political and psychological experience. *Le laid est beau mais le beau est plus beau*: in the same manner the departure from an Eidos is itself an Eidos, but it is less of an Eidos than the Eidos from which it departs. The approximate study of the perversions of ideal polity is due to the fact, further, that in their case we are in the realm of the Infinite (cf. the mention of the intermediate forms of government in 544d): a few critical points can be sketched, but not all forms of deviation can be dealt with. Exhaustiveness only applies to the simple, prime Eide.

If there are any doubts as to the eidetic character of Books VIII and IX, these are laid to rest by the famous mathematical passage of 546. All deviations in the state are genetically caused, and these genetic changes point back to cosmic changes which are rooted in the Numbers on which every human and natural instance necessarily is built. The elaborate and difficult Pythagoreanism of the passage has led some to think that it cannot have been serious: it is, however, more serious than the exoteric state-pathology which follows. For it sketches what Socrates-Plato hoped could be ultimately worked out at the dianoetic level of science, and fully justified at the noetic level, whereas the exoteric pathology that follows plainly belongs to the realm of πίστις, Assured Belief, and is as remote from true science as is modern sociology. The details of the Pythagorean passage need not be dwelt on here: Adam, in his great edition of the *Republic*, has perhaps given as satisfactory a treatment of them as can be given. Suffice it to say that they build on the charismatic properties of the right-angled, Pythagorean triangle, whose hypotenuse of 5, and sides of 4 and 3, very simply show that the square on the hypotenuse of a right-angled triangle is equal to the sum of the squares on its two sides. Multiplication, always a more fundamental procedure in the Pythagorean-Platonic philosophy than addition, yields 60 as the product of these three numbers, and sixty multiplied by itself thrice over (in due deference to the cubic solidity of such triple multiplication) yields 12,960,000, which can equally be regarded as a regular square number 3600^2 or as an irregular, 'oblong' number, the product of 4800 and 2700. The number 12,960,000 is approximately the number of days in a cycle of 3600 years, the Great Year of Pythagoras-Plato, the time it allegedly takes for all the planets to start together in a given stance towards one another, and to return to an identical stance. Making use of data in the later Dialogue *Statesman*, the regular square number 3600^2 represents a period in the life of the cosmos when eidetic order and consequent uniformity (ὁμοιότης) prevails, when Units regularly mature into Lines, Lines systematically burgeon into regular Figures and Solids, and regular Solids into Solids regularly moving, and all into the completed patterns of organic life and life in society. The irregular oblong number 4800×2700 then arguably represents a subsequent period in which all this fine structure slowly disintegrates, in which ἀνομοιότης, non-uniformity, replaces uniformity, in which, in short, the blind, instantial forces prevail, and in which God, to use the language of the *Statesman*, has abandoned the tiller of the Universe, and has let Necessity rather than Mind direct. (The use of data from a late Dialogue to illuminate an earlier one is justified by the fact that *all* Plato's exoteric writings express but a single teaching, which was probably more monolithic and unquestioningly accepted when the earlier Dialogues were written, than when the later ones were, a decline of confidence which went with greater willingness to divulge detail.) The Great Year of the Universe, with its two cyclically recurrent variants, corresponds to two gestation periods in the life of the human embryo, the seven months period of roughly 210 days, and the nine months period of 270 days, and, as Adam puts it,

the Great Year of the Universe may therefore be denoted by a rectangle whose sides are respectively the longer period and the sum of the longer and shorter period of gestation in the race of man, after it has been multiplied by the square of the Pythagorean perfect number 10. As the Universe is a 'magnus homo', and man a 'brevis mundus', these and similar analogies may well have seemed significant to the Pythagoreans, whom Plato is certainly copying here (op. cit., vol. II, p. 302).

And not only significant to the Pythagoreans, but also to the modern 'structuralist' who sees possibilities of numerical combination in all physical, psychological and social phenomena.

The decline from the arrangements of the ideal state is therefore rooted in the cyclical changes of the universe, and these in the eternal relations of Numbers, which include the oblique, the oblong and the irrational as much as the straight, the rational and the square. The coming to an end of the good, uniformly structured period of the cosmos, and the start of a bad, irregularly structured period, will be marked by spiritual as well as physical disorders. The rulers of the state will make incorrect calculations, and marriages will no longer be arranged so as to yield the right ratios of intelligent, belligerent and menial persons. As the mating arrangements deteriorate, there will no longer be a sufficient number of gifted intellectuals to take charge of the state: intellect and music will be pushed into the background, and a state will arise in which the class of auxiliary guardians takes over the lead, and war, honour and a rigorously disciplined life, resting on a foundation of helotry and a secret lust for wealth, will become the chief notes in the social pattern. The corresponding timocratic man will typically be the son of a high-minded intellectual leading a retired life in an honour-geared state, who moves in a timocratic direction as the result of the exhortations of a status-seeking mother and family entourage, and becomes a man of honour and temper, rather than a man of insight and calm self-control. In much the same manner the oligarchic, property-oriented state arises when the hidden tendencies towards accumulation and acquisition take over, and a property-qualification is made necessary for full citizenship. The whole state then becomes divided into the state of the rich and the state of the poor, and new laws abolish all limits to the impoverishment of the latter. The state becomes full of paupers, on the one hand, and criminals, on the other. The corresponding transition in the individual man is accomplished by the financial and political ruin of the young man's father, which leads a young man to resolve that he will at all costs always preserve a bastion of wealth to stand between him and similar ruin. In such a man, all the higher interests of intellect and temper are subordinated to amassing and hoarding tendencies, and so are the lower, non-necessary lusts and appetites, which, however, in the absence of higher and more musical control, wax extraordinarily in secret. Turning to the oligarchic state, it is clear that the poor, whether passively feeble or actively criminal, must increase in misery and in numbers, and must end by throwing up champions who will promote a democratic revolution. All will then become as piebald and as various as a much-decorated garment, in which all shapes and colours are set side by side (557c, d). Society will become infinitely egalitarian and permissive, and not only the young, but even animals, will enjoy extraordinary liberties and privileges (563c). The corresponding democratic man arises when the non-necessary appetites, which tend to display and expense, overcome the necessary appetites, which tend to careful accumulation: obviously the son of a too careful, accumulative father will tend in this spendthrift direction. A superficial dilettantism in the arts and philosophy, and a playful interest in bodily exercise, mixed with lapses into self-indulgence, will become part of the democratic man's attitude.

What all this unmathematicized descriptive dialectic is however leading up to is the state in which the champion of the people and its liberties gradually converts himself into a tyrant, at first protected by a bodyguard given him by his popular supporters to protect their liberties, and then employing that bodyguard to take away those liberties, surrounding himself by mercenaries and freedmen, and destroying all who can in any way criticize or resist him, the brave, the high-minded, the wise and the rich (467b, c). What corresponds to such tyranny in the individual person is the person dominated by some senseless master-lust, who has to sacrifice and override all high-minded and low-minded interests and sentiments in the interest of this lust. Such a man is obviously wretched in any case, but his wretchedness reaches a pinnacle when circumstances allow him to become an actual tyrant. Of necessity he then becomes more and more envious, treacherous, unjust, friendless, impious, hospitable to all evils, and is not only rendered supremely miserable by all this but also makes all those near him just as miserable (580a).

The Dialogue then goes on to give two 'proofs' that the tyrannical man does not, as Thrasymachus claimed that he does, live in the happiest and most profitable manner. The first proof rests on the ground that while each element in the Soul has its characteristic pleasures, the lower appetites the intense pleasures of food, drink and sex, the money-loving desires the pleasures of acquisition, the victory- and honour-loving desires the pleasures of victory and honour, and the wisdom- and knowledge-loving desires the pleasures of discovery and knowing – and while to each element in the Soul its own pleasures seem greatly superior, there is yet a sense in which the intelligent, reasoning side has a better standard of judgment (κριτήριον) than the other parts. For the man who knows the satisfactions of rational thought necessarily has had experience of the satisfaction of appetite, acquisition and ambition, while the reverse is not necessarily the case, so that his preferences are for that reason more justifiable, and they are also more justifiable because what we are in quest of is not a blind, but a reasoned preference, one based on reasons (λόγοι) or objective grounds, and such reasons are essentially the objects of the reasoning faculty, which accordingly has better grounded preferences. In all this Socrates-Plato is not really considering pleasure as momentarily and elusively instantiated, but pleasure justified for an overall vision that sees it as contributing to an ordered pattern of life. It is in fact a value for the person that is being assessed, rather than any vanishing state of pleasure, a measurable permanence and object of πίστις, rather than something felt and guessed at. Obviously reason will be the faculty that will assess such pleasure rightly, and it will also evince an almost necessary self-love in virtue of which the reasonable man will take pleasure in his own reasonableness.

Socrates-Plato moves on, however, to an even profounder line of argument. He argues that the vanishing instantial experiences of pleasure derive what sense and substance they have from the eidetic status of the objects to which they are directed or from the eidetic attitudes that they exemplify. A state of mind that 'clings to the ever-uniform and undying and to the truth, and which is itself such and arises as such' (585a) will have a higher ontological status than a state of mind of which the contrary is true, and this means that the instantiations of Knowledge and its satisfactions rank higher in their approach to true Being than the instantiations of bodily activity and *their* satisfactions. 'If, therefore, being satisfied with what accords with one's nature is sweet, what really satisfies us with what is more real will cause us to rejoice more truly and really, and with a truer joy, than what shares less in real being' (585d, e).

In the realm of Nature or Eidos, there is, moreover, an absolute above, below and middle position (584a): relative Being, though eidetic, presumably merely attends upon the prime Being which belongs to Eide in and for themselves. Those who fail to see the superiority of rational pleasures over all others are, however, subject to an illusion or confusion: they confuse the *relative* superiority of an absolutely middle over an absolutely lower position with the absolute superiority of a truly high position in and for itself. (This passage is immensely important: it shows how there can be sophistry and falsehood and non-being even in the realm of the Eide, as the *Sophist* will afterwards discuss.) The life of desire is always subject to this illusion: we mistake the grey of relief from true pain for the white of true pleasure (585a). Almost all the bodily pleasures exploit this relativistic illusion: relatively they represent a move in the direction of true pleasure, but they do not achieve the absolute pleasantness found only in a few sensuous pleasures, for example those of fragrance (584b), as they are also found in those of mind and thought. Socrates-Plato's arguments have a strain of surface-sophistry veiling profounder insight: they are invalid if what we are talking of, and think worth talking of, is a vanishing, affective state, they are valid if what we are talking of is a state of satisfaction, that depends on our own true nature and the nature of what we are concerned with.

The outcome of these ontological arguments is now applied to the tyrant. The tyrant is placed third from the oligarchic man, from whom he is separated by the democratic man, while the oligarchic man is by a similar reckoning placed third from the philosopher-ruler, being separated from him by the timocrat. 3×3 is therefore a measure of the inferiority of the tyrant's well-being to that of the philosopher-ruler, and this number cubed, for reasons probably connected with the three-dimensional character of fully concrete being, yields the portentous number 729. The joys of the tyrant are only worth $\frac{1}{729}$ of the joys of the philosopher-ruler. This inexact guess at a proportion which a true development of the Platonic Dialectic would have been able to prove, is succeeded by a Pythagorean picture of the threefold soul, one that may very well have hung on the walls of the Pythagorean lodges in South Italy. The soul is a strange, composite beast, outwardly human, but harbouring within itself a vast, insatiable, many-headed monster of appetite, a smaller lion of temper and courage, and a yet smaller man of reason. Those who hold the injustice of the tyrant to be more profitable and pleasant than the justice of the philosopher-ruler are really saying that it is more profitable and pleasant to gratify the monster at the expense of the lion and the man than vice versa (589d, e). These merely edifying pictures have no force apart from the 'Numbers' behind them. These alone will describe the true constitution of Soul and City, which Socrates-Plato indifferently locates in discourse (ἐν λόγοις) or in heaven (ἐν οὐρανῷ: 592a, b).

V

The tenth book of the *Republic* rounds the Dialogue off with a renewal of the destructive criticism of the imitative arts, followed by an argument for immortality and an Orphic-Pythagorean picture of the life to come. In the former, Socrates-Plato takes up the fascinating theme of appearance, of the being which is no being, or the no-being which is not nothing, a theme to be carried further in the *Sophist*: it is of the essence of the Eide that their true, substantial being proliferates in the wholly dependent being of instances which derive all that they have of sense or substance from the eidetic being they enshrine. But the dependent being of instances itself proliferates in the doubly dependent being of the appearances which derive their simulated reality from the instances they copy, and so stand at a second remove from the Eide examplified in those instances and from other Eide exemplified elsewhere. Socrates-Plato does well to explore the gradations in the ontological hierarchy, and to reject as absurd that one-level ontology which, itself rooted in philosophical confusion, has always been infinitely productive of others: he assumes, as Aristotle will later explicitly assert, that there are several senses, primary, secondary, tertiary etc., in which something may be said to be or to be something and not nothing. (It is a pity that he did not see that an infinity of such senses readily conjures itself up: it can for example appear to A that it appears to B that it appears to C etc.) The discussion limits itself to considering the case in which an Eidos E is instantiated in a perceived object O, and in which this perceived object appears to instantiate another Eidos A, and this appearance is not one that arises spontaneously by refraction, reflection or some other form of deceptive transmission, but occurs in an artefact, the work of a manufacturer of appearances, in other words a creative artist.

Socrates-Plato finds it convenient to consider the case of artificial rather than natural 'natures', i.e. what it is to be a table or a bed rather than what it is to be a mountain or a fig-tree.

There are, he argues, three categorially different sorts of tables or beds, the eidetic sort which is that of being a table or a bed Itself or as Such, the instantial sort which is that of being a case of being a table or a bed, and the phenomenal sort which is that of only seeming to be a case of being a table or a bed. The first way of being a table or bed is, contrary to the usual assumption, the primary way, since only being a table or bed has that entire identity with being a table or bed, at which instantiated tableness or bedness merely tries to arrive. Being an instance of tableness or bedness merely mimics this true identity of tableness or bedness with itself, just as merely seeming to be a table or a bed merely mimics this true mimicry. Socrates-Plato, talking exoterically, says that God is the maker of the eidetic table or bed, while the ordinary table-maker or bed-maker only makes something table-like or bed-like, or, what is the same, *a* table or *a* bed. And there is moreover a necessity which renders it impossible for God, who does not wish to make merely *a* table or *a* bed, to make more than one eidetic table or bed. For were he to make more than one, a new eidetic table or bed would at once spring into being, which would be the Eidos of both of the prior tables or beds, and which alone would be what it is to be a bed (597c). The contradictions in this account reveal its exotericism: if God were an instantial Maker, he could very well make a plurality of instantial tables and beds, and the fact that he *can* only make one table or bed shows that he is not an instantial Maker at all. Plainly God is nothing but a name either for an eternal Thinkingness correlated with the whole system of thinkables, and as eidetic as they are, or for that Absolute which lies behind Thinking and Thinkables alike. In either case the conception of a possible multiplication of one self-identical Eidos obviously founds an argument *per impossibile*: the absurdity of the conclusion makes nonsense of the whole conception in question.

Socrates-Plato further obscures his account by connecting Eide with the use of general names: we are wont (εἰώθαμεν), he says, to postulate a single Eidos for each group of many things to which we apply the same name (596c). This account suggests that if we were, as Aristotle suggests, to make the name 'cloak' stand for what we now mean by a pale physician or a goat-stag, there would automatically be Eide of the sorts of being in question. This grotesque interpretation runs counter to the deep connection of the Eide with what is natural and good and real (*Metaphysics*, 1070c), and it also ignores the fact that Socrates-Plato only says that we *usually* postulate Eide corresponding to common names, which implies that to connote Eide is what common names *mainly* are for, but does *not* exclude the possibility of making up meaningful names, like those above, which correspond to *no* Eide. Of course, as we have argued, there is a *secondary* sense in which there are Eide of *anything* thinkable or nameable, in the sense, that is, that an Eidos includes whatever it excludes, or even what it remotely renders possible. In this sense even the most distorted or arbitrarily constructed meaning has an interstitial place in the realm of the Eide. The passage before us is not, however, concerned with such deviant or factitious forms, but with excellent, standard ones, and its contrast is between *The* Bed or Table, and *a* bed or table, and a *seeming* bed or table, and nothing else. Some of the Aristotelian evidence suggests, however (*Metaphysics*, 991b, 1080a), that there were no Eide of artefacts, for example of a house or a ring, which would rule out the beds and tables of the present example. But even if Plato were so foolish as to deny a 'nature' to the necessary instruments and embellishments of civilized living – he would perhaps rightly have denied it to certain modern gadgets which prove their inauthenticity by their refusal to function reliably – he might still have found it expedient to talk as he does in the present context, since he wishes to compare three makers, God, the craftsman and the imitative artist. If there were human makers of fig-trees or mountains they would have provided a better illustration. Plato, it is clear, was capable of infinite mental reservation: he wrote all the Dialogues with his tongue in his cheek.

The distinction of the three types of bed leads, however, to a depreciation of seeming beds and of those who make them. No one, he argues, would make a seeming bed if he were capable of making a genuine case of Bedness as Such. Seeming instances of beds exploit the differences of apparent size and shape due to the varying situation of the observer, changes in medium etc: they do not dig down to the quantitative invariances which only reveal themselves to the arts of measurement, counting and weighing (602d). The art of the painter is therefore a magical art of illusion, and it does not even produce the half-realities of the instantial realm. It is moreover easier to counterfeit what is uncontrolled by reason than what is rationally controlled: hence the bad influence on behaviour represented by tragic and comic poetry. It is not worth our while to devote more time to all this puritanism, which is surely not of the essence of Platonism. If the Good as universal source of all, and the Eide as its specific forms, necessarily overflow into the endless richness of instantiation, it is likewise necessary that instances should overflow into the endless richness of variable, qualitative appearance. If we value an Eidos for being one over many instances, we should value its instances for being one over many appearances: in either case the many are required as that in which the one exercises its efficacy. And it is quite arguable that the appearances of nature and art often come closer to pure Eide than the actual things of sense which only feebly instantiate them. A writer like Plato who has used so much art to suggest in words what transcends instantiation, should surely know that this is so. If the imitative artists are to be expelled from the state, the writers of Dialogues will have to go with them: only the formal logicians and the pure mathematicians can be allowed to remain. It is further plain that, since an Eidos can as much be approached by what it excludes as by what it covers, eidetic knowledge being always of opposites, there can be no reason why undisciplined characters should not be used in drama to inculcate virtue. To prohibit such representation would be to prohibit all the marvellous pathology of the soul and the state in Books VIII and IX of the *Republic* itself.

Socrates-Plato, having proved virtue to be its own reward, even if concealed by false appearances throughout our present life, now goes on to give a Pythagorean picture of the rewards of virtue which take account of what he regards as the Soul's demonstrable immortality. Everything in the world not only has a nature that it instantiates, and a characteristic good that preserves and assists that nature: it also has, built into its nature, a characteristic evil which will corrupt that nature, and in the end utterly disrupt and destroy it. Ophthalmia corrupts the eye, sickness the body, mildew corn, rot timber, and rust iron. Nothing can, however, be destroyed by anything but its proper evil, or by what is productive of that proper evil. The proper evil of the Soul, on the eidetic analysis given in the previous books, is, however, Injustice, which bodily evils, including bodily destruction, do not tend to produce. The Soul will, therefore, only be capable of destruction if its own evil, Injustice, tends to destroy it. Empirically, however, this would not appear to be the case, since liveliness, the essential character conferred by Soul, is as much or even more characteristic of the unjust than the just (610e). It would, therefore, seem that, since its own evil, Injustice, wholly fails to destroy the Soul, nothing else can do so. The soul is accordingly deathless.

This argument is by no means demonstrative, since Souls are certainly only *instances* of the Life, Mind and Justice which are plainly deathless, and since an empirical premise, that Injustice has no tendency to diminish liveliness, has been brought into the argument. On Platonic assumptions it is, however, far from a worthless argument. For a Soul in its capacity to understand the total eidetic order comes far nearer to transcending time and change, and is far more authentically expressive of the supra-essential Good, than any other sort of instance. If there are instances which persist through time, and gather more and more of the total sense of things into themselves than other instances do or can, then Souls plainly are such instances. In a cosmos which depends on Eide, it is not plausible that greater permanence should be found in instances which exemplify much more one-sided, limited Eide than Souls do, or that Souls should depend for their persistence or dissolution on these. And if we think that Plato had the sense and the consistency to affirm the existence of a single Mind, Life and Knowledge, which not only stands over against all eidetic objects, but is itself wholly eidetic and paradigmatic, and is instantiated in all the intelligences to whom it lends the capacity to think all true Eide – a view of which Aristotle retains the traces in his doctrine of the Active Intelligence – then it is plain why Souls, rather than any other instantial realities, should be indestructible. For what they instantiate is bound up with the existence of all instances whatever, and not merely with some of them.

Socrates-Plato's proof of immortality leads on to an Orphic-Pythagorean apocalypse in which we are told how Er the Pamphylian, killed in battle, was allowed, after a ten days' visit to the world of disembodied souls, to return to his body at the moment when it was about to be burnt on a pyre, and to report to men the rewards and pains of the after-life. The account continues that of the *Phaedo* and was very probably written not long after. But it describes the manner in which the discarnate souls, having taken a path to the right to the heavenly regions on the true earth, or a path to the left to the infernal regions – where their agonies are further described, culminating in the great horror of the bellowing mouth of hell which compelled some souls to return again and again to the same torments – at last returned, after a thousand years, to the meadow from which they had first started on their after-life journey, and from which they were due again to return to incarnate existence on earth. And it describes the choice they there have of earthly lives, some eminent and some obscure, and the infinite danger of choosing amiss among such lives, preferring lower satisfactions, or those of honour and power, to the true good of the Soul, and its everlasting communion with the Absolutely Good. All human life becomes a preparation for that existential moment of choice, so that we shall be able to spurn the shadow for the substance, and see no profit at all in anything that puts a distance between us and the one true source of whatever is beautiful and well-formed and excellent. And, whether or not we make our choices in the manner and situation described in the Dialogue, it is certain, we may say, that we do make such choices, and that their consequences, even if the initial acts and circumstances are trivial, may be in every way immeasurable. We may either make ourselves into trivial marginal detritus in the accomplished significance of the eidetic whole, or into glorious elaborations of standard eidetic possibilities. All this assumes, what Socrates-Plato does not plainly spell out, that instantiation not only springs from the Eide, but also sinks back into, and permanently enriches the latter, so that what has been, after its moment of actual instantiation, becomes part of what eternally is.

The magnificent end of the Dialogue also contains an excursion into astronomy. The souls, journeying to earth from their otherworld meadow, see a light which is both the axis of the universe and also holds it together from without, like the undergirders of a trireme: we are reminded of Dante's account of the love which binds all the substances and accidents and trappings of the world into a single volume. And, as in Dante, one vision yields inconsequently to another which none the less carries the same meaning, so the white light binding the universe together becomes the distaff of Necessity, in whose whorl the orbital spheres of the eight planets are compressed as into a nest of circular boxes, each moving according to its own numerical rhythms, and generating a harmony whose mathematical exactitude far surpasses its sensuous beauty. Here Lachesis, Clotho and Atropos sing as they weave the historical web of instantiation into which the past, present and future of the Souls is inwoven. They sing, presumably, because their hearts are light, and because they know that instantiation, however far it may stray from its eidetic guide-lines, must always return to them in the end. Possibly the distaff of Necessity, with its contained planetary circuits, was some model seen in the lecture-room of Philolaus or Archytas, and now given the incomparable shading and colour of Plato's poetic genius. The *Republic* is in many ways a strange book, certainly not a manual of practical politics, yet one understands as one reaches the end of it how Benjamin Jowett and others were able to make it, for a brief period, the keystone of an education which produced the best government for the greatest number of persons that our confused world has ever witnessed.

VI

THE STOICHEIOLOGICAL DIALOGUES: THE *CRATYLUS*, *THEAETETUS* AND *PARMENIDES*

I

From the Dialogues of Plato's 'middle period', which we have called 'ideological' since the Ideas, the Eide, furnish the main pivot upon which the argument turns, we proceed to another set of Dialogues, presumed to be later in date, which we may call the 'stoicheiological' or 'principial' Dialogues, since their emphasis is not so much on the Eide as on the Elements (στοιχεῖα) or Principles (ἀρχαί) of the same Eide. The Elements or Principles of the Eide are said by Aristotle to have been the One, the Principle of οὐσία, substantial reality, on the one hand, and the Great and Small, or Principle of the Indefinite or Infinite on the other, the former being both a good and an active Principle, and the latter a bad and passive one, and the second being operative in the instantial as well as in the ideal realm (*Physics*, 203a). But the notion of 'Elements' or 'Principles' obviously can be applied further than to the basic dualism underlying the architecture of the ideal realm: it can be applied to all the general features of that architecture, and to what would now be thought of as notions of higher order, which characterize or describe the ideal order as such, and its internal and external relations, without being actually part of its content. Not only the key notions of Goodness and Unity, on the one hand, and Badness and Indefinite Multiplicity, on the other, belong to this chosen band of transcendentals, but also such higher-order notions as those of Being and Beauty (and their excluded opposites), of Sameness and

Otherness, of Likeness and Unlikeness, of unchanging Stability and active Movement, of being absolutely or καθ' αὐτό something, and of being something relatively (πρός τι), including among these last the relations of Participation, Imitation or whatever, which connect sensibles and mathematicals with certain Eide, or certain Eide with one another. Everything that can truly be said *about* Eide, but which, since it is predicated *of* Eide, makes Plato hesitant, though not plainly unwilling, to rank it *among* the Eide which it characterizes, can be put into a slightly stretched version of the class of Principles which Aristotle mentions. (Plato fortunately never says that in talking of such eidetic Principles he is introducing a new class of Principles more archaic than those Principles themselves.) What is very remarkable is, however, that notions antagonistic to the Eide should receive such higher-order treatment at Plato's hands: the Formless and Bad has a status as a Principle as well as the Well-formed and Good, the Moving has a higher-order status as well as the Stable and Resting, the Presence and Self-communication which the Eide have to sensibles has its analogue in the relations that Eide have to other Eide. And the instantial knowledge which particular minds have of the Eide has its eidetic representation in the relation of Knowledge Itself to those same Eide. Plato was of course only dimly conscious of the many difficult type-problems that he was thus uncovering.

Many of these higher-order developments of the ideal theory are more or less adequately documented in such later Dialogues as the *Cratylus,* the *Theaetetus,* the *Sophist* and the *Statesman,* and some of the more technical sides of Plato's all-pervasive mathematicization of the Eide are almost explicitly expounded in the *Parmenides* and the *Philebus.* Some of the unclearness of purport of these later Dialogues is best explained, however, as not merely due to the tension of new ideas breaking through the mould of earlier conceptions, but to internal resistances in the Academy. Plato in his later thought was moving further and further away from any notion of the Eide as things rigorously to be held apart from the instances in which they were actively present, or from the thoughts that envisaged them, and they were becoming less and less isolated atoms of meaning for him, and more and more elements in a pervasive sense-making structure, in which they threw light on one another by their contrast, and even interpenetrated and pervaded one another. We may say that Plato was tending to bring both Parmenidean and Heraclitean notes into his ideal theory, strange as it may seem to couple these tendencies in a single context. On the one hand, the distinct Eide were becoming mere differentiations of superior Principles, which was a move in the direction of Elea, while, on the other hand, the rich inter-mixture of Eide, at one time seen as a sign of the impurity of the instantial realm, was being paralleled in the realm of the Eide, even the forms of Movement and Active Thinking being given a place there, and this plainly was a movement in a Heraclitean direction. None of these thought-tendencies really involved a blurring of the pure content of each Eidos, everlastingly what it is in whatever instance or complex eidetic context it may find itself, but it may very well have appeared dangerous to an Old Guard in the Academy, who having once risen to the pure intrinsicality of the Just Itself, the Equal Itself etc., were loth to see their clear-cut units lost in a larger mosaic, or, worse still, in a continuum or fluxion of ideal points of distinction. Who this Old Guard were we need not here determine: they are plainly referred to and criticized as the Friends of the Eide in the *Sophist*, 248a–249a.

But plainly there was also an Academic party who tended more and more to think of the Eide as only present in their mathe-matical, or, going further, sensible instances, and so indissolubly wedded to the Principle of Multiplicity. These last are arguably the Giants, the materialists mentioned in the *Sophist*, who are described as maintaining that what they cannot squeeze in their hands, for example the Justice or Wisdom present in virtuous souls, is just nothing at all (*Sophist*, 247c). One would not need to be very materialistic to qualify as a materialist in the Academy, and it is quite arguable, though of course not at all certain, that Aristotle was a member of this wing. Certainly, however, the members of this wing were the authors of the 'Third Man' and other ingenious arguments destructive of belief in the prime reality of the Eide, which arguments had become so familiar that their mere name sufficed to call them to mind. And Plato may very well be imagined to have occupied a middle place among all these acute-minded, logically precise younger men, at times investing himself, with a somewhat tired tolerance, in the mantle of Parmenides, at other times verging towards the flux-doctrine of

Heraclitus, which to many of them must have been anathema. It is only on some such hypothesis that we can explain the tenor of Plato's 'stoicheiological' Dialogues. They point beyond the Eide to Principles more fundamental than they, and they do so in the face of a varied opposition of those who either wished to return to an older, pluralistic idealism, or to revise it quite radically in various ways, and to do so in either case with a faith in exact argument which was quite alien to a man of insight like Plato, who could make brilliant use of exact argument when he chose, but who knew that it was never stronger than its premises or its working conceptions.

The *Cratylus* is an important Dialogue which carries to the limit the view that linguistic rules and distinctions are not the foundation for the connections and distinctions among the things referred to by language, but rather follow the latter, and that it is our insight into the natures of things and the connections among such natures that determine the establishment of linguistic conventions, and not vice versa. Not only the weaving together of linguistic expressions runs parallel to the ways in which really existent items are woven together, but there is an inherent appropriateness of certain primitive features or elements in language to certain features of reality, so that the one may be said to be *truly* representative of the latter. The Dialogue further suggests that an immense number of variations in the stream of speech mirror corresponding variations in the stream of real Becoming: there is a philosophy of flux built into our language that corresponds to the pervasive mutability of instantial being. But it also stresses that there are Eleatic aspirations in our language, and that, without the ability to construct a system of stable meanings in which to capture the very flux that we are trying to talk about, discourse and understanding will alike be impossible. This immutable aspect of language depends, of course, on the Eide and their immutable relations.

The Dialogue begins with the statement by one Hermogenes, the brother of Callias the host of sophists, of the view of Cratylus the Heraclitean that 'the correctness of names has its natural roots in each thing that is, and that a name is not something which some men agree to use as appellation, letting forth some inflexion of voice, but that there is a certain natural rightness in names, that is the same for all Greeks and all barbarians' (383a, b). This view does not recommend itself to Hermogenes who cannot believe that there is any other correctness to names beyond convention and agreement: whatever name anyone gives to anything is *ipso facto* a correct one. Names do not rest on nature, but on rule or prescription. Socrates resists this opinion by arguing that a complete saying (λόγος) can be true or false, and that a true saying declares things that are, and that this can only be the case if its smallest parts are as true as it is, and correspond to things that have a certain stability of being (386a). To accept complete conventionalism in regard to ultimate names is to side with Protagoras, and to make truth a matter of what seems so to each, so that no man can rightly be said to be wiser than another (386c). But if we admit that things have their own firm being and nature, not dragged hither and yon by our private fancies, then we must admit that to this firm natural being and its differences there will correspond names that declare them suitably. Things have to be named conformably to their natures and not as we choose, and the giving of the right names to things must therefore be the role, not of every man, but of a specially insightful, name-giving legislator. Such a legislator must look towards what we may call the eidetic name of each nameable thing (βλέποντα πρὸς αὐτὸ ἐκεῖνο ὃ ἔστιν ὄνομα). This eidetic name, or Name as Such, will not necessarily be instantiated in exactly like syllables in different languages, any more than an instrument of use is necessarily made of the same materials in exactly the same way, but it will necessarily have the same function and will declare the same ontological elements or features (389d, e). Socrates is not therefore arguing absurdly that a name like ἄνθρωπος is the one true name of Man as Such, but only that *any* name that picks out the same genuine Eidos, and that has vocal inflexions which vaguely mirror the Eidos's make-up or general content, is an instance of the True Name of that Eidos.

The Dialogue now passes on to an immense number of fanciful etymologies in which the suitability of certain names to the things they name is shown by showing their affinity – often only clear when certain additions, subtractions or other twists have been made – to certain other more primitive names or combinations of names, the ultimate names being left unexplained for the moment, or attributed to some godlike or non-Hellenic legislator. By 'names' Socrates covers adjectival and verbal as well as concretely nominal expressions. The theory is really a theory of all expressions short of complete sentences, and it covers logical expressions like 'being' as well as more concrete expressions, and it roams more or less systematically over the linguistic regions of theology, physics, psychology, epistemology and ethics. Everywhere Socrates discovers a Heraclitean tendency in the name-giving acts of the primitive legislators, but this Heraclitean tendency is everywhere balanced by an Eleatic tendency towards the stationary which is held to be more basic philosophically.

It is impossible to give more than a selection from the inconsequent, somewhat tediously prolonged etymologies with which Socrates sports. The gods or θεοί are so called, because their most obvious cases, the heavenly bodies, are always 'on the run' (θέοντα), a Heraclitean touch, the daemons are so called on account of being δαήμονες or very understanding, the heroes (ἥρωες) are love-children (from ἔρως, love) of gods and men, or alternatively are good speakers and questioners (from εἴρειν, ἐρωτᾶν), while a *man* (ἄνθρωπος) is held to be one who looks up (ἀναθῶν) to what he sees (ἃ ὄπωπε), a primitive exercise in existentialism. The Hearth-goddess Hestia is held to be identical with ἐσσία, an old form of οὐσία or being, which by a further transformation becomes ὠσία, the principle of pushing (ὤθειν), an identification which again suggests Heracliteanism and looks forward to the characterization of being as power (δύναμις) in the *Sophist*. Likewise Heraclitean is the name of Rhea, the following principle, from ῥεῖν, to flow, and 'Cronus', 'Ocean' and 'Tethys' have similar connections with flux. The name Selene, the moon, can be expanded into Selainoneoaeia which can be taken to mean 'what always has new and old light' (409e), and which can then be interpreted as hinting at Anaxagoras's view that the moon borrows its light from the sun. Epistemological terms again are given almost Bergsonian meanings connected with the Heraclitean flux: Wisdom (φρόνησις) is a noesis of φορά and ῥοῦς, streaming motion; insight (γνώμη) is consideration (νώμη) of generation (γονή), while another name of wisdom, σοφία, indicates for various dark reasons an even darker connection with the reality of flux. The good (ἀγαθόν) is unplatonically interpreted as what is admirable (ἀγαστόν) in speed, while bravery (ἀνδρεία) obviously means upstream motion (ἡ ἄνω ῥοή). When Hermogenes protests against the sheer lack of principle or

scruple in all these derivations, Socrates pleads that any penetration to the original form of names must involve the difficult
undoing of all the attrition and complication and euphonic
elaboration that words have undergone in the lapse of time (414e).
Sometimes all his ingenuity fails him, and the obscure origins of
a word like κακόν (bad) are relegated to the speech-efforts of
pre-Hellenic barbarians.

The explanation of names by other names which has hitherto
been attempted must, however, end up by revealing names which
do not permit of such explanation, which are elementary and
primitive. On what principles shall we successfully attribute
correctness to such primitive names? The answer which at first
suggests itself is that a name must be a vocal likeness of the thing
it names (423b), a theory which has as a consequence that those
who imitate the bleating of sheep or the crowing of cocks are
naming the animals in question. Plainly names are not likenesses
of the *sensuous* qualities of things, otherwise they would fall
within the province of the musician or the poet: what they must
be likenesses of is the οὐσία, the substance or essence or being of
each thing (423e), they must, it would appear, imitate the eidetic
style of what they name. And the imitation of total expressions
must be dependent on the more basic imitation of syllables and
letters, which resemble the pigments which a painter has on his
palette, and which he mixes to form the represented colours of
objects. It seems ridiculous, Socrates admits, that the being of
things should be mirrored in our syllables and our letters, but such
is necessary if we are not to refer everything to quite mysterious
sources such as the barbarians or the Gods, and if our derivative
explanations are not to be without an absolute foundation
(426a, b).

Socrates then advances various confessedly 'way-out' suggestions as to how primitive names may be linked to unanalysable
aspects of being. Movement, variability is the basic characteristic
of instantial particularity, and the sound of the letter *rho* (ῥ, r), in
whose utterance the tongue vibrates most rapidly, is naturally
fitted to express the flow and rush of things. Socrates instances
verbs such as τρέχειν (run), κρούειν (strike), θρύπτειν (break), in
whose case, we may observe, English equivalents often oblige by
using the same semi-vowel as the Greek. The ee-sound of the
Greek iota is said to have a peculiar fitness to express the subtle

essences which most readily penetrate everything (426e), while the l-sound of the Greek lambda is intrinsically expressive of smooth motion, and, by the addition of a gamma as, for example in γλισχρός, becomes arrested into the sticky. Consonantal stops such as delta (δ, d) and tau (τ, t) are likewise intrinsically geared to the expression of arrest and stationariness. It is not necessary to pursue these onomatopoeic fancies further. Plato has slipped back from his previous understanding that it is not the sensuous make-up of the spoken noise which can lend it its significance, but the typical intention or use which lies behind it. We cannot, however, blame Plato for not rising to the subtleties of Husserl and Wittgenstein.

Plato sees, however, that if resemblance is made the sole criterion of the suitability of a name, then the best names will be exact replicas of the things named (432d). The further conclusion is not drawn that on this view the best name of anything would be the thing itself. These tempering reflections lead, however, to some slight concessions to custom (ἔθος) and convention (συνθήκη) as having a part to play in the use of names. Letters, for example, that do not resemble anything in things named can be incorporated in names provided we have made an agreement thus to include them, and provided it would be impossible to find exact resemblances of the things named (for example in the case of very large numbers).

From these concessions to conventionalism Socrates however reverts to a firmer realism. The legislators who prescribe the primitive names should also be guided by a true and consistent ontology, and for them the discovery of things and names should go hand in hand, the essentially similar always falling under the same art or science (435e). We have reason, however, to think that the first prescribers of names were not guided by such a true and consistent ontology: their inconsistency is shown by the fact that the same names which can be justified by a Heraclitean flux-philosophy, can also be justified by an Eleatic doctrine of unchangeables. Thus the word ἐπιστήμη, Knowledge, interpreted as a following (ἔπεσθαι) of the movement of things (412a), also permits interpretation as a stopping or standing still (στῆναι) of the soul in the presence of things (437a). The best explanation of the contradictory tendencies of ordinary language is that the first imposers of names were in part the victims of a false ontology, a belief in the reality of universal flux and process, and that, whirled round in a vortex themselves, they tried to drag us into it (439c). We have, however, plainly the power to investigate things by themselves (τὰ πράγματα δι' αὐτῶν) without the assistance of names, and it is only because we possess this capacity that we can see whether the names have been suitably given. Using this capacity, we see at once that there is a Beautiful Itself and a Good Itself and so on in the case of each other essence, and that it does not make sense to suppose that these eternal natures are ever other than they are, or are ever intrinsically in flux or capable of departing from their own Idea. If they were, one could never have knowledge of them, nor knowledge of anything as exemplifying them. There must, moreover, also be an Eidos of Knowledge, which is as unchangeable as the things that can be known: only on this assumption can there be instantial knowers in the flux-realm and things instantially known. (This is the only way in which I can interpret 440a, b, which concedes the existence both of an Eidos of Knowledge, and of something *else*, i.e. instantial knowledge, which it renders possible.) Whatever the deliverances of such eidetic insight may be, it is plain that we must bow to it, and not hand ourselves over to the power of established names, and to the perhaps false and inconsistent ontology which those names embody.

The *Cratylus* may therefore be regarded as an early and not wholly successful criticism of conventionalism, which, however, is cogent on its main points: that insight into natures or meanings and their relations pre-exists and conditions the actual use of names and linguistic expressions, and that a false and inconsistent ontology may very well be part and parcel of ordinary usage. It rejects the basic premiss of the Wittgensteinian theory of language: that there is no understanding or percipient grasp of ideal natures prior to the use of linguistic expressions. Platonism further involves a thoroughgoing revision of our ordinary ontology: instead of regarding ideal characters or natures as mere appendages of instantial concreta, it regards instantial concreta as mere appendages of ideal characters or natures. All this reversal of ontology demands, however, a total revision of language: we must cease to speak as if there were things other than the Eide, since the Eide have now become the only true things, all else being no more than a qualification of them. Those who have rejected Platonism have generally been those who have never been fully willing to adopt its language. That this language was imperfectly elaborated and operated at many points by Plato in part excuses this unwillingness.

II

The *Theaetetus* is a Dialogue in many ways similar to the *Cratylus*, and was conceivably set down, in part at least, at about much the same time. There are the same preoccupations with flux and Protagoras and subjectivism in both, and in both too there are meditations upon ultimate elements and our apprehension of them. The *Theaetetus*, however, also has an interest in the pervasive notions of Sameness, Difference etc. which cover the general ordering of the realm of Eide rather than any specific Eidos in it. As such, it expresses the stoicheiological orientation of Plato's later writings, which the *Parmenides*, *Sophist* and *Philebus* carry further. But its curious admixture of vivid Socraticism assimilates it to the earlier Dialogues, and very possibly there were distinct layers in its composition.

The *Theaetetus* has a prologue, possibly written long after the main Dialogue, in which the speakers are Eucleides and Terpsion, the philosophers of Megara with whom Plato stayed after the death of Socrates, and from whom he must have derived his increasing tendency to stress the identity of Goodness with Unity, and the dependence of all the Eide on this supreme Principle. It also, through them, connects the main Dialogue which follows, cast in the past before the death of Socrates, and involving Socrates and Theaetetus, with the recent death of Theaetetus, which probably took place in 369 B.C., not long before Aristotle joined the Academy. Theodorus of Cyrene, one of the great mathematicians of the Academy, and a supporter of Protagoras in his early days, also takes part in the main Dialogue, and thereby brings out the brilliant mathematical gifts of the young Theaetetus, who was at a later date to advance the theory of Irrationals and of Regular Solids in the Academy. The Dialogue also mentions a meeting of Socrates with Parmenides, and is for this reason held to have been written *after* the Dialogue *Parmenides*, which paints the picture of such a meeting. It would appear not impossible, however, that this meeting was a piece of history, responsible for Socrates's friendly relations with the Megarians, though the superstructure built on this meeting in the Dialogue *Parmenides* is entirely Platonic. Certainly there is a deep gulf between the *Theaetetus* and the *Parmenides*, and if this does not prove that the former was written before the latter, it does justify us in treating it first.

In the main Dialogue Theodorus first describes the brilliant mind of Theaetetus as running effortlessly like 'a stream of oil' through the most complex and obscure investigations, a description which enables Socrates to inveigle him into a perfectly conducted Socratic enquiry into the nature of Knowledge ($\grave{\epsilon}\pi\iota\sigma\tau\acute{\eta}\mu\eta$). Knowledge is at first identified by Theaetetus, in customary fashion, with the whole round of geometry, cobbling and other arts and sciences, until Socrates shows that these are each merely a knowledge of this or that, which cannot be understood until we know what Knowledge Itself may be. We must know this as we know that clay, to whatever uses it may be put, is in all cases earth mixed up with moisture. Theaetetus shows that he understands what is wanted by providing a brilliant account of the difference between rational and irrational magnitudes, the former being the roots of such Natural numbers as are factorizable in terms of a single natural Number and therefore said to be square, cubic Numbers etc., whereas the latter are the geometrically real roots of natural numbers which are *not* factorizable in terms of one single natural number, and which are therefore to be called 'oblong' or corresponding solid numbers. Thus the square root of the natural number 15, the product of the natural numbers 1 and 15, or 3 and 5, and no others, is an irrational magnitude, not commensurable with these Numbers, since 15 is not a square but an oblong number (147d–148a). If such be the sort of reasoning on which Theaetetus founded his remarkable definition, he had indeed much mathematical and logical acumen. He displays above all the capacity exhaustively to divide the whole territory of being into separate segments on one single pervasive principle, the ability distinctive of the dialectician above all others. In philosophy, however, he is unable to effect such an organization of the total field, and Socrates has to egg him on with the perhaps historically authentic comparison of himself, Socrates, to a man-midwife, barren himself of ideas but able to bring the ideas of others to birth, and to test them for validity or invalidity. He does not say that the effect of his midwifery will be to suppress as invalid and drive from the mind all positive characterizations whatsoever. Theaetetus, however, is unfamiliar with Socrates and his manifold ruses, and is simple enough to identify Knowledge with αἴσθησις, direct sensing or feeling or experience or unreflective judgment, the sort of cognition in which we seem up against the very thing itself. This enables Socrates, now plainly Socrates-Plato, to embark on a long refutation of a type of epistemology which he connects with Heraclitus and Protagoras, but which is plainly a philosophical Eidos rather than an historical instance.

In this philosophical Eidos everything is related to the individual man as a standard: a thing is what it is, not absolutely nor by itself, but for a particular man in a particular state. A wind is cold to a shivery man, which does not prevent it from being not cold to one who is not shivery, or to the same man when he ceases to shiver (152b). The true being of things is accordingly in a perpetual flux: nothing is anything in isolation but only in the endless, changing intermixture (κρᾶσις) of one thing with another (152d). This view is elaborated in the conception, far too subtle for the historical Protagoras, that the qualities of sense are all generated in the commerce of sense-organ with some external motion: the eye, acted on by a sort of external motion, becomes momentarily white-perceptive, and the object momentarily white, which does not prevent other types of eye being otherwise affected, and what we call the same man otherwise affected at different times (153e–154a). Such relativity of being is met with even in the mathematical world of numbers and measures, where 6 can be greater than 4 by a third, and at the same time less than 12 by a half, while Socrates may in one year be taller than Theaetetus, and in the next year, without change in himself, less tall than Theaetetus. The thesis we are considering makes such relativity universal: nothing is anything by itself, but is always anything for or to something. Being, if meant stably and non-relatively, must simply be expunged from our speech, together with all designations that imply stability and non-relativity, even though custom and ignorance may render this very difficult (157a, b). We must therefore never talk in terms of persistent agents or patients such as Socrates or this wine, but only in terms of innumerable independent agents and patients involved in innumerable independent interactions, none of which justify an inference from one to the other. The Heraclitean flux and the Protagorean subjectivism are therefore shown to be one and the same. We may note with interest Socrates-Plato's analysis of a being the case which is essentially relative: the whole theory of Plato amounts to holding that there are quasi-things, the particulars of sense, which are nothing absolutely, but only as embodying or reflecting natures which absolutely are. It is not such relativity of being that is rejected as absurd – as it would be by many contemporary thinkers – but the project of universalizing it, of working solely with relativities which do not point to absolutes of some sort, in contrast with which they are merely relative.

The first criticism of experiential relativism is an *argumentum ad hominem*: what right has Protagoras to pretend to discern anything better than anyone else, and to exact large fees for his instruction? If his own view is correct (as it is undoubtedly correct for him) why should anyone else prefer it to *his* own view, or why should Protagoras expect him to do so (161c–e)? It is also refuted by the argument that it clashes with our view that there is such a thing as memory-knowledge: if a man has seen and has thereby known something, and now ceases to see it, but only remembers it, we shall have to say that he has ceased to know what he saw, even though he perfectly remembers seeing it (164). These arguments are, however, acknowledged by Socrates to be trivial and eristic: we must treat relativism as regards truth and being with more seriousness, and this Socrates does by putting an imaginary defence in the mouth of Protagoras, which retains relativism while contending that a sophist like Protagoras may have something to teach us. For a sophist is not someone who can give men or societies a truer view of being – this is impossible since being is wholly relative to the passing perceptions and discriminations of individual persons – but he is certainly someone who can give men a better and more healthy and more expedient view of what is the case, and one in which things which appear and are good take the place of things which appear and are bad (166d–167c). Protagoras is not, be it noted, represented as arguing that he is able to change men's view of what they are experiencing from bad to good, for example learn to see toothache as delightful, but that he is able, by his persuasion, to make men change their experience from what seems and is bad to them, for example one of social disorder, to what seems and is good to them, i.e. one of social order. The defence has, however, merely shifted the ground from being and truth to value and expediency, and Socrates has no difficulty in showing that what *is* expedient is in this defence rightly taken to be other than what seems expedient to someone at a given time, and that this acceptance of a true or real expediency is as much a violation of the relativistic thesis as the acceptance of absolute truths of being. For the expedient is not concerned with the time at which we seem to discern it, but with a time to come, and whether or not something which seems expedient *is* expedient will be decided, not in the present, but the future. Just as memory points back for its justification to past experience, so the judgment of expediency points forward to future experience, and of such future experience not everyone is an equally good judge. There may, for example, be legislative experts who are better judges of the expediency of certain proposed laws and regulations than those who pass them or persuade others to pass them. If Protagorean relativism is correct, all this looking to the future and trusting those who can anticipate it goes by the board: we have no reason to prefer any expert opinion to our own.

The previous *argumentum ad hominem* is further strengthened by pointing out that, while Protagoras may think himself a wiser counsellor than others in all matters, other men do not take such a view of themselves. They believe that, while they are better judges in some matters, others are better than they are in certain other matters, and so have recourse to these latter in unpropitious situations (170a). On the view of Protagoras, the perceptions of such men are not therefore the measures of truth and being for them, and since such men are a majority, and since Protagorean relativism should see superiority, if anywhere, in majority – the argument seems quite feeble – then Protagoras too should admit that he himself is not the measure of truth and being even for himself (171e). The refutation of Protagoras is rounded off by a magnificent digression justifying the true philosopher, who may not be a success when persuasion is bandied in the law-courts, but who becomes an expert when Justice and Injustice Themselves are in question, and how they differ from all other things and from one another (175c). Such a true philosopher may seem infinitely inferior to political and legal advocates when petty affairs are in question, but he comes into his own when matters of principle are raised, and for him the great issue is not to avoid trivial disadvantages, but to rise above the evils inseparable from instantial being, and to assimilate himself, as far as may be, to the God who embodies Justice supremely (176b, c). By this God he plainly means the Goodness Itself which the justice of men merely exemplifies.

Socrates-Plato then proves generally that the Protagorean relativism cannot be extended to cover general natures and significant contents or our apprehension of the same, for, if it is so extended, all statements become confounded in a common non-significance. For if things and what things are, are everywhere totally in flux, we both can, and cannot say that anything is thus and not thus, or even that it is becoming thus and not thus, and we shall need a new language altogether, if there can indeed be such a language, to embody this total permissiveness which is just as much total prohibition (183a–c). The defects of such a relativistic flux-doctrine point in the direction of Parmenides, whom Socrates met and admired in youth, but whose splendidly deep philosophy of unmoving Unity would too much complicate the investigation of Knowledge that they are undertaking now. One thing, however, is clear: that there is more to knowing than the use of the senses which is the most obvious case of what is covered by the word αἴσθησις. For the Soul can take cognizance of things *common* to the various senses, the Being of both colours and sounds, the Sameness of each with each, and the Difference of each from the others, the Numbers which they severally or jointly instantiate, and the Likenesses and Unlikenesses that they may have to one another (185a, b). These common matters would not appear to be revealed to the sense-organs, nor to some special organ, but rather to the Soul itself and by itself (185d). The Beautiful and Ugly, the Good and the Bad, fall into the same non-sensuous group, all of which are discerned, not by the immediate use of the senses, but after long effort and much training. It would appear then that, however much Knowledge, taken in a wide sense, may have to do with what we perceive by the senses, it must also necessarily range beyond what the senses offer. It must see such offerings in the logico-mathematical framework of all being, if it is to be able to say anything about them. The specific Eide are not, in this context, mentioned, but it is plain that they are involved in the stable meanings which enable us to identify this or that on numerous occasions, or to say that it has passed from being thus to being thus. The Protagorean-Heraclitean account of the sense-qualities is, we know from Aristotle, Plato's own view of them. We can, he believes further, only rise to rational assurance even about the instantial sphere as we pass beyond the vanishing, inconsequent shows of the senses to natures that do not vanish and are rationally connected. That these are of the nature of Numbers and numerical Ratios is not stated in this painfully exoteric Dialogue, but a reading of comparable passages in the *De Anima* (Book III, para. 2), at countless points close to Platonism, will show that this is so.

The Dialogue now takes an eristic turn, and enters into a confused and confusing discussion of various obviously unsatisfactory definitions of Knowledge. The first is that Knowledge is simply True Opinion, a definition that was shown up as inadequate as far back as the *Meno*, and that immediately sidetracks the discussion into a treatment of the sophistical problem: How is false opinion possible? False Opinion would seem to involve the identification of an entity with which one is acquainted with some other entity with which one also is acquainted, which seems impossible, or the identification of an entity with which one is not acquainted with another entity with which one is not acquainted, which is even more impossible, or the identification of an entity with which one is acquainted with one with which one is not acquainted, which is likewise impossible. It also seems the case that, whether we think something about ($\pi\epsilon\rho\acute{\iota}$) something or think of something by itself ($\alpha\mathring{\upsilon}\tau\grave{o}$ $\kappa\alpha\theta$' $\alpha\mathring{\upsilon}\tau\acute{o}$), we are in either case thinking one definite unified content ($\mathring{\epsilon}\nu$ $\tau\iota$) which is something and not nothing, and which therefore has the being which should make our opinion true and not false (189a, b). This straightforward recognition of what would now be called 'purely intentional objectivity' is then watered down by the suggestion, often to be revived in philosophy, that false belief is never of singles, only of a number of entities, and consists always in taking something for something else, for example mistaking the Ugly for the Beautiful, or Theaetetus for Theodorus. The soul, it is argued, even when not talking aloud, converses silently with itself, and this silent speech is always an identification of something with something, it being taken for granted that what we would now call 'predication' is some sort of weakened form of identification. But the notion of a misidentification of, for example, being two with being one, or being an ox with being a man, remains inconceivable (190c), and it is only by imagining that, beside the present clear impression of something, we also have a vague memory-imprint of it left by former impressions, that we can explain how we can fit a present clear impression into the wrong memory-imprint and so achieve a misidentification, taking Theaetetus for Theodorus of whom we have only memories, or taking the Ugly which we see instantiated before us for the Beautiful of which we have only a notion.

This type of explanation, while very satisfactory if applied to instances, is however unsatisfactory if applied to the misidentification of notions. Yet such misidentification occurs; a man who miscalculates may misidentify the number 11 with the sum of the numbers 7 and 5, and yet here we are dealing with pure notions, direct confrontations with essences, and not with vague memories fitted to clear notions (196a, c). The explanation is bettered by supposing that we do indeed have something which corresponds to vague memory in the case of notions: in addition to the actual *having* (ἔχειν) of knowledge, we have something vaguer, which may be called the possession (κεκτῆσθαι) of such knowledge, which amounts more or less to the power to have it whenever we want. As a man who has imprisoned birds in an aviary, does not always actually hold them, but can do so when he cares to, so a man who possesses knowledge can raise such possession to knowledge actually had (197c, d). Such mere possession may, however, give rise to mistaken catches, and a man may catch hold of the number 11 when the number 12 is really what he wants. Socrates points out, however, that such miscatching is inexplicable if the man really possesses knowledge of anything, and equally inexplicable if, following a suggestion of Theaetetus, we imagine that there are non-knowledges as well as knowledges in the possession of the soul, and that one may be miscaught in place of the other. The whole suggestion would lead to an infinite regress, as there would have to be knowledges and non-knowledges of knowledges and non-knowledges without end, and the whole discussion is, moreover, futile, since there obviously is more to Knowledge than True Opinion, there being many cases where men are truly persuaded of something, for example by good lawyers, which they have never witnessed and of which they can therefore not have knowledge (201a–c).

The whole discussion is indeed futile, since it fails to break Knowledge into the species distinguished in the *Republic*, and since it confuses the so-called instances of Knowing which all have possibilities of error built into them with Knowledge as Such, the eternal Eidos of adequate apprehension of what absolutely is, which Plato increasingly saw (e.g. *Parmenides*, 134d, e) that no mere instance of Life and Thought could perfectly rise to. Not only can there be no instances of Knowledge of the imprecise vanishing instances of Eide around us, but there can be no perfect instantial knowledge of the Eide themselves: we can only see them imperfectly, struggle to revive our pre-instantial grasp of them, at most momentarily lay hold of them. Error in regard to the Eide is therefore as much written into our apprehension of them as it is written into our apprehension of the things of sense. It can hope, at best, to be *less* erroneous than the latter, since in the former case the object itself is not shifting, nor as such incapable of notional capture, whereas in the case of the things of sense both apprehension and object are congenitally in flux.

From Knowledge as True Opinion Theaetetus proceeds to the historical Socratic view of Knowledge as True Opinion plus a definitory λόγος. If we were in possession of the full account of what it is to be beautiful, we should never be in error as to the beauty of anything, nor should we misidentify being beautiful with being convenient etc., as often happens in Dialectic. This Socratic formulation had been made hard to hold by the careful analysts and exact reasoners in the Academy, who argued that this view of knowledge involved the curious consequence that there must be ultimate elements of knowable things that are quite beyond knowledge. They are involved in the analysis of explanation of other natures, but of themselves, as ultimate natures, there is no such analysis possible. We know things through them, but we cannot know them themselves. Even to predicate Being of them, or to identify them as this or that, is to go beyond their intrinsic content, which is essentially beyond reason and knowledge, though accessible to direct perception (αἴσθησις;

201e–202c). Ultimate meanings such as those of Unity, Being, Difference, Sameness, Movement etc. are probably in this supra-epistemic category, and the opinion is quite in harmony with what Plato says in several contexts. There is, however, Socrates points out, some difficulty in denying that there can be knowledge of the ultimate elements or Stoicheia of things. For it is paradoxical to maintain that one can know something about a number of things taken together if one has no knowledge of any of them singly (203d). The whole which things form can, on reflection, be nothing but the elements in the totality of their relations, and, if we know something about the whole, we *ipso facto* know something about all the parts. Or if, alternatively, the whole is something new and simple which supervenes upon the related parts, then it too will be an element, and unknowable as the elements of which it is held to consist. The drift of the whole argument is to discredit the strict separation of elements from complex unities which we may imagine the exact young reasoners of the Academy to have pressed for. Socrates-Plato implies, we may suggest, that the ultimate and unutterable is none the less that without which the derivative and utterable would not be utterable at all, and that it therefore, in a manner, shares in the utterability of the latter, just as the latter after a fashion shades into the unutterability of the former. The Idea of Good, for example, is and is not an Idea. Those who try to talk very lucidly about it and those who adopt a strict policy of mystical silence, are alike mistaken. All talk is only relatively clear and relieves itself from a background of hinting reserve.

The Dialogue ends in the conventional Socratic manner, with a failure of definition. Knowledge may be True Opinion justified by a λόγος or Account, but this Account cannot merely be a putting of the True Opinion into words, nor a mere enumeration of the ultimate elements of what it talks about, nor a mere specification of its differentiating features, since all these can be accidentally correct and so not cases of Knowledge, and since it is hard to see how one can be talking of anything definite if one does not know the analysis or the differentia of what one is speaking of. The eristic quality of the whole latter part of the Dialogue is very disheartening: one seems back among the self-refuting exactitudes of the early Socratic Dialogues. It seems a plausible hypothesis to ascribe these re-crudescent exactitudes, either to some old piece of writing 'revamped' for a special occasion, or to the influence of some of the younger men, very possibly Speusippus and Aristotle, who promoted such argument in the Platonic assemblies, to which Plato, the man with long experience of such Dialectic, gave a distantly sympathetic, but increasingly disaffected response.

III

The *Parmenides*, to which we now turn, is the most important and philosophically revealing of all Plato's writings. In it Plato, who has identified himself with Socrates in all the previous mature Dialogues, finds a new *persona* for his utterances in the Eleatic philosopher of the One and the Unchangeable, Parmenides. At the same time Socrates appears as the defender of the earlier Ideology or Eidos-theory, while Plato-Parmenides becomes the exponent of a new Stoicheiology, a doctrine of the Elements or Principles which lie behind and are generative of the Eide. The occasion of a perhaps historical encounter of the young Socrates with Zeno and Parmenides, casually mentioned in the *Theaetetus* and fitting in with the date 450 B.C. – it is a matter of absolutely no interest whether there was such an encounter or not – is now used as the setting of a Dialogue which certainly did not occur, but which undoubtedly mirrors controversies in the Academy at about the time when Aristotle first joined it. At that time there were those who were content with the old notion of the Eide as pure paradigms of character and good form, having none of the irrelevant interwovenness with things and happenings and one another that they have in their instances, and as free from all that contrariety of aspect which those instances constantly exhibit. They would have accepted the general identification of these Eide with Numbers, which the *Republic* consistently adumbrates, and they may have accepted their derivation from Principles more ultimate, but they none the less saw in them firm bases rather than shaky underpinnings of discussion, and things explanatory rather than requiring explanation. Now, however, a new band of critics of the Ideology had grown up in the Academy, young men who saw in it a nest of problems rather than a set of illuminating solutions, who doubted whether the postulation of Eide was justified, who found difficulty in the relation of Eide to their instances, who doubted whether things so transcendent could be either knowable or theoretically helpful. To this band of critics Aristotle may not have belonged at the time of his entry into the Academy, but there is no reason to question the old tradition that he did in the end belong to it: the fact that, as late as 354, he wrote a school-exercise imitative of the *Phaedo* on the occasion of the death of his colleague Eudemus, does not prove that his mind failed to react to the criticisms of the Eide which must have been all around him when he entered the Academy, and which he rehearses in so routine a fashion in the *Metaphysics*. It is, in fact, amusing to conjecture that the Aristoteles mentioned in the Dialogue, and said to have been one of the Thirty Tyrants, was given that name to suggest the presence of Aristotle in the discussion, a reference that perhaps so offended Aristotle that he never afterwards referred to the Dialogue.

Be that as it may, the reply of Plato to his young critics was immense and characteristic: in the person of Parmenides he propounded the new difficulties and recognized their extremely thorny character. But he then went on to show that all the problems in the relations of Eide to their instances were repeated in the relations of Eide to one another and to the First Principles in terms of which the Eide were to be understood. And he developed the exhibition of difficulties into a vast dialectical exercise which flailed out in all directions and which was as destructive of the assumptions of the critics of the Eide as of those who accepted them. This magnificent exercise, with its two basic hypotheses, each seen in two distinct, equally fundamental lights, and each worked out along two lines of relevance, and so yielding eight packed parcels of argument, may contain quite a number of fallacies, but on the whole it shows, what the *Republic* only put forward as a programme, how the vast range of the Eide must be thought of as logically 'flowing', in ordered fashion, from a basic First Principle or Principles beyond them, and how these basic Principles must be conceived of as standing to one another. And it comes closer to suggesting the *mathematical* manner in which this derivation of the Eide from their Principles was conceived as taking place than any other Dialogue bar the *Philebus*. And the Dialogue suggests, though it does not work it out, that the same techniques which explain the Eide in terms of their Principles, will explain the realm of instances in terms of the Eide, that the latter will in fact repeat the fecund oneness-in-manyness characteristic of the former at a lower level. The effect of these arguments is, we may suggest, to turn criticisms into confirmations, and objections into positive reasons for acceptance. All we have said is, however, by way of preliminary orientation in the interpretation of a document where all statements are in the last degree controversial.

The main Dialogue, in which Socrates, Parmenides, Zeno and Aristoteles are the speakers, is reported by one Cephalus of Clazomenae as having been written down by Antiphon, Plato's brother, from accounts furnished by Pythodorus, a pupil of Zeno, who heard the original discussion in the middle of the previous century, a set of complications perhaps indicating the flatly unhistorical character of the reported discussion. Zeno has been reading a set of arguments against the possibility of there being a plurality of things, with which he intends to buttress the arguments of Parmenides for the Unity of Being, showing that many more ridiculous and self-contradictory consequences flow from the postulation of such pluralism than have been held to flow from the Parmenidean monism (128d). If there are a plurality of entities, Zeno has argued, they must be both like and unlike, which is impossible: possibly the argument ran that the 'many alike' of sheer numerical difference is a distinction without a difference (127d, e). Socrates advances the Platonic plea, used in the *Phaedo, Republic* and elsewhere, that there is nothing absurd in the meeting of contraries *in an instance*: this is in fact one of the things which distinguishes being an instance from being an Eidos. What would be absurd would be if the Eide themselves were to sustain such contrariety of predication, if it were to be possible for both Likeness and Unlikeness, Multitude and Unity, Motion and Rest etc. to nest in one another or in the same Eidos just as they do in sensible things (129b, e; 130a). Parmenides-Plato is, however, about to show that just such a marriage of contraries is to be found among essences as such as among the instances of those essences, and that, in the case of the essences, it is moreover a marriage of necessity and not of chance: the whole Second Part of the Dialogue will enforce that message. For the time being, however, he is content to enquire into the relatively unreflective view of the Eide that obtained in the early Academy, and to raise those objections against this that had been made familiar by later criticism.

Socrates, Parmenides-Plato says, believes simply that Eide, Essences, exist *apart* (χωρὶς) from the instances that share in them. Likeness, just mentioned, is of their number, and so are the Just, the Beautiful and all such natures, each taken itself by itself (αὐτὸ καθ' αὐτό). Does he also believe in such separate being for the essences of Man, Fire and Water, which seem more highly concrete and closer to sensible nature, and to which Plato himself was more and more coming to give a high place among the Eide (*Metaphysics*, 1070a)? Socrates, representing the earlier, highly generic interests of the ideal theory, replies that he is uncertain on this point (130c), and he is even more hesitant to accord any ideal essentiality to ignoble things such as hair, mud and dirt: these he argues are just as we see them to be and it would be grotesque to suspect them of embodying something ideal (130d). Parmenides-Plato remarks sagely that a philosopher should not defer so much to human prejudice nor despise what is merely *thought* mean (130e): the implication is that even the meanest possibility has a place in the eidetic order, even if only as representing an impoverishment or an aberration from its central points of paradigm. How would Socrates, however, conceive that things share in (μεταλαμβάνειν) the Essences from which their names are derived, and which make them what they are, becoming great through Greatness, beautiful through Beauty etc.? Does Socrates think that the *whole* Essence of Greatness resides in each great thing or only a part of this Essence? On the former assumption, will not Greatness Itself be absurdly parted from itself, and as it were pluralized (131a)? And, on the latter assumption, will we not have such absurd consequences as that something is made great by a mere fragment of absolute Greatness, or equal by something less than absolute Equality, or small by something smaller than the absolutely Small (131d, c)? Parmenides-Plato further shows that if Essences or Natures are ranged along with their instances, and are treated as being what they are in precisely the same manner in which the things which share in them are what they are, then we shall be involved in an infinite, senseless multiplication of such Essences. For, when we have been led to postulate one ideal Essence of the Great as present in or extending over many great things, and then range this Essence Itself beside the many things that it renders great, then a second Essence of Absolute Greatness must by parity of reasoning seem needed to impart Greatness both to the first Essence and its instances, and a third Essence of Greatness to impart Greatness to this second Essence and *its* instances, and so on indefinitely, so that Greatness Itself will be pluralized into types as well as into instances (132a, b). This famous argument is identical with one cited by Aristotle in his lost treatise *On the Ideas* and called that of the 'Third Man' (see also *Metaphysics*, 990b and 1038b), a name also given to other arguments. It is tempting to hold, as Socrates suggests, that the Eide are merely thoughts in the mind, and so avoid this seemingly necessary pluralization, since nothing is added to a set of great things when a common Greatness is merely *thought* of as pertaining to them. Parmenides-Plato does not pursue the infinite regress into the sphere of thought, but merely points out that all thoughts point beyond themselves to entities of some sort, so that if the Great Itself is thought of as the same for all great things, then there must be a Great Itself as well as the things which share in it. The thought-solution would, further, only work if we were to reduce the whole world to thoughts, either existing in thinkers everywhere present, or not existing in thinkers at all, both of which are absurd. It is taken for granted that the Greatness needed to make great things great cannot depend on anything so intermittent as thoughts and thinkers.

Parmenides-Plato then shows that our problem is not bettered if instead of thinking in terms of the 'sharing' most characteristic of Platonism, we revert to the 'imitation' most characteristic of Pythagoreanism. It will not help to conceive of the Eide as paradigms set up in nature, of which other things are merely the likenesses, for, if instances are like Essences, then Essences will be like instances, and both alike will need to be made what they are by their common likeness to further Essences, and so on *ad infinitum* (132c–133a). But all difficulties pale beside the great difficulty that if the Eide are thus set wholly apart from their instances, it is impossible that there should be any instances of the Knowing of them or about them, and if there is a Knowing of them or about them, then this Knowledge will itself be a divine, supra-instantial Knowledge. For to hold that *we*, in our acts of thinking or knowing, can either think of or know the Eide themselves and their attributes and relations, is like holding that a slave can be an instance of Slavery not to a master, who is an instance of Mastery, but to absolute Mastery as Such, or that a master can be an instance of Mastery, not to a slave who is an instance of Slavery, but to absolute Slavery Itself. It is, however, mere nonsense to suppose that anyone can enslave Slavery, or be mastered by Mastery: the commerce of instances is with instances, and not with the Essences they exemplify. In the same way it is nonsense to suppose that any person or thought can know of anything but of instances of Eide: only Thought Itself or Knowledge Itself, being itself an Essence, can be of Being Itself, or of any of the Essences into which Being is subdivided. And only a God who is Knowledge Itself, as well as other related excellences, can enjoy that Knowledge of the Essences themselves which is for ever denied us. The strange consequence further obtains that there can be no absolute knowledge of instances, and that God, the absolute Knower, can know nothing of us and our concerns (133b–134e).

Such strange consequences might at a later date have been acceptable to Aristotle or to some of Plato's mystical successors: Parmenides-Plato, however, sees them as a difficulty. The Eide must in some sense be genuinely present *to*, as well as present in, the minds which reason about them, and see other things in their light: otherwise all power to discourse on anything with anyone will be wholly destroyed (135c). How are these difficulties regarding the Eide and our knowledge of them to be evaded? Parmenides-Plato says that the sort of one-sided superficial discussion that they have just been carrying on must be carried much further. They have been quite right in extending philosophical puzzlement from the world of instances to the instantiated Eide themselves (135d, e), but they must investigate these latter much more systematically. It is not enough to postulate that there *are* such and such Eide, or Eide in general, and then see what consequences flow from such a postulation: they must also see what consequences would flow from a corresponding denial, and that both for the entities in question and for anything else with which they may be contrasted. Only at the end of such a methodical working out and survey of consequences can we hope to see where truth lies. And Parmenides-Plato is then persuaded, after some resistance, to offer a specimen of the new hypothetical method in the case of the Unity Itself which is his own supreme Principle: we must see what consequences are involved, both for Unity Itself and for anything else, of assuming both that there is and that there is not such a Unity.

The difficulties raised against the Ideal Theory have often been seen as really demolishing it, of revealing the absurdity involved in treating Eide as if they were things having bona fide natures, instead of descriptive features of things, whose so-called names only describe, and do not really name. The reification of the Eide is then, on this view, complicated by the independent error of self-predication: they are treated as if they were, not merely characters of real or imagined things, but perfect instances of those characters, things such-and-such as their instances are, only more pre-eminently such-and-such. These errors lead to the supposed necessity of parcelling Eide as their instances are parcelled, and to the ranging of them beside their instances so that further Eide are required to account for them, and to the setting of them apart from their instances so that they cast no light on the latter, and are moreover inaccessible to a knowledge like our own which is essentially instantial and of instances. Some of these objections are ancient and Academic or Aristotelian, some modern and recent, and all have substance: all, however, are vitiated by an instantial ontology of which Platonism is the negation, and will appear in a very different light if the world is seen Platonically. For Platonism is the view that there are no instances, except in a more or less legitimate *façon de parler*: Eide alone are, and Eide are instantiated, but such instantiation does not create a shadowy world of Eidos-copies, in any other but a transformed reducible sense, the sort of sense in which there is a replica of a room behind a mirror or in my imagination. The Eide are the living Meanings or Natures whose force is felt in all instantiation, and whose sense creates all understanding, and in neither existence or experience is there anything substantial to be laid hold of apart from them. The sense, therefore, in which each of them *is* the Essence it is, is the true paradigmatic sense of being anything, and predications which fall short of this, whether relating Eide to other Eide, or to their instantiations, or instantiations to Eide, all presuppose and enrich this primary, essential sort of predication. The Just Itself is more absolutely just than any case of being just, and this is precisely why it must always infinitely transcend the instances of Justice which are only what they are derivatively, and at a second remove. The error of the arguments set forth in the First Part of the *Parmenides* does not therefore consist in supposing that the characters of things have the genuine reality of the things they characterize and that they therefore must behave as these things do, but rather that so-called things have genuine reality and that characters are not real because they do not behave as these things do. It is the assimilation of multiply-present, reidentifiable characters to their variable instantial efflorescences in which the error consists, together with the error of supposing that firm reality and knowability are to be found in the latter. On Platonic premises, an Essence instantiated here and there is not separated from itself: it does not, except at a second remove, have the modalities of its modes, and it is consequently not rent apart because they are. It is essentially a One-over-many, and cannot be deprived of its own being in characteristically exhibiting it. On Platonic premises, likewise, an Eidos is not the Nature it is in the manner in which its instances only are *of* that nature, and so provides no basis for the infinite regress of the two forms of 'Third Man' argument. And while Parmenides-Plato shows great insight in arguing that instances of Knowledge of the Eide are never the perfection of that Knowledge, which pertains to Knowledge as Such, yet instances of Knowledge may none the less approach the Eide imperfectly through the instances of the latter: there is, moreover, nothing else that they could cognitively approach, since everything that is firm and graspable in instances is only their Eidos. The medicine which the difficulties demand is the realization that the Eide and the eidetic Knowledge of them are essentially two-sided: being what they are, and being all that anything is or could be, they have not only a side intrinsic to themselves, but also one that is extrinsic or for other things, and this second side can, on profounder reflection, be seen to be entirely dependent on the first side, so that knowing what an Eidos is goes with knowing how it could be instantiated and vice versa. This is, however, the lesson to be learnt from the dialectical exercise in the Second Part of the Dialogue to which we now must turn.

IV

The dialectical exercise in Part Two is built around the notion of Absolute Unity or the One Itself, the key-notion of the Eleatics, and two basic Postulations or Hypotheses are tried out for their consequences, the first that there is such a One Itself, and the second that there is no such One. The One is presumably meant as a fundamental Eidos or eidetic Principle, not merely as one that represents a complication of, or deviation from, more fundamental Eide, and as such it requires a postulate asserting its existence, since not every random conception occupies such a paradigmatic position. That there is or is not such an absolute Unity is, however, considered in two regards: in regard purely to its intrinsic content, to what it is in and for itself, and in respect of its wider or fuller nature, which allows us to predicate other notions of it or relate them to it. If the former treatment reduces it to a minimum, the latter expands it to the widest extent. That there is or is not an absolute Unity is further considered in its bearing on what are called 'the Others' (τὰ ἄλλα), the remainder-class or negation of Absolute Unity, as well as in its bearing on Unity *qua* Unity. And these 'Others', always a notion very important in Plato whether covered by the term ἄλλος or ἕτερος, are likewise seen in two distinct lights, either as participating in absolute Unity or at least embodying some trace of it, or, in the second place, as being utterly free from any sort of presence or derivation from Unity. The eight Hypotheses to be considered can accordingly be summarized as follows, though the scheme does not work out with perfect smoothness:

I. If there is such a thing as Unity Itself, what follows for Unity Itself, considered in the narrowest manner and solely in and for itself?

II. If there is such a thing as Unity Itself, what follows for Unity Itself, considered in the fullest manner and not merely in and for itself?

III. If there is such a thing as Unity Itself, what follows for what is (or are) other than Unity Itself, considered as possibly having a relation to Unity Itself?

IV. If there is such a thing as Unity Itself, what follows for what is (or are) other than Unity Itself, considered as having no relation at all to Unity Itself?

V. If there is no such thing as Unity Itself, what follows for Unity Itself, considered in the fullest manner and not merely in and for itself?

VI. If there is no such thing as Unity Itself, what follows for Unity Itself, considered in the narrowest manner and solely in and for itself?

VII. If there is no such thing as Unity Itself, what follows for what is (or are) other than Unity Itself, considered as having some vague trace of Unity Itself?

VIII. If there is no such thing as Unity Itself, what follows for what is (or are) other than Unity Itself considered as having no trace of a non-existent Unity?

Of these eight Hypotheses the first and second are the most interesting, and the second, despite many false steps, may be adjudged more interesting than the first. The eightfold method could further, it is suggested, be applied to the postulation of Eide other than Unity, and it could also be applied to the postulation of Eide *in general*, in which case it might remove, in one great seeming contradiction (which was really merely a statement of what the being of Eide amounts to), the difficulties raised in the first part of the Dialogue.

Hypothesis I (137c–142a) postulates the being of an essential Unity, and considers that Unity only in respect of its being the Unity that it is, and not in regard to its possible participation in Essences other than itself, or in regard to its relation to such other Essences either considered in themselves or in their actual or possible instantiations. Unity, so considered, conveys no suggestion of multitude of any sort; in it there is no suggestion of parts, nor of the wholeness which implies the presence of parts. Nor, consequently, is there in Unity Itself any suggestion of a beginning, a middle or an end, nor of any limits in any direction: in a sense different from the ordinary, Unity Itself may be said to be indefinite or infinite (ἄπειρον). Having nothing of division in what it is, Unity Itself can in consequence have nothing of the round or the straight or any other more complex spatial pattern in it, and is accordingly, in a special sense, wholly amorphous. It can, moreover, include nothing of location in what it is, whether this be the relative location of something encompassed by something else (ἐν ἄλλῳ) or the absolute location of something just where it is or in itself (ἐν ἑαυτῷ), since both of these types of location involve multitude and division and contact: in a special sense, Unity Itself is therefore nowhere. Not including plurality, parts and location in what it is, and being just what it is and no more, Unity Itself can have nothing of alteration or translation or even of rest in it: it is, in a special sense, un-alterable, unmoved and unresting. Difference and sameness in relation to itself or anything else can likewise play no part in it: difference from self, i.e. from Unity, and sameness with what is other than self, are obviously ruled out, but so also are sameness with self and otherness than what is other than self, the latter because it is plainly not by being one that anything is made other than what is other, the former because sameness with self is a character other than Unity, and because Unity Itself can include no such different character in itself. Unity Itself can likewise include nothing of likeness or unlikeness, whether to self or others, in itself, since likeness involves sameness of affection (τὸ ταὐτόν που πεπονθός) and unlikeness difference of affection (τὸ ἕτερον πεπονθός) and sameness and difference have already been excluded from what it is to be one. Equality and inequality are, on similar grounds, excluded from absolute Unity: Unity Itself, having neither division nor plurality nor sameness in what it is, can include nothing which corresponds to having more measures, or less measures, or the same number of measures with anything, whether itself or anything else, and these are what it is to be greater or less than or equal to anything. For similar reasons absolute Unity neither is nor becomes older or younger nor of the same age with itself or anything else, since all these predications have a content other than Unity Itself, and also involve equality and likeness and their opposites, which we have acknowledged not to be part of what it is to be one. All of which entails that Unity Itself has nothing of temporality in it. It differs essentially from its instances which are 'in time', and which are always (*qua* present) growing older than their (past) selves, or, *qua* past, growing younger than their (present) selves, or, *qua* present, keeping pace with their (present) selves. Unity Itself displays none of these paradoxical temporal differences, and so cannot be said to be in time. And, not being in time, it cannot appropriately be said to have existed or to have arisen, or to be in existence or to be in process of arising, or to be about to exist or arise. In none of its modalities is being therefore part of being one, and this leads to the further paradox that the being which we include in being one is itself excluded by its pure unitariness, so that Unity Itself, having no sort of being, can neither be named nor have anything said of it, nor can there be knowledge or opinion or even dumb perception of it. Asked whether he thinks that all this can be so, Aristotle, the down-to-earth man, replies that he does not think so (142a).

We have, in the above restatement, somewhat refashioned Plato-Parmenides's language, so that it becomes plain that, though he is talking *about* the inner coverage of an Eidos, what he says of it is not itself part of that inner coverage. It is not part of being one that it excludes all the characters that it, as a character, is said to exclude. Unity Itself is only simple, shapeless, timeless, non-metric etc. as *all* Eide are: it does not include simplicity, shapelessness, timelessness etc. as part of what as an Eidos it covers or is, and is quite as hospitable to the contrary of these characters as to them. This will in fact appear in the Second Hypothesis. But what Plato-Parmenides is stressing in this First Hypothesis is that, in addition to their instantiability or eidetic causality, and in addition to their higher relations with one another, Eide also have an own-being, or narrowly intrinsic content, which distinguishes them from all other Eide, and which, in the case of the simpler, more ultimate Eide, can be simply enjoyed, but not further elucidated or talked about. To penetrate to this eidetic nucleus, through the penumbra of instantiation, and the corona of eidetic interrelations, is necessarily to perform a mystical or transcendental act *par excellence*, and almost necessarily to experience the characteristic aura of mysticism. To think clearly of Divisibility by 107 is at a low level to have such an experience, but one has it with infinitely enhanced intensity when the Eidos or Principle enjoyed is one so basic or so fecund as the One, the Beautiful or the Good. The 'mysticism' of the First Hypothesis is therefore only an intensification of the unavoidable mysticism that at all times lies beneath the surface of all thought and all speech and all life.

In the Second Hypothesis, Parmenides-Plato now shows that if Unity Itself is postulated, all other Eide whatever are likewise postulated: the whole eidetic cosmos, given a numerical interpretation, and developed in the dimensions of space and time, can be seen to flow from it, or to be truly 'caused' by it. And the trick is done, not by showing, as might have been done, that Unity requires all these other Essences if it is to have effective application or instantiation, and so to *be* the creative Eidos or Principle that it is, but rather that all these other Eide have application to Unity Itself, can be found to nest in the apartness of its eternal self-existence, as well as participating in its fecund development into an instantial world. Parmenides-Plato begins by arguing that if there *is* such a thing as Absolute Unity, then it must be a case of, participate in the Being that is predicated of it, and which is necessarily other than the Unity which it enriches. The Unity which is, will therefore necessarily have two sides or aspects, the Unity which it essentially is, and the Being which attaches to this Unity, and it will be a *whole* in which these two sides can be distinguished. But once we have thus dichotomized it, each of its aspects will ask for a similar dichotomy: its Being-aspect will have unity as well as being, and its Unity-aspect being as well as unity. And this sort of cellular fission will go on indefinitely, all the multiples of Two arising concurrently with the products of such fission. A trichotomy will also necessarily arise alongside of our dichotomies, since there will necessarily be a *difference* between the Being-aspect and the Unity-aspect of the Unity which is, and this difference will constitute a *third* aspect of the Unity which is, since it is not because this Unity is a Unity that it is thus differentiated, nor because it has a Being-aspect, but solely on account of the difference or differentiation present in it. Triplicity or Thriceness having been thus generated, it is easy to see that, by a due repetition of one's previous dichotomies and trichotomies, one can advance to cases exemplifying all the multiples of Two and Three, and if, by processes not further specified, one can find some peculiar relation holding among a set of terms less by one than any prime number, one can, by adding this relation to the set of terms in question, get a case of the prime number in question one will then, if one is indefinitely assiduous, be able to generate all the prime numbers and all the multiples of the prime numbers out of Unity Itself and what is primitively true of it. It is no mean discovery, even if here worked out in a somewhat makeshift, exoteric way, that the whole Number-series can be developed out of the simplest of our notions. And Parmenides-Plato has also shown that the separation from self and the unity-in-multiplicity held peculiar to the realm of instantiation, and seen as a mark of its defectiveness, is also to be found in the realm of the Eide, and is in fact more thoroughly the norm there. Truly understood and accepted, such a realization will, by a vaster homoeopathy, remove the difficulties raised in the first part of the Dialogue.

The infinitely diversified whole constituted by the Unity which is, can now be argued to contain, in principle at least, all the possibilities of definite shape and size that can be encountered in space. Parmenides-Plato does not generate Points or Indivisible Lines from Monads, Surfaces from Lines, and Solids from Surfaces in the manner in which we gather they were actually generated in the Academic Stoicheiology, but a brief paragraph (144e–145b) implies that it *could* be done. In the differentiated wholeness of Unity Itself there is, moreover, a formal representative of absolute location or being-in-itself, the parts in their distributive totality (πάντα) being encompassed by the whole which, considered collectively, is but another version of themselves, and also a formal representative of relative location or being-in-another of which Parmenides-Plato gives a somewhat unconvincing demonstration (145c–e); he could quite well have held that each part of Unity Itself, being itself a case of Unity, is contained in the context of the remaining parts. The variability and invariance whose instantial, sensuous forms are Motion and Rest, will also obviously have been represented in the all-encompassing, differentiated Unity, absolute Unity being both eternally in itself, and so 'at rest', while also, by a somewhat unsatisfactory argument (145e–146a), eternally dodging from another to another *qua* the totality of its parts. It is important to note that Movement, Becoming, formerly the mark of the instance, have here taken up residence in the eidetic world: though its content, Movingness, may be that of the typically imperfect and instantial, it is, *qua* Eidos, part of the changeless, paradigmatic order. Everything instantial could undergo the same transformation, remaining what it is but in a transfigured manner.

Long reasonings now follow to show that Unity Itself can be said to be both the same and also different from itself and others, or both like and unlike itself and others, or both equal and unequal to itself and others. They contain fallacies, but a simple, valid argument could always be substituted. The first conclusions could simply have been reached by arguing that Unity Itself is always Unity and so selfsame, like and equal to itself, yet that its distribution among infinite parts also makes it other than, unlike and unequal to self, and same as, like and equal to others. Parmenides-Plato prefers to base himself on the doubtful disjunction that anything is either the same as anything, or other than it, or a part or a whole in relation to it. Not being other than itself, or a part or a whole to itself, Absolute Unity must be the same as itself, and being, as previously admitted, both in itself and in what is other than self, it is also, to that extent, other than self. But it is also other than all others by the nature of Otherness, and yet, since Otherness is essentially external to the terms that it 'others', there is nothing intrinsic to prevent Unity itself from being the same as such others, since it cannot stand in the relation of whole or part to them. The second conclusion, that absolute Unity is both like and unlike others and itself, is then proved by arguing (i) that the very difference between absolute Unity and what is other than absolute Unity, being symmetrical, creates a likeness between them, and that (ii) since difference establishes a resemblance, sameness, being opposed in force, will create an unlikeness among them (147c–148c), an argument so silly as to be worthy of Socrates, and (iii) that likeness and unlikeness to self are a mere consequence of the sameness and otherness previously concluded. The third conclusion – that Unity itself is both equal and unequal to itself and others – is established by arguing that inequality between anything and anything involves the presence of Greatness in one thing and a correlated Smallness in another, but that there are grave difficulties in believing in a Greatness which is *less* than the whole of that in which it is, and a Smallness which pervades a whole, and is therefore *more* than some parts of it. It follows that Unity Itself, being incapable of being greater or smaller than itself or than anything else, must in this sense be equal to either. This argument fails to see that being greater or smaller is not the same as being Greatness or Smallness Itself, and that there is no absurdity if Greatness Itself is in some contexts smaller than something, or Smallness Itself greater than something. But its interest lies in its showing that the very difficulties which, in the first part of the Dialogue, have been used to discredit instances, recur at the eidetic level, and so are not really difficulties nor discreditable at all. It is further argued that Unity Itself can, despite the above argument, be shown to involve both the encompassing and encompassment of itself by itself, and of others by itself, which amount in principle to inequality. *Qua* whole it encompasses itself *qua* all its parts, and as Unity it encompasses all the other Ratios which arise in it by division as well as the divisible continuum out of which all such Ratios are carved, and is encompassed by all the same Ratios in inverse form in so far as they arise from it by multiplication and addition, and is also encompassed by the infinitely expansible continuum in which all such Ratios arise (see Cornford, *Plato and Parmenides*, 1939, pp. 177 ff.). Unity, it is plain, is at once the most elementary and the most comprehensive of notions, and there is nothing genuinely self-contradictory in its Protean shifts of position.

Parmenides-Plato, having exhausted all possibilities of qualitative, quantitative and local differentiation, proceeds to consider the differentiation of time. Can absolute Unity be said to be or to become older or younger than itself or others, or to be of the same age as either? Immensely tortuous arguments are devised to deal with these questions. The being of anything is, in the first place, held to be identifiable with a participation in being in the present tense, as having been is a similar participation in being in the past tense, and aboutness to be with a similar participation in the future tense (151e–152a). Parmenides-Plato here takes an immense step, which could be very readily misinterpreted: he is holding that tense-modification, though not, of course, affecting the essential core of meaning of each Eidos, must none the less have an eidetic representation. The changing and developing states of growing organisms and of planets in motion, are all regularly prefigured in the Eide of those entities, and so is the great logical web of changing modalities which is none other than the eternal Eidos of Change Itself. What it is to change, to pass from being about to be something, to actually being that thing and then going on to having been that thing, is of course an absolutely changeless pattern in the eidetic realm: it will in the *Sophist* be studied as one of its supreme Kinds. And of course even the being of the Eide also has an extrinsic relation to the *instantiation* of such change: considered in relation to changing instances even an eternal Eidos was, is and will be, and Plato cannot have been so foolish as not to see this. Since it is of the essence of time to be always 'going on' (πορευόμενον), the being of anything always involves a perpetual growing older of something *qua* present related to a perpetual growing younger of the same thing *qua* past: it also involves a perpetual being of the same age as itself at any present time, over the whole time in which it can also be said to be growing older and younger than itself. It can therefore be said, with only an appearance of paradox, always to be and to be becoming older and younger than itself, and also always *not* to be becoming either. Its relation to the Others will generate other pseudo-paradoxes: Unity Itself must always be prior to the Others, since they are confessedly many, and since Unity is always presupposed by Multitude, but on the other hand, the whole formed by a number of things always terminates in Unity, which is therefore posterior to the others. Any distinguishable member of the Others is likewise a case of Unity, which is therefore neither prior nor posterior to the Others, but always contemporary with them. This argument may be criticized as transforming logical into temporal order, but such is not the case: both in the timeless pattern of changing modalities and in the relation of timeless things to things in time, we have Unity present alike in the origin, the progress and the final outcome of the pattern of change. Plainly Unity is primordial, permanent and also final, and Parmenides-Plato only puts this in a funny way. The question is further put whether Unity Itself can be said to be, and also not to be, *becoming* older and younger than the others, and the answers are reached (i) that in terms of absolute distance Unity is never becoming more primordial or more final than anything other than itself, but that (ii), relatively speaking, as we move away from primordial Unity or towards final Unity, distance does increase or decrease, and absolute Unity can therefore be said both to be speeding more rapidly towards primordiality or finality, or, on a reversed point of view, limping more slowly towards them, than it did before or will do afterwards. These kaleidoscopic conclusions, whose dizzy complexity is much more confusing than their uncertain ballast of fallacy, lead on to the statement that Absolute Unity, having been thus shown to have a relation to time, and to permit past-, present- and future-tense talk, can be made a subject of characterization and a term of relation (καὶ εἴη ἂν τι ἐκείνῳ καὶ ἐκείνου), and an object of knowledge, opinion and perception, and that there can be naming and saying practised upon it (155d).

Parmenides-Plato completes this analysis of formal temporality by introducing the new and important notion of the instant or point of transition (τὸ ἐξαίφνης). In Ḥypothesis II, and in Hypothesis I and II taken together, we have been constantly faced with a predication of contraries of absolute Unity, and this nesting of contraries in a single point is precisely this notion of the point of transition of which a temporal instant is the instantial representative. Unity Itself combines Not-being (Hypothesis I) with Being (Hypothesis II): this combination of contraries in a single point is what is temporally realized in coming to be and passing away. 'There must surely be a time when it takes on being and a time when it loses it . . . the One, it would therefore seem, taking on and losing being, becomes and passes away' (156a). But this unity of contraries itself is a unity of contraries in its relation to time: the transitional point in which a contrary passes over into a contrary has been said to be and now is said not to be in time. The instantaneous 'is a certain extraordinary nature which lies betwixt movement and rest, without being in any time: into it and from it a moving thing changes to rest and a resting thing into movement' (156d, e).

This final paragraph of Hypothesis II on the instantaneous in a sense furnishes us with the lesson of both the Hypotheses: that Unity Itself (and by implication all the Eide) obey a different logic from their instantiations and that what would be destructively self-contradictory if said of an instance is not destructively self-contradictory if said of Unity Itself (or of any other Eidos). The realm of Eide is not a realm of independent entities set side by side with the seeming externality of their instantiations; it is rather a continuum of sense in which the elements shade into one another in varying ways, and in which the distinctiveness of each depends on its place in the continuum, and on the way in which the whole continuum 'looks' from that place. Each can be said in varying manners to be no more than an aspect of every other, Being being capable of being seen as an aspect of Unity, and Unity of Being, and that even in the case of contraries, as the example of the 'instantaneous' has just shown. And nothing prevents what is intimately an aspect of one thing from being just as intimately an aspect of what is most contrary to that thing: it will not be dirempted by such contrariety. Diversity and contrariety in fact assume a new meaning at the level of the Eide, being merely the unopposed, undivided eidetic residue of what, at the level of instantiation, involved opposition and division. The arguments of Hypotheses I and II are in no sense satisfactorily carried out. What is satisfactorily established is their principle: that a seminal notion like Absolute Unity both contracts into a nucleus in which naming and saying cease, and expands into a fully-developed structure in which all the possibilities of Being are distinguished and yet held together indissolubly. What is also established is the ultimate nugatoriness, even for the realm of instantiation, of that separation of being into those hard, resistant counters in which reliance on the senses might tempt us to believe. It will be objected by some that we are here merely reading Hegelianism into Platonism, but this is to forget that the basic principles of the Hegelian Dialectic were in large part mined from the Platonic *Parmenides*, which Hegel described in 1807 as 'the greatest work of art of the antique Dialectic and the authentic expression of the divine life'. The basic notion of a unity of differents or contraries is not, however, original to Plato: it is to be found in Anaximander and Heraclitus, and is in fact deeply a part of common sense, which has never practised that diremption into innumerable entities to which a too rigorous, exhaustive use of negation readily leads. The Neoplatonists were later to stress the unitive aspect of the thought-world, and that in it 'each is all, and all each, and the glory infinite', but the greatness of Plato is perhaps that he let a little of this higher glory trail down even into the world of the senses. For in saying, for example, that Being specifies itself into having been, being now and being about to be, he is recognizing, *sub specie aeternitatis*, the very principles on which the flux is built. There is, in fact, no further content to the realm of the Eide than those permanent possibilities of instantiation which, in it, are raised above instantiation.

V

The remaining six Hypotheses are sketched more sparely, but are none the less very interesting. Hypothesis III marches with Hypothesis II in considering Absolute Unity in an expansive manner, while Hypothesis IV marches with Hypothesis I in considering it contractively. Both Hypotheses have to do with the relation of the being of Absolute Unity to 'the Others', which again is seen in a double light.

Hypothesis III starts by saying that things other than Unity cannot *be* absolute Unity, but that they may none the less not be altogether deprived of it, but may share in it after a fashion ($\pi \hat{\eta}$ – 157c). As other than Unity, they will contain parts, but these parts will be parts of a whole, 'a certain single idea and unity which out of all the parts becomes perfectly one' (157d, e), and will therefore share in both wholeness and unity, and *their* parts, not being absolute Unity, will likewise be wholes, and will each share in absolute Unity. So far we have been considering 'the Others' as participants in absolute Unity: there is, however, another way of regarding them in which we consider merely what it is to be other than one, without considering this as participating in absolute Unity. So considered, 'itself by itself', the 'Other Nature' reveals itself as essentially one of unlimited multitude, which is only capable of being parcelled into parts in so far as something other than itself sets bounds to it, and this other than itself which bounds the second nature can be none other than absolute Unity Itself. 'In the Others a joint product therefore arises out of absolute Unity and themselves, which sets bounds to them in relation to one another. Their own nature only confers Boundlessness on them' (158d). We here have the first clear appearance of the second transcendental Principle in Plato's philosophy of Number: the principle of the continuum, of indefinite magnitude, of that which can be expanded or contracted without limit, and which requires the co-operation of absolute Unity to give rise to the Eide, which are all specific Numbers or Ratios of numbers or sets or patterns of Ratios of Numbers. The co-operation of the two Principles is not properly to be described as one of participation of the one in the other, but of their joint presence in a single species which as it were com-promises between them.

Parmenides-Plato does not, however, dwell for more than a few lines on the emergence of the Eide out of the union of the One and the Great and Small, but uses his double view of 'the Others', as both participating in Unity as Such and also as capable of an eidetic isolation from it. As capable of this double allegiance, cases of the 'Other Nature' will both be one and infinitely divided, and so like one another and themselves in respect of one of these properties, and yet utterly unlike and opposed when one is considered in respect of one of these properties and the other (or the same one) is considered in respect of the other (159a). They will therefore be as omnirecipient of 'affections' as Unity was found to be in the Second Hypothesis. The Fourth Hypothesis, however, considers 'the Others' not merely as joint products of Unity and Indefinite Multitude, nor as the latter seen in isolation, but as something utterly apart (χωρίς) from absolute Unity and even from the possibility of having anything to do with it. 'The Others' so conceived share neither in the whole nor in any part of Unity, nor have anything in them which savours of Unity. They cannot have many parts since each such part would have unity, and they cannot form a unitary whole of parts. They can have no similarity or dissimilarity with one another or with absolute Unity, since they cannot participate in one definite property. Nothing whatever is therefore sayable of the Others seen in this last isolation. What the Fourth Hypothesis then really establishes is the complete monism of the Platonic Stoicheiology. Absolute Unity requires a contrasting principle of Indefinite Multiplicity if there is to be any emergence of the Eide out of the two factors. The second factor, however, reveals itself as being nothing at all if held apart from the supreme Unity. Only as the mere formlessness which is an invitation to unitive forming, and that everywhere suggests clear boundaries which melt away on examination, and only acquire definition when bounded by Unity (as in Hypothesis III), can it be anything at all. But that Otherness-than-Unity, held resolutely apart, reduces to absolute vacuity, does not mean that it has no position in the Platonic ontology. Even as what isn't real or isn't thinkable, it still is the something excluded by these negations. The mere shadow cast by the substance of Absolute Unity has at least the substance of being that shadow.

Hypotheses V and VI now make the apparently drastic assumption that there is no such thing as absolute Unity. This assumption, except in the contracted sense of Hypothesis I, is of course nonsensical, and Plato shows his sense of the logical character of such pure nonsense by pointing out (V) that it leaves everything as it is, since the possibility of the being of Unity and of discourse about it rests on a necessary foundation, and cannot be undermined by what we may choose to assume, and yet (VI) that it utterly destroys the possibility of Unity's being, or of any discourse about Unity. V and VI are not, however, two reconcilable sides of a positive conclusion, but amount to the negative conclusion that it cannot be the case that there is no such thing as absolute Unity, except in the special, contracted sense of Hypothesis I.

Parmenides-Plato starts by pointing out that we say something quite different if we say that non-Unity does not exist, than if we say that Unity does not exist: Unity Itself has to be the specific Essence that it is, and not another, in order that it can be significantly said *not* to be. (Compare Meinong's opinion that *Sein* presupposes *Sosein* and not vice versa, and that it is only if one has an object of definite character before one, that one can presume it *not* to be.) A Unity which is said not to be, must accordingly be knowable, and differentiable from other natures, and from the knowledge which is of it, and it must be a subject of many predications, and a term in many relations, despite its non-being. It must further, despite its non-being, be like itself and unlike other things, and be unequal to other things and equal to itself, and it must finally, after a fashion ($\pi \hat{\eta}$), share in being. For there must be a *being* of its non-being which acts as its bond ($\delta \epsilon \sigma \mu os$) to non-being, and prevents it from slipping over to being, just as there must be a non-being of the non-being which binds what *is* to being, and keeps *it* from slipping over into non-being. What is, therefore, participates indirectly in non-being, and what is not, in being. And this involves, in the case of what is not, a curious mixture of non-being and being formally analogous to the mixture we had in the case of the instant: the one that is not must be envisaged as trembling on the verge between being and non-being, yet remaining fixed in its transience, like Zeno's arrow. Whatever the meaning of this last, most obscure contention (162b–e), the outcome of the whole Hypothesis is plain: that a denial of being to so absolute a thing as Unity Itself, suffers shipwreck on the rocks of its own senselessness: we cannot, whatever we like to suppose, get away from Unity, Being etc. and all their inevitable developments.

There is, however, an alternative strategy of pure negation which is explored in Hypothesis VI. We assume, not that what is not after a manner ($\pi \hat{\omega}s$) is not, and after a manner is, but rather that it nowise and in no manner and in no respect has any part in being ($o\dot{v}\delta a\mu \hat{\omega}s$ $o\dot{v}\delta a\mu \hat{\eta}$ $\ddot{\epsilon}\sigma \tau \iota \nu$ $o\dot{v}\delta \acute{\epsilon}$ $\pi \hat{\eta}$ $\mu \epsilon \tau \acute{\epsilon}\chi \epsilon \iota$ $o\dot{v}\sigma \acute{\iota}as$ – 163c). When we refuse to allow what is not to be even thus parasitic upon being, the Unity which is not passes beyond the limits of discourse altogether. Such a Unity can neither have nor lose nor take on being, nor can it be in motion nor at rest, nor can it be more or less than, or equal to anything, nor resemble or be different from itself or anything else. It will be impossible to make it a subject of predicates or a term of relations, or to refer to it as something, or as this thing, or as related to this or that thing, or as pertaining to anything else, or as having been, or going to be, or as now being, or to make of it an object of knowledge, opinion, perception, meaning or saying (164a, b). The completely contracted non-existent Unity of Hypothesis VI therefore becomes indistinguishable from the completely contracted existent Unity of Hypothesis I, which was said at the end of the Hypothesis not to have being. (Just as the expanded non-existent Unity of V became indistinguishable from the expanded existent Unity of II.) We have reached the same mystical terminus, where silent grasp takes over from ordered utterance, but we have reached it from another starting-point.

Hypothesis VII is deeply interesting as sketching the other mystical ultimate of the eidetic system, but in a purer manner than was possible in Hypothesis III. It gives us a portrait of the Pythagorean ἄπειρον, or the Platonic Great and Small, as the indefinite continuum of flowing quantity, which is deliberately held apart in thought from the limiting action of absolute Unity, and which is accordingly void of all emergent forms and numbers. Plato-Parmenides asks: If (*per impossibile*) there were no such thing as absolute Unity, then what would happen to 'the Others'? They would cease to be other than Unity Itself, since such Unity would have been blotted out. Their otherness would therefore have to confine itself to being that of others to others, and it would have always to be an otherness of *many* others to *many* others, and never of *one* other to *another*. The others will always be present in mass, and active as a crowd, and if, as in a dream, one fancies one has picked out one minimal other in the crowd, it will at once dissolve into a vast number of distinct units liable to further dissolution. What one has before one will always have an appearance of simplicity, of an exact ratio of the greater to the less, of a precise beginning, middle and end, but all these appearances will dissolve on closer examination. The smallest unit will burgeon into as many component units as the largest, and another beginning will always emerge before any beginning, another end after any end, and another middle in the middle of every middle. To a distant, blunted view, units will constantly make their appearance, but to a closer, sharper vision each will appear indefinitely numerous. And the characters of things will vary as much as their size and number: they will change as scene-paintings change with a change in distance (164e–165d). This magnificent description of the multiplicative, 'evil' aspect of the eidetic system is of course an abstraction, just as the description of the ineffable One of the First Hypothesis is also an abstraction. Ultimate Unity and Ultimate Disunity are nothing apart from their mutual work of fecundation, except as Principles which, in their contracted nature, can be silently understood, metaphorically gestured at but never lucidly talked about.

Hypothesis VIII now gives the notion of the non-being of Unity its final *coup de grâce*: the Others are now too enfeebled to show even the vain simulacrum of Unity that was theirs in Hypothesis VII. Unity not being present to these Others, plurality vanishes also. And the nullification of Unity will be so total, that the Others will not even be able to muster an appearance of unity or multiplicity, and it will be quite impossible to think that they are one or many, or like or unlike, or the same or different, or in contact or set apart, or any of the other things considered in previous hypotheses. If there is no Unity, then there can be nothing, and the Others will be part of this nothing. The Other Nature from Unity, pushed to the extreme of separation from Unity, simply vanishes. It is the bounding line of the eidetic system, and with the last vanishing of that system it vanishes also, retaining only its residual sense as what that system completely excludes.

It will not be maintained that the surveys we have given of the various sections of this inexhaustible Dialogue cover all its details fairly and accurately, and do not simply skate over many of its obscurities. The lesson of the whole eightfold exercise carried out by Parmenides-Plato is, however, sufficiently clear: that talk about the Eide, as of some iridescent object, constantly challenges us to change our point of view, so that what is truly said at one position, and from one angle, has to be recanted at the next, the whole truth of the situation somehow lying in the complete round of our utterances. To quote the famous last sentence of the Dialogue, to which the Aristotle of the Dialogue agrees as he did not agree to the conclusion of the First Hypothesis: 'Let this then be said, and let us add that it seems to be the case that, whether there is or is not a One, itself and the Others all stand, and do not stand, in all possible relations to themselves, and to one another, and that they all also both appear, and do not appear, so to stand – very, very true' (166c). It is clear that for Plato, as for many other Greek philosophers, contrariety and tension enter into his conception of what ultimately is, and that without disrupting its unity, or involving anything like the head-on, self-destructive contradiction which Plato and Aristotle alike condemn and eschew. But the importance of the eightfold exercise must also lie in the way in which it invites us to dispose of the difficulties raised in the First Part of the Dialogue. What it invites us to argue is, first of all, that each Eidos has a contracted self-being which is beyond utterance, and involves nothing of what may be predicated of it, or of what it may be predicated of with or without other Eide. In such abstracted self-being any Eidos is cut off from instances and from knowledge and mention. It invites us further to argue that, despite such august isolability, each Eidos is the possibility of boundless instantiation, with or without other Eide, and is essentially explanatory of such instances as being their one true cause. This explanatoriness can be understood if we consider how all the more specific Eide are the necessary specifications of the more generic Eide, and so on to the highest: we do not need to step outside of the charmed circle of the Eide to understand the lesser mysteries of instantiation. And in the charmed circle in question we see all the cases of identical essences present in widely different and incompatibly developed species which raise such a pother when we are dealing with instances. No one finds it hard to understand how Five and Seven and Nine should all be cases of Oddness, nor supposes that Oddness must somehow be severed from itself in all of them. Nor does anyone suppose that Oddness Itself and the Oddness of five are two separate Essences and that the second uses the first as a paradigm or a source. In a sense it does indeed do so, but the asymmetry of the relation does not mean that the same term may not stand at either end of it. Nor does anyone suppose that if Unity is predicated of Unity, whether as being what Unity is, or as what it shares in as one Eidos among others, that there must be two Unities involved in the matter, or that any multiplication of an ideal Essence is therefore thinkable. And we also see how Eide may function at a given level, and may in that context share in themselves and in other Eide, which in that case belong to another level, without thereby suffering any schism from themselves or from these other Eide. In terms of the descents and ascents possible in the eidetic realm, the ascents and descents from the eidetic to the instantial realm present no special difficulty. There are, of course, type-difficulties and contradictions of which Plato was unaware, but, had he known of them, he would probably have regarded them as curious, limiting excrescences in the eidetic landscape, ornamental rather than vexatious, and self-sterilizing in virtue of their own peculiar structure rather than to be cast forth by a general exorcism. In a system already involving the built-in absurdity of the Great and Small, the addition of this curious species of double-edged absurdity would have presented no special problem. We cannot, for the rest, say how Plato would have worked out Hypothesis II in the case of the particular Eide, since instantiation involves issues of contingency not present at the eidetic level. And the lessons to be drawn from Hypotheses III to VIII in relation to the specific Eide and their instances are too obscure to be touched on here.

VII

THE STOICHEIOLOGICAL
DIALOGUES: THE *SOPHIST*,
STATESMAN, *PHILEBUS*
AND *EPISTLES*

I

The *Sophist* is a Dialogue concerned with the structuring principles of the eidetic realm: the various manners in which Ideal Natures, while maintaining their distinctness of content, can none the less come together in a number of intimate ways, sometimes being shared by, and so sayable of one another, sometimes coinciding or being unable to coincide in the area of lower Eide which share in them, sometimes having to one another the semblance of a relation which turns out to be *other* than what is true. This communion of the Eide is not worked out in a completely satisfactory manner, nor one that disposes of all ambiguities, but is none the less an illuminating treatment of the Oneness-in-manyness essential to being an Eidos. And, as in the *Parmenides*, the interrelations of the Eide are used to throw light on the obscurities of instantiation: it is as wrong to seek to tear the Eide from their involvements with the realm of flux as it is wrong to seek to tear them from one another. The interrelations among the Eide are also used to throw light on the innumerable exclusions and negations among them, and on that peculiarly difficult form of exclusion or negation when what is excluded has no being at all, when it represents a *wrong* or *erroneous* way of construing the relation of Eide to Eide, or of Eide to their instances. Plato seeks to understand, as he did in the *Theaetetus*, how misconstructions and false appearances have somehow a place in the pure world of being, and how the mind can be so misguided as to mistake them for the authentic contents and connections of that realm. Plato's solution to this problem has at least the merit of seeing that the non-existent and false are in no sense extraneous invaders of the realm of being, but in their very exclusion a part of its structure: what he says has, however, to some had the air of reducing them to things not thus excluded, and so bemusing and perplexing whole generations of commentators, whose standards of reality are less finely graded than Plato's. All this treatment of the fundamental architecture of Being is set in an exoteric discussion of the utmost banality, an attempt to discuss the nature of Sophistry by likening it to Angling. The dialectical divisions worked out in the Academy, in which the alternative ways of being an organized multitude were made to flow from the general notions of Unity and Unorganized Multiplicity, are here travestied in a set of bifurcations based on trivial empirical familiarity and the current divisions of language, and not on any deep perception of what is essential. There are signs throughout the Dialogue of adjustment to a double audience, the wider public who would read it or hear it read aloud, and experience vague titillation of their philosophical memories, and the narrower Academic group who would see its own special controversies reflected in some of its references. These preliminary indications will take on more substance in what follows.

The Dialogue portrays a discussion supposed to have taken place the day after the discussion sketched in the *Theaetetus*, and a little while before the trial and death of Socrates. Theodorus of Cyrene is again present, but says remarkably little: Socrates is also present, but drops out of the discussion altogether. Theaetetus makes the responses, but the direction of the argument is in the hands of an Eleatic Stranger, plainly a successor to the Parmenides-Plato of the Dialogue *Parmenides*. The discussion is not one that could have occurred in the lifetime of Socrates, but mirrors controversy in the Academy, with some adjustment, as we have said, to the broad notions of philosophy entertained by a cultivated public.

The problem is posed by Socrates before he falls silent: the Stranger is to tell them what sense the names 'Sophist', 'Statesman' and 'Philosopher' have in Elea. The present discussion is to be devoted to the nature of Sophistry, while the nature of

Statesmanship and Philosophy will be discussed later: there is in fact a later Dialogue devoted to the Statesman, but the proposal to discuss the Philosopher is not carried out. The Stranger says that it is not enough if we have the same thing privately in mind when we utter the name 'Sophist': it is necessary for us to pin down this shared understanding with a λόγος, a clearly set out account of what that difficult customer, a Sophist, really amounts to. How such a λόγος is to be arrived at is shown in the trivial case of an angler: an angler is a technician (τεχνίτης), and being a technician covers the two possible cases of being a producer (ποιητικός) and being a getter (κτητικός), under the second of which angling plainly falls. Being a getter then divides into being a purchaser or exchanger (μεταβλητικός) or being a seizer (χειρωτικός), and the latter into being an open contender (ἀγωνιστικός) or a stealthy hunter (θηρευτικός). The latter divides according as what are hunted are lifeless or living things, and the latter according as the living things hunted live on land or in a fluid medium, of which air is one case and water another. Fishing is plainly the form of hunting under which being an angler falls, and it is fishery which wounds rather than captures in a net or other enclosure, and wounds by day rather than by night, and round the head and mouth with a barbed hook rather than anywhere else with a spear. To be an angler is therefore to be an artist who forcibly but stealthily seizes living prey belonging to the water and does so by day with the use of a barbed hook which wounds the head and mouth. This λόγος is arrived at by dichotomous division, but the alternatives covered are not the exact negations of one another, nor is any criterion of exhaustiveness provided. The definer in fact knows what an angler is, and is empirically familiar with its alternatives at various levels of generality, and so steers the division until it comes down just in the right place. It is strange that such a jejune procedure should have been thought by some to represent an important *Entwicklung* of Plato's mature thought, and a great advance on the vaguer methodology of the *Republic*.

The Sophist is now fitted into a number of serially dichotomizing divisions based on the same scheme as the angler: the fact that the Stranger gives so many alternative accounts of the Sophist shows that he is not really serious about any of them. The Sophist is a hunter of land animals rather than of such as inhabit a fluid medium, and he is a hunter of tame land animals rather than wild ones, and he hunts by cunning persuasion rather than violence, and he persuades his prey to give him money in return for discourses about virtue, instead of giving them gifts for favours of another kind. Alternatively the Sophist is an exchanger, and as an exchanger a seller rather than a giver, and a seller of other men's wares and not of his own, and of wares imported from foreign parts rather than locally produced, and of wares of a spiritual rather than a bodily kind, and of wares consisting in the learning of an art rather than a display of the same, and in a learning about virtue rather than any other subject-matter. In the same way the Sophist is an open contender who fights rather than competes, and who fights with words rather than with the body, and who fights in brief, private questions and answers, rather than in long public speeches, and who is concerned with Justice and Injustice themselves and similar topics, rather than with the justice and injustice of particular transactions. The Sophist is also, finally, seen as a separator (διαιρετικός, διακριτικός), separation being a new art which is neither productive nor acquisitive, and which therefore disturbs the dichotomy of the previous divisions. He is, further, a separator of the better from the worse and hence a purifier, and a purifier of the living rather than the lifeless, and a purifier of the soul from a deep ignorance which causes it to swerve from the truth towards which it is striving (28c, d), rather than from the baseness (πονηρία) which consists in a general measurelessness (ἀμετρία) and consequent conflict (στάσις) among the elements in the Soul. The baseness and measurelessness of the Soul goes together with the deeper ignorance and tends to reinforce it, but is not identical with it. Its cure lies in the art of corrective punishment (κολαστική), whereas the cure of ignorance lies in moral teaching (διδασκαλική), which can either be of the old-fashioned, ineffective, admonitory sort practised by parents and other authorities, or of the new-fashioned Socratic sort which shows up the self-contradictions involved in various systematic immoralisms, and so makes a man angry at himself and his own stupidity and ashamed of the psychic asymmetries that consort with his folly. The purification of the Soul from such deeper ignorance is the noble Sophistry (ἡ γένει γενναία σοφιστική) from which common-or-garden Sophistry is a mere declination.

In understanding what it is to be Socratic we understand the falling short of Socraticism which is Sophistry.

Neither the several characterizations of Sophistry in terms of production or acquisition, or the final characterization in terms of purification, are, however, satisfactory, for the very reason that they are multiple. Obviously they have not penetrated to the common target of all the skills they describe (εἰς ὃ πάντα τὰ μαθήματα ταῦτα βλέπει). If, however, Socratic Sophistry has been rightly described as a technique which purifies the soul of a false conceit of knowledge, and thereby enables its real insight to function, then Sophistry in the pejorative sense can plainly be described as a technique which, by the disputing of all opinions, creates a false belief in the boundlessly superior insight of the universal disputer. Like the painter, who can in a sense 'make' everything, but only in counterfeit or in imitation, so the Sophist can make likenesses of everything in words or in argument, can turn Justice into the advantage of the stronger or anything else whatever, and so create a firm impression of his own unlimited sagacity. To pin down the Sophist dialectically we shall therefore have to carry out divisions in the genus of thaumaturgic likeness-making, until at length we find one species that exactly fits him (235a–c). Of such likeness-making there are two main sub-species: the making of approximately exact images (εἰκόνες) of some original, which may be called Eicastic, and the making of things that will merely *look* like some original, when seen in some peculiar light or fashion, and which do not, when seen in a good light or straightforward fashion, really resemble it at all. The second form of likeness-making may be called Phantastic, or the art of illusion, and the question arises whether the Sophist is to be classed as an eicastic or as a phantastic artist, as a fairly accurate model-maker or a cunning illusionist.

The investigation is, however, interrupted by a far more serious question: How is illusion, whether substantial or merely suggestive, really possible at all? How can there even be an appearance, in dialectical dispute, that Justice is the interest of the stronger, when this is not what Justice really is at all? To say that there *is* such a momentary appearance seems to give some sort of substance to what confessedly has no substance and being, and so to violate the Parmenidean rule that one should keep oneself from supposing that what is not in some way is. Of what is not we cannot legitimately speak in the singular or the plural, since Number is above all something that has Being, and which cannot be attributed to what has no Being at all (238a, b). What is not, is in fact essentially unthinkable (ἀδιανόητον), ineffable (ἄρρητον), unutterable (ἄφθεγκτον) and indescribable (ἄλογον – 238c). Even to make these statements is to make what is not, a single thing, and to give it some sort of being, which should not be possible. The Sophist has therefore escaped into an infinitely secure hide-out. The likenesses he is supposed to create are not seizable pictures or models or reflections but likenesses set before us in discourse alone (240a), likenesses which are not truly what they are the likenesses of, and yet truly are the likenesses of it, and so combine being and non-being in a thoroughly mystifying manner, without anything seizable to give substance to the distinctions we try to draw. All we have is a something which in some way isn't, and which therefore *is*, in being just this sort of something. It will not do to say that it is *we* who have false opinion about such a something, for false opinions must opine something opposed to what really is, and must see this as really being, or must see what really is as not being, and all this involves a not-being which is truly thinkable, or has a being in thought, which is quite contrary to the complete exclusion of not being from being that was previously asserted (241a, b). It is plain that, to escape from our difficulties, we must impiously question the central pronouncement of our father Parmenides, we must dare to assert that what is not, the false and merely semblant, after a manner (κατά τι) is, and conversely that what is, after a manner (πῇ) also is not (241a). Only when this has been established, shall we be able to return to the problem of the classificatory position of the Sophist.

The Dialogue now passes to a wonderful characterization of philosophical differences which, exoterically speaking, ranges over the differences among the early Greek philosophers, while it also has a readily fathomed reference to contemporary idealism and the quarrels of the Academy. The early philosophers, the Stranger says, discoursed rather too complacently (εὐκόλως) about the number of ultimate entities they admitted, and constructed children's stories about them, instead of building them into a scientific ontology. Some accepted a triad of ultimate

principles, at times warring with one another, at times contracting marriages and begetting offspring: others accepted a
dualism of basic contraries. The Eleatic tribe, whose origins lie
with Xenophanes or further back, are unwavering monists. The
severe thought of Heraclitus, and the more relaxed thought of
Empedocles, believe in a union of many principles, bound
together by love and enmity, a permanent union of impermanents
in the case of the severer school, and an alternation between close
union and extreme disunion in the case of the more relaxed
thinkers. What, however, all these mythologists fail to ask is
what is really to be understood by the 'Being' which they attribute to the one or many entities that they acknowledge, a Being
which assembles differing and disparate things under its covering
sense. If the Hot and the Cold are said to be all the things that
there are, what do we mean by saying of each and both of them
that they *are*? Is Being some third, distinct thing common to the
Hot and the Cold, or is it the same as one or both of them, in
either of which cases all that is will be confounded in unity? On
the other hand, if we follow the Eleatic line, and say that all is
one, or that one thing alone *is*, we are plainly saying of something both that it is one and also that it *is*, thereby applying two
names to the same object. It would be ridiculous to admit *two*
names in a strictly monistic ontology, and even to admit a single
name flies in the face of reason. For, if the name differs from
what it names, we shall have two things, and if it does not differ,
it will either name nothing or name only itself. In the latter case,
the one reality will be the name of the one reality, and also the
name of this name (244a), and presumably so on. And what are
we to make of the notion of the indivisible *whole* which features
so largely in Eleatic utterance? If what is, is such an indivisible
whole, it may indeed *have* unity as an affection ($\pi\acute{\alpha}\theta os$), but it
cannot *be* Unity Itself, which must have nothing of parts about it.
If reality is a whole, Unity must be distinct from it, though
qualifying it, and all the things that are, will be many. But if, on
the other hand, what is, is not a complete whole of distinct parts,
then Wholeness Itself, which we take to be something, will fall
outside of Being, which will accordingly fall outside of itself, and
will yield a plurality of entities. But if there is no such thing as
Wholeness, there neither is, nor can come to be, a complete
entity anywhere, and Being and Becoming are alike senseless

without completeness (245 d). It is plain that the early cosmologists have lost all relevance to the argument. The Stranger is
talking about the eidetic cosmos and its structure, and showing
that it is as absurd to break it up into a number of unrelated,
mutually exclusive entities – he talks in 246b of those who would
shatter everything into tiny particles in their discourses – as to
lose all its varied aspects in a quite undifferentiated unity.

In the next reference to the myths of past philosophy, the
Stranger speaks of a doctrinal war between Giants and Gods, the
former dragging all invisible, heavenly things down to earth, and
identifying real Being with body and with what resists touch,
while the latter identify true Being with certain bodiless, thinkable
patterns of which so-called bodily Being is merely a dispersed,
inconstant expression. The surface-reference in the first case is
to the pre-Socratic cosmologists in general, but it is arguable that
who are more pregnantly the target are what may be called the
'immanentalist' wing in the Academy, of which Aristotle later
became the spokesman, a wing which refused to countenance
(except in a few privileged cases) any apartness of the Eide from
the matter or body with which they were united, while the
surface-reference, in the second case, is to the Academic Platonists
in general, though Plato's critical stance taken up towards them
shows that they were rather in the nature of an Old Guard, who
believed in a stark separateness of Eide from Eide and from
sensibles, which Plato was finding more and more unacceptable.

The argument against both wings lies basically in pointing to
the Soul whose activities bridge the gulf between visible and
invisible, and which is as much bound, on the one hand, to the
realm of eternal significance, as it is, on the other hand, to the
realm of bodily instantiation. The reply to the protagonists of
body is that there surely are such things as animated bodies,
bodies exhibiting the self-movement and intelligent discernment
which mark the presence of Soul, a presence unquestionably of
something that *is*. But even if Soul could in part be thought of in
corporeal terms, there are sides of its being which cannot be
thought of in this manner. Soul takes cognizance of, and can also
follow out, what is Just Itself and Wise Itself, and these no one
would allow to be visible, bodily realities, so that the Soul
which takes cognizance of them, and acts upon them, cannot be
a purely visible, bodily reality either (247a, b). Even those who

fancy that there is a bodily side to Soul (δοκεῖν σῶμά τι κεκτῆσθαι –247b) – arguably a reference to a nascent form of the views expressed in the *De Anima*, a very Academic document – would never dream of ascribing bodiliness to Wisdom, Phronesis Itself, the eternal Eidos of all those acts of intelligence that souls can perform.

The argument is capped by another contention that can readily be misinterpreted: that whatever has such a nature as in the slightest degree to do something or be acted on by something, even if only on one occasion, must truly have Being, and that things that are can even have as a provisional ὅρος or definition that they are nothing but power (δύναμις – 247e). On such a definition, the power of the bodiless Eide to effect genuine changes in Souls, and through Souls on bodies, stamps them as being indubitably as real as the bodies on which they act, and whose Being is not questioned by those to whom the argument is addressed. Despite the use of the term ὅρος, the definition of Being as Power does not indicate a completely new orientation to Being as Such: a philosopher so refined as to distinguish between Being and Unity, or Being and Wholeness, is unlikely to identify Being with so derivative and complex a notion as the Power to do or suffer, which is only one of the things that there are, and which is, moreover, arguably, a power to *be*, and so involving the notion it is used to elucidate. Plainly what Plato is here recurring to is the old doctrine of the true causality of the Eide, that they make a difference, and in fact all the difference, in the realm of bodily visibility, and for those to whom the ontological claims of this realm are paramount, it is an argument carrying immense persuasion. It is in fact even today a quite decisive argument against many forms of neuralistic mechanism, for it cannot be doubted that ideal relations of meaning are operative in many cases of cerebral action and direction, and that such an influence on motivation, or whatever one may choose to call it, is not such as anything corporeal, or in fact anything instantial, could readily exercise. Universals acting as naked universals are plainly the operative agents in some cases of intelligent, perhaps even unconscious, cerebration. It is therefore only as a mark of true Being that Power is here selected, and the mark is chosen because it suits the man to be persuaded.

The same mark is employed against the one-sided, separatist

protagonists of the Eide, who pulverize Being into a vast number of unchangeable Essences, which are what they are without any capacity or need to do or undergo anything whatever, while all interweaving of such Essences or all seeming action or suffering among them, is entirely a matter of 'Becoming', of the changeable, instantial world (248c). These friends of the Eide admit, however, that we have commerce with such Eide through the thinking discourse of our Souls, just as we have commerce with instantial becoming through our senses, and such admission implies that there is indeed a dynamic relation between our thinking selves and the eternal Eide, and that they do something to us, or, perhaps more acceptably, we do something to them (248d, e). To deny such commerce is to remove Motion, Life, Understanding and Soul from what most absolutely is, and to turn the latter into a solemn, sacred fixture, in which there can be neither Understanding nor Movement (248e–249a). The friends of the Eide do not wish to make the Eide quite alien from, and inaccessible to our changeable, instantial thinking, and they must therefore concede that both what changes (τὸ κινούμενον) and also change (κίνησις) really *are*, and to make all that is, be immobile, is in effect to banish Mind from reality (249b). The friends of the Eide would, however, be going too far if they denied the being of what always are the same, and are just as they are, for without such unchangeably stable entities to know, Knowledge, Wisdom and Mind would be ruled out (249c). What is, must therefore neither be placed wholly in the unchangeable, nor in the changeable, but must in all cases combine change with changelessness (249c, d).

The statements in this passage are as open to misinterpretation as in the former passage regarding Being as Power. Plato *cannot* be saying that changeable instantiation has the same foothold in absolute Being as unchanging eidetic content: this is shown by the fact that, in the next section, he does not go on to discuss the relation of the unchanging Eide to changeable instances of knowing or anything else, but the relation of the *Eidos* of Stasis or Unchangeability to the *Eidos* of Kinesis or Change. Plato is only asserting that changeable instances do have *some* foothold in the realm of absolute Being, and that, in particular, the pure Eide of Wisdom, Knowledge, Belief, Life etc., whose absolute status is never in question, would be nothing except as imparting instantial insight and instantial life to instantial minds and souls, of which, of course, the directive, divine Soul of the Cosmos is the chief. The Active Intelligence, we may say, to pass over into the language of Aristotle, possibly in formation at this very time, requires passive intelligences to act upon, in order to be the Active Intelligence that it absolutely is. Plato is here making an immense, but necessary, concession to instantialism: he is saying that, since the Eide *alone* have Absolute Being, not even that simulacrum of Absolute Being that we call the realm of instantiation can be anything but a mode of the Eide, an outflow, if one likes, of their power. Though we may seem to act on the impassive Eide in knowing them, it is really the Eide (of Knowledge, Wisdom etc.) that are active in all our knowledge, and without such activity none of these august Eide could be what they are. And so much is a relation to the world of Becoming and to the knowing of that world, built into the Eide, that there necessarily is, among those Eide, the very Principle of that world: Kinesis, Movement, no less than Stasis, Rest, must be one of the highest genera in the eidetic sphere. It will be observed that *t*'s have been crossed and *i*'s dotted in my comments on this famous passage, but I have, it may be claimed, done so less audaciously than most other commentators.

The Stranger now points out that, in conceding Being both to Stasis or Stability as Such, and to Kinesis or Movement as Such, two of the most irreconcilable of the Eide, we are not identifying Being with either of these irreconcilables, but conceiving both as having a communion or commerce (κοινωνία) with Being, a communion which Being, in its own nature (κατὰ τὴν αὐτοῦ φύσιν), does not reciprocate, since it can neither be said to be at rest nor in motion (250c). But this last involves a seeming antinomy, since it appears evident that what is not at rest *must* be in motion, and what is not in motion at rest (250c, d). (In reality, we may note, the Stranger's antinomy is quite confusedly based, since Stability and Movement are only irreconcilable in what participates in them, while Movement as Such, being an Eidos, certainly participates in the Stability characteristic of all Eide, including Being and Stability.) The case of Being, an Eidos one-sidedly shared in by both Movement and Stability, which do not share in one another – a better-chosen example would be Being or Motion in relation to Fastness and Slowness, which are not mutually predicable – is, however, used to raise the whole question of the communion or non-communion of the Eide. It has long been accepted that there is nothing absurd when a sensible thing has the names of several Eide predicated of it, when a variety of shapes, sizes, colours and virtues are said of it: only very young or very silly old men want to argue that Man is only Man, Goodness only Goodness etc. The question, however, is whether it is not equally sensible to predicate the names of certain Eide of other Eide, so that Stability and Movement, while not being Being, can none the less both be said to *be*. And we have also to ask whether Eide *never* share in or commune with other Eide, or do so in all cases, or in some cases do so, and in some cases not (251a). Obviously, it is absurd to hold to a doctrine of universal non-communion, which would not only destroy all the philosophies of changeless Unity, changing Multiplicity etc. detailed above, but would also even conflict with its own utterance and acceptance, since to say that nothing can have any part in anything else, is to connect several Eide in a single utterance (252c). But a doctrine of universal communion is equally unacceptable, since this would imply, for example, that Movement is stable and Stability is in motion, which we have agreed to regard as absurd. (In reality, Movement, being an Eidos, *is* stable, while Stability, also being an Eidos, is stable and *not* in motion.)

We are therefore led to a view of eidetic communion in some cases, and non-communion in others, which points to the necessity of a special art or science which will tell us *when* we have a case of eidetic communion and when not. Just as there are arts of grammar and phonology which tell us how words may be combined into sentences, and how sounds may be combined into words, so there is an art called 'Dialectic', not perhaps that of the Sophist, but certainly that of the Philosopher, which will show us how the Eide may be fitted together in the constitution of the realm of sense. (Justice, for example, cannot be fitted together with the interest of the stronger, even if a Sophist may persuade us that it can.) The philosophical dialectician will then be able to sort out the eidetic realm into Kinds (γένη), and will never imagine the same Eidos, however referred to, to be one that is different, nor imagine different Eide to be one and the same. He will, further, see some Eide which are, as it were, the connective tissue of the whole system, which render communion possible, for example the Eidos of Participation, and others which everywhere underlie division, for example the incapacity for joint exemplification which Movement has to Stability (253c). He will also be able to see one Eidos spread through numerous quite separate individual cases, and many distinct Eide held together in the embrace of a single, comprehensive Eidos, and again many Eide wholly set apart (253d). (The last are probably cases of corruption or deviation, and even cases of the false and the absurd which the Dialogue is in fact investigating, and which, though excluded from eidetic Being, necessarily share in it, in and through that very exclusion.)

To illustrate the articulations which have been thus marvellously described the Stranger elects to examine the character and eidetic relations of a few highly generic Eide: such an examination will, it is hoped, not only throw light on the Being which pervades all the Eide, but also on the Non-being, the element of shifting illusion, which also haunts them all, and which constitutes our present problem. Stability and Movement are two of the major Kinds to be considered, and, on the Stranger's view, they cannot be 'mixed' with one another, but Being, the third major Kind, 'mixes' with both of them, since either of them can be said to be. Obviously, however, two other major Kinds are essential to a fully described eidetic picture: each of the three major Kinds has Sameness to the Kind in question, and Difference, Otherness to each of the remaining Kinds. Are such Sameness and Difference two other major Kinds, necessarily mixed with the three Kinds under examination, and as it were holding them apart, or can either of them be identified with one or other of these three Kinds? The second alternative is obviously absurd, and leads to absurd consequences, for example if Sameness is identical with Being, then the common Being of Motion and Rest will also be their common Sameness. The essentially relative character of Otherness (τὸ ἕτερον), in virtue of which nothing can be other in isolation, but only in relation to some other other, also forbids us to identify Otherness with the non-relative character of Being (255d).

Otherness now assumes a very important place among the five Kinds under consideration: it is not in virtue of being what they are that eidetic Kinds differ from one another, but in virtue of an Otherness and a Difference which, as it were, supervenes upon what they are and is the truly differentiating factor (255e). The Stranger might equally have observed that an Eidos is not the same as that Eidos in virtue of being the Eidos that it is, for example Movement, but in virtue of a supervenient Sameness which is always and necessarily (ἐξ ἀνάγκης ἀεί – see 254e) consequent upon what anything is. The relations of the five eidetic Kinds to one another are now gone through in some detail. Movement is, in the first place, other than Stability, and does not, as has been previously held, share in it, but the Stranger admits that it would not be self-contradictory to say that it *did* share in it, while not *being* it (256b). Movement is also other than Sameness, and yet is the same as Movement, in virtue of a share in the Same. Movement is also other than Otherness, and yet shares in Otherness in virtue of the very fact of being other than Otherness, and likewise in virtue of the fact of being other than Sameness and other than Stability. Movement, finally, is plainly other than Being, and yet unquestionably shares in Being: in different senses therefore Movement is and is not a case of Non-being (256d).

It is now argued that the nature of Otherness engenders a sort of Non-being throughout the whole realm of the Eide: every Eidos is, in the sense of participating in, many other Eide, but every Eidos is not, in the sense of being other than, countless other Eide, and even Being shares in this sort of Non-being, inasmuch as it is other than every Eidos but Being as Such. This sort of Non-being is not in any way opposed to Being: it merely differs from it, and it is divided into countless specific forms according to what it negates or is other than. Thus Not-being-lovely is one species of this pervasive Non-being, whereas Not-being-large or Not-being-just are others (257d–258b). Being Itself has countless specific forms, according as this or that Eidos shares in it, and each of these countless specific forms is also a case of Not-being-all-the-other-specific-forms-of-Being (259b). Not-being is therefore so far from being an unmentionable alternative to Being that it pervades all Being. It is also involved in all discourse, since in all discourse Eide are always being combined with Eide which are *not*, i.e. other than, themselves, and an attempt to eliminate the contrast which always presupposes, yet always overleaps Not-being, would destroy discourse altogether (259e). The question, however, arises whether discourse may not involve Not-being in a sense more pregnant than that of a mere contrast of existent elements, whether things as they occur in discourse may not in some unique sense be other than things as they occur outside of discourse, and so yield us a case of that pregnant falsehood or Non-being of which the Sophist denied the thinkability (260c–e). It is to this more fundamental enquiry that the Dialogue now turns.

Discourse and Thinking (διάνοια) are seen by the Stranger as one and the same sort of thing, except that Discourse involves a stream of sound proceeding from the mouth, whereas Thinking is the soul's silent dialogue with itself which is the soundless source of Discourse (263e–264a). The assertion and denial that are present in Discourse are likewise present in the silent Thinking that inspires Discourse, and are called Opinion (δόξα) or Sensuous Seeming (φαντασία), and so will be distinctions corresponding to those that occur in Discourse. Basic among such distinctions are those of the noun and the verb: a mere string of verbs such as 'walks', 'runs', 'sleeps' will not constitute Discourse, nor will a mere string of nouns such as 'lion', 'stag', 'horse' do so. For Discourse to exist verbs must be *mingled* with nouns: unless this is done, no action or inaction or being or anything that is or is not can be shown forth by verbal noises (262c). It must, however, be in this mingling of nouns and verbs, and in the corresponding mingling of the thoughts of agents and actions, that the character-istic saying or thinking what is not, and the consequent falsehood of Discourse and Thought, will be found. This possibility is explored, not as one might expect in the context, in regard to the relations among the names and thoughts of Eide, but in regard to the relations among the names and thoughts of instantial agents like Theaetetus, and the names and thoughts of such actions as sitting and flying. To understand the passage fully, one must transpose what is said from such banal examples to the eidetic contexts which are principally in question, since the best Sophists do not try to persuade us that Theaetetus is flying. If I say or silently think that Theaetetus, to whom I am now speaking, is sitting, I say or think something about Theaetetus that is true, whereas if I say or silently think that Theaetetus is flying, I say or think something about him that is false. But such truth of my first assertion or thought plainly means that I am saying or thinking about Theaetetus things that are *as* they are regarding him, whereas the falsehood of my second assertion or thought plainly means that I am saying or thinking about Theaetetus things *other* than the things which *are* in his case, and I am thus treating what *are not* in his case, as if they *were* in his case. A false statement is therefore a combination of nouns and verbs which states what are different, as being the same, and what are not, as being what are (263d), and a false thought or belief or imagination is merely a corresponding piece of the silent Discourse of the soul. In either case, what is not, merely means something *other* than what is, and we are no longer in the dilemma posed by the Sophist of having to say of someone who says or believes something false, that he is saying or believing nothing.

It is very easy to misunderstand the subtle argument here put forward, and to see in it only the jejune plea that, though someone who says or believes that Theaetetus is flying, or, more interestingly, that Justice is the interest of the stronger, is combining thoughts and words wrongly, the separate thoughts and words do at least correspond to things that are. Such a being of mere elements would do nothing to solve the problems of false thought and utterance, since what these concern is elements *combined*, not elements isolated, and it is elements combined which, in falsehood, seem to have no being. It is not Theaetetus as Theaetetus, or flying as flying, or Justice as Justice, or the interest of the stronger as the interest of the stronger, that are not, but Theaetetus as flying, or Justice as being the interest of the stronger, that are not, in other words things that are as otherwise than they are. And what the Stranger's solution amounts to is that, in the case of combinations, there is an Otherness or an Otherwiseness which is *no more than* an Otherness or an Otherwiseness, which does not imply any straightforward Being for the combination it is other or otherwise than, though it does draw content from the real elements of that combination. In other words, everything, in being as it is, and being combined as it is combined, delimits a sphere of alternatives, sometimes nonsensical, which represent what it isn't, and which as thus other and excluded, are merely the other side to what it is, and are indissolubly wedded to its sense. They have the being of Not-being, to which Plato, accepting a graded ontology, has not the aversion so common in modern thinking, but sees as the essential obverse side of Being taken simply, much as, for Wittgenstein, even tautology and contradiction, though in a sense 'saying' nothing, are still parts of 'the language'. And the combinations which thus, after a fashion, are, in being straightforwardly excluded by what straightforwardly is, or is the case, also after a fashion are, in being believed, or in being verbally asserted. The Sophist, therefore, as a naïve ontologist, is left without a leg to stand on.

The Dialogue now returns to the serial dichotomizing which, it is hoped, will yield a λόγος of the Sophist. What is now divided is, however, the genus of productive, not acquisitive, art. There is held to be a divine production responsible for natural existents, and a human production responsible for artificial objects. Each of these forms of production is further divided into a form which makes the things themselves, and a form which makes images, eidola, of things. In divine production the images produced are such things as reflections, shadows and dreams, whereas, in human production, they are either instrumentally constructed works of art, or images shaped in words, in which Justice, Virtue etc. appear as other than they are. If such images are constructed with conscious irony, given every semblance of full reality, yet known to be the unreliable things that they are, then we undoubtedly have before us what it is to be a Sophist.

II

The *Statesman* is a very different Dialogue from the *Sophist*, and has little of its fine exploration of the principles of the eidetic theory, but is rather a belated reappraisal and revival of themes and methods found in the *Republic*: it has, at the same time, the external setting and pattern of the *Sophist*, of which it is the sequel, being set on the imaginary day after the imaginary day of the discussion conducted in the *Sophist*. The Stranger from Elea is again the principal speaker, while Socrates and Theodorus sit silent among the audience. Only the answerer is changed from Theaetetus to the younger Socrates; the change betrays no discoverable motive, except perhaps the desire to compliment some younger member of the Academy, whose interests were political. The Dialogue seeks to achieve a definition of the Statesman and the Divine King by the same tedious, arbitrary method of dichotomic division that was used in the *Sophist*, illustrated by the supremely uninteresting case of Weaving. There is, however, some criticism and apology for this travesty of a method. The division of polities, into three sorts of good and bad states as set forth in the *Republic*, is revived, but a new ideal of human and divine Monarchy assumes the position of the politically best, while Democracy, in a restrained form, is deemed to be the least evil of the inferior polities. There is also a remarkable concession of the need for unprogrammed improvisation in the endlessly inexact realm of practice: precise, mathematical law may hold in the realm of the Eide, but is a mere *faute de mieux* in the realm of flux and the instance. There is also a stress on the Mean, and on the need to effect compromises between differing trends in Virtue, which became the foundation of Aristotle's immensely concrete ethical phenomenology. And there is, finally, the fascinating disclosure of a Pythagorean doctrine of the periodic reversal of the direction of time which has much relevance for modern scientific and philosophical speculation.

The Dialogue begins with an attempt to pin down what it is to be a Statesman, which is taken to be the same question as what it is to be a King. It is thought clear that being a Statesman or being a King consists in the mastery of an appropriate science, whether one is in fact called upon to apply such a science or not. A private person may be kingly if he knows what ought to be done in political situations. It is also thought clear that the householder (οἰκονόμος) must be in possession of the same science: that he wields it in a restricted sphere is not important. This science is not narrowly practical like Architecture, nor yet wholly theoretical like Arithmetic: it passes judgment (κρίσις) on various matters, but it also prescribes (ἐπιτάττει) courses of action that depend on these judgments. The prescriptions put forward by the Kingly Science are, moreover, last prescriptions, not prescriptions mediated by subordinates from some higher authority (261a), and they are prescriptions not only addressed to living beings but also concerned with living beings (261c, d), and with their begetting and their nurture. They are, further, prescriptions concerned with living beings taken in herds (ἀγελαί), and not as isolated individuals. At this point the young Socrates wishes at once to divide herd-management into the management of beasts and the management of men, and to associate the Kingly Science with the latter. The Stranger, with strange scruple, counsels against such ill-considered dichotomy: we must not take for granted, in scientific division, that the small class of men deserves to be set against the whole vast class of other animals. To assume this is to be dialectically chauvinistic, as are the Greeks when they rank all other peoples as barbarians, and as wise cranes might be who dismissed all other animals as non-cranes. Dichotomically we must proceed, since Duality is in some sense the fundamental opposite of Unity, but our dichotomies must take account of some genuine, centrally placed difference, which divides a genus into two approximately equal species, such as occurs in the case of the Odd and the Even, or the Female and the Male (262d, e).

The Stranger proceeds, therefore, to divide the group-management of animals into the group-management of wild and of tame animals, and of solitary and gregarious animals: the group-management of tame, gregarious animals is obviously the right *cadre*, and divides into the group-management of water- and land-animals, while the latter divides into the group-management of horned land-animals and of hornless land-animals, and, in the latter case, of hornless land-animals that interbreed with other species, and of hornless land-animals that do not so interbreed. Finally we have the divisions into quadrupeds and bipeds, and into winged and wingless bipeds, so that the Kingly Science becomes one which prescribes the group-management of tame, gregarious, land-living, hornless, non-interbreeding, two-footed, wingless, living beings. It is not clear that there is anything genuinely eidetic in this long division, and it is not clear why the Kingly Science might not have exercised itself on the Houyhnhnms or on the wise cranes that the Stranger has mentioned. The objection is not, however, to the grossly empirical character of these divisions, but to the fact that it has not singled out the Ideal Monarch, who controls all political life, from the innumerable, independent authorities who, in an actual state, *try* to exercise such control, the merchants, farmers, grocers, gymnasts, doctors, accoucheurs etc., who all seek to direct human life without taking a lead from a further authority (267e–268b). It is only as setting the tone for all these subordinate performers, that the true King, as eidetic schema, can make his emergence. Since such a true King reveals himself only to eidetic intuition, and is not now to be found in the realm of instantiation, we may turn to an old tale which will explain why this is so.

The Stranger now unfolds the magnificent story of a past age of the world when everything happened in reverse, but when Divinity was also in complete charge of the tiller of the world, so that it also was an age of gold. God, by whom undoubtedly is meant Mind as Such, the comprehensive vision eternally correlated with the Eide and itself an Eidos, systematically varies his grip upon the world, sometimes helping it on and circling about it, sometimes so relaxing his grip that the cosmos and its intelligent Soul are at once forced by an inherent necessity (διὰ τί ἐξ ἀνάγκης ἔμφυτον – 26c, d) to reverse their motion. The reason for this alternation lies in the bodily nature of the Cosmos – which is plainly not different from its instantial nature, its essential, dispersed changingness – it cannot realize the total changelessness of the Eide, but, since it is the highest of instances, change is in its case reduced to a minimum. It continues to move in a circle exactly where it is, but it reverses the direction of that motion. It cannot be the Divine Nature as Such that moves it thus oppositely, nor can it be a second Divine Nature opposed to the first: it is the nature of the world, as an instantial, bodily existence, that forces it from time to time to depart from its single uniform direction, as at other times it forces it to conform to it (269d–270a).

At present we live in a period of relaxation of divine guidance, or, what is the same, of spontaneous self-direction by the forces of body or instantiation. But there was another time when all this was different, when the sun and stars rose in the west and set in the east, and when living creatures were not begotten by parents nor grew up from infancy to maturity and on to old age and burial in the earth, but rather sprang from the earth (γηγενεῖς) and then regressed through what we now call age, maturity and infancy and then vanished altogether. (The Stranger has not the audacity to suggest that they ended up in their 'mothers'' wombs.) In that other time, we may hold, divine Daemons were Kings and Shepherds over various naturally docile herds, and God, or Divine Reason Itself, was the Shepherd and King of them all. But at an appointed time, fixed by changeless mathematical relations, the divine direction of the world ceased, and the random forces of instantiation were liberated. These random forces, full of obstruction and injustice (χαλεπὰ καὶ ἄδικα), stemmed from an earlier dispensation, and must have been held in check in the golden period just mentioned. Now, however, they infected the heavens, and from these spread to the living inhabitants of the Cosmos. The time-order of human and animal development became as it is at present. Men were no longer sown in the earth, to emerge therefrom full-grown, and undergo gradual diminution, but were begotten as at present, and, like the self-regulated Cosmos, achieved maturity through their own exertions. The resourcelessness and misery of early human existence were mitigated by the compassionate cultural gifts of Prometheus, Hephaestus, Athene and other divinities, but by and large men were left in what modern existentialist philosophers would call a 'thrown' condition, left wholly in all circumstances to fend for themselves. It is on account of the 'thrown' condition in which men now subsist, and the corresponding 'thrown' condition of the Cosmos, that the Kingly Science has no instantial wielders and possessors, and is for us merely an eidetic Shape.

The myth just sketched must have been seriously intended, and fits in with accounts of cycles in the *Republic*, even if not quite in harmony with the teachings of the *Timaeus*. It is also remarkable for its anticipation of modern musings on the complete reversal of the time-order of happenings, or scientific musings on the variable direction of entropy. And it suggests a rational eschatology which, while recognizing vast possibilities of corruption, yet gives comfort to human despair. Its major importance lies, however, in its clear view of the instantial as so wholly dependent on the invariantly eidetic that even its cyclical variations have an eidetic foundation: it is not something external and fortuitous that causes the rhythmical pulsation of the cosmos, but an element of accident which is as such inherent in its Eidos, its essential pattern. No one who reads Plato carefully can doubt that in his doctrines dualism is as much 'overcome' as it is deeply recognized.

After recounting his myth, the Stranger goes on to add refinements to his conception of the royal Statesman. He will have a general care of wingless bipeds rather than being in charge of some precise need like their feeding, and his care of them will be voluntarily rather than compulsorily accepted. This is still felt to be too vague and wide a characterization, and the Stranger

tries to show what he is striving for by working out a circumscription of Weaving. This circumscription will not only throw
light on the Royal Science, but on the nature of analogy
($\pi\alpha\rho\alpha\delta\epsilon\hat{\iota}\gamma\mu\alpha$): we shall see how the soul can come to discern the
basic identity of elements which, well-known in one simple
context, pass quite unrecognized in another (278a–e). The many
steps of the division which leads to a pinning down of Weaving
may here be ignored, though they bring out the deeply 'natural',
i.e. eidetic character of many distinctions found in human
technology. The Stranger admits to the full that no one would
wish to analyse Weaving for its own sake, but he argues that the
discernment of Eide in a comparatively humble, sensuously
presented case will make it easier to discern quite bodiless Eide
which only yield themselves up to argument and discourse
(285d–286a). One must not fear to be long-winded (or the
reverse), if this leads in the end to a more perfect division among
the Eide (286d).

What emerges from the analysis of Weaving is, however, that
it involves both separation ($\delta\iota\acute{\alpha}\lambda\upsilon\sigma\iota s$, $\delta\iota\alpha\kappa\rho\acute{\iota}\sigma\iota s$) and combination
($\sigma\upsilon\mu\pi\lambda o\kappa\acute{\eta}$, $\sigma\upsilon\gamma\kappa\rho\acute{\iota}\sigma\iota s$): the intertwined, clotted fibres must be
twisted into separate threads, and the separate threads must then
be woven together into one fabric. The separated threads must,
moreover, be of two sorts: the tightly drawn threads of the warp,
and the more loosely and softly knit threads of the woof. In all
this it is important to notice the part played by metric considerations. There is a Greater and a Less throughout the process
of weaving, and there is also a Mean of this Greater and Less
which is essential to its finished artistry. Greater and Less are
essentially relative to one another, but they are also essentially
relative to the well-measured ($\tau\grave{o}$ $\mu\acute{\epsilon}\tau\rho o\nu$), the Mean, and the
adherence to this Mean makes the difference between a good man
and a bad (283d, e), and is a condition of the success of all arts,
and of the excellence and beauty of their products. The notion of
the Mean has in fact the same importance in the realm of practice
that the notion of Non-being has in the realm of theory (284b, c).
What Plato, through the Stranger, is here asserting is that the
true line in theory, and the correct line in practice, are lines that
essentially include (by excluding) all the false and incorrect lines
that exceed them or fall short of them: they are a precise, simple,
numerical Ratio or structure of some sort, and they define, by not

straying into, the infinity of endlessly varying structures or Ratios which represent excess, defect, ugliness or irrationality. 'If the Mean exists, the Greater and the Less will do so too, and, if the Greater and the Less exist (reading ὄντων for οὐσῶν), the Mean will exist also, and if no Mean exists neither of the others will, nor will either of the others exist if one of them does not' (284a). It would be giving a poor appraisal of this, Plato's central philosophical conception, the mathematical character of all being and all value, to say that it comes close to the Aristotelian doctrine of the Mean.

The notion of the metric Mean must now be made central in Royal Science, which cannot be defined in terms of the uniqueness, the paucity or the multitudinousness of the governors, or in terms of their riches or poverty, their government according to fixed laws or without fixed laws, and with or without the consent of the governed (292c). 'Even if they kill certain persons and expel others, and so purge the city for its own good, and even if they reduce it by sending out colonies like swarms of bees, or increase it by admitting new citizens from abroad, as long as they abide by what is wise and just, and guard against deterioration, and make things as good as possible, the state which they rule over, and which has these marks, should be said by us to be the one true state' (293d, e). The legitimacy of dispensing with laws is questioned by the younger Socrates (293e), but the Stranger points out that no law can do justice to the dissimilarities of men and actions, and to the fact that nothing human keeps constant for a moment (294b). Government by laws is essentially a *pis aller*: it is like following a set of rules left by some doctor in his absence, but which he will not hesitate to alter when he returns and finds circumstances have altered. To act contrary to established laws, and to use force in doing so, cannot be regarded as a genuine case of wrongdoing, provided that it is done wisely and skilfully, and for the good of the citizens, and by a correct application of Royal Science (297a). It seems clear, however, we may remark, that the difficulty of applying Royal Science to the infinite detail of fact and practice must also mean that Royal Science in such an application can only amount to opinion, and that it therefore necessarily involves the possibility of differences of opinion, and the consequent wrongness of merely overriding one such 'scientific' opinion by another. Plato does not see that it is only at the eidetic limit that the evidently true and correct can correctly claim to override the incorrect and untrue, but that at this limit there will also cease to be all those varying circumstances to be reckoned with, that make it necessary to override rigorous laws. The notion of a science which operates in conditions which preclude the possibility of strict science, and which overrides all rules in deference to such conditions, has plainly something self-contradictory about it, but perhaps it indicates some relaxation and deepening of the Platonic conception of science.

The Stranger points out that, in the absence of Royal Science and a royal scientist, it is far better to adhere to fixed laws which reflect the wisdom of the royal scientists of the past, than to reject such laws altogether (300b). No large body of people can hope to master any science, and forms of government dominated by the numerous rich or by the yet more numerous mob, would do well never to stray beyond their own fixed written laws and traditional customs (300e–301a). When a single individual ruler, who is not a royal scientist, follows such laws, we have Monarchy, when he rules without such laws, Tyranny. And when the whole body of rich, who are of course not royal scientists, follow such laws, we have Aristocracy, when they rule without such laws, Oligarchy. Democracy, too, divides into a good and a bad species, according as it defers or does not defer to laws that have been handed down by royal lawgivers. And we may hold that, while Monarchy following good laws is the best of the imperfectly good polities, and Democracy following such laws the least good, while Aristocracy is intermediate, Democracy without good laws is the least bad of the three bad polities, Tyranny the worst, and Oligarchy of an intermediate degree of badness. Living under a royal scientist, and beyond the need of any laws, remains the best of political conditions (303a, b). Plato, we may note, attaches no Numbers to the good and bad polities thus distinguished; contrary to a widely-held opinion, his enthusiasm for precise numerical values seems to have waned since the time of the *Republic*.

The Dialogue ends by developing an interesting analogy between the Royal Art and the art of Weaving. Weaving, as we saw, involves a different and separate construction of the warp and the woof, and the weaving of both into one fabric: the

Royal or Political Art likewise involves the different and separate cultivations of two types of virtue, which must be interwoven in the political virtue of individual and community. The Stranger, echoing a passage in the *Charmides*, suggests that there is an incisive (ὄξυς), powerful (σφοδρός) species of virtue, seen both in bodily and mental performance, which is readily covered by the notion of Courage, while there is also a quiet (ἡσυχαῖος), orderly (κόσμιος), slow, gentle (μαλακός), rhythmic species of virtue, which is readily summed up in the notion of Orderliness or Temperance. These types of virtue are in a sense antagonistic to one another and resist mixture: those who exemplify the one type tend to be hostile and critical towards those who exemplify the other. Yet either type of virtue, if cultivated intensively and separately, becomes evil: the peace-loving, rhythmic moderates end in slavery, and so often do the over-daring activists who promote wars. The Royal Art will consist precisely in weaving together the warp of Courage and the woof of Self-restraint, in the correct manner and proportions, so as to yield the fabric of individual and social virtue (309a, b). In those capable of science, this weaving will involve, as an eternal, divine bond, firm and true opinions regarding beautiful, just and excellent things and their opposites, implanted by a suitable education. This will tone down the otherwise rude nature of the Courageous Element, while it will also prevent the element of Self-restraint and orderliness from degenerating into mere simplicity (εὐηθεία, 309e). But a fleshly, vital bond will also be needed in the weaving, and this will be provided by the intermarriage of audacious, assertive natures with gentle, temperate ones, and not exclusively, as too often tends to happen, with those of their own type (310e–311a). It is in the right blending of these two natures, involving always a Mean between excess and defect, that the Kingly Science has its task and function. What is interesting in the whole treatment is the relaxed character of the mathematicization which remains central to Plato's thought. It is an imprecise differentiation of the more than right, the less than right and the just right, dependent in the last resort on personal judgment and decision and the needs of the situation, as well as on timelessly exact eidetic relations, that is now what Plato deems truly scientific, and attributes to his divine king. He must know the eternal alignments of the Eide, but he must also know how to modify them and depart from them in the infinite intricacies of instantiation. In a sense, Plato hints, one does not depart from the Eide in applying them to an approximate world; one only fulfils them, gives them their due function.

III

The *Philebus* is a late Dialogue in which the role of the two basic Principles of the Platonic Stoicheiology, the Principle of Limit, variously identified with the Good, the True, the Measured or that which involves bounds (τὸ πέρας ἔχον) (but not with the One of which it is none the less plainly a variant), and the Principle of the Infinite (ἄπειρον), of the not marked-off Continuum, of indefinite Excess and Defect, are both clearly distinguished. And the two Principles are shown at work, first in the delimitation of the Eide (15c–18d), and then in the delimitation of instantial phenomena (23c–26d), the second being as it were an inferior reflection of the first. Part of the difficulty in understanding the Dialogue has been due to the ignoring of the plain statements of Aristotle that the *second* Principle, the Infinite or Great and Small, played a role in *both* generations, both as what Aristotle calls the indeterminate but determinable 'matter' or ὕλη of the Eide – Plato of course never uses this term – and then again as the corresponding 'matter' of their sensible instances (see for example *Metaphysics*, 988 10–15, and *Physics*, 203a with comment of Simplicius). Having been limited at the eidetic level, and so having had as an outcome the various specific Ideas, it then reappeared at the instantial level as the boundless emptiness or non-being of Space (see Simplicius on *Physics*, 209b 11, 35), and was again limited to give rise to the instances or 'copies' of the Ideas. Instantiation would, on this account, have many analogies with specification: both involve the self-differentiation of Unity into a diversity of forms, and the indefinite 'matter' or medium of either process would appear to be no more than a name for the specifiability of Unity and the instantiability of its specifications. The Dialogue is also important as clearly pointing to the role of the Cosmic Mind, instantiated in the World-Soul, and so a divine being and a God, as what is responsible for the imposition of eidetic Limit on the indefiniteness of the sense-order, and in distinguishing this Cosmic Mind, grandiose as it is, from a yet more august eidetic Mind or Mind as Such, which, eternally correlated with all the Eide, and a Godhead rather than a God, is responsible for all order, beauty and exact measure everywhere. The role played by the One or Good in generating the Eide (as in, for example, the *Parmenides* and the Unwritten Doctrines) is also the role played by this eidetic Mind, by way of the World-Soul, in generating the world of instances, and so *both* can be covered by the term Πέρας or Limit: the one is simply a more ultimate Limit than the other.

All this can be discerned in the Dialogue, which is, however, not primarily concerned with the Eide or their Principles or their relation to the instantial world, but with the question of the good life for man, and the position of pleasure and thought in that life. The old question, touched on in the *Republic*, as to whether pleasure or wisdom were the supreme good for man, and there lost sight of in the metaphysical consideration of the Good as Such, as the source of the Eide and of everything else through them, is here again taken up and given a remarkable solution. Just as sensation is something infinitely variable and standardless, which yet can acquire bounds of Number and Measure which enable us to advance through it to the firm truth regarding instantial realities, so pleasure, which in itself is infinitely variable and standardless, also can acquire bounds of Number and Measure which enable us to feel where the true eidetic joints lie, whether in our own thinking nature, or in the nature of anything else. There are true pleasures which are consonant with eidetic structure, and register the accommodation of our own eidetic patterns to them, just as there are false pleasures attuned to the infinite deviations in the way of Excess and Defect which are possible both in ourselves and the things that we have to do with. Plato goes far in showing how, in a world where the instantial always strives towards the eidetic, and has all its sense in doing so, there can be truth in some of the feelings and needs we experience, as much as in our perceptions and judgments, and that we can have true as well as false satisfactions, which acquaint us with real as opposed to merely seeming values. One can only regret that Plato ascetically sees the most truly pleasant in the most narrowly pure pleasure and the least admixed with pain, instead of seeing it, as moderns might prefer, in the widely ranging, the complexly structured and the not unmixed with overmastered pain. Eidetically structured pleasures are, however, subordinated to the structurings of mind which they accompany, and which represent the psychically enjoyed knowledge or understanding of those structures. And all of course are subordinate to Goodness or Measure or Ratio or Patterned Unity as Such.

The main speaker in the Dialogue is a revived Socrates, brought back to dramatic life since the central themes of the Dialogue are Socratic, and are indeed those which have been raised in such largely Socratic Dialogues as the *Gorgias* and the *Protagoras*. Socrates defends the superiority of the life of thought (τὸ φρονεῖν) to the life of mere enjoyment (τὸ χαίρειν), though he is willing to allow, as has been said, that there are rationally structured pleasures which assort well with the life of reflective reason. The defender of unstructured, source-irrelevant enjoyment, good only to the extent that it is enjoyment, and as such protracted, intense etc., is the young Philebus, a man of a few or indeed only of one idea, who is not interested in arguments for or against his goddess. The case for unstructured hedonism is therefore left in the hands of his less dogmatic friend Protarchus. The discussion is not to be confined to the possibility that enjoyment or thought, each by itself, is the sole determinant of human well-being, but must cover the possibility that one or other of these is the dominant factor in some third, better form of life (11a, e–12a).

Socrates argues against the hedonistic view by pointing to its eidetic difficulty: how can anything so piebald (ποικίλος) in its specification, and so mixed up with differences of person and action, be held to be the sole determinant of the goodness of life, and not differently assessed in each case? Is the satisfaction of folly and self-indulgence to be rated as highly as that of wisdom and self-restraint? Protarchus replies that, as satisfactions or enjoyments, none of these differs from, or can be opposed to, any other: it is only in what they are *of* or *from*, that they can differ or be opposed (12a). To this Socrates-Plato replies that enjoyment, as enjoyment, may, like colour, be specified in many different and opposed ways: Protarchus denies that this can be so in so far as they are enjoyments (12e–13c). This leads on to a consideration of the problems of oneness-in-manyness as applied to each eidetic case: in what circumstances are differences irrelevant to what something truly is, and in what circumstances relevant? Every-one concedes that there is no problem in the oneness-in-manyness of changeable individual instances: that Protarchus, who is one, should have many limbs, share in many properties etc. (14c, d). Many purists, however, see difficulty in the case of eidetic unities, Man as Such, Ox as Such, the Beautiful and Good as Such, and so on. Are such unities genuine entities, one in all their species, and let alone one in their infinitely numerous, dispersed cases? It is here, Socrates-Plato says, that Pythagoras, like Prometheus, kindled a new fire for men to see by, holding of all things that we say *are*, that they spring from the One and the Many, and that they contain both a Limit and a certain Boundless-ness (ἀπειρία) in themselves (16c). Such being the order of things, it is in all matters necessary that we should first look for and find a single Idea present in our field, that we should next see whether there are not two or more than two species of this Idea, and that we should go on doing this in the case of each successive unity, until we have reached, not a unity embracing indefinite plurality, but one articulated into a definite number of species, and per-mitting descent into indefinite plurality only when the process of specific articulation can go no further (16d, e). It is the ex-haustive articulation of a single generic Eidos into sub-species and sub-species of sub-species, till no further Eide are discernible, that distinguishes the true dialectician from the logic-chopping eristic. It is clear that Socrates-Plato does not mean the articulation of the Eide to be something that *we* do – he is not considering how we articulate our 'concepts' or apply them to experience or reality – he is saying that Eide as Essences are themselves exhaustively specified and ordered, and that we find them so arranged, and that if anything is responsible for their arrange-ment, it is not ourselves, but the Divine Reason or the more Ultimate Unity behind everything. Socrates-Plato gives examples of the detailed self-specification of single Eide: thus the sound which issues from our mouths orders itself first into the high, the low and the medium, then into all the notes that can be discerned in each of these divisions, and which are each so much higher or so much lower than one another, or stand to one another in various harmonic relations. In like manner the same sound which issues from our mouths differentiates itself into vowel-sound, voiced consonantal sound, and voiceless consonantal sound, and each of these into the numerous elementary vowel-sounds, voiced consonantal sounds, and voiceless consonantal sounds respectively. The descent from the single generic Eidos to the many quite specific ones, can also, as Socrates-Plato perceptively notes, be regarded as an *ascent* from the undifferentiated continuum of cases to various partial differentiations, and thence on to the all-embracing differentiation which corresponds to the quite general notion of an 'element' or 'letter' (18a, b). The effect of the whole argument is to stress the articulated, organized character of the eidetic realm, and the need of considering each Eidos in all its articulations before making general pronouncements that link it, or that refuse to link it, to other Eide. Some species of enjoyment may be good, and others not good or less good, and the same would apply to the species of insight and knowledge. And it may be in the relations of such species to one another, or to something better and more fundamental than either, that the human good will be found to consist. Chopping of the field into separate notions not seen as parts of a vertically and horizontally arranged order, will never yield answers to important philosophical questions. It is therefore only by the searching out of a necessary, eidetic unity-in-plurality, wholly different from the chance, changing unity-in-plurality of empirical cases, that we may hope to put these questions to rest.

It is in the direction of such a solution that Socrates-Plato now moves. He says that there may be something better than either enjoyment or insight by affinity with which either is made good, and one of them may have a greater affinity with this third thing than the other. He also says that the human good must be wholly perfect, sufficient and supremely choiceworthy ($\alpha i\rho\epsilon\tau\delta\nu$) and that neither enjoyment alone or insight alone is in this position. A life of continuous enjoyment without the accompanying exquisite consciousness *that* one was enjoying oneself, or that one had enjoyed oneself, or would or might enjoy oneself in the future, would plainly not be at all choiceworthy, nor would a life full of the most perfect wisdom, insight, knowledge and memory which was wholly void of any feeling of enjoyment (21d, e). Plainly only a mixed life could be good, and the only question would then be whether enjoyment or insight or some third thing was the constituent which made such a life good.

To this question Socrates-Plato turns, again appealing to the

Pythagorean doctrine of elements: God, through Pythagoras, has pointed up an Infinite element in all that is, and also an element of Limit, and it is necessary for us to postulate a third species of being which arises out of the mixture of these two, and also to postulate a fourth nature, which brings the first two elements together, and is the Cause (αἰτία) of their mixture. These four species have already been shown by implication at the level of the Eide, where an unbounded continuum was given and a Unity opposing it, and this continuum was then broken up, step by step, into subordinate unities, until indefiniteness had quite vanished from the articulate Eide, and been pushed back into the darkness of instantiation. This process or rather timeless procession is now to be carried on further, and we are to see how the same limitation of boundlessness which generated the Eide, can now generate their infinitely many good and bad instances. Plainly there is an element of Indefiniteness or Infinity which meets us over and over again in the realm of instantiation. Thus the hotter and the colder, and likewise the drier and wetter, swifter and slower, greater and smaller, always permit of a More and a Less, and would not be what they are if bounds could be set to them as such: they are brought to an end wherever a precise Measure or a definite Quantity is imposed on them (24b–d). It is, in fact, wherever we can talk comparatively, and employ such adverbs as 'more' or 'less', 'extremely' or 'slightly' or 'excessively', that we must recognize this element of indefiniteness or infinity. Wherever, on the other hand, no such adverbs are applicable, as in the case of the exactly equal, or double, or what stands in any other precise proportion, we have cases of the element of Limit (25a, b). And the mixed species of case arises wherever a case of Limit is applied to a case of the Unlimited, thereby putting an end to the latter's conflicting tendencies towards indefinite expansion and contraction, and creating a well-balanced, harmonious, definitely proportioned unity. Bodily health undoubtedly involves such a definite, proportionate mixture of the bodily elements (warm and cold, moist and dry etc.), and harmonious music likewise involves a proportionate mixture of the high and the low, the swift and the slow. Wherever in fact we have a case of the sound, the beautiful or the strong, whether in body or soul, we have a case of Limit in the form of a definite Ratio imposed on the Unlimited, and so creating law and order (νόμον καὶ τάξιν – 6b). The effect of the imposition of Limit or Ratio on the Unlimited is further said to be a coming into substantial being (γένεσις εἰς οὐσίαν – 6d): what is not characterizable as this or that, owing to its ceaseless deviations from pattern, comes to be definitely this or that, a healthily functioning eye, a symmetrically structured particle of Fire etc.

The passage we have been studying is of immense interest. Socrates-Plato is indeed discussing goings-on in the instantial world, the constant reimposition of definite sets of Ratios on confusedly variable natural characters. But what he is discussing has a prologue in Heaven: the being of the Eide, as dependent on the interfused presence in countless specific unities of Unity as Such, which as Unity limits, and various forms of flowing Quantity, which are as such capable of limitation, or, figuratively speaking, taking a plastic impression. The 'processes' described are in either case mythic, and stand for a union of distincts rather than for any actual act of union. This myth is, however, greater in the case of the Eide where there is no Becoming of true Being, whereas, in the case of instances, something of the sort can at times be discerned, for example when a man recovers from an illness. What it is also important to note is that the species of the mixed kind are always good, beautiful or healthy. Socrates-Plato does not enquire into the proportions characteristic of various diseases, causes of discord, various forms of aesthetic or moral baseness. Yet these are cases of limitation, often having a highly characteristic profile or set of symptoms: in them τὸ Πέρας is certainly at work, even if pouring out the wrong dose, like the doctor in Aristotle. It is clear, as we have often had occasion to say, that here is a place where a little dotting of *i*'s and crossing of *t*'s is necessary: we must distinguish between the good, prime forms of the Πέρας, which amount to the Eide, and its secondary, interstitial forms of which no separate science is necessary, and which form a mere background to the good Eide, though they are given separate rein in the realm of instantiation. Only so can we understand why Socrates-Plato here only cites *good* examples of the mixed class, when so many bad examples were freely available.

The Dialogue goes on to argue that the good life for man obviously falls into the mixed class of existences, and that its enjoyments fall into the class of the Unlimited, of that which in itself has no precise bound, but which can be bounded by Ratios, proportions, an order and laws derived from some higher source, and not a part of enjoyment itself (27e). Enjoyment so bounded can have a place in the mixed class, but then it is not purely enjoyment. The only question that arises is in what class we are to place Wisdom (φρόνησις), Knowledge (ἐπιστήμη) and Mind (νοῦς), the other candidate for second place in the good life, the first being the mixed life itself, and enjoyment being the competing candidate. Are Mind and its activities themselves cases of Ratio or Limit, or are they, on the other hand, a member of the more august and mysterious class which has not yet been investigated, and which *causes* Limit to be imposed on the Unlimited? Socrates-Plato argues that Mind – its activities are temporarily lost sight of – is to be placed in the supreme, causative class. Mind, the wise agree, is the King of Heaven and Earth, and this view is borne out by the whole spectacle of the Cosmos and the majestic revolutions of sun, moon and stars (28e). The only alternative, which is quite unacceptable, is to subordinate the whole universe to the power of the irrational and fortuitous and merely contingent (τὴν τοῦ ἀλόγου καὶ εἰκῇ δύναμιν καὶ τὸ ὅπῃ ἔτυχεν – 28d). But just as the elements in our bodies are but poor specimens of the eternal natures which those elements instantiate, whereas similar elements in the Cosmos at large are much better and purer specimens, and are the source and the replenishment of those elements in ourselves, even so the soul and mind in ourselves will be but poor specimens of Life and Mind as Such, and point to better specimens in the Cosmos at large, and above all to one supreme specimen, which, acting as Limit, arranges the years and the seasons and the months, and is the source from which the Soul and Mind in ourselves are replenished. But Zeus, the Soul which directs the Cosmos, derives both Soul and Mind from 'the Power of the Cause' (διὰ τὴν τῆς αἰτίας δύναμιν), which also dispenses similar gifts to other divinities. The Cause is therefore both productive of instantial Mind and is also itself of the nature of Mind: it is plain that the Cause can be none other than Mind as Such or Mind Itself, incorporating Knowledge Itself and all possible forms of Knowledge, and wrought up with Life Itself from which Mind Itself is inseparable, all other instances of Life and Mind, whether in the cosmic Soul, the star-souls or the souls of men and animals, being mere participants in this supreme Cause.

Where are the innumerable Eide in this picture, it has often been asked, and what is their place in this fourfold classification of Limit, Unlimited, Mixture and Cause? The answer is that the Supreme Mind is itself an Eidos in which all other Eide can for many purposes be regarded as included, since it is the eternal cognizance of them all. But the Eide not only live secure, in fainéant fashion, in the Supreme Cause: they are also involved in its instantial involvements, and as such they become cases of the Limit, what sets bounds to instantial indefiniteness and continuity. But it is plain that for Plato there is a yet further Cause of the Eide and their structures, and of the Mindfulness which has all the Eide for its object, and this is the final Unity Itself, of which all-embracing Mindfulness is merely the most embracing specification. This ultimate Unity is the final Πέρας which lies even beyond Mind as Such, and from the perspective of this Unity all the Eide, including Mind as Such, are wholly secondary. Just as, in a Platonic ontology, there are really no instances, only instantiations, so also, in a Platonic ontology, there are really no species, only specifications. In all the Eide, including Mind as Such, we have only 'the Power of the Cause' variously operative, not anything with an independent subsistence. The reason, therefore, why the Eide play so small a part in the *Philebus* is that, shocking as it may seem, Plato does not, from an ultimate standpoint, really believe in the Eide at all. But from this standpoint he also does not believe in the Mind of Zeus, or in Mind as Such, which he here uses as representing the Cause whose power it concentrates. The Eide and the eidetic Mind are alike merely the One in Action, a truth for ever incommunicable to those whose minds only function, like those of the friends of the Eide in the *Sophist*, by tearing everything into little bits.

The Dialogue now turns from these stoicheiological intricacies to the question of the good for man. Socrates-Plato attempts to show, by an immensely winding set of arguments, whose general drift we can only unfold inadequately, that Enjoyment or pleasure necessarily occupies an inferior place in the life of man, since it is essentially part of the *movement* of the bodily and psychic life of man towards a final goal, whereas Knowledge and Insight achieve something of the finality and unchangeability of that goal.

Enjoyment belongs essentially to genesis, Becoming, while Knowledge in its highest reaches touches the eternal οὐσία, Being as Such, towards which Becoming essentially tends. The Being towards which Enjoyment and Knowledge alike tend of course transcends either, and involves no such thing as Enjoyment, but this does not mean that Enjoyment may not be an essential element in the good of a changeable, instantial being such as man. This view (see particularly 53c–55a) is led up to by an attempt to analyse Enjoyment as an aspect of man's bodily and psychic existence. The nature of a living creature involves a characteristic harmony of qualities and elements, and when this harmony suffers disturbance or dissolution, pain results: pleasure or Enjoyment results, on the other hand, when there is a return to the shattered harmony of the creature's nature, to its specific limitation of the Unlimited. It is plain why pleasure and Enjoyment have the nature of a genesis, and why, being what a creature is, its fulfilled οὐσία is not as such pleasant. Such processes of 'rationalization', gradual restoration to a Ratio, are also called 'replenishments' (πληρώσεις), since they involve, in the simplest bodily cases, the filling up of the creature with materials, for example liquids, coming from without. But there are cases of psychic depletion and replenishment which require a more complex analysis into which memory (μνήμη) and desire (ἐπιθυμία) enter: the thirsty man suffers sensations due to the depletion of water in his body, but he remembers, and in consequence desires, a state of bodily replenishment through drinking which is opposed to his state of depletion, and this ultimately leads to the drinking itself. What all this proves is that our bodies *qua* bodies never suffer desires of any sort, which are always psychic accompaniments pointing beyond the body's present state (35d). And what it also proves is that there will normally be an admixture of the pain due to bodily depletion and psychic desire in the state of replenishment which forms the basis of a pleasure on the theory in question. There will have then to be very special conditions for enjoyments to involve no pain at all; such enjoyments will obviously be choiceworthy constituents of the human good.

Socrates-Plato now develops an ingenious set of arguments designed to show that there are 'false' as well as 'true' enjoyments, and that the former have a badness which makes it impossible to include them in the wholly choiceworthy 'good for man'. Enjoyments are not merely vanishing states regarding which we can only say that they are or are not, any more than opinions are in this position: in some sense, like opinions, they admit of certification as correct and incorrect, and, if repeated and stabilized, can be said to reveal Being. Socrates-Plato points out, in the first place, that there are enjoyments in which the enjoyed is not as the enjoyment conceives it as being, and in which the falsehood on which the enjoyment is built, can be said to pollute or infect the latter, so that it becomes truly 'false', or, as modern philosophers would put it, 'unjustified'. Such 'falsehood' of enjoyment is particularly met with when the enjoyment is of something in prospect, as in a dream of bliss over unlimited gold and possibilities of spending it (40a), but it is equally possible as regards the past or the present, of which Socrates-Plato gives no examples. But obviously there is something empty and hollow, and felt to be such, in nostalgic recalls of an unduly glamourized past, and there is a similar inner hollowness in the comfort we sometimes take in empty assurances and thinly disguised pretences. It is not merely that we are intellectually in error while genuinely pleased, but that the possibility of error corrupts the enjoyment: it is fraught with the suppressed sense of its own future disconfirmation, of its inherent mere wishfulness. This obviously is even more the case when we appease our consciences by one-sidedly conceiving that the facts are as they very well may not be: a conscience thus appeased has an inner, felt fragility. Only a repeatable satisfaction, like a repeatable judgment, has the solidity that makes it a *true* satisfaction. In other words, enjoyment always makes claims as to the being and character of its object, and can only be true, as opposed to merely existent, if those claims are themselves true.

In addition to the objectively 'unjustified' enjoyments just mentioned, there are others that are false in virtue of felt comparisons with other enjoyments or pains, an enjoyment being felt as greater or less than it intrinsically is, in virtue of its close association with other enjoyments and pains. Here again it is the sustainable, repeatable feeling that is the true one, whereas the one that is bound up with very particular contexts has something 'false' about it. The possibilities of such falsehood are augmented when distantly recalled, remotely felt satisfactions are emotionally compared with more immediate ones: the distant enjoyment may, we may say, be 'underfelt', but equally the close enjoyment may be 'overfelt' (see 41e–42c). Socrates-Plato here sees through the facile error of arguing that a pleasure in anticipation (or recollection) is merely an anticipation (or recollection) of pleasure, an intellectual experience perhaps coloured with present pleasure. Obviously our life of feeling has its own tense-modifications, and we feel proleptically as well as retrospectively, and may be wrong in so feeling. One of the possibilities of comparative feeling-error is that of those who confound painlessness with pleasantness. When bodily replenishment takes place very gradually and gently it does not work through to the Soul, nor produce genuine pleasure, desire or pain. But philosophers who then see or feel pleasantness in this neutral state, and who say that the pleasantest of all things is to be free from pain, are falling victims to a feeling-confusion as well as to an intellectual error. They are feeling their neutral state as other than merely neutral, and so falsely and as it is not (43c–44a). Socrates-Plato is perhaps slyly hinting that Speusippus, his nephew, a convinced protagonist of the neutral state, was covertly identifying the neutral with the agreeable or vice versa. It is plain that there is a genuine feeling-error of the kind indicated, and that some death-wishes or exalted Nirvanic wishes are special cases of it.

The main feeling-errors lie, however, in the case of mixed feelings, states where there really are very great and intense pleasures, which depend, however, on concurrent release from very great and intense pains: the element of falsehood in such pleasures lies in the feeling of a liberation from pain as if it were an intensification of pleasure. It is a regrettable fact that pleasures in which this intensity, this σφοδροτής is evident, are, in the main, badly mixed pleasures, wrongly felt as purely agreeable, cases of the 'unrest which men miscall delight', a view that would seem to assort ill with the ecstatic delights held to arise from contemplating Absolute Beauty and other Eide, as dwelt on in the *Symposium, Phaedrus* and elsewhere. Socrates-Plato is, however, an older man than when he wrote those ecstatic Dialogues, and he has also had to live with the anti-hedonistic persuasions of his dour (δυσχερής) nephew Speusippus, who varied between holding the true good to be a relief from *all* feeling, and holding pleasure to be a mere illusion resting solely on the relief from pain. Plato has come to believe that the true eidetic delights are sane and measured, rather than unmeasured and a little mad. He draws a firm, but somewhat unclear, distinction between the pleasures which are intensest (σφοδροτάτας), greatest (μεγίστας) and highest (ἀκροτάτας), and those which are simply more (πλείω) enjoyed (45c), and he holds that we are always enjoying things *less* when we are enjoying them *more intensely*. For the intensest pleasures all involve an admixture of need or pain misfelt as pleasure, and such need or pain goes with an abnormal or diseased condition of body or Soul or both, whereas in the healthy state of Souls or bodies there is a built-in Never-too-much which limits the intensity of pleasures and pains alike, and makes life *more* pleasing though *less intensely* so (45a–e). Socrates-Plato then gives a series of finely etched pictures of various misfelt intensities of pleasure: the delights of scratching in the case of the body (46a), and the delights of anger, derision, malice, grief etc. which are often intensest when least appropriate to their objects (47e–50e). In all these cases it would be *more* pleasant not to experience such effects at all, though their intensity as pleasure cannot be gainsaid. And as cases of pleasure in which there is no admixture of pain, and no consequent falsity, Socrates-Plato lists aesthetic delights in simple geometrical patterns, the straight, the round, the cubical etc. (not, he explicitly says, the delight in living bodies or paintings of them), the delight in smells, and simple delights in learning new facts and truths. In all these cases there may be previous depletions, but these are wholly insensible, and so the sudden fulfilment presents itself as something exquisite and uncovenanted, and not as involving any element of struggle and pain (51b–52b). It is in purity of pleasure that we must see an indication of the truth of pleasure – pure pleasure is most truly pleasant just as pure white is most truly white (53a–c) – while the mere intensity of either character is no indication of its truth. It must, of course, be said that modern sentiment, steeped in romanticism, would not agree with Socrates-Plato. A contrast with pain, and a relation to struggle, might for many be a sign, not only of the intensest, but also of the truest satisfactions, the most revelatory of eidetic structure in ourselves and the world. A wholly painless life would not present itself to such moderns as either perfect, sufficient or at all choiceworthy.

From the varieties of pure and impure, or true and untrue,

pleasure, Socrates-Plato passes to consider the sciences and the arts. There are some of these where numbering, measuring and weighing, and consequently accuracy (ἀκρίβεια) are at a minimum, and where experience, practice (τριβή) and mere guesswork (στοχαστική) achieve results. Such 'knowing how', unaccompanied by any lucid 'knowing that', is the most diluted, form of science. There are other arts and sciences in which accuracy increases and guesswork declines: architecture, ship-building, and furniture-making fall into this category. We go on to approximate numbering and measuring, where there is no concern to achieve exactly equal units: these lead on to pure arithmetic and geometry where units, being pure and mathematical, cannot be other than equal, and where lines, angles etc. have all the metric properties presupposed or demonstrated in proofs. Finally we have the Knowledge which moves beyond mathematics and investigates the pure structures, ever single and invariant, that are multiply exemplified even in arithmetic and geometry: this is obviously a truer Knowledge, and hence also a truer sort, than even mathematical knowledge (55e–58a). It is plain, from Socrates-Plato's grading, that knowledge is esteemed high and pure according to the exactness, directness and reliability with which it apprehends the nuances of eidetic structure, and that the life of feeling, of enjoyment and displeasure, though it also strives to be true to such nuances, and is never merely vanishing and subjective, represents an altogether lower, much more blurred and unreliable expression of such structure, which derives such value as it possesses from the Knowledge with which it is associated. The delights of Knowledge are important according as the Knowledge is important.

The Dialogue ends, as it began, with some attempt to sum up the human Good, and to relate it to what lies beyond human and instantial existence. Purely eidetic Knowledge, such as is achieved in dialectical analysis and which more remotely irradiates mathematics, must obviously be the most totally satisfying thing for a being whose enjoyments and satisfactions are all concerned with a fulfilment of nature, and whose nature, *qua* capable of Knowledge, is related to the natures or Eide of all other things (61d, e). (The above sentence expands what is a plain presupposition of Socrates-Plato's unhesitating transition from the purity of certain forms of Knowledge to their wholly sufficient, perfect and choiceworthy character.) But it is impossible to exclude from the wholly self-sufficient Good the less pure and perfect forms of art and science which depend on inspired guesswork and know-how: provided we also have the purely eidetic form of Knowledge, there can be no harm in having the less accurate forms as well (62d). (One would have thought that it would only be worth having them where purely eidetic Knowledge was not available or failed to apply, and it is not clear why they should not in such cases have a value in their own right, and not as a mere addition to eidetic Knowledge.) As regards pleasures, the unmixed and true forms obviously must be elements of the good for man; the pleasures of smell are given an importance which they do not deserve, and the pleasures which go with health and self-restraint may, even if going with painful urgency, and no doubt on account of their eidetic content, be given a place in that good. But all pleasures of an intense and unrestrained sort are to be excluded from the human good, since they obviously violate that containment and control by Eide or natures, in which that good must consist (63d, e). That the human good may embrace, as one of its highest forms, the overcoming of certain grave evils and violations, is not a proposition which Socrates-Plato, nor G. E. Moore, his disciple on this point, can in any way entertain. Socrates-Plato concludes by holding that the mixture of Enjoyment and Knowledge just considered must have truth (ἀλήθεια: 64b): the elements just mentioned must belong together eidetically, themselves constitute an eidetic unity. That they have such truth, and that delight by nature accompanies the realization of an Eidos and the knowledge of this realization, is, as we saw, the unspoken presupposition of the whole treatment.

The examination of the human good leads us, however, beyond the human good to a Cause which explains its goodness. This Cause can be nothing but a character of Measure (μετριοτής) and Symmetry (συμμετρία) which everywhere gives rise to beauty and virtue; if we add Truth to this character, we can say that Symmetry, Beauty and Truth generate goodness in the blend of characters constitutive of the human Good, and it is in relation to this trinity-in-unity that the worth of different factors in the blend must be considered. As regards Truth, Wisdom is obviously superior to the frequent deceits of Enjoyment, and especially to those of the stronger, passionate enjoyments. The same holds as regards Measure: Enjoyment, especially in its intenser forms, tends to exceed Measure, while Knowledge dutifully takes the measure of things. And as regards Beauty, Knowledge even of a thing malformed can never be ugly, while Enjoyment of some things certainly can be so.

The Dialogue ends with a solemn passage indicating reserves of doctrine that it does not elucidate. Five possessions ($\kappa\tau\acute{\eta}\mu\alpha\tau\alpha$) distinguish the Good Life, the first of which is not strictly a possession, but an eternal Essence which the good life only exemplifies, and whose nature floats about such things as Measure ($\mu\acute{\epsilon}\tau\rho o\nu$), the Measured and Timely ($\tau\grave{o}$ $\mu\acute{\epsilon}\tau\rho\iota o\nu$ $\kappa\alpha\grave{\iota}$ $\kappa\alpha\acute{\iota}\rho\iota o\nu$). It is not hard to conjecture that here we have an alias for the Limit, or the One, or the Good, the Nature or Supranature exemplified in all the eidetic unities. The second 'possession' is said to float about such things as the Symmetrical, the Beautiful, the Perfect, the Self-sufficient etc.; obviously what are meant are the innumerable facets in terms of which, like the myriad Divine Names, the Supreme Unity can be regarded. Alternatively, the second 'possession' is the innumerable species of Beauty, Perfection, Self-sufficiency etc., i.e. the Eide. The second possessions are, on either view, an eternal treasure laid up in heaven. But the third possession is Mind or Wisdom, the fourth the Sciences, Arts and correct Opinions, and the fifth pure and painless Enjoyments, all real possessions of the human soul. The human good is therefore unintelligible in terms of what people like and find pleasant: it is only intelligible in terms of basic Principles which altogether transcend human and instantial existence, whether bodily or psychic, and which even transcend the specificity of the Eide. Neither Enjoyment nor Knowledge is to be found in such an Ultimate, but Knowledge specifies it better than Enjoyment, and the instances of Knowledge instantiate it better than the instances of Enjoyment. And this Ultimate, while not a Number or Ratio of Numbers, is in essence the pure Diversity-in-unity which Number and Ratio specify in infinite ways. And Plato's stress on the $\mu\acute{\epsilon}\tau\rho\iota o\nu$ and $\kappa\alpha\acute{\iota}\rho\iota o\nu$ makes plain that his Ultimate is not the blank Unity of Neoplatonic exaggeration: it is blank, but only because it can be infinitely filled in, because it is Number or Ratio or Unified Pattern as Such rather than any specific form of them.

IV

It will be convenient to couple the solemn passage at the end of the *Philebus* with a set of similar passages which occur in Plato's *Epistles*, and which must have been written at approximately the same time in Plato's life. The first of these is the very cryptic passage in Epistle II, on which the Neoplatonists built their doctrine of the Three Hypostases, and which proves the Epistle to be spurious for many interpreters, simply because it is cryptic and because it even tries to justify its own cryptic quality. Dionysius of Syracuse had been using one Archedemus as a travelling go-between in his intercourse with Plato, who had gone back to Athens after his first Syracusan visit. Dionysius had continued to philosophize after Plato's departure, with some aid from other philosophers like Archytas, and wished to keep in touch with Plato in regard to his various notions and difficulties. Dionysius had sent Plato, through Archedemus, a model of the various planetary circles which encompass the spherical Cosmos, and Plato tells him that his diagram or model is not quite right and that Archedemus will explain what is wrong about it (312d). Dionysius had also, however, been meditating on a worthier and more divine topic, on which he had not received sufficiently cogent demonstrations, the nature of the First Principle. Plato says that he will have to talk about the whole matter in riddles (δι' αἰνιγμῶν), so that, if his letter goes astray, the chance reader may fail to understand it. Everything, he declares,

> revolves about the King of All, for whose sake all things exist and who is the Cause of all lovely existences. But secondary things revolve about a Second Principle, and tertiary things about a Third. The human soul yearns to know what all these things are like, likening them to that with which it is akin, but which is quite inadequate for its purpose. As regards the King and what I (Plato) said to him, nothing of the sort is possible, so that the soul is thereupon moved to ask: What on earth can He be like? This question, or rather the pang stirred up by it in your soul, are the cause of all your troubles, son of Dionysius and Doris, and you will never get to the truth of things until you get rid of it (312d–313a).

What is here obviously being said is that the First Principle from which everything derives, can only be characterized in a higher-order, negative manner, which rejects all first-order definite circumscriptions, such as are possible in the case of other Natures: it is specified in all the Eide without being reckoned among them. But it can be characterized indirectly as what is thus specified in all the Eide: each is It, and nothing but It, *in* a specific guise. It must be noted that while Plato makes the First Principle that for whose sake everything is, and that which is causative of everything, he makes this 'everything' peripheral to the First Principle, whose nature it is to have an exalted In-itselfness as well as an infinitely ambient outflow. No one who has read crucial passages in the *Republic* will fail to feel their perfect concordance with the passage before us. The Second and Third Principles in our passage are less readily identifiable, but can it be doubted that the 'Seconds' are the Eide or specific essences which specify the supreme Unity, while the Second Principle about which they cluster is necessarily the archetypal, eidetic Mind, or Mind as Such, which includes in itself specified 'Knowledges' of all the Eide. This archetypal eidetic Mind, which is what is instantiated in the Mind in our Souls and in the Soul of the cosmos, but which transcends all its instances, is the only unity which, at the eidetic level, holds all the 'Seconds' together: it has been more or less explicitly referred to in the *Parmenides*, *Sophist* and *Philebus*, and can, with some readiness to cross *t*'s and dot *i*'s, be found in the Sun-passages in the *Republic* as well. The Neoplatonists were quite right in making Mind their Second Hypostasis, but they went astray in sometimes talking of it as if it were some sort of instantial mind, a Divine Thinker instead of the pure Idea of such a Thinker, which is far more of a Platonic reality than any such Divine Thinker could possibly be. All this being conceded, the Third Principle can be none other than the World-Soul, the all-embracing, instantial, ordering Principle, and the things that are about it are *both* the higher eidetic unities as they enter its conception and their infinite progeny of instances, mathematical or sensible, in which it illustrates and applies them. One is not being presumptuous in saying that Plato's riddles are, for the discerning reader of the Dialogues, very readily solved.

Plato, however, dwells on the psychological difficulty of accepting a transcendent Indefinite, characterizable only through negations or seeming contradictions, as the Ultimate Horizon in which all the definite, lucid Eide are contained. Some see and accept the reality and truth of such a Principle at one moment, but are in doubt about it the next, and continue to see it in ever varying lights (313b): others, after thirty full years of meditation upon it, suddenly become as certain regarding it as they were formerly certain of other things, which now in their turn appear doubtful. The verdict of history has shown how many, who have moved with ease and pleasure through what Plato has to say about the Eide, have been utterly ill at ease when confronted with the mysticism which for him is the circumambient background of all lucidity, and have invented every reason to consider it un-Platonic. It is connected with too much in Plato to be thus regarded as spurious, and those who feel mysticism and lucidity to be merely two sides of the same coin, and mysticism neither illogical nor illucid, but merely lucid and logical in an extraordinary manner, will feel happy that Plato's mind worked similarly. They will only regret that he gave comfort to those who identify the mystical with the unutterable, when it has been shown to be wholly utterable in a language which builds upon, but also systematically transcends, our *ordinary* ways of speaking. He holds indeed that the 'educated' will have no difficulty regarding the whole doctrine, and will embrace it with wonder and enthusiasm (314a).

Very solemn, too, is the passage at the end of Epistle VI addressed to King Hermias of Atarneus, together with the Platonists Erastus and Coriscus, who, like Aristotle, lodged with Hermias for a while. After recommending that Hermias should value good friends above cavalry and military alliances, and that Erastus and Coriscus should trust to other ways of resisting evil than the beautiful wisdom of the Ideas, he counsels both to get over whatever little rubs and differences may have arisen among them. They must do so by reading Plato's letter together, or at least in pairs, as often as may be, and by pledging themselves to keep up their philosophical friendship in a manner which combines deep seriousness with playfulness, at the same time invoking the God who sways all things present and to come, and who is the Supreme Father of the Ruling Causative Principle (323c, d). The God who sways all things present and to come is obviously the Supreme Unity, and the Ruling Causative Principle the ordering principle of Mind as Such, which is instantiated in our souls and in the Soul of the Universe. That causality is here made an attribute of the *Second* rather than the Primal Principle does not signify: obviously causality is transmitted from the highest to all lower principles, and the First Principle is intrinsically so beyond everything that *its* causality is, as it were, extrinsic to it.

The most celebrated solemn passage in the *Epistles* is, however, that from 341a to 344c in Epistle VII. Plato explains to various friends and companions of Dion, who was originally responsible for his invitation to Sicily, why the Doctrine of Principles given out by Dionysius, and derived from various second-hand sources, is not authentically Platonic. Plato did not divulge all his teachings to Dionysius, and has written no work on the highest subjects and never will do so. For it is not verbally expressible as are other topics, but after a long time spent in considering such matters, in the close company of others, light suddenly bursts forth in the mind, and becomes a steady flame (341c, d). The results of such philosophical illumination can only be communicated to a few: if attempts are made to communicate it to wider circles, it will only arouse scorn, or puff men up with a vain conceit of extraordinary knowledge. One has only to think how, in quite recent times, Wittgenstein restricted attendance at his gatherings and access to his manuscripts, and how the half-known contents of these writings caused some to scoff and others to indulge in vain boasting, to have a perfect analogue to the Platonic situation. Both philosophers had astonishing and deep ideas to disclose, both held these ideas in an inchoate form which did not lend itself to finished exposition, and both had good reason to keep them from those who, unable themselves to think to any purpose, live wholly on their 'encounters' with those who can and do.

Plato goes on to explain in detail why written accounts of eidetic matters and their Principles, necessarily fail of their purpose. The knowledge of any true Eidos involves at least five existences – the non-mention of the mathematical objects has no particular significance – that of a name, of a definitory account (λόγος), of a picture, of the Knowledge or Opinion or Intuitive Grasp (νοῦς) itself, and of the Eidos that is known. Names, definitions, and pictures are more or less remote from the Eidos that is known: the *Noûs* or intuitive grasp of the Eidos comes closest to it. Plato gives an interestingly comprehensive list of the Eide of which there is such an intuitive grasp: Straightness and Curvature of Shape, Colour – presumably given some mathe-maticized definition as in the *Meno* – the Good, the Beautiful and the Just, the Natures of all natural objects and all artefacts – that these last are not excluded shows that there was only a contro-versial *tendency* to exclude them – the elementary Natures of Fire, Water etc. and the Nature of every animal and psychic habituality, and of every kind of action or undergoing (342d). The only candidates for eidetic status *not* mentioned are deviant and defective forms: the passage confirms the view that they were in some fashion secondary, derivative, interstitial members of the realm of the Eide. Plato suggests that unless a man is willing to struggle through the three inferior members of his pentad to the fourth intuitive member, he is very likely to mistake some inessential mark of an Eidos for its true essence and constitution: the weakness of words is shown in their tendency to fish up an accident or mere quality ($\pi o\iota \acute{o}\nu$) when the essence is to be found. The tendency to fix meanings initially, when all must be left un-fixed till the essence is seized, is the besetting sin of verbal dis-course, and particularly of written discourse. Names must be used shiftingly if they are to serve as a basis for eidetic insights, and the same applies to definitory accounts (343b, c). If a pretended exact-ness is sought too early, we shall always have counter-examples crowding in on us from the realm of sensible cases (343c). It is only in the long pull of analysis, in which we rub names, defi-nitions and sensible illustrations together, among interlocutors concerned with truth rather than victory, that insight and grasp regarding each eidetic entity will on a sudden blaze forth, flooding consciousness with superhuman light (344b). The sort of eidetic grasp of what everything *itself* properly is, cannot be creditably set down by a creditable ($\sigma \pi o\upsilon \delta a \hat{\iota} os$) person: it is the sort of understanding that a man enjoys, but that he will not try to formulate too exactly in writing. The inadequacies of writing are of course at their maximum when one is dealing, not with some specific Eidos, but with the First Principle or Principles of all such Eide. What can be said of these should be said once and quite briefly – for example, Nothing whatever can be predicated of Absolute Unity considered in and for itself. If, like Dionysius, one professes to base a whole articulate philosophy on a single utterance of this sort, one is bringing the Ultimates of Philosophy into total discredit (345a–c).

It will be noted that Plato in these passages does not hold philosophical insight to be ineffable and private, only that it cannot be shared while words are used in a routine manner based on examples culled from the commerce of the senses. A particular revisionary or penetrative urge must be awakened in a number of co-operating enquirers, and it must go beyond ordinary examples till a truly accurate yet also shared vision is achieved. What they see and say to one another will not be in any way obscure to those who share the vision, but it will be obscure and even laughable to those who have not tried to rise to such a vision. Plato in these passages is not discouraging the use even of highly precise expressions; what he is discouraging is thinking according to rule, leaving the smallest tract of one's thought without constant revision. What he says in these memorable passages has nothing of mystery-mongering: he is merely uttering the common sense of all who attempt to rise above common diction.

VIII

PLATO'S PHILOSOPHY OF
THE CONCRETE: THE
TIMAEUS, CRITIAS, LAWS
AND *EPINOMIS*

I

In this penultimate chapter of our book we shall deal with Plato's treatment of what moderns call 'concrete reality': the infinitely mixed, inexact, dubious, chance-ridden, shifting web of the instantial which, though utterly dependent on the might of the Eide, and having no sense or substance other than what is eidetic, none the less has a seeming solidity and a significance for us as instantial beings, which it does not and cannot have in and for itself.

The works we are about to comment on have the same place in Plato's system as the so-called *Realphilosophie*, the philosophies of Nature and Spirit, in the system of Hegel. The *Timaeus* sets forth Plato's theory of the natural world in which the Eide appear, in infinite reduplication, in the two great multiplying yet distorting media of Space and Time, while the *Critias, Laws* and *Epinomis* yield us the inexact, more or less arbitrary mirroring of the exact norms of the ideal society in the realm of instantiation. The *Laws* gives us a series of prescriptions for a society which will come reasonably close to eidetic standards, and includes a treatment of the religion necessary to structure such a society, while the *Epinomis* sketches this religion a little further, and the *Critias* shows us, in an imagined historical perspective, how a society based on the correct eidetic norms could defeat a much vaster and apparently stronger society based on this-world mechanisms, and on forced collocations rather than eidetic affinities.

The works we are about to study are further of extreme

importance since the full sense of a philosophical system is only clear when it is seen in relation to physical realities and to the exigencies of practice, as those who seek to understand Aristotle while ignoring his *Physics*, or Descartes while ignoring his *Système du Monde*, or Hegel without studying his *Naturphilosophie*, amply prove. The same applies to the practical political recommendations of these writers. And the works of this last period have the further importance of showing what Plato's reduction of the Eide to Numbers really meant in practice: the purely geometrical structure of the physical elements, the harmonic structure of the heavens, and the reduction of the Psyche and its virtues and activities to the same Numerical Ratios which govern the objects that it knows and over which it has practical control. We see how the mathematicization of the Eide was not a set of numerological fantasies as in the thought of some Pythagoreans, but a determined attempt to see Measure and Ratio everywhere, burgeoning into many dimensions, but never yielding anything irreducibly qualitative. The works we are about to deal with are further interesting in that they represent a return to the inspiration of Plato's great Middle Period, only with a stress on the concrete and instantial, rather than the abstractly eidetic. The much closer affinity of these last Dialogues to the writings of the Middle Period have led some, for example G. E. L. Owen, to place a Dialogue like the *Timaeus* in that earlier time, its differences of style being explained by the very different sort of Dialogue that it is. It is, however, better to locate that Dialogue, both on account of its stress on notions like Sameness and Difference much stressed in the *Sophist*, as well as for general reasons, not in that earlier time, but in that earlier time regained, in a *temps retrouvé* in which the whole force of the Written and Unwritten Doctrines, which had inspired Plato since the foundation of the Academy, were for the first time given an application to this approximate, half-real world. This background ideology of the *Timaeus* has for this reason a condensed, almost scholastic character, which points to repeated meditation, and which is not at all like the argumentative exploration of the *Republic*. The writings of this time regained have also a detailed character which places them in the realm of the scientific and the practically political rather than the philosophical and eidetic. For this reason there is a great deal of the natural philosophy of the *Timaeus*, and practically all of the political recommendations of the *Laws*, that we shall only touch on in passing, our concern being with the Eidos of Platonism, rather than with the minutiae of its elaboration. The *Laws*, of course, belongs undoubtedly to the last period of Plato's writing, since we know that it was not made public till after his death.

The *Timaeus*, to which we now turn, may best be regarded as a comprehensive study in eidetic causation: the self-differentiation of Unity or Ratio or Goodness – it does not matter what we say – in the system of the Eide, is now seen as active in a wider sweep, in the inexactitude, the mutability and the repetitive multiplicity of the realm of instantiation. To all those who believe in the real being of instances, not as mere outflows and manifests of Eide, but as solid, self-existent entities, and who strengthen this belief by thinking that they alone can exert efficient causality – the 'formal causation' of the Eide being something totally ineffective and idly descriptive – the *Timaeus* must necessarily seem a tissue of mere myth and riddle. But to those who accept the Platonic insinuation that there are not, in the strict sense of 'are', any such things as instances at all, and that, in the strict sense, they can do nothing whatever, being mere 'strengthless heads' or modalities of the Eide in a medium even more insubstantial than themselves, the treatise will be throughout of the most extreme illumination, even if much of its detail may be of merely historical or technical interest. In the *Timaeus* the self-instantiating causality of the Eide is, however, seen in an aspect of *unity*, rather than one of diversity or difference, and in the former aspect it figures as the embracing Thinkingness and Knowingness, the eidetic Intellection Itself of which all psychic acts of thought and knowledge are the instances, and which stands in coeval correlation with the ranged Eide of which it is the Thinking and the Knowing. This eternal, timeless Mind as Such, dimly adumbrated in the *Republic*, but given clearer standing in the *Parmenides*, *Sophist* and *Philebus*, now takes its place as an active, creative Demiurge, responsible for the existence of the Cosmos and of the Soul that presides over it. The Soul of the World, which fulfils all that can be demanded of a God by most worshippers, is here plainly seen as subordinate to an elder God, the timeless Mind or Vision of which the Eide are summarily the objects, and which, being Vision Itself and Direction Itself, is more absolutely percipient and directive than the Soul to which it gives existence.

With the descent into instantiation is involved the functioning of what would now be called the two great media, Time and Space, Time in which eternal, eidetic Being takes the form of perpetual reassertion and reinstantiation, and Space in which there emerges a possibility of endless numerical duplication not based on true eidetic difference. That Time and Space are nothing in themselves beyond the two species of reiteration involved in instantiation should be clear to anyone who even reads the text of the *Timaeus* carefully, without seeking to interpret it profoundly. But with the necessary descent into instantiation also goes a necessary descent into imperfection: the indefinitely numerous, defective and deviant forms which merely fill in the holes and gaps of the eidetic order will be given a new charter in the realm of instantiation. We shall have all the irregularities and inexactitudes and conflicting realizations of which the world of instances is full, and which *appear* to give it a being which is cut off from its only source. Of these degradations the *Timaeus* gives a fascinating treatment in its doctrine of the Works of Necessity as opposed to the Works of Mind. The eidetic realm is a realm of Life and Intelligence as Such, specified in the forms of Life and Intelligence characteristic of the World-Organism and of various types of celestial and earthly organism, but its organic, intelligent aspect presupposes an inorganic aspect, the eternal patterns of the bodily elements, the Fire, Air, Earth and Water of which the Cosmos and all its contained organisms are made. In the instantial realm these elements not only fall short of their types in various ways, but they also move and combine in ways that have nothing concerted or organic about them: they represent the element of chance, of unregulated causality in the Cosmos, which both assists, and also often impedes, the operation of its organic patterns. The Cosmos is, accordingly, a compound of blind mechanism and organic purpose, and there are situations and even epochs in which the former predominates, and which form the real basis for Plato's talk of an original chaos, and epochs in which it is brought to heel by the latter. The alternation of periods dominated by Mind and Purpose, and periods dominated by blind Mechanism, had been taught in the *Statesman,* and is probably to be read, with lowered emphasis, into the *Timaeus* as well. But Platonism does not permit us to fear the final submergence of life and thought and goodness in blind mechanism, of which modern experience and alienated science would readily persuade us: the structure of the elements is eidetically subordinated to the structure of organisms, as not only the *Timaeus* but also Aristotle's accounts of Academic teaching inform us, and convinced Platonists may accordingly remain of good cheer in regard to the human future. All these generalities must, however, be tested by their success in throwing light on the actual pattern of the Dialogue, to which we accordingly turn.

II

The setting of the *Timaeus* is also the setting for the incomplete Dialogue *Critias*, and the merely projected *Hermocrates*, of which mention is made in its exordium. Actually it sets the stage for the whole set of Dialogues dealing with nature and culture in the concrete, including the *Laws*, which possibly took the place of the unwritten *Hermocrates*. Socrates is shown conversing with Timaeus of Western Locri, Hermocrates of Syracuse and Critias an Athenian. Critias is not the relative of Plato who was one of the tyrannical oligarchs of the late Fifth Century, but some earlier ancestor, Hermocrates is a great political leader of Syracuse, not in favour with its democracy, while Timaeus seems an invented figure, like the Eleatic Stranger, who will do well as an exponent of Plato's eclectic, but basically Pythagorean cosmology. The Dialogue is connected with the themes of the *Republic*, since Socrates is represented as having summarized some of these themes the previous day; today Timaeus will give an account of the origin and nature of the Cosmos, while on the next day Critias will tell how the prehistoric Athenians, schooled in the disciplines of the *Republic*, were able to defeat the bloated, mechanistic Atlanteans 9000 years ago; what Hermocrates was to say on the third day is not stated. What the exordium strongly brings out is that Plato regarded nature and culture as of one piece: the prescription of good but imperfect political institutions merely carries one step further the excellent, but imperfect, institutions of nature. Both pointed to a source 'above' in eternal mathematical Ratios, and to an instantial carrying-out in the 'lower' realm of the approximate and the deviant.

The discourse of Plato-Timaeus begins by drawing a distinction between what always is, and has no origin, on the one hand, and what is always arising, but never really is, on the other. The former is graspable by thought with the help of a verbal definition, since it does not alter, whereas the latter is grasped by belief based on unreasoning sensation, and is always arising and perishing, and never stably is (27d–28a). When we think, an Ideal Nature presents itself to our gaze with clearly circumscribed outlines: when we perceive, we see only an inconstant illustration or suggestion of numerous, jumbled Ideal Natures, which elude precise and certain circumscription. What is always thus flickeringly illustrated or suggested, cannot, however, sustain itself in its uncertain half-being: it always requires a Cause, by implication not itself flickering, to keep it on the go (28a). This Cause, it is assumed, must be a Demiurge or Maker who belongs to the eternal, and not to the changeable order.

Plato-Timaeus now turns to our world, and asks whether it exemplifies patterns of changelessness or patterns only of change – it is assumed that there will be such secondary patterns, as the ideal detritus surrounding the Eide. If the latter is the case, the world will be confused and ugly, if the former, beautiful. Now the world itself is obviously a visible, tangible, bodily existence, a flickering thing that can only be apprehended by sense-guided guesswork, and that requires an unflickering Cause to keep it going: this Cause is, however, not easy to find, nor easy to declare to men at large. Leaving it aside, however, we may say that, if our Cosmos is good, its Maker must have been a good Maker, who looked to eternal patterns in his making, whereas, if it be ugly and bad, the reverse must have been the case. The world is, however, the most beautiful of all possible generated existences; it must exemplify eternal originals, and its Maker must accordingly have been the best of all Causes (28b–29a). The world, however, only flickeringly illustrates eidetic originals: cases of Eide only are, as it were, likenesses (εἰκόνες) of certain Natures, rather than those Natures themselves. Since we are dealing with *likenesses*, we may expect what we say of them to be merely *likely*: on the firm, fixed contours of Being we can discourse with firmness and fixity, but on their inconstant instantiations we can at best hope to talk with inconstant likelihood. Plato-Timaeus is therefore not to be faulted if his accounts of theogony and cosmogony fall short of absolute accuracy and consistency: a likely tale (εἰκὼς μῦθος) is all that he

can be expected to provide (28c). The passage we have summarized is quite clear: Instantial Being is also illustrative being,
being that has all that is clear and graspable and substantial in the
content that it illustrates. There can be no knowledge of it as
such, since, if it can be said to be anything at all, it is so only as
approximating to something firmer and clearer than itself. Of
such inexact approximation exact statement is impossible: we
can only talk vaguely of such vagueness.

After this apology, Plato-Timaeus returns to his assault on the
Cosmos. We have established that its Maker was good, and a
good being is incapable of grudgingness ($\phi\theta\acute{o}\nu os$): being un-
grudging, he necessarily wished the instantial world to be as like
him as possible. He found the whole visible world, not at rest,
but in disorderly, inharmonious motion, and he brought it into
order out of disorder, thinking it would be better so. It would in
fact have been impossible for the Supremely Good to do anything
but what was loveliest. Considering, too, that no mindless work
can as a whole be lovelier than the work of an intelligent being,
and that Mind only exists in Soul, he put Mind in Soul when he
fashioned the universe, which is accordingly an animated,
intelligent being (29e–30b). This paragraph tells us that the
Instantial is such as essentially to deviate from the Eidetic, to
overshoot it, or to fall short of it: with seeming paradox, we
may say that it is the Eidos of the Instantial thus to deviate from
its Eidos. This means that, however ungrudgingly instantiation
may proceed, it necessarily involves an element of the defective
and the deviant. This element is held in check by the Eide, and
by the eidetic Mind which is their total Vision, but it cannot, in
virtue of what it is to be an Eidos or an instance, be perfectly held
in check. Nothing in the world can put an instance on a level
with what it instantiates: its inferiority is an irremoveable
inferiority of type. This logical fact is expressed in Plato's queer
statements about an Ungrudgingness which has limits set to it
by what is 'possible'. Even a quite orderly Cosmos would be a
one-sided illustration of the infinite riches of the Eidetic Order,
and would, in that sense at least, be imperfectly ordered.

The nature of the Maker's model is now discussed. It must be
a model which embraces *all* possibilities of Life and Mind, rather
than anything abstractly generic or too narrowly specific. It must
weld into intensional unity what in the instantial realm can only

be realized dispersedly: it must be an Eidos comprehending possibilities that would in fact clash in instantiation. There is no contrariety in being the possibility of contrary things: contrary possibilities are as compatible as their actualities are not. Life as Such is an eidetic content which is undividedly itself in the disparate forms of celestial, human and animal life in which it must specify itself: it conjoins in itself what in instantiation must be disjoined. The glorious, many-sided Ideal of Livingness and Thinkingness is what we see inadequately exemplified in our Cosmos and its sets of living inhabitants, each separately realizing a single facet of this Ideal. This is the clear meaning of Plato's remarkable words: 'for we should not imagine that the Maker made the Cosmos in the likeness of any living nature of a merely partial sort – resembling what is imperfect it could never become beautiful – but he made it in the closest possible likeness of the Living Creature of which all other living creatures are severally and collectively the parts' (30c). This Living Creature is not, of course, some polymorphous monster of mythology, but rather Animality as Such, the Genus in which all the alternative ways of being living and conscious are as such necessarily comprehended. It was what Hegel was later to call a 'Concrete Universal', a notion of great commodiousness and perspicuity, yet enigmatic to many. It is clear why Plato found it necessary to speak so enigmatically: the logic of abstracted intensions is to this day as far from being clearly worked out as it was in his own time.

The necessary singleness of the world's all-comprehensive model leads to the further contention that, contrary to the Milesian opinion of numerous worlds, our world must be unique and single (31a, b). There might, from a general point of view, have been worlds other than our own, since the realm of instantiation is the realm of boundless, baseless multiplicity, but in the case of the highest of all instances, the World and the Soul that informs it, this possibility must be ruled out. It must have the perfect uniqueness of the pattern that it instantiates.

Plato-Timaeus next tells us that organic structure presupposes elementary inorganic structure, the details of which will be later worked out in what is said of the 'Works of Necessity'. The unique instantial Cosmos, and the many instances of Living Creatureliness that inhabit it, must have both the luminous visibility and the tangible solidity of bodily being: otherwise they would not be distinguished from the undispersed essence of the Eide. But to be visible implies the presence of the luminous element Fire, just as to be tangible implies the presence of the solid element Earth. An instantial world is, further, necessarily extended in *three* dimensions in virtue of basic eidetic requirements – the sacred Tetractys of Unit, Line, Surface and Solid is here hintingly gestured at – and this means that each bodily element will occupy these three dimensions somewhat differently, Number and Proportion being, here as elsewhere, the complete key to eidetic difference. Quite obviously, Earth must have the least extensive, most concentrated representation in a Cosmos, and Fire the most extensive and pervasive. If now we conceive of Earth and Fire as having extensions representable by the simple cubic magnitudes m^3 and n^3, there plainly will be two mean magnitudes m^2n and mn^2 between these limiting magnitudes, and as m^3 is to m^2n, so m^2n will be to mn^2, and mn^2 will be to m^3. There is therefore a place in the Cosmos for the interstitial representation of two elements, of Water which verges towards Earth, and of Air which verges towards Fire. These elements will therefore be present in the Cosmos to an extent corresponding to these Numbers. Such at least is a plausible interpretation of 31b–32c, where it is simply said or implied that Means of some sort, and preferably Geometric Means, are necessary to bind extremes together, and that, while there is *one* geometric mean mn between the two *square* numbers m^2 and n^2, there are *two* geometric means, m^2n and mn^2, between the *cubic* numbers m^3 and n^3. What is important is not the detailed interpretation of the Magnitudes and Ratios postulated, but the belief that Ratios are everywhere operative in the Cosmos, and that in no important case are there merely random differences of magnitude, not subject to proportionate governance.

The Cosmos thus duly constructed, with Life and Intelligence everywhere organizing its elements, is now said to be utterly self-contained, like the 'Wholes' of Xenophanes and Parmenides. Holding all Fire, Air, Water and Earth in itself, there will be nothing outside it to disturb or afflict it, or to induce disease or age in it. And it will also have the perfectly rounded shape of the 'Spheres' of the Eleatics and Empedocles, without organs of sense needed to perceive an external environment, nor organs of movement needed to deal practically with it. It will have no need either to breathe in or to breathe out (as even the Pythagoreans thought needful), and will nourish itself entirely on its own detritus (33c). And its movement, finally – for, as belonging to the inconstant realm of the instance, it cannot be wholly immobile – will be uniform circular motion in one spot. Plato-Timaeus says nothing of the periodic reversal of such uniform circular movement of which he spoke in the *Statesman,* but nothing rules it out.

The treatment now shifts to the 'making' of the Soul by the eidetic Cosmos-maker. This soul, with its built-in Mind, has been made by the Cosmos-maker both to pervade, and also to contain, the revolving Cosmos, since, doubtless in a non-spatial sense, it is said to extend 'beyond' it (34b). Plato-Timaeus points out that, while he must talk as if the body of the world was first prepared, and the Soul then made to animate it, in reality Soul is an 'elder' existence both in origin and in virtue (34c). Plato, as the Academic tradition held, did not believe in his construction-myths at all, being in this respect vastly superior to Kant, who seems really to have believed his: neither the world nor its animating Soul are fabricated in time, but are 'generated' only in the sense in which an eternal, eidetic pattern is causative of its instantiations in time. The chaos *before* Soul was put into body merely indicates a tendency towards deviation which is inherent in instantiation, and which at times threatens to break down all eidetic ordering.

III

The construction of Soul is one of the most difficult in its beauty in Plato: it is at once a construction of a musical scale, a planetary order, and of a supreme instantial Mind which is attuned to both, and which is capable of realizing and maintaining both. All arise about the eternal fixtures very much as an exquisite wake for ever forms and reforms itself about a moving ship. The details are obscure and matter for controversy: there is little obscure or controversial regarding the principles. Soul, we are told, is a curious blend of three blends: of a blend (1) of the undivided ever constant Essence (οὐσία) and of the Essence divided and becoming among bodies, of a blend (2) of the eternal Self-sameness (of the Eide) and of the long-drawn-out, reiterated

Self-sameness of instantial things, and lastly of a blend (3) of the sharp Difference and Otherness that obtains among the Eide and the blurred, relaxed Difference which half-distinguishes instantial things. These three blends are themselves blended into a single compound Nature, a certain violence being exerted to force the stark note of Difference into harmony with the note of Sameness (35a). What is here being asserted is the amphibious, intermediate nature of Soul, a point also greatly stressed in the *Phaedo*. For the Soul, like the Objects of Mathematics – which are in fact its essential familiars – has its feet both in the eidetic and the instantial camp: it can, on the one hand, open itself to the riches of the noetic Cosmos, in doing which all souls will presumably lose themselves in Mind as Such, or it can turn towards instances, in doing which it will itself become instantial, and have its private and often lowly sphere of care and interest. But the Soul is not merely an extraneous conscious link between Eidos and Instance: it is also a living channel through which the one impinges on the other. The eidetic of the bodily elements may or may not be exhausted by the role they play in the Eide of various forms of Life, but the forms of Life we see in the world, whether in stars or crawling maggots, are all expressions of Psyche, the Self-movingness which mediates between eidetic Immobility, on the one hand, and the enforced Motion characteristic of unorganized elemental masses, on the other.

The Soul being thus attuned to Identity and Diversity, to Unity and Division, whether in the eidetic or the instantial sphere, now becomes attuned to the main modes of Diversity represented by certain salient numbers, which necessarily make their appearance when Identity is forced into union with Difference, at once permitting the emergence of innumerable Sums, Products, Ratios and other structures, while also hiding in their interstices all that rabble of secondaries and irrationals which are the necessary detritus of the numerical world. For Platonic mathematics is not egalitarian, but believes always in well-formed, well-born Prime Forms, from which a whole host of less advantaged forms in devious ways descends. Soul will necessarily carry in itself those nodal differentiations from which all other species of Number are descended, and this Plato represents by imagining Soul rolled out in a long strip along whose length various psychic distances are marked off. These distances will be

those of the powers of Two and Three: in a three-dimensional
world they will advance to cubes, and, starting with unity, we
shall accordingly have the two progressions 1, 2, 4 and 8 and
1, 3, 9 and 27, which together yield the series 1, 2, 3, 4, 8, 9, 27.
The Soul will be attuned to work in these forms of the Double
and Triple, and all else that it thinks and does will, as it were,
follow from, or be bred by, these fundamental differentiations.
(Whether the Double and Triple are as totally fecund, without
the special creation of the other Prime Numbers, is, of course,
questionable.) A rich crop of further differentiations now
appears in the interstices of the divisions thus arrived at, by the
device of looking for their Harmonic and Arithmetic means: if
this takes us into the sphere of the fractional, it yet avoids the
irrational. We thus obtain the series 1, 4/3, 3/2, 2, 8/3, 3, 4, 9/2,
16/3, 6, 8, 9, 27/2, 18, 27 whose proportions are those of the
lengths of strings needed to give us four octaves plus a fifth and
a tone, with fourths and fifths intercalated in each octave. Further
manipulations will enable us to break up our octaves into what
are recognizable intervals of one tone (9/8) with a residual
part-tone of 256/243. All that this shows is that all the possibilities
of musical harmony and disharmony, or of whatever follows
parallel numerical principles, can be arrived at by further interpolations and extrapolations, governed in each case by a Ratio
of some sort. The Soul will be attuned to all such extensions or
densifications of its fundamental equipment, and so, it is suggested, to all the patterns of which instantial harmonies are only
one illustration.

The Soul-strip is, however, put to other uses besides the
musical: it is cut along the middle into two narrower strips,
which are then bent round into two circles. These will cross
each other at two opposed points, the one circle being fixed
inside the other, and moved on by it, while having its own
contrary motion at an angle to that of the other encompassing
circle. The outer, dominant circle is said to be that of 'the Same':
it is responsible for the uniform diurnal motion of the whole
heavens from East to West, while the inner circle, carried round
by the outer, is said to be that of 'the Other', and is responsible
for the steady backward slip of the zodiacal signs in relation to
the sidereal equator: the latter carries them round protesting,
as it were, as they cross and recross this equator and negotiate

their own opposed path at an angle to that of this equator. This zodiacal circle presides over seven subordinate circles, three of which (those of the Sun, Venus and Mercury) practically run together with it, while of the remaining four, one, that of the Moon, hastens ahead of the zodiacal circle in its backward shift, while those of Mars, Jupiter and Saturn lag behind the zodiac, and accordingly seem to slip less. It is not our concern to analyse or improve on all the carefully phrased sentences in which Plato-Timaeus communicates this complex astronomy. It is important, however, that we should realize that these circles are for him realities, far more real than the stars which are moved by them, or than the material circles with which Aristotle replaced them, or than the brass circles of actual models. If not themselves Eide, they are the psychic, mathematical instantiations of Eide, the blue-prints by which the Soul steers, and far nearer to ultimate Being, and far more capable of effecting change, than are crystalline spheres or brass circles. And Plato believes that the same organizing numbers 1, 2, 3, 4, 8, 9, 27 which organize the distances from the centre of the various planetary circles, also organize the psychic processes which take place in the Cosmos. There are processes which register what is uniform and eidetic and processes which register what is variable and instantial, and these involve the working of the same 'circles' as move the stars in their circuits, so that Celestial Dynamics and Rational Psychology become one and the same. If one likes, one can say that starry distributions and psychic structurings represent one and the same structuring of 'logical space', which would be a very wonderful and illuminating truth if it were a truth at all. For Plato-Timaeus the Circle of the Same which carries the contents of the Universe uniformly from East to West, is also the organ through which the World-Soul is able to cognize all the eternal natures and verities, while the Circle of the Other, with its subordinate planetary circles, is also the organ through which this Soul has assurances touching all mere matters of contingent, changeable fact (37a–c).

The generation of the organic Cosmos is then perfected by the generation of Time. Instances, however perfect, cannot have the date-indifference of the paradigms that they instantiate. They are always in a process of coming into being and passing away out of being, of being brought into being by eidetic power, and ceasing to be sustained by such power. The best that eidetic power, or the eternal Thinkingness that sums it up, can do for an instance, is to maintain instantiation of a certain sort continuously, to keep it from being the vanishing gleam that it essentially is. This in a privileged set of cases the eternal Thinkingness can and does effect, in the case, that is, of the various stars and planets, and it thus is responsible for Time, which for Timaeus-Plato, as for Kant, involves permanence as well as flux, the one making no sense apart from the other. Instantiation as an abstracted possibility is the mere flux of meaningless novelty that is metaphorically said to antedate the Cosmos, but Time proper only arises when that senseless flux is limited, when it falls within regularly recurrent, recognizable patterns, and this background of recurrence and permanence is what the heavenly bodies are there to provide. They are the august predecessors of Kant's substances, the transcendentally necessary points of permanence in the flux of instantiation. Time then is a case of the heightened analogy of Instance with Eidos which occurs in certain limiting instances: just as the one Cosmos, in its uniqueness, is an analogue of the necessary uniqueness of its original, so the regularly recurrent cosmic order is an analogue of the necessary invariance of its original. We see, accordingly, why and how the eternal demiurgic Thinkingness made 'an everlasting likeness going on numerically of the everlastingness which abides in unity' (37d), and also why 'Time arose with the heaven, that, begotten together, they might be dissolved together, if ever there were to be a dissolution of them, and that Time is patterned on the everlasting Nature so as to be as like it as possible. For the pattern is something which is throughout eternity, whereas heaven has been and is and shall be throughout all time' (38b, c).

What we must remember at this point is that the analogy also works in reverse, and that, just as Eternity has its reflection in the drawn-out persistence of Time, so this drawn-out persistence has an eidetic feed-back in the Eide of Movingness and Becomingness, and of Slowness and Swiftness, of which Plato, both in the *Republic* and the *Sophist*, magnificently takes account. The eidetic order may lavish itself in instantiation, but the possibility, and indeed the necessity, of such self-lavishment is intrinsic to the eidetic order. What we must further remember is that Time, though it is said to have arisen, is not for Plato anything substantial, a flowing medium or whatever: it is, if we may venture to spell it out, no more than an aspect of the permanent possibility of there being instances, of which Space or Place is afterwards shown to be the other aspect. Eternity, likewise, is no specific Eidos among Eide, but a transcendental character of Eidetic Being as Such, which it has, of course, in contrast to the Becomingness of the Instance. Plato certainly felt these higher-order subtleties from time to time, even if he has no consistent stance towards them.

From the heights of metaphysics we descend to the fretted sky: cosmic Time is measured by the Moon, the Sun and the five other planets which are fitted into the subordinate circles, like jewels into rings, and have incredibly complex relations to each other's movements. These Plato-Timaeus in part covers with carefully dark phrases, in part refuses to cover with phrases, as being too complex to be set forth in the present context. It is important to note that some of these movements involve an inherent contrariety, suitably attributed to self-moving responsibility. Conspicuous among the jewels thus set into rings is the shining Sun, responsible for the sequence of day and night, illuminating the whole planetary system, and making the study of celestial dynamics possible for such as are capable of it. The especially gifted will pass beyond the periods of the various planetary bodies to the Great Year, at the end of which all bodies will have returned to their initial relative position. Plato-Timaeus here again makes no mention of the periodic reversal of the whole cosmic movement taught in the *Statesman*: this, however, is not excluded by the present account, and is not at odds with the whole doctrine of Time and Eternity. The jewels set in the rings are, as has been said, endowed with a life which explains their various captious, contrary movements, and this applies also to the Earth which, at the centre of the Universe, of its own proper motion counteracts the swirl of the cosmic circuit – we follow Cornford's convincing interpretation – and so enables us to take cognizance of the latter. Had the Earth been a mere Work of Necessity, carried around by the Circle of the Same, we should never have become aware of the most impressive, uniform feature of the cosmic order, which both establishes Time and gives it a likeness to Eternity.

IV

The Dialogue now turns to consider a great metaphysical fault which runs through the whole Cosmos, the antithesis between those features of it which are 'Works of Mind', and which reflect the Thinkingness systematically correlated with the Eide, and those features of it which are 'Works of Necessity', and which reflect the directionless mechanism characteristic of the instantial as such. Before this is directly dealt with, Plato-Timaeus considers a few last details of demiurgic activity, the creation of the Gods and the manufacture of human Souls and bodies. Earth and Heaven, Ocean and Tethys, Cronos and Rhea, Zeus and Hera and the rest, are allowed to be the offspring of the celestial star-souls previously acknowledged. Plato has left it open to Proclus in a later age to fill in this outlined theology. The eternal demiurgic Thinkingness now turns to the task of finishing off the instantial being of man and of other embodied psychic beings. This Thinkingness itself will be responsible for their Souls, of which the immortal part will be compounded on the same recipe, the same blend of blends of eidetic and instantial Being, Sameness and Difference as the World-Soul, and will accordingly have the same sort of capacity to compare Eide with instances, and to impose patterns derived from the former on the latter (41d). This immortal part of Souls is located by the Gods in the head, whose spherical shape is made to resemble the shape of the Cosmos. Two revolving circles of the Same and the Other, analogous to those in the Cosmos, then acquaint the Soul with the eternal round of the Eide through the revolutions of the former circle, while the second circle acquaints it with instantial situations surrounding it, and with others inferred from these. The head, the receptacle of these sacred circles, is then placed for security, and for commodious locomotion, on the lower parts of the body, in the interior of which special Soul-functions will afterwards be located. The stream of nourishment and the sensations and desires stemming from the lower bodily members are, however, such as to perturb for a long time the functioning of the two divine circles, so that clear thought and reliable perception are impossible in infancy and in adolescence. Only when growth is completed are the circles able to function with integrity and can a man truly come to his senses. In this 'coming to his senses' the sense of sight plays a pre-eminent part, since without it we should never become aware of the divine recurrences of the heavens, nor of the eidetic invariances which these instantiate. Without sight to acquaint us with visible shapes, we should likewise never be able to advance to those Notional Shapes, the Eide, just as without hearing to introduce us to audible harmonies, we should never progress to the pure Ratios of Numbers which they sensibly illustrate (46c–47d).

Plato-Timaeus now says (47e) that he has hitherto considered only the 'things fabricated by Mind' (τὰ διὰ νοῦ δεδημιουργημένα): he must now complete his account by setting beside these 'the things that come to pass of Necessity' (τὰ δι'ἀνάγκης γιγνόμενα). For the origin of our Cosmos is mixed: it is a joint product of Necessity and Mind, Mind having used intelligent (ἔμφρων) persuasion to overrule Necessity, and so making it direct things for the most part to the best. If anyone wishes to say how things arose, he must make a new start and bring Necessity, the 'Wandering Cause' (ἡ πλανωμένη αἰτία), into the picture. He must consider what Fire, Water, Air and Earth may have been like, what their nature may have been, *before* the Cosmos came into being. There is a tendency simply to take them for granted as elements (στοιχεῖα) or Principles (ἀρχαί) of the Universe: the true elements of the Universe must, however, be infinitely more elementary than these, and one's views regarding them could not well be set forth in a discourse like the present, which is not primarily concerned with Stoicheiology. The best one can hope for is that one may talk no less probably than has been possible hitherto, invoking some God to guide one through such bizarre and unfamiliar subject-matters (48a–d). Plainly what Plato-Timaeus is now exploring are the features which differentiate instantial from eidetic being, which cause it to deviate from eidetic simplicities and symmetries, and to achieve confused, complex results which have no plain roots in the eidetic order. They are features characterized by 'wanderingness', since they fall randomly in a great number of different directions. But they are also features characterized by Necessity, since the possibility of deviation and chance collocation is inherent in the Instance, and since each particular deviation or collocation will no doubt have its warrant in what went before, and in the nature of the instances concerned. They are also features characterized by Necessity since they spring from no single Principle, no ordering, eidetic design: a variety of Eide are instantially, not eidetically, connected, and hence each instance has a merely external, imposed connection with the instances of other Eide. Such contingent collocations there must be if there are to be instances at all: there are, however, necessary limits to such permissiveness, and this is what Plato-Timaeus means by the 'persuasion' exercised by Mind over Necessity. We may here note that Plato-Timaeus in his treatment simply takes up no stance in regard to the modern issue between determinism and indeterminism. He gives absolutely no indication, in regard to either purposive or mechanistic causation, whether there is or is not a single predictable course which Becoming must take. The difference between the Works of Mind and the Works of Necessity is that of integrated, eidetically based causation, on the one hand, and eidetically irrelevant, instantially compresent causation, on the other. It is an axiom of Plato's cosmological theory that both must be present when Eide are instantiated, but he simply never raises the question as to whether either form of causation may or may not involve its own quota of unpredictability. Such questions lie in the future, when the notion of Law will largely have replaced the notion of Eide, and when Laws will be thought to have a much firmer sway over the course of instantiation than Eide are ever given by Plato.

The realm of instantiation, however, requires something more fundamental than the blindly necessary tendencies of which Timaeus-Plato has been speaking: it requires a universal Receptacle (ὑποδοχή) or Nurse (τιθήνη) of Becoming, a Nature (εἶδος) of great difficulty and obscurity. So far we have been satisfied with a twofold ontology of unchanging eidetic Natures, on the one hand, and their changing, visible analogues, on the other: now we find it necessary to introduce a third ontological category, having the peculiar receptive function that has just been indicated. The need for postulating such an omnirecipient Nurse lies in the universal transformability of the so-called bodily elements. We should like to call something we have before us 'Water' but we see it promptly solidifying into Earth and stones or being sublimated into wind and Air, which achieves combustion as Fire, gets extinguished into Air, becomes mist or fog which condenses into Water, and again solidifies into Earth and stones. To apply the name of any one elementary Nature to such changeable phenomena is plainly repugnant. Instead, therefore, of calling our phenomenon 'Fire' we should rather say that it is of a fiery nature, or such as Fire, and so likewise in the other cases. But what we can genuinely pin down as this or that, is not such a variable phenomenon, but something *in which*, as we say, the phenomenon arises or passes away. What we mean may be best elucidated by an analogy.

If someone were moulding a piece of gold into a number of shapes, and were asked what he was thus moulding, it would be safest to give the simple answer 'Gold', rather than to mention any of the particular shapes, 'Triangle' etc., into which he was moulding it. He might, if he wished, say that the gold was now triangular or was such as a triangle, but it would be misleading to call it 'This triangle'. The same holds of the omnirecipient Nature of our consideration, though of course this is not a sort of stuff like gold, nor capable of being moulded at all. The Nurse of Becoming, in which there come to be appearances of Eide, receives them impartially, but never takes on the nature of any form that enters it. It lies there, a plastic base (ἐκμαγεῖον) for everything, seemingly changed by whatever enters it or leaves it, such entrants being, however, the merest simulacra of true Being, derived marvellously from their originals in a manner that passes all utterance (50a–d). The recipient Nature must be void of all form in order to be able to receive all form: if it instantiates any Eidos to whatever degree, and carries the faintest scent or savour of it, it will at once have difficulty in instantiating contrary Eide. It must be like the scentless bases which perfumers use in manufacturing their perfumes: in order that it may show forth the sensuous characters of Earth, Air, Fire and Water it must itself have none of these characters. It must, in short, be an invisible shapeless sort of thing, in some unintelligible manner sharing in the intelligible (μεταλάμβανον δὲ ἀπορώτατά πῃ τοῦ νοητοῦ – 51a, b).

Plato-Timaeus once more runs through and elaborates the grounds for his threefold ontology. Have we, he asks, any good ground for believing in something which is 'Fire in itself' (πῦρ αὐτὸ ἐφ᾽ ἑαυτοῦ), or which is any other sort of thing thus spoken of? Or must we, on the contrary, confine genuineness (ἀλήθεια) to the things perceived through the bodily senses, turning our 'in itselfs' into mere words (51c)? He replies that we have good ground in the generic difference between Intellectual Insight (νοῦς) and True Opinion, the former being imparted by instruction (διδαχή), the latter by persuasion, the former grounded in a reasoned account (λόγος) and the latter reasonless, the former, consequently, being quite unsusceptible to persuasion and the latter highly susceptible. This cognitive difference points to an ontological difference between the unbegotten, indestructible, imperceptible Eide, on the one hand, which never themselves receive anything else into themselves, nor go forth into anything else, and their perceptible, changeable, fabricated namesakes on the other, which arise in, and depart from, a given place, and which we grasp through Opinion and Sense-perception. Besides these two categorially different sorts of things there is, however, plainly the eternal, indestructible nature of Space (χώρα), providing a seat (ἕδρα) for all generated things, and grasped without the use of the senses by a sort of spurious argument (λογισμῷ τινι νόθῳ), a thing barely credible and seen by us as in a dream. The argument is to the effect that whatever is, must somehow be in some place or occupy some region, and that what is not to be found anywhere in the heaven or on earth is simply nothing (52b). And if we are to reformulate this argument in a fully lucid, waking manner, we must say that, since an illustrative image (εἰκών) has its principle of Being in something else, and is merely the floating appearance of something else (ἑτέρου δέ τινος ἀεὶ φέρεται φάντασμα), it must for that reason arise *in* something else, from which it will precariously cling to Being, if it is not to be nothing at all. Whereas what authentically is, has its accurate support in the true general statement that, wherever things are distinct, none will come into being in the other so as to be at once one and the same, and also twain (52c).

This immensely complex, highly analogical, confessedly spurious argument, for an entity confessedly eluding description, and only known by us in a confessedly obscure manner, requires careful examination. It must not, any more than Aristotle's list of categories, be misread as a mere classification of the sorts of things we *find* in the world, or feel it necessary to suppose are present in it, and which are there, and contribute to the world, in one and the same univocal manner. Plato was not such a dolt as to suppose that reality consisted of three species of things, one unchanging, contentful but invisible, one changing, contentful and visible, and one unchanging, contentless and invisible, the second having some obscure dependence on the first, which in some unintelligible way forces it to seek support in the third. Plainly the sense in which there *are* Eide, and the sense in which there are sensible instances, and the sense in which there are spaces for sensible things, are entirely different senses, and the whole business of ontology is simply to see and show how they differ and how they fit together, a business of which Plato was more than a master, even if he often used pictures and metaphors without going on to an unpictorial, non-metaphorical statement. It is of course wholly axiomatic that for Platonism only Eide can have Being in a strict and unqualified sense: all else merely hangs on to the Being of the Eide in one or another way, and merely *is* the Eide thus or thus functioning or thus or thus circumstanced. And sensible things are, as stated above, the floating appearances of something different (52c), the simulacra of things that truly are (τῶν ὄντων ἀεὶ μιμήματα), modelled marvellously on what truly are in a manner which (being unique) passes expression (50c). For Platonism, we may note, the *appearance* of an Eidos does not even involve the real being of an appearance as such: it only points, if to anything, to something *not* apparent, of which appearing is no more than a mode. It is, we may say, of the essence of Eide to appear, to illustrate themselves, to body themselves forth here and here and again and again: so much is part and parcel of the Ungrudgingness, which is equally an ἀφθονία, an infinite abundance, and which Plato-Timaeus has attributed to the Absolute Thinkingness.

But if sensible appearances are thus insubstantial, what are we to think of the great receiving mirror or screen on which they are all projected? Is this to be supposed to exist without qualification, to be a solid cosmic fixture, a wet-nurse taking over a strange by-blow of the eternal Eide? Plainly the language in which Plato speaks of the Nurse Chora forbids any such assumption. Though she is momentarily compared to the gold which we mould into ever varying shapes, it is soon made plain that she has no shape at all, that she has not even the analogical link with qualified stuff which Aristotle uses to give a more solid status to *his* Nurse, Hyle. It is true that we are allowed to call Chora 'This' or 'That', even if we may not call her 'Water' or 'Air' or 'Earth' or 'Fire', but since our only access to her person is by way of a confessedly fishy argument, it is not clear what good this permission does us. We argue that whatever is, must be in some place, or must occupy room, in order *not* to be nothing, but what we are arguing *for* remains unbelievable, a mere vision seen in a dream. If we try to wake up, and find what lies behind this rigmarole, we can only reason unconvincingly that what wholly depends on something else for its being, must of necessity attach to a third thing, since it cannot exist on its own. Surely the correct answer is that what wholly depends on something, wholly depends on what it wholly depends on, and requires no third thing for any purpose. If Chora is therefore necessary as a support for the dependent instance, it can only be because she too depends on the Eidos instantiated in it, because Instance and Space are merely two sides of the same mystery or necessity, that what is one in essence should be multiply bodied forth. If instances are the actuality of such bodying forth, Space is no more than the perpetual possibility of the same bodying forth: we have indeed endless 'room' for cases which do nothing but repeat the same single Nature or Character. And it is plain that, in the ontological stakes, Chora runs behind, and not ahead of, the Instance. She has less assignable character to lay hold of, a less clear mode of making her presence known, and much less analogy with what is eidetic than the instance: it is only in the most hopelessly difficult way (ἀπορώτατα – 51b) that she participates in intelligibility. There is good reason to think that she is merely τὸ πάντως μὴ ὄν, the utterly non-existent, of *Republic* 478, masquerading under an alias, of which ἄγνοια, total Unknowingness, is the non-apprehension which counts for an apprehension. If modern analysts hesitate to treat Nothing-at-all as in some sense something, we must remember that the Greeks had no such scruples, and Plato, we are told by Aristotle and the Aristotelian commentators, identified That-which-is-not with the principle of Movement and Otherness in the world (*Physics*, 201b), which was identical with the Great and Small in the world of the senses, and he also identified χώρα, Space, with the Great and Small (Simplicius on *Physics*, 209b), from which it follows that Space, and the Great and Small, and the Principle of Motion, were all quite intelligibly identified by Plato with That-which-is-not. If the Atomists gave Not-being a sort of derivative, separative function in the physical world, Plato gave it a similar function both in the physical and the metaphysical sphere.

Though Chora, Space, underlies the possibility of the instantial order, we must avoid supposing that Spatiality, as opposed to Space, will have no representation in the eidetic realm. Plainly it will, as the whole science of geometry bears witness. Just as sheer numerical multiplicity, which is a mark of the Instance, has an eidetic echo in the eternal essence of the Numbers, which though not multiple, yet are patterns of multiplicity, so the sheer repetitiousness of instantial spatiality will have its eidetic reflection in eternal, unextended patterns of spatiality, the Circle as Such, the Square as Such etc., all pointing back to the generic spatiality of the Long and Short, the Broad and Narrow and the Deep and Shallow. Chora, Space, in fact occupies precisely the same place in the realm of instances that the Great and Small, the Principle of unlimited Quantitative Advance or Shrinkage, has in the realm of the Eide. They are in fact one and the same Principle, only working at different levels, as Aristotle tells us over and over again. The same indefinite specifiability which, when subjected to bounds, yields all the Eide, themselves Numbers or many-dimensional Ratios of Numbers, also goes on to yield all the instances of such Eide: everywhere we have the notion of So-much-and-no-further in creative combination with the notion Always-a-little-more-or-a-little-less. The use of the term ἐκμαγεῖον, plastic medium, by Plato in the *Timaeus*, and by Aristotle in talking in the *Metaphysics* (987b) of the genesis of the Numbers, shows how closely Platonism identified the two media, as Aristotle himself did in his doctrine of Intelligible Matter, and Plotinus in his treatise on the Two Matters.

The identification of Chora with Non-being has a further, very acceptable result. The dualism of ἀρχαί, of basic Principles, which runs through Plato, and which is solemnly documented by Aristotle, really reduces to a monism. One of the ἀρχαί is really no ἀρχή at all, but a mere shadow of the other. The One is really responsible for everything, and the Indefinite Dyad which opposes it is merely what it needs to be itself. As Parmenides, the ultimate source of Plato's revised, critical Eleaticism, puts it (Diels 8), 'Men have made it their custom to name two forms of which it is not right to name one – that is where they have gone astray'. The negative or empty Principle which in the eidetic sphere specifies, in the instantial sphere instantiates, is merely the extrinsic side of absolute Unity, a side as necessary to it, as what it is καθ'αὐτό or in and for itself. It is as much one with absolute Unity as the diminishing shadow is one with the spreading light, or as the concavity of a curve is one with its convexity, an infinitely illuminating analogy from Aristotle, which may very well have a Platonic origin.

V

From this point (52d) the Dialogue becomes more and more detailed, and we shall need to practise the same compression in restating the gist of Timaeus-Plato's teaching that Timaeus-Plato has exercised in stating the same teaching in elegantly undecipherable sentences. The state of the Receptacle, the Nurse of Becoming, *before* receiving her comprehensive restructuring by the Demiurgic Thinkingness, is eloquently described:

> She was moistened and inflamed, had received the shapes
> of Earth and Air, and the other affections that go with
> these, and presented a very motley appearance, since she was
> filled with forces (δυνάμεις) which were neither homogeneous
> nor in balance, so that she was unevenly tossed and shaken
> by them in all directions, and through her movements shook
> them in their turn (52d–53c).

The bodily elements had even then some rudiments (ἴχνη) of their present structure and powers, and the shaking of the Receptacle, presumably within rough limits, that confined its contents in a narrow space, had the effect of sorting the roughly different elements into regions where like consorted with like: the pre-Socratic vortex is not made use of for this purpose. On this disordered scene, the Demiurgic Thinkingness imposed an order of Forms and Numbers (διεσχηματίσατο εἴδεσί τε καὶ ἀριθμοῖς: 53b), an ordering which in fact helps us to understand what Plato meant by the mathematical nature of the Eide. The story of the Tipsy Nurse rehabilitated by the Divine Doctor need not be taken too seriously, since that Nurse is, as we have seen, That-which-is-not, the Nothingness which the Demiurgic Thinkingness has only to exclude and annul. Her original condition is mythic:

though there are times when the hegemony of the Eide is relaxed, there are no times in which it vanishes altogether. And her original condition, if not mythic, would be wholly indescribable, as Timaeus-Plato in fact makes plain by describing it as a shaking of emptiness, and as a presence of rudiments of structure of which no account should be possible in the absence of all. No serious heed need therefore be given to the state of Chora before the Divine Doctor took her in hand. Her weaknesses were the weaknesses of the impotently possible which is nothing apart from its structuring Eide.

The manner in which the rudiments of elementary structure were refined into fairly exact representations of Eide and Numbers is of absorbing interest: Timaeus-Plato employs for the purpose the Regular Solids, of which Theaetetus, Plato's outstanding pupil, had triumphantly proved that there could only be five, thereby fulfilling those finitist hopes of which the keeping of the Numbers within the Decad, or making them the products of the first even and odd numbers, were other expressions. Timaeus-Plato makes no use of the Dodecahedron, the most impressive of the Regular Solids, in his physical Stoicheiology: as in the *Phaedo*, it was reserved for the shape of the Cosmos as a whole, or of some many-faceted, many-coloured jewel set in the crystalline round of the Cosmos, though Timaeus-Plato does suggest (55c–d) that, had more than one Cosmos been conceivable, other Solids might have been used in their constitution. This conveniently leaves the four-sided Tetrahedron, the six-sided Cube, the eight-sided Octahedron and the twenty-sided Icosahedron for the four physical elements. Obviously sharply pointed, dissolving Fire fits the structure of the Tetrahedron, stable, closely packable Earth the structure of the Cube, the light and nimble, but not penetrating Air the structure of the Octahedron, and readily rolling Water the practically spherical Icosahedron (55d–56c).

The allocation of the Regular Solids to the elementary bodies has interesting consequences. The Tetrahedron, the Octahedron, and the Icosahedron have sides which are equilateral triangles: the Cube has sides which are squares. From this it follows that, while Fire, Air and Water are mutually transformable, the triangles being dismembered and recemented, Earth, whose sides are square, and which cannot be resolved into equilateral triangles, can also not be transformed into the other elements. There is a Heraclitean Way Up from liquid Water through vaporous Air to burning Fire, and a corresponding Way Down, but, despite appearances (49b, c), Earth stands aside from the cosmic merry-go-round, and can at most be dissolved into component planes by the pressure of other elements. The doctrine is somewhat more complex than has been stated, each equilateral face of Tetrahedron, Octahedron and Icosahedron being subdivided into *six* smaller triangles, whose angles of 30°, 60° and 90° stand in the charmed ratio of 1:2:3, while the four faces of the Cube are each divided into *four* isosceles triangles, with one angle of 90° and two of 45°.

Cornford has brilliantly shown (*Plato's Cosmology*, 1937, pp. 230–9) that this constitution of the faces out of smaller triangles has the effect of making it possible to have a finely graded set of sizes of different elementary particles, it being a property of both classes of triangles that they can be resolved into, or cemented into, smaller or larger triangles (respectively) of the same kind. The requirement of 57c, d that the bodily elements should come in a number of distinct sizes is also clearly met, and with it an understanding as to why the compacting of finer structures into larger should lead to an increase of volume, whereas a forced decrease in volume leads to the breaking up of coarser structures into finer ones. If we now conceive of the finer forms of Fire as the main disintegrators of coarser structures, while the coarser forms of Earth are the main agents of solid compacting, we have a fine pair of explanatory principles on which to hang the cosmic changes. Aristotle has gravely reprimanded Plato for attempting to construct mobile Nature out of insubstantial geometrical solids which at times permit disintegration into mere planes: stuff of some sort, he insists, is necessary to give concreteness to the picture, and to make its elements have true causal effect on one another. For Plato, however, Eide are the true causes of motion and interaction, and require as little help from his disorderly Nurse of Becoming as they might derive from the equally empty Aristotelian Prime Matter, which is infinitely removed from any stuff of common sense. Plato and Aristotle were alike in removing quality from the purely eidetic and the natural order, and in making them the vanishing offspring of sense-object rubbing on sense-organ. But, if sensible qualities are to be left out from cosmic objects or their patterns, only Numbers, Lines, Planes and Solids remain as the materials from which they may be constructed. And there is nothing wrong in such a construction, provided possible instantiation is seen as inherent in the Eide, and provided quality is also seen as inherent in instantial illustration.

Timaeus-Plato next gives an account of that derivative aspect of motion which is a Work of Necessity, of the chance interaction of instances, rather than the direct effect of Eide and the minds informed by them. Where instantiation is quite homogeneous, motion will not arise: it will arise only when instances have come to differ, to be in some respect 'unequal' (57e). The segregation of instances into zones of fiery tetrahedra, airy octahedra, watery icosahedra and earthy cubes is always in process of taking place, owing to the inhomogeneity otherwise resulting: it is, however, always being impeded by the corseted tightness of the Cosmos, confined within its spherical limits, and pushing the finer structures into the interstices of its coarser ones. Fire and Air are its finest structures, leaving the least space between them, and they therefore force themselves into the interstices of Water and Earth, constituting a dissident minority within their bounds, which must always either suppress the coarser, environing masses or be suppressed by them. In the former case there will be expansion, and what we feel as a warming up, in the latter case contraction and what we feel as a cooling off, and both directions of change lead to further mass-movements (58a–c). These movements and changes also effect changes in the different varieties and sizes of the elemental structures involved: the departure of Fire makes the small octahedra of liquids freeze into the packed masses of the coarser octahedra of the corresponding solids, whereas normally frozen liquids, the metals which are made of very coarse octahedra, melt on the advent of Fire into the finer octahedra of the corresponding liquid forms (58d–59a). Earth, compacted unbrokenly into the largest cubes, becomes stone: made finer, and permitting Fire, Water and Air into its interstices, it becomes various more attractive, less obdurately solid substances, for example salt, earthenware etc. (60b–e).

All this leads on to the treatment of the sense-qualities, in which Timaeus-Plato has obviously learnt much from the Atomists, both in his willingness to allow the sense-qualities to be merely subjective products of purely quantitative space-time differences, and in the ingenuity of the materialistic hypotheses by which he accounts for them. The 'hotness' of Fire is obviously due to the sharpness of its pyramidal angles, its penetrative fineness, and its power to pierce and rend (61d, e). Whereas the 'coldness' of Water is due to the shivering resistance of particles of different sizes, forced by its voluminous presence into finer uniformity (62a, b). Processes in which there is a sudden disturbance of a peaceful and stable arrangement of particles are painful (cuts and burns), whereas processes in which there is a sudden return to such a stable state are pleasant. Gradual disturbances of stability or returns to it occasion no feelings (64d–65b). The explanation of tastes and odours (65b–67a) and of sounds and colours (67a–68d) are too ingeniously complex to be set forth here.

The Dialogue now goes on to consider the lower structures of Soul and body, a consideration interrupted by the long consideration of the 'Works of Necessity'. These lower structures are, as said before, the creation of an outlying part of Divinity, enmeshed in instantial multiplicity as the Demiurgic Thinkingness is not. As in the *Republic*, there are two inferior parts of the Soul, separated by the diaphragm like the men and women in a Greek household, and both separated from the intelligent, immortal part of the Soul by the isthmus of the neck. The upper part of the inferior Soul inhabits the breast; it receives directives from the upper acropolis of reason, and forces the burgeoning appetites to defer to them. It is brave, full of spirit and a lover of victory, and operates mainly through the heart, the place where the veins are knotted together, and from which the blood is sent coursing all over the body, instantly responding to all dangers and all insults to dignity or propriety. It also requires the lung as a cooling mechanism, to keep the heart's boiling indignation from running to excess (69d–70d). Passing beneath the diaphragm, we come to the Appetitive Soul, feeding on the stomach like a beast at a manger, deaf to the discourse of reason, except to such as employs the fantastic symbolism of the liver, an organ which dispenses both happy and painful dreams, the best being the divinatory insights of seers, whose interpretation is best essayed by those who are not seers at all. And, as the lung is there to quieten the excesses of the heart, the spleen quietens and purifies those of the liver (70d–72c). The sexual apparatus and impulse is to be assigned to a yet lower Soul-part, and is not dealt with till the end of the Dialogue.

The Dialogue then proceeds to a discussion of various bodily substances and performances, more from the mechanistic standpoint of the Works of Necessity than the teleological standpoint of the Works of Mind. The substance of the cortical and spinal nerve-cells is singled out as the most unwarped (ἀστραβής) in the body, and consisting of all the best triangles. It is understandably identified with the substance of the bone-marrow and also with that of semen, which is held to flow by a special channel to its sexual outlet. Other substances, such as bone, flesh, sinews, hair etc., give protection and assistance to the divine brain-marrow-seed, and are compounded out of the four elements in various arrangements and proportions.

Respiration and digestion are jointly explained in an infinitely ingenious legend, whose inspiration is in Empedocles, according to which we live surrounded by a sort of network of Air containing a centre of Fire, and having as openings the mouth and nose on the one hand, and the pores of the skin on the other. Inspiration and expiration have a purely mechanical explanation, due jointly to the sorting action of affinity, and the mingling action of cosmic compression. The Fire at our centre strives to move out from among the packed substances where it is situated: if it is expired through the nose or mouth, an equal amount of Air is drawn in through the pores, the former becoming cooled and the latter heated. This heated Air has to retreat through the pores, and an equal amount of cooler Air is drawn in then through the mouth or nose, thus setting up an alternation of exhalation and inhalation (79c–e). The main agent in breathing is therefore the compressive action of the Universe, which at once forces something to take the place of any substance that is moved. Timaeus-Plato has been as much a mechanist in his account of the behaviour of the lungs as Descartes was afterwards to be in his account of the behaviour of the heart. The digestion of food, and its dispersal in the form of blood to the remoter parts of the body, is all due to the action of Fire in the belly, and so ultimately to the cosmic compression. Growth is explained by the dominance of the new, fresh triangles in the organism's brain and marrow over worn-out ones that stem from outside:

when the organism's own triangles become worn, decay sets in (81b–d). Disease in its various species is treated in a masterly manner, showing great knowledge of contemporary medicine.

Near the end of the Dialogue sexual differentiation receives a brief paragraph (90e–91b), in which the behaviour of phallus and womb are vividly set forth and explained. Both are living organisms in their own right, though dependent on the larger organisms to which they are attached, and both accordingly show a self-will and a violence which merits indulgence rather than censure (86c–e). The uncontrolled incontinence of many men, and the hysteria of some unsatisfied women, are not voluntary failings, but to a large extent the result of bodily structure and the exigencies of the marrow-semen. The Dialogue ends with a fine sentence in which Timaeus-Plato says that the visible Cosmos has now come to incorporate in instantial form all the specifications of Life which were contained in the divine blue-print of the Demiurgic Thinkingness. The discourse, though at best probable, is now as perfect as it well can be. We may value it extremely, since it shows us how Plato thought that purely eidetic causality, on the one hand, and its confused, imperfect, fortuitous, instantial outcome, on the other, may be held to fit together, and to be accommodated to one another. It is also extraordinarily valuable since it shows us Plato's mathematicization in action. The Eide are not merely Natural Numbers, but Numbers distinguished as to dimension, and having complex Ratios to one another which would have been best expressed in differential equations, had Plato had such tools at his disposal.

VI

After the discourse of Timaeus on the construction of the Cosmos by the demiurgic Thinkingness, we go on, according to the prearranged plan, to Critias's discourse regarding the proto-Athenians of 9000 years previously, and their victory over the power of decadent Atlantis. Atlantis, as related by the Egyptian priests to Solon, was an island as large as Lybia and Asia together, set beyond the pillars of Heracles in the true Ocean, in comparison with which the Mediterranean and its surroundings are a mere puddle in a cow-byre. As in the *Phaedo* Plato gave us a true

Ocean of Air in which the world of the philosophers floats, and beneath which our earth is a submarine simulacrum, so here he gives us a true Ocean of Water, in both cases sketching us a map designed to express moral and spiritual, rather than geographical differences. Egypt, which relies for its waters on inundations from below, rather than rain from above, was able to preserve itself from the watery and fiery cataclysms which destroyed all other cities and civilizations of men, and so to preserve traditions regarding the 9000-years-old Atlantean civilization and its contemporaries.

The island in the Atlantic began, Solon was informed, as a model of all the virtues, founded by Poseidon and his mortal spouse Cleito, and presided over by ten Kings who were his descendants, and who were frugal in all things except the gorgeousness of their garments and the splendour of their architecture. After a time, however, no doubt owing to one of those periodic relaxations of demiurgic control mentioned in the *Statesman*, the virtue of the Kings was lessened, and their kingdom became an example of the greed, luxury, violence and other vices of the decadent polities sketched in the eighth and ninth books of the *Republic*. Meanwhile, according to the same reliable tradition, an earlier Athens, flourishing in a much richer Attica, came close to exemplifying the virtuous arrangements sketched in the early books of the *Republic*, and described by Socrates the day before Timaeus gave his cosmological exposition. Critias was astonished, when Socrates was developing his ideal arrangements, by their resemblance to the accounts he had received from his grandfather Dropides, who had them from Solon, who had them from the Egyptians, but so necessarily does history, and particularly prehistory, mirror the results reached by eidetic insight. The ancient Athenians had class-divisions, an aristocracy of 20,000 guardians, common meals for their aristocracy and shared military and other duties for men and women alike. It is, however, to be presumed that some of the more audacious and controversial recommendations of the *Republic* represent some of the many points in which discourse went beyond the bounds of practice.

It is not, however, possible for us to pursue Plato's picture beyond this point: like some spectacular film it snaps off quite suddenly, leaving it unclear precisely what was Plato's design in starting it all. Socrates-Plato said, at the beginning of the *Timaeus* (19a), that he desired to see the wonderful, ideal picture of his community, not frozen and static, but set in appropriate motion, and engaged in a contest suitable to the human 'livestock' in question. Plainly the Dialogue would have shown the genuine advantage, in war and in other contests, of the Athenian πόλις, like some well-formed, well-cemented Solid, over the amorphous, inflated, irregularly expanding shape represented by Atlantis, and so would have shown that it is not merely a matter of numbers and structure but of palpable effectiveness that puts the Athenian above the Atlantean ideal. The fragmentary Dialogue before us is, however, only of poetic, not of philosophical, value, and we shall not therefore consider it further, beyond noting the great convenience of the inundation which submerged both Atlantis and Athens and so erected a screen behind which Plato could do his poetic conjuring.

The writing of the *Critias* was, however, followed by a cataclysmic disturbance far more serious than the mythic flood mentioned in the Dialogue. Plato's philosophical and literary genius was overwhelmed by an inundation whose precise nature we can only conjecture, but whose final effect is evident in the writing called the *Laws*. It is the fashion to conceive crises in the life of Plato, for which the evidence is largely insufficient, but here is a crisis for which the evidence is surely sufficient: the descent from works of incomparable literary and philosophical excellence, even in their most wayward excesses, to a performance so inferior that it is really a punishment to read it. Zeller attributed the identification of the Eide with Numbers to the encroachments of senility in Plato's seventh decade: it was not, however, the intricacies of Number-theory that were then Plato's main preoccupation, but endlessly rambling political recommendations, which are the antithesis of anything mathematical or otherwise exact, which lack the excuse of being adjusted to practical exigencies, which are for modern, and even ancient, taste, deeply unattractive, and for which, except in the case of some platitudes which provide their own reason, no good general reason, let alone a good philosophical reason, is ever given. The writing of the *Laws* bears witness, not to some slow, senile fading, but to a stroke or seizure which, even if it may not have destroyed Plato's smooth style, certainly disrupted his higher powers of judgment.

There is, however, no need for special hypotheses where the facts are so plain: something happened to Plato, in his last years, whether of a clinically certifiable type or not. The one thing that runs counter to this diagnosis are the theological discussions in the tenth book of the work. These, like some isolated Peak of Teneriffe, are all that bears witness to the Atlantis of Plato's sunken genius. And of their non-immersion several explanations are of course possible.

It may be thought, in view of the attempts of some distinguished students of Plato to rehabilitate the *Laws*, not only as a genuine, but as a great work of Plato's, that I have been unduly harsh in these statements. I can only refute the charge by quotation, from which I shall go on to consider the arguments of the tenth Book. Possibly the work may have importance from some non-philosophical angle, as a slight improvement on the contemporary Attic code, and so on: such considerations are not in place in this book. We shall choose three widely different, but representative passages from different parts of the work, from which the character of its contents will be apparent to all who are not past persuading.

Our first citation is from Book II (661c–663b), where the Athenian Stranger is discussing the case of a man who possesses health, wealth and a tyranny, surpassing strength and bravery plus immortality, who is in fact free from all evil but arrogance and injustice: such a man, the Stranger opines, cannot be happy, but must be miserable. Living basely, he will be living in a bad way, and this cannot be agreeable or advantageous to him. From these empty utterances, paradoxical or tautological as interpreted in one way or another, and once given dignity and content by the moral earnestness of Socrates, the Stranger proceeds to the following:

> How can this be? May a God bring us into harmony, since we are now fairly far from it. To me these things are as inescapably plain, my dear Cleinias, as that Crete is an island. And if I were a legislator, I would try to force all poets and everyone in the city to sing in this style, and I would impose almost the worst of penalties on anyone in the country who ventured to say that there were some wicked men who yet lived pleasant lives, or that the juster

course differs from the profitable or the advantageous. I
should in fact persuade my citizens to put many things
quite differently from what is now said by the Cretans and
the Spartans and (so it would seem) by the rest of mankind.
Best of men, I would say, by Zeus and Apollo, suppose
we ask the very Gods who gave you your laws 'Is the
justest life the sweetest, or are there two lives, one
sweetest and the other justest?'. If they answered 'Two',
and if it seemed proper to enquire further and ask, 'Which
of the two should we say are happier, those living the
justest, or those living the sweetest life?', and they were
to answer, 'Those living the sweetest', they would be
making a very strange reply. I do not like attributing such
a statement to the Gods. I would rather put the question
to a parent or a lawgiver, and, if he answered that the one
who lived most sweetly also lived most blessedly, I would
then say, 'My dear father, so you did not wish me to live
as happily as possible, since you never laid off telling me
to live as justly as possible?'. The rule-giver, whether
legislator or parent, would then be embarrassed, and would
not know how to prove his consistency. But if he said that the
justest life was also the happiest, everyone who heard him
would wonder what marvellous good, quite superior to
pleasure, the law was commending as present in this life.
For, in the absence of pleasure, what good could the just
man enjoy? Shall we say that a good standing in the eyes
of men and Gods is a fine but painful thing, and that a bad
standing is the reverse? Dear Lawgiver, we can say nothing
of the sort. . . . An argument, therefore that refuses to
separate the delightful from the fair and fine will at least
persuade a man to live piously and justly, while an argument
that denies this will be the most objectionable and base of
arguments from the standpoint of the legislator.

The coincidence of Justice with Pleasure, once proved by
reasonings of some nobility, if of doubtful validity, is now
proved by showing it to be an expedient doctrine for a legislator
to teach in order to hold a community together, for which end
there is of course no longer any acceptable justification.

My second quotation runs from 746d to 747, and illustrates the senselessness to which even Plato's mathematical interests could fall. Numerical ratios no longer have a cosmic or ontological significance: they are tied up with a doubtful, low-grade, social utility.

> Having decided on a twelvefold division, we must now consider how twelve parts will be internally divisible in a maximal number of ways and will lead on to similar divisions till the number 5040 is reached. We must consider how the law must adjust the size of its fraternities, demes and villages, military columns and cohorts, as well as its coinage, weights, liquid and dry measures, so as to fit in with the number in question and with one another. One should further have no fear of being thought small-minded, if one insists that every instrument should have its precise measure, believing in the general usefulness of common Ratios in numerical divisions and further developments, whether in the arithmetical or the geometrical field, or in the field of tones or of rectilinear and circular movements. The lawgiver intent on these principles should demand of the citizens that they should do all they can never to depart from these numerical patterns. Nothing learnt in infancy is so effective in the household or the state, or in all the arts, as the study of Numbers. Most important of all, it rouses a man from his ignorant slumbers, and makes him bright, retentive and keen-minded, raised above himself by a divine art.

My third quotation deals with assault and battery (879b, c).

> All the injuries so far mentioned involve violence, and the whole class of assaults is likewise violent. So that what every man, woman and child should always hold in mind on such matters, is that the senior ranks far above the junior in honour, whether among the Gods, or among such men as desire a secure and happy life. To see a younger man assault an older man in the city is an evil, a god-detested sight. A young man should put up patiently with the blows and rage of an old man, laying up for himself a similar honour in old age.

If the propriety and expediency of these recommendations is unquestionable, they are also worthier of a gnomic poet than of a philosopher.

The tenth book of the *Laws* is, however, concerned with the social and political dangers of atheism and bad theology, and merits closer attention. It is led up to by the treatment of assaults just cited. Assaults are a form of violence, of which by far the gravest form is sacrilegious violence against the religious property of tribes and other civic associations: violence against private religious property comes second in gravity. We have, it is held, to institute a series of penalties for those who blaspheme against the Gods in word or deed, for it is plain that none who believe in the Gods would willingly behave impiously or lawlessly. The impious and lawless must either believe that there are no Gods, or that, though they exist, they care nothing for men, or that they can be readily won over by sacrifices and prayers. (The possibility of demonic beings, trembling in awful, unrepentant faith before an unwavering God, is obviously unknown to the Athenian Stranger.)

The Stranger, however, puts a reply into the mouth of his impious opponents. Some of us, they say, indeed think that there are no Gods, others that the Gods are such as you have said. We have, they say, to be persuaded that there are Gods, and that these Gods cannot be cajoled into condoning injustice by gifts. Arguments based on the wonderful order of the heavens and the seasons do not weigh with such persons, since they have read books that persuade them that Sun, Moon and stars are compounded of earth and stones, quite bereft of divinity and incapable of minding human affairs. It is abominable to have to argue with such persons, who have rejected the tales told them regarding the Gods at their mother's knee, and who have not been persuaded to believe in Gods by the faith and devotion shown by their parents in their prayers and sacrifices. None the less we must try to restrain our rage, and to reason with these warped intelligences. We must point out to them how few men persist in these mad opinions in later life, and must at least persuade them to defer to the wisdom of the legislator until they have garnered more sense. The most dreadful of their opinions is one that holds the bodily elements to be products, not of divine art, but of nature and chance, and conceives that, without

337

a trace of mind, they have given rise to Sun, Moon and stars and to all plants and animals. The products of art are for them all late developments, and merely pretend to have a natural foundation and truth. The laws of society are among such artificial creations, and from those laws stem the dogmas of religion and the precepts of morality. The enlightened young scorn all these artefacts, and believe only in the natural morality which identifies Right with Might. The root-error of these young moderns springs from their failure to see that Soul is an elder reality than anything bodily, and that its thought, care and understanding are of more account in settling the arrangement and course of things than the Hard and the Soft, the Heavy and the Light, or any other bodily attributes (892a, b). They must therefore be given a proof that will compel them to accord seniority and priority to the Soul.

This proof is now sketched, and begins with the admission of almost universal motion in the Cosmos, sometimes involving translation from one place to another, sometimes circular rotation in a single spot. The wonder of cosmic motion lies above all in the manner in which the circular rotation of the outer heavens is communicated as a proportionately swifter and slower movement to the various other circles which it encloses. Other motions are mentioned, some of simple translation, others blending translation with rotation, some involving disruption (διάκρισις) through the resistance of inert bodies, some combination (σύγκρισις) as the result of an impact, some involving increase, some diminution, some the destruction of a bodily pattern, some the genesis of a new bodily pattern. Behind all these motions, the Stranger darkly hints at a more transcendental set of motions which rather generate genesis (894a) and its phenomenal expression, than anything in the realm of Becoming. These transcendental motions are those by which the dimensions are generated, the motion through which Linearity emerges out of absolute Unity, two-dimensional Superficiality out of Linearity, and three-dimensional Solidity out of Superficiality: at this point those bodily impacts become possible with which sensible quality can be associated. The *Laws* shows a curious interest in these timeless eidetic precursors of instantial motion and generation, and has another reference in 819e–820a to the irreducibility of the various dimensions, which is tantamount to postulating an eidetic leap from one to the other. It is as if Plato were trying to preserve the memory of his former excursions into profundity even when they are not relevant for his present purpose, since it is certainly not Soul that is responsible for the dimensional generations of which it is itself an offshoot.

From the welter of motions, real and transcendental, thus distinguished, two types of motion alone remain over for consideration, as relevant to Plato's theistic proof: motions, on the one hand, which can give rise to other motions, but which are not self-originating but started by other motions, and motions, on the other hand, having the wonderful property of self-origination, whether as regards combination or dissolution, growth or diminution or coming into being or passing away. (The 'transcendental' motions are not again mentioned, since their originative source is by implication higher than Soul.) These latter, self-originative motions are obviously first in genesis and in force. For, if all were at rest, things unable to start motion would never be moved: they could only be moved, and pass motion on to other things, if something whose motion is self-originated started them all off. When, however, a thing is capable of self-originated motion we say that it is alive, and we also say that there is Soul in it: the very definition of Soul is, in fact, to be capable of self-originated motion (895e–896a), and wherever we have an instance of such a capacity we have an instance of Soul. To query it would be as nugatory as querying whether we have an instance of Evenness where we have an instance of a Number divisible into two equal parts. It cannot therefore be doubted that Soul, with its essential Self-movingness, must be the ultimate cause of all the motion and change that we meet with in the world. Its habits, attitudes, inclinations, reasonings and true opinions, its memories and concerns, must always take precedence over the length, breadth, thickness and strength of corporeal things, and must in fact use them, or at worst circumvent them, in what it causes to be.

So far the argument merely harks back, with lessened eloquence, to the passages in the *Phaedrus* which expound the Soul's essential Self-movingness, and to the passages in the *Phaedo* which expound its essential Livingness: now, however, a strange novelty is introduced, of which interpreters have not known what to make. Since Soul is the ultimate cause of all that occurs or arises in the

changeable world, it must be the ultimate source of *evil* as well
as of good, of ugliness as well as of beauty, of disorder as well
as of order, of the unjust as well as the just. Can there, however,
be one instance of Soul responsible both for the elements of
goodness and order, and the elements of badness and disorder,
that we find in the world? The Stranger answers that this is
impossible. There must be at least two instances of Soul in the
Cosmos, one at least responsible for its elements of goodness,
and one at least for its elements of badness. A greater number of
good or bad souls is not excluded, but two at least are postulated.
It is then argued that there is a profound analogy between the
regular movement of the outer heaven, on the one hand, always
turning in exactly the same manner about the same centre and in
the same place, and preserving a single set of orderly relations
to the bodies it encloses, and the procedure of Mind or Reason
(νοῦς) on the other hand, which is always subordinating multi-
plicities of fact to dominant unities of idea: we in fact get the best
notion of what Mind and Reason Themselves are like by going
beyond ourselves to their images in the cosmic order (897d–898b).
Whereas motions which lack all uniformity, and which perpetually
change their location and all their relations, and have no sort of
exact proportion in them, plainly assort best with Unreason and
Mindlessness (ἄνοια – 898b). It is therefore absurd not to attribute
the orderly motion of the heavens to one or more supremely
good and rational Souls: an evil Soul could not be responsible
for such order.

The number and character of evil souls now drops out of
sight: the Stranger touches on the mystery of the manner in which
Soul is known to us. None of the senses reveals it, but an act of
mind (διανόημα) alone shows it to us. And in the case of the good
Soul or Souls responsible for heavenly movement, we are faced
by difficult alternatives not arising in our own case. Does the
Sun's Soul live in the Sun as our own Soul lives in our body, and
does it propel the Sun from place to place? Or does it inhabit
an airy or fiery body, through which it impinges on the bodily
Sun? Or is it wholly disembodied but capable of exerting
immaterial pressures on body (898e–899a)? Whichever of these
alternatives we adopt, we cannot avoid placing marvellous virtues
in the Soul or Souls responsible for cosmic order. They are at the
very least what we understand by 'Gods' (899a, b). The young

atheists in our state are thereby refuted: either they must find a flaw in our arguments, or abide by their conclusion.

There are, however, a great number of flaws in the Stranger's arguments, which abound in vagueness and obscurity. No good ground has been offered for the alleged impossibility that Reason and Unreason should consort in a single cosmic Soul, as they do in our own. It has merely been thought unplausible that movements so accurately regular as those of the heavenly bodies should spring from the same source as those which involve a great deal of confusion. The unplausibility, treated as unplausibility, may be granted: a Soul capable of directing the perfectly accurate movements of the Universe cannot be at all like our own soul oscillating inconstantly between the eidetic and the instantial. It must be a different, because a different sort of soul. But Plato's proof is not based on the structure of the eidetic Cosmos and the necessary dependence of everything on that Cosmos: the God of which it proves the existence is an instantial agent in the instantial world, not anything whose non-being is unintelligible and unthinkable. And the existence of this God rests on contingent facts of astronomy, of which the *Republic* taught us to be not a little disdainful, and which our own Copernican revolution has entirely reinterpreted. If *Laws* X, barring some subtleties of argument, is the real beginning of Rational Theology, it is indeed a poor beginning.

Plato's treatment of the other two contentions of irreligion are less interesting. God, having been proved to be able and willing to mind the stars, is not likely to want to take a holiday from our poor human affairs, which, though difficult to size up, are yet most easy to manage when sized up (902e–903a). The notion that God neglects man would, further, disappear, were we able to survey all the various incarnations and disembodied wanderings of the soul, and the rewards of virtue and punishments of vice in all these transmigrations. God leaves us free to do as we will in respect of being good or bad but, once we have made our choice, he will not neglect to requite us. If one makes oneself little enough to sink into the depths of the earth, or tall enough to soar up to heaven, one will still have to pay the due penalty for one's misdemeanours, either on earth, or in Hades, or some yet more sinister place (905a, b). The other-worldly stories which in Plato's early writings merely reinforced the supreme claims of virtue, here assume the minatory character that they have in popular religion. And that the Gods can be bribed or cajoled by wicked men so as to remit their penalties is arguably to put them on a level below that of good watch-dogs, or of most of those who take part in chariot-races, and certainly below that of generals, doctors, farmers or shepherds, who would not betray the interests of those of whom they are in charge for the sake of bribes and cajolements (907a).

This preamble of argument leads on to the recommendation of more compelling legal pressures towards piety. Everyone who hears impious opinions expressed should inform the authorities, and those who fail to give such information shall be themselves held guilty of impiety. And there should be three state-prisons in this near-ideal community that is being established, one a mere Place of Detention for ordinary offenders, one near the meeting-place of a body called the Nocturnal Council, and amiably called the Sophrontisterion or Place of Softening Up, and one in a wild and deserted region and called a House of Punishment (τιμωρία) proper. Atheists who lead tolerable social lives should only be incarcerated in the Sophrontisterion for five years, unvisited by their friends, but receiving visits from the members of the Nocturnal Council 'for their soul's salvation' (ἐπὶ τῇ τῆς ψυχῆς σωτηρίᾳ: 909a). If these visits and discourses have, after five years, failed in their enlightening and reformatory effect, the obdurate atheists are to be punished by death. But those who, on the other hand, are not atheists, but who believe in negligent and venal Gods, and who perhaps practise priestcraft and magic, should go to the House of Punishment in the desolate place indicated, and should be allowed to die in solitary confinement, fed only by slaves, and to be cast out on death unburied. These savage dispensations are not, however, to be visited on their non-dissenting offspring. Further laws rule out the setting-up of private religious rites or shrines of any sort: those who wish to pray or sacrifice should do so at the public altars and through the public priests. Socrates, it is plain, would not have been allowed his private prayers, nor his daemonic communications, in Plato's Cretan city, and it is doubtful whether the punishment for his alleged impiety would have been a simple draught of hemlock, taken after a marvellous talk with his friends. He would have died listening to the discourses of the Nocturnal Council in the

Sophrontisterion, or have been cast forth from the House of Punishment unburied, after years of solitary confinement.

VII

The *Epinomis*, a sort of addendum to the *Laws*, and classified in the past as its thirteenth Book, is either Plato's last piece of writing or the writing of Philip of Opus, his pupil. As the *Laws* is undoubtedly the work of Plato, and as the *Epinomis* is, on the whole, a worthier philosophical effort than the *Laws*, and also continues the themes of the latter, we may with uninterested hesitation attribute it to Plato: despite the glassy structure of its re-entrant sentences, it is what Plato, in some happier moment in his last phase, may have written.

The Dialogue is an attempt to discuss the nature of the Wisdom (φρόνησις, σοφία) which is the necessary background to law-giving, and which the State Officials and Members of the Nocturnal Council will have to cultivate, if they are to legislate and to apply laws desirably. This Wisdom was perhaps the intended theme of the Dialogue *The Philosopher*, which was to have succeeded the *Sophist* and the *Statesman*, and it may contain material that was to have been incorporated in the *Hermocrates*, the Dialogue that was to follow the *Critias*. Be that as it may, it gives us the astronomical transformation which Plato's firmament of Eide underwent in its last phase: if we can no longer soar to the eidetic empyrean on the wings of mathematics and mathematicizing Dialectic, we can at least rise to something consolingly like it in the subtle invariances of the heavens. In it the Athenian Stranger continues to dogmatize, the Cretan Cleinias to assent, while the Spartan participant stands silently by.

The Athenian Stranger first expresses what must have been Plato's own sense of the vanishingly short, moderately easy period, set between the torment of growing up, and the torment of growing old, in which scientific thought is possible at all, and from which there can spring any clearness as to its nature. It seems, in fact, as hard to catch hold of as is human well-being. There are, however, certain sciences which, though important and necessary to life, confer absolutely no Wisdom on the person who knows them. There is, first of all, that growing Pythagorean sense of the impropriety of eating one's fellow-creatures (ἀλληλοφαγία – 975a) which leads men gradually to adopt a purely cereal diet. But, while the cultivation and eating of wheat and barley may make men pure, it will not make them wise. All farming and agriculture is similarly unproductive of Wisdom and its cognate virtues, as are also the profitable arts of building, carpentering, bronze-work, moulding, weaving and the manufacture of tools. No glorious Wisdom accrues from hunting, nor is any to be found in divination, which is unable to interpret what it divines. If we pass from the necessary to the imitative arts, we have much that is casual and unseemly, but even the seemlier arts, which employ words, tones or outlines, variously decorated and in moist or dry media, cannot be held to impart Wisdom. The very useful art of the general, productive of courage, is yet not productive of the Wisdom which perfects courage, and the doctor exercises a merely empiric art, snatching at chance cures for chance disorders, in which Wisdom and Measure play no part. Pilots may guide themselves by the heavens, but there can be no science of the ways of storms, while the advocates in the law-courts have only a repertoire of tricks and ruses which influence men's minds, and bypass the requirements of true justice. There is further a quickness of wit (ἀγχίνοια: 976c) which is readily confused with Wisdom, but which is obviously quite different from it.

After this odd rehearsal of ancillary forms of knowledge, a rehearsal at once reminiscent of Socratic treatments, yet always introducing a note of the bizarre, the Athenian Stranger asks if there is not one element in human knowledge which, if removed, would make of men the most witless of beings. The answer is plain. Excise Number from men's understandings, and they at once sink to the witlessness in question. The source of men's understanding of Number is likewise plain: it is Uranus, the Divine Heaven, which by decorating itself with starry jewellery that it turns and twists continually so as to create the seasons on which our nourishment depends, puts Number sensibly before us and induces us to penetrate it still further (977b). Courage and temperance may be possible without the knowledge of Number – we may, it is implied, live according to Numbers without knowing what these Numbers are – but the crown of virtue involves the ability to give a true account (λόγος), a true Ratio or Rationale, as to how we are acting, and this is impossible without a knowledge of the Dyad and the Triad, or of the Even and the Odd (977c, d). All music depends on numerically related notes and the movements of the same, and all movement which is senseless, disorderly, unrhythmic and inharmonious obviously lacks Number, and is thereby accounted evil. And, in a less obvious fashion, our sense of the just and noble always depends on a subtle numbering that we use to persuade ourselves and others (διαρίθμησις πρὸς τὸ ἑαυτόν τε καὶ ἕτερον πεῖσαι – 978b): without this we should only have correct opinion, and could convince no one. (It is, however, a pity that while harmony and morals are thus both held to rest on Numerical Ratios, which we feel rather than understand, the Athenian Stranger fails to say why we gained such a good understanding of the Numerical Ratios underlying harmony, while this is not so in regard to those that underlie morals. Here Aristotle provided the Wisdom: the Ratios underlying morals are felt by the good man, but they have the essential *inexactness* of the Ethical as Such.)

The whole capacity to grasp Numbers and numerical Ratios was, however, implanted in us by Divinity, and it is Divinity too that has constantly supplied food and stimulus for that capacity by regularly replacing the one-starred Day by the illuminated numerosity of Night, and, like a schoolmaster, by holding up illustrations of every conceivable Number before us, some drawn out in time like the fifteen days in which the moon waxes and in which it again wanes. Some of these Numerical Patterns and Ratios impose themselves on the merest dolt, others require infinite penetration to puzzle them out. And they underlie all the natural goods of this life, but may also be held to underlie all the human virtues, which are all arguably attempts to imitate the mathematical perfection of the heavens, and the mathematicizing Thinkingness behind it. Such at least would appear to be the drift of the Stranger's discourse (979a–d), which is tendentious rather than clear.

After a brief interval devoted to silent prayer, the Stranger develops his astral theology further. Soul, always senior to body, has been seen to be ultimately responsible for such movement as goes on in the heavens, and there must accordingly be Souls living in, and inwardly directing, the movements of various types of body in the Universe of which the Stranger says that there are five. These are the bodily forms of Fire, Water, Air, Earth and Ether (981c). One wonders why Plato has added a fifth element to the four distinguished in the *Timaeus*. Quite conceivably he has decided to shift the Dodecahedron from its vague role as the shape of the whole Cosmos, to having its own element to preside over, but perhaps he has yielded to the materializing tendencies in the Academy which led Aristotle to postulate a special matter for the heavenly spheres. The Cosmos is, however, increased by a vast population of living beings beyond those familiar ones in which earth is the dominant element. The stars of Heaven are a fiery class of living beings: their complete regularity, while by us readily associated with lack of Soul, is really a true mark of Soul's presence: inferior Souls like ours may be essentially mutable, but the heavenly Souls show their essential superiority in their immutability, which is also superbly choreographic and performed as a perpetual service towards the world at large (982d). The vast bulk of the heavenly bodies, and their effortless translation through the heavens, afford, moreover, an unanswerable proof of their manipulation by Soul. In addition, however, to the visible classes of living creature, earthly or stellar, we may suppose the existence of other invisible classes, who inhabit or propel ethereal, airy or watery bodies. Zeus, Hera and the rest may be recognized as among these invisible divinities, who are, however, always staging temporary appearances to men in dreams, visions and at the time of death, and it would ill beseem the legislator to ignore these intimations, or to invent doctrines and rites which lack such a divine sanction. But the legislator ought not to ignore the visible in favour of the invisible Gods, and the divine beings visibly present in, or active through, the heavenly bodies must be given equal honour with the Gods known only through report. Plato and his entourage were obviously building up a burgeoning theosophy and theurgy such as we are wont to associate with the Neoplatonists.

The number and order of the visible, stellar Gods is now briefly sketched, and the Stranger gives them godlike names corresponding to those given them by the Egyptians and Syrians, whose countries, he says, afford much better opportunities for observing the stars than the climate of Hellas. There are, the Stranger tells us, eight powers operative in the heavens, one for the Sun, one for the Moon, one for the fixed stars and five for the remaining planets: of these last, two with the Syrian names which correspond to Aphrodite and Hermes, keep pace with Sun, one pre-eminent in slowness bears a name which corresponds to Cronos, another less slow a name equivalent to Zeus, and a third, the ruddiest, a name which corresponds to Ares. The power of the fixed stars dominates that of all the other heavenly bodies, and carries them around with itself. The manner in which the Earth, as obscurely taught in the *Timaeus*, exactly counters the movement of the fixed stars, instead of being carried with it, is not here spelt out, but possibly a hint of it is intended in the Stranger's reference to those who see no difficulty in holding that the fixed stars drag *all* the planets (including the Earth) along with them (987c). The astronomy of the Dialogue involves many problems, which are not, however, of philosophical interest. The Stranger hopes that, with encouragement from Delphi, the revelations of astronomy will be allowed to stand beside the reports of encounters with the less visible Gods. The new divinities have at least the superiority that they can be reasoned about mathematically, and their open encouragement of such reasoning forbids the plea that it would be wrong for men to busy themselves with such divine matters (988a, b).

The manner in which astronomy will promote piety, and through piety all virtue, is then sketched, and it is suggested that those who have understood and admired the operations of the celestial Gods, will be able to carry out similarly splendid operations in the state (989c). But understanding of the divine workings demands a mathematical training, which must begin with the disembodied patterns of Arithmetic, and must study the origin and powers of the Odd and the Even. From such Arithmetic, which is plainly meant to be dialectical and not merely mathematical, the trainee must proceed to the science ridiculously called Geometry or earth-measurement: what it really imparts is a reduction of mutually disparate sets of Numbers (τῶν οὐκ ὄντων δὲ ὁμοίων ἀλλήλοις φύσει ἀρίθμων) to Numbers of the same sort, which assimilation (ὁμοίωσις) rests on the part they play in surfaces. What the Stranger is here teaching would seem to be a dialectical reduction of the dimensional differences and incommensurabilities which are taken as ultimate at the level of mere mathematics. At the dialectical level Numbers are not idealized groups, but the universal eidetic *operations* (doubly doubled, half way between being doubled and being tripled etc.) by which such groups are generated. At this level the double doubleness which is the Number Four does not differ *in type* from the self-multiplication which is specifically tantamount to Twoness, in other words from the square root of the Number Two, which is also the length of the diagonal of a square whose side is one unit in length. If the former is an eidetic Number, so may the latter be also: we achieve on the level of pure intension what modern mathematics has achieved with such painful devices as infinite classes, imaginary numbers and the like.

The same intensional assimilation occurs in the next step towards Solid Geometry, where we have triply complex Numbers which correspond to solid realities, but which are put on a level with the other Numbers through the new science of eidetic Stereometry. A mathematical or sensible Solid may not be commensurable with a mathematical or sensible Line or Surface, but the eidetic operations which generate either, and which *are* what it is to be a Number in either case, do not differ basically. Both are defined in terms of timeless generative operations, which are all that Numbers are eidetically. The student of mathematical foundations will gain an understanding of all these things, and will thereby have more and more light thrown for him on the deepest secrets of being and action. On the plane of the Eide he will explore all the notional relations which lead from the simple doublings etc. and interpolations which lead to the series of Integers, to the doubled doublings and corresponding interpolations which lead to the procession of geometrical patterns, and thence to the doubly doubled doublings and corresponding interpolations which lead to the procession of tangible and solid forms. What we will have will of course only be the ghost of the solidly instantial, but it will give the trainee intellectual mastery over the latter. And having discovered all these primary patterns, he will also examine the interstitial proportionalities, which may at first have attracted the ire of the philosophical mathematician as fragmenting the integral numbers, but which come to be seen, at the eidetic level, as Numbers no less legitimate than the Eide among which they hold. We have the proportionality of being just as much greater than being of one Number as one is less than being of another (the Arithmetical Mean), or as being as much proportionately greater than being

348

of a certain number as being of another number is proportionately greater than being of the number in question (the Geometrical Mean as Such: 991a, b). The specific forms of these proportionalities will themselves be eidetic Numbers, Numbers being understood simply in terms of the generations which set them up. The man who sees all this will also see the source of all the excellent harmonies which render life beautiful and delightful (991b), and which can render a man or a society well-ordered and just. This manner of instruction, the Stranger asserts, will make a geometrical diagram, an arithmetical problem, a musical set-up or a starry revolution yield up its secret, which is one and the same in all cases, since a single natural bond binds all these things together (δεσμὸς γὰρ πεφυκὼς πάντων τούτων εἶς: 991e–992a). The man who has all this deeply founded knowledge of the eternal mathematical verities will be a truly wise man in this world and a blessed one in the next.

We may note, as a sign of Plato's great scruple, that he is not willing to exaggerate the affinity of the mathematical and the ethicopolitical into a dogmatic identity. Time on time he comes close to asserting their identity, but time on time he veers away from it. The mathematical passages in the *Epinomis* are probably the belated expression of attempts to solve the problem of dimensional differences within the bounds of the theory of eidetic Numbers, attempts which Plato had made over many years, but which he had laid aside owing to their immense unsuccess. The glosses we have put on his words in our last few paragraphs are inadequate attempts to get closer to the sense of his immensely obscure, immensely deep-delving pronouncements on these all-important issues. We can see both how deeply penetrating his ideas were, and also how impossible that, with the tools and skills at his disposal, he should have brought them to a lucid outcome. There is not, in fact, even at this moment any well worked out intensional theory of Arithmetic, nor any well worked out intensional theory of any topic whatever. We may, however, be glad that, almost at his last gasp, Plato blurted forth all these aspirations whose very entertainment uniquely enhances his stature.

IX

APPRAISAL OF PLATONISM
AND ITS INFLUENCE

I

We have now completed our interpretative survey of the Platonic writings, trying to show that their content is throughout reconcilable with the reports of Unwritten Platonic Teaching to be found in the writings of Aristotle, the Aristotelian commentators and others, and that the two strands of teaching, suitably interpreted, are such as to throw light on each other at every point. We have worked on the hypothesis that the doctrines attributed to Plato in Aristotle's *Metaphysics* and other works – quite distinct doctrines are attributed to Plato from those attributed to the Platonists – were in fact those that Aristotle encountered when he joined the Academy in 367, and that had been in process of development as far back as the time of the writing of the *Republic*. We have not found it hard to explain why the Dialogues are not straightforward expressions of Plato's philosophical insights: being such writings as they are, they could hardly be the straightforward expression of any opinions whatsoever. Plato's doctrines are certainly *in* them, but they have to be freed from Socratic incrustations, from the exaggerated Socratic inconclusiveness, and from the various brilliant reflexes of the Socratic manner: they have to be disentangled from opinions put into the mouths of many pitched controversialists, and discerned only through hints, pictures, suggestions and packed utterances which point to reserves of doctrine deliberately left inexplicit. The reason why these reserves of doctrine were not divulged is also plain: they were a project rather than a finished performance, and a project that Plato, with his infinitely fine critical sense of the inadequacy of all his linguistic and conceptual devices, could well see would never be more than a project, an inchoate vision of absolute perspicuity that could never receive perspicuous written expression. We may, however, be deeply grateful that the Aristotelian reports, firm and consistent in their main lines, though obscurely self-contradictory in their details, and more to be trusted because what they report so often surpasses Aristotle's powers of misunderstanding, should throw the one, necessary, quite revealing light on the nature of the project behind the Platonic writings, and should enable us to form an integrated picture of what Plato really intended.

The nature of the Platonic view of the world is to be an outlook in which concrete instances, whether they be things, events or situations or whatever, are seen as in the deepest sense parasitic upon what may be called 'Ideal Contents', and not, as is commonly thought, vice versa. It is, further, a view in which such Ideal Contents form an integrated Order, ranging from Contents of the most generic to the most highly specific, arranged according to affinities, distances and dependences which spring wholly from what they are, and could not at any point be otherwise. All these Ideal Contents and all their ideal relations are such as to reveal themselves perspicuously to a thought which looks for them in the right manner, though they are not in any sense constituted by or for such a thought. Acts of thought have, however, their own ideal representation: there are Ideal Contents corresponding to all the acts of intellection in which other Ideal Contents are represented, and together they form an ideal vision of everything which actual thoughts only dimly adumbrate. The Ideal Order has, further, a Prime Membership of well-formed Contents, between and around which cluster a vast Secondary Membership of Contents that exceed them or fall short of them in infinite ways, or which are completely formless, negative and indefinite. This Secondary Membership of the Ideal Order is throughout parasitic upon the Primary Membership, something which the latter explicitly excludes, and, by excluding, includes in its sense, but in the realm of instantiation the Secondary Membership works loose from such primary dominance, and acquires a seeming independence. It is one of the basic characteristics of what is instantial that it can thus deviate from its Ideal Original. Platonism, further, involves the revolutionary assumption that all Ideal Contents are, in their intrinsic essence, pure forms of Number and Quantity. They may involve qualities in their instances, colour, warmth etc., but in themselves they are pure structures of Numbers and Magnitudes having varied relations, mainly proportional, to one another. The quantitative structures in question may be composed out of Natural Numbers, or out of continuous Linear Magnitudes, or out of two-dimensional Superficial Magnitudes, or out of three-dimensional Solid Magnitudes, or out of Magnitudes involving a dimension of Duration and Movement. The Ideal Contents of Mental Activity are at every point parallel to those of Ideal Number and Spatio-temporality, and everything qualitative in mental life falls in the field of instantiation. It is impossible to overestimate the importance of Plato's comprehensive 'mathematicization' of Ideal Contents, which Aristotle has misleadingly simplified into a plain identification of such Contents with Natural Numbers. It evinces Plato's profound grasp of the fact that it is only in the realm of the logico-mathematical that complete intellectual perspicuity is achievable, that everything complex reduces to the same interchangeable simplicities, that nothing has to be introduced from outside or hypothetically assumed or taken to be or not to be the case, that all relationships are such as cannot be otherwise. Even the Being or Supra-Being of the Supreme Unity, from which everything else follows dialectically, is for Plato nothing but an ultimate, self-justifying, logico-mathematical fact or truth: in the sense in which 'content' means empirical quality, it is quite without content. This mathematicization of the Ideal Contents points to yet another astonishing insight, which connects it with the seemingly quite different doctrine of the unenviousness of God in the *Timaeus*. For Number, Space and Time are the very forms of instantiation: instantiation is nothing if not numerical multiplication, spatial externalization, a drawing of things out into change and time. In making his Ideal Contents basically numerical, geometrical and chronometrical, Plato is in effect declaring that Ideal Contents are nothing beyond the eternal possibilities of instantiation, instantiation seen *sub specie aeternitatis*, and that, if instances have no sense or substance apart from the Eide they instantiate, Eide equally have their whole life in the instances in which they display themselves, or in the intellectual acts in which that display becomes fully consummated. This is why our insight into Eide emerges, and must emerge, out of a rubbing together of illustrations, names, tentative notions and definitions, as detailed in the Seventh Epistle: it is in seeing an Eidos at work, or in putting it to work, that we become apprised of what it is. And such a doctrine does not make Eide depend on things or acts which stand outside of them: it reduces these so-called things and acts to dependent (if essential) modalities of eidetic Being. No one who has read the *Sophist* and some other writings carefully can doubt that Plato was well aware of all the points made above.

Platonism then goes on, in a somewhat hesitant way, to consider *another* set of Ideal Contents of higher order, which are *instantiated* by the Ideal Contents just mentioned, and which can be invoked to throw light on *their* nature and structure. Whether such Contents of higher order are or are not to be included in an enlarged class of Ideal Contents, is a point on which Platonism never achieves a firm decision. These higher-order Contents are, for example, what is characteristic of an Ideal Content as Such, and what distinguishes it from an Instance as Such, or they are what distinguishes particular sorts of Ideal Contents from one another, or what is involved in the various relations of Ideal Contents to one another or to their instances etc. These higher-order Ideal Contents make up the membership of the Realm of Ideal Principles which is built upon, and therefore represents an extension of, the more narrowly conceived Realm of first-order Eide. Among such Principles are those of being One or Good on which Platonism lays such stress, and the opposing Principle of being Indefinitely Multiple or Bad, but other Contents, such as those of being a Genus or a Species or an Instance or a Number or a necessary or an accidental feature, are equally fundamental. All purely formal, logico-mathematical Meanings, as they would now be called, qualify for admission to the Realm of Principles. Platonism does not, however, entertain the notion of a higher set of Meta-Principles in which the character and structure of Principles displays itself, and much less of an infinite hierarchy of such Meta-Principles. The quest for Principles terminates in the notions which characterize and structure the common run of Eide, and by implication such Principles would appear to suffice to give a clear account of their own characters and structure, and so in a sense act as Principles to themselves. All the Principles of the Ideal World further terminate in a pair of Principles of which the one is merely the contrasted shadow of the other, so that there is in effect only one, single, supreme eidetic Principle on which all Ideal Contents and all instances are in various ways parasitic.

The account we have given of Platonism is not one that will be found written out in Plato's writings, nor in any of the writings of those who have hitherto interpreted him. Our long absorption in the Dialogues, coupled with a restrained willingness to dot a few *i*'s and cross a few *t*'s, and to consider the joint force of many dispersed utterances – without which willingness all scholarship reduces to idiocy – have justified us in saying what we have just said: while our formulations have made some points more explicit than they can ever have been for Plato, it can none the less be held that he tends unambiguously in their direction. We now turn to consider a number of genuine objections to Platonism, to all of which he shows some sensitiveness in his writings, even if he does not manage to deal with any of them conclusively.

The first is an objection which can be held to capture the real *gravamen* of Aristotle's largely misplaced criticisms of the Eide: the objection to a form of talk or thought which turns general Meanings whose whole sense lies in their illumination of the instances in which they live, into a new set of inert subjects of predication, having the same surd character as the instances which they were meant to supersede. If we refuse to believe in particulars as the substantial pegs on which predication hangs, if we have opted for a theory of instantiation without such peg-like instances, then we must not be tempted to turn instantiated or instantiable Natures into a new set of higher-order instances which inertly underlie what we say of them, and so become dead vehicles of sense rather than living senses themselves. Such a treatment further tends towards an infinite regress: if the substance and sense of instances lies in what we say of them, then the substance and sense of what we say of them lies in what we say of that sense and so on indefinitely, a regress far more ruinous than any stated in the *Parmenides*.

On reflection, however, this objection is seen to rest upon the misleading effects of abstract *language*, especially on those given to instantial thought. For an Eidos does not change from being an intrinsically instantiable Nature, which *is* some character rather than has it, because we take it out of some predicative setting – where it is, for example, the equality of this piece of wood with that – and talk of it in and for itself, and in so doing predicate various higher-order Eide of it. What is essential to the great Platonic revolution is not the erection of predicates into a new sort of logical subjects, though we *may* seek to express it by doing just this: it is rather the recognition that predicates, senses, universals are the primary stuff, if one may so put it, of experience and reality, that so-called particulars are as such unidentifiable and undiscoverable, their whole being consisting, if one may so phrase it, in instantiating Natures or in having things said of them. Whether we talk abstractly or concretely, we must see the substance of discourse in what we say of things rather than in the things we say of them. And we may leave Eide functioning predicatively in concrete instantial settings, while yet managing to make higher-order assertions about them *adverbially*, as when we say such commonplace things as that something is of a certain character in a very unique or unusual or ordinary or uniform or highly intermittent or diversified manner.

There is also an objection to Platonism based on the difficulties of making it cover all the problems of falsehood. It would seem that the realm of Essence, of Ideal Significance, lacks all distinction between reality and unreality: it is only when we consider the relation of Ideal Contents to possible instantiation that distinctions between reality and unreality, truth and falsehood, enter the picture. This leads to the traditional view that Existence is something more than Essence, and that instantiation must be brought in to account for it. Plato himself has, however, made clear, both in the *Theaetetus* and the *Sophist*, that there is error and falsehood in the realm of Ideal Contents quite as much as in the realm of instantiation. A poor mathematician may be persuaded that the Number which sums up Six and Five is Twelve, so that we have as Ideal Content the Equality of Six and Five to Twelve, and a Sophist may persuade his listeners that Justice is the Interest of the Stronger so that we have, as an Ideal Content, the Identity of Justice with such Ruling Interest. It would not appear, however, that Plato's general view that science is of contraries, and that an Ideal Content therefore includes its contrary as the reverse of itself, is unequal to the task of explaining such high-level falsehood. 'False' Ideal Contents can be held to be essentially secondary and parasitic upon those that are 'true' and real, and to have being only in the sense of being excluded by what is true and real. Such Contents secondarily *are* in being essentially *other* than anything that is, the doctrine obscurely set forth, and much misunderstood, in the *Sophist*. Being and Truth do not, therefore, take us beyond the realm of Ideal Contents, and that even when the Being and Truth is that of the instantiation of certain Contents. And the Being of an Ideal Content is simply its straightforwardly being an Ideal Content, and not merely being one in some secondary, derivative way. And even if we bring in 'false' Ideal Contents in which a simulacrum of Being is expressly included – being the *true* and *real* Identity of Justice with the interest of the stronger is a case in point – yet, being themselves parasitic upon what we redundantly call 'true' and 'real' cases, they are powerless to communicate what we may call a true truth and a real reality that they do not themselves possess. Secondary Contents bracketed in other Primary Contents can in a sense be removed from their brackets through the ignoring or abstractive action of thought, but nothing that they are *within* such bracketing containment ever amounts to what they would be *without* it. This is not, however, the place to negotiate all the symbolic and other hazards involved in talking about falsehood and error.

A third serious objection to Platonism, revealed only in the present century, lies in the paradoxes involved in self-instantiation. If we are not to have an infinite series of Ideal Contents bearing the same name, we shall have to allow that some Ideal Contents instantiate *themselves*, while others do *not* do so. Thus Being Instantiated in more than three cases is itself instantiated in more than three cases and so instantiates itself, whereas Being an instance of Beauty is not an instance of Beauty and so does not instantiate itself. But, as is now well known, if we ask whether Being Non-self-instantiating is or is not self-instantiating, the answer is that, if it is not, then it is, and if it is, then it is not. It is this supra-absurd situation which led Russell to hold such Ideal Contents to be 'meaningless', a solution obviously unacceptable, since it is only by immersing ourselves in what they mean, or rather are, that we become aware of their paradoxical nature. It would appear that Platonism could meet this paradoxical situation by adding yet another way in which Ideal Contents can be merely parasitic to the ways previously distinguished. If there are Ideal Contents which in a sense *are* because falling short of, or because being wholly excluded by, what primarily is, there may be Ideal Contents which *are* only as excluded in a yet more absolute manner, as being Contents in short from whose absurdity it is not even possible to argue to some positive outcome. They are the lepers of discourse, at whose approach a warning bell must be rung, which is the force of what Russell meant by calling them 'meaningless'. But lepers or non-lepers, they are still, in their peculiar, damned fashion, a part of discourse, and as necessary to the Being of the Eide as are its most respectable and eminent members.

A fourth grave objection to Platonism lies in its too austere mathematicization, its rigid exclusion of Quality from the true essence of anything. It is more than merely arguable that logico-mathematical structure means nothing in isolation: in its deepest essence, it demands connection with at least *possible* qualitative contents, such as could be given in contingent experience, and it seems necessary that it should even have a relation to some *actual* qualitative contents. Logico-mathematical structures may represent the necessary skeleton of pure Being, but such a skeleton can be nothing without contingent, qualitative flesh to clothe it. There is a necessary presence, therefore, of contingent, qualitative distinctions, not only in the field of instantiation, but also in its ideal sources. Red and Green, Warm and Cold, cannot have their whole being in mere Ratios: they must also retain the familiar, qualitative side which depends on such Ratios. The Eide must set standards to something, and be illustrated by something, and all this means that recognizable, specific, qualitative manifestation must be of their essence. Qualities cannot therefore occupy a place in the world of instances without also occupying a place in the world of Ideal Patterns, a point readily granted by all those who have ignored Plato's mathematicization of the Eide. But even we, who regard mathematicization as essential to Platonism and to philosophy, may still accord to the qualities contingently connected with logico-mathematical structures a true place in Ideal Being. For Ideal Being, being all in all, must certainly have its contingencies as well as its necessary structures.

None of the objections we have mustered therefore basically shakes Platonism, and it is probable that other objections will prove equally undisturbing. Platonism is therefore a workable, legitimate thought-outlook on the world. This does not, however, give us any conclusive ground for preferring it to other thought-outlooks, which might seem equally tenable. We have therefore to consider Platonism in its relation to such forms of thought as Empiricism, Naturalism, Materialism, Nominalism, Theism, Existentialism which are in many points un-Platonic. We have to decide whether it has decided notional and interpretative advantages over these other outlooks. But to do so profitably will involve us in a consideration of the part played by Platonism, conceived somewhat widely, in the whole subsequent history of philosophy. We shall have to see how Platonism, not necessarily invoking the name of Plato, but seeing things in his manner, was powerful either in directing, modifying or resisting, the various thought-tendencies, and consequent practical and emotional tendencies, of ancient, medieval and modern times. Only when we see what Platonism has done, both in predominantly religious and predominantly scientific ages, will we be able to see what it is truly good for, and what it therefore truly is.

II

In sketching the history of the influence of Platonism, we shall, of course, have to begin with the two Scholarchs who immediately succeeded Plato in the Academy, Speusippus and Xenocrates. Of these there is, however, very little to say. The writings to which they entrusted their reflections have unfortunately perished, and hence, apart from some brief references in Aristotle, Theophrastus and others, these reflections are no longer accessible to us. What it is important to note is that Aristotle always emphasizes the points of difference of their views from Plato's – see, for example, *Metaphysics*, 1028b 16–32, 1080b 4–33, 1090b 5–1091a 29 – and so does Theophrastus, and so also do others (e.g. Stobaeus), so that they quite exclude any facile view that would attribute the arithmetization of the Eide to members of the Academy other than Plato.

Speusippus, we are told, rejected the eidetic Numbers, and

hence the Eide, and believed only in the Objects of Mathematics: he believed in short in all the nines which occur in mathematical reasonings, without believing in the Threefold Threeness which is the common Eidos behind them all. He took, we would say, an extensional or class-view of number-concepts, only the members of his class were the imaginary instances that have a status for thought, rather than the concrete instances that are real and perceptible. If he was restrictive in respect of the Eide, he was, however, liberal in respect of the classes of Mathematica: each had their own Principle, one for Numbers, one for Spatial Magnitudes and another for Soul (*Metaphysics*, 1028a 22–5). Aristotle complains that his theory made the Universe a mere series of episodes like a bad tragedy (*Metaphysics*, 1076a 1–5), since the existence or non-existence of its substances has no influence on that of other substances: we may well doubt whether Aristotle was in a position to cast such a slur on Speusippus. Speusippus was also an early believer in evolution. He believed that the supreme Goodness and Beauty were not present in the sources or origins of things, but in their final outcome. They were not automatically associated with Unity, but made their appearance only when the nature of things had advanced to some extent (*Metaphysics*, 1072b 30–5, 1091a 30–6).

If we turn to Xenocrates, we find that he *identified* the Eidetic with the Mathematical Numbers, probably treated them, in short, as Unities-in-manyness carrying a built-in reference to possible cases in themselves as Eide. This view Aristotle regards as one for which nothing at all can be said (*Metaphysics*, 1083b 1–8), but there may have been profound, anti-abstractive insights behind it. For the rest, Xenocrates is remembered for his statement that the Soul is a self-moving Number, a statement to which Aristotle takes grave exception (*De Anima*, 408b 32–409a 4), but which perhaps encloses an early realization of the way in which flux blended with recurrent pattern is of the essence of our psychic life. All the Eide are causative, but the psychic Eide are causative in a medium of perpetual change.

If we now turn to Aristotle himself, we may neglect, as sufficiently dealt with, the various maladroit criticisms of the Eidetic Theory, framed in terms of an instantialist ontology to which Aristotle himself only partially adheres. Aristotle accepts the Platonic view of the Eide as causative factors in instantial generation: they are present in the male parent, they are also present as a formative factor in the offspring, and they represent 'that for the sake of which', i.e. the final cause, of organic development. It is, however, a merit of his view that he recognizes the necessity of other conditions of generation than the purely eidetic: men do not spring fully formed from the mere Eidos of humanity, but require prior instantiations of humanity to bring them into being. Even in the case of so-called spontaneous generation, there must be rudimentary realizations of an Eidos to kindle other realizations (*Metaphysics*, 1032b 22–30). Plato would certainly have recognized, even if he did not stress, these supplements to eidetic causality: causation in the changeable medium of instantiation for him points back, not merely to eidetic fixities, but also to previous changes. Aristotle further recognizes the restrictions upon the Prime Eide current in the Academy and harps on them in his criticisms: there are, for him, in a basic sense, only Eide of the natural species and their component elements and natural properties (*Metaphysics*, 990b). Negations are merely the definitory boundaries of positives, there is no science, because no Eide, of the accidental, the perishable or the composite (1029b 24–30a 17), and there are no true Eide of artificial objects, as is witnessed by the fact that a bed planted in earth may burgeon into leaves but hardly into bedposts (*Physics*, 193b 7–12). It is only in a secondary sense that there are definitory essences, and hence Eide, of accidentals (*Metaphysics*, 1030a 17–31). The great Aristotelian distinction of Potency and Act further hangs together with Aristotle's conception of Eide, the connection of full actuality with instantiation revealing his typical emphasis. Eide invisible and merely virtual are present in potency, but if they are fully and visibly instantiated, they are present in act. Aristotle lays peculiar emphasis on the principle that actualization always springs from previous actualization and never from mere potency, a doctrine probably framed to counter the 'evolutionism' of Speusippus (*Metaphysics*, 1072b 30–73a 1), but not excluding the recognition of a tendency towards self-actualization even in the merely potential (for example Fire moving towards its 'natural Place' in the Cosmos). All in all, there is the fullest realization of the active and explanatory role of Eide, conceived as moving goals of excellence, quite as much as scientific concepts, in the movement and change of the Cosmos.

There is nothing here that basically opposes Aristotelianism to Platonism.

The belief in eidetic causality and the explanation of changing instantiation by way of it, are however supplemented by two great Aristotelian innovations: a radically new, non-Platonic conception of Matter, and a largely non-Platonic conception of Mind. Plato in the *Timaeus* gives no sort of real being to the Substrate of instantiation: it is the all-receptive emptiness of Space, the uncharacterizable irregularity of chaotic motion, it can be apprehended by nothing but a spurious argument, which tries to give insubstantial instances a certain substantiality by imagining a medium, a general recipient, to which they attach (*Timaeus*, 52b, c). The Great and Small, as it functions in the instantial realm, is in fact no more than a name for the permanent possibility of instantiation, and for all the random repetition and defective exemplification that instantiation involves. Aristotle does not, however, think of his Matter, his ὕλη or Timber, in this wholly negative manner. Though it is sometimes characterized in an extremely negative way (*Metaphysics*, 1029a 26–33), it is none the less one of his candidates for substantial being, and is certainly that which underlies all the substantial being of things in nature, and though it can only be known analogically, as standing to all formed being as the wood stands to the bed, and the bronze to the statue, there can be no doubt that Aristotle thinks of it as a genuine, even a solid factor, in natural reality, and one of which we not only have confused intimations but certain knowledge (*Physics*, 189a 34–b 5; 190a 34–b 5). Aristotle is, in fact, a dualist, which Plato is not, and he believes in Matter as some sort of real stuff on which eidetic activity is exercised, thus constituting the realm of Nature.

Aristotle counterpoises to his doctrine of Matter, a doctrine of Mind which bears some signs of a like origin. Plato, in so far as he has a clear theory of Mind, tends to think of it in active, intentionalist terms. To difference in object there corresponds difference in mental powers or faculties, each being characterized by the capacity to apprehend a certain sort of object (*Republic*, 470a, b, 509e–511e; *Sophist*, 248e). There is in the main no view of the object of thought as *in* the mind, even if, as we are given to understand by Philoponus, the characterization of the Mind as the Place of Ideas (*De Anima*, 429a 26–28) is in origin Platonic.

There is only one field in which Plato verges towards a mental containment of objects, and that is in his theory of sense-perception. If we read *Theaetetus*, 156a–157a, and *Timaeus*, 61e–69a, we encounter the view that the sense-qualities are conjured into being by the interaction of our sense-organs with external bodies, and that they certainly have no being outside of our minds. This theory is taken over by Aristotle, even if it assorts ill with his view of the Hot and the Cold, the Moist and the Dry, essentially qualities given to sense-perception, as the basic contraries which help to constitute natural reality. But he believes that our material sense-organs receive the pattern or form of external bodies apart from their Matter, and that there is a unitary experience in which, from different points of view, we experience ourselves as thus or thus sensuously affected, and the external object as thus and thus sensuously affecting us (*De Anima*, 425b 10–426a 26). It is hard to know whether this view should be characterized as the extreme of materialism, or as a profound statement of intentionalistic mentalism, or as a confusion of both. On the one hand, the qualities of sense are affections of a material sense-organ, while on the other hand they make us aware both of ourselves as undergoing such affections, and of the remote sources which cause them. It is, however, this theory, whether profound or confused, that Aristotle makes use of in his theory of Mind. Thinking is the reception into the Mind, the immaterial part of the Soul, of the Eide of objects without their Matter, which makes of this a materialistic-sounding theory of Mind, but thinking is also an awareness both of the Eide concerned, and also of our own reception of them, and it can further, in cases where images are present, become broadened to a general awareness of the *instances* of the Eide in question, which makes it the very reverse of a materialistic theory. By receiving Eide into ourselves as thinkers, a very materialistic-sounding proceeding, we not only become cognizant of those Eide, but also of their possible instances and of ourselves as thinkers. And if Aristotle starts by comparing the reception of Eide by the Mind to the reception of characters by a blank tablet (*De Anima*, 429b 29–430a 2), he ends by comparing it to the action of a hand (*De Anima*, 432a 1–2) which employs the Eide as tools, presumably to reach out to further objects. Images, while utterly disparate from thinking, are held to be the factors which enable thought to reach out beyond what is thus abstractly general. The immaterialism of the theory is further shown in the view that in the mind opposites cease to be mutually exclusive: though the Mind may 'become' the Whiteness and Non-whiteness that it thinks, they will not drive one another from its comparative purview. It seems plain that Aristotle's Theory of Mind, while it may be full of insights, is also full of confusions: it is thus very hard to say how far it diverges from that of Plato. Long familiarity with the fact that there is nothing basically original in Aristotle may here tempt us to think that there may have been detailed discussions of Mind in the Academy of which Aristotle's views represent a one-sided excerpt.

On one point, however, Aristotle would *appear* to have diverged rather widely from Plato. Plato, as we have seen reason to think in interpreting the *Timaeus* and other late Dialogues, believed in an eidetic Mind which was eternally correlated with the whole system of the Eide, and which was in fact the Idea of the comprehensive vision of them all. The Demiurgic Thinking-ness of the *Timaeus*, which is responsible alike for the being of the Soul and its actual thoughts in time, and for the objects, intelligible or sensible, which those thoughts concern, was transformed by Aristotle either into a single mind, or an assemblage of single minds, which he tried to conceive of as instantial, so as to be able to preserve instantiation even when he had to depart from the field of concrete, natural reality. One has the remarkable passage in *De Anima*, 430a 10–25, in which Aristotle says that *even in the Soul* there must be a factor which stands as full actuality does to potency, and which *makes* all the Eide – presumably *qua* objects of thinking – and so is able to raise our ordinary, inferior intellect from mere potency to full actuality. The notion of a private, monitoring, intellectual daemon, to whom intellectuals can turn when faced by problems, and who, it would seem, is capable of answering all questions, may be phenomenologically descriptive, but is none the less philosophically difficult, and one marvels at the intellectual levity, especially in one supposedly more hard-headed than Plato, which can conjure such a daemonic host into existence, against which there are so many obvious objections. The strange doctrine here set forth seems, however, to hang together with the statements regarding the thought of God set forth in *Metaphysics*, XII, and one is overwhelmingly moved to think, with a great number of deep students of Aristotle, that it is the Divine Intellect which is also, as affecting the Soul, the Active Intellect of that Soul, which always envisages the total spread of the Eide. The objection to this view is not only the relatively trivial statements that the Active Intellect is *in* the Soul, but the curious characterization of the Divine Thought (*Metaphysics*, 1074b 32–35) as being merely concerned with *itself* and as being no more than a thinking on *thinking*. Aristotle has, however, made it plain at a previous point in his discussion of the Mind of God (1072b 17–23) 'that thought thinks about thought because it shares the nature of the object of thought, for it becomes an object of thought in coming into contact with and thinking its objects, so that thought and object of thought are the same'. There is therefore nothing to prevent the Divine Mind, while thinking only of itself, from eternally enjoying, and, on an Aristotelian view, *being* all the Eide: if one objects that it ought not to think of anything alien or inferior to itself, the answer surely is that the Eide in their full systematic development, with what is defective only included *qua* excluded, *are* the Divine Mind itself. It would indeed be a strange state of affairs if the Divine Intellect, the most perfect of all, did not extend to the thoughts enjoyed by our several Active Intellects and the passive intellects which these inspire, but was as it were potential in comparison with them. And it would be a strange state of affairs if God were able, through inspiring love and desire for himself, to raise the heavens to their highest activity of circular rotation (*Metaphysics*, 1072a 18–b 4) and even humble creatures to reproduce their kind (*De Anima*, 415a 25–b 2), though the perfection of such beings was not in some eminent form present in Deity himself. We therefore associate ourselves with the opinion of those Aristotelian interpreters who believe he believed in a single all-embracing Active Intellect, which, considered in itself, is the self-thinking Divine Thought, but which becomes as it were multiplied by its relation to various thinking Souls. Such a view is in fact suggested by Aristotle's own statement (*Metaphysics*, 1074a 32–8) that things that are many in number involve Matter, and that the Unmoved First Mover (who is also an immaterial First Thinker) is therefore one, both in definition and in number. But when this view is taken, the difference between Aristotelianism and Platonism becomes blurred. For what is this immaterial Thinking

Being, unique because it is immaterial, and a thought of itself in so far as it is a thought of anything, if it is not the same as the Demiurgic Thinkingness which, on Plato's view, is an all-comprehensive Eidos standing over against, and so holding together, all the Eide. It would appear arguable that both philosophers are here dealing with Mind as Such, the eternal pattern of all instantial, imperfectly developed Minds and acts of thought.

Aristotle, of course, neither understood nor tolerated Plato's arithmetization of the Eide, being unable to see how the basic patterns of the organic and inorganic world can be identified with Numbers, or even with Ratios of Numbers. Nor could he grasp the notional generation of the world's basic patterns from Unity Itself and Indefinite Duality, and he could see nothing peculiarly dignified in Unity or in Ratios. And he tried to dispense with the Platonic Objects of Mathematics, the many conceived Units, Lines, Figures, Solids etc. of the mathematician, by identifying them with ordinary objects abstractly treated: we can, he holds, effect a separation in thought to which no separation in reality can correspond (*Metaphysics*, 1077b 11–1078a 31). But he ignored the Platonic difficulty that such ordinary objects do *not* really illustrate mathematical properties. But despite this anti-arithmetical bias, Aristotle's writings are full of semi-arithmetical analyses of the natures of things, most of which point to an Academic origin. Thus in the *De Anima* Straightness is identified with Duality (429b 20), and the essence of the sense-qualities is sought in each case in a Ratio (426a 26-b 29; 424a 17-24). It is plain, further, that one of the doctrines most intimately associated with Aristotle, the notion of a virtue as the mean of two vices, is a simple relic of the Platonic mathematicization of the Eide, the pretence of an unattainable ἀκρίβεια or accuracy having been wisely abandoned. There is nothing basic in the *Nicomachean Ethics* that is not anticipated in the *Philebus* or in the Aristotelian summary of Platonism, *On the Good*. Aristotle may, in fact, be held to have brilliantly 'cashed in' on the basic insights of Platonism by freeing them from some more contentious and speculative elements.

It is not necessary to lay stress on some other brilliant contributions of Aristotle to the eidetic theory of Platonism. Conspicuous among these is the wonderful theory of *Noῦs* as intuitive

Reason, the intuition which among other things reveals the existence and defining formulae of Eide, in and through the syllogistic process of trying to explain one fact by another. In and through such a process we become aware of the Eidos which is the true middle term in all our reasonings, the Eidos of Eclipse as being the exclusion of light by an intervening body which explains the absence of shadows (*Posterior Analytics*, 90a), or the Eidos of a triangle as necessitating that its external angles should be equal to four right angles (86a). It is not by a remote withdrawal from sensible instances, but in the attempt to understand *why* those instances are as they are, that we become aware of the Eide that are the true causes of their being thus. And Aristotle draws no distinction between the intuition of the man who would now be called the inductive scientist and that of the geometrician: both penetrate to Eide and eidetic connections beneath the casual surface of things. If we are to regret anything in Aristotle, it lies in his willingness to remain contented with an enumeration of separate concepts and principles and not to press onwards to the highest conceptual integrations. It is this stopping short at a list that makes him into a clipped, truncated, dismembered Platonist, with a queer desire to parade instantialist convictions with which he is not deeply in accord, even if superb Platonic insights are always shining forth in his writings.

III

From Aristotle we shall speed over five centuries to the time of Ammonius Saccas and Plotinus, and the beginnings of Neoplatonism in Alexandria. If our view of Aristotle has been modified by the view that we have taken up in regard to Plato, the same will apply to our view of the Neoplatonists who are for us much more truly Platonic than they are usually taken to be. The age between Plato and Plotinus has many features of deep interest, and among the 'ways of life' by the search for which the period is mainly characterized, a way of life inspired by Plato and Pythagoras continued to hold its own as against the equally noble, spiritual stands of Stoicism, Epicureanism and Scepticism, though the Academy was no longer the place in which this Platonism was principally maintained. There was, however, a continuing tradition of Platonic interpretation and reinterpretation throughout the period, even though we may doubt whether it had great influence on the main Neoplatonists, who derived their central ideas, not through historical infection, but through the direct study of the Platonic writings, helped out by those of Aristotle, the Stoics and the pre-Socratic philosophers. It would not, however, do not to mention Philo the Jew who lived and wrote in Alexandria about the time of Christ, and who Platonized Judaism, declaring God to be the most generic ($\gamma\epsilon\nu\iota\kappa\dot\omega\tau\alpha\tau o\nu$) of beings, but outdoing Plato in making Him superior not only to Virtue and Knowledge, but also to Beauty and the Good, and declaring Him to be known only through an inward lucidity ($\dot\epsilon\nu\dot\alpha\rho\gamma\epsilon\iota\alpha$) which transcends all demonstration. From God thus conceived radiate many distinct powers of whom the most exalted is the Divine Word or Logos, the place ($\tau\dot o\pi o\varsigma$) in which the total range of Eide stands arrayed, and which is also the instrument through which everything that was made was made. We may also mention such Platonists as the first-century Eudorus of Alexandria who wrote a commentary on the *Timaeus* and who attempted to derive the Indefinite Dyad from the Primal Unity, Dercylides responsible for the very important citation from Hermodorus, the contemporary of Plato, regarding Plato's three categories of the Self-subsistent, the Opposite and the Relative, Theon of Smyrna, who expounded the Platonic Number-theory, and Plutarch of Chaeronaea (d. A.D. 125) who located the Eide between God and the material world, and who played around interestingly with the Platonic hints in the *Laws* regarding an evil World-Soul. We may also mention the second-century Platonists Maximus of Tyre, Apuleius of Madaura, Atticus who commented on the *Timaeus*, and Numenius of Apamea who, though not a Jew, sufficiently approved of Judaism to speak of Plato as 'Moses talking Attic', and who devised a Trinity which differs from that of Platonism and Neoplatonism. Plotinus was acquainted with these Numenian theories, and was in fact accused of having plagiarized his own doctrines from them, an accusation which his pupil Amelius, writing indignantly for three days on end, was able to refute conclusively. It seems clear in fact that the profound revitalization of Platonic ideas that began with Ammonius Saccas owed little to all this intermediate Platonism.

Ammonius Saccas is said to have believed in the essential homodoxy or agreement of opinion between Plato and Aristotle, and, in addition to this mark of insight, was sufficiently arresting to hold the passionate interest of Plotinus from A.D. 232 to 243. After Ammonius's death, Plotinus did not feel free to put any of his teachings into writing until his fellow-pupils, Erennius and Origen (probably *not* the contemporary Christian father), had violated a pact of silence regarding them. After that he began the writing of his famous Tractates, afterwards grouped by his pupil Porphyry into sets of nine, and for that reason called Enneads. This delay in writing powerfully suggests that the main body of his ideas were those of Ammonius, and certainly the comparative lack of development in the successive Treatises – Porphyry has given us their order – confirms this opinion, which is not otherwise of great interest. The central dogma of the Ammonian-Plotinian system is that of the 'three Primal Hypostases', the three Principles, of which only the First is absolutely self-subsistent and non-parasitic, though it is said to be beyond Thought and Being, the Second being the Principle of Timeless Thought and Being, which exists as an irradiation from, and interpretative commentary on, the First, while the Third, the Principle of conscious life and activity in time, is as much a drawn-out irradiation from, and commentary on, the Second, as the Second is in respect of the First. This central doctrine is referred by Plotinus to the dark passages in Epistle II, 312e and Epistle VI, 323d, but it is also referred more generally to the Mixing-bowl passages in the *Timaeus*, to the passage about the transcendence of Being in *Republic*, VI and to the Platonic *Parmenides*. 'These doctrines', Plotinus says, 'are not novel, but ancient, though not put with full explicitness (ἀναπεπταμένως), and our present words are merely their interpreters, calling on Plato's writings to bear witness to their antiquity' (*Ennead*, V, 8). And, as our long study of the Platonic writings has shown, they *do* bear witness to a triple ontology of a Supreme One or Good, of secondary Eidetic Being correlated with eternal Eidetic Understanding and Knowledge and of a tertiary Soul, parcelled out into psychic units, living in the Time which is the moving image of Eternity, and always hovering amphibiously between the eidetic and the instantial. The doctrine of the Three Primal Hypostases is, in fact, what any intelligently interpretative, not

brutally literalistic, student of Plato *must* derive from a close
study of his principal writings.

The First Hypostasis bears the two Platonic names of the One
and the Good, though, strictly speaking, neither name truly
describes it, but merely indicates its relation to ourselves, or to
other things that 'come after it', and derive from it. We talk around
and about it, and can say what it is not, but It Itself we do not
and cannot put into words. If it is called the Good, it is so called
as being the supreme Good, the object of desire and delight of all
that comes after it (V, iii, 16). And if it is called the One, it is so
called, not because it is one and single, as are all the intelligible
Eide, and the Mind which contemplates them, and the Soul
which is guided by them, and as are likewise all the instantiations
of the eidetic unities, but because it is the Principle of all these
specific or instantial unities, because it is that in virtue of which
they have unity, and, having unity, such Being as is possible for
them. 'For what could have being, if it were not one? If Unity
is taken away from anything, it forthwith ceases to be what it is
said to be' (VI, ix, 4).

Being Unity Itself rather than any species or case of Unity, and
being the generative source of all such species and cases, the
First Hypostasis is further unlike anything that it generates: it has
neither quality, nor quantity, nor psychic nor mental status, nor
has it a place, nor a time, nor is it in motion nor at rest: it is in
itself the utter uniformity or rather formlessness which precedes
all form (αὐτὸ καθ' αὐτὸ μονοειδές, μᾶλλον δὲ ἀνείδεον πρὸ εἴδους
ὂν παντός – VI, ix, 4), and in referring to it we in effect only
register our own vain attempts to approach it. But though thus
eluding ordinary characterization, the First Hypostasis is also the
most inescapably familiar of objects: differing absolutely in type
from its species or instances, it is also what each has as the central
core of its identity and existence, and to which each can therefore
revert by a sort of self-simplification, a despecification of the
species or a disinstantiation of the instance, which ends by leaving
us with that which all species and instances, no doubt one-sidedly
and imperfectly, but also authentically *are*. And the experience
of thus coming into coincidence with the Supreme Unity,
through despecification and disinstantiation, is an ecstatic limit
towards which our experience may advance, and from which it
may later retreat, and about which it may in a relative fashion

think and talk, though what lies at the limit must transcend all thought and talk. The First Hypostasis can, further, be talked about inasmuch as, though it contains nothing specific and instantial, nor any specific or instantial consciousness of anything, it is none the less all these things *in power* (δυνάμει): it is in fact the universal power (δύναμις πάντων – V, iv, 2) which no subsequent Hypostasis possesses, owning only a derivative, after-power of which the First Hypostasis is the disposer (κύριος – V, v, 12). This universal existence-in-power is superior to the actuality (ἐνέργεια) which streams from it: Plotinus does not therefore fully endorse the Aristotelian dogma that Actuality is, in all senses and at all times, prior to Potency.

It will be plain that almost everything that Plotinus says of the First Hypostasis simply dots the *i*'s and crosses the *t*'s of what Plato said of the Good or One in *Republic*, VI and in the First Hypothesis of the *Parmenides*. The only apparent exception lies in the mention of a self-transcendent, self-simplifying mode of direct touch with the Supreme Point of Unity, but this is surely implicit in what Plato says in the *Republic*. What transcends Being, which is the object of Knowledge, must surely be reached in a manner which transcends Knowledge. And very arguably the Socratic trance described in the *Symposium*, which led to the 'reported' sermon on Absolute Beauty, was an experience that was more than the mere understanding of what it is to be beautiful. Nor, apart from a few lapses into rhetoric, is there anything illogical or absurd in the Platonic-Plotinian One beyond Being and the Union with It that transcends Knowledge: the recognition of anything as such and such, is an implicit recognition of eidetic entities of another type, and the explicit recognition of these, is likewise the implicit recognition of Something of a yet higher type, which can be enjoyed only in an important, characteristic, limiting experience. If propositional discourse fades away at this limit, it fades away in an orderly and acceptable fashion, which can be propositionally described, even if its finishing outcome cannot.

From the First Hypostasis, however, species and instances and the consciousnesses of them proceed by what Plotinus calls an ἔλλαμψις or irradiation, whose description has many features of the poetic and pictorial, and has accordingly been condemned as wholly such. Thus *Ennead*, V, i, 6 declares that

all beings while they last, necessarily give rise, out of the
substance and the power present in them, to an existence
which is dependent upon them, and which faces out
towards what is around them, being an image of the origins
it grew out of. Thus Fire gives out its own warmth, and
snow does not keep all its cold within itself. Fragrant
things bear particular witness to this principle, for, while
they exist and are established, something goes forth from
them in which all near can take delight.

A passage like the above seems grossly empirical, but it is clear
from other passages, and from the whole drift of the system, that
Plotinus does not base his doctrine of Irradiation on a doubtful
induction from physical facts, but regards such irradiation as
logically necessary. Thus he writes in *Ennead*, II, ix, 3:

It is a necessity that each thing should also impart what is
its own to something else. The Good will not be the
Good, nor Mind Mind, if there were not something which
enjoys a secondary life while its predecessor enjoys a
primary one. It is a necessity that all should thus always
descend from one another, being 'generated' in the sense
of depending on other things.

This necessary accompaniment by dependencies is simply the
strictly logical account of what Plato in the *Timaeus* called the
unenviousness of God. The necessity (ἀνάγκη) just spoken of
must not, of course, be confused with need (δεῖσθαι): the Supreme
Unity is not in *need* of any of the inferior Hypostases which flow
from it, and can even be said not to *care* if they should not arise
(οὐ δεηθεὶς οὗτος τῶν ἐξ αὐτοῦ γενομένων οὐδ᾽ ἂν ἐμέλησεν αὐτῷ
μὴ γενομένου – V, v, 12). Nor is Plotinus arguing that in a
Universe where the instantial includes much that has broken loose
from ideal measures and patterns, everything will be somehow
deducible from the Supreme Unity (see for example I, viii). He is,
however, arguing that the Supreme Unity cannot be the supra-
existent Unity that it is, if it is not the centre of a system of
distinct and divergent Eide, which in their turn are multiply,
imperfectly and changeably instantiated in the sensible world.
Like Plato in terms of the metaphor of Unenviousness, he

concedes all the claims of the individual and the concrete which could legitimately be made by an entrenched nominalist.

From the First Hypostasis of Absolute Unity, the Second Hypostasis of Mind or Intelligence, eternally correlated with the system of the intelligible Eide, necessarily proceeds: this is arguably not different from the Eternal Thinkingness which enacts the role of the Demiurge in the *Timaeus*, and which is also adumbrated in the Sun-passage in *Republic*, VI. (Not of course as the Sun.) Plotinus certainly does a little dotting of *i*'s and crossing of *t*'s in conceiving of the 'generation' of this Second Principle, which in some passages is conceived as itself generating the ordered, eidetic Being that confronts it, in some passages being coeval with it. Thus in V, ix, 5 Plotinus says that the Eternal Mind truly *is* the real existences that it thinks, that they do not come to it from without, and do not exist before it or after it, and that it is itself the first Lawgiver or rather Law of their being. But in the same Tractate (ix, 7) Plotinus warns us against any 'constitution-theory' of the intelligibles. They are not set up by any act of thinking them. We must in fact conceive of what is thought as *prior* to the act of thinking it (ταύτης γὰρ τῆς νοήσεως πρότερον δεῖ τὸ νοούμενον εἶναι) on pain of making thought a wholly random matter. But in the infinitely vivid V, i, 7, the Eternal Mind is simply said to be the One's return to itself, in which it sees in quasi-separation all the things of which it is the Power (ὧν οὖν ἐστι δύναμις ταῦτα ἀπὸ τῆς δυνάμεως οἷον σχιζομένη ἡ νοήσις καθορᾷ· ἢ οὐκ ἂν ἦν νοῦς). The Mind in short is the self-consciousness of the Supreme Unity, which depends upon and yet falls short of that Unity, in so far as it is a mere consciousness, having the essential weakness of consciousness of distinguishing itself from its object, and of breaking that object into an infinite number of distinct aspects. In VI, vii, 15, even more vividly, the multiplication of the Eide is attributed to the Mind's inability to envisage the dazzling unity of the Supreme One. Unable to hold the single power it received from this One, it broke it up and multiplied it so that it could deal with it piecemeal. What really underlies all these apparently conflicting, mythic accounts is that infinite specific possibilities necessarily radiate from one single, supraspecific Source, and that with this radiation necessarily goes that of the possibility of an Intelligence at once directed on each of them specifically, and on all of them together. In all this we have no doctrine of the Mind of God which has some sort of ontological priority over what it envisages: since it is only abstractly distinguishable from the Eide, it must be as much an Eidos as they are. It is Mind as Such, as the Eide are each This or That as Such: it is the infinite, unifying Thinkingness, which is just another side to thinkable Being. There might be some doubt as to this interpretation, since Plotinus in V, ix, 13 questions whether there can be Eide of Soul and Mind. On examination, however, what the passage really says is that Souls and Minds are less definitely distinguishable from their eidetic originals than are sensible instances.

Plotinus's account of Thinkingness and Thinkableness at the eidetic level is, in some points superior to Plato's, in some points inferior. Plotinus stresses, what in Plato is so much less emphatic as almost to be forgotten by certain Platonists, the systematic unity of the Eide, their necessary interconnection as the diverse specifications of one supreme unity, their integration into a single synoptic science. Even if they seem widely different and mutually irrelevant, they necessarily have their place in what we may call the same eidetic space, and to understand one is to understand all. 'Mind', says Plotinus (V, ix, 6), 'is all things together and yet not together since each thing has a separate power', and he compares the interpenetrating unity of the Eide in thought to the way in which λόγοι, or as we should say 'genes', are co-present in a single seed. In some later Tractates (for example V, viii, 4) the unity of the Eide spread before a total mental vision is given lyrical expression: in the noetic sphere, Plotinus tells us,

> all things are transparent, and nothing is dark and resistant, and each thinker and object is clear down to its inmost depths as light is transparent to light. And each thinker holds everything in himself, and sees everything in what is other, so that everything is everywhere, and all is all, and each all, and the glory infinite. . . . Each thing has some one special thing that predominates in it, but also reveals everything.

This magnificent description no doubt gives voice to the feeling of the momentarily dazzled soul as it rises to the complete vision of timeless Thinkingness: what is risen to is, however, merely the connected spread of the Eide and the eidetic vision that matches them. It is this logical unity of the interpenetrating Eide in an encompassing unity that gives them all the reality that Plato has hinted at in the *Republic*, *Timaeus*, *Parmenides* and *Sophist*, which here comes to full statement, unintelligible to all such as cannot see beyond the half-truth that 'everything is what it is and not another thing'. It will be noted that Minds in the plural (νόες or νοῖ) play a part at the eidetic level as well as thinkables (see VI, vii, 17): there is presumably a typically Socratic or Aristotelian mentality of each of which we have encountered an instance down here. Plotinus goes even further and completes Platonism by holding that there may even be Eide of particular souls, for example Socrates himself, which will however apply to more than one bodily incarnation. We must not, says Plotinus, object to an infinity of Soul-types at the eidetic level, since such an infinity collapses into a point, and is not drawn out into endless series.

In other respects, however, the Plotinian theory of Mind and the Eide falls beneath the Platonic. Though Plotinus often mentions the Platonic reduction of Eide to Numbers, and their generation by the One and the Great and Small, he has no true understanding of this aspect of Plato, which accordingly has no impact on medieval or later philosophy. In the long Tractate on Numbers (VI, 6) there is much discussion of the *plurality* of the Eide, or of the specific Eide of Numbers, but there is no attempt to conceive the *being* of the Eide as in some pervasive sense numerical. Plotinus is likewise ignorant of Plato's three fundamental categories of the Self-existent, the Opposite and the Relative: in so far as he deals with the Platonic categories as Kinds of Being, he confines himself to the five Major Kinds of the *Sophist* (see VI, ii). He therefore fails altogether to give a subordinate place among the Eide to negative and defective forms, though he is willing to concede the presence of a sort of intelligible Matter in the eidetic sphere, an indeterminate substrate presupposed by eidetic difference (III, v, 4, 5). There are, as Plotinus says (V, ix, 9), no Eide of things evil: evil arises here from privation, deficiency and need, and is a malady of unhappy Matter, and whatever resembles it. This view of the purely positive, excellent character of the Eide conforms to the strand of Academic opinion to which Aristotle himself belonged, but, as we have seen, Plato himself adhered to the wiser doctrine which makes the Eide two-edged, including in themselves, and in the Knowledge of themselves, whatever falls short of them, or is basically opposed to them. So that for Plato the ideal world is not all *ordre et beauté, luxe, calme et volupté* as it is in Plotinus.

The generation of the Third Hypostasis, Soul, necessarily coincides for Plotinus, as for Plato, with the generation of Time. Just as the Eternal Mind arises out of the Supreme Unity in and by the holding apart of the various Eide of which it is the Power, so Soul and Time arise out of Eternal Mind by a departure from the *completeness* of the eidetic sphere, which permits neither addition nor subtraction. This departure from completeness is identical with the life of Soul, an essentially unquiet faculty, like Martha busy over many things (πολυπράγμων – III, vii, 11), and forced to decode the total message of the Eide into a long string of separate messages, each of which it laboriously fits into a growing whole. Plotinus is not, however, regarding this declension into temporality as an unfortunate accident: plainly it is as logically necessary for the Ultimate Unity to give rise to the moving, questing Soul, and to the Time which is its pervasive form, as it is necessary for it to differentiate itself in the Eide. It is, in fact, in the life of Soul that the Eide and the Supreme Unity beyond it live and move, and it is absurd to scorn the life of Soul for pointing to something higher. Soul, further, involves a less transparent pluralization than exists at the level of Mind and the Eide: our souls do not interpenetrate as do the eidetic Minds above them, and have something of the separateness of the bodily masses in which they are active (IV, ix), and there is also somewhat of a gulf between them and their Great Sister, the All-Soul. But, though thus separated in their lower being, Souls remain linked together at their highest points, much as light divides itself among separate dwellings while remaining undivided and truly one (IV, ii, 4). This beautiful statement, reminiscent of a passage in Plato's *Parmenides*, well shows how Plotinus was able to reconcile gulfs of difference with more basic identity and unity. The All-Soul is, of course, responsible for the unending turning of the heavens as in Plato's *Timaeus*, *Phaedrus* and the *Laws*, and as done by the Unmoved Mover in the *Physics* and *Metaphysics* of Aristotle.

Beneath Soul lies Matter (ὕλη), into which Soul pours the

λόγοι, the Ratios, which form the essence of the various species of natural being. Regarding Matter, Plotinus has a long, interesting Tractate (II, iv), in which the Aristotelian accounts of ὕλη are subtly combined with the accounts of the Receptacle in the *Timaeus* and the Aristotelian accounts of the Great and Small. Plotinus follows Plato, and also Aristotle, in recognizing an eidetic as well as an instantial Matter: the indefinite substrate, which is what is common to all the Eide, reappears, at another level, in the basic indefiniteness which underlies sensible instances. Sensible Matter, we are told (II, iv, 6), is required to give bulk to the being of sensible things which cannot consist of pure form, and to explain the continuous transformation of sensible things into one another. To this omnirecipient Prime Matter Plotinus denies, not only every sensible quality, but even bulk (ὄγκος) and size, thereby going beyond Plato's treatment of χώρα in the *Timaeus*, but Prime Matter, though not intrinsically bulky, nevertheless has an intrinsic aptitude (ἐπιτηδειότης) for size and distance. How is such Matter apprehended? Plotinus follows Plato in holding that we apprehend Matter not so much by an act of thought as by the failure of such an act, an indefinite Unthinkingness (ἄνοια) in which no clear content comes to light (II, iv, 10). But Plotinus disagrees with Plato in seeing in the indefinite material Principle the *sole* source of evil in the Cosmos (II, iv, 16; I, viii), and by ignoring the various quite definite forms of Excess and Defect presupposed by an Eidos, and so in an extended sense part of its content.

Why do Souls descend from the intensive parcelling involved in temporal process, to the extensive parcelling involved in bodily extension and existence? The Plotinian answer is simply because they are Souls, and because, stemming from Absolute Unity, and having in themselves an image of that Unity which abides through flux, they necessarily desire to preside over and impose unity upon a disunity which is *further* from Absolute Unity than themselves. To decorate and arrange, to inform and control and order, are part of what it is to be a Soul, and these involve the possibility of a domain of things spread out in distance and bulk, and capable of being so ordered and arranged. Necessarily the descent of Soul into the otherness of body entails endless possibilities of defect, miscarriage and corruption – which do not, however, touch our august Sister, the World-Soul – and necessarily the Soul must seek to raise itself to the Patterns yonder, and to the Unity from which they radiate. Yet it is only by descending from the Supreme Unity that it is possible for a Soul to return to it, and the descent is in consequence not something misjudged or wanton, though it may at times metaphorically be said to involve τόλμα or wantonness. 'For it was not possible for everything to stand still at the level of the intelligible, it being possible for something else to arise, inferior indeed, but as necessarily existent as what came before it' (IV, viii, 3). Plotinus makes a magnificent defence of the natural world against those who, like certain Christian Gnostics, would regard it as the evil product of a fallen power. Being an instantial image, it necessarily falls short of its eidetic original, but nothing can exceed the accuracy and beauty of its major arrangements (II, ix, 4).

We have summarized the Platonism of Plotinus at some length, because, with a few exceptions, it is so utterly true to its paradigm. It is simply what one arrives at if one meditates on the major speculative passages in Plato's written work with a willingness to carry eidetic thinking to the limit, a willingness which has not been present in many of the empiricists, pluralists, nominalists, sceptics, formal logicians, anti-mystics and pure scholars who have ventured to interpret Plato. Hardly at any point does Plotinus say anything that cannot fairly be regarded as a relatively slight bringing together or carrying further of drifts that are found in Plato. The treatment of the two philosophers *together*, which prevailed until Schleiermacher altered the fashion at the beginning of the nineteenth century, was therefore fully justified. It is also only in the light of a Plotinian interpretation that Plato assumes his full stature, and that the drift of his doctrine can be fully assessed. There were sides of that doctrine that Plotinus could not understand, and in which we may do better then he did, but on those that he did understand his guidance is not merely useful, but mandatory.

We shall give little space to the various followers of Plotinus. Of Porphyry, who died at the beginning of the fourth century, we shall say only that his introduction to the *Categories* of Aristotle, in the Latin translation of Boethius, introduced the whole question of the status of the Eide to medieval thought. Of Iamblichus, who lived later in the century, we may mention that his *Protrepticus* or *Exhortation to Philosophy* contained large fragments of a similarly oriented, Platonic work of Aristotle. Of Julian the Apostate (d. A.D. 363) we may say that he fought nobly, tolerantly, philosophically and quite vainly against the ignoble fanaticism sadly shown by the newly established Christian religion. In the fifth century which followed, Platonism once more established itself in the Academy, and numbered among its exponents the great Proclus (411–485) who, in addition to writing commentaries on the *Timaeus*, the *Republic*, the *Cratylus*, the *Parmenides* and on Euclid, also produced an imaginatively theosophical *Platonic Theology* translated by Thomas Taylor in 1816, and a very excellent *Elements of Theology* ($\Sigma\tau o\iota\chi\epsilon\acute{\iota}\omega\sigma\iota\varsigma$ $\Theta\epsilon o\lambda o\gamma\iota\kappa\acute{\eta}$), which summarizes Platonic and Plotinian doctrine with the accuracy of a treatise on set-theory, and which, in Latin translation via the Arabic or direct from the Greek, was deeply studied by Albert the Great, Aquinas, Eckhart, Cusanus and many others. It contains the valuable distinction of the Noetic and the Noeric, the latter standing for the Eide of mental activity. It exists in an excellent English edition and translation by Professor E. R. Dodds.

IV

In passing on to consider the influence of Platonism in the Christian ages of philosophy we shall attempt only to be illustrative, and to show how the iridescence of Platonism again and again gathers on the surface of theories even where a misunderstood Platonism is not acknowledged or is explicitly disavowed. The Christian religion, in its earlier phases, was not disposed to deny its debt to Platonism, even if that debt had to be disguised by supposing that the theology of Moses had by Divine Providence filtered through to Plato. And Platonism, despite surface-semblances to the contrary, is in fact the only philosophy tailored to fit the Judaeo-Christian religious need for a unique, single, absolutely surpassing, all-disposing source of everything. For an instantial God, even if emptily said to have made Heaven and Earth and Man out of nothing and even if expressing His being in the superb blankness of 'I am that I am', will always remain one among others, a particular being jealous of possible rivals, who might very well not have existed, and exhibiting a particularity in his disposition and his dispensations such as leaves many admirable possibilities unrealized, and makes it perfectly proper to turn one's back on Him. There can indeed be nothing sacrosanct about any particular. Whereas a God who is in no sense one among others, and whose being and association with every power and excellence is in no sense capable of being otherwise, is necessarily what it is after the fashion of a Platonic Eidos, and not after that of its quirkish instantiations, or better still, is what it is after the fashion of the Supreme Arche of all the Eide, in which all eidetic possibilities, even if contrary, are present together, in perfectly thinkable unison. God, in short, to deserve the self-prostration accorded Him by the Jews, or the unreserved love demanded for Him by Jesus, would have to be, not a particular case of Justice, or Understanding, or Power or Beauty etc. but the Justice Itself, the Understanding Itself, the infinite Might and Loveliness etc. which are necessarily unique and surpassing, in that they are of a different logical type from their parasitic instances. And they exist necessarily since it is quite unmeaning to think them away, and it is further possible to see them as merely different sides of the Supreme Goodness which they all are, sides disjoined in instantiation, but necessarily cohering in what is the Power of them all. Whatever is truly said of this Unity merely brings out a side of Itself, rather than a Genus or Species under which it falls, and whatever is excluded from it, or falls wholly beneath it, becomes part of its sense in being thus excluded or inferior. If it be argued that such a notion is emptily abstract, the answer is that this view rests on a false view of the highest Universals; on them lower Universals and instances depend, and not vice versa, and there is nothing in one-sided Species or instances which is not present in power in the highest Universals. And if it be argued that such a thing of thought cannot evoke the highest religious passion, the answer is that religion is precisely the passion which can be satisfied by no contingent and one-sided object, but which necessarily tends to a focus defined solely in terms of Omnitude, Necessity, Excellence, and Pure Being, and other notions of the most rigorously logical character. Of such an object, and not of any finite, one-sided expression of it, is it possible to say with St Catherine of Genoa: *Non voglio cose che sono da Te: sol voglio Te, o dolce Amore.* True religion, it may be argued, is the logical passion *par excellence,* and the logical pattern into which it breathes that passion tends to have a Platonic tinge.

Such Platonism, we may say, was implicit in the deepening religious experience of the Jews, when the object of their absolute reverence began to lose its instantial particularity, and became associated with such things as Mercy, Justice and Humility rather than with specific ritual performances. The vivid particularity of their initial religious myths and pictures performed the great service of lending life to Platonic Universals which might readily seem empty and strengthless to the uninverted outlook. And the characteristic personality of Jesus, and the vivid poetry of his Messianic outlook, likewise gained an entry for that necessary but underemphasized aspect of Platonism, veiled in talk of Divine Unenviousness and the Causality of the Eide, according to which it is eidetically necessary that the Pattern of Patterns should 'come down' from its logical elevation, and should involve itself in the generation and redemption of an instantial world. It would not be nonsensical, though perhaps too partially Christian – in view of other great exemplars – to conceive of an evangelical preparation in which the Concept, the Eidos, came down to meet the Person, and the Person was raised up to meet the Concept, and both achieved their completed sense thereby. If the utterances of Jesus arrange themselves along a spectrum terminating at one end in sayings and stories of a hard, harsh and arbitrary kind, they terminate at the other end in utterances of Platonic universality, as when, e.g., the sectarian workers of miracles and casters forth of devils are passed over in favour of those who, without sectarian affiliations, have done signal acts of mercy. And in the fine Greek phrases of Paul something like a Platonic leaven is powerfully at work, through which Christ becomes something which it is grammatically possible to live and to die, and in which we are exhorted to pursue everything that is true, just, pure, lovely and of good report. But Providence or the Logos – it does not matter how we phrase it – soon removed Christianity from Jerusalem to the more intense civilization of cities like Alexandria, Athens, Constantinople and Rome, and later to such centres as Cologne, Paris and Oxford, thereby Hellenizing or Latinizing or Europeanizing it. In the process it became ever more deeply tinged with the fortified Platonism of Plotinus or the more diluted

Platonism dispensed by Aristotle. There is in consequence little in Christian theology or eschatology in which a Hellenic, Platonic tinge is not discernible. More recent attempts to de-Hellenize Christianity have merely succeeded in barbarizing it.

It is not possible to pass over without mention Clement (d. A.D. 213) and Origen (d. 254), the Christian Platonists of Alexandria. Largely derivative in their thought, they brilliantly and patiently applied Platonic concepts to the illumination of the stories and pictures of the Jewish and Christian scriptures, acting throughout on the principle that nothing detrimental should be attributed to Deity. When Scripture suggested something of the kind, it had to be reinterpreted allegorically, though such reinterpretation should be reserved for the philosophical, and kept from the vulgar. To Clement God the Logos was an Educator as well as a Saviour, and a Hierophant of the Greater Mysteries. The knowledge of Himself that He communicated was the true eternal life, which would necessarily result in a dying away of the lower passions. There was a celestial after-life, described with many touches borrowed from the *Phaedo*, *Republic* etc. in which the illuminated would be gathered together and all will then terminate in a Nirvanic Rest in God, in which God Himself will have achieved a Pauline all-in-allness. God Himself is tiered in two Hypostases – the Spirit is for some reason little mentioned – and beyond the Word with its conscious embrace of all the Eide, lies the Supreme Divinity who can only be known by a breaking down (ἀνάλυσις) or stripping away (ἀφαίρεσις) of all physical attributes and spatial dimensions, until even the position which makes a point a point is eliminated. Clement surpasses Plato in placing God beyond the One and beyond the Unit Itself. In Origen God the Father is the αὐτοαγαθόν or Goodness Itself, of which God the Son is essentially an image, not as immovably good as His parent, as is shown by Christ's rejection of goodness in Mark 10:17. The Eide are then all contained in the Logos or Second God, and as so contained are given the Stoic name of λόγοι, which Plotinus also employs in similar contexts. The Logos is coeval with the Father on Whom He timelessly depends, and lives absorbed in the vision of the paternal depths. He is, further, surrounded by a whole world of dependent Minds (νόες), substances (οὐσίαι) or powers (δυνάμεις), the sort of court that the Gnostics had made *de rigueur*. The origin of the material cosmos is in part due to the fall into materiality of these attendant powers, who had grown weary of contemplating the Paternal Depths. Origen's theory of the human soul is sufficiently Platonic to admit pre-existence without reincarnation: God's preference for Jacob over Esau could not otherwise be justified. The human soul continues its progress after death: it is always subject to Divine persuasion, but is always in a position to resist it, until in the end it must weary of perversity as the original Powers wearied of contemplating the Divine Depths. When all have achieved this rational ennui, the Great Restitution will ensue, and all souls will be lost in the Paternal Depths. What is most characteristic of all this theology is its deep indoctrination by the Platonic inversion: universals, rather than instantial persons, are the true agents and substances behind the particular things and events in this world.

In the next century Gregory of Nyssa (331–94) produced a Catechetical Logos comparable to the *De Principiis* of Origen, and to some extent derived from the latter. Plato is not often mentioned in Gregory's work, but of the degree of his Platonism Harold Cherniss has said that 'but for some few orthodox dogmas, which he could not circumvent, Gregory has merely applied Christian names to Plato's doctrines and called it Christian theology' (*Platonism of Gregory of Nyssa*, 1930, p. 62). Gregory of Nyssa approaches Platonism in his constant connection of Divinity with a Goodness which is not in any way a thing shared in (κατὰ μετοχήν) or acquired as a possession (ἐπικτητόν), or is possessed of goodness only on certain occasions or in certain parts or on certain grounds. In other words, he comes close to asserting, though he does not with perfect clarity assert, that Divinity is not some supereminent instance of Being, Goodness and Beauty, but that it is rather these ultimate characteristics themselves, by participation in which instances are said to be, or be good, or be beautiful. And Divinity is these perfections in some wholly unspecific, indefinite, deeply simple and quite incommunicable manner, which our knowledge and the differing energies of things splinter into many distinct features or attributes. Beneath the ultimate, indefinite, simple Unity, is a Logos which is one in nature with it, but which constitutes a Second Hypostasis because it ramifies into all the distinct energies that will become operative in the world. The human soul has the paradoxical unity-in-multiplicity of Divinity, and it is also capable of becoming luciform, and losing itself in the pure light of Divinity Itself. Gregory's main conceptions are as unclear as the vanishing into light just mentioned, but their Platonic affiliations are none the less quite evident.

A very different influence of Platonism, beginning in the same century, comes before us if we pass from Asia to Africa, and consider the shattering philosophical and human phenomenon of Augustine (354–430). Deeply different from the Platonic is, however, the origin of his thought in the subjective experience of the individual, though this has some anticipations in certain Tractates of Plotinus. Even if nearly everything is as doubtful as the sceptical successors of Plato in the Academy thought it was, we cannot, says Augustine, doubt one truth, that which concerns the being of the inner man of thought and his doubts. We need not go abroad, but need only retreat into ourselves to be aware of this truth, and this truth instantiates Truth Itself, whose being as an Eidos is therefore beyond all doubt. This quite certain knowledge of Truth Itself is, however, such as to remove all doubt concerning our knowledge of a whole interconnected family of cases of Truth, concerning eternal natures or Eide, which interconnected family does not differ from the Divine Intelligence or God Himself. To know even truths concerning changeable instances is to be made aware of the truths regarding the unchanging natures that they presuppose. God, however, is not merely the Truth specified and articulated in all truths: He is also the Goodness of every good thing, and the Unity which constitutes the beauty of every unified existent. Augustine even carries his Platonism into the citadel of the Aristotelian categories: God is said to be what is categorial in all categories, rather than a Case falling under any of them. He can be said to be the Good without having a quality, the Great without having a quantity, the Everlasting without having a date, the Simply Substantial without being a substance, the Omnipresent without having a location, the Source of all mutability without being Himself mutable etc. (*De Trinitate*, V, VII and *passim*). The recognition of essential type-differences entails the further paradox that God, being that in virtue of which all intelligibles are intelligible, must Himself transcend intelligibility: we come nearest to knowing Him in recognizing this necessary, categorial ignorance, which a modern would express by saying that God is simply not the sort of thing that one can in an ordinary sense be said to know or know about. The paradoxical trinitarian properties of God are dealt with very masterfully, and the human soul is recognized as manifesting many of these paradoxical properties, as well as certain analogues to the free creativity of Divinity. The latter, however, enable the human soul to fall short of Goodness and Pattern in ways in which, in virtue of its limited constitution, it need not fall short: it has a secondary power to use or withhold its powers, and to use them in ways which depart from the limited goodness of which it is capable. Such a falling short from Absolute Goodness in the mutable realm can, however, be variously compensated, and is accordingly acceptable from the Divine Standpoint.

All this mainly Platonic doctrine is wonderfully and persuasively set forth in Augustine's writings *On the Trinity*, *On True Religion*, on *The City of God*, in his *Confessions*, and in many other works, and Augustine concedes that the Platonists alone, of all previous philosophers, had worked out what may be called the eidetically understandable side of Christian doctrine. There was, however, another darkly important side to Divine Being, covered by its freely chosen edicts, arrangements, dispositions, which was and ought to be eidetically unfathomable. There is nothing basically un-Platonic in this way of regarding things, for there is no Platonic doctrine to the effect that the way in which this instantial world is arranged is the only way in which it could be: there can be only one world, the *Timaeus* tells us, but what it will be like in detail, and how far departing from its eidetic originals, is not said to be eidetically determinable. The contrary is in fact suggested. Where Augustine, however, goes astray, is in his willingness to accept Divine Arbitrariness even when it runs counter to our no doubt faulty, flickering eidetic insight, rather than in seeking to accommodate the former to the latter. Origen and Clement thought we must so interpret Scripture that it accords with what our poor insight finds acceptable. Augustine, as later Kierkegaard, almost glories in affronting that insight. Prevenient grace, majority damnation, absolute insistence on nugatory ceremonial performances, refusal to recognize pagan virtues etc., all give the thought of Augustine what can only be called its monstrous character, that could certainly never recommend itself to a Platonist. Origen deprived himself of his virile parts, but became more rational and gentle in consequence. Augustine suppressed his carnality, but could only do so by coming to feel something like a settled hatred, overlaid by a concern for Justice and Goodness, towards the majority of the human race.

If Providence behaved somewhat unsearchably in letting the great, perverse African loose upon mankind, it was more obviously provident in the next century, when it permitted the fraud of an unknown, probably Syrian monk, who pretended to be the Dionysius the Areopagite whom Paul converted on his momentous visit to Athens. By so doing it allowed a stream of the purest Platonism to irrigate the whole subsequent course of medieval thought. This deceiving monk had perhaps heard Proclus lecturing at Athens, but had certainly studied his and other Platonic writings, and was able to set forth a basically Platonic theology in several treatises that had all the merits of an excellently written modern paper-back, backed up with a pleni-tude of pious citations, and with the added nimbus of an author-ship deemed to belong to apostolic times. Platonism could there-fore penetrate areas, and overcome resistances, that would not yield to unconsecrated suspects like Origen. The reputation of Dionysius took some centuries to overcome initial questions, but by the ninth century he had become the St Denis of the Parisian abbey, encrusted with far more legends than he had originally propagated. He was translated by John the Scot, paraphrased by Albert the Great, respectfully commented on by Aquinas, and had a profound influence on Meister Eckhart, Denys of Chartres, and Nicolaus of Cusa.

In his short work *On Mystical Theology*, Denis begins by in-voking the superessential Trinity, which is more than Divine and more than Good, to raise him and his readers, not only beyond all Light, but also beyond Unknowingness, till the mysteries of Theology become revealed in the luminous darkness of Silence. He also adjures the scriptural Timothy to strip himself of sen-sation and thought, and to unite himself in ignorance with the One who is beyond all Essence and beyond all Knowledge. In previous treatises he has dealt concisely with various descriptions of God as Supreme Cause, which became more and more atten-uated as one advanced to the summit: now at the summit all words and thoughts and ideas wilt away in one's mute union with the Unspeakable. This Unspeakable has neither figure nor form nor quality nor quantity, nor bulk, nor position, nor mutability nor any other sensuous affection. Being devoid also of conceptual determinations, it has no connection with Science, Truth, Kingship, Wisdom, Unity, Godhead, Spirit, Sonship or Paternity (*On Mystical Theology*, ch. v). These effusively multiplied statements of the Divine Emptiness recall the First Hypothesis of the *Parmenides*, but are followed in the treatise *On Divine Names* by an equally effusive treatment of the countless inadequate but *positive* ways of designating the Supreme Unity. It can be called Good, Beautiful, Adorable, Intellectually Luminous etc., in virtue of its relation to us, but these terms do not express its intrinsic features, and it is not to be conceived of as in any ordinary sense knowing or loving itself or anything else. Interesting in this connection is Denis's teaching of the value of contradiction in saying what God is for us. 'In the One all beings exist and are subsistent in advance, and this is so even when those beings are most completely opposed' (*On Divine Names*, ch. v, 19). God is the Greatness of all great things in virtue of His universal extension, but He is also the smallest of all small beings in virtue of bulklessness and infinite subtlety. He is in a sense infinitely stable and stabilizing, but also in a sense infinitely motile and mobile, and so on. We remember the Second Hypothesis of the *Parmenides*. Nicolaus of Cusa founded his doctrine of the Divine Coincidence of Opposites on these Dionysian passages. And while Plotinus had enriched the realm of the Eide by planting among them an infinity of νόες or eidetic Minds, each of which mainly minded a given Eidos, and while Proclus had believed in a race of pure Henads or numerically distinct offspring of the Primal One, Denis turned these eidetic creations into a Heavenly Hierarchy of Angels, Archangels, Seraphim and Cherubim, and also added Thrones, Dominations, Princedoms, Virtues and Powers, whose distinguishing features could be fascinatingly imagined. Another pendant treatise discusses the ecclesiastical hierarchy and its ceremonial performances which mirror the arrangements of the Heavenly Hierachy: it is a misfortune that this earthly hierarchy and its ceremonies were as yet undeveloped in the times of the historical Dionysius. All in all, the works of the false Denis form an exciting farrago: vividly pictorial, they none the less bring out the essentially logical character of the Platonic theology.

We shall barely make mention at this point of the brilliant and fascinating thought of John the Scot (born in Ireland in the ninth century) who derived his main inspiration from Denis. His *Division of Nature* is in some ways the purest statement of Platonism ever put forward, in that he accords no shadow of independent substantiality either to the Eide, through which God's creativity operates, or to the instances in which these Eide terminate, while making God *also* so above everything of which He is the creative essence, and so set in His own uncreative Self-abidingness, as to give a new and strangely pregnant meaning to the creation of all things out of Nothing. He also anticipates Spinoza and Hegel in making man's knowledge of God be God's *self*-revelation in them, thereby giving man a theological function. The medieval world was, however, successful in for the most part turning its back on John the Scot, and for this reason (though we admire him) we shall also turn our back on him.

We cannot, however, turn our back on the great Anselm, whose famous Ontological Proof of the Divine Existence, put forward in his *Proslogium* in the eleventh century, has been gravely misunderstood – by myself among others – because not read in the Platonizing context of the *Monologium* which preceded it. In the *Proslogium* (ch. ii) Anselm has declared belief in God as 'the Good than which there can be nothing more good' (*Et quidem credimus te esse bonum quo maius bonum cogitari nequit*), and has argued that it is self-contradictory to imagine that such a being can only exist 'in the intellect', i.e. as an intentional object of our thinking, and not independently and 'in reality'. For if something, conceived as being such as God is conceived as being, existed merely 'in the intellect', there would of necessity be something greater and better than this merely intended God, a God, namely, that existed in reality and not merely in thought. There is therefore something which, being conceived as the greatest and best of all things, is also necessarily conceived as really existing, and not as something that merely might exist (*Proslogium*, ch. iii). Gaunilo, Anselm's contemporary, pointed out that the argument, as it stands, proves too much, since it could be used to prove reality of a most perfect island, or of anything else perfect, and Kant, at a later date, drew a distinction between what the application of a concept implies, *if* and *when* it can be so applied, and the momentous fact of its actual application, which requires sense or some similar faculty to attest it, and cannot be established by examining concepts alone. These criticisms, however, ignore the *sort* of being that Anselm was trying to establish, which was *not* the being of some instance which merely exemplified Divine Maximality, and which was distinct from the nature or essence it exemplified. Such a being, whatever it was, would not have the absolute Goodness of a God, and we can help Anselm further by saying that, being an instance, it could not be the greatest of conceivable beings, since every exemplification can be exceeded, and since, in addition, not all exemplifications can be combined.

If we now turn to the earlier *Monologium* we see all this spelt out. For Anselm argues that, if there were a plurality of unsurpassably perfect beings, they would have to be perfect through participation in a single essence of perfection, and that this, rather than the several instantiations of perfection, would be the unsurpassably perfect being (ch. iv). God's being is therefore the being of an Eidos, or of the Principle of all Eide, and no instance is anything apart from the Eide it instantiates. At a later point Anselm says that God is not just as just men are just, but is Justice Itself, and that Justice in God is identical with every other perfection, all entering into a single, many-sided perfection (*Monologium*, chs. xvi, xvii). It is clear, therefore, that to prove that God has being, we have merely to prove that He represents a genuine eidetic Principle, and not some arbitrary, perhaps self-contradictory notional assemblage that *we* have dreamt up, like being the last of all Natural Numbers or the most perfect of all islands. But that the supreme point of unity in the whole eidetic structure should be thus arbitrary or incoherent, is not anything that can be entertained. The Ontological Proof is, therefore, entirely valid, if seen in its Platonic background, only it does not prove the existence of the self-contradictory, instantial God in which some have tried to believe.

V

We may now ignore the many streams, deriving from Platonism – including the major stream concerned with the Realist-Nominalist-Sermonist controversy – that thread the major and minor valleys of medieval thought. Varying our metaphor, we shall proceed straight to the major elevation of Aquinas, where, in the thirteenth century, the transmitted light of Platonism, reflected from Denis, Augustine, Gregory and more remotely Proclus, struck at last on a very great understanding, and, with some refraction in Aristotelian directions, illuminated it centrally. Superficially no one could be more critical of Plato and the Platonists than Aquinas: their 'image' in his writings is with very few exceptions a poor one. Plato, he says, was led to his position by epistemological considerations: he accepted the doctrine of the 'early naturalists' (Heraclitus, Cratylus etc.) that knowledge of bodily things was impossible, since everything (bodily) was in flux and the senses constantly deceived us, and he therefore postulated the existence of certain natures separated from flux, regarding which there could be a fixed truth which our minds could come to know. Plato also imagined that the unchanging natures he was positing would be in some way capable of explaining, and of giving rise to, the existences, characters and changes that we meet with in the sensible world (*Commentary* on *Metaphysics*, I, 15, *Metaphysics*, VII, 7 and elsewhere). And he imagined that his separated natures would be able also to give rise to knowledge in the mind by some sort of direct influx and participation, in which the sensible encounter with particulars would merely have an inciting or reminiscent role (*Comm. In De Anima*, 15; *Summa contra Gentiles*, II, ix, 8). In all these lines of argument, Thomas argues, Plato went badly astray. The sensible world is not so fantastically restless as he believes it to be: every change in it necessarily involves something unchanging, a substance or at least basic matter, and even such a posture as Sitting endures for some time, and can give rise to unchanging truth and knowledge (*Summa Theologica*, I, 84). And though it is indeed true that knowledge of bodies, and of anything, involves the reception into the mind of certain 'natures' in an immaterial, universal, necessary and stable manner, and that the mind can consider these natures in abstraction from other natures present in a body or other entity, such abstraction and separation is nothing but the manner of the mind, and one must not allow oneself to suppose that it is feeling the influx of immaterial, universal, stable, separate entities in the manner of being (*Summa Theologica*, I, 84 and elsewhere). It is the root error of Platonism to confuse intentional with real being, and to suppose that what can be separated in the manner of the mind (*secundum intellectum*) can also be separated in the manner of being (*secundum esse*: *De Veritate*, 21, and elsewhere).

But even if there were all these separated universals that the Platonists believe in, they could throw no light on the being or knowledge of anything. For they would be motionless, while that which they were required to explain was in motion, useless for knowledge since they were not the substance, nor intrinsic to the things they were required to explain, nor the models on which things in the world were constructed, since the latter could have arisen without them (*Comm.* on *Metaphysics*, I, 15), and they would be general and without matter, whereas what they were required to explain might be individual and involving matter (*Summa Theologica*, I, 76, 5). The human intelligence is, further, such as to have to collect its explanatory universals from sensible instances, and is therefore not accidentally embodied (*Summa Theologica*, I, 76, 5), and it need not be supposed to derive its full knowledge of these from some direct contact or influx, but from the action of an Agent Intellect, which is well qualified to contain without matter specific natures whose real existence necessarily is in matter (*In III De Anima*, 10). Thomas further industriously reinterprets all the statements of his predecessors which would seem to regard God as a Supreme Platonic Eidos in which all finite things in some plain sense participate. God can have no relation to finite things other than being their Principle: He cannot be a nature actually inherent in them nor be literally their essence or substance. Dionysius is mildly censured for saying profoundly that the *esse* of all things is the *superesse* of God, thereby making immanence and transcendence two sides of the same coin: such talk, says Thomas, requires explanation, rather than further propagation (*Comm. in Librum I Sententiarum*, 18, 1, 5).

It will be plain, from the material cited, that Aquinas gives the impression of inveterate anti-Platonism: Platonic doctrines are for him either poor inferences, or based on false premisses, or they are loosely worded expressions of truths better stated in quite another language. But it will also be plain that his picture of Plato and Platonism rests throughout on Aristotle's hostile characterization, in which it is conceived as the unnecessary postulation of a second world of entities set alongside the good material particulars that we are all so sure of, and that we daily see and handle, new entities which make no difference to, and throw no light on, what we thus see and handle, since they are held to be quite apart from them. Whereas the real point of Platonism is that, beside the true being of the Eide, there is simply no room for the material particulars in question, or for the gross form of cognition which supposedly establishes their being, much less for the matter supposed to underlie them, for which Plato has absolutely no place at all. The truth of these matters is only that Eide are instantiated, and that we, instantiating thought, thereby instantiate the cognition of these Eide. Eide have of course the relation of Principles to their instances, and to the instances of the knowledge of them: they have the immense prerogative of *being* the very things of which their instances are only the cases. And Eide themselves yield what prerogative they have to their own First Principle of Unity or Goodness, which they in their turn instantiate rather than specify, so that the *esse* of the Eide can very well be said to be, following Dionysius, the *superesse* of the Principle they exemplify. On a Platonic basis, therefore, the Eide have a sense distinct from, but necessarily related to, the qualifications and natures of their instances, and the Principle of the Eide has a sense which so utterly transcends even the specificity of the Eide, that it is rather the living possibility of the latter, than their unfolded difference. And in Platonism there is no doubt about these higher-order entities being active in their lower-order extensions, however much, in the case of instantiations, this may involve the mediations of previous instantiations ('Man begets man'): power and eidetic status go together, nor is there anything else to exercise power. All this never was understood by the man from Stagira, correctly as he might report the minutiae of Platonic teaching, and the man from Rocca Sicca had not the materials to alter the Aristotelian misinterpretation, which succeeding ages have likewise swallowed whole. But the Thomist theology can none the less be called truly Platonic, even if it quarrels with what Thomas *thought* was Platonism.

We shall here briefly consider a few points in this remarkable theology, which are all that are relevant for our purpose. Aquinas, as we saw, refuses to accept an establishment of the Divine Existence based on such a circumscription of His Essence as is proffered by Anselm. He is ready to point out the distinction between 'that than which nothing greater can be thought' as itself an object of thought, and the same as existing *in rerum natura* or reality: even if we include existence *in rerum natura* in an object of thought, it is still an existence *in rerum natura* which is itself only an object of thought, as opposed to an existence *in rerum natura* which itself exists *in rerum natura*. Aquinas is not, however, unwilling to concede that, *if* one could fully understand what it is to be God, one could at once see that He *must* exist *in rerum natura*, since His essence simply *is* His existence and since He cannot therefore not exist. The reason why we cannot make use of such an essentialist approach is simply that we do not have the full understanding of what it is to be God, which would make such an approach possible to us: the Divine Essence cannot itself be given to us, and is known only through its effects on us, through likenesses, and so on (*Summa contra Gentiles*, ch. xi). The main proof that there must be something of a Divine Nature has therefore to be an Aristotelian proof based on the empirical facts of motion, and on what we can see to be necessary in the ultimate source of such motion. In actual fact, however, Aquinas shows himself extraordinarily familiar with what we call the logical pattern of Godhead, what it takes to be God, even if he rightly distinguishes this from what can only be given to a beatific vision which utterly transcends natural cognition. In the beatific vision, Godhead will act directly upon us, and will not only be the Essence *that* we perceive, but will also be the Essence through which we perceive it (*Summa contra Gentiles*, ch. lix). But nothing prevents us, even in this life, from knowing what we may call the logical place of Divinity among other sorts and senses of being: this is in fact arguably what Aquinas means by the analogical knowledge of Godhead, of which he shows himself such an accomplished master. And this knowledge is, despite disclaimers, a knowledge in and through essences, and terminating in essences, and hence through and through Platonic.

God, first of all, simply *is* His Essence (*Summa contra Gentiles*, I, xxi): in other words, God and Godhead are the same, a theorem than which nothing more Platonic can be conceived. This leads on to another theorem: that God's existence does not differ from His Essence (*ibid.*, ch. xxii): in Godhead properly understood Existence is included. The kind of diremption between Essence and Existence that is meaningful in the case of an instance, meaningful even in the case of some specific or complex Essence, loses all meaning in this Sovereign Supracase. These theorems are made to follow, in Aquinas's exposition, from the prior theorem of the Divine Simplicity (ch. xviii), which in its turn is connected with the eternity necessary for a 'Prime Mover', but, considered apart from this no longer acceptable starting-point, this simplicity simply is another way of regarding a being whose essence it is to be, or whose being simply is this essence. Obviously, we are here not far from the Unity of the Second Hypothesis in the *Parmenides*, except that here we have a perfect coincidence of what in all other beings falls apart. And what is really the *reason* for this extraordinary conception is stated in the following theorem that, in this coincidence of Essence and Existence, lies the *perfection* that is, as Anselm showed, the inmost core of the notion of Deity (ch. xxviii): the something moreness that other Essences achieve by being embodied in actual cases, is intrinsic to the Supreme Essence, and is in fact only conferred on other Essences through it. They in fact only *have* the capacity which it alone truly *is*. The Being which God or Godhead essentially is, is not, however, Aquinas is careful to tell us, the real being or *esse formale* of all things in the world, for their *esse formale* is only to be the acci-dental instances of that which *is* essentially (ch. xxvi). Aquinas, in short, brilliantly preserves the *gulf* between creatures and Godhead in and through the very truth that they *derive* all they have and are from Godhead, and so, in a sense, fall entirely *within* it. The Goodness of God then simply consists in the coincidence of Essence and Existence which God is, and which rules out the alien intrusion in which evil consists. God is not merely good by participation in, or relation to, anything, but simply *is* His Goodness, and is also, in secondary fashion, the Goodness of all cases of Goodness (chs. xxxviii–xl). God, further, cannot be anything but unique, for if, *per impossibile*, there were a plurality of cases of Godhead, there would be nothing to distinguish one from the other, and so they would be one only (ch. xli). Nothing can be more Platonic than this argument.

It is, however, in Thomas's account of the Divine Intelligence and Will that the austerity of his Platonism really comes out. For while Plato, in his later Stoicheiology, tended to *subordinate* the Eide to a Supreme Principle or Principles which in some trans-cendental sense give rise to them, Aquinas takes the further step of making his Eide more or less vanish in his First Principle, so that even his Second Hypostasis or Word or Wisdom of the Godhead, which intellectually embraces all the Eide, becomes a more or less equivocally conceived, unreally isolated, aspect of Deity (see, for example, *Summa contra Gentiles*, ch. xii). God's intelligence amounts, on the view of Aquinas, not to any reception of alien patterns into Himself, but simply to the fact that He is the Essence He is, being an Essence being, as it were, a more consummate form of the reception of Essence involved in intelligent cognition. Being what one is thinking of is, in fact, the perfection that all thinking of anything tends towards, and so, in an entirely analogical and supereminent manner, God, the essential Existent and existent Essence, can be said to think Himself (ch. xlvi). Here the Divine Analogy is nothing unintelligible: we can see, in formal terms, just how and why this sort of 'intellection' both resembles, and also utterly differs from, our ordinary intellection. But God, in thus perfectly understanding the Essence He is, by simply being it, also understands, in virtue of His unlimited powers of instantiation, all the ways in which He might be instantiated. He understands them supereminently by being the power of them all. We should not, however, suppose that the natures of instantial things exist in clear distinction in this Divine Intelligence, as even Plato and Plotinus supposed: their existence is merely that of the infinite virtualities of instantiation involved in the one undivided Divine Essence (*Omnia autem quae Deus cognoscit una specie cognoscit quae est sua essentia* – ch. lv).

In much the same way, the Divine Will is simply the Divine Essence willing its own perfection in the consummated form of actually being it, and, in a secondary and non-necessary manner, willing this perfection to be instantiated in this or that imperfect set of actual instances by in fact *being* thus instantiated (chs. lxxv–lxxvi). God, being the perfect Essence, also is the active Power which can and does realize itself in innumerable, distinct, limited fashions, the creatures which dimly participate in, or imitate His perfection, without, however, being able to import real division into His essential simplicity (chs. vi–xiv). It is not necessary for us to pursue this fascinatingly skilful development any further: Aquinas is obviously performing the same ideal and real 'generation' of Forms from an ultimate source that Plato and the Platonists attempted: the hands, one may say, are Aristotle's, but the voice is that of Proclus or Plato. Only Aquinas goes further than Plato in making Essence, in its supreme form, the active cause of everything, in making it quite transcend ideal as well as real Being, and transcend Mind and Power and Will, as something better than all of them. Aquinas, we may say, represents a Platonism in which the Idea of Good has become absolutely all-in-all so that all inferior Hypostases are lost in its light.

The supreme merit of this medieval Platonism lay, however, in its preservation of the rational values and excellences from an arbitrary, instantialist taint. For a God who wills His own essence, and whose essence is Truth and Goodness, cannot will the self-contradictory or the intrinsically immoral, what is contrary to Reason or the 'Natural Law'. The free exercises of the Divine Power will, without constraint, fall *within* those essential limits. In later theologies those essential limits were violated, and God became an instantial being whose arbitrary edicts could determine everything, but in so doing also undermined all validity and all value. Only a sad travesty of religion can be built up on such a basis, and it is because Aquinas, with his essential Hellenism, derived ultimately from Plato, stood out against such a travesty, that he can be said, in a sense different from the ordinary, to have defended the Catholic, the Universal, Faith.

VI

From this point onwards our tracing of Platonic influences will have, with one exception, to reduce to a series of allusive impressions, in which we shall stress only what is essential to Platonism, its belief in the reality and power of Eide and eidetic connections, rather than any explicit interest in the letter of Plato. For us the Cambridge Platonists will be Russell and G. E. Moore rather than Cudworth and Henry More, and Hegel will rank as a Platonist rather than Ficinus or Thomas Taylor. In the two late medieval centuries that followed the century of Aquinas philosophy mainly swung away from Platonism in an instantialist direction, Scotus making Will, the faculty of the Last Instance, superior to Intelligence, the faculty of the Universal, and declaring universals to require an extra enrichment to sink to the full reality of the individual, an enrichment which, we may wryly observe, received such universal-sounding names as 'Thisness' (*haecceitas*) or 'Socraticity' (*Socratitas*). Belief in God became the will to believe in an indemonstrable Prime Instance, as acceptance of His commands became blind obedience to unjustifiable decrees. In Ockham the process goes further, and the Logic of the Instance, and the intuitive Confrontation with instances and the Realization of instances through acts of Volition, are subtly explored, while it is not seen that all this is an eidetic, and not an instantial enquiry, and that no adequate justification of any theoretical or practical principle can be achieved on instantial foundations. It is in Meister Eckhart, more or less a contemporary of Scotus and Ockham in time, that we must see, as in the case of John the Scot, one of the most perfect workings-out of the Platonic theology, inasmuch as in it the whole power to descend into instantiation not only becomes part and parcel of the Supreme Principle of Essence, but also becomes *necessary* to the Principle in question. It is in relation to creatures of which He is the indwelling Essence, that God is the utterly transcendent Essence that He also is, and His being therefore involves an essential procession or process from and to Himself, in which the *world*, as well as the personnel of the Blessed Trinity, plays an essential part. The Divine Essence, on Eckhart's view, further is the Divine Essence only in and for the *finite spirits* in which it reveals itself to itself, and its highest works are performed through the medium of human agency. This is the famous Germanic Theology, which Eckhart and his associates lived as well as uttered: it is not, however, remarkable that, unlike the orthodoxly worded utterances of Aquinas, twenty-eight of Eckhart's paradoxical-poetic pronouncements were condemned by a Papal Bull in 1329. The Platonism of Eckhart's Germanic Theology is in principle the same as the later Germanic Theology of Hegel: the latter was not, however, as a matter of history, borrowed from the former.

We shall merely touch on the explicit revival of Platonism in the fifteenth century which is associated with such names as Marsilio Ficino in his Florentine Academy producing his admirable translations of Plato and Plotinus, Pico della Mirandola, with his nine hundred Platonizing theses whose disputation was soon forbidden, and Nicolaus of Cusa, who identified the Divine Essence with the Same which admits of no Difference, who saw in Number the pullulating First Principle of Nature, and who also saw in the Divine Essence a Coming together of Opposites, which harks back to Dionysius, and ultimately to the Platonic *Parmenides*. And in the next century we shall merely mention, as more remotely Platonic, Bruno, who saw in the world the necessary self-unfoldment of an ultimate Unity, and Campanella who made the Divine Essence first generate the Eide, and then all inferior creatures through successive injections of Non-being. The immense movement of these centuries was, in part, a revolt against the intolerable burden laid upon thought by the categorizing and syllogizing genius of Aristotle; in part, however, it was a revolt against the stress laid on the particular *qua* particular which, though resisted by philosophers, was yet deeply characteristic of the whole Judaeo-Christian heritage.

In the next centuries, however, the part played by Platonic residues was not so much a mitigation of the arbitrary and instantial in religion, as a dilution of the drift towards a boundless empiricism of brute fact, through the injected belief in a framework of eidetic connections without which it would be impossible to learn anything from experience. Bacon refused to be a scholastic spider spinning nature syllogistically out of his intellectual entrails, but what he looked for in his methodical investigations was still Forms, Eide, entities of an undoubtedly Platonic stamp. Hobbes saw human society as the brute result of warring individual wills, but the result itself involved the emergence of a set of Laws of Reason or Nature, which both in their content and necessary emergence had something eidetic about them. Descartes, like Augustine, started with his solitary, subjective instantiality, which involved, however, a built-in reference to other instances of the same predicament, but soon he was accompanied by an Ideal perfection whose ancestry dated back to the Platonic Idea of Good, and, from this, justification descended on a host of propositions connecting various 'simple natures' with one another, as well as on various deeply-set natural likelihoods not unlike those in the Platonic *Timaeus*. Spinoza, despite explicit rejections of many Platonic concepts, may be said, none the less, to have made the eidetic order, and its principles, so all-pervasive as to have left small room for an inexact realm of instantiation: the order of events in time did not for him differ from the sequence of propositions in a geometrical proof. And Leibniz, we may say, articulated the Eidetic Cosmos into a beautiful total system of possible worlds, presided over by a Divinity who decided among them on grounds of a Goodness referred explicitly to the *Phaedo*, and for whom these worlds were each in their turn beautifully articulated into sub-worlds repeating the same general pattern of contents from a specific, subjective point of view, thereby constructing the first eidetic map of Subjectivity, Intersubjectivity and Shared Objectivity.

If we turn to the empiricists, the official stress, as in Ockham, is on sheer submission to the assaults of particular fact and existence, and the derivation of all universal patterns from their patterns. But the programme itself is built on eidetic insight into the origin of all ideas, rather than on the particular encounters in which, on its own showing, its origin should be placed, and it is carried out to include many insights into relations of essence to which the empiricist axioms do not serve as premises. Even in Hume there is an acknowledged body of 'relations of ideas', principally centred in the mathematical sciences, which are not readily squared with his empiricism, but there is also an unacknow-ledged body of such relations, such as the mysterious identity of 'the thought' which slides with ease or difficulty from one idea to another, and which is assumed to be paralleled by the existence of similar gliding 'thoughts' in the readers to whom Hume addresses himself. Hume's essays in radical empiricism serve only to bring out the eidetic framework of Consciousness as Such, its continuity, its unity-in-difference, its replication in separated but mutually recognitive centres, etc., etc. To have provided such a vivid refutation of the dogmatic exaggerations of his own position, and to have frankly acknowledged its self-refuting character in a remarkable Appendix, are among Hume's most magnificent achievements.

Kant, who followed on his heels, was the first to work out, with some fulness and great insight, the necessary gearing into one another, and the necessary mutual accommodation, of the forms of Subjectivity, on the one hand, and those of Objectivity, on the other, thereby completing that eidetic correlation of faculties of Mind with levels of Being which was first attempted in Plato's *Republic*. Kant was, however, too much under the spell of empiricist dogmas to accept this correlation of Thought and Being for what it gave itself out to be, a necessity of Being which was also a necessity for Thought. He had to explain our power to anticipate the character of not as yet examined particulars on the assumption that we do not really possess such a power, that the encounters of sense were not true encounters with things as they are in themselves, but dreamt-up encounters with things built to suit our own intellectual requirements through processes whose descriptions are among the most addled passages in all philosophy. Strangely enough, Kant who despaired of giving an account of what things-in-themselves must be like, did not despair of correctly describing the complicated machinery and the un-witnessable workings through which seeming things come to be set before us. The crypto-psychologism and crypto-empiricism of these extraordinary doctrines, unique in their power to confuse and blur the insights with which they were associated, were set aside by Kant's successors, and in Schelling we have an Absolute that is as much expressed in natural Objectivity as in conscious Subjectivity, and a continual mirroring and remirroring of the structure of the one in that of the other. The Platonism of Schelling is at many points profound, but cannot be explored in the present context.

It is, however, in Hegel that we may see the supreme modern developer of the eidetic teaching of Plato: if Plotinus plays the part of the interpretative *Noûs*, the Second Hypostasis attendant on Plato as First Principle, Hegel may be said to have played the part of Soul, the Third Hypostasis, which brought all the eidetic structures to life, and worked out their necessary descent into the particularity of Nature and History. The attempt to 'generate' Specificity and Instantiality out of ultimate eidetic Principles, of course goes back to Plato's *Parmenides* and *Timaeus* and to the Unwritten Doctrines reported by Aristotle, but both Proclus, and later Meister Eckhart, had seen that we can only establish the complete parasitism and non-being of the Instance by making it something into which the Eidetic Order, and its Principle, necessarily goes forth, and from which it as necessarily returns, such going forth and returning being as much of the essence of the Eidetic Order as any intrinsic character that it has by contrast. And the very structure of the Eidetic Order then becomes an eidetic anticipation of the descent into Number and Particularity, a conceptual manœuvre which finally absorbs Particularity into the Eidetic Order, so that in all instantiation we can see nothing but that Order 'in action'. In other words, Universality is essentially active, and the only activity, and it essentially lives in its instantiations, and in the instantial cognition of the same, and is the Universality it is in and through such instantiations. It is this notion of the Concrete, Active Universal which is the central doctrine of the Hegelian system as of the Platonic.

Hegel, in the introductory *Phenomenology of Spirit*, leads up to his Absolute Idealism by both describing to his readers, and also leading them through, a series of successive illuminations called 'Shapes of Consciousness' in which they more and more come to recognize the presence of the same patterns which guide their minds in the phenomena of natural and social reality, until in the end, in various moral, religious and philosophical experiences, they realize the identity of the Principle of all these patterns, whether in their thought, or in the whole realm of being. Kantian fears of an ultimate inadequacy of the patterns of thought to the patterns of real being having melted away, we then embark on a Logic which is not merely a study of the Categories of subjective thinking, but of Being in all its superficial and deeper moods, and which is further described by Hegel as 'the presentation of God, as He is in His eternal essence, before the creation of Nature and finite Spirit' (Introduction to *The Science of Logic*, par. 21). But though thus metaphysically described, the Logic deals with nothing but the categorial structures of Quality and Number, of the Dynamic, the Dispositional, the Phenomenal, the Substantial and the Causal, and finally with the categorial structures involved in Propositions and Syllogisms, in the Mechanical and Teleological arrangements of material objects, and in the relations of Life and Consciousness to an environing objective world. Hegel's 'Greatest Kinds' are not, however, like Plato's, placed more or less on a level, but are seen as forming a Sequence, in which the more elementary and abstract have to be embraced in the later and richer, a procedure also followed by Plato in the *Timaeus*, where the ultimate Eide are those of Living Creatures, and the Eide of the Natural Elements only serve as the necessary materials of the former. Hegel's logical progression ends like Plato's in an Absolute Idea, which is that of Living Unity and Truth and Goodness, but which is more clearly conceived than in Platonism as only being itself in the absorption into self of an 'Other' which has at first the semblance of the wholly alien and disparate.

This absorption of Otherness into self which occurs on the

eidetic plane, then necessarily translates itself, in order to be what it is, and of course without temporal transition, into the immense self-alienation of the natural world, in which every instance lies inertly outside of every other instance, and appears to have nothing to do with what thus lies outside of it. The process through which there is this immense, eidetically necessary descent into instantiation, then leads to a gradual reduction of alienation and mutual externality in various physical and organic forms, where the Universal performs an ever more active, integrative role, until in the end the bonds of natural externality are broken altogether, and we have the Universal instantiated in the new, detached forms of Conscious Mind or Spirit. The Eternal Idea behind the whole process then abolishes and transforms natural objectivity, and finally, after working through various social and cultural forms, becomes fully present to itself in the self-consciousness of the Hegelian philosopher, who is for Hegel the highest embodiment of Absolute Spirit. It is not our aim to treat Hegelianism more fully in this place, but only to make plain its deep affinity with Platonism and its notional derivation from the latter. In both the Universal, and the Universality of Universals, occupy a supreme place, in both they are seen as being something active and concrete on which particular forms and instances wholly depend, rather than contrariwise, and in both they are seen as transcending both natural realities and conscious states of mind.

VII

From Hegel we may leap over the many confused, diversely wandering thought-movements of the most eclectic, syncretistic of centuries, the nineteenth, to the brilliant Platonism which flowered at its close and in the opening years of the following century, and which was in evidence both in Germany and in England. In the German world Franz Brentano in 1874 produced a 'Psychognosy', an eidetic study of the basic dimensions of conscious experience, strangely miscalled *Psychology from the Empirical Standpoint*. Based upon, but going quite beyond, the Aristotelian intentionalism of the Schoolmen, Brentano saw in states of mind alternative ways of directing oneself to objects different from oneself, a basically Platonic conception and an orientation which inspired immense analysis and discrimination and systematic interrelation of the species of conscious self-direction, as also of the species of objectivity which such self-direction apprehends or constitutes. These eidetic researches were carried further in the Psychology, the Value-Theory and the Object-Theory of Alexius Meinong (d. 1920), and, more famously, in the Phenomenology of Edmund Husserl (d. 1938), who anatomized Consciousness and the Objectivities to which Consciousness directs itself, and the processes through which Consciousness sets up every item and nuance in its world and in itself, and in the many fellow-consciousnesses essential to its consciousness of the world and itself, with a subtlety and a brilliance which sets him far above all the other philosophers of our age. The basic methodology that he followed is, moreover, at all times eidetic and Platonic.

Turning to England, the opening of this century witnessed the production of Bertrand Russell's datelessly excellent *Principles of Mathematics* (1903), which states the doctrine and the programme of which the *Principia Mathematica* of 1911 represented the more limping execution. In this work Russell saw all Logic and all Mathematics, and all present and future sciences in which a formal structure is discernible, as exhaustively derivable from a quite exiguous set of primitive ideas and principles, capable of further simplification and extension, and not as yet thought to be arbitrary linguistic creations or empty tautologies, but substantial certainties setting forth a framework for possible being and significant thought. He declared in the *Principles* (par. 4):

> By the help of ten principles of deduction and ten other premisses of a logical nature (e.g. 'implication is a relation'), all mathematics can be strictly and formally deduced, and all the entities that occur in mathematics can be defined in terms of those that occur in the twenty premisses. In this statement Mathematics includes not only Arithmetic and Analysis, but also Geometry, Euclidean and non-Euclidean, rational Dynamics, and an indefinite number of other studies still unborn or in their infancy.

And obviously, with the introduction of new concepts and definitions, as well as further axioms or hypotheses, 'these other studies' could be widened, and have in fact been widened, to include an axiomatized Biology, an axiomatized Psychology, whether of an intentionalist or a behaviourist stamp, an axiomatic Deontology and Axiology, and an axiomatic Theology whether of a Thomistic, Spinozistic or Proclean type, and even an axiomatized version of the Hegelian Dialectic (see, for example, M. Kosok's article in the *International Philosophical Quarterly* of 1966).

In all this the project of Russell agrees fully with the mathematicizing project that lay behind the mature thought of Plato, and the agreement went further, in that Russell articulated the realm of sense, of significant discourse and eidetic reality, into a vast, branching family of Platonic entities, all timelessly there, and all quite independent of the thought that apprehended them or that pieced them together. There were, in addition to Individuals, Propositions both True and False, and Propositional Functions harbouring gaps filled by the very queer entities known as Variables, which could serve as place-holders for ordinary constant Terms, there were Concepts, whether Predicative or Relational or Denotative, the last referring non-psychologically to objects in about eight different manners of which modern Quantification Theory recognizes only two, there were Classes-as-Many and Classes-as-One, and there were Aggregates reachable through enumeration without the benefit of common properties. The early thought of G. E. Moore, Russell's great contemporary and associate, was likewise brilliantly Platonic: not only did he populate his Universe with many of the entities distinguished by Russell, but he added to them the Good of Plato, conceived in a very unanalytic, Eleatic manner. And his system of Common-sense Certainties can not unreasonably be characterized, not as a mere rag-bag of things that we *happen* to know, but as a set of certainties that can be defended as constituting the categorial background of all reasoned knowledge: the certainty of a common world, of other persons with whom we share it, of an ordered past and of memory that reveals it, of sense-data that reveal material objects without compromising their essential independence, and of Ideal Meanings of different sorts that can be successfully pinned down by ordinary and extraordinary language, communicated to others, and put together in tentative 'analyses' of our ordinary notions and certainties. These Moorean certainties have much in common with those that form the background of Plato's writings and methods. And, in anticipation of much later work, we may here mention the pervasive Platonism of A. N. Whitehead, who worked with Russell on *Principia Mathematica* and was responsible for its later geometrical sections, and whose *Process and Reality*, published in 1930, is in many respects a modern version of the Platonic *Timaeus*.

The Platonism of the early twentieth century did not however survive the shock of the war which effectively maimed all Western civilization. In Europe, after this war, it passed over into an elaborately eidetic statement of predicaments too special to be of central interest to Platonists: the predicament of the Spiritual Peasant overwhelmed by modern commercial civilization, the predicament of the defenders of the finest of European cultures against the most bestial of encroachments, the predicament of the religious person prepared to believe something at the cost of any injection of nonsense, myth, etc., etc. The interest of such eidetic pathology is undoubted, but a Platonist would wish to see it as a set of παρεκβάσεις on a background of standard-setting, normal forms. And in England Platonism was practically dead in the second decade of the century. The spirit of Ockham, with its misplaced appeal to 'economy' in the conceptual realm – an 'economy' of course valuable in the sphere of empirical hypothesis – soon made short work of Russell's multitudinous array of types of entity. Most of these were held to be mere 'logical constructions', while the symbols that seemed to denote them had only a meaning in context, or a definition in use. It was thought that we could very well do with a very small number of types of ultimately simple entities – not unfortunately known to experience – linked together in a small number of types of simple fact. In more complicated forms of diction, the notion of a Class, a complex whole which was not really complex, nor really a whole, would prove less noxious than other seeming types of Platonic entity. The process of ontological decimation was accelerated by Russell's discovery of a whole crop of paradoxical propositions, generally involving some sort of direct or indirect self-reference, which can be shown, by accepted logical rules, to be true if they are false, and false if they are true. To a Platonist the presence of such maverick propositions and notions in discourse is profoundly interesting, and there would be no difficulty in making *ad hoc* restrictions to avoid their use in argument. To Russell, however, they had to be excluded as 'meaningless', which they certainly were not, but by their suspect character they cast a doubt on the entities referred to in them: the Propositions, Classes and Predicative Concepts that they seemed to concern.

It was, however, in Wittgenstein that the liquidation of Cambridge Platonism culminated. Rather like a mischievous child, he soon wrecked the structure that his teachers had laboriously built up in the course of two decades, under the impression that it represented *Philosophia Perennis*. The nature of Meaning was then set forth in three successive simplifications: Meaning consisted in the mere mirroring of the elements and structures of Fact in the elements and structures of Language, Meaning consisted in the array of tests necessary to justify the use of an expression in a sentence, Meaning consisted in the correct and justified use of expressions in situations where speakers have been *taught* that use by simple, public methods of teaching, in which showing, ostension, played a pivotal part. Necessary truths of essence became on these views mere reflections of the rules governing the use of expressions in our language, and were of profit only as guarding against the use of such expressions in a self-destroying or self-refuting manner. The examination of use, and the procedures by which use is taught, had, however, the further profit of exposing the senseless, idle use of expressions in statements and questions, of which the whole history of philosophy was full, and certainly that part of it that is concerned with Platonic entities, and their relations to ordinary things. One can use Platonic talk if one likes, but one cannot separate it from ordinary sense-giving procedures, which would make it equivalent to quite ordinary statements. And it is highly misleading, because it ignores the ever shifting, open use of words in varying contexts, which excludes from the start the sort of eidetic circumscription practised by Socrates and Plato.

It is not possible in this place to provide a Platonic refutation of Wittgenstein. Suffice it only to say that no Platonist could accept the inconceivably simplified accounts of the manner in which our basic terms are given meaning: however we arrived at our understanding of notions of great philosophical importance, notions such as Temporality or Infinity or Subjectivity or

Potentiality or Number etc., it was not in and through those simple performances, through which we are said to have been taught them. Not only are Wittgensteinian teaching-analyses inadequate: they are often painfully and grotesquely circular. In so far as we were taught such meanings by others, the teaching was a form of hinting and gesturing eked out by something more like Platonic reminiscence than Wittgensteinian ostension. The stress on ostension is in fact here a mere recrudescence of the old empiricism: that held that every idea must have originated in a corresponding impression, this holds that it must have originated in an act of public showing. The value of such radical empiricism is its complete self-refutation: whatever may be unclear, it is clear that none of our importantly basic meanings have been acquired in this manner.

We may, however, turn to another development which concerns Platonism, and which takes us right back to the beginnings of the nineteenth century, when Schleiermacher made a detailed study of the Platonic Dialogues the sufficient prerequisite of a true understanding and assessment of Plato. This approach meant that a mode of philosophical expression suitable to the vivid recreation of the inconclusive discourses of Socrates, and not, as such, fitted to express anyone's definite stance on any issue whatever, and persisted in by Plato mainly from habit, and from a besetting lack of certainty in regard to his central convictions, would be taken as the sole evidence of what he really thought and believed, and that the immensely strong evidence in Aristotle and elsewhere, that he had centrally significant Unwritten Doctrines not adequately reflected in the Dialogues, should be wholly set aside. It also meant that the centuries of impassioned interpretation of Platonism which began with Plotinus, and which were nothing beyond an attempt to make sense of the more exciting statements in Plato's Dialogues, should be likewise discounted. The notion of a two-tier Plato, who thought in terms of a programmatic mathematicization of the Eide, but wrote for the general public in a manner that harked back to Socrates, was thereby abandoned: whatever was not present in Plato's literary performances was held to be unPlatonic. So far did this restriction of Plato to the Dialogues go, that Zeller, in his great *History of Greek Philosophy*, could suppose that Aristotle's carefully documented accounts of Plato's central opinions only reflected senile aberrations of the great philosopher.

In the present century, with the increasing development of analytic empiricism, the movement has gone yet further. Attempts have been made to restrict the basic eidetic doctrines of Plato to a short 'Middle Period' in his life, in which the *Phaedo*, the *Symposium*, the *Republic*, the *Phaedrus* and on some views also the *Timaeus*, were written, while in later life Plato acquired advanced analytic convictions as to the semantic errors involved in the whole eidetic theory, and expounded these in the *Cratylus*, the *Parmenides*, the *Sophist* and other late Dialogues. These opinions shatter themselves against the demonstrably late date, indicated by many cross-references, of the *Timaeus*, and also against the solid weight of the testimony of Aristotle, whose picture of the points of doctrine central to Platonism cannot be set aside. This is especially clear since Harold Cherniss wrote his two vastly learned, stylistically delightful examinations of Aristotelian Platonism: *Aristotle's Criticism of Plato and the Academy* (1944) and *The Riddle of the Early Academy* (1945). These works only succeed in showing how incredible it is that Aristotle should have derived the doctrines he attributes to Plato from an incredibly perverse reading of the Platonic Dialogues taken alone, and that they should not represent the teaching that was actually current in the Academy when Aristotle joined it.

It is also clear, as a result of all the labours of those who have sought to base their conception of Plato's doctrine exclusively on the Dialogues and particularly on modern interpretations of the later Dialogues, that the Plato who emerges from these researches is not, after all, a deeply coherent thinker at all. The Dialogues are works of incredible philosophical merit, but only because, in addition to all they make explicit, they also hint at depths of insight that range far beyond what they say. If Plato's insights ended in the portentously inconclusive, confused fashion that the Dialogues alone would suggest, he would deserve the relegation that Popper and some others have meted out to him. The enigmatic doctrines sketched by Aristotle certainly involve many problems, but their unriddling is by no means as difficult as has been believed. Taken together with the general view to be found in Plotinus and Proclus, they alone afford us an integrated, worthy view of a great philosopher.

VIII

As to the merits of Platonism as an ultimate view of reality we may here say a few final words. Platonism, we may say, is an attempt to understand the world in terms of a single notion or principle, which we may call that of Universality or Eidetic Sense as Such. For Platonism the Particular or the Instance is wholly parasitic upon some well-rounded Sense, some Eidos, that it, with greater or less imperfection, instantiates, and that could be instantiated in other instances as well. These Eide have their own eidetic relations which can be explored in Dialectic, and these relations include, after a fashion, their relations to all the deviant forms that are yet part of their sense, and to the absurd or worse than absurd forms that they wholly exclude. But the Eide are not the last word in the ideal structure, and their structure and interrelations and relations to instances, themselves instantiate Principles of higher order, the most august of which is Unity as Such, Goodness-Beauty-Measure as Such, Eidetic Pattern as Such, the Supra-Essence instantiated in all specific essences, and through them present in even the most deviant and misshapen particulars, and also instantiated in all patterns of Mind and Subjectivity, and through them in all thoughts, sensations and instantial experiences, however remote from the ideal. The whole philosophy of an Ideality, a generic, inclusive Eidetic Sense, which none the less goes forth, and must go forth, to the most abandoned reaches of instantiation, makes its appeal to us, not merely as a unified logical pattern, but as something that echoes our 'idealism' in the non-technical, value-tinged sense of the word. It is not a matter of shame to see in this value-tinged 'idealism' the ultimate recommendation of Plato's eidetic theory. We are at all times exposed to an influence which makes for purification and elucidation of content, and for a universality which more utterly pervades and unifies whatever falls under it, and it is not wrong to say that this Principle moves us at all times, though particularly in exercises of penetrative thought, or detached enjoyment of surface appearance, or deeply engaged practical endeavour. That everything in the world exists to make sense in terms of dominant, eidetic universality, is a way of regarding things that itself makes supreme sense, and leaves nothing unexplained. It is certainly something in terms of which we, as largely frustrated instances, can not only hope to think, but also to live, in this vanishing instantial world.

The Platonic Idealism has, however, its main rival in the Idealism which encapsulates all ideal meanings in a comprehensive Subjectivity, which, whether it be called the subjectivity of God, or the Transcendental Ego or what not, is very often a real, concrete thinking being of some kind, an instance of Cogitation rather than Cogitation Itself. Platonism has nothing to say against the eidetic hypostatization of Thought Itself: it recognizes, with Proclus, that there are noeric as well as noetic universals, patterns of subjective awareness as well as correlated patterns of objectivity, and that the former can be integrated into a supreme pattern of Mind as Such. It has also nothing to say against the belief in a Supreme Soul or Word or Logos which perhaps instantiates Consciousness in some supremely inclusive, directive manner, and which prevents the frail ship of eidetic Sense from foundering among the rocks, shallows and confused drifts of instantiation. But for Platonism there is some inherent imperfection in the conscious as much as the unconscious instance, which does not vanish however much the conscious instance increases its vision or its strength. A Mind or a Soul is always one Mind or Soul among others; incapable of rising to the categorially different eminence of being Mind as Such. Hence the best Christian theologians have always located Godhead beyond God, the Divine Dark beyond the luminous creative Wisdom, and similar distinctions have often been made by the theologians of the East. We may therefore hold that, if we are to be idealists, it is better to be idealists of the Platonic, than of the transcendentally subjective, or theistically subjective, type.

Platonism has, however, other rivals of a non-idealistic stamp, and of these the philosophical orientation which refuses to absolutize anything is, at first sight, the most formidable. This is the philosophical orientation which is quite willing to adopt different principles in different fields, and to adopt a plurality of principles and methods in a single field, without attempting to reduce them all to something simple and single. It is the orientation which is quite willing to use eidetic insights in some fields, but which is crassly empirical in dealing with other questions, and which does not expect either its insights or its empirical findings to be all capable of being seen as radiating from a single centre, or as making a single structure or sense. Aristotelianism in antiquity, Scotism and Ockhamism in medieval times, and certain of the best forms of modern analysis, exemplify the orientation we are trying to characterize, and all are resolutely opposed to the speculative simplification or reduction or misplaced craving for universality. Philosophical problems, it is said by the most perceptive of such thinkers, are a widely diverse assemblage of difficulties: it is quite wrong to expect there to be one treatment which will solve or dissolve them all. There is nothing in the philosophical orientation just indicated which is inherently opposed to Platonism, except its wilful self-disassociation from the latter. There are problems of the middle distance which are best treated in isolation, and in terms of their own concepts and methods, and which would lose all their characteristic slant and force if removed to some generally blurring horizon. There is also a point at which an eidetic descent into particularity becomes altogether too unrewarding: Sartre may be able to conjure eidetic meaning into two eyes regarding each other through the same keyhole, but such confrontations are for the most part best seen as embarrassing accidents, over which no great eidetic pother should be made. It is not, however, feasible to give our sense-making instincts scope in the small, and to rein them in in the great. The same notional transformations which simplify and order special fields must necessarily tend to take place in our view of things as a whole. This is merely not seen when, for certain thinkers, disjunction, pluralism and absence of inclusive sense become themselves dogmas in terms of which the world at large is viewed. Thus Heidegger's comparison of human life to a series of tracks which momentarily meander about and then lose themselves in a forest, is not itself a tentative exploration of such tracks: it journeys along a well-paved highway of despair, towards a predetermined frustration. If one is going to be systematic, one might as well be systematically systematic, as in Platonism or some other absolutist system.

The most truly formidable rival of Platonism is not, however, any of the orientations we have mentioned, but the materialistic instantialism of a mechanistic science, which throughout makes the Works of Mind parasitic upon the Works of Necessity. This rival of Platonism might seem to be based throughout on eidetic absurdities: organized unity is to be explained by a chance relation among elements which involves no organization, temporal succession to be based on relations violating all the axioms which define temporality, conscious reference to objects to be based on the functioning of elements which in no sense can take cognizance of anything whatever, and so on. A certain structure of a molecule can reproduce with exactness the lineaments and personal traits of an Aristotle, the time in which we make our vital decisions could run backwards, or be something long past on a suitably chosen standard of reference, an arrangement of neurones which neither know or care about their own electric potential, or the conduct of their neighbours, can mediate the most far-flung, intelligent comparisons or the most penetrating insights. All these monstrous basings of high-grade eidetic connections on the lowest-grade interactions of dumb particulars, go against the grain of reason: only there are more 'facts' that can be interpreted to tell in their favour than can leave us entirely without a qualm. That those who report or interpret these facts are incoherent thinkers does not wholly make for our comfort: the world, we feel, may be as incoherent as they are.

That a close attachment of Sense to Symbol or Sense-vehicle can be used to explain the apparent entanglement of the eternal Eide with mechanical arrangements, that work for them or against them, can, of course, be accepted by the Platonist. An arrangement of molecules or a process of neurones may well be the Means through which certain eidetic patterns instantiate themselves, whether in external reality or in the Soul's inner discourse. Our deep slavery to such 'Means', and the possibility of their manipulation by barbarized scientists and politicians, remains, however, the gravest of philosophical and practical problems, far graver than any that Plato and Aristotle, with their belief in the freedom of thought from bodily instrumentation, ever encountered. The present work cannot deal with the issues raised by such a barbarized science and politics, which may well discover and abuse more and more of the mechanistic truths which are all that they know how to look for and use. Platonism can at least counter them by a supreme argument which, like all supreme arguments, is practical rather than purely theoretical. If, *per impossibile*, the mechanistic views of a barbarized science should turn out to be the proveable truth of things, this would be a truth by which we, as practical, inventive, value- and pattern-oriented beings, could not live, and on which we should have, in all but the lowest instrumentalities, to turn our backs. Truth of this type would neither be worth knowing or applying, and the suasions of a Nocturnal Council might not be too much in order to secure its suppression. These suggestions need not, however, be taken too seriously. For the science which sees all things in terms of manipulative mechanism is arguably the product of a transient, manipulative phase of human society, which, even as we think and write, is busily in process of destroying itself, and creating an order in which the unified and the purposive will have as irreducible and as firm a place as the mechanically conditioned and manipulable. In the infinitely well-ordered, stably progressive societies of the future, something like Platonism may well dominate science and practice, and the figure of Plato, with his index finger pointing skywards, and the *Timaeus* under his arm, may very well occupy the same central place that he takes up in Raphael's *Schools of Athens*.

APPENDIX I

TRANSLATED PASSAGES ILLUSTRATING PLATO'S UNWRITTEN DOCTRINES

1 Diogenes Laertius, III, 46.

Plato's pupils were Speusippus of Athens, Xenocrates of Chalcedon, Aristotle of Stagira, Philip of Opus, Hestiaeus of Perinthus, Dion of Syracuse, Amyclus of Heraclea, Erastus and Coriscus of Scepsis, Timolaus of Cyzicus, Euaeon of Lampsacus, Pytho and Heracleides of Aenus, Hippothales and Callippus of Athens, Demetrius of Amphipolis, Heracleides of Pontus and many others, among whom were two women, Lastheneia of Mantinea and Axiothea of Phlius who, Dicaearchus tells us, affected masculine ways. Some say that Theophrastus was among his auditors. Chamaeleon says, and Polemo agrees, that the orator Hyperides and Lycurgus attended him.

2 Aristoxenus, *Elements of Harmony*, II, 30-1, Meibom.

Aristotle was wont to relate that most of those who heard Plato's Discourse (ἀκρόασις) on the Good had the following experience. Each came thinking he would be told something about one of the recognized human goods, such as Wealth, Health or Strength, or, in sum, some marvellous Happiness. But when it appeared that Plato was to talk on Mathematics and Numbers and Geometry and Astronomy, leading up to the statement that the Good was Unity (ὅτι ἀγαθόν ἐστιν ἕν), they were overwhelmed by the paradox of the whole matter. Some then pooh-poohed the whole thing and others were outraged by it,

413

3   Simplicius on Aristotle's *Physics*, 187a 12.

Alexander says that 'according to Plato the One and the Indefinite Dyad, which he spoke of as Great and Small, are the Principles of all things and even of the Eide themselves. So Aristotle reports in his work *On the Good*'. One might also have got this from Speusippus and Xenocrates and the others who attended Plato's Lecture on the Good. For all of them wrote down and preserved his opinion and say that he made use of these same Principles. It is very likely that Plato made the One and the Indefinite Dyad the Principles of all things, since this was the doctrine of the Pythagoreans whom Plato followed at many points. And Plato made the Indefinite Dyad a Principle of the Ideas also, calling it Great and Small to signify Matter. . . .

Aristotle, *Metaphysics*, 987a 29–988a 17.

After the philosophies we have mentioned, the Platonic approach arose, following the Italian Pythagorean philosophy in most respects, but adding certain characteristic doctrines of its own. Having been made familiar from youth with Cratylus and the Heraclitean opinions – to the effect that all sensible things are in flux and that knowledge of them is impossible – he adhered to these views even in later life. Socrates meanwhile was concerning himself with moral issues, in utter neglect of Nature as a whole, and was in quest of universals in the moral sphere, and was the first to turn men's minds in the direction of definitions. Plato accepted his approach but was led by it to think that it must be concerned with things other than the sensible. For it is impossible to formulate a general definition of any sensible thing, since all is in flux. These other entities he called Ideas, and held that sensible things lie beyond them and are called after them. For it is in virtue of Participation that the many things having the same name share this name with the Eide. The term 'Participation' represented a mere change of name. For the Pythagoreans had made things *be* through an Imitation of Numbers, whereas Plato said it was by Participation, making a change of name. But what such Participation or Imitation of the Eide might be, both left unexplained.

This passage makes clear that it was the Pythagorean, i.e. the mathematical affiliations of Platonism that first struck Aristotle when he joined the Academy in 367. It also makes plain that the criticism of the flux-doctrine, while most clearly stated in fairly late writings like the *Cratylus* and the *Theaetetus*, went back to Plato's earliest development. It also makes plain how subordinate the ethical analyses of Socrates had become for the Academic Plato.

> In addition he placed the Objects of Mathematics beyond Sensibles and Eide, and in between them, differing from Sensibles in being eternal and immoveable, and from Eide in being many alike, whereas each Eidos is one alone.

This clear statement is of the highest authority, and counts for more than all the hints and evasions of the Dialogues. It tells us what Plato really thought and taught. And it makes perfect sense.

> And since the Eide are the causes of other things, he thought that their Elements would be the Elements of all other things. For Matter the Great and the Small were his Principles, for Substantial Being (οὐσία) the One. From these Principles through a participation in Unity, the Eide or Numbers came into being. For that the One is a substantial Reality, and not something else of which Unity is predicated, they held very much as the Pythagoreans did, and that Numbers were causes of the substantial Being of other things was also similar to the Pythagorean doctrine. But to turn the one Infinite of the Pythagoreans into a Dyad, and to make the Infinite consist of the Great and Small was peculiar to the Platonists. And Plato put the Numbers beyond sensible things, whereas they say that the things themselves are Numbers, and do not introduce Objects of Mathematics in between Numbers and things. The putting of Unity and the Numbers beyond things (as the Pythagoreans did not) and the introduction of the Eide arose out of the quest for definitions – Plato's predecessors knew nothing of Dialectic – and Plato made the Dyad be his Other (basic) Nature, because the Numbers, apart from the Primes, could be simply produced from it as from some plastic medium.

All these Aristotelian statements are authoritative, and tell us what Plato taught and thought in 367 and earlier. But their interpretation is, of course, difficult, and has been attempted in Chapter II above.

> But what happens is the opposite: it could not reasonably be thus. For the Platonists make many things out of their single Matter, and the Eidos generates once only, but evidently one table is made out of one lot of Matter, while the man who imposes the Eidos on Matter makes many tables. The same holds in the case of male and female. For the female is fecundated in a single connection, while the male fecundates many females. Yet these are modelled on our Principles.

Aristotle is perhaps pointing out, in this obscure objection, that most Eide point back recursively to prior Eide on which they are built, and only ultimately to the formless Great and Small. In the eidetic sphere, therefore, prior Eide in a sense serve as part of the Matter of posterior Eide, if Plato had chosen to think in terms of Matter at all. It is only when the Natural and Complex Numbers have all been evolved, that sheer spatio-temporal difference furnishes a basis for the multiplication of instantial tables and men. It would appear, therefore, that the generation of the Eide, each of which is unique and unlike any other, is not exactly analogous to the making of tables or the procreation of children, and Aristotle is pointing this out.

> Plato therefore declared himself thus on the matters in question. It is plain from what has been said that he made use of only two causes, the Cause of Essential Nature and the Cause which is Material – for the Eide cause the Essential Natures of other things, and the One causes the Eide. And as to the nature of the underlying Matter of which the Eide are predicated in the case of sensible things, but of which the One is predicated in the case of the Eide, it is plain that this is a Dyad, the Great and the Small. Plato further assigned a cause of Goodness and a cause of Badness to each of his Elements, one to one, and one to the other, something attempted by some of the earlier philosophers, such as Empedocles and Anaxagoras.

Aristotle brings out the often forgotten point that Indefinite Multiplicity and Badness are as much involved in the structure of the eidetic as of the instantial sphere.

5   Alexander on Aristotle's *Metaphysics*, 987b 33.

> Plato and the Pythagoreans made Numbers the Principles of Realities, since they thought that what comes first and is uncompounded is a Principle, and since Surfaces come before Bodies – things that are simpler than other things and that are not destroyed by the destruction of the latter, taking natural precedence over those other things – and since Lines by parity of reasoning come before Surfaces, and Points before Lines. What the mathematicians call Points they called Units (μονάδες), things wholly incomposite and preceded by nothing. But Units are Numbers, and Numbers are therefore the Primal Realities. And since for Plato the Eide are Primal Realities and the Ideas come before everything that is relative to them, and

owes its being to them – this he tried to prove in many ways – he said the Eide were Numbers. For if a simple Nature comes before what is relative to it, and nothing comes before Number, the Eide must be Numbers. He accordingly identified the Principles of Number with the Principles of the Eide, and made Unity the universal Principle of everything.

The Eide are the Principles of other things, and since they are Numbers, their Principles are the Principles of Number. These Principles he said were Unity and the Dyad. And since in Numbers we meet with Unity and with what surpasses Unity, and since this last is Many and Few, the origin of what surpasses Unity lies in the latter, and he made this the Principle of the Many and Few. The Dyad comes first after the One, containing both the Much and the Little in itself. For the Double is much, and the Half little, and both are contained in the Dyad. And the Dyad is opposed to the One, being divided, whereas the One is undivided.

Plato also tried to show that the Equal and Unequal were universal Principles both of self-existent things and their opposites, for he tried to reduce everything to these as being most simple. He connected Equality with the Unit, and Inequality with Excess and Defect. For Inequality is to be found both in the Great and the Small, in what surpasses and falls short. For this reason he spoke of his Dyad as indefinite, as being as such determined neither to what exceeds nor to what is exceeded, but as being indefinite and unbounded.

When given definition by the One, the Indefinite Dyad became the Numerical Dyad. This Dyad was a single Eidos, and the first of the Numbers. Its Principles were the Exceeding and the Exceeded, since both Double and Half are present in the first Dyad. The Double and Half are Exceeding and Exceeded respectively, but the Exceeding and Exceeded are not as yet Double and Half, and are therefore Principles of the Double. And since, when bounded, the Exceeding and Exceeded become Double and Half (for these are not indefinite any more than the Triple and the Third, or the Quadruple and the Quarter, or any other case of definite Excess), it must be the nature of Unity which effects this bounding (each thing being one since it is this definite thing). The Elements of the Numerical Dyad are therefore the One and the Great and Small. But this Dyad is the first Number, and so these are the Elements of the Dyad (and of every Number). Such, more or less, are the reasons why Plato made Unity and the Dyad the Principles of the Numbers and of all realities, as Aristotle tells us in *On the Good*.

This long-winded, unintelligent account none the less lifts the curtain on Aristotle's lost treatise *On the Good*, to which Alexander plainly had access, and on the Oral Teachings which that treatise reported.

6　Aristotle, *Physics*, 302b 34–303a 16.

> It is proper for a physicist to consider the Infinite, both whether or not it is, and, if it is, what it is. That it is an appropriate object of physical study is shown by the actual consideration of it. For all those who are thought to have made worthwhile contributions to Physics, have discoursed about the Infinite and all have made it a Principle of things, some, like the Pythagoreans and Plato, as something self-existent and a substantial reality, and not as an accident of anything else. But the Pythagoreans put the Infinite among sensible things (for to them Number did not exist apart), and said that what lay outside the Heavens was infinite, whereas Plato denied that there was any body outside of the Heavens, not even the Ideas, which were nowhere, but held, none the less, that there was an Infinite both in sensible things and in the Ideas. And the Pythagoreans identified the Infinite with the Even, for this, cut off and shut in by the Odd, gives things their infinity, as is plain by what happens in the case of Numbers, for when gnomons are fitted tightly round the One or stretching beyond it, in the latter case one gets a shape that is always different, in the former case one single shape.

7　Simplicius on Aristotle's *Physics*, 202b 36.

> Plato denies that the Ideas are beyond the Heavens, since they are not located in space at all, but he asserts none the less that there is an Infinite Element both in sensible things and in the Ideas. Aristotle says that Plato made the One and the Indefinite Dyad the Principles of sensible things in his discourses on the Good, but he also located the Indefinite Dyad in the noetic realm, and made the Great and Small into Principles there, saying they were a case of the Infinite. Aristotle and Heracleides and Hestiaeus and other friends of Plato were present at these discourses, and wrote down Plato's enigmatic utterances. And Porphyry, expounding their reports, has this to say about them in his writing on the *Philebus*:
> 'Plato made the More and the Less, and the Strong and the Mild, of the nature of the Infinite. For, wherever they are

present, and become intensified or reduced, they do not stand still nor set bounds to what shares in them, but progress into the indefinitely Infinite. The same is true of the Greater and Smaller, or, as Plato calls them, the Great and Small.

'Let us take a limited magnitude like a cubit and divide it into two parts, leaving the one half-cubit undivided, and dividing the other and adding it bit by bit to the undivided portion: we shall then have two parts of the cubit, one proceedingly infinitely towards increased Smallness, and one towards increased Bigness. For we shall never reach the Indivisible by such partial division, since a cubit is continuous, and a continuum always divides into divisibles. This gapless segmentation reveals a certain Infinite Nature locked up in the cubit, or rather more than one such Nature, the one proceeding towards the Great, the other towards the Small. In these the Indefinite Dyad shows up as constituted by a factor (μόνας) which tends towards the Great and a factor which tends towards the Small.

'These properties are found both in continuous bodies and in Numbers. The first Number is the even Number Two, and in the nature of the Even both Double and Half are embraced, the Double being in excess and the Half in defect. Excess and Defect are therefore present in the Eide. The Dyad is the first among even Numbers, but in itself it is indefinite, and receives bounds by participating in Unity. For the Dyad is limited in so far as it becomes a single Eidos. Unity and the Dyad are therefore the Elements of Number, the one limiting and formative, the other indefinite in its Excess and Defect.'

This is more or less what Porphyry says in the cited work, setting forth in order the enigmatic utterances made at the seminar (συνουσία) *On the Good*, and maintaining that these were perhaps in accord with what was written down in the *Philebus*.

And Alexander himself has written as follows in agreement with the statements of Plato in his talks *On the Good*, as reported by Aristotle and the other friends of Plato:

'Plato was in quest of the Principles of real things and considered that Number came before all other things in nature, for the limits of Lines are Points, which are Units having position, and without Lines one can have neither Surfaces nor Solids, whereas Number can exist without these. Since then Number came before all other things in nature, he thought it to be the Principle of all, and the Principles of the first Number to be the Principles of all Numbers. But the first Number is the Dyad, whose Principles he said were the One and the Great and

Small. Being a Dyad, it holds both Multitude and Fewness in itself. In so far as there is Doubleness in it, it includes Multitude – for the Double is a case of Multitude and Excess and Magnitude – and in so far as Halfness is in it, it includes Fewness. Excess and Defect and the Great and the Small are accordingly in it. But, inasmuch as each of its parts is a Unit, and it itself is the single Eidos of Duality, it shares in Unity. He therefore said that the One and the Great and Small were the Principles of the Dyad. He called it the Indefinite Dyad in so far as it shared in the Great and Small, or the Greater and Smaller, and so was more or less. For these go on expanding or contracting unceasingly, and in progression towards the indefinitely infinite. Since then the Dyad is the first of the Numbers, and Its Principles are the One and the Great and Small, these are the Principles of all Number. But Numbers are the Elements of all other things. So that the Principles of all things are the One and the Great and Small (or Indefinite Dyad). And each of the Numbers, to the extent that it is this definite single Number, shares in Unity, but to the extent that it is divided and is a multitude, in the Indefinite Dyad. Plato also said that the Ideas were Numbers, and therefore plausibly made the Principles of Number be the Principles of the Ideas. But he said the Dyad was of the nature of the Infinite, since neither the Great and Small nor the Greater and Smaller have bounds, but involve the More and Less, which go on to infinity.'

8   Aristotle, *Physics*, 206b 16–20, 27–33.

There is therefore a potential Infinite by Addition which is, as we have said, after a fashion the same as an Infinite by Division. For it will always be possible to lay hold of something lying outside of it, without however exceeding every magnitude, just as in division one can always go beyond every magnitude in smallness. . . . For this reason Plato made his Infinities two in number, since it is possible to go beyond something and go on infinitely both in the direction of increase and that of diminution. But having thus set up two Infinites Plato fails to use them. For in the case of Number there is neither an Infinity by Diminution, since the Unit is the smallest element, nor yet an Infinity by Increase, since Plato constructs Numbers only up to the Decad.

Aristotle supposes that the numerical analysis of the Eide amounts to their simple identification with Natural Numbers, and that it does not extend to cover the Ratios and many-dimensional Patterns, which he himself introduces as possibly covered by the analysis, and with which Plato's practice accords. He also misinterprets the restriction of the Numbers to the Decad (= the Tetractys), which is a doctrine of basic numerical dimensions, as a doctrine concerning the Natural Numbers.

9   Aristotle, *Metaphysics*, 1073a 3–5, 13–21.

> It is clear from what has been said that there is an eternal, unmoved Substance, separated from sensible things. . . . But whether one such Substance must be posited or many, and how many, is what we must be clear on, and we must also remember the positions of others, inasmuch as they said nothing or nothing clear about such numbers. The theory of Ideas has no special consideration of the problem, but at times talks of such Numbers as infinite, at other times as bounded by the Decad. But as to the question why this should be the Number of the Numbers they devote no demonstrative care.

This passage shows that the restriction of the Eide within the Decad was not the fixed Academic dogma that some have taken it to be. And Plato did devote some 'demonstrative care' to connecting the numbers 1, 2, 3 and 4 (which add up to 10) with the basic dimensions of Being.

10   Aristotle, *De Anima*, 404b 16–27.

> In the same manner Plato in the *Timaeus* makes the Soul out of the Elements. For like is known by like, and things arise from their Principles. In the same way in the discourse On Philosophy it was laid down that the Living Creature Itself came from the Idea of Unity Itself together with the first Length, Breadth and Depth, and other things in similar fashion. And in yet another fashion they make Mind or Intuition be the One, Knowledge the Dyad (since it proceeds in a single line to one point), Opinion the Number of the Surface, and Sensation the Number of the Solid. For Numbers are said to be the Eide themselves and the Principles and arise out of these Elements. Things are judged by Intuition, Knowledge, Opinion and Sensation, and these Numbers are the Eide of things.

The importance of this passage lies in its application of arithmetical and dimensional concepts to the forms of Subjectivity in precisely parallel fashion to their application to Objectivity. The Eide develop themselves perspicuously out of Pure Unity, but in four tiers of dimensional complexity, and the corresponding structures of Mind are simply the ways in which these four tiers become perspicuous. The passage, of course, poses endless further problems.

11   Philoponus and Simplicius on the above.

Aristotle here gives the name 'On Philosophy' to his treatise *On the Good*. In this treatise Aristotle says what went on at the unwritten Seminars of Plato. The book is genuinely Aristotelian. He there tells us the opinion of Plato and the Pythagoreans regarding real things and their Principles.

By 'On Philosophy' he means what he wrote down from the Platonic seminars On the Good. In such writing he sets down Pythagorean and Platonic opinions on real things.

12   Aristotle, *Metaphysics*, 1085a 7–14.

In the same way difficulties arise in regard to the things which are posterior to Number, the Line, the Surface, and the Solid Body. For some manufacture them out of species of the Great and Small, Lengths out of the Long and Short, Surfaces out of the Broad and Narrow, and Bodily Masses out of the Deep and Shallow. These are the species of the Great and Small. And the Principle of such things which corresponds to the One is differently described by different Platonists.

13   Pseudo-Alexander on the above.

He tells us what are the later Kinds of Number, the Long and Short, Broad and Narrow, Deep and Shallow. Since we wish to deduce Magnitudes from these two Principles, he says that the Line receives Length and Shortness from this Dyad, the Surface receives Breadth and Narrowness from it, and the Solid Depth and Shallowness from it. Length and Shortness and the rest are obviously meant to be species of the Great and Small in the Indefinite Dyad. But he tells us that not all thinkers brought in Unity in the same manner, but some held that the Numbers themselves imposed species on Magnitudes, the Dyad on the Line, the Triad on the Surface, the Tetrad on the Solid. This is what Aristotle says of Plato in his *On Philosophy*, for which reason he here sets forth the opinion of these persons very briefly and pithily. Some Platonists, however, made the specification of Magnitudes depend on participation in Unity.

14 Aristotle, *Metaphysics*, 1028 16–28.

It seems to some that the limits of Body, such as Surface and
Line and Point and Unit, are Substances and more so than
Bodies and Solids. And some think that there is nothing
substantial beyond the sensuous sphere, but others that there are
several eternal and more real Substances, as Plato supposed that
the Eide and the Objects of Mathematics were two sorts of
Substances, while a third was the Substance of sensible bodies.
Speusippus believed in yet more Substances beginning with
Unity, and assigned Principles to each sort of Substances, one
for Numbers, one for Magnitudes and one for Soul. And in this
way he extended the range of Substances. Some held that the
Eide and the Numbers were of the same nature, and that others
followed on them, Lines and Surfaces, until one came to the
Substance of the Heavens and sensible things.

Aristotle here distinguishes Plato's views from those of Speusippus,
and dwells on the gradations of Being recognized by Plato. But he
has not fully understood that for Plato the Eide were much more
absolutely real, ontically ontic, than the other so-called Substances,
which only had Being in a secondary and derivative sense.

15 Aristotle, *Metaphysics*, 1090b 13–1091a 14, 23–9.

One might, however, be a little less complacent and inquire into
the implications of the fact that, in the case of Number generally
and the Objects of Mathematics, prior things contribute nothing
to what comes after them. For, if Numbers did not exist, Magnitudes would still be there for those who believe only in the Objects
of Mathematics, and if Magnitudes did not exist, there would still
be Souls and sensible bodies. But the appearances belie any view of
Nature as a series of episodes like a bad tragedy.

The reference in this passage is to Speusippus.

The believers in the Eide avoid this difficulty, for they construct
Magnitudes out of Matter and Number, Lengths out of the Dyad,
Surfaces perhaps out of the Triad, Solids out of the Tetrad or
out of other Numbers – it makes no difference. But are these
Magnitudes Ideas, or what is the manner of their being, or what
do they contribute to things? Nothing at all, as the Objects of
Mathematics contribute nothing. But neither is there any theorem
regarding them unless one is prepared to change the Objects
of Mathematics and invent opinions of one's own. For it is not

hard to lay down what one likes by way of hypotheses and
then string out a long set of conclusions. People who thus
assimilate Mathematical Objects to Ideas go astray.

The last reference in this passage is to Xenocrates who tried to
identify Mathematical Objects with Eide.

But the first Platonists who distinguished two sorts of Numbers,
eidetic and mathematical, are quite unable to explain how and
from what source Mathematical Number arises. For they place
it in between Eidetic and Sensible Number. But if it springs
from the Great and Small, it will be the same Number as that
of the Ideas – for from what other Great and Small will Plato
construct the Magnitudes? – but if he postulates some other
source, he will be multiplying his Elements. And if Unity is the
Principle of both sorts of Number, it will be common to both,
and we shall have to ask how (according to Plato) Unity can be
thus twofold since Number cannot arise otherwise than from
Unity and the Indefinite Dyad. All these are unreasonable theses,
in conflict with one another and the likelihoods, and they seem
to contain something like the Simonidean 'circumlocution', as
when slaves go on and on without saying anything sensible. It
would seem that even our elementary Great and Small cries
out at the way it gets dragged about. For it can generate no
Numbers except those got from Unity by doubling. It is,
moreover, an impossibly strange thing to assign an origin to
things that are eternal. . . . They say there is no generation of
Odd Number, so that there must plainly be a generation of
Even Number. And some construct the first even Number from
unequals, the Great and Small, when these have been equalized,
so that, on their view, Inequality exists prior to such
equalization. For, if Great and Small had always been
equalized, they could not previously have been unequal –
nothing being prior to what has always been – so that it is
plain that they do not generate Number as a theoretical fiction.

Equalization, finding the just right point where the excess of
Greater over this point is equal to this point's excess over the Lesser,
is the source of the first even Number Two. It is obviously a different
sort of Equalization, perhaps given a different name and certainly not
understood by Aristotle, which pins down the first Odd Number
Three between Two and Four, and which operates in similar fashion
in the generation of all the Prime Odd Numbers. Following Robin,
we have talked of a 'splitting the difference' in this case of Equalization.

16   Simplicius on Aristotle's *Physics*, 192a 3.

Since Aristotle frequently says that Plato spoke of Matter as the
Great and Small, one must note what Dercylides, according to
Porphyry, has written in the XIth Book of his *Philosophy of Plato*,
where Matter is under discussion. Dercylides, Porphyry says,
cited a statement from a book on Plato by one Hermodorus,
Plato's friend, from which it is clear that Plato put Matter in the
class of the Infinite and Indefinite, and showed it to be one of the
things that admit of the More and the Less, among which the
Great and the Small are to be reckoned. His statement runs:
   'Of realities some, he says, are self-existent, like Man and Horse,
some relative to other things (πρὸς ἕτερα), of which some stand
relatively to Opposites, as Good to Bad, and others in comparison
with something (ὡς πρός τι) and of these last some are definite,
others indefinite.' He continues: 'The things that are called
Great in comparison with the Small, all involve the More and
the Less. For it is possible to be yet greater and yet smaller *in
infinitum*. In the same way being broader and narrower, or
heavier and lighter, and all such comparatives will go on
infinitely. But what is said to be equal and abiding and
harmonized has nothing of the More and the Less in it, but
rather their opposites. For one case of Inequality is more
unequal than another, one case of Motion more mobile than
another, one case of Discord more discordant than another, so
that all, with the exception of one element, that falls on either
side of such relations, admits of the More and the Less. All this,
in virtue of a negation of Being, can be said to be unstable,
shapeless, boundless and unreal. For such negativity there is
neither Principle nor Essence, but it rushes about in a
certain unjudgeable condition. . . .'

17   Sextus Empiricus, *Against the Mathematicians*, X, 248–83.

Since Number is also one of the things that go yoked with Time,
it being impossible to measure Time except by counting hours,
days, months and years, it seems fit that we, having completed
our study of Time, should also treat of Number, and that
particularly since the wisest of natural philosophers attribute so
great a power to Numbers as to think them the Principles and
Elements of all things whatever. Such were those who hung about
Pythagoras the Samian.
   These men say that genuine philosophers should be like
linguists who first investigate the expressions of which speech

consists, and then, since such expressions consist of syllables,
first consider these syllables, and then, since from the
analysis of syllables come the letters of written speech, first
investigate these letters. Just so the Pythagoreans say that the
philosophers who really wish to investigate Nature as a
whole, should first examine the things in which that whole has
its analysis.

To make the Principle of all be something phenomenal is a bad
move in Physics. For everything phenomenal must be constituted
by things which are unapparent; what is constituted out of this
or that, cannot be a Principle, but only what constitutes it.
Phenomenal things cannot therefore be said to be the Principles
of the whole, but only what enters into the constitution of
phenomena, while not being itself phenomenal. They
therefore assume the Principles of things to be occult and
unapparent, though not in the common manner. For those who
make atoms or homoeomeriae or massive points (ὄγκοι) or
rationally conceived Bodies be the Principles of things, were
right in one respect but wrong in another. They were right in
making their Principles unapparent, but wrong in making them
corporeal. For as rationally conceived, unapparent Bodies
[atoms etc.] take precedence over those that are sensible, so
incorporeal things serve as Principles to rationally conceived
Bodies. And with reason. For just as the elements of expressions
are not themselves expressions, so the Elements of Bodies are
not bodies. But they must either be Bodies or incorporeal. There
is therefore every reason to hold them to be incorporeal.
It is no good saying that atoms may be everlasting, and so,
though bodily, may serve as Elements of the whole. For those
who first made homoeomeriae or point-masses or indivisible
minima their Elements, also made them everlasting, so that
atoms are in no better position as Elements than they are.
Suppose that we grant everlastingness to the atoms. Then, just
as those who believe the Cosmos to be ungenerated and
everlasting, nevertheless try to find out the first Principles that
constitute it, so we, say the Pythagorean physicists, try to find
out the elementary constituents of these everlasting, rationally
conceived Bodies. These constituents must either be Bodies or
incorporeal. And we should not say they are Bodies, since it will
then be necessary for them also to be constituted by Bodies,
and so an infinite thought-regress will leave us with a whole
which has no Principle. We must therefore hold that rationally
conceived Bodies have incorporeal constituents, as Epicurus also
recognized, saying that Body was dreamt up through the

crowding together of Shape, Size, Resistance and Weight.

It is clear from what has been said that the Principles of rationally conceived Bodies must be incorporeal. But it is not the case that if certain incorporeal entities preside over Bodies, these must necessarily be the Elements of things and first Principles. For consider how the Ideas, which Plato deems incorporeal, preside over Bodies, and how all that comes into being follows their pattern. But they are not the Principles of all Realities, since each Idea, taken by itself, is said to be one, but in company with another or others is said to be two or three or four, so that there is something which transcends their existence, and this is Number, through which other things have Unity, Twoness, Threeness and higher Numbers predicable of them. And Solid Shapes precede Bodies conceptually, having an incorporeal nature, but again they are not the Principles of all Bodies. For Surfaces precede them conceptually, since it is out of Surfaces that Solids are put together. But not even Surfaces can be regarded as the Elements of Being. For each of these is constituted by assembled Lines, and the Lines presuppose Numbers, in so far as the Figure made by three Lines is called a Triangle, and the Figure made by four Lines a Square. And since a simple Line is not conceived apart from Number, but, leading from one point to another, has connection with a Dyad, and all Numbers themselves fall under Unity, for the Dyad is one definite Dyad, the Triad one definite thing, the Triad, and the Decad one completion of Number. Starting from this the Pythagoreans made the Monad the Principle of Realities, for by sharing in it each thing that is is said to be one.

This Monad, conceived in identity with self, is thought of *as* a Monad, but, combined with self in the mode of Otherness (καθ᾽ ἑτερότητα), it produces the so-called Indefinite Dyad, since none of the counted and defined Dyads are the same, all being conceived by participation in the Dyad Itself, and so also as bearing witness to Unity. There are, accordingly, two ontological Principles, the Primal Monad, by participation in which all counted Monads are conceived as Unities, and the Indefinite Dyad, by participation in which definite Dyads are Dyads.

That these are in truth the Principles of everything the Pythagoreans prove variously. For of real entities some are conceived by way of Difference, some by way of Opposition, some by way of Relation. By way of Difference we conceive of self-existent things, substrates having their peculiar description, such as Man, Horse, Plant, Earth, Water, Air, Fire. Each of these we consider absolutely, and not in its relation to anything else. By way of Opposition we conceive things in virtue of their opposition to one another, such as Good and Bad, Just and Unjust, Profitable and Unprofitable, Holy and Unholy, Pious and Impious, Moving and Stationary, and other similar cases. By way of Relation we conceive things in relation to something else, such as Right and Left, Above and Below, Double and Half. For the Right is conceived in its relation to the Left, and the Left in its relation to the Right, the Below in relation to the Above and *vice versa*, and the same in other cases.

The Pythagoreans say things conceived in Opposition differ from things conceived in Relation. For in the cases of opposites, the destruction of one is the coming to be of the other, as in the case of Health and Disease, Motion and Rest. For the arising of Disease is the ceasing of Health, the arising of Health the ceasing of Disease, the existence of Motion the destruction of Rest and *vice versa*. The same argument holds of Pain and Painlessness, Good and Bad, and in general of all that have an opposed nature. But relatives involve the joint presence and removal of one another. For nothing is right unless something is left of it, and every double presupposes a half of which it is the double. In addition there is in general no mean of opposites, for example of Health and Disease, of Life and Death, of Motion and Rest. But in the case of things which have a relative determination, there is such a Mean. For the things determined as greater and less in relation to something may have a Mean in what is equal, and in the same way the Sufficient is the Mean of the More and Less, and the Well-tuned of the Sharp and Flat.

But these three Kinds of Being, that of things that exist by themselves, of things conceived as Opposites, and of things conceived relatively, must have a Kind ranged above themselves, which is first in Being since every Genus exists before the Species ranged under it. If this Genus is destroyed, all its Species go to destruction with it, but if a Species is destroyed, the Genus remains undismantled. The Species depends on the Genus and not *vice versa*.

The sons of Pythagoras then placed the One in a position of transcendence over the class of Things Conceived by Themselves. For it is through this One that this class has self-existence, so that each distinct entity is a single thing and can be contemplated on its own. And over the things spoken of oppositely, they placed as ruling Genus the Equal and Unequal. In these the whole nature of all opposites displays itself; the nature of Rest, for example, in an Equality which admits neither

of More or Less, and of Motion in Inequality, since it admits
of both of them. In the same manner what is natural is seen in
Equality – the summit cannot be surpassed – while what is
unnatural is seen in Inequality, since it admits the More and Less.
The same rule applies to Health and Disease, and to Straightness
and Crookedness. Relatives, however, fall under the Genus of
Excess and Defect. Great and Greater, Many and More, High
and Higher are conceived by way of Excess, whereas Small
and Smaller, Few and Fewer, Low and Lower are conceived by
way of Defect. But since things Self-existent, Opposite and
Relative are Genera that have been found to be subordinate to
other Genera, i.e. to Unity or Equality-Inequality or Excess-
Defect, we must consider whether those higher Genera cannot
be referred to yet higher ones. Plainly Equality is subsumed under
Unity – for Unity is the prime case of Self-equality – while
Inequality is seen in Excess and Defect, since unequal things are
those of which one exceeds while the other is exceeded. But
Excess and Defect are ranged under the account of the Indefinite
Dyad, since the prime Excess and Defect occurs among two
terms, the exceeding and the exceeded term. The highest
Principles of all therefore emerge as the First Monad and the
Indefinite Dyad.

From these Principles the Number One arose and the Dyad
which succeeded it, from the Prime Monad the Number One, and
from both Prime Monad and the Indefinite Dyad the Number
Two. Twice One are Two, and since there was not as yet a Two
or a Twice among Numbers, the Number Two arose out of the
Indefinite Dyad, and so was the offspring of this Dyad and the
Monad. In the same way the other Numbers were constructed
out of these, the One always setting bounds, while the Indefinite
Dyad doubled and so extended Numbers *in infinitum*.

For which reason they say that of these Principles the one
which has the character of an active cause is the One, whereas
that which has the character of passive Matter is the Dyad. And
in the same way in which they built up the Numbers which
came from these Principles, they built up the Cosmos and all
that is in it.

Plainly the Point is ranged under the rubric of Unity. For as
the Monad is indivisible, so also is the Point, and as the Monad
is a Principle in the case of Numbers, so the Point is a Principle
in the case of Lines. So that the Point has the logical position
of the Monad, whereas the Line is conceived under the Idea of
Duality. Both Dyad and Line are conceived through a
transition ($\mu\epsilon\tau\acute{\alpha}\beta\alpha\sigma\iota\varsigma$). And again, the breadthless Length

conceived between two Points is a Line. The Line therefore falls under the Dyad. The Surface falls under the Triad, since one does not only consider its Length as in the case of the Dyad, but it also has Breadth as a third distance. If three Points are posited, two at opposed ends of a distance, and a third Point in the middle of a Line which joins these Points, a Surface is generated. A Solid Figure and a body such as the Tetrahedron are ranged under the Number Four. For where there are three Points, as just laid down, and another Point above them, a pyramidal form of Solid Body is forthwith produced. For it already has the three dimensions of Length, Breadth and Depth.

Some say that Body arose from a single Point whose flux produced a line, whose flux in its turn produced a Surface, and, when this moved into depth, three-dimensional Body was generated. This position differs from that of the earlier Pythagoreans. These generated Numbers from two Principles, the One and the Indefinite Dyad, and from Numbers Points, Lines, Surfaces and Solids. These later thinkers build up all from one Point from which a Line arises, from the Line a Surface, from the Surface a Body. Except on this view, Solid Bodies are constructed under the hegemony of Numbers. And from them lastly sensible things arise, Earth and Water and Air and Fire, and the Cosmos as a whole. The Cosmos, they say, is arranged in harmony, again following upon Numbers, whose Ratios are the concords which introduce perfect harmony, the Fourth and the Fifth and the Octave, the first being a Ratio of $4/3$, the second of $3/2$, the last of $2/1$.

This long passage is ostensibly concerned with the 'Pythagoreans', but references to Unity and the Indefinite Dyad (which are not basic Pythagorean names) stamp it as indubitably referring to the Platonic Number-theorists, in the main to Plato, but sometimes to his successors. The threefold Category-doctrine – Self-existent, Opposite, Relative – which is explicitly cited as Platonic in the Hermodorus extract above (16) – is set forth in uncomprehending fashion in the middle portion of the passage, while Parts I and III deal respectively with the dialectical pathways leading up to, and leading down from, the Platonic Principles. There is good reason to follow Wilpert (*Zwei aristotelische Frühschriften über die Ideenlehre*, 1949) and see in this citation a poor summary of the content of the three Books of Aristotle's lost treatise on Academic doctrine, *On the Good*. Sextus has not grasped that it is the Bad, rather than the Good, which is 'opposite', and that Relatives are opposed to Absolutes rather than to correlatives. I have attempted to interpret the passage in terms of the notion of a three-tier membership of the

Eidetic Order, which harmonizes many conflicting drifts in the Dialogues.

18 Aristotle, *Metaphysics*, 1003b 33–1004a 2.

There are therefore as many species of Being as there are species of unity. And there is a science, one in kind, whose task it is to investigate the essence of all these, i.e. of Identity and Similarity and other such notions. For almost all Opposites can be referred to this Principle, as we can be taken to have done in our List of Opposites.

19 Alexander on the above.

He makes a Principle out of the opposition of the One and what is contrary to it, i.e. Multitude. The former is one selfsame thing, the latter Multitude and multitudinous. Similarly, being Like and Equal falls under Unity, being Unlike and Unequal under Multitude. In order that we may know how almost all Opposites lead back to Unity and Multitude as their Principles, he refers us to his List of Opposites, the List in which he himself dealt with them. He talked of such a list in the Second Book of his *On the Good*.

20 Aristotle, *Metaphysics*, 1004b 27–1005a 2.

The one side-list of Opposites is privative, and all Opposites are reduced to Being and Non-being, and to Unity and Multitude. Thus Rest is a case of Unity, and Movement of Multitude. And nearly all philosophers agree that existents and existence consist of Opposites. All at least have opposing Principles, some the Odd and Even, the Hot and the Cold, the Limit and the Unlimited, Love and Strife. And we may take it for granted that all other reductions are into Unity and Multitude, since all the Principles of other thinkers fall under these as Genera.

21 Alexander on the above.

By talking of such a reduction, he is again referring us to what he proved in the Second Book of *On the Good*.

22 Aristotle, *Metaphysics*, 1054a 30–32.

To the One belong, as we showed graphically in our Division of the Opposites the Same and the Like and the Equal, to Multitude the Different, the Unlike and the Unequal.

23   Pseudo-Alexander on the above.

Aristotle performed this division in his *On the Good*, as we have
said elsewhere, reducing all Opposites to Multitude and the One:
the Same, Like and Equal to the One, and the Different, Unlike
and Unequal to Multitude.

24   Aristotle, *Metaphysics*, 990a 32–990b 18.

Let us now leave the Pythagoreans, for we have said quite
enough about them. Those who made the Ideas into causes
(the Platonists) tried first to assign causes to real things by
bringing in other causes quite as numerous as they were, just
as if someone were to think that he could not count things
when they were fewer, and so multiplied them in order to count
them. For the Eide are equal in number, or not less, than the
things from which those in quest of causes had recourse to them.
For in each such case there is an Eidos bearing the same name,
and there is a One-over-many in other cases, whether instantial
or eternal.

Aristotle is saying that there is an Eidos for every recognized
Natural Kind and for other classes of things instantial and ideal, and
he is regarding such Eide as a senseless, non-explanatory reduplication
in a separate medium of what for him are or may be existentially
self-sufficient.

The ways in which we prove that there are Ideas are, moreover,
not cogent. For some yield no necessary inference, and others
prove the existence of Eide in cases where we do not think there
are any. For the Argument from the Sciences will prove that
there are Eide in the case of all things of which there are
sciences, and the Argument from the One over Many will prove
that there are Eide of Negations, and the Argument from the
Knowledge of what has Perished that there are Eide of perishable
things. For there is an image of such things. And the more
accurate of the Arguments imply that there are Ideas of Relatives
of which we admit no separately existent class, and others
involve the Third Man.

For the restriction of the Eide see Syrianus in the last three excerpts
in this Appendix. For Platonism there are no Prime Ideas of mere
Negations, e.g. Impiety, or of Relatives (i.e. Comparatives), e.g.
Inequality, Superiority, Greater Intensity, or of perishable instances,
yet Aristotle argues that since Knowledge extends generally to these

things there should be Eide of them also. The Platonic view is that in knowing an Eidos we implicitly know what it differs from, what comes close to it, what instances it might have. Aristotle also argues that the doctrine of the Eide leads to the formation of an Infinite Regress, but this will only happen if we think of Eide as always instantiating themselves (which they only sometimes do) and then absurdly identify the Eidos that they instantiate with something like-named but different from themselves.

> The arguments for the Eide in fact destroy certain things whose existence is more fundamental to us than that of the Eide. For they put, not the Dyad, but Number first, and the Relative before the Self-existent, and they have all the consequences which have been brought against the Principles by those who developed doctrines concerning the Ideas.

Aristotle stresses the important point that for mature Platonism the Principles of the Eide had become more fundamental than the Eide themselves, and he argues that these Principles, e.g. Indefinite Duality, being special cases of more general notions, e.g. Number in general, ought, on the Ideal Theory, not to count as Principles.

> The basic conception on which the existence of Eide rests, entails further that there will not only be Eide of substantial things, but of many other things as well. For we do not only have a single conception in the case of substantial things but in other cases as well, and there are not only sciences of substantial things but also of what is not substantial, and countless other similar objections can be raised. But the necessity of the case and the opinions concerning the Eide suggest that, if the Eide are to be shared in, there can only be Ideas of substantial things. For Ideas are not shared in incidentally, as happens, for example, when something incidentally shares in Eternity because it shares in the Double Itself, which happens to be eternal, but Eide must be shared in non-incidentally, and not in virtue of belonging to some (other) substrate. This makes the Eide substantial, and the same terms that mean Substance down here must also mean Substance in the Ideal Realm. If this were not so, what would it mean to say that there is something beyond these many cases, and one in them all? But if there is one and the same Eidos of Ideas and things that share in them, there will be something common to both. For if the Dyad is one and the same in all perishable Dyads, and one and the same in the (Mathematical) Dyads which are many but imperishable, it will be one and the same in itself and in a particular Dyad. For, if it is not the

same, the two Dyads will be one in name only, as when someone calls both Callias and a wooden image a 'man', not looking to any community between them.

Aristotle is here implying the mature Platonic view that the Prime Eide are those of perfect Natural Substances, Man, Fire etc., not of separate properties of these. He is arguing that it is not *indirectly*, by instantiating separate properties which together constitute a complex Eidos, that a particular instantiates that Eidos, but by instantiating it *directly*. In other words, a man instantiates Humanity as a single, unitary structure, not as a bundle of properties which happen to constitute being human. But Aristotle is also arguing that the general arguments for the Eide are not such as to accord a necessary prerogative to the Eide of substantial realities over against their abstract attributes. Yet the Ideal Theorists want the Eide to be the deepest Being, the Substance of their instances, not some accidentally supervenient pattern.

> One might above all wonder what in the world Eide do for everlasting sensible things [stars etc.] or for those that come into being and pass away. For there is nothing in them to cause movement or change. Nor do they assist us to know anything about other things of which, not being in them, they are neither the Substance nor the Essence, nor about the being of things which share in them, although they are not present in them. Some might conceive that they are causes as white by admixture makes a thing white, but such a view, of which first Anaxagoras, and then Eudoxus made use, is easily upset. We can in fact readily marshal many impossibilities which rule it out.

Aristotle here refuses to concede that it is possible for Eide, not being instances, but separated by a type-gulf from instances, to be none the less present in those instances, though neither as a part or even an aspect of them, in the manner of the white in a pigment-mixture.

> But there is further no ordinary sense in which other things can be said to come from the Eide. For to say that they are Patterns, and that other things share in them, is to talk emptily and make use of poetic metaphors. For what is it that operates, looking towards the Ideas? For it is possible for something to be or become like something without being modelled upon it, as a man like Socrates might arise whether Socrates existed or not, and this might be so even if Socrates were eternal. It will further mean that there will be several patterns of the same thing, and so several Eide of it: Man will be modelled on Animal and

Biped as well as on Man Himself. The Eide further are not
merely patterns for sensible things but for themselves also, as
the Genus is a pattern for its Species. The same thing,
therefore, may be both Pattern and Image.

Aristotle fails to see that, on the Ideal Theory, only Eide are in any
true sense causative: the so-called agencies that help to bring about
their instantiation, or the instantial minds which make them into their
goals, are only causative in a derivative and secondary sense. One
cannot hold it as an objection to the Eide that they are not causative
in this essentially occasional manner.

It would also seem to be impossible that the Substance (οὐσία) of
something and that thing should exist apart. How then could
the Ideas, being the Substance of things, exist apart from them?
In the *Phaedo* it is said that the Eide are causes both of Being
and Becoming. But, though the Eide exist, we do not see their
participants arising if there is nothing to initiate movement, and
many other things arise, such as a house or a ring, of which we
hold that there are no Eide. So that it is plain that other things
can be and become through such causes as have just been
mentioned.

Plato does not deny, but explicitly affirms, the existence of occasional
causes which help on the 'true causality' of the Eide. The *Phaedo* and
the *Crito* both deal with instrumental causes of this sort. In the case
of some artefacts, to whose deep artificiality Prime Eide do not correspond, there must none the less be the material for their instantiation
in the eidetic realm. All causation is ultimately eidetic, but one eidetic
product may certainly help to occasion another, or co-operate with
another in a curious joint product.

And if the Eide are Numbers, how will they be causes? Perhaps
because things are other Numbers, this Number being Man,
this Number Socrates, this Callias. But for what reason are the
former Numbers causes of the latter? It will make no difference
if the former are eternal, while the latter are not. If it means
that things down here are Ratios of Numbers like a harmony,
there must be some one thing of which they are the Ratios.
If this is Matter, it is clear that the Numbers themselves will be
Ratios of some one thing to another. I mean, for instance, that if
Callias is a numerical Ratio among Fire, Earth, Water and Air,
the Ideal Number must also be a Ratio of certain subjects. And
Man Himself, whether he be a Number or not, must be a
numerical Ratio of certain things rather than a Number, nor
will he be a Number because he is a Ratio of Numbers.

This passage is important as showing that Plato's identification of Eide with Numbers could at least be given the looser interpretation of identifying Eide with numerical Ratios or sets of such Ratios, rather than with particular Natural Numbers. Aristotle contends that Ratios entail definite terms between which they hold, but does not see that, while actual terms are necessary for instantiated Ratios, merely the possibility of such terms is sufficient for purely eidetic Ratios. The Ratio 3/2 instantiates itself in countless instantial pairs, but as a pure Eidos pointing to such pairs is sufficient for it. The qualified items between which Ratios hold are part of their outlying mechanics of instantiation, not of their eidetic core. Only a committed instantialist would fail to see this.

One Number, moreover, arises out of many, but how does one Eidos arise out of many Eide? If it does not arise out of component Numbers but out of the Units in them, as in the case of Ten Thousand, what will these Units be like? If they are of the same kind, there are many difficulties, and so too if they are not of the same kind, whether in each Number or in different Numbers. For how will they differ, being immune from influence (ἀπαθεῖς)? These are not reasonable views, nor in accord with our notion of things.

Aristotle persists in thinking that since the eidetic Number Fourness *presupposes* Duality, and is in fact Duality doubled, it must *consist* of the actual couples and Units which would be found in its instances. He cannot see that while two things and two things make four things, there is no sense in holding that Twoness and Twoness, or Oneness and Oneness and Oneness and Oneness, make Fourness. Since Plato explicitly denies that different eidetic Numbers can be associated with one another as their instances can be, Aristotle can only understand this denial by supposing that Plato believes that each of the eidetic Numbers has its own peculiar Units or even that each distinct Unit in each distinct eidetic Number is incomparable with every other. Whereas no eidetic Number, not even Unity Itself, consists of Units of any sort.

They are also compelled to set up another sort of Number for Arithmetic, and all the other Intermediates which some mention, but how can there be such entities, and what are their Principles? How can there be Intermediates between things here and the Things Themselves? It is further impossible that each of the Units in the numerical Dyad should come from a prior Dyad. And why is a Number a Unity when taken together?

Aristotle having made the eidetic Numbers quasi-instantial has obviously no use for the Mathematica, which have precisely this role. The other objections reflect similar misunderstandings.

> In addition to these objections, if the Units (in different Numbers) are different, Platonists should have talked like those who make the Elements four or two in number. For these people do not make what is common into an Element, for example Body, but rather Fire and Earth, whether or not these have Body in common. The Platonists, however, speak as if Unity were made of like parts just like Fire or Water.

Aristotle rejects a Unity of Kind as being a true Unity of Principle, a typical instantialist objection. But for Plato the Instance is parasitic on the Species, and the Species on the Genus, and a Principle is, if anything, supra-generic.

> Wishing to reduce Substances to their Principles, we make Lengths come from the Short and Long (a certain Small and Great), Surfaces from the Broad and Narrow, and Body from the Deep and Shallow. But how can the Surface contain a Line, or the Solid a Line and a Surface? For the Broad and Narrow and Deep and Shallow differ in kind. So that since Number is not present in these, and since the Much and Little differs from them, it is clear that none of the higher Kinds will be present in the lower ones. And the Broad, moreover, is not the Genus of the Deep; if it were, Body would be a certain sort of Surface. And whence do Points come? Plato was opposed to this class of entities as being a fiction of the geometers, but said over and over again that the Line had its Principle in the Indivisible Line. Yet Lines must have limits, and so what proves Lines, proves Points.

Aristotle here shows that Plato so regarded Numbers as to think what are now called Complex Numbers represented a necessary extension of them. In Number we have the possibility, not only of Natural Numbers and Ratios, but also of the basic dimensional differences. But this is unintelligible to Aristotle to whom the Genus is always poorer than the Species in its extensions and applications. And while Plato sees a Point as the first breath or last gasp of a Line, Aristotle likes to feel more substance in it.

> Our Wisdom looks for the cause of phenomena, but we have abandoned our task, since we say nothing of causes as sources of motion: intending to state the substantial reality of phenomena, we assert the being of non-phenomenal substances and indulge in empty talk as to the manner in which they are that

substantial reality: 'sharing', as we said previously, means
nothing. Nor has the (final) causality which we acknowledge
as fundamental, and which we see operative in the arts and in
all mental and natural construction, anything to do with the
Eide. The moderns have turned Philosophy into Mathematics,
though they pretend Mathematics should be studied for the
sake of other things. And the Substance which they make their
underlying Matter is altogether too mathematical, and is rather
a predicate and a difference of Substance and Matter, than
Matter. The Great and Small are like the Rare and Dense of the
natural philosophers, who make them the first differences of
something that underlies them: they represent a certain Excess
and Defect. And if these are identified with Movement, the
Eide will plainly be in movement. If this is not so, whence did
Movement come? The whole of Natural Science is overthrown.
And we cannot succeed in the seemingly easy task of proving
all things to be one. For by ranging instances under Unity we
do not prove all to be one, but only that there is such a thing
as Unity Itself, if we accept all their assumptions. And even this
we do not prove, if we do not concede, as we cannot in certain
cases, that Being a Universal is a Genus. Nor can we show any
good reason for the existence, actual or possible, of the Lengths,
Surfaces and Solids after the Numbers, or what their force can be.
For, not being Numbers, they can neither be Eide nor
Mathematical Intermediates nor perishable things, and must
plainly constitute a fourth distinct class.

Aristotle wants solid substance in instances: Plato is content to see
in them a functioning of the Eide, a more or less disorderly spatio-
temporal multiplication of Eternal Meanings, whose possibility is
part and parcel of the Eternal Meanings themselves.

25   Alexander on Aristotle's *Metaphysics*, 990b 17.

They (the Platonists) have a greater or the greatest concern for
the existence of the Principles. For the Principles are also for
them Principles of the Ideas themselves. These Principles are
the One and the Indefinite Dyad, as he himself told us a little
before in his work *On the Good*. But on their view the Principles
are also Principles of Number.
    Aristotle says that the arguments for the Ideas destroy these
Principles, and their destruction involves the destruction of
what comes after them (as coming from the Principles) and hence
also of the Ideas. For if in each case of general predication,

there is a separate something and an Idea, and Duality is predicated of the Indefinite Dyad, then Duality will be a First Thing and an Idea. So that the Indefinite Dyad will no longer be a Principle. But not even the Dyad will be a First Thing or a Principle. For Number will again be predicated of it as being an Idea – the Ideas being taken by him to be Numbers. So that Number will come to be first for them, being a certain Idea. If this is the case, Number will come before the Indefinite Dyad which is its Principle, and not the Dyad before Number. If this is the case, it will no longer be a Principle, if it is such by participation in something. Yet it is set before us as a Principle of Number, and yet Number on the above argument comes before it. But if Number is something relative – since each Number is a Number of something – and if Number is the first of all realities, it will also come before the Dyad which is supposedly its Principle, and so they will be allowing that what is relative comes before what is self-existent. A strange conclusion, since whatever is relative is secondary. For a relation signifies the standing (σχέσις) of some prior Nature, which must come before the standing which accrues to it. A relation is like an outgrowth (παραφυάς) as is said in the *Ethics*. But if someone says a Number is a Quantum and not a Relation, the consequence will hold that for them Quantity precedes Substance. But the Great and Small Itself is a case of Relativity. And so it still follows that they must admit something relative to be a Principle prior to the Self-existent, since an Idea to them is a Principle of Substances, and since being an Idea means being a paradigm, and a paradigm is relative to that of which it is the paradigm. And if the being of Ideas lies in their being paradigms, and if the things that are modelled on them, and of which they are the Ideas, are their images, this will make all natural products relative on their view. For all things are images and paradigms. And if the being of Ideas lies in their being paradigms, and a paradigm exists for the sake of what is made on its pattern, and if, further, what is done for the sake of something else is less worthy than the thing itself, then the Ideas will be less worthy than the things made on their pattern.

26 Asclepius on Aristotle's *Metaphysics*, 990b 15.

Of bad things we say there are no Ideas. For bad things exist subordinately and without real substance (τῷ ὄντι ἀνυπόστατα ὑπάρχουσι καὶ παρυφίστανται) as was said in the Platonic seminars. Pure evil has no place in the Universe.

27 Aristotle, *Nicomachean Ethics*, 1096a 17.

They refused to admit Ideas in cases where there was a distinction
of Prior and Posterior, and hence they admitted no Idea of
Numbers.

The meaning is not that there are no numerical Ideas – all Ideas are
numerical – but there is no *single generic* Idea of Number as Such.

28 Aristotle, *Metaphysics*, 1091b 13–15, 26–35.

Of those who admit non-moving Substance some say that the
One Itself is the Good Itself. But they make its Essence consist
mainly in its Unity. . . . Again, if the Eide are Numbers, all the
Eide will be particular cases of Goodness. A man may, however,
postulate Ideas of anything he chooses. For if there are Ideas
only of good things, the Ideas will not be substantial realities,
and, if they are also of substantial realities, all animals and plants
and all participants in Ideas will be good. These are strange
consequences, and it also follows that the opposed Element,
whether called Multitude or the Unequal or Great and Small,
will be Evil Itself. For this reason one thinker [Speusippus]
refuses to connect Goodness with Unity, since this would
identify Evil with the nature of Multiplicity, it being the case
that things arise from their opposites. But they [the original
Platonists] make the Unequal the essence of Evil.

29 Aristotle, *Physics*, 207a 29–32.

If the Great and Small is the all-containing element in the case
of sensible things, it should also be all-containing in the case
of intelligible things. But it is bizarre and impossible that what
is unknowable and indefinite should contain and bound things.

30 Simplicius on the above.

Having shown that the Infinite is rather something contained
than a container, and that it is unknowable by Nature, Aristotle
examines the ordinary acceptation of Plato's views. Plato in his
utterances *On the Good* said that the Great and Small were
Matter, and also said that this Matter was infinite, and that all
sensible things were contained by the Infinite, and were
unknowable on account of their material, infinite and fluid
nature. Aristotle says it follows from these opinions that the
Great and Small as present in the noetic sphere, that is the

Indefinite Dyad, should likewise, in company with Unity, be a
Principle of all Number and of all entities. For the Ideas are also
Numbers.

31 Aristotle, *Physics*, 209b 11–17.

For this reason Plato identified Matter and Space in the *Timaeus*.
For the participating Principle and Space were one and the same.
He talked in a different manner regarding the participating
Principle in the so-called Unwritten Doctrines, but none the less
identified Place and Space. For all philosophers say that
Place is something, but what it is he alone undertook to say.

32 Philoponus on the above.

The name he gave to Matter in the *Timaeus* was different from
the name he gave it in the Unwritten Doctrines, i.e. in the
Unwritten Seminars. For in these Seminars he called Matter the
Great and Small, as Aristotle said above – and we have explained
why Matter is great and small – but in the *Timaeus* he called
Matter the participating Principle ($\tau\grave{o}$ $\mu\epsilon\tau\alpha\lambda\eta\pi\tau\iota\kappa\acute{o}\nu$) since it
shared in the Eide. Aristotle himself made written records of the
Unwritten Seminars of Plato.

33 Simplicius on the same.

He says that Plato gave Matter a different name in the *Timaeus*
and in the Unwritten Seminars. In the *Timaeus* he called it the
participating Principle (which shares in some very puzzling
way in the intelligible) whereas in the Unwritten Seminars he
called it the Great and Small.

34 Themistius on the same.

Plato identifies Matter and Space in the *Timaeus*, for what shares
in the Eide (the Matter) and Space (which is Place) are said to
be the same. None the less the reception of the Eide by Matter
is differently described in the *Timaeus* and the Unwritten
Doctrines. For in the *Timaeus* it is a case of participation, but a
case of assimilation in the Unwritten Doctrines.

35 Aristotle, *Physics*, 201b 16–26.

That we have spoken soundly about Motion is clear when we
consider what others say about it, and from the fact that it
is not easy to define it otherwise. That Motion and Change

cannot be placed in another Genus, is clear when one considers where others place it when they say that Motion is Difference and Inequality and Non-being. None of these things is necessarily a case of Motion, whether a thing be different or unequal or non-existent. Nor is it change to a greater extent to or from these things than to or from their opposites. The reason why Motion is ranged under these heads, is that it seems to be something indefinite, and the Principles in the Second Column (of Opposites) are indefinite on account of their privative character.

36 Simplicius on the above.

He [Alexander] says that if Plato and the Pythagoreans had said that Difference, Inequality and Non-being were *causes* of Motion, their view would have been a possible one, but that they do not suffice to define Motion. For the cause is not the same as what it causes. And their mention of Non-being, even if it strikes truth, none the less states an accident of Motion and not what Motion itself is.

And that Plato talks of Inequality as a cause of Motion, will soon be clear if we bring forth Plato's own words. It must be noted that, even before Alexander, Eudemus set forth Plato's opinion on Motion and controverted it. He writes as follows: 'Plato says Motion is the Great and Small or Non-being or the Unequal, and other things which amount to these. It seems odd that he should identify Motion with these. For when Motion is present, that in which it is present is moved. But it is ridiculous to make Inequality and Irregularity necessitate Motion. It would be better to follow Archytas and speak of these as causes.' And a little further on: 'The Pythagoreans and Plato very properly associate the Indefinite with Motion – no one else has written about it. For what is not is also defined by its imperfection, and imperfection is a case of Non-being. What is imperfect is coming to be, and what is coming to be, *is* not'.

37 Aristotle, *Metaphysics*, 1083a 20–b 19.

Nor is what others have said about Numbers at all well said. There are some who deny the existence of Ideas, either as such, or as being certain Numbers: they say that the Objects of Mathematics and the Numbers are first of existent things, and make Unity itself their Principle [Speusippus]. It is strange that there should be, as they say, a One which is first of

all Units, and not a Dyad which is first of all Dyads, nor a
Triad which is first of all Triads. For all fall under the same
argument. If such is the case in regard to Number, and
Mathematical Number alone is held to have Being, their One
will not be a Principle, since a One which is a Principle will
differ from all the other Units. If it does so differ, there must
be a Dyad which is first of Dyads, and similarly in the case of
successive Numbers.

But if the One is a Principle, then the facts about Numbers
must rather be as Plato stated them, and there must be a first
Dyad and a first Triad, and such Numbers will not be
comparable with one another. But if this is supposed, much that
is impossible has been shown to result. One or other of these
possibilities must obtain, and, if neither of them does, Number
can have no separate existence.

It is clear from this that the third way of stating things [that
of Xenocrates] is the worst: that Eidetic and Mathematical
Number are the same. For this combines two errors in a single
opinion. For Mathematical Number cannot exist eidetically, and
to suppose it can means spinning out arbitrary assumptions,
and one has also to accept all the consequences that attend on
those who make Number eidetic.

The Pythagorean approach has from one point of view fewer
difficulties than those just mentioned, but has other
difficulties of its own. To deny the separateness of Numbers
removes many impossibilities: Bodies then consist of Numbers,
and it is impossible that such Numbers should be mathematical.
But one cannot assert the existence of indivisible Magnitudes,
and, even if such existed, Units could have no magnitude.
How then could Magnitude consist of indivisibles? Arithmetical
Number however, is made up of Units. The Pythagoreans
identify Number with things. At least they apply theorems
to Bodies, as if Bodies consisted of Numbers.

38 Aristotle, *Metaphysics*, 1086a 2–13.

Those who hold that the Objects of Mathematics alone exist
beyond sensible things, and who see the difficulty and artificiality
of the theory of Ideas, abandoned Eidetic Number and
postulated Mathematical Number [Speusippus]. But those who
wished to make the Eide Numbers as well, not seeing how, if
one posits such Principles, one can explain how Mathematical
Number exists alongside Eidetic Number, made Eidetic and
Mathematical Number identical [Xenocrates]. They did so

verbally, but in fact destroyed Mathematical Number, for what they suppose is their own fabrication, and not mathematical at all. But the first man to say that the Eide were also Numbers [Plato] very properly separated them from the Objects of Mathematics.

39   Syrianus on the above.

Aristotle admits that he has nothing to oppose to the Platonic hypotheses, and that he does not understand their Eidetic Numbers. This is shown by this sort of passage in the Second Book of *On Philosophy*: 'So that, if the Ideas are some other sort of Number, and not mathematical, we could have no understanding of them. For of what other sort of Number do most of us have understanding?' So that his refutations are now being framed for the benefit of the many who know none other than Numbers composed of Units, and he has not touched on the Principles from which flow the notions of our divine men.

40   Aristotle, *Metaphysics*, 1080a 12–30, b 4–33.

Since we have pronounced on these points, it will be well to consider once more what happens in the field of Numbers for those who make them separated Substances, and the First Causes of existent things. It is necessary, if a Number is a certain Nature, and its Being is none other than this very Nature, as some hold, then either there is a First in Number, and a next, each being different in Species, and this either applies directly to the Units involved, each being incomparable with every other, or the Units follow on one another and each is comparable with every other, as they say is the case in Mathematical Number, where no Unit differs from another, or, lastly, some Units are comparable and some not. The last obtains on the supposition that the Dyad comes first after the One, then the Triad, and so each other Number, and that, while the Units in each Number are comparable, the Units in the first Dyad with one another, the Units in the first Triad with one another, and so on in the case of the other Numbers, the Units in the Dyad Itself are not comparable with those in the Triad Itself, and so on in the case of successive Numbers.

This passage only reflects Aristotle's basic misconception of the eidetic Numbers. He cannot conceive of Triplicity Itself without imagining it to consist of three Units. Since the eidetic Numbers are said by Plato to be incomparable, Aristotle can only conceive that the

Units of which one eidetic Number consists must be incomparable with those of which another eidetic Number consists, instead of seeing that it is an ontological as well as a grammatical howler to make any of them consist of Units at all.

> These are the only ways in which Numbers can exist, and practically everyone who made the One the Principle and Substance and Element of all things, and Number its joint product with another Principle, has spoken in one of them, though no one has made *all* the Units incomparable. This is an appropriate result, since the ways we have mentioned are the only ways possible.
>
> Some say there are two sorts of Numbers, those having Priority and Posteriority being the Ideas, while Mathematical Number lies apart from Ideas and Sensibles, and both sorts of Number are separate from sensibles [the opinion of Plato]. There are also those who say that Mathematical Number alone exists, the first of real beings and separate from sensible things [the opinion of Speusippus]. And the Pythagoreans believe in Mathematical Number alone, only not separated, since they say sensible things consist of such Numbers. For they construct the whole Heavens out of Numbers, only not out of Numbers that consist of Units, but think that Units have size. How the first One was put together so as to have size they do not seem able to say. And another philosopher thought the first Number was that of the Eide alone, while some [i.e. Xenocrates] think that Mathematical Number is the same as this.
>
> The like holds in regard to Lengths, Surfaces and Solids. For some [i.e. Plato] distinguish between the mathematical cases of these and the cases that follow upon the Ideas. And of those who pronounce otherwise, i.e. those who do not make the Ideas Numbers or admit the existence of Ideas, some talk of Mathematical Objects in a mathematical manner [Speusippus], while others talk of mathematical Objects but not mathematically [Xenocrates]. For they say that not every Magnitude divides into Magnitudes, and deny that any two Units form a Dyad.
>
> And all who make the One the Element and Principle of existent things, say that Numbers consist of Units, save only the Pythagoreans, who think that Numbers have magnitude, as said before.

41   Aristotle, *Metaphysics*, 1081a 5–29, b 10–33.

> If all Units are comparable and undifferentiated, we have Mathematical Number as our only sort of Number, and the

Ideas cannot be Numbers. For what sort of Number could Man Himself or Animal Itself or any other Eidos be, the Eidos being unique in each case, i.e. a single Idea of Man, and another single Idea of Animal? There are infinitely many undifferentiatedly similar Mathematical Numbers, so that *this* Triad will no more be Man Himself than any other. But if the Ideas are not Numbers, they cannot exist at all. For what will be their Principles? Number comes from the One and the Indefinite Dyad, and these Principles and Elements are said to be those of Numbers, and the Ideas can neither be ranked as prior or posterior to Numbers.

Aristotle is saying that, *on Plato's theory of Principles*, the Eide must be Numbers of some sort, and that, as being Mathematical Numbers would violate their uniqueness, they must be Eidetic Numbers.

But if the Units are incomparable, and no Unit is comparable with any other, then this Number [with which the Ideas are identical] cannot be Mathematical Number, since Mathematical Number consists of undifferentiated Units, and mathematical demonstrations are adjusted to this fact. But neither can it be Eidetic Number. For the First Dyad will not spring from the One and the Indefinite Dyad, to be followed in the stated order of Dyad, Triad, Tetrad, for the Units in the First Dyad will be generated at the same time – whether as unequals subsequently equalized, as the view's first author [Plato] held, or otherwise – so that one Unit will be prior to another, and also to the pair they form, since, wherever one thing is prior to another, the resultant whole will be prior to the latter and posterior to the former.

Aristotle cannot make the theory of eidetic Numbers work because he is determined to hold that they consist of component Units. The reference to 'equalization' is important, but does not mean that, for Plato, Duality Itself first consisted of two unequal units which were then equalized. It only means that Duality itself is the Pattern of Doubled Unity which instantial pairs imperfectly and approximately instantiate, and which can be described as 'equalized' because it stands opposed to the rough Pattern of Indefinite Plurality which is not similarly precise.

It is also plain that, if all Units are incomparable, it will be impossible for there to be a Dyad Itself or a Triad Itself or similarly in the case of the other Numbers. For, whether the Units are undifferentiated or differentiated from one another,

it is necessary that Number should be counted additively
(κατὰ πρόσθεσιν); a Dyad is counted by adding one Unit to
another, a Triad by adding another Unit to two, and the same
with the Tetrad. Such being the case, it is impossible for
Numbers to be generated as they say they are out of the Dyad
and Unity. For the Dyad becomes a part of the Triad, and the
Triad of the Tetrad, and the same happens in the case of the
subsequent Numbers. But they say that the Tetrad arose
from the first Dyad and the Indefinite Dyad, two Dyads in
addition to the Dyad Itself. If this does not happen, the Dyad
Itself will be a part of the Tetrad, and another Dyad will be
added to it. And the Dyad Itself will consist of the One
Itself and another One. If this is the case, the second Principle
cannot be the Indefinite Dyad. For it generates a single Unit, and
not a definite Dyad. And how, beyond the Triad Itself and the
Dyad Itself, can there be other Triads and Dyads? And in what
manner will they consist of prior and posterior Units? All these
notions are bizarre and fantastic, and there cannot be a First Dyad
and thereupon a Triad Itself. But this would have to happen if
the One and the Indefinite Dyad were Principles. If the
consequences are absurd, the existence of such Principles also
is absurd.

This passage, in its tortured subtlety, only exhibits the absurdity
of imagining that an eidetic Number can contain its eidetic predecessors
as its parts. It also exhibits Aristotle's preference for Addition over
Multiplication. Numbers *can* be generated additively, e.g. Fourness
is a Number which amounts to the Augmentation of Being Three by
Being One – Numbers are basically operations – but Addition has no
prerogative over Multiplication, i.e. Fourness is Double-strength
Duplication.

42   Aristotle, *Metaphysics*, 1083b 23–1084b 2.

Does each Unit in the Number Two arise from the Great and
Small brought to equality, or does one Unit arise from the Great
and the other from the Small? If this last be the case, each Unit
will not spring from all the Elements, nor will the Units be
undifferentiated, since the Great is present in one, and the
Small, antithetical in nature to the Great, in the other. And
what of the Units in the Triad Itself? One of them is odd, for
which reason they probably give Unity a middle position in
Odd Numbers. But if either Unit in the Dyad consists of Great
and Small equalized, how will the Dyad be a single Nature

447

emergent from the Great and Small? Or how will it differ from the Unit? The Unit, further, is prior to the Dyad, since its destruction entails the destruction of the Dyad. It must therefore be an Idea of Ideas, since it is prior to an Idea, and must have arisen before it. But from what? For the Indefinite Dyad only doubles.

It is further necessary that Numbers should be infinite or finite. Number is thought by the Platonists to exist apart, so that it is impossible for one of these alternatives not to obtain. That it cannot be infinite is plain, since an infinite Number is neither odd nor even, and the generation of Numbers is always that of an odd or an even Number. If Unity operates in one way on an even Number an odd Number results, if the Dyad operates in one way on an even Number we get the Numbers got from Unity by doubling, if odd Numbers operate on an even Number we get the other even Numbers. If every Idea is an Idea of something, and the Numbers are Ideas, the Infinite also will be the Idea of something, whether sensible or of another sort. Yet this is not possible on their theory, nor is it reasonable, and yet this is how they conceive Ideas. But if Number is finite, how far does it go? One must here not only state facts but give reasons. But if Number only goes as far as the Decad, as some say, the Eide will soon be exhausted. If for example the Triad is Man Himself, what Number will be Horse Itself? The Numbers of Each-thing-Itself go up to Ten, and it will have to be one of these Numbers. (For they are Substances and Ideas.) But these Numbers will be exhausted, for the species of Animal will exceed them, and it is also clear that if the Triad is Man Himself, the other Triads, which are alike in the same Number, will be so too, so that an infinity of men will each, if each Triad is an Idea, be Man Himself, and if not, they will at least be men. But if a smaller Number is part of a greater, as when both are composed of comparable Units in the same Number, and if the Tetrad Itself is the Idea of something, for example of Horse or White, Man will be a part of Horse, if Man is the Dyad. It is also strange that there should be an Idea of Ten and none of Eleven, nor of the succeeding Numbers. And if certain things exist and come into existence though there are no Eide of them, why are there no Eide in their case? It seems that the Eide cannot be causes. And it is also strange that the series of Numbers up to the Decad has more eidetic reality than the Decad, although there is no generation of this series as a whole, and there is a generation of the Decad. They try to make out that Number up to the Decad is complete. For they at least try to generate consequent notions such as Gaps, Proportions, the Odd, and others within the Decad. Some they connect with the Principles, for example Motion and Rest, Good and Bad, the others with Numbers. This is why the One is the Odd. For if Oddness were in the Triad, how could the Pentad be odd? Magnitude and suchlike also only go up to a point, for example the first Indivisible Line, the Dyad. These also go no further than the Decad.

This passage continues to unwind the difficulties involved in thinking of the Eidetic Numbers as composed of Units or of other Numbers. It also canvasses the difficulty of locating all the Eide within the limits of the first ten Natural Numbers. But it is clear at the end of the passage that the Decad sums up, not such specific Eide as Man and Horse, but the basic dimensions of the Eide, i.e. Units = One, Lines = Two, Surfaces = Three and Solids = Four, the sum of 1, 2, 3 and 4 being 10.

43 Aristotle, *Metaphysics*, 1070a 13–19.

In some cases a particular thing has no reality apart from its composite substantiality, for example the Eidos of House exists only as an Art, and as such it is neither generated or destroyed. A House without Matter, Health and all ideals of Art both exist and do not exist in different senses. But if there is any particularity apart from composite substantiality, it is to be found in Natural Objects. Plato therefore was not wrong when he said that there were as many Eide as there were Natural Objects (if indeed there are Eide at all) but not of things down here such as Fire, Flesh and Head.

This passage attests the Organicism of mature Platonism, and fits in with accounts of the Ideal Living Creature in the *Timaeus*. There are, on such an approach, no Prime Eide of the mere Parts and even, it would seem, of the Elements of Living Beings, but such Eide are parasitic upon Organic Eide.

44 Aristotle, *De Anima*, 429a 22–9.

The part of the Soul called Mind (I mean by Mind the part with which the Soul thinks and conceives) is nothing actually till it thinks. For this reason one cannot reasonably suppose it to be mixed up with Body. For it would take on some quality, for example Cold and Warm, or have an organ as its sensitive part has, but none of these things obtain. Those speak well therefore

449

who call the Soul the place of Eide, save that, not the whole
Soul, but only its thinking part is in question, and this is
not the Actuality, but only the Potency of the Eide.

45   Philoponus on the above.

Aristotle is praising Plato. For he said above that the Soul
receives the Eide of intelligible things and so achieves
Actuality, and on this account he praises Plato for calling it the
place of Eide. But he blames him on two scores, first for making
the whole of the Soul the place of the Eide, and not solely the
reasoning Soul. One could, however, say, on Plato's behalf,
that for him the reasoning Soul is the only Soul, while the
other Souls are for him 'animations' (ἐμψυχίαι). He therefore says
that 'all Souls are immortal'. He may, therefore, call the Soul
the place of the Eide but he means only the reasoning Soul.
Aristotle also blames Plato on another point, i.e. for saying that
the Eide exist actually in the Soul and not potentially. For
Aristotle compares the Soul to a blank slate, and is correct in
talking of learning, whereas Plato likens the Soul to an
inscribed slate, and speaks of learning as Reminiscence.

46   Aristotle, *De Caelo*, 279b 32–280a 10.

Some try to rescue their accounts of the world as being both
indestructible and also generated, by a false excuse. They say they
are speaking of generation as people do who draw up diagrams,
not implying that the world really had a beginning, but for the
sake of instruction, in which understanding is improved by seeing
a diagram in actual formation. But, as we have said, the two cases
are not parallel. In the construction of diagrams, when all has
been drawn, the very things result, whereas in their proofs the
result is not the same but something impossible. For the
things said to be prior and posterior are in conflict. They say
that Order arose from Disorder, but the same thing cannot be
both disordered and orderly, and there must necessarily be a
generative process and a lapse of time between them. But in
diagrams nothing is temporally separated.

Surely one can see that, *qua* distinct from its ordering Eide, Instantiation is without order, and that, subject to its ordering Eide,
Instantiation is ordered. One can also express this fact by talking as if
Disorder was succeeded by Order in time. Aristotle must have understood all this: he is merely being contentious, after the manner of
many young philosophers who affect accuracy.

47   Pseudo-Alexander on Aristotle's *Metaphysics*, 1091a 12.

Xenocrates defended Plato, as reported in Book I of *De Caelo*, by
saying that it was for the sake of instruction, and in order to
ascertain how the Ideas might have arisen if they had in fact had
an origin, that he supposed that they would have sprung from
an equalization by the One of the Great and Small. In reply to
these statements of Xenocrates, Aristotle showed that Inequality
must have been prior in time. It is clear he infers that the
generation of the Eidetic Numbers was not thought up for the
sake of understanding or instruction, but because those who
made these pronouncements really believed they were generated.

48   Syrianus on Aristotle's *Metaphysics*, 1078b 32.

The Ideas are universals, if one may predicate universality of the
causes of our most eidetic accounts which in all cases precede
their creative execution. For the Platonists do not say that there
are Ideas of all that is universal in our thought. There are no
Ideas of evil and base things, since it is rather by privation and
departure from Eide that such things are added to nature, for
which reason they are said to be unnatural. Nor are there Ideas
of negations, since these destroy the definition and limit given
by the Eide to everything; being indefinite is rather a plight
of Matter than of the Eide. Nor are there Ideas of things that are
different at different times. These things receive their chopping
and changing from a moving cause, and not from the constant,
steady irradiation of the Eide. Nor do the Platonists leave room
for Ideas of parts which are not also wholes, for example of a
hand or a head or fingers or a nose. For, being the complete
causes of things, they bring up their total forms undivided in
respect of parts in their definition of what is natural. Nor do the
Platonists posit distinct causes in Mind Itself for the accidents
which first accrue to bodies, for example sweetness and whiteness,
but think that natural ratios are sufficient to produce such bodily
accidents. Nor are there Ideas of compounds such as 'wise man'.
For the Eide, being simple, are each the artificers of a simple
essence, but the things that share in several Eide move our
understanding to combine Eide together or separate them from
one another. Concerning such things there is affirmation and
denial, and also combination and division, but the Eide and the
thoughts correlated with them are freed from all this through
their sheer simplicity. Nor should one suppose there to be Eide
of things which arise through a congress of dissimilars, such as

mules, stunted mules and the grafts of different trees. These
things are all posterior in origin, the episodic works of more
than one nature, not at all the expression of their own nature
running its course, but of that nature violated, stultified and forced
into meddlesomeness. From this it is clear that every art that
imitates nature, and that only lends perfection to mortal life, is
without an eidetic cause. The same applies to the works of
mental choice or to things brought about by a concourse of
several causes. These things we say are due to chance, and are
not by us connected with eidetic causes. For what springs from
such causes always exists in the same state and is exempt from all
that is contingent. It remains then that there are Ideas of universal
and perfect substances and of what perfects the natural disposition
of such substances. There is for example an idea of Man and of
what perfects Man, e.g. wisdom and virtue. For the Ideas, being
the generators and perfectors of all, are constitutive of
substances, and perfect these by making them turn towards
themselves. For it is clear that Ideas from the start have the
cause of such being and perfection in themselves. We have it,
therefore, in brief, that there are Ideas of some things and not of
others, and that there are no ideas of all the universals of which
our critic has made mention.

This passage, written by Syrianus, the Academic scholarch, eight
centuries after the time of Plato, can none the less be regarded, in
view of its intelligibility and inner coherence, as a fairly authentic
expression of the views of that party in the early Academy, several
times referred to by Aristotle, who thought that there were not Ideas
of everything. Plato himself, we have seen reason to argue, accorded
a secondary, interstitial place in the eidetic realm to the deviations and
privations which this tradition sought to exclude, and framed categorial
distinctions to render this possible.

49   Syrianus on Aristotle's *Metaphysics*, 1079a 11.

We say there are no Ideas of unessential relations nor of
those pertaining to movements nor of those realized in some
non-natural position, such as the relations of the above and the
beneath, the right and the left, and of what is akin to these. But
of the relations things have owing to their participation in a
single Eidos, for example likeness or equality or difference, some
share in ultimate kinds of being while others express ways in
which each Idea stands to all others. Is it then remarkable that
some of the relationships down here are effected by the relations
yonder, since we even leave room for such relationships yonder?

50 Syrianus on Aristotle's *Metaphysics*, 1079a 19.

On these points Aristotle has been somewhat ponderously
difficult. Our predecessors have laid down, and we agreed with
them above, that there are Ideas of some things and not of
others. We have agreed that there are Ideas of universal substances
such as Man or Horse, or of anything that perfects such
substances, such as virtue and knowledge. And of anything that
pertains to souls and bodies and natures alike, such as similarity
and equality and magnitude and the like. What pertains to bodies
alone has, according to Iamblichus, its determined cause in
natural ratios, since the divine Plotinus insists that we ought not
to locate an Eidos of whiteness in Mind Itself. It is not therefore
the case that where one notion applies to many things, it
corresponds to an Idea: at that rate there would be Ideas of
monstrosities. But while there are general definitions of the
things of which there are Ideas, the converse does not hold. Nor is
it the case that there are Ideas of all the objects of the sciences,
if these are not sciences in the full and true sense. If there are
such ideal substances, things down here may rightly be said to
share in them, but a thing which shares in substance is not for
that reason substantial. For we say that Knowledge Itself and
Justice Itself are substances, but not the corresponding
dispositions in ourselves. It must further be said that nothing
in the realm of Ideas is present in a substrate, but all achieve
substantiality. Even Aristotle admits that eternity is not accidental
to the Double Itself. For he clearly proved, in the First Book
of the *Metaphysics*, that nothing is accidentally destructible or
indestructible. One must rather say that every immaterial and
divine essence hides vastly many powers in the unmultiplied,
uniform supersimplicity of its being, and that things down here
do not share in all of these powers. For the Double Itself
essentially possesses indivisibility, intelligibility, creativity and
eternity, and none of them attributively. The Soul Aloft shares
in more of its powers, ours in less, and bodies and bodily
powers may be allowed to share in one or two. But the things
which share in substances need not in all cases be substantial,
as we have often pointed out. Some things share divisibly in
indivisibles, some unintelligently in intelligibles, and just so there
is an insubstantial sharing in substance. The talk of a One over
Many did not mean that the One fell under the same category as
the Many, but rather that it unutterably outsoared the multitude
that proceeded from it, and that was modelled upon it and
depended on it.

This passage illustrates the splendour and subtlety of one of the most admirable and Platonically understanding of the Aristotelian commentators, in his defence of Plato against the criticisms in those books of the *Metaphysics* where Aristotle has most gravely misrepresented him. In comparison with Syrianus, even a commentator like Alexander, privileged beyond all others in being able to read Aristotle's lost treatises, writes like an illiterate person, missing the point, reiterating it unnecessarily, and being beyond all measure superficial. The commentary of Syrianus should be made more accessible in translation.

APPENDIX II

CRITICAL NOTE ON THE VIEWS OF HAROLD F. CHERNISS

As many people, even without having read them, believe that Harold Cherniss's two brilliant and learned books, *Aristotle's Criticism of Plato and the Academy* (1944) and *The Riddle of the Early Academy* (1945), have performed the (to them) welcome service of relegating Plato's Unwritten Doctrines to the limbo of Aristotelian misinterpretation, so that all philosophical and philological effort can now be transferred to the smooth study of the Dialogues, I have been reluctantly persuaded by the Editor of this series to add the following Appendix to my volume, in criticism of the opinions just mentioned. I am, however, far from confident that my few stones of philosophy, garnered from the brook of an eidetic experience which is, I believe, similar to Plato's, will be able to prevail against this Goliath of truly wonderful, but at times wonderfully misapplied, erudition. I believe that Professor Cherniss, with his immense learning, has, however, placed a huge block in the path of research by delaying recognition of what is undeniable and obvious: that some of the Aristotelian statements as to Platonic teachings not quite in harmony with what is said in the Dialogues, are much too circumstantial, much too distinctive and 'odd' – they are not at all odd when deeply meditated upon – to have been arrived at by the tortuous processes which gave rise to Aristotle's more curious misinterpretations, and particularly not by the lines of misinterpretation that Professor Cherniss has tried to construct. I should have preferred to counter Professor Cherniss's damming-up of research by simply circumventing it, by showing, as I have tried to show, that the Aristotelian material, though confused and confusing, does admit throughout of a worthwhile interpretation, and that, as so interpreted, and treated as the Unwritten Programme (not finished doctrine) behind all Plato's mature writing, it casts immeasurable light on the content of the Dialogues themselves. It has, however, been urged upon me, in view of the considerably discredited character of my whole approach, at least in Britain and some parts of America, that I ought to take on Cherniss more directly, and this I have in the present brief Appendix attempted to do, at the risk of raising a whirlwind in which I shall unjustifiably perish.

At the very beginning of Cherniss's first work he stresses the need for *interpreting* the Platonic and Aristotelian texts, and for doing so in their 'full philosophical intention', while restricting himself to interpretations for the support of which specific passages can be cited (*Criticism*, p. xxii). I entirely approve and have tried to follow this policy, though my view of a 'full philosophical intention' involves far more implications than his does, but if the hypothesis around which my work is founded involves some dotting of *i*'s and crossing of *t*'s, so too, in a much more negative way, does his. He has reduced Plato's opinions to the barest bones of any account of Platonism known to me, and through those bare bones the winds of Aristotelian criticism will certainly blow for evermore, though we may rejoice that he has left them white and antique, and has not covered them with an irrelevant flesh of Neo-Kantianism or Anglo-Hegelianism or Wittgensteinian linguistic therapy. The cardinal propositions of Plato's doctrine of Ideas are held (*Riddle*, pp. 5–6) to be that:

> the apparently disparate phenomena of human conduct, of mental activity and of physical process can each and all only be accounted for on the assumption that there exist quite outside of the phenomenal process real entities which are the standards of conduct, the termini of process, and the objective correlates of knowledge. These entities are the Ideas, and for every phenomenal multiplicity to which a common name is applied one of these Ideas exists as the real correlate. Each of these Ideas is an immutable and eternal unit. Each is a perfect individual because, not being involved in the restrictions of place, its existence is not a consequence of its being *in* something other than itself, and being unaffected by process and motion, its existence is timeless, transcending all duration; but each is a universal with respect to all the similar phenomena which are only transient reflections or imitations of it in space.

This doctrinal summary is unimpeachably documented from the Dialogues, though the use of the word 'individual' is question-begging and the term plainly misleading. But Cherniss does *not* mean by calling the Ideas 'individuals' that they are perfect cases of certain universals in comparison with which other cases are only inadequate 'imitations', but rather that they are *identical* with those universals, that they are, in other words, those universals *themselves*. Cherniss quite correctly sees that Plato is wholly immune from the kind of 'paradeig-matism' which would at once expose him to eristic 'Third Man' refutations. Plato believed, he says, 'that since the Idea *is* that which the particular *has* as an attribute, the "third man" is illegitimate as an argument against the Ideas because Idea and particular cannot be treated as homogeneous members of a multiplicity' (*Criticism*, p. 298). Cherniss also correctly says, in criticism of Vlastos, that such statements as 'Justice is just' or 'Beauty is beautiful' need not be taken to mean that Justice and Beauty *have* the characters indicated but that 'Justice' and 'just', or 'Beauty' and 'beautiful' are *identical* (*Studies in Plato's Metaphysics*, ed. Reginald E. Allen, 1965, p. 370). (The whole doctrine of the inaddible Ideas of Number in which, though not in the universal Idea-Numbers, Cherniss believes, likewise shows that Plato did not regard the Triad Itself as a perfect instance of Threeness, for if he did it would certainly consist of two perfect units added to a third perfect unit.) Cherniss correctly points out that a rejection of this sort of paradeigmatism as leading to an infinite regress is already present in the argument of *Republic*, 597c that if God had, *per impossibile*, been able to make two Beds Themselves, the third bed that they both had as a paradigm would have been the real Bed Itself. In other words, the multiplicity of many like things has no application to Ideas, and for this reason the 'likeness' of beds to the Bed Itself is a unique sort of analogy and not at all the same as the purely derivative likeness of one bed to another, and not therefore leading to any further postulation of Beds Themselves.

One may go further with Cherniss and agree both that Aristotle thought that the Platonic Ideas were meant to have a real existence apart from or separate from phenomena and that he cannot be shown to have been mistaken in this interpretation (*Criticism*, pp. 206–7). For not only is an Idea a different sort of entity from its participants, and not only is it the Perfection which they never fully exemplify, but it would plainly not cease to enjoy its perfect kind of being, and to be what it is, if it never had any closely approximate illustrations. What can, however, be questioned is whether the *sort* of separateness that Ideas were meant to have from phenomenal instances was the sort of separateness that meant that Ideas could not *also* be really present in those instances, and truly operative in them, and truly present to the mind in knowledge, and also truly present in and sharing their entrails with one another, and overlapping and interpenetrating one another in a continuum of sense. Yet some or all of these possibilities are rejected by Aristotle as contradicting the very notion of ideal apartness, and are rejected by Cherniss for the same reason, and were probably rejected by a body called the Friends of the Ideas which grew up in the Academy, and of which Speusippus probably was at first a member, with whom Cherniss in his interpretations admiringly ranges himself. It is arguable that Plato *never* assented to any crude antithesis of transcendent apartness and indwelling presence as mutually contradictory – he in fact tells us that the Forms themselves *appear* many in their instances – and the acceptance of such an antithesis would plainly have destroyed the possibility of discourse and knowledge for the justification of which the Eide were at first introduced. We may, in fact, say that the very separateness of the Ideas from their instances, being quite unlike the separation of one instance from another, need imply no sort of remoteness or disconnection from those instances, but *rather the contrary*. For it is a profound gulf of *type* which rests on the disparate roles of Idea and Instance in predication, the one being the predicate itself, while the other is no more than a case or instance or likeness or participant of it. We may, in fact, say that the sort of separateness which the Idea has from its instances is one which, differently regarded, *entails* their mutual inseparability. For while an Idea could, on Platonic premisses, exist even if it had no instances, it is none the less always the sort of entity of which there could, with some degree of approximation, be instances – the notion of an Idea incapable of having such instances is undocumented in Plato since it is wholly meaningless – and the instantial sharers in Ideas are plainly thought by Plato to be abjectly *dependent* on the Ideas they approximately exemplify, and without whose efficacious presence they would be wholly uncharacterizable as well as non-existent.

I do not imagine that Professor Cherniss would wish to question the sort of inseparability or profound connectivity that I have just been emphasizing: plainly it is as much part of the eidetic theory as the gulf of type which he rightly emphasizes. But something in his whole mental slant makes him, like Aristotle, push the sort of separateness that he rightly recognizes further than it ought to go, so that it encroaches upon the rights of the sort of connective inseparability that is simply its other side. And this encroachment, as in many similar cases, is justified by an invalid appeal to the Law of Non-Contradiction, the divinity that is wrongly made to preside over all bad philosophy. Thus Professor Cherniss is particularly harsh to Eudoxus who held that the Idea Whiteness might be admixed with a white thing, and so render it white, a view that sounds remarkably like the statement in *Republic*, 476a referred to above, that Ideas through their communion with actions and things and one another might appear to be many. To this view Aristotle says that it is easy to assemble many insuperable objections (*Metaphysics*, 991a 16–18), the most important of which, taken by Alexander from Aristotle's Περὶ ἰδεῶν, amounts to holding that the mixture of Ideas with particulars *contradicts* the Platonic conception of Ideas as imperishable, independent, immobile 'models' of particulars.

This criticism is endorsed by Cherniss, who says that Eudoxus had tried to explain the relation of Ideas to particulars as one of immanence, and had thereby made of the Ideas a self-contradictory conception, 'either unconsciously or at least without express recognition of the consequences and commensurate alteration of the theory to avoid them' (*Riddle*, p. 79). He also suggests that Plato in the *Parmenides* is disassociating himself from these immanentalist views of Eudoxus and their consequences. Yet it is hard to see how the intimate παρουσία or κοινώνια of the Ideas with their cases, which cannot be very different from the admixture of Eudoxus, and which in *Phaedo*, 100d is said to be that through which these cases become what they are, is in any way incompatible with the utter difference of type between them and their cases in which their 'separation' alone can consist. Of course, if Eudoxus meant by the admixture of White with a white thing, the presence of something like an individual lump of white in that thing, then his theory confused type and instance, and was utterly non-explanatory and self-contradictory, but is there any reason to suppose that he believed anything so absurd? Was he doing more than making clear the essential two-sidedness, the amphibious straddling of two realms, involved in any case of predication?

Professor Cherniss also reproves all those interpreters of Plato who have made the Platonic Ideas 'productive agents' of any kind (*Criticism*, p. 452), but here he not only collides with the statements of Plato but also with those of Aristotle. For not only are the Ideas regarded as the true causes of their instantiations in *Phaedo*, 100, but the Idea of the Good is plainly said in *Republic*, 509 to be that through which being is itself dispensed to the Ideas and hence to all things. And in the *Parmenides*, Hypothesis II, the Idea of Unity can quite fairly be said to 'generate' a whole set of related Ideas. And Aristotle's attempts to show that the Idea of Man does not by itself account for the being of a man without an instantial father as cause of motion, show that Plato *did* think it was the real, operative cause, though the instantial father and his acts might of course be that without which it could not act. That Aristotle believed that eidetic causes must be impotent and formal, unless helped out by sources of motion, does not mean that Plato thought so. The Aristotelian 'formal cause' is a mere shorn relic of Platonism. And though, from the time of the writing of the *Phaedrus* onwards, Soul and Souls become the universal dispensers of motion to the universe, this does not imply that eidetic causality has been done away with. For Souls are plainly instances of Life Itself, Knowledge Itself, Self-motion Itself, integrated in all probability into the true Demiurge, Very Mind Itself, and it is from these, which are all ideal entities, that the power of Souls to initiate motion is derived.

And yet another very extraordinary conclusion is deduced by

Cherniss from his dogma of total separateness: that the hierarchical arrangement of Ideas into Genera and Species 'does not portray the relational arrangements of the world of Ideas' but is only an 'instrument of analysis' (*Criticism*, p. 46). The various Genera and specifying Differentiae of Ideas are not to be thought of as entering into their 'construction' or 'constitution', but as merely expressive of their logical relations of implication, compatibility and incompatibility with other Ideas. They are merely aids to *reminiscence*: by placing an Idea in the right context, they remind us what it is. If any interpretation is without support in anything Plato anywhere says, this surely is in that case. Again Professor Cherniss says (*Riddle*, p. 54) that Plato nowhere 'makes the distinction of genus and species among the ideas, but what Aristotle calls genus, differentia and species are for him all distinct ideal units, each other than the others, each having aspects which imply the existence of the others or are compatible with them, but each being an independent nature which cannot be exhaustively analysed into the others'. And again (*loc. cit.*) that the Ideas which in the *Sophist* are said to blend or pervade one another are still separate, unmixed and indivisible units, the relations between them being really those of implication and compatibility. No Idea can be a constituent part to any other. Of all accounts of the realm of Ideas this surely is the most flagrantly paradoxical. For it would turn that realm into an assemblage of entities not only individual but wholly simple, Wittgensteinian 'objects' in short, and it is hard to see how λόγοι or definitions, the very soil out of which the theory of Ideas grew, could retain any meaning when all they do is connect such senseless atoms with one another. We are asked to believe that when Plato defines Justice as doing one's own job and not meddling with that of others, he is not discerning any structured complexity of sense in the Idea thus defined, but merely connecting one unstructured simple with others. Why take the trouble to do anything so senseless? And how do the unstructured simples assist reminiscence? Why not simply dwell on the profound simplicity of Justice without connecting it with anything? Whatever these views are, they are not Platonic.

Speusippus, it is said, was led by the difficulties of logical division into Genera and Species into abandoning the doctrine of Ideas. He could not conceive that one could define any Idea without locating it in the whole hierarchy of Ideas (*Posterior Analytics*, 97a 6–22 and commentators), and this seemed to involve the multiplied presence of generic Ideas in their varied species, and involved separation of the generic Idea from itself, and its association with incompatible differentiae (see *Riddle*, p. 40). These difficulties indicate that Speusippus suffered from the fragmenting disease reprobated in the *Sophist*, a disease from which Plato himself was apparently immune, realizing that it was no true problem but only a platitude of essence that a generic Idea should be inseparable, not indeed from a single specific Idea, but from one or other out of a range of specific Ideas, whose inseparability from the generic Idea does not entail their inseparability from one another. Thus in the *Phaedrus* (265d–266a) madness is treated both as a single Idea and also as a continuum of sense which extends over, and can be divided into, various left-handed and right-handed species, and where it is all-important that this continuum should be cut 'at the joints', and not at wrong and unnatural places. The whole tenour of the passage is not to encourage the notion of Ideas as simple, mutually external units, but as natural segments in a continuum of sense, a continuum which can be wrongly and arbitrarily cut, and as segments, moreover, which, while utterly distinct from other well-cut or badly-cut segments, may very well overlap or include, quite as much as exclude, one another, the generic segments always necessarily including the specific. Such a belief in a continuum of sense accords well with what Aristotle says of the Ideas as begotten by the action of Unity on the Great and Small: the Great and Small is the continuum which as such is jointlessly extensive, while Unity is the joint-introducing factor, which splits it up into well-formed segments, cut off at natural nodes. It is only by accepting such a jointed-continuum view of the Ideas that we can understand Plato's superior interest in the Genus, to which Aristotle throughout testifies: for the Genus extends over its species and sums them all up. If anyone doubts whether Plato really viewed the Genus in this inclusive manner, let him read *Timaeus*, 30c where the Ideal Living Creature on which the cosmos is modelled is one of which the Ideas of more specific living creatures are all parts, which embraces them just as the instantial cosmos embraces all the instances of animality. Yet on the unit-view of Cherniss the Genus of Living Creature would in no sense take precedence over its many species, but they, on account of their greater number and more specific content, would rather take precedence over it. The passage in the *Timaeus* is not signalled as an innovation: it is meant to state the conception of the generic universal, the One over Many, in terms of which Plato has continuously thought. And Dialogues such as the *Sophist* and *Parmenides* do not bring in a new doctrine of eidetic interpenetration to which Plato had lately come: they merely make explicit the view implicit in the definitory endeavours from which the doctrine of Ideas had sprung, and which were now being challenged by the 'Friends of the Ideas'. The language of the much-studied sentence in *Sophist*, 253d, where one Idea is said to be completely extended through many that lie apart from one another, or to embrace many different from one another, or to be continuous in many wholes while only some lie wholly apart etc., plainly yields us an eidetic continuum where the same territory is pervaded by several Ideas. If the coincidence were complete, as it is in the case of such supremely generic Ideas as Unity, Being and Goodness, it would hardly matter whether, with the Megarians, one regarded them as the same Idea differently spoken of and approached, or as distinct Ideas, and this explains why Plato shows a differing allegiance to Being, Unity, Goodness and also Beauty in different Dialogues. And if the conjunction of the two parts of the Dialogue *Parmenides* has any lesson to teach us, it is that the mutual embrace and coverage of Ideas by Ideas which is not paradoxical at their own level, even if it leads to seemingly self-contradictory formulations, removes the paradox of the mutual embrace and coverage of Ideas by Ideas which occurs more wildly in their scattered instantiations. An Idea is no more hindered from being its distinct self in and through the shadow-involvements of instantiation, than it is hindered from being its distinct self by overlapping and even coinciding with other Ideas in the region of ideal contents. Professor Cherniss argues that the blendings and sharings of the Ideal realm can have no parallel in the sharings of Ideas by instances, since relations of Ideas are all symmetrical while the sharing of Ideas by Ideas is not (*Riddle*, p. 54). But surely, when one Idea embraces and pervades many Ideas which lie apart from one another, this is as asymmetrical a relation as any: the embracing Idea is *not* embraced by the Ideas which merely fall within it. And when the Idea of Motion shares in that of Being, since it eternally is, the Idea of Being surely does not therefore share in that of Motion, being eternally at rest.

If one may now specify a basic objection to all Cherniss's reasonings, it is that they turn Ideas into instance-like entities, and so make their universality meaningless. It may be said that Professor Cherniss throughout ignores the ontological difference of kind which Plato expresses by calling the Ideas 'ontically ontic', whereas no other *soi-disant* entities, whether these be instances or souls or mysterious media like Space, have such an ontically ontic status. Professor Cherniss thinks, as all instantialists think, that Plato could not really have meant to deny that there were particular things and activities in space and time, or particular souls that caused motions in space or the great empty medium Space itself in which all this phantasmagoria was displayed, and to which it was compelled to cling. What he really meant was that, *in addition* to all these second-class entities, which can yield no accurate knowledge and moral guidance, there are *other* remarkable, separated entities which do have these prerogatives, and it is only this superior *dignity* we try to express when we call them really real. But perfection and timelessness and perspicuity, etc., etc., plainly would not give the Ideas the faintest ontological advantage if instances, souls and space existed in the same sense as they do, and were in fact so ontologically self-sufficient that they existed quite outside of the Ideas and did not *owe* their being to them. Plainly Plato's theory of Ideas was the first essay in that Analogy of Being which Aristotle first formulated semantically, while completely inverting its application, and of which almost all medieval philosophy is an elaboration. The Ideas only really are, and instances and souls are merely an outlying, variable accident of their being, a way in which they overflow in display, souls being of course an infinitely more honourable and Idea-like overflow than bodily manifestations, while Space is no more than the confusedly hypostatized range or field in which we have to imagine that the overflow takes place. Plato like Aristotle believes that Being is spoken in many senses, and that some have a linguistic and ontological prerogative over others, only while for Aristotle individuals and their essences have this sort of prerogative, for Plato the Ideas (and afterwards their Principle(s)) have this sort of prerogative, all else being variously dependent on them. Plato could not, of course, say that instances, Soul and Space were *in* the Ideas as Aristotle could put other categories variously in Substance, but he made use of talk of efficacy, communication, presence, reflection etc. which have the same logical role. Things other than Ideas exist only πῇ, after a fashion: they are ways, and peripheral ways, in which Ideas are what they are, but they are much less central for philosophy than what Ideas are in and for themselves.

When Plato says in *Republic*, 478e that instances participate in both being and non-being and can have neither straightforwardly predicated of them, and when he says in *Timaeus*, 50c that they are likenesses of what eternally are, modelled by them in a wonderful manner which is hard to express, he is certainly not making of them anything that can exist apart from the Ideas of which they are the flickering exhibitions. And when he says that we have to locate these exhibitions in something in order to give them a tenuous hold upon being, he is not giving an ontological certificate to the shadowy spatial medium which has just been said to have been arrived at by a spurious argument. He is merely indicating the manner in which the flickering category of the instantial points to the unflickering nothingness to which it is a halfway house. And souls, though almost raised above the instantial through their instantiation of such pervasive universals as Life and Knowledge, are none the less also instances, whose efficacy derives from the force of the whole ideal realm which is always impinging on them. Yet, as we have seen (*Criticism*, pp. 207, 452), Professor Cherniss is content to deny all efficacy to the Ideas, souls only having this prerogative, while Space is taken so seriously that he can call it (*Criticism*, p. 103) an object of reason, even if admittedly 'bastard', and can say that its being is genuinely necessary if there are to be instances at all. Plato does indeed say in the *Timaeus* that Being, Space and Becoming, all three, exist, but the very opposition of Being to Space and Becoming shows that he does not believe that all members of the trio exist in the same manner, and there is plainly a tongue-in-cheek attitude in talking of the being of Space and Idea-copies that is not present in talking of Ideas. Professor Cherniss repudiates as an Aristotelian misunderstanding any identification of Space with Non-being or Falsehood (*Criticism*, pp. 99–104): all that has been rendered impossible by the *Sophist*, where Non-being has been shown to be Otherness, and Falsehood to be the mistaken combination of really existent factors. The *Sophist* has not, however, abolished Non-being but enriched it and given it positive content: it has been made to embrace all that is other than what a thing is, the flying of Theaetetus, the identity of Justice with the interest of the stronger etc., things which, in being other than what is, are more than a merely mistaken combination of existent factors coming to be only in the ψυχή, wherever that may be. They are combinations which, because other than what is, have a hold upon being, whether mistakenly believed in or not. Space may well be falsehood or Non-being in this sense, the empty expanse which real being abhors, and in whose nullity instantiation has room to flicker. Such at least appears to be a better interpretation than Professor Cherniss's of what must be conceded to be very puzzling passages.

I must, however, turn from these irreconcilable differences of general interpretation, which are, however, quite relevant to our discussion, to the specific issue of Plato's alleged identification of the Ideas with Numbers. Professor Cherniss thinks that he never did make the identification in question, though he certainly had a detailed theory of the Ideas of Numbers which Aristotle has garbled: the general identification is, in its entirety, an extraordinary piece of Aristotelian garbling, based on Aristotle's determination to force the notions arrived at in his own philosophy on earlier thinkers. I, of course, believe that Plato did make the identification, and I also think that it is necessary to the complete rounding out of the Platonic theory, and to the understanding of the Dialogues. Here at the beginning I must however agree with Professor Cherniss that Plato certainly had conceived the doctrine of the Ideas before he came to believe in any arithmetization of them, and that the many arguments for them which Aristotle summarized in the Περὶ ἰδεῶν and the *Metaphysics* are quite independent of any identification of Ideas with Numbers. I believe myself that Plato compounded the Ideas out of Cratylean, Pythagorean, Socratic and Megarian elements during the life-time of Socrates, perhaps with the ironically encouraging or wryly discouraging midwifery of his teacher. Certainly the whole doctrine was well-established and argumentatively buttressed when the Academy was founded, and represented the basic material of its teaching and discussion, though not in the sense of a mandatory dogma. The giving of a completely numerical analysis of the Ideas was, however, the exciting project with which Plato had been fired on his first Italian visit by contact with the Pythagoreans, and he expounded it in oral gatherings and in private conversations in which only a few auditors persisted, and in which incomprehension made him withdraw into increasing reserve and tentativeness.

The recommendation of the project is, however, plain, and it is extraordinary that Aristotle, who makes so much of Cratylus and his flux, should not have mentioned it. It is that the qualities of sense, redness, warmth etc., belong wholly to the great instantial flux, varying from moment to moment and from man to man, and that no reliable statement or knowledge can be made or had regarding them. All that is reliable are measures, quantitative data of some sort: this is what the *Republic* implies throughout, the *Theaetetus* justifies and the *Timaeus* illustrates. Quite obviously, if the Dialectic is to begin, proceed and end with Ideas, as stated in the *Republic*, it cannot do so if any of these Ideas involve an infusion of sensuous quality or the vague sentiments of common morality: they must be formal, mathematical, rigorous, reasoned from beginning to end. Some sort of rudimentary formalization, a reduction of all notions to mathematical manifolds, is plainly on the cards. This formalization was not, even on the Aristotelian evidence, the silly identification of Ideas with isolated Natural Numbers which kept within the Decad. The identification was with patterns of ratios rather than with isolated Natural Numbers, and with ratios covering many distinct dimensions which the Decad was introduced to delimit, and sense can be made of their coverage of the psychological, the biological and the axiological. In a sense Plato anticipated the whole pattern of formalization which modern logic has in many fields implemented. It is a pity that Professor Cherniss never published the second volume of his *Aristotle's Criticism* in which we might at least have had his detailed treatment of Plato's Ideas of Numbers, whether or not one agreed that these were only *some* of Plato's Ideas. The war which claimed Professor Cherniss's services interrupted his life-work, and one has only the polemical *Riddle of the Early Academy* to go upon. What one has there is really only a project, as incomplete as the Unwritten Doctrines which they criticize.

Why then, according to Professor Cherniss, did Aristotle credit Plato with a comprehensive identification of Ideas with Numbers, when he only believed in the reality of certain Ideas of Numbers? Professor Cherniss thinks, in the first place, that it would be wrong to think that Aristotle simply *heard* Plato expounding his arithmetizing doctrine on a number of occasions, and that what he heard formed the basis of his reports. He holds that there is only reliable evidence of *one* lecture on the Good given by Plato, of which several present took notes, and he admits (*Riddle*, p. 12) that Aristotle certainly worked up his notes into the published treatise *On the Good*, which was accessible to Alexander and from which he quoted in many places. It is not, however, clear why, if Plato only gave this one totally enigmatic lecture on the Good and then shrank into silence, Aristotle should have devoted a three-book treatise to its contents. Surely the pervasive references to a Platonic identification of Ideas with Numbers point to more than a single occasion on which Plato held forth on the subject? Surely all that Aristotle says could not all have been based on a single obscure lecture and a long chain of precarious inferences?

Cherniss says (*Riddle*, pp. 14-15) that the Unwritten Doctrines of Plato are at best referred to by Aristotle in two places, and that in one of these (*De Anima*, 404b) Aristotle may have been referring to his *own* treatise *On Philosophy* and not to one of Plato's, and that he may have been drawing material from Xenocrates's treatise *On Nature*. Equally, however, he *may* have been referring to a writing of Plato, who alone is mentioned in the passage, and whose own treatise would have been a vastly better authority for Plato's views than one of Aristotle's. And if the unmentioned Xenocrates has really crept into the picture, his interpretations of the *Timaeus* would hardly have been dragged in without mention unless they largely agreed with what Plato was wont to say. To one reader at least the message of the Psychogony in *Timaeus*, 35ff. is that the contrast between Selfsameness and dispersed Variety which obtains between eidetic and instantial being and the soul's cognition of either, is *also* reproduced in the contrast of Selfsameness and Difference in either form of being, so that we have a contrast of parallel contrasts, as in the *Republic*, and not a simple threefold mixture. Such an interpretation brings the *Timaeus*-passage closer to its traditional interpretation, which alone makes worthwhile philosophical sense, and which is also more in accord with Aristotle's account of Plato's elements. And to one reader, also, the Xenocratean account of the Soul as a self-moving Number is quite fairly based on the later parts of the Psychogony, in which account is taken of the spatial dimensions and of time, and where the continuum of the Great and Small is represented by the rolled-out Soul-strips, on which demiurgic Unity infixes delimiting ratios. If this is Xenocrates, it is Plato also, and Plato as he may have on various occasions orally explained himself. The characterization of a Soul as a self-moving Number is, moreover, apposite as well as profoundly Platonic, especially when one considers the varied life-styles of the people one knows.

The other passage cited by Cherniss (*Riddle*, pp. 15-16) is one from

Physics, 209b which says that Plato in the Unwritten Doctrines identified the Material Principle with the Great and Small, whereas in the *Timaeus* he identified it with Space. Cherniss says that the reference does not imply that Plato gave ordered lectures on these topics, and that the Unwritten Dogmas referred to may have been mere opinions that Plato expressed in conversation. If he expressed such opinions in conversation, the conversations in question must have been so frequent and so memorable as to be not very different, in effect at least, from an ordered series of lectures. Certainly they stamped themselves on the memory of Aristotle. The passage, moreover, shows the key-significance of the term 'Great and Small' in these memorable conversations, and though the arithmetization of the Ideas is not referred to in *Physics,* 209b, it is so closely connected with this term in what Aristotle says in other places, as to authenticate, in an indirect manner, the bulk of what is said in those places. The term 'Great and Small' is certainly singular, it is not Pythagorean, and presumably Plato gave it a peculiar sense and used it in peculiar contexts, which Aristotle has correctly reproduced. And that Aristotle thinks that the Great and Small is not very different from Space or from his own Matter, will not prove that it did not *also* have important eidetic functions for Plato, for, whether mysterious to Aristotle or Cherniss or not, it is for Plato the *same* Principle which specifies in the ideal world and individuates in the sensible.

One should not, however, build on Aristotle's *explicit* references to unwritten Platonic teachings: his whole account of Plato's doctrine presupposes such teachings, and is honeycombed with their deposits. Cherniss thinks that the fact that we almost certainly have *all* Plato's authentic written work is a relevant point against Unwritten Doctrines: the point would be relevant were the Dialogues the sort of composition in which anyone's doctrines could be plainly set forth. He thinks (*Riddle,* p. 13) that statements in the Seventh Epistle, *if* authentic (which he does not think they are), would render it doubtful whether Plato would have endorsed as accurate any of the reports we have of his unwritten conversations or discourses. Perhaps he would not have endorsed them, but evidence of his teaching they would none the less remain: the auditors of his discourses certainly claimed to have garnered certain doctrines from him, even if he would have held that they had misunderstood him totally. Plato's objections to his reporters read like Wittgenstein's explosions against those who, he said, had vulgarized his doctrine: they do not prove that the reporters or the vulgarizers misunderstood everything. Even Dionysius of Syracuse may have got some things right. Cherniss thinks it remarkable (*Riddle,* pp. 71–2) that, if Plato talked freely on his doctrines, he should never have been asked and should never have answered all the questions on, for example, the physics of the *Timaeus*, on which Academic interpretation differed. Anyone who has consorted with philosophers knows, however, how apt they are at deflecting the direct and unwelcome question: Wittgenstein in such predicaments became positively scriptural, and asked how, having been with him so long, one could dream of raising such a question. There is therefore no reason to doubt that Plato discoursed fairly systematically on a wide number of philosophical questions, and that parts of what he said seemed too tentative or too transcendental or too readily misunderstood to be given a place in the publicly circulated and perhaps publicly performed Dialogues. And there is no reason to doubt that what he said is the basis of the Aristotelian reports. One can believe otherwise if one is determined to do so – everything in this field is hypothesis, as Cherniss himself concedes (*Riddle*, p. 29) – but such a determination is wilful, and the evidence tells against it.

How then, according to Cherniss, did Aristotle come to attribute to Plato a comprehensive identification of Ideas with Numbers? He came to do so because he was enamoured of his own new concepts of the contraries and of Matter and Form, and was determined to see them everywhere. He had successfully foisted these doctrines on the pre-Socratic thinkers (*Criticism*, p. 83), and thereupon went on to foist them on Plato (p. 84, *et seq.*), first identifying his own Material Principle with the Platonic Recipient, Space, which is by no means thought of by Plato as a Matter on which forms are imposed, and also perversely reading his doctrine of contraries into Plato's term 'Great and Small', which it is plain really had a unitary rather than a dual significance. Plato, Cherniss says, may *possibly* have used this phrase of the permanent substrate of generation in his 'conversations' (*Criticism*, p. 87), and may *possibly* have substituted the word 'Dyad' for it. That these key-terms of Platonism were actually used by Plato is therefore conceded by Cherniss. Aristotle then went on more or less gratuitously to identify Plato's pure Space-Matter with Non-being, an identification that could not stem from Plato, since Plato in the *Timaeus* accords eternal existence to Space – what, however, could be more eternal in its being than that which is not? – and since in the *Sophist* he has shown himself unwilling to have anything to do with absolute Non-being (*Criticism*, p. 92), which he has replaced by Otherness. But Plato, according to Aristotle, was led to this identification by his acceptance, in Eleatic fashion, of Being as quite undifferentiated, and by the consequent demand that something other than Being, i.e. Non-being, was needed to differentiate it. Having got so far, and having identified Plato's Space with Matter, and his Matter with Non-being, Aristotle went on to identify Plato's Non-being with the False, again taking his stand on passages in the *Sophist*, and bringing in a reference to the use of false premisses in certain geometrical proofs (*Posterior Analytics*, 49b). Having made all these inadequately motivated identifications of Matter with all these Platonic concepts, Aristotle went on to look for some variant of Matter even in the case of the Platonic Forms (*Criticism*, pp. 172–3). Plato, Cherniss argues, could not have thought in terms of such a variant, for the Space which Aristotle identifies with his sensible Matter is expressly excluded by *Timaeus*, 52 from the intelligible world. Being thus unable to find a concept which answered to Matter in the case of the Forms, Aristotle was forced to suppose that the *same* factor, i.e. the Great and Small, which served as Matter in the sensible world *also* served as Matter (for Plato) in the world of Forms. The *Sophist* assisted this hypothesis, for, by teaching that Otherness pervaded the intelligible world, and by identifying Otherness with Non-being, which Aristotle had already identified with Matter and Space, it suggested that something like Matter and Space was present in the intelligible world (*Riddle*, p. 25). In association with the One this Material Principle generated the Forms, and then proceeded to have an incestuous affair with its own offspring and generated the sensibles: to such straddling of two spheres by the Great and Small, and to such incestuous commerce with its own offspring, Aristotle and Cherniss have the gravest objections, Aristotle to Plato for thinking it, and Cherniss to Aristotle for thinking Plato thought it. Unity, according to Cherniss, is an important but by no means pivotal member of the world of Forms, and it certainly confers unity on all the Forms, but it would be quite un-Platonic to treat it as some sort of formative factor which shapes the Forms out of some sort of Matter: this is entirely an Aristotelian interpretation, which leads to the un-Platonic belief that the Forms must have a Matter as well as a Form (*Riddle*, p. 51). Certain modern interpreters, Cherniss says, have tried to defend the Platonic character of the ideal Material Principle by appealing to the *Philebus*, taking it that Plato meant the Forms to be the products of Unity, the Limit, sporting with the Unlimited, i.e. the Great and Small. Cherniss retorts that the *Philebus* identifies the mixtures of Limit and Unlimited with sensible things, while the Ideas are spoken of as eternally immutable and unmixed (*Riddle*, p. 18). And those modern interpreters who venture to suppose that 'different species' of the Great and Small might be present in the intelligible and sensible worlds are soundly trounced by him for trying to see even an analogy between the spatial recipient of the *Timaeus*, and anything which can be alleged to be a Material Principle in the case of the Ideas (p. 22).

As one reads through this terrible tissue of argument, which I may very well have misunderstood or misrepresented at certain points, one cannot help wondering whether Professor Cherniss can be really reconstructing a great philosopher's progressive misunderstandings of another great philosopher, or whether he may not rather be giving expression to a non-philosopher's misunderstandings of the mis-understandings of a great philosopher, motivated throughout by entrenched theoretical *parti pris*. The concepts of Matter and Form may be Aristotelian, but are they not concepts that *anyone* must form and use, when he thinks deeply on any material, and were they not truly present and operative in the thought of the pre-Socratic philosophers, and might they not also be present and operative in the thought of Plato, even in regard to so exalted a matter as the being of the Forms? Aristotle himself believed in an ideal Matter for geometrical abstrac-tions, and conceived of the Genus as a sort of ideal Matter to which a differentia gives form, and thereby perfects a Species: could Plato not also have thought in this manner? Was any interpretation in terms of Matter and Form, whether of the pre-Socratics or of Plato, necessarily an alien and violent Aristotelian imposition? Cherniss is forced to suppose such things only by his own view of the Forms as timeless, ideal, unanalysable 'individuals', as separate from one another as from sensible things: all talk of blending, presence, communion, imparting etc., must be so interpreted as to fit in with these choristic prepossessions. But other readers of Plato do not read him in this manner, as we have indicated, and to them such an account as that in the *Phaedrus* where the dialectician is required to cut at the joints, have every suggestion of an eidetic continuum in which certain points of salience distinguish themselves. And if Plato's Space in the *Timaeus* is not properly conceived as a kind of material, some of his arguments for it, i.e. those which have to do with the different shapings of gold, certainly bring out some analogy between pure Place and Stuff, which Aristotle laid hold of, and we must then remember that since some of the most important inhabitants of the world of Forms are geometrical figures and solids, there must, despite the rigorous exclusion which Cherniss tries to cull from the *Timaeus*, be something like Spatiality Itself or Very Space Itself in the realm above. And if one asks for specific passages where something like an ideal Material Principle is mentioned, one has but to think of the rolled-out soul-strips previously mentioned, on which demiurgic Thinkingness pricks out crucial points of ratio. Truly, it is a Soul that is being constructed, but surely its construction may point to something in the 'Intelligible Animal' on which it is modelled? And one has further but to think of 'the Others' throughout the *Parmenides*, and particularly in the seventh Hypothesis (164–5), where, in the absence of Unity, they always evanesce into an indefinite multiplicity which defies all numeration, in which even Cornford recognizes the presence of the Great and Small. Surely it is meaningful to conceive of such an indefinite continuum as a sort of ἐκμαγεῖον or raw material on which unity is imposed as a Limit, thereby helping to constitute the Natural Numbers, the Ratios among them, and all measurable multi-dimensional patterns? The 'generation' thus involved can be conceived as a logical constitution rather than as a fabrication in time.

We may note further that the *Philebus* uses its Principles of Limit and Unlimited in *two* contexts and manners just as the Aristotelian reports declare: they operate eidetically in *Philebus*, 16, and phenomenally in *Philebus*, 25-6, and if Plato does not very clearly distinguish between these two operations, it is because they are in fact for him parts of a single shadow-play, in which Unifying Limit as Such first begets the specific Form-unities, and these specific Form-unities then beget their sensible instances, the operation proceeding analogously in the two cases. Cherniss calls on the *Timaeus* to witness that the Space which makes possible the instantiation of the Eide, cannot have any identity or analogy with anything in the realm of the Eide, where all is unmixed and enduring. But Plato is the sort of thinker who, while *admitting* the deep gulf of difference between the Great and Small functioning in its two contexts, would also be capable of believing in the *identity* of the Great and Small in and through its two modes of operation, just as he would believe both in its difference *qua* constituting the various geometrical dimensions in the eidetic realm and its profound identity in all these various constitutions. Plotinus tells us that in the ideal realm each is all, and all all, and the glory infinite, and he tells us also that everything that is yonder is also here. Plato may not have expressed himself with such Alexandrian lyricism, but this is what his statements at every point presume, and what is presumed by all who know the difference between meanings and peanuts or between a Type and its cases.

The use of the principles of Identity and Contradiction to establish the rigid exclusions favoured by Cherniss had fortunately not as yet established itself in Plato's time, and the last sentence of the *Parmenides* is an eloquent warding-off of all the nonsense that was to come. Plato, though he was capable of using bad arguments to prove that the Soul had parts, shows that he was well capable of locating Ideas multiply, and inducing them to blend, without incurring anything like genuine self-contradiction. And the various notions which Cherniss painfully connects by a series of Aristotelian confusions, can be seen as indicating a genuine eidetic progress. The continuum of Space which separates the half-being of distinct instantiations is a total non-being in comparison with their half-being, and is a condition of their movement as well as their multiplicity. Otherness in the world of Forms is rather like the non-being of Space: it covers the interstices between the prime Forms where all corruptions and deviations nestle, and in which a skilful Sophist, by squinting *raisonnements*, can induce us to see the prime Forms in question. Instead of seeing Justice where and as what it is, the fulfilment of function in a well-ordered society, we can by the sophist Thrasymachus be induced to see it where it is not and as what it is not, in the place reserved for the oligarchical or tyrannical society, where Justice is distorted into being the interest of the stronger. This squinting Aristotle interestingly likens to the squinting practised by geometers who displace lines where they are not and cannot be, in order to make clear where they absolutely and necessarily are (*Posterior Analytics*, 49b). In this sense Non-being or Falsehood pervades the whole realm of the Forms, since there are gaps there that will harbour them, just as illusion pervades the whole realm of the senses since there are empty spaces in which they may be projected. And neither form of Non-being really commits us ontologically, since neither the eidetic nor the material recipient exists except in a so-to-speak manner. If one were not too afraid to shock textualists and literalists, one might say that, in the last resort, only Unity Itself, which is also Being and Goodness and Beauty Itself, is given anything like an ontological status by Plato, all else being only its specifications or instantiations, whether material or psychic, and even though Plato, like his remote disciple, the pseudo-Dionysius, prefers to think of it in terms of a *superesse* rather than an *esse*.

There are a great number of further points of interest in Professor Cherniss's treatment of Plato's doctrine of the *numerical* Eide, which he seems to allow may have had a conceptual derivation from Unity Itself, even though not the one sketched by Aristotle. Had Cherniss written the projected second volume of his *Criticism* all these points would have come up for detailed discussion. He has also sketched an imaginative picture of the personalities and activities in the Academy, which, however, only proves that the Cherniss-view of the early Academy is as much a projection of Cherniss as everyone else's picture necessarily is a projection of themselves. The loss of Aristotle's books *On the Good*, Xenocrates,s books *On Nature* and other writings, render certain problems permanently insoluble: one can at best hope to construct a credible over-all picture out of all the evidential material, including both the Dialogues and the Aristotelian and other reports. Professor Cherniss has chosen to construct a somewhat arid, limited picture of Plato's doctrine, open to all the classical, Aristotelian objections, by interpreting most of Plato's utterances in terms of a few, chosen others, and employing canons of strict entailment and non-contradiction which are not applicable to any great philosopher, and certainly not to Plato. He has also defended his interpretation against any discrepant reports of Aristotelian thought by *any* hypothesis, however far-fetched, that will enable him to discount those reports. Professor Cherniss has argued a case, and has argued it ingeniously, but he has not argued it convincingly. His whole elaborate structure of inferences is in fact little more than a house of cards. The whole body of Aristotelian statements regarding Plato's number-analysis of the Forms cannot be discounted as due to the perverse identifications and inferences of Aristotle, based on a slanted reading of the Dialogues, nor can it all be fathered upon Xenocrates who, though very Platonic, undoubtedly diverged from Plato in many points in this sort of doctrine. The only way to assess the probable truth of the Aristotelian reports of the Platonic Number-analysis is to try to make sense of them, to show that they are not a nonsensical farrago, and that they do accord with, and throw light on, the statements of the Dialogues. This is what I have attempted to do in this book, though conscious of my own inadequacies for doing it, and in the hope that others would go on to do it better.

It must not be thought that there are not respects in which I profoundly admire the work of Cherniss. Quite apart from his almost superhuman scholarship, he is utterly right in holding that Plato never deviated from his doctrine of the Ideas, and did not end up in a phase of negative criticism in which he was little different from a modern analytic philosopher writing Attic. He is entirely right in holding that Plato's doctrine was at all times firmly realistic, and can at no point be interpreted in neo-Kantian or other idealistic terms. He is also right in recognizing that Plato's treatment of the forms as being Each Thing Itself does not expose him to silly charges of self-predication, nor to the shallow antinomies of the first part of the *Parmenides*, and that his recognition of the eidetic Numbers as not made up of units, nor as mutually conflatable, represents no more than a lucid piece of common sense. I only wish that Cherniss had used his incomparable grasp of all the evidence to forge a path of understanding to this, the central citadel of Platonic doctrine, rather than to build up a massive structure of obfuscating objections, which have, for a time, rendered such understanding more difficult.

INDEX

Absurd (paradoxical) Eide 356–7
Academy 22–5, 211–13, 229, 256, 260, 262, 350, 358–9, 366, 378
Accuracy (ἀκρίβεια) 162, 293, 365
Active Intelligence 7, 25, 186, 207, 265, 363–4, 390
Adam, J. 197–8
Addition 68, 447
Adeimantus (Plato's brother) 166
Advantage (συμφέρον) 162–3, 166
Affinities of Eide 2, 143
Affinity of Soul with Eide 135–6
Agathon 145, 147
Albert the Great 378, 385
Alcibiades 145, 150–1
Alcmaeon of Croton 10, 138, 146
Alexander of Aphrodisias (Aristotelian commentator) 60, 64, 67, 73, 416–19, 431, 438, 454, 458
Allen, R. E. xiii, 457
Ammonius Saccas x, 184, 366–8, 457
Analogy of Being 34–6, 235–6, 321–2, 462–4
Analytic Philosophy 407, 410, 473
Anamnesis, see Remembrance
Anaxagoras of Clazomenae 10, 138–9, 215, 416, 434
Anaximander 247
Anselm of Canterbury 387–8, 391, 393
Anti-absolutism 409–10
Anytus 128
Apart(ness) (χωρίς, χωρισμός) 24–9, 36–7, 233–4, 236, 249, 435, 457–9
Apology 9, 16, 82, 120–1
Appearances 203–6, 259–60, 271
Aquinas, Thomas 378, 385, 388–95
Archelaus of Athens 138

Archytas of Tarentum 17, 28, 209, 442
Aristippus of Cyrene 231
Aristocracy 278
Ariston (Plato's father) 8
Aristophanes (dramatist) 145–7
Aristoteles 230–1, 253
Aristotle ix–xi, xiii, 4, 7, 16, 21–2, 24–5, 32–7, 42, 45, 47–8, 52, 55–7, 60–5, 67, 69–70, 72–3, 75, 77, 80, 157, 160, 184, 185–7, 195, 203–4, 207, 210, 212, 219, 229–30, 233, 253, 261, 265, 272, 277, 286, 298, 303, 306, 321, 324–5, 345, 350–2, 358–66, 375, 380, 413–14, 417–21, 423, 455–61, 464–73
Aristoxenus of Tarentum 23, 49, 413
Arithmetic 192–3, 293, 336, 344–5
Arithmetization (of Eide), see Mathematicization
Artefacts 42, 44, 203, 205, 271, 276, 300, 435, 448
Assos 25
Atheism 337, 341–2
Augustine of Hippo 383–5

Bacon, F. 397
Bastard argument (λογισμὸς νόθος, *Timaeus*) 35, 321, 323, 463–4
Beauty 86–9, 148–50, 210, 218, 240, 285, 294–5, 370
Becoming (γένεσις) 264, 286, 289
Being 14, 34, 154, 180, 184, 210, 221, 240–1, 245, 261, 263–8, 321–2, 387–8, 393
Bergson, H. 215
Biology 48, 72–3, 195, 309, 449
Bolzano, B. 47

475

Boundlessness 248, 283
Bracketing, mental 356
Brentano, F. 401–2
Broad-and-narrow (τὸ πλατὺ καὶ τὸ στενόν) 64, 71–2, 195, 324, 422, 437
Bruno, G. 397
Buddha, Gautama 150
Burnet, J. 5

Callippus 23, 73
Categories 55
Categories (Aristotelian) 32, 34; (Platonic) xii, 35, 74–5, 374
Catherine of Genoa 379
Causality of Eide and their Principles 33–6, 38, 131, 137–8, 140, 263, 285, 287–8, 298–9, 304, 307, 318–19, 380, 416, 432, 434–5, 459
Cave 189–91
Cebes 10, 129, 131, 133, 137
Cephalus 160–1
Charmides 8
Charmides 15, 82, 91–5, 105, 279
Change 244–5; *see also* Becoming; Movement
Cherniss, H. F. xi, xiii, 10, 22, 80, 381, 407; canon of interpretation 456; 'individuality' of Eide 456–7; Eide rightly held to be self-identical rather than self-predicated 457; Eide separated from instances by a gulf of type, but such separateness wrongly taken to preclude 'immanence' 458–9; Eide wrongly held to lack productive efficacy 459; Eide wrongly held to be mutually exclusive 460; continuity and mutual interpenetration of Eide wrongly denied 461–2; relations of Eide not always symmetrical 462; differing sense of the 'being' of Eide and non-Eide, e.g. space, not properly recognized, and the Non-being-otherness of the *Sophist* misunderstood 464; correct that many arguments for Eide irrele-

vant to their identification with numbers 464–5; but identification rooted in Plato's attested belief in the impossibility of knowledge of fluctuating sensible qualities 465; if Plato only gave one discourse on the Good Aristotle would hardly have devoted a treatise to it 466; if Plato held oral 'conversations' rather than lectures, they must have been many and impressive 466–7; quite apart from explicit references to Unwritten Doctrines, Aristotle's accounts of Plato's doctrine are honeycombed with much the same reported material: if Plato queried such reports, this will not prove them quite inaccurate 467–8; the tortuous steps by which Aristotle is held to have achieved his misinterpretations exceed Aristotle's powers of mis-understanding and the reader's belief 468–70; the *Philebus* quite in harmony with the Aristotelian reports 471; a great mistake to apply formal logical rules to fluid concepts like those of Plato 471–2; case for thoroughgoing Aristo-telian misinterpretation ingeni-ously but unconvincingly argued, but includes some valid points 473
Chora (χώρα, Space, the Nurse of Becoming) 321–4, 376
Classificatory hierarchy of Eide 47–8, 155–7, 189, 266–7, 283–4, 460–2
Clement of Alexandria 381, 384
Communion (κοινωνία) of Eide 49, 265–6, 460–2
Complex Numbers 416, 437
Concrete Universal 309, 400
Continuum 248, 461–2, 470
Contradiction, use and abuse of Law of 175–6, 238, 246, 253–4, 298, 386, 458–9, 471–2
Contrariety 40, 231, 246, 253
Convention (συνθήκη) 214, 217–18

Cornford, F. M. 244, 316, 327
Cosmologists, early 10, 138–9
Courage (ἀνδρεία) 95–8, 107–8, 111–12, 171, 176, 279
Cratylus 11, 414, 464
Cratylus 302, 306, 331–3
Criterion 201
Critias 8, 306
Critias 11–13, 33, 211, 213–19
Crito 16, 26, 82, 121
Cudworth, R. 395
Cusanus, Nicolaus 378, 385–6, 396

Dante 208
De Anima 51, 55, 64–6, 72, 225, 262, 361–5, 421, 449–50, 466
Decadic restriction of Eide 60, 63, 66, 326, 420–1, 448–9, 465
De Caelo 450
Deduction 47–8, 141
Deep-and-shallow (τὸ βαθὺ καὶ τὸ ταπεινόν) 64, 71–2, 324, 422, 437
Deontic Logic 191
Demiurgic Thinkingness 304, 325, 363, 365
Democracy 196, 199–200, 272, 278
Dependence of Instance on Eide 35–6, 181, 236, 449, 458
Dercylides 367, 425
Descartes, R. 303, 397
Desire 148, 175
Determinism 319
'Development' of Plato's thought ix, 24, 47, 257
Deviant Eide 35, 42–4, 90, 161, 196–203, 300, 439, 451–2
Dialectic 82, 155–6, 158, 189, 194–6, 237, 247, 266–7, 283
Dialogues 4–6 *and passim*
Dichotomy 273
Difference (τὸ ἕτερον) 4, 224, 242–3, 267–8, 312, 464
Digestion 330
Dimensions 60, 64, 195, 339, 348–9, 437
Diogenes of Apollonia 108
Dion 17, 27–8
Dionysius I of Syracuse 17, 27

Dionysius II of Syracuse 27–8, 53, 159, 296, 299–300, 467–8
Dionysius the Areopagite (Pseudo-) 385–6, 390–1, 472
Dionysodorus the Eristic 82
Discourse (τὸ διαλέγεσθαι) 269–70
Division (διαίρεσις) 47–8, 155–7, 189, 257, 266–7, 283–4, 460–2
Dodds, E. R. 378
Double audience 256
Dualism xi, 324–5
Duality 68–9, 88, 273
Duns Scotus 395–6
Dyad, Indefinite (ἀόριστὸς δύας) 68, 414, 416–20, 422, 438, 468

Eckhart, Meister 378, 385, 396
Ecstasy 369–70
Eide (Ideas, Forms, εδῖη, ἰδέαι), meaning of Greek terms 29–30; standard arguments for 20–1, 432–3; prime ontological and epistemological status of 31–2, 235–6, 321, 462; causal efficacy of 33–6, 38, 72, 192–4, 360; relation to instances 36–40; of deviant or factitious types 290, 351, 360, 439, 451–2; hierarchical arrangement of 45–7, 141, 155–6, 283–4, 351; intellectual apprehension of 48, 65, 156–7, 227, 421; relation of, to natural types 50, 360, 434, 449; of individuals 50; of Numbers 55–6, 66–70, 88, 193, 241, 344–5, 347–9, 472; interpenetration of 460–2, *see* Communion; Arithmetization of *see* Mathematicization; of mental acts and Mind 351–2, *see also* Mind as Such; of higher order 353; as either subjects or predicates 354–5; in *Hippias Major* 86; in *Euthyphro* 30, 119; in Middle Period Dialogues 122; in *Meno* 123, 125–6; in *Phaedo* 130–1; in *Symposium* 149–50; in *Phaedrus* 154, 155–6; in *Republic* 180–5, 189–90, 194–5, 196–7, 203–6; in *Cratylus* 217–18;

Eide–*cont.*

in *Theaetetus* 223–5, 227; in *Parmenides* 229–30, 232–6, 238, 240, 253–4; in *Sophist* 255, 262–9; in *Statesman* 272–6; in *Philebus* 280–6, 288, 295; in *Epistles* 297–300; in *Timaeus* 302, 304, 307–8, 319–21; as criticized by Aquinas 391–2

Eleaticism 13–14, 34, 212, 213, 215, 217, 261, 310

Elements (στοιχεῖα), *see* Principles (ἀρχαί)

Elements, natural (earth, air, etc.) 305, 310, 319–20, 326–8, 346

Empedocles of Agrigentum 138, 146, 261, 310, 416

Empiricism 46–7, 190, 256, 294, 307–8, 357, 366, 371, 397–8, 401

Enjoyment (ἡδονή), *see* Pleasure

Epinomis 23, 66–7, 72, 302, 343–9

Epistle(s) 4, 6, 22, 296–301; Second 52–3, 158, 179, 186, 296–8, 352, 368, 467; Sixth 298–9, 368; Seventh 27, 299–301

Equality 135, 417, 428–9

Equalization (ἰσάζειν) 62, 67, 69–70, 424, 446–8

Er, myth of 207–8

Eternity (αἰών) 315–16, 375

Ethics 184, 191, 415

Etymology 215–16

Eucleides of Megara 13, 47, 129, 219

Eudemus of Rhodes 24–5, 78, 442

Eudoxus of Cnidos 23, 93, 434, 458–9

Eurytus of Tarentum 17, 79

Euthydemus 16, 101–5

Euthydemus the Eristic 82

Euthyphro 15, 30, 43, 82, 118–20

Evil 42, 206–7, 340, 374, 376, 393, 416, 439–40

Evolution (Speusippus) 359–60

Fallacies (Socratic) 83–5, 103, 108, 243

Falsehood, of Eide 355–6, 464, 468,

472; of statements and opinion 44, 202, 255–6, 270; of pleasures 289–93

Feeling-error 290–2

Ficino, M. 395–6

First Principle 296–8

Flux 12, 33, 364

Fluxion (of points, lines, surfaces) 70–1, 430

Formlessness 182

Fractionalization 67, 193, 348–9

Frege, G. 76

Freud, S. 176

Friends of the Eide (academic party) 24, 212, 264, 268

Gaiser, K. ix, xiii, 63, 73, 79–80

Gaps (eidetic) 451–2

Gaunilo 382

Genera (kinds, γένη) 45–7, 267–8, 283–4, 309, 400, 460–2

'Generation' of Numbers and Magnitudes 66–78, 241–7, 440–1, 469–70

Geometric magnitudes, *see* Magnitudes

Geometry 192–3

'Giants' (academic party) 24, 212, 262

Glaucon (Plato's brother) 165–6

Gnosticism 377, 381

'Gods' (academic party), *see* Friends of the Eide

God(s) 7, 154, 204, 224, 234, 274, 280–1, 298, 337, 341, 345–7, 363–4, 373, 378–80, 383–4

Good, lecture on the 23, 59, 466

Good, On the (Aristotle, Περὶ τοῦ Ἀγαθοῦ) 59, 61, 64, 68, 73, 210, 417–19, 422, 430–2, 466–8, 472

Good, the 10–11, 14, 46, 52, 114, 120, 139–41, 150–1, 160, 179, 183–5, 189–90, 193, 218–19, 224, 228, 240, 281–2, 295, 353, 369, 379, 387, 391–5, 413–40

Gorgias 16, 112–18, 282

Gorgias of Leontini 9, 81, 122, 124, 147

Great-and-small (τὸ μέγα καὶ τὸ μικρόν) 59, 61-3, 65, 77-8, 168, 210, 248, 251-4, 280, 376, 414-16, 418-20, 422, 440-1, 469-70
Gregory of Nyssa 382
Guesswork (εἰκασία) 186-7
Gymnastics 170-1

Happiness 164
Harmonics 192, 194
Harmony 11, 136, 146, 312-13
Hegel, G. W. F. 247, 302-3, 309, 387, 395-6, 399-401
Heidegger, M. 410
Heraclitus of Ephesus 11-13, 33, 55, 131, 146, 212-13, 215, 217, 221-2, 247, 261, 327, 414
Hermocrates 306
Hippasus of Metapontium 59
Hippias of Elis 106
Hippias Major 15, 55, 82, 86-9
Hippias Minor 15, 89-90
Hobbes, T. 397
Homosexuality 144, 146-7, 150-2, 155
Hume, D. 4, 398
Husserl, E. 30, 76, 189, 217, 402
Hypostases (Neoplatonic) x, 296-8, 368-75
Hypostatization 3, 13
Hypothesis (postulation) 127, 140, 156, 187-8, 194-5, 234-5, 237, 468

Iamblichus of Chalcis 377-8
Ideal meanings 5, 7, 9, 11-13
Idealism (realistic or subjective) 408-9, 473
Ideas, On the (Aristotle, Περὶ Ἰδεῶν) 33, 59, 233, 465
Ideological dialogues xii
Images (εἴδωλα) 271
Imitation (μίμησις) 37, 53, 133, 211, 233, 414
Immanence of Eide 459
Immortality 11, 141-2, 206-7
Incommensurability 58, 65, 338
Incomparability of Ideal Numbers (τὸ ἀσύμβλητοι εἶναι) 56, 60, 436

Indefinite Dyad, *see* Dyad
Individuality of Eide (Cherniss) 457
Ineffability of ultimate elements 228, 252, 298, 301
Inequality 428-9
Infinite, the (τὸ ἄπειρον) 58-9, 197, 210, 248, 251-2, 280, 285, 353, 418-19; by addition and division 420
Infinite Number 448
Insight (νοῦς), *see* Intuition
Instant (τὸ ἐξαίφνης) 377-8
Instantiation, parasitic nature of 34, 36, 40
Intensional view of Numbers 348-9
Intentionality 134-5, 188, 190, 389-90
Intermediates 312, 436, 438, 443-7
Intuition, intellectual (νοῦς) 48, 65, 156-7, 421
Ion 15, 90-1
Irradiation (ἔλλαμψις) 370-1
Irrationals 58, 67, 219

Jackson, H. 25
Jaeger, W. xi, 24
Jesus Christ 379-80
John the Scot (Erigena) 385-7
Joints in Dialectic 156
Jowett, B. 209
Judgment (πίστις) 187
Julian the Apostate 378
Justice 187-8, 114-18, 161-4, 165-7, 172-3, 176-7, 334-5

Kant, I. 25, 315, 387, 398-9
Kierkegaard, S. 384
Kingly science 272-3
Knowledge(ἐπιστήμη, φρόνησις, etc.) 10, 15, 65, 154, 180-3, 185, 201, 218, 220-1, 233-4, 264-5, 289, 293-5, 421; of knowledge 93-5; and Virtue 83-4; and Welfare 103
Krämer, H. J. ix, 80

Laches 15, 82, 91, 95-8
Laws 277

479

Laws xi, 21, 23, 27, 65-6, 72, 302, 304, 333-43, 375

Leibniz, G. 397-8

Lepers of discourse 357

Life 72, 143, 308-10

Likelihood 307

Likeness = Resemblance 211-307; = Image 259-60

Limit (πέρας) 57, 61-2, 280-1, 283, 285-8, 295, 469

Line(s) 70-1; divided 186-9; indivisible 71, 124, 437

Living creature itself (αὐτόζῳον) 309, 421

Logical paradoxes 404-5

Long-and-short (τὸ μακρὸν καὶ τὸ βραχύ) 67, 71, 195, 324, 422, 437

Longer road (μακρότερα περίοδος) 174, 182, 185

Love 144-52

Lysias the orator 151-2

Lysis 15, 82, 91-2, 98-101

Machiavellianism 163

Magisterial character of Soul 137

Magnitudes (eidetic) 17-18, 57, 60, 423-4

Mahayana Buddhism 144

Many-and-few (τὸ πολὺ καὶ τὸ ὀλίγον) 65, 195

Mathematica (Objects of Mathematics) 56-7, 76-7, 126, 131, 187-8, 312, 365, 415

Mathematical Understanding (διάνοια) 187-9

Mathematicization of the Eide 6-7, 17-18, 21-2, 26, 39, 54-80, 82, 111, 117, 122-4, 130, 138, 140, 147, 184, 192, 197, 211, 229, 272, 279, 303, 331, 336, 347-9, 357, 365, 374-5, 413, 432, 438-40

Mathematics xiii, 192

Matter (ὕλη) 62, 280, 327, 361, 364, 374-6, 415-16, 468, 470

Mean (ratio) 71, 74, 276-7, 279, 310, 313, 325, 352

Meanings, Ideal 5

Mechanistic materialism 410-12

Medical writers 146-7

Megarian school 13, 219-20

Meinong, A. 76, 250, 402

Meno 15-16, 18, 122-9, 225

Meta-Eide 53

Metaphysics (Aristotle) ix, 11, 21, 24, 33, 35, 41, 55-6, 62-5, 68, 70, 72-3, 77, 141, 188, 205, 230, 232-3, 280, 324, 358, 360-1, 363-5, 375, 414-16, 421-3, 431, 439-41, 444-9, 451-4, 464

Meta-principles 353

Methexis, *see* Participation

Middle period Dialogues xii, 122

Midwifery, intellectual (μαιευτική) 220-1

Mimesis, *see* Imitation

Mind (νοῦς) 10, 183, 281, 287, 308, 340, 421, 449-50

Mind as Such 50-2, 60, 72, 139, 144, 154, 185-6, 207, 274, 287-8, 297, 299, 304, 363, 372-3, 459

Mind, works of 27, 35, 50, 198, 305, 317-19, 330

Monad 429

Monarchy 272, 278

Monism of Plato 231, 249, 324-5, 354

Moore, G. E. 3, 30, 192, 294, 403

More, H. 395

Movement (κίνησις) 211, 242, 264-6, 268, 315, 328, 338-9, 441-2

Multiplicative emphasis in Plato 68, 447

Names, eidetic 214, 261; divine 386

Natural numbers 416

Natural objects 50, 360, 434, 449

Naturalistic 'fallacy' 192

Nature (φύσις) 177-8

Necessity, distaff of 209; works of 27, 35, 50, 98, 305, 309, 317-19, 328-30

Negations 42, 270, 432

Nicomachean Ethics (Aristotle) 53, 141, 365, 440

Neo-Kantianism 473

Neoplatonism xiii, 62, 186, 247, 295–7, 346, 366
Nocturnal Council 342, 412
Noeric and noetic Universals (Proclus) 51, 378
Non-being (τὸ μὴ ὄν) 78, 81–2, 249–50, 260, 267–70, 280, 323–4, 387, 442, 464, 468
Number, notion of in Plato x, xi, 6–7, 11, 39, 55, 61, 67, 88, 278, 344–5, 347–9, 415–17
Numenius of Apamea 367
Nurse (τιθήνη) of Becoming (Chora) 319–20, 325, 327

Ockham, William of 3, 396, 404
Oligarchy 196, 199, 202, 278
One, the (τὸ ἕν), *see* Unity; One-over-Many 236, 255, 282–4, 432
One-in-Action 288
Ontological proof 387–8
Opinion (δόξα) 10, 14–15, 65, 128, 180–2, 225–6, 321, 421
Opposition xii, 35, 43, 74, 108, 425, 427–30
Origen (Christian Father) 368, 381–2, 384–5
Other, circle of the 313–14, 317
Otherness (others) 210, 243, 237–8, 267–8, 468
Overfeeling 291
Owen, G. E. L. 18, 303
Own-being of Eide 240

Paradeigmatism 457
Parasitism, logical, of instances on Eide 32, 34–6, 181, 236, 449, 458
Parmenides of Elea 13–14, 219–20, 224, 310, 324
Parmenides xi, 5, 14, 16, 21, 26–7, 36, 38, 41, 49, 51, 63, 70, 150, 196, 211–12, 219–20, 229–54, 255–6, 281, 297, 304, 354, 368, 370, 393, 459, 461–2, 470–1
Parousia (Real Presence) of Eide in instances 33, 38, 100, 458
Participation (μέθεξις, μετάληψις etc.) 33, 37–8, 53, 211, 232–3, 414

Particulars 1, 2, 32
Parts of Soul 174–7, 329
Paul the Apostle 380, 385
Pausanias 149
Perictione (mother of Plato) 8
Perishables, knowledge of 432
Phaedo 6, 10–11, 16, 18, 21, 24–5, 40–1, 55, 78, 121–2, 129–44, 208, 230–1, 312, 326, 331, 381, 398, 459
Phaedrus 145
Phaedrus 16, 18, 47, 121, 151–8, 174, 291, 375, 459, 470
Philebus 21, 26–7, 47, 51, 61, 66, 78, 95, 211, 230, 280–95, 297, 304, 365, 418–19, 469, 471
Philip of Opus 23, 67, 343, 413
Philo of Alexandria 367
Philolaus of Tarentum 10, 17, 129, 209
Philoponus (Aristotelian commentator) 66, 361, 422, 441, 450
Philosophy, On (Περὶ Φιλοσοφίας, Aristotle) 64, 82, 421–2, 466
Physics (Aristotle) 35, 60, 62–3, 68, 70, 73, 75, 77–8, 210, 280, 360–1, 375, 414, 418, 420, 425, 440–1, 467
Piety 107–8, 118–20
Planets 314, 316, 346–7
Plato, writer of Dialogues x–xi, 4–6, 15–18, 25–7; of Epistles x, 4, 6; as Number-theorist x–xi, xiii, 6–8, 21; as monist xii, 231, 249, 324–5, 354; as theorist of categories xii, 35, 53–4, 74–5, 374; as Socratic portraitist xii, 15–16; as mature Eidos-theorist xii, 1–4; as critical stoicheiologist xii, 1–2, 21, 25, 54, 210–13; as oral teacher 4, 6–7, 19–20, 22–3, 54, 466–8; as value-theorist 9–10, 40–1; as mystic xiii, 6, 145, 240, 251, 298; as classifier of Eide 2–3; as hypostatic realist 3–4, 13, 31; birth and descent 8; association with Socrates 8–10; association with the sophists 9; student of the cosmologists 10; association with

Plato—*cont.*

Pythagoreans 10–11, 17–18; association with Cratylus and Heracliteanism 11–13; association with Eleaticism and Megarianism 13–15; abandonment of politics 15; first visit to Italy and Sicily 17–18; foundation of Academy 19; activities in the Academy, *see* Academy; second Italian visit 27–8; *et passim*

Pleasure (ἡδονή) 87–8, 109–11, 117, 183, 201, 281–2, 284, 287, 289, 292–5, 329, 334–5

Plotinus ix–x, 50, 184, 324, 366–78, 380, 383, 407, 471

Pluralism 231

Points (σημεῖα, στιγμαί) 70–1, 124, 416, 429–30, 437

Polemarchus 160–1

Popper, K. R. 407

Porphyry of Tyre 68, 368, 377, 418–19, 425

Posterior Analytics (Aristotle) 366, 427, 468

Postulations (of Existence = ὑποθέσεις) 127, 140, 156, 187–8, 194–5, 234–5, 237

Potency and Act (Aristotle) 360, 370, 450

Poverty and plenty 148, 150

Power(s) (δύναμις, δυνάμεις) 180–2, 263–4, 370

Pre-existence 134

Prime Eide 75, 194, 312

Prime Numbers 69–70

Primitive names 216–17

Principles (ἀρχαί) = elements (στοιχεῖα) 1, 11, 25–7, 53–4, 61–2, 149–50, 210–11, 415, 417, 421, 426–7, 435, 438

Probability (likelihood) 331

Proclus 4, 24, 51, 378, 385, 407

Prodicus of Ceos 106

Propositions, unemphatic in Platonic theory 47–8, 370

Protagoras 15, 17, 192, 282

Protagoras of Abdera 9, 12, 54, 82, 214, 219, 221–3

Pseudo-Alexander (commentator) 422–3, 451

Psyche, *see* Soul

Psychogony (in *Timaeus*) 311–14, 466

Pythagoreanism 10–11, 17–19, 37, 57–9, 61, 121, 129, 169, 171, 174, 176, 197–8, 233, 283, 285, 311, 414–15, 418, 425–6, 443, 445, 461

Qualities, sensible 12–13, 18, 39, 54–5, 184, 225, 303, 327–9, 357, 362, 464

Quantity 55, 439, 464

Ratio (λόγος) xi, 55, 60, 67, 72, 136, 139, 147, 168, 180, 184, 192, 195, 225, 244, 285–7, 295, 310, 344–5, 435–6, 465

Rationalization 289

Reason, intuitive (νοῦς) 366

Receptacle (ὑποδοχή) 78, 319–20

Reification 235

Relativity (τὸ πρός τι) xii, 35, 73, 141, 201–2, 221–3, 425, 427–30, 432, 439

Reminiscence (ἀνάμνησις) 91, 126, 128, 137, 450

Republic xi, 9, 13, 16, 18, 21, 27, 34–5, 40–1, 43, 46, 52–3, 55, 66–7, 80, 93, 95, 121–2, 140, 153, 159–209, 227, 229, 230–1, 271–2, 275, 278, 281–2, 297, 303–4, 306, 315, 329, 332, 341, 350, 361, 368, 370, 372, 381, 420, 457, 458–9, 466

Respiration 330

Reversal of time 275, 316

Revolution (of heavens) 311

Rhetoric 112–14, 155–8

Right Opinion 128, 148

Robin, L. x, 67, 69, 79, 424

Ross, D. x–xi, 22, 179, 188

Royal Science 276–8

Russell, B. 25, 402–3

Ryle, G. 9, 16

Same, Circle of the 313–14, 317

Sameness 4, 210, 224, 242–3, 267, 311–12

Index

Sartre, J.-P. 410
Schelling, F. W. J. von 398
Schleiermacher, F. E. D. 406
Sciences, Argument from the 432
Self-existence (καθ' αὐτὸ εἶναι) xii, 35, 74, 253, 425–30
Self-knowledge 93–5, 105
Self-movement 153, 312, 339
Self-predication (of Eide) 38, 235–6, 356–7, 457, 473
Sense (significance) 1, 31
Sense (sense-organs and their function) 31, 65, 221, 321, 421
Sex 331
Sextus Empiricus xii, 4, 35, 45, 61, 64, 73–5, 425–30
Simmias (Pythagorean) 10, 129, 133, 136
Simplicius (commentator) xii, 45, 61, 68, 70, 75, 77, 78, 280, 414, 418, 422, 425, 440–1
Social unity 160
Socrates 3, 8–10, 11, 13, 15–18, 30, 47, 414 and passim
Socratic dialogues xii, 15–16, 228
Socratic problem 5
Socratic sophistry 83–5, 165, 211–12
Solids, regular 46, 71–2, 193, 219, 326–7; in motion 72, 193
Sophist xi, 14, 24, 26, 44, 47, 49, 51, 63, 66, 131, 203, 219, 244, 255–72, 288, 297, 303–4, 315, 343, 353, 355–6, 361, 374, 460, 461, 464, 469
Sophists 9, 106, 128, 256–9, 271
Sophrontisterion 342–3
Soul 11, 35, 51, 72, 129, 132, 134, 141–2, 153–4, 206–7, 262–3, 308, 311–14, 329–30, 338–40, 345–6, 359, 375, 459, 466
Space 35, 39, 64–5, 77–8, 182, 280, 305, 321–4, 441, 464, 468–9, 471
Spatiality 324
Speusippus (academic scholarch, Plato's nephew) 22, 24, 188, 229, 291, 358–9, 413, 423, 442–3, 445, 457–8, 460
Spinoza, B. de 387, 397
Stability (στάσις) 211, 265–6, 268

Statesman 26, 47, 198, 211, 271–80, 305, 311, 316, 332, 343
Stenzel, J. 79
Stoicheia (Elements), see Principles
Stoicheiology 50; stoicheiological dialogues xii, 210
Substantial being (οὐσία) 415, 435–6, 453
Suitability (τὸ πρέπον) 87
Sun 183–4, 189–90, 314, 316
Swift-and-Slow 195
Symmetry 294–5
Symposium 16, 18, 121–2, 144–51, 291, 370
Syrianus (academic scholarch and commentator) 42, 53, 60, 75, 432, 444, 451–4
Systoichia (list of opposites) 57–8

Taylor, A. E. 378, 395
Taylor, T. 378, 395
Temperance (self-restraint, σωφροσύνη) 91–3, 107–8, 171, 176, 279
Tense-modifications 244–5, 291
Tetractys (Pythagorean-Platonic) 63, 66, 310
Theaetetus 23, 46, 67, 193, 219, 326
Theaetetus 11–12, 26–7, 54, 211, 219–29, 256, 355, 362
Themistius (commentator) 441
Theodorus of Cyrene 67, 219, 256
Theophrastus of Lesbos 4, 59, 358, 413
Thinking, thought 269, 282; on thinking 364
Thinkingness (Eidos of thought) 27, 51, 143, 204, 304, 363, 372–4
Third Man 33, 212, 233, 236, 432, 457
Thirty Tyrants 8
Thomism xii
Thrasymachus of Chalcedon 161–4, 200
Timaeus xii, 4, 18–19, 27, 34–5, 39–41, 46, 50–1, 57, 60, 63, 66, 70–2, 76–8, 98, 131, 150, 153, 173–4, 182, 191, 194, 275, 302–31, 352, 361–3, 368, 371–2, 376, 384, 421, 441, 461, 463, 466–7, 468–71

Timarchy, timocracy 196, 199, 202
Time 39, 66, 272, 274–5, 305, 314–16, 375
Trances (of Socrates) 143
Transcendentals 25
Truth 128, 225, 294, 320
Two–world misinterpretation of Platonism 78
Type-gulfs 25, 254, 458

Underfeeling 291
Ungrudgingness or lack of φθόνος 308, 322, 353, 371, 380
Uniqueness of Cosmos 309
Unity (τὸ ἕν) 14, 18, 57–9, 61, 77, 150, 160, 179, 184–5, 195, 288, 295, 353, 369–70, 413–14, 420, 438, 440, 469, 472; of Virtue 97, 109
Unknowingness (ἀγνωσία, ἄγνοια) 180–2
Unlikeness 211
Unlimited (ἄπειρον) 61–2, 210, 248, 469
Unwritten Doctrines (ἄγραφα δόγματα) xiii, 4, 6, 76–8, 80, 157–8, 160, 182, 281, 350–1, 441, 455, 466–8
Ur-Phaedo 16
Usefulness (τὸ χρήσιμον) 87, 98, 162

Value-meanings 9–10, 40–1
Value-theory 101

Virtue, as knowledge 83–4, 127–8; teachability of 101, 106–7, 127–8; unity of 97, 109
Vlastos, G. 437

Wandering Cause (ἡ πλανωμένη αἰτία) 318
Wantonness (τόλμα) 377
Welfare (εὖ πράττειν) 102, 164–5
Whitehead, A. N. 404
Wholeness 261
Wilpert, P. 64, 73, 79–80, 430
Wisdom (σοφία, φρόνησις) 107–8, 171–2, 176, 343
Wittgenstein, L. 4, 217, 270, 299, 405–6, 460, 467–8
Women 177–8
Work (ἔργον) 164–5, 177
Works of Mind and Necessity 27, 35, 50, 198, 317–19, 329–30
World-Soul 280, 297, 304, 311–14, 375

Xenocrates of Chalcedon (academic scholarch) 22, 24, 62, 188, 358–60, 413, 424, 443, 445, 451, 466, 472–3
Xenophanes of Colophon 261, 310
Xenophon (historian) 11, 129, 138

Zeller, E. 333, 406
Zeno of Elea 155, 229–31, 250
Zeus 287